J. Meites

CRC SERIES IN AGING

Editors-in-Chief

Richard C. Adelman, Ph.D.
Executive Director
Institute on Aging
Temple University
Philadelphia, Pennsylvania

George S. Roth, Ph.D.
Research Chemist
Gerontology Research Center
National Institute on Aging
Baltimore City Hospitals
Baltimore, Maryland

HANDBOOK OF BIOCHEMISTRY IN AGING
Editor
James Florini, Ph.D.
Department of Biology
Syracuse University
Syracuse, New York

HANDBOOK OF PHYSIOLOGY IN AGING
Editor
Edward J. Masoro, Ph.D.
Department of Physiology
University of Texas
Health Science Center
San Antonio, Texas

HANDBOOK OF IMMUNOLOGY IN AGING
Editors
Marguerite M. B. Kay, M.D. and
Takashi Makinodan, Ph.D.
Geriatric Research Education and
Clinical Center
V.A. Wadsworth Medical Center
Los Angeles, California

IMMUNOLOGICAL TECHNIQUES APPLIED TO AGING RESEARCH
Editors
William H. Adler, M.D. and
Albert A. Nordin, Ph.D.
Gerontology Research Center
National Institute on Aging
Baltimore City Hospitals
Baltimore, Maryland

SENESCENCE IN PLANTS
Editor
Kenneth V. Thimann, Ph.D.
The Thimann Laboratories
University of California
Santa Cruz, California

CURRENT TRENDS IN MORPHOLOGICAL TECHNIQUES
Editor
John E. Johnson, Jr., Ph.D.
Gerontology Research Center
National Institute on Aging
Baltimore City Hospitals
Baltimore, Maryland

Additional topics to be covered in this series include Cell Biology of Aging, Microbiology of Aging, Pharmacology of Aging, Evolution and Genetics, Animal Models for Aging Research, Hormonal Regulatory Mechanisms, Detection of Altered Proteins, Insect Models, Lower Invertebrate Models, Testing the Theories of Aging, and Nutritional Approaches to Aging Research.

CRC Handbook of Physiology in Aging

Editor

Edward J. Masoro, Ph.D.
Professor and Chairman
Department of Physiology
University of Texas Health Science Center
San Antonio, Texas

CRC Series in Aging

Editors-in-Chief

Richard C. Adelman, Ph.D.
Executive Director
Institute on Aging
Temple University
Philadelphia, Pennsylvania

George S. Roth, Ph.D.
Research Chemist
Gerontology Research Center
National Institute on Aging
Baltimore City Hospitals
Baltimore, Maryland

CRC Press, Inc.
Boca Raton, Florida

Library of Congress Cataloging in Publication Data
Main entry under title:

Handbook of physiology in aging.

  (CRC series in aging)
  Bibliography: p.
  Includes index.
  1. Aging—Handbooks, manuals, etc. 2. Human physiology—
Handbooks, manuals, etc. I. Masoro, Edward J. II. Series.
QP86.H345   599.03′72   80-19983
ISBN 0-8493-3143-9

  This book represents information obtained from authentic and highly regarded sources. Reprinted material is quoted with permission, and sources are indicated. A wide variety of references are listed. Every reasonable effort has been made to give reliable data and information, but the author and the publisher cannot assume responsibility for the validity of all materials or for the consequences of their use.

  All rights reserved. This book, or any parts thereof, may not be reproduced in any form without written consent from the publisher.

  Direct all inquiries to CRC Press, Inc., 2000 N.W. 24th Street, Boca Raton, Florida 33431.

© 1981 by CRC Press, Inc.

International Standard Book Number 0-8493-3143-9

Library of Congress Card Number 80-19983
Printed in the United States

PREFACE

The aim of this handbook is to provide an encyclopedic coverage of currently available data and knowledge regarding physiologic changes occurring with age from young adulthood on to and through senescence. It is further aim that bibliographic documentation be provided for all such data and knowledge. These aims have been achieved.

All such data and knowledge have been presented in this handbook either in the form of tables or figures prepared by experts in the subject areas. The entries in the tables are one of two types or a combination thereof: (1) numerical data and (2) statements of fact.

The subject areas covered primarily involved the classic organ systems usually covered in textbooks of physiology such as nervous system, cardiovascular system, endocrine system, etc; in addition, coverage was given to topics that transcend the organ systems such as body composition, exercise, and thermal regulation. There is some overlap with other handbooks in this series, but every attempt was made to keep this to a minimum. For example, in so far as this handbook covers neurophysiology and the neuromuscular system, there is overlap with the Neurobiology Handbook. However, such areas as neuroanatomy, neurology, neuropharmacology, neurochemistry, and behavioral science were avoided since they are important coverage areas in the Neurobiology Handbook. The extent of the overlap that occurs is the minimum needed for a complete coverage of physiology to be effective. The potential overlap with the Cell Biology, Biochemistry, and Pharmacology Handbooks was in each case handled in a similar fashion.

In the aging literature, possibly more than most fields of biology, there are conflicting reports; e.g., it is not uncommon to find in three reports that *Process A* decreases with age, in one report that it increases with age and in two reports that it does not change with age. Of course, the data from any of these reports with obvious technical deficiencies were not reported in this handbook. However, all data that appeared to be free of technical error were reported. Consequently, in the same table the reader will sometimes find diametrically opposed statements or numerical data. Since literature references are provided for each entry, the reader is free to draw his or her own conclusion from the original works.

Another problem encountered when surveying the aging literature is the fact that many reports are limited to the time span of birth to young adulthood. In most instances, such studies were considered to be in the field of developmental biology, and therefore, not included in the handbook. Indeed, by and large, only those studies that involve a substantial span of adult life are included.

The editorial assistance of Gretta Small and Linda Clark is greatfully acknowledged.

Edward J. Masoro
San Antonio, Texas

EDITORS-IN-CHIEF

Richard C. Adelman, Ph.D., is currently Executive Director of the Temple University Institute on Aging, Philadelphia, Pa., as well as Professor of Biochemistry in the Fels Research Institute of the Temple University College of Medicine. An active gerontologist for more than 10 years, he has achieved international prominence as a researcher, educator, and administrator. These accomplishments span a broad spectrum of activities ranging from the traditional disciplinary interests of the research biologist to the advocacy, implementation, and administration of multidisciplinary issues of public policy of concern to elderly people.

Dr. Adelman pursued his pre- and postdoctoral research training under the guidance of two prominent biochemists, each of whom is a member of the National Academy of Sciences: Dr. Sidney Weinhouse as Director of the Fels Research Institute, Temple University and Dr. Bernard L. Horecker as Chairman of the Department of Molecular Biology, Albert Einstein College of Medicine, Bronx, N.Y. His accomplishments as a researcher can be expressed in at least the following ways. He is the author and/or editor of more than 70 publications, including original research papers in referred journals, review chapters and books. His research efforts have been supported by grants from the National Institutes of Health for the past 10 consecutive years, at a current annual level of approximately $300,000. He continues to serve as an invited speaker at seminar programs, symposiums, and workshops all over the world. He is the recipient of the IntraScience Research Foundation Medalist Award, an annual research prize awarded by peer evaluation for major advances in newly emerging areas of the life sciences; and the recipient of an Established Investigatorship of the American Heart Association.

As an educator, Dr. Adelman is also involved in a broad variety of activities. His role in research training consists of responsibility for pre- and postdoctoral students who are assigned specific projects in his laboratory. He teaches an Advanced Graduate Course on the Biology of Aging, lectures on biomedical aspects of aging to medical students, and is responsible for the biological component of the basic course in aging sponsored by the School of Social Administration. Training activities outside the university include membership in the Faculty of the National Institute on Aging summer course on the Biology of Aging; programs on the biology of aging for AAA's throughout Pennsylvania and Ohio; and the implementation and teaching of Biology of Aging for the Nonbiologist locally, for the Gerontology Society and other national organizations, as well as for the International Association of Gerontology.

Dr. Adelman has achieved leadership positions across equally broad areas. Responsibilities of this position include the intergration of multidisciplinary programs in research, consultation and education, and health service, as well as advocacy for the university on all matters dealing with aging. He coordinates a city-wide consortium of researchers from Temple University, the Wistar Institute, the Medical College of Pennsylvania, Drexel University, and the Philadelphia Geriatric Center, conducting collaborative research projects, training programs, and symposiums. He was President of the Philadelphia Biochemists Club. He serves on the editorial boards of the *Journal of Gerontology, Mechanisms of Ageing and Development, Experimental Aging Research,* and *Gerontological Abstracts.* He was a member of the Biomedical Research Panel of the National Advisory Council of the National Institute on Aging. He chairs a subcommittee of the National Academy of Sciences Committee on Animal Models for Aging Research. As an active Fellow of the Gerontological Society, he was Chairman of the Biological Sciences section; a past Chairman of the Society Public Policy Committee for which he prepared Congressional testimony and represented the Society on the Leadership Council of the Coalition of National Aging Organizations; and is

Secretary-Treasurer of the North American Executive Committee of the International Association of Gerontology. Finally, as the highest testimony of his leadership capabilities, he continues to serve on National Advisory Committees which impact on diverse key issues dealing with the elderly. These include a 4-year appointment as member of the NIH Study Section on Pathobiological Chemistry; the Executive Committee of the Health Resources Administration Project on publication of the recent edition of *Working with Older People — A Guide to Practice;* a recent appointment as reviewer of AOA applications for Career Preparation Programs in Gerontology; and a 4-year appointment on the Veterans Administration Long-Term Care Advisory Council responsible for evaluating their program on Geriatric Research, Education, and Clinical Centers (GRECC).

George S. Roth, Ph.D., is a Research Chemist at the Gerontology Research Center of the National Institute on Aging, Baltimore City Hospitals, Baltimore, Md.

Dr. Roth received his B.S. in Biology from Villanova University, Pennsylvania in 1968 and his Ph.D. in Microbiology from Temple University School of Medicine, Philadelphia, Pa. in 1971. He received postdoctoral training in Biochemistry at the Fels Research Institute in Philadelphia, Pa. Since coming to the National Institute on Aging (NIA) in 1972, Dr. Roth has also been affiliated with the Graduate Schools of Georgetown University and George Washington University, Washington, D.C.

He is an officer of the Gerontological Society of America, a co-editor of the CRC series, *Methods of Aging Research,* an associate editor of *Neurobiology of Aging,* and a referee for numerous other journals. Dr. Roth has published extensively in the area of hormone action and aging and has lectured throughout the world on this subject.

THE EDITOR

Edward J. Masoro, Ph.D., is Chairman of the Department and Professor of Physiology at the University of Texas Health Science Center at San Antonio.

Dr. Masoro obtained his training at the University of California, Berkeley, receiving the A.B. degree in 1947 and the Ph.D. degree in 1950. He served as an Assistant Professor at Queen's University (Kingston, Ontario) from 1950 to 1952, as an Assistant Professor and an Associate Professor at Tufts University School of Medicine (Boston, Mass.) from 1952 to 1962, as a Research Associate Professor and Research Professor at the University of Washington (Seattle) from 1962 to 1964, as a Professor and Chairman of the Department of Physiology and Biophysics at the Medical College of Pennsylvania (Philadelphia) from 1964 to 1973. It was in 1973 that he assumed his present position.

Dr. Masoro is a member of the American Association for the Advancement of Science, American Association of University Professors, Canadian Physiological Society, American Physiological Society, Society for Experimental Biology and Medicine, Canadian Biochemical Society, American Chemical Society, New York Academy of Sciences, American Society of Biological Chemists, Gerontological Society, Association of Chairmen of Departments of Physiology, and the honorary society Sigma Xi. He is a Fellow of the American Association for the Advancement of Science and of the Gerontological Society, and has served or is serving on the Council of the American Association for the Advancement of Science, the Gerontological Society, and the Association of Chairmen of Departments of Physiology. He served as Vice President of the Gerontological Society in 1978 and 1979. He has received the Christian R. and Mary F. Lindback Distinguished Teaching Award as well as two Golden Apple Awards from the Students American Medical Association. He has been the recipient of many research grants from the National Institutes of Health and the National Science Foundation and is currently the Program Director of a Program Project Grant entitled "Nutritional Probe of the Aging Process" from the National Institute on Aging.

Dr. Masoro is the author of more than 100 papers and has been the author or coauthor of three books. His current major research interests relate to the modulation of the aging process by nutritional intervention.

ADVISORY BOARD

Edward J. Cafruny, Ph.D.
Professor of Pharmacology
Dean, Graduate School of Biomedical
  Sciences
College of Medicine and Dentistry
Newark, New Jersey

Charles W. Daniel, Ph.D.
Professor of Biology
Cowell College
University of California
Santa Cruz, California

Caleb E. Finch, Ph.D.
Professor of Biology and Gerontology
Ethel Percy Andrus Gerontology Center
University of Southern California
Los Angeles, California

James W. Leathem, Ph.D. (deceased)
Bureau of Biological Research
Rutgers University
New Brunswick, New Jersey

Warren W. Nichols, M.D., Ph.D.
Head, Department of Cytogenetics
Institute for Medical Research
Camden, New Jersey

George A. Sacher (deceased)
Division of Biological and Medical
  Research
Argonne National Laboratory
Argonne, Illinois

D. Rao Sanadi, Ph.D.
Director
Department of Cell Physiology
Boston Biomedical Research Institute
Boston, Massachusetts

Nathan W. Shock
Scientist Emeritus, NIH
Gerontology Research Center
National Institute on Aging
Baltimore City Hospitals
Baltimore, Maryland

Marc E. Weksler, M.D.
Wright Professor of Medicine
Department of Medicine
Cornell University
Medical College
New York, New York

CONTRIBUTORS

Ellen Bragg Arnold, Ph.D.
Environmental Manager
Arapahoe Chemicals, Inc.
Boulder, Colorado

Hermann Bader, M.D.
Professor and Chairman Abteilung
Pharmakologie und Toxikologie
Universitat Ulm
Ulm, Germany

Helen A. Bertrand, Ph.D.
Assistant Professor
Department of Physiology
University of Texas Health Science
 Center
San Antonio, Texas

Maria A. Biedenbach, Ph.D.
Associate Professor
Department of Physiology
University of Texas Health Science
 Center
San Antonio, Texas

Nils W. Bolduan, M.D.
Research Physiologist
Institute of Environmental Stress
University of California
Santa Barbara, California

Barbara A. Brooks, Ph.D.
Associate Professor
Department of Physiology
University of Texas Health Science
 Center
San Antonio, Texas

Robert A. Bruce, M.D.
Professor of Medicine
Co-Director, Division of Cardiology
Department of Medicine
University of Washington
Seattle, Washington

Hugh G. Donahue, B.S.
Graduate Student
Ethel Percy Andrus Gerontology Center
University of Southern California
Los Angeles, California

Devendra P. Dubey, Ph.D.
Research Associate
Associate in Pathology
Harvard Medical School
Division of Immunogenetics
Sidney Farber Cancer Institute
Boston, Massachusetts

Caleb E. Finch, Ph.D.
Professor of Biology and Gerontology
Ethel Percy Andrus Gerontology Center
University of Southern California
Los Angeles, California

J. Harold Helderman, M.D.
Assistant Professor of Internal
 Medicine
Director, Renal Immunology
 Laboratory
University of Texas Health Science
 Center
Southwestern Medical School
Dallas, Texas

Jeremiah T. Herlihy, Ph.D.
Associate Professor
Department of Physiology
University of Texas Health Science
 Center
San Antonio, Texas

Steven M. Horvath, Ph.D.
Director and Professor
Institute of Environmental Stress
University of California
Santa Barbara, California

Hive-Ho Huang, Ph.D.
Research Associate
Neuroendocrine Laboratory
Department of Physiology
Michigan State University
East Lansing, Michigan

Dianne Impelman, Ph.D.
NEI Postdoctoral Fellow
Department of Physiology
University of Texas Health Science
 Center
San Antonio, Texas

John M. Johnson, Ph.D.
Associate Professor
Department of Physiology
University of Texas Health Science
 Center
San Antonio, Texas

Dike N. Kalu, Ph.D.
Associate Professor
Department of Physiology
University of Texas Health Science
 Center
San Antonio, Texas

Michael D. Kaye, D. M., M.R.C.P.
Associate Professor of Medicine
Department of Medicine
The University of Vermont
Burlington, Vermont

Robert R. Kohn, Ph.D., M.D.
Professor of Pathology
Institute of Pathology
Case Western Reserve University
Cleveland, Ohio

Richard S. Kronenberg, M.D.
Professor of Medicine
Head, Pulmonary Section
Department of Medicine
University of Minnesota Medical
 School
Minneapolis, Minnesota

Edward G. Lakatta, M.D.
Head, Cardiovascular Section
National Institute on Aging
Gerontology Research Center
Assistant Professor of Medicine
Division of Cardiology
John Hopkins Medical Institutions
Baltimore, Maryland

Robert D. Lindeman, M.D.
Professor of Medicine and Associate
 Dean for VA Affairs
University of Louisville School of
 Medicine
Louisville Veterans Administration
 Medical Center
Louisville, Kentucky

Joe L. Mauderly, D.V.M.
Physiologist
Inhalation Toxicology Research
 Institute
Lovelace Biomedical and
 Environmental Research Institute
Albuquerque, New Mexico

Roger J. M. McCarter, Ph.D.
Associate Professor
Department of Physiology
University of Texas Health Science
 Center
San Antonio, Texas

Joseph Meites, Ph.D.
Professor of Physiology
Department of Physiology
Neuroendocrine Research Laboratory
Michigan State University
East Lansing, Michigan

Terry M. Mikiten, Ph.D.
Associate Professor
Department of Physiology
University of Texas Health Science
 Center
San Antonio, Texas

Charles W. Miller, Ph.D.
Associate Professor
Department of Physiology and
 Biophysics
Collaborative Radiological Health
 Laboratory
Colorado State University
Fort Collins, Colorado

Thomas G. Pickering, M.D., D. Phil.
Associate Professor of Medicine
Cardiovascular Center
Cornell University Medical Center —
 New York Hospital
New York, New York

Sanford M. Rosenthal, M.D.,
Scientist Emeritus
National Institute of Arthritis,
 Metabolism, and Digestive Diseases
National Institute of Health
Bethesda, Maryland

Douglas L. Schmucker, Ph.D.
Associate Professor
Department of Anatomy
University of California San Francisco
  and Assistant Chief
Cell Biology and Aging Section
Veterans Administration Hospital
San Francisco, California

James A. Severson, Ph.D.
Postdoctoral Fellow
Laboratory of Neurobiology
Ethel Percy Andrus Gerontology Center
University of Southern California
Los Angeles, California

Richard W. Steger, Ph.D.
Assistant Professor
Department of Obstetrics and
  Gynecology
University of Texas Health Science
  Center
San Antonio, Texas

Antonia Vernadakis, Ph.D.
Professor
Departments of Psychiatry and
  Pharmacology
University of Colorado School of
  Medicine
Denver, Colorado

Rose Koe-Jui Wang, M.A.
Research Associate
Department of Anatomy
University of California San Francisco
Cell Biology and Aging Section
Veterans Administration Hospital
San Francisco, California

Myron L. Weisfeldt, M.D.
Professor of Medicine
Director, Division of Cardiology
The Johns Hopkins Medical
  Institutions
Baltimore, Maryland

Hartmut Wohlrab, Ph.D.
Senior Staff Scientist
Department of Cell Physiology
Boston Biomedical Research Institute
Boston, Massachusetts

Robert D. Woodson, M.D.
Professor
Department of Medicine
University of Wisconsin
Madison, Wisconsin

Byung Pal Yu, Ph.D.
Professor
Department of Physiology
University of Texas Health Science
  Center
San Antonio, Texas

Edmond J. Yunis, M.D.
Professor of Pathology
Harvard Medical School
Chief, Division of Immunogenetics
Sidney Farber Cancer Institute
Boston, Massachusetts

TABLE OF CONTENTS

NERVOUS SYSTEM
Nerve Cells 3
Peripheral Somatosensory Mechanisms 7
Special Senses 13
Central Nervous System Integrative Functions 31
Non-Neuronal Elements of the Central Nervous System 35

NEUROMUSCULAR SYSTEM
Motor Unit 45
Skeletal Muscle 47

BLOOD
Plasma Components 53
Red Blood Cells and Erythropoiesis 55
Leukocytes and Lymphocytes 61
Platelets and Blood Clotting 63

CARDIOVASCULAR SYSTEM
Heart 69
Blood Vessels 83
Hemodynamics 137
Neural and Humoral Regulation of Cardiovascular System 151
Microcirculation and Lymphatics 155
Coronary Circulation 159
Other Special Circulations 161

KIDNEY AND BODY FLUIDS
Kidney 175
Body Fluids 189
Acid-Base Regulation 191
Micturition 193

RESPIRATION
Lung-Thorax System 197
Gas Transport 217
Utilization of O_2 by Tissues 221
Chemical Regulation of Ventilation 225

GASTROINTESTINAL PHYSIOLOGY
Motility 231
Oral Cavity 235
Esophagus 239
Stomach 241
Liver 243
Small Intestine 255
Large Intestine 263
Gastrointestinal Secretion 267
Absorption 273

ENDOCRINE SYSTEM
    Adenohypophysis 289
    Adrenal Cortex 295
    Thyroid 317
    Neurohypophysis 325
    Hypothalamic-Hypophysial System 329
    Reproduction 333
    Adrenal Medullary Hormones and Sympathetic Neurotransmitter 383
    Pancreatic Hormones 391
    Parathyroid Hormone, Calcitonin, and Vitamin D_3 397

BODY COMPOSITION — METABOLIC SYSTEM
    Metabolic Rate 411
    Lean Body Mass 413
    Adipose Tissue 417
    Bone 423
    Connective Tissue 433

EXERCISE
    Survey of Exercise and Aging 443
    Human Data from Seattle Heart Watch and Network Registeries, 1971—1977 ... 457

TEMPERATURE REGULATION
    Terms, Constants, Symbols, and Equations Used in Thermal Physiology 475
    Age-Related Changes in Thermal Physiology 483

INDEX 489

Nervous System

NERVE CELLS

Terry Mikiten

Table 1
NEURAL CELLULAR CHANGES WITH AGING

		Ref.
1.	Gross atrophy of the brain with aging is accompanied by neuronal loss in many, but not all, species.	1—4, 15, 22, 26
2.	Cell loss in the aged human cortex may involve some areas to a greater extent than others, with greatest effects seen in the superior temporal gyrus, precentral gyrus, visual cortex, and postcentral gyrus.	10, 25, 26
3.	In the human cortex, neuron loss is marked in cortical layers 2 and 4.	10
4.	Human ventral cochlear nucleus and facial nerve nucleus do not show significant changes in cell population with aging.	11—13, 15
5.	In human, the inferior olivary nucleus fails to show significant changes in cell number with aging even though the neurons are sites of significant accumulation of lipofuscin.	10, 22, 25
6.	Trochlear and abducens nuclei in humans fail to show changes in cell number with age.	10
7.	Locus ceruleus in human shows a decrease in cell number with aging.	10
8.	Cells in the human cochlear nuclear show a decrease in size with advancing age.	15
9.	Phylogenetically older sections of the cortex appear to show atrophic changes with aging before neocortical areas.	15
10.	Some species (rabbit, mouse, rat, hamster) fail to show obvious atrophic changes of the cerebral cortex with age. They many even show an increase in cortical mass.	15
11.	The brain of the senescent housefly fails to show neuron loss, but does exhibit cellular changes, such as lipofuscin inclusions.	21
12.	Nissl substance may show changes suggestive of a decrease in RNA content with progressive aging.	7—9
13.	In aging humans, there was progressive loss of cortical dendritic spines with ultimate loss of horizontally disposed dendrites. The cytoplasm of the pyramidal cells was choked with abnormal tubular material.	28
14.	Pyramidal cells from the visual cortex of rats 3—36 months of age show progressive decrease in perikaryal size and dendritic diameter, associated with progressive loss of dendritic spines. No loss of dendrites was noted.	29
15.	Lipofuscin accumulations directly relate to age and are prominent in the olivary and dentate nuclei.	1
16.	By age 70, 100% of inferior olivary nucleus cells contain lipofuscin, but this is not accompanied by a change in cell content of the nucleus.	10
17.	It has been suggested that several mutant strains of mice that show both premature aging and lipofuscin accumulation may prove useful in the study of neurocytological correlates of aging.	14
18.	Lipofuscin accumulates in neuroblastoma cells in tissue culture. Pigment formation was enhanced by procedures that reduced cell division (papaverine, prostaglandin E_1), and was reduced by centrophenoxine.	16
19.	Lipofuscin accumulation with age in rhesus monkeys was seen in all cortical laminae of Brodmann's area 3, but the highest correlation between pigment accumulation and age was found in cortical layer IV.	17
20.	Lipofuscin accumulates more rapidly in some brain areas than others during aging.	17, 18
21.	Lipofuscin may be extruded from neurons into CSF or the bloodstream in some animals. It may even appear associated with adjacent glial cells.	18

Table 1 (continued)
NEURAL CELLULAR CHANGES WITH AGING

		Ref.

22.	Intracellular lipofuscin accumulation can be modified by various means. The following agents antagonize accumulation:
	  1. Magnesium arotate
	  2. Kavain
	The following agents promote accumulation:
	  1. Vitamin E deficiency
	  2. Acetanilide
	  3. ACTH
	  4. Perchlorphenazine
	  5. Tetanus toxin
		18

23.	Neurons of aged brains may contain: neurofibrillary tangles, twisted tubules, basophilic granules in vacuoles, lipofuscin, eosinophilic rods (Hirano's bodies), degenerating mitochondria, and virus particles.	1, 23
24.	Extracellular "senile" plaques contain nerve terminals, glia, and amyloid.	1, 23, 26
25.	Psychometric changes associated with aging were positively correlated to the incidence of senile plaques.	2, 23, 26
26.	It has been hypothesized that plaque formation may be related to disruption of axoplasmic flow.	3
27.	Senile plaques are well seen in senile dogs and monkeys but not in rodents.	1
28.	Lipofuscin accumulation is directly related to age and is prominent in the olivary and dentate nuclei.	1
29.	Neurofibrillary changes resembling those occurring in Alzheimer's disease are seen in aged brains, with those having most severe changes being associated with dementia.	1, 23, 26
30.	The neurofibrils of Alzheimer's disease show pairs of helical filaments (PHF). Although possibly related to neurofilaments or neurotubules, they lack the characteristic side projections. Isolation of presumptive PHF protein suggests neurofilament origin.	23, 27
31.	In animals, intracranial injection of aluminum ions induces neurofibrillary degeneration, disrupts axoplasmic transport, and alters a broad variety of electrophysiological and behavioral parameters. Since aluminum was present in greater concentration in brains of patients with Alzheimer's disease, it is suggested that this ion may play a role in its etiology.	24

REFERENCES

1. Terry, R. D. and Wisniewski, H. M., Pathology of the aging nervous system, in Survey Report on the Aging of the Nervous System, Maletta, G. J., Ed., DHEW Publ. No. NIH 74-296, National Institutes of Health, Public Health Service, U.S. Department of Health, Education and Welfare, Washington, D.C., 1975, 125.
2. Roth, M., Thomlinson, B. E., and Blessed, G., Correlation between scores for dementia and counts of "senile plaques" in cerebral gray matter of elderly subjects, *Nature (London)*, 209, 109, 1966.
3. Suzuki, K. and Terry, R. D., Fine structural localization of acid phosphatase in senile plaques in Alzheimer's presence dementia, *Acta Neuropathol.*, 8, 276, 1967.
4. Hoch-Ligetti, C., Effect of aging on the central nervous system, *J. Am. Geriatr. Soc.*, 11, 403, 1963.
5. Buetow, D. E., Cellular content and cellular proliferation changes in the tissues and organs of the aging mammal, in *Cellular and Molecular Renewal in the Mammalian Body*, Cameron, I. L. and Thrasher, J. D., Eds., Academic Press, New York, 1971, 87.
6. Brody, H., Organization of the cerebral cortex. III. A study of aging in the human cerebral cortex, *J. Comp. Neurol.*, 102, 511, 1955.
7. Appel, S. H., Brain macromolecular synthesis and aging, in Survey Report on the Aging of the Nervous System, Maletta, G. J., Ed., DHEW Publ. No. NIH 74-296, National Institutes of Health, Public Health Service, U.S. Department of Health, Education and Welfare, Washington, D.C., 1975, 93.

Table 1 (continued)
NEURAL CELLULAR CHANGES WITH AGING

8. Commermyer, J., Cytological manifestations of aging in rabbit and chinchilla brains, *J. Gerontol.*, 18, 41, 1968.
9. Hyden, H., The neuron, in *The Cell*, Vol. 4, Brachet, J. and Mirsky, A., Eds., Academic Press, New York, 1960, 215.
10. Brody, H., Aging of the vertebrate brain, in *Development and Aging in the Nervous System*, Academic Press, New York, 1973, 121.
11. VanBuskirk, C., Seventh nerve complex, *J. Comp. Neurol.*, 82, 303, 1945.
12. Konigsmark, B. W. and Murphy, E. A., Neuronal populations in the human brain, *Nature (London)*, 228, 1335, 1970.
13. Konigsmark, B. W. and Murphy, E. A., Volume of the ventral cochlear nucleus in man: its relationship to neuronal population and age, *J. Neuropathol. Exp. Neurol.*, 31, 304, 1972.
14. Russell, E. S. and Sprott, R. L., Genetics and the aging nervous system, in Survey Report on the Aging Nervous System, Maletta, G. J., Ed., DHEW Publ. No. NIH 74-296, National Institutes of Health, Public Health Service, U.S. Department of Health, Education and Welfare, Washington, D.C., 1975.
15. Feldmand, M. L. and Peters, A., Morphological changes in the aging brain, in Survey Report on the Aging Nervous System, Maletta, G. J., Ed., DHEW Publ. No. 74-296, National Institutes of Health, Public Health Service, U.S. Department of Health, Education and Welfare, Washington, D.C., 1975.
16. Nandy, K. and Schneider, H., Lipofuscin pigment formation in neuroblastoma cells in culture, in *Neurobiology of Aging*, Terry, R. D. and Gershon, S., Eds., Raven Press, New York, 1976, 245.
17. Brizzee, K. R., Ordy, K. M., Housche, J., and Kaack, B., Quantitative assessment of changes in neuron and glia cell packing density and lipofuscin accumulation with age in the cerebral cortex of a nonhuman primate *(Macaca mulatta)*, in *Neurobiology of Aging*, Terry, R. D. and Gershon, S., Eds., Raven Press, New York, 1976.
18. Brizzee, K. R., Kaack, B., and Klara, P., Lipofuscin: intra- and extraneuronal accumulation and regional distribution, *Adv. Behav. Biol.*, 16, 463, 1975.
19. Brizzee, K. R., Gross morphometric and quantitative histology of the aging, *Adv. Behav. Biol.*, 16, 401, 1975.
20. Brizzee, K. R., Klara, P., and Johnson, J. E., Changes in microanatomy neurocytology and fine structure with aging, *Adv. Behav. Biol.*, 16, 425, 1975.
21. Sohal, R. S. and Sharma, S. P., Age-related changes in the fine structure and number of neurons in the brain of the housefly, *Musca domestica, Exp. Gerontol.*, 7, 243, 1972.
22. Brody, H., Structural changes in the aging nervous system, *Interdiscipl. Top. Gerontol.*, 7, 9, 1970.
23. Wisniewski, H. and Terry, R. D., Neuropathology of the aging brain, in *Neurobiology of Aging*, Terry, R. D. and Gershon, S., Eds., Raven Press, New York, 1976, 265.
24. Crapper, D. R., Functional consequences of neurofibrillary degeneration, in *Neurobiology of Aging*, Terry, R. D. and Gershon, S., Eds., Raven Press, New York, 1976, 405.
25. Brody, H., An examination of cerebral cortex and brainstem aging, in *Neurobiology of Aging*, Terry, R. D. and Gershon, S., Eds., Raven Press, New York, 1976, 177.
26. Tomlinson, B. E. and Henderson, G., Some quantitative cerebral findings in normal and demented old people, in *Neurobiology of Aging*, Terry, R. D. and Gershon, S., Eds., Raven Press, New York, 1976, 183.
27. Iqbal, K., Grundke-Iqbal, I., Wisniewski, H. M., Korthals, J. K., and Terry, R. D., Chemistry of neurofibrous proteins in aging, in *Neurobiology of Aging*, Terry, R. D. and Gershon, S., Eds., Raven Press, New York, 1976, 351.
28. Scheibel, M. E., Lindsay, R. D., Tomiyasu, U., and Scheibel, A. B., Progressive dendritic changes in aging human cortex, *Exp. Neurol.*, 47, 392, 1975.
29. Feldman, M. L., Aging changes in the morphology of cortical dendrites, in *Neurobiology of Aging*, Terry, R. D. and Gershon, S., Eds., Raven Press, New York, 1976, 211.

PERIPHERAL SOMATOSENSORY MECHANISMS

M. A. Biedenbach

REMARKS ON THE INTERPRETATION OF THE TABULAR DATA

Three kinds of structures participate in generating the somatosensory message before it enters the central nervous system. They include: (1) nonneural tissue (skin, muscle, tendon, etc.) through which somatic stimuli must be transmitted to reach the embedded receptors, (2) the somatic receptors which consist of terminals of sensory axons, some free-ending, others surrounded by organized structures, and (3) myelinated and unmyelinated sensory axons and their ganglion cells.

The question of whether the peripheral somatosensory message is altered due to aging could be answered ideally by direct anatomical and functional studies on the three structures in subjects ranging from young through old age. To date, no such definitive aging studies are available, except for isolated anatomical studies on skin thickness,[1,2] axon myelination,[3] and density of Meissner corpuscles, one of the many cutaneous tactile receptors.[1,4]

A series of psychophysical studies, listed in Table 1, provide the only suggestive, but not conclusive, evidence for peripheral age changes in somatosensation. In different human age groups, sensation thresholds were determined for touch, two-point discrimination, vibration, pain, temperature, and kinesthesia. The observed age-dependent changes in somatic sensation threshold cannot, of course, be pinpointed to peripheral mechanisms, but could arise from changes in any of the structures interspersed between stimulus site and the subject's verbal response: (1) nonneural tissue surrounding the receptor, (2) the various somatic receptor categories, (3) peripheral sensory axons, (4) central structures involved in somatosensation, and (5) central structures involved in verbal response decision. Conclusive evidence for peripheral age changes could emerge only from such definitive studies on peripheral somatosensory mechanisms, as have been conducted in experimental animals and to some extent in humans, but without regard to age. In these studies, the functional characteristics of each somatic receptor category were established by applying a range of natural stimuli and recording the responses from single peripheral axons.[5-10]

Findings of the psychophysical studies, in Table 1, are probably best taken as qualitative indicators of age changes in sensation thresholds. The reported magnitudes of age changes vary from minimal to marked, and seem to reflect the fact that factors other than age influence sensation thresholds. It was noted that particularly pain threshold varied with socioeconomic status, ethnic background, sex, test-site on the body surface, etc. In different studies, age groups were only partly, or not at all, matched for these other factors. Furthermore, mean threshold values of unequal age groups are often compared, e.g., in one study, "old" subjects may be comprised of ages 30 to 65, in another of ages 70 to 90.

Two studies[11,12] analyzed sensation threshold data according to signal detection theory. This theory assumes that each psychophysical response consists of two components, a sensory one (representing peripheral and central sensory structures) and a "decisional" one (representing subject attitude, anxiety, response bias, motivation, etc.). From experimental data, two factors can be calculated, d' for the sensory and β for the decisional components. Both factors can contribute to an age-dependent increase in sensation threshold. A decrease in d' indicates reduced sensory capability but does not distinguish peripheral from central sensory mechanisms. An increase in β indicates more caution or reluctance in reporting a sensation. As yet unsettled controversy, however, questions whether the interpretation of signal detection theory is applicable to pain studies.[13,14]

Table 1
AGE-DEPENDENT CHANGES IN PERIPHERAL SOMATOSENSORY MECHANISMS

	Ref.
Nonneural tissue	
Two studies described age changes in the skin that could affect transmission of mechanical, thermal, or noxious chemical stimuli. In subjects over 60 years, the epidermis is thinner, has fewer cell layers, and epidermal cells are irregularly arranged. The ground substance of the dermis is also decreased and collagen bundles are disarranged.	1—2
Within any age group, skin is thicker in exposed than nonexposed areas. Age changes occur in both areas, but are less pronounced in nonexposed skin.	
Peripheral sensory axons	
In the central nervous system, accumulation of lipofuscins and formation of neurofibrillary tangles in neurons are age-dependent phenomena. With lipofuscin accumulation, ribosomal RNA decreases but does not necessarily result in cell degeneration. To what extent function of such neurons is impaired has not been established. Neurofibrillary tangles presumably interfere with neurotubular transport.	15—17
In spinal ganglia, age-dependent accumulation of lipofuscins, but no formation of neurofibrillary tangles, has been reported.	
In myelinated axons, internodal length is normally proportional to axon diameter but over the age of 65 this relationship becomes increasingly obscure. Abnormally short internodal lengths become frequent, evidently due to demyelination and remyelination of axons which are in the process of degeneration and regeneration. Large myelinated axons seem to be more affected than small ones (age range studied 18—80 years).	3
Between ages 30 and 90 years, a small, but continuous, decline in conduction velocity, by 0.4% per year, has been established by transcutaneous recording in human ulnar nerve.	18
A significant reduction in the number of axons in dorsal and ventral roots and in the number of neurons in spinal ganglia was observed in material from human subjects over the age of 80. A similar reduction in number was not demonstrable in animals; however, their equivalent ages were somewhat younger than 80 years.	19, 20
Somatosensory receptors	
Anatomical studies restricted to glabrous human skin were conducted on specimens representing an age range from birth to 93 years. Histologic techniques visualized primarily organized receptor endings, whereas free ending nerve terminals, especially those of small myelinated or unmyelinated axons (thermo- and nociceptors) were not studied. There is a continuous age-related decrease in the number of Meissner corpuscles. For females, the number of corpuscles per square millimeter digital skin were 69 at age 3, 27 at age 32, 15 at age 65, and 4 at age 83. The remaining corpuscles in aged skin often showed morphological changes; the enlarged, internal nerve endings were disarranged, and they separated from the epidermis to which their elastic capsule is normally attached. A similar decrease of Meissner corpuscles occured in skin of toes where their density is less at all ages. Throughout the studied age range, density of Meissner corpuscles was slightly greater in females than in males.	1, 4
A continuous age-related decrease in the number of Pacinian corpuscles in the dermis was also noted. Meissner and Pacinian corpuscles, both rapidly adapting low threshold mechanoreceptors, are probably involved in touch and vibration and Meissner corpuscles in two-point discrimination as well.	
In contrast, the number of Merkel corpuscles in digital skin appeared unchanged over the studied age range (decades 1—8). Merkel corpuscles are slowly adapting low threshold mechanoreceptors.	21
In the oral cavity, the density of organized receptor endings decreased markedly in the tongue and gingiva; less so in hard palate (age range 3—78 years).	1
Touch	
Touch threshold varies over the body surface of a given individual at any age. When comparing equivalent skin areas, touch threshold increases as function of age.	19

Table 1 (continued)
AGE-DEPENDENT CHANGES IN PERIPHERAL SOMATOSENSORY MECHANISMS

	Ref.
Over the tip of the nose and cornea, sensation threshold measured with von Frey hairs increased two- to threefold between 50—75 years.	22
Equivalent threshold increases in both cornea and skin is of interest since the cornea is innervated only by free nerve endings, whereas skin possesses in addition organized nerve endings.	
When measured with short (< 50 msec) air puffs, sensation threshold of the cornea increased little up to age 50, but thereafter increased more rapidly and nearly doubled in old age (age range 11—81 years). The threshold increase became less apparent as air puff duration was increased.	23
On digits and palm, two-point threshold (related to ability to resolve spatial detail) as well as sensation threshold were significantly greater in old (63—78 years) than in young subjects (20—36 years).	24
The number of touch spots per unit area of skin (volar side of hand near wrist) decreased by approximately 50% between second and seventh decade. This study reported, however, a slight decrease in touch threshold with age which was ascribed to marked thinning and easier mechanical deformation of the tested skin area. The anatomically demonstrated loss of Meissner corpuscles may in part be responsible for deficits in number of touch spots and two-point threshold.	25

Vibration

Diagnostic clinical tests employing tuning forks indicate a general decrease in vibratory sensitivity with age, more so in lower than upper extremities.	19
Systematic testing employing vibratory frequencies from 30—600 Hz revealed increased thresholds for all frequencies. The effect was slight by middle age (51 years) and quite apparent in old age (age range tested 18—87 years). The overall threshold increase was small in upper extremities but nearly double in lower extremities. No significant difference in thresholds was noted between males and females.	26
A psychophysical study employing only one frequency (100 Hz) found the vibratory threshold on the index finger nearly constant through the seventh decade, but on the toe it increased markedly (age range 5—75 years).	22

Pain

Several psychophysical studies indicate that the threshold for cutaneous pain increases with age. Heat dolorimetry (application of radiant heat to blackened skin and measured in millicalories revealed a rather constant pain threshold up to age 50. Thereafter, it rose continuously into old age reaching a maximum increase of 25% (age range tested 12—83 years). These age groups were matched for sex, racial origin, and socioeconomic status.	22
Three distinct ethnic groups from the Montreal area (French, Jewish, and Anglo-Saxon) were divided into young (20—30 years) and old (65—97 years) subjects. Heat dolorimetry on the skin of the forehead showed that thresholds for both pain sensation and "wincing" (a reflex response involving muscle contraction near the corner of the eye) increased with age in each of the three groups. Comparison of threshold for pain sensation at a given age showed no significant difference between French and Jewish subjects, but a higher threshold in the Anglo-Saxon subjects, at least in the young group. There were no significant differences between the three groups for the reflex response.	27
Heat dolorimetry on volar skin of forearm, determined separately in males and females, revealed in both sexes progressive age-related increases in pain threshold to a maximum of 12 % (age range 12 to over 70 years). The threshold for women was somewhat lower throughout the age range than for men. Threshold increase was interpreted to arise from both change in receptors and greater heat dispersion in aged skin.	28

Table 1 (continued)
AGE-DEPENDENT CHANGES IN PERIPHERAL SOMATOSENSORY MECHANISMS

	Ref.
In contrast to human studies, a rat population was divided into five age groups (10, 21, 42, 90, and 440 days old) and two kinds of noxious stimuli, mechanical and electrical, were delivered. Electrical or mechanical stimuli were applied to the hindfoot dorsum in order to determine the intensity that would evoke vocalization (squeak threshold). On mechanical stimulation, the forces at squeak threshold were 30, 30, 50, 80, and 300 mm Hg in the five age groups, respectively. For electrical stimulation, squeak thresholds were constant in the four youngest groups and increased only in the oldest age group approximately twofold. (Electrical stimulation has two effects: it produces a more synchoronous sensory input and probably bypasses the receptors, exciting axons directly).	29
Two studies on age-dependent changes in human pain threshold employed signal detection theory for analysis of their data.	
Heat dolorimetry on the volar surface of the forearm revealed higher pain threshold in an older (28—67 years) than in a younger group (18—30 years). Computations, according to signal detection theory indicated it was due to increased β.	11
The dental pain threshold was determined in two age groups, mean ages 22.9 and 67.3 years, age range 20—81 years. Both age groups contained equal numbers of males and females. Increasing intensities of electrical stimuli were delivered to the tooth pulp. (Such stimuli may, however, bypass receptor terminals and stimulate tooth pulp axons directly). In both sexes, the older group required somewhat greater intensities to reach pain threshold than the younger group. According to computations, this was due to increased β. (The elderly would seem to be more cautious before identifying a signal as painful.) In both sexes, an age-dependent decrease in d' did, however, occur when distinguishing different intensity levels of pain. Since d' was not affected during threshold measurements, this change was ascribed to central sensory effects rather than to receptor changes (if receptor thresholds were indeed measured).	12

Temperature

A psychophysical study using heat dolorimetry on the volar surface of the forearm found slightly higher detection thresholds for warm sensation in "old" (30—67 years) than in "young" (18—30 years) subjects. Computations according to signal detection theory showed a small decrease in d', implicating either peripheral or central thermosensory, but not decisional, factors in the age change.	11

Kinesthesia

Functional characteristics of joint and muscle receptors have been studied, but as in the preceding somatic submodalities, little is known about the effect of age on peripheral sensory functions. A psychophysical study determined thresholds for detection of passive joint movement and for identifying the direction of movement in old (50—85 years) and young (17—35 years) subjects. The modal values for movement detection were similar in both groups, although the values in the older group showed greater variability. In identifying movement direction, the error frequency was significantly greater in the old than in the young group.	10, 30

REFERENCES

1. **Winkelmann, R. K.,** Nerve changes in aging skin, *Adv. Biol. Skin,* 6, 51, 1965.
2. **Montagna, W.,** Morphology of the aging skin: the cutaneous appendages, *Adv. Biol. Skin,* 6, 1, 1965.
3. **Lascelles, R. G. and Thomas, P. K.,** Changes due to age in internodal length in the sural nerve in man, *J. Neurol. Neurosurg. Psychiatry,* 29, 40, 1966.

Table 1 (continued)
AGE-DEPENDENT CHANGES IN PERIPHERAL SOMATOSENSORY MECHANISMS

4. **Cauna, N.**, The effects of aging on the receptor organs of the human dermis, *Adv. Biol. Skin,* 6, 63, 1965.
5. **Burgess, P. R. and Perl, E. R.**, Cutaneous mechanoreceptors and nociceptors, in *Handbook of Sensory Physiology,* Vol. 2, Iggo, A., Ed., Springer-Verlag, Heidelberg, 1973, 29.
6. **Darian-Smith, I., Johnson, K. O., and LaMotte, C.**, Peripheral neural determinants in the sensing of changes in skin temperature, in *The Somatosensory System,* Kornhuber, H. H., Ed., Georg Thieme Verlag, Stuttgart, 1975, 23.
7. **Dubner, R., Price, D. D., Beitel, R. E., and Hu, J. W.**, Peripheral neural correlates of behavior in monkey and human related to sensory discriminative aspects of pain, in *Pain in the Trigeminal Region,* Anderson, D. J. and Matthews, B., Eds., Elsevier/North-Holland Biomedical Press, Amsterdam, 1977, 57.
8. **Iggo, A. and Young, D. W.**, Cutaneous thermoreceptors and thermal nociceptors, in *The Somatosensory System,* Kornhuber, H. H., Ed., Thieme Publishing Sciences Group, Stuttgart, 1975, 5.
9. **Kenshalo, D. R.**, The dynamic response of cold units of the cat, in *The Somatosensory System,* Kornhuber, H. H., Ed., Thieme Publishing Sciences Group, Stuttgart, 1975, 38.
10. **Skoglund, S.**, Joint receptors and kinaesthesis, in *Handbook of Sensory Physiology,* Vol. 2, Iggo, A., Ed., Springer-Verlag, Heidelberg, 1973, 111.
11. **Clark, W. C. and Mehl, L.**, Thermal pain: a sensory decision theory analysis of the effect of age and sex on d', various response criteria and 50% pain threshold, *J. Abnorm. Psychol.,* 78, 202, 1971.
12. **Harkins, S. W. and Chapman, R. C.**, Age and sex differences in pain perception, in *Pain in the Trigeminal Region,* Anderson, D. J. and Matthews, B., Eds., Elsevier/North-Holland Biomedical Press, Amsterdam, 1977, 435.
13. **Rollman, G. B.**, Signal detection theory measurement of pain: a review and critique, *Pain,* 3, 187, 1977.
14. **Chapman, C. R.**, Sensory decision theory methods in pain research: a reply to Rollman, *Pain ,* 3, 295, 1977.
15. **Wisniewski, H. M. and Terry, R. D.**, Neuropathology of the aging brain, in *Neurobiology of Aging,* Vol. 3, Terry, R. D. and Gershon, S., Eds., Raven Press, New York, 1976, 265.
16. **Bondareff, W.**, The neural basis of aging, in *Handbook of the Psychology of Aging,* Birren, J. E. and Schaie, K. W., Eds., Van Nostrand Reinhold, New York, 1977, 157.
17. **Terry, R. D.**, Ultrastructure of senile dementia and of experimental analogs, *Adv. Behav. Biol.,* 3, 89, 1972.
18. **Norris, A. H., Shock, N. W., and Wagman, I. H.**, Age changes in the maximum conduction velocity of motor fibers of human ulnar nerves, *J. Appl. Physiol.,* 5, 589, 1952.
19. **Kenshalo, D. R.**, Age changes in touch, vibration, temperature, kinesthesis and pain sensitivity, in *Handbook of the Psychology of Aging,* Birren, J. E. and Schaie, K. W., Eds., Van Nostrand Reinhold, New York, 1977, 562.
20. **Birren, J. E. and Wall, P. D.**, Age changes in conduction velocity, refractory period, number of fibers, connective tissue space and blood vessels in sciatic nerve of rats, *J. Comp. Neurol.,* 104, 1, 1956.
21. **Iggo, A.**, Cutaneous receptors with a high sensitivity to mechanical displacement, in *Touch, Heat and Pain,* DeReuck, A. V. S. and Knight, J., Eds., Little, Brown, Boston, 1966, 237.
22. **Corso, J. F.**, Sensory processes and age effects in normal adults, *J. Gerontol.,* 26, 90, 1971.
23. **Jalavisto, E., Orma, E., and Tawast, M.**, Ageing and relation between stimulus intensity and duration in corneal sensibility, *Acta Physiol. Scand.,* 23, 224, 1951.
24. **Axelrod, S. and Cohen, L. D.**, Senescence and embedded-figure performance in vision and touch, *Percept. Psychophys.,* 12, 283, 1961.
25. **Rong, H.**, Altersveränderungen des Berührungssinnes, *Acta Physiol. Scand.,* 6, 343, 1943.
26. **Perret, E. and Regli, F.**, Age and the perceptual threshold for vibratory stimuli, *Eur.Neurol.,* 4, 65, 1970.
27. **Sherman, E. D. and Robillard, E.**, Sensitivity of pain in the aged, *Can. Med. Assoc. J.,* 83, 944, 1960.
28. **Procacci, P., Bozza, G., Buzzelli, G., and Della Corte, M.**, The cutaneous pricking pain threshold in old age, *Gerontol. Clin.,* 12, 213, 1970.
29. **Nicák, A.**, Changes of sensitivity to pain in relation to postnatal development in rats, *Exp. Gerontol.,* 6, 111, 1971.
30. **Laidlaw, R. W. and Hamilton, M. A.**, A study of thresholds in appreciation of passive movements among normal control subjects, *Bull. Neurol. Inst. N.Y.,* 6, 268, 1937.

SPECIAL SENSES

Barbara A. Brooks and Dianne Impelman

Table 1
AGE-RELATED CHANGES IN GUSTATION

	Ref.
I. Physiological Changes in the Gustatory System	
There is a decrease in the number of taste buds in old age compared to young adults.	1—3,5,9,12, 16,19
The gustatory papillae are fully developed at puberty and begin to atrophy in women at age 40—45, in men between ages 50 and 60. The mineral content of the papillae and calices increases with age after puberty.	1
Young adults possess approximately 250 taste buds in each circumvallate papilla. "A striking decline" of taste buds was noted in individuals aged 74—84 (less than 100 buds per papilla).	2
The number of circumvallate papillae delines slightly with age, with large individual differences.	16
There is a reduction of taste buds in the foliate papillae of elderly Japanese.	19
The gradual reduction in number of taste buds which accompanies age may be associated with inhibition of alkaline phosphatase in the epithelium overlying the taste buds.	9
General changes may be encountered in the tongue which include a differential hypertrophy of fungiform, foliate, and circumvallate papillae in older patients. There is decreased salivary secretion with reduced pytalin, mucous gland secretion thickens and has a high mucin content, salivary pH changes towards slight alkalinity, and muscle tone is decreased.	3,5
II. Tests of Gustatory Sensitivity	
Some decrement of taste sensitivity is found in older age groups, compared to young adults.	4,6—8,10,11, 13—15,17, 20
Thresholds for all four primary taste qualities (salty, sweet, bitter, sour) increase in older age groups.	8,14
Threshold increases in the elderly for the primary tastes may be so slight as to be insignificant.	6,7
Thresholds for sucrose are three times higher for the age group 52—85 years, as compared to 15—19 year olds.	20
No sex differences are found in sensitivity for the primary taste qualities in older people.	8
Thresholds for sucrose increase in older (60—93 years) men and women, but salt sensitivity declines only in men.	4
Sensitivity to phenylthiourea declines with age.	13,17
Women are slightly more sensitive than men to phenylthiocarbamide.	10
After the ages of 16—20, women are more sensitive than men to 6-n-propylthiouracil, quinine, and hydrochloric acid.	11,17
Elderly males show a higher error than elderly females in taste identification for the primary qualities.	7
Thresholds for the "taste" of a mild galvanic current increase with age and are not correlated with smoking habits.	15
No significant increases with age are found in thresholds for the "taste" of an electrical current applied to the tongue.	18

Table 1 (continued)
AGE-RELATED CHANGES IN GUSTATION

REFERENCES

1. **Allara, E.,** Investigations on the human taste organ. I. The structure of taste papillae at various ages, *Arch. Ital. Anat. Embriol.,* 42, 506, 1939.
2. **Arey, L. B., Tremaine, M. J., and Monzingo, F. L.,** The numerical and topographical relations of taste buds to human circumvallate papillae throughout the life span, *Anat. Rec.,* 64(1), Suppl. 1, 1936.
3. **Balogh, K. and Lelkes, K.,** The tongue in old age, *Gerontol. Clin.,* 3, 38, 1961.
4. **Bourliére, F., Cendron, H., and Rapaport, A.,** Modification avec l'age des senils gustatifs de perception et de reconnaissance aux saveurs salée et sucrée chez l'homme, *Gerontologia,* 2, 104, 1958.
5. **Burket, L. W.,** Oral pediatrics and geriodontics, in *Oral Medicine, Diagnosis and Treatment,* 2nd ed., Burket, L. W., et al., Editors, Lippincott, Philadelphia, 1952, 429.
6. **Byrd, E. and Gertman, S.,** Taste sensitivity in aging persons, *Geriatrics,* 14, 381, 1959.
7. **Cohen, T. and Gitman, L.,** Oral complaints and taste perception in the aged, *J. Gerontol.,* 14, 294, 1959.
8. **Cooper, R. M., Bilash, I., and Zubek, J. P.,** The effect of age on taste sensitivity, *J. Gerontol.,* 14, 56, 1959.
9. **El-Baradi, A. and Bourne, G. H.,** Theory of taste and odors, *Science,* 113, 660, 1951.
10. **Falconer, D. S.,** Sensory thresholds for solutions of phenylthiocarbamide, *Ann. Eugen.,* 13, 211, 1947.
11. **Glanville, E. V., Kaplan, A. R., and Fischer, R.,** Age, sex and taste sensitivity, *J. Gerontol.,* 19, 474, 1964.
12. **Harris, W.,** Fifth and seventh cranial nerves in relation to the nervous mechanism of taste sensitivity: a new approach, *Br. J. Med.,* 1, 831, 1952.
13. **Harris, H. and Kalmus, H.,** The measurement of taste sensitivity to phenylthiourea, *Ann. Eugen.,* 19, 24, 1949.
14. **Hermel, J., Schonwetter, S., and Samueloff, S.,** Taste sensation and age in man, *J. Oral Med.,* 25, 39, 1970.
15. **Hughes, G.,** Changes in taste sensitivity with advancing age, *Gerontol. Clin.,* 11, 224, 1969.
16. **Jurisch, A.,** Studien über die Papillae Vallatae beim Menschen, *Z. Gesamte Anat.,* 66, 1, 1922.
17. **Kalmus, H. and Trotter, W. R.,** Direct assessment of the effect of age on P.T.C. sensitivity, *Ann. Hum. Genet.,* 26, 145, 1962.
18. **Kranz, D., Berndt, H., and Wagner, H.,** Studies on age-dependent changes of the taste threshold, *Arch. Klin. Exp. Ohren-Nasen-Kehlkopfheilkd.,* 192, 258, 1968.
19. **Mochizuki, Y.,** Papilla foliata of Japanese, *Folia Anal. Jpn.,* 18, 337, 1939.
20. **Richter, C. P. and Campbell, K. H.,** Sucrose taste threshold of rats and humans, *Am. J. Physiol.,* 128, 291, 1940.

Table 2
MEAN TASTE THRESHOLDS
ACCORDING TO AGE AND SEX

Threshold (solution number)[a]

Age group (years)	N	Males Mean	σ_d	N	Females Mean	σ_d
6-n-Propylthiouracil						
1—5	2	8.50		3	10.67	
6—10	37	9.62	2.27	46	9.52	2.47
11—15	34	9.59	2.23	50	9.66	2.24
16—20	78	9.28	2.25	98	9.37	2.62
21—25	72	9.43	2.51	45	9.42	2.37
26—30	22	9.45	2.40	21	9.05	2.58
31—35	23	9.74	2.53	21	10.38	2.04
36—40	13	10.00	2.86	21	9.52	2.56
41—45	20	10.45	2.33	30	9.63	2.77
46—50	3	13.00		18	10.28	1.93
51—55	4	11.00		15	9.73	2.96
	308			368		
Quinine						
1—5	2	5.00		3	5.67	
6—10	37	5.38	1.72	46	5.48	1.87
11—15	34	4.85	2.28	50	5.04	1.56
16—20	78	5.05	1.73	98	4.89	1.91
21—25	72	5.18	1.69	45	5.29	1.41
26—30	22	5.23	1.82	21	5.76	2.26
31—35	23	5.83	1.72	21	5.86	1.80
36—40	13	7.38	2.36	21	5.91	1.69
41—45	20	6.45	2.44	30	5.80	1.61
46—50	3	6.67		18	6.67	1.71
51—55	4	7.00		15	6.13	2.84
	308			368		
Hydrochloric Acid						
1—5	3	11.33		2	10.50	
6—10	28	10.54	1.43	37	9.73	1.25
11—15	24	10.46	1.02	32	9.72	1.02
16—20	26	10.19	1.24	21	9.86	1.59
21—25	34	10.18	2.45	9	9.89	1.45
26—30	8	10.38	1.69	6	9.67	2.00
31—35	12	11.08	1.17	11	10.00	0.78
36—40	9	12.11	1.06	9	10.67	1.15
41—45	14	11.43	1.61	15	10.73	1.34
46—50	3	11.33		7	10.43	1.27
51—55	2	14.00		6	9.67	1.37
	163			155		

Table 2 (continued)
MEAN TASTE THRESHOLDS ACCORDING TO AGE AND SEX

^a Solutions were ranked from lowest to highest molar concentration in 15 steps, in the following order:

Solution number	Molarity	Solution number	Molarity
1	7.32×10^{-7}	9	1.88×10^{-4}
2	1.46×10^{-6}	10	3.75×10^{-4}
3	2.93×10^{-6}	11	7.50×10^{-4}
4	5.86×10^{-6}	12	1.50×10^{-3}
5	1.17×10^{-5}	13	3.00×10^{-3}
6	2.34×10^{-5}	14	6.00×10^{-3}
7	4.69×10^{-5}	15	6.00×10^{-2}
8	9.38×10^{-5}		

From Glanville, E. V., Kaplan, A. R., and Fischer, R., *J. Gerontol.*, 19, 474, 1964. With permission.

Table 3
AGE-RELATED CHANGES IN OLFACTION

	Ref.
I. Physiological Changes in the Olfactory System	
Anatomical studies of elderly cadavers reveal atrophy of the olfactory glomeruli and nerves, at least partially due to loss of sensory cells in the olfactory mucosa.	5,13
Anatomical degeneration is loosely but positively correlated with age and may be partly due to long-term inhalation of toxic agents such as tobacco smoke and other pollutants which affect the peripheral analyzer. Some elderly human olfactory bulbs show no atrophy.	5,7,13
Decline in olfactory sensitivity with age may be partly the result of a general degeneration of brain cells and independent of peripheral change in the olfactory apparatus.	3
Rats show structural degeneration of the olfactory system after 1 year of age.	14
The olfactory epithelium is capable of regeneration in healthy animals. This process may decline with age.	8,15
II. Tests of Olfactory Sensititivity	
There is a general decline of olfactory sensitivity with age.	1,3,9,11, 12,16
A London sample of people over 65 showed increased thresholds to domestic gas. Some of these subjects, however, had illnesses which may have biased the results.	2
There is a marked decrease in sensitivity to camphor with age.	16
There is no significant change in ability to smell camphor with age.	7
There is an increase in olfactory threshold for n-butanol and iso-amyl acetate with age, the effect reaching an asymptote at age 70. Large individual differences are noted.	4
The threshold for coffee and citral is highest in a sample population from 70—90 years of age.	6
Subjects over 60 are more sensitive than younger persons to the odor of n-propanol.	10
Women are markedly more sensitive than men to camphor odors at all ages.	16
Elderly women are not significantly more sensitive to camphor than elderly men.	7
Elderly women are more sensitive to domestic gas odors than men.	2

Table 3 (continued)
AGE-RELATED CHANGES IN OLFACTION

REFERENCES

1. Bartalena, G. and Bocci, C., L'acutezza e la fatica olfactoria in relazoine alla'etta anagrafica e biologica, *Clin. Otorinolaringol.*, 16, 409, 1964.
2. Chalke, H. D., Dewhurst, J. R., and Ward, C. W., Loss of sense of smell in old people, *Public Health*, 72(6), 223, 1958.
3. Hinchcliffe, R., Aging and sensory threshold, *J. Gerontol.*, 17, 45, 1962.
4. Kimbrell, G. McA. and Furchgott, E., The effect of aging on olfactory threshold, *J. Gerontol.*, 18, 364, 1963.
5. Liss, L. and Gomez, F., The nature of senile changes of the human olfactory bulb and tract, *AMA Arch. Otolaryngol.*, 67, 167, 1958.
6. Megighian, D., Variazioni della soglia olfattiva nelleta senile, *Minerva Otorinolaringol.*, 8(9), 331, 1958.
7. Mesolella, V., L'olfatto nelle diverse età, *Arch. Ital. Otol. Rinol. Laringol.*, 46, 43, 1934.
8. Moulton, D. G., Cell renewal in the olfactory epithelium of the mouse, *Ann. N.Y. Acad. Sci.*, 237, 52, 1974.
9. Rous, J., Effect of age on the functional state of the olfactory analyser, *Cesk. Otolaryngol.*, 18, 248, 1969.
10. Rovee, C. K., Cohen, R. Y., and Shlapack, W., Life span stability in olfactory sensitivity, *Dev. Psychol.*, 11, 311, 1975.
11. Schiffman, S. S., Moss, J., and Erickson, R. P., Thresholds of food odors in the elderly, *Exp. Aging Res.*, 2(5), 389, 1976.
12. Shiokawa, H., The clinical studies of the olfactory test using standard odorous substances. The change of olfactory acuity due to ageing (Author's Transl.), *J. Otolaryngol.*, 78(12), 1258, 1975.
13. Smith, C. G., Age incidence of atrophy of olfactory nerves in man, *J. Comp. Neurol.*, 77, 589, 1942.
14. Smith, C. G., The change in volume of the olfactory and accessory olfactory bulbs of the albino rat during postnatal life, *J. Comp. Neurol.*, 61, 477, 1935.
15. Takagi, S. F., Degeneration and regeneration of the olfactory epithelium, in *Handbook of Sensory Physiology*, Vol. 4, Beidler, L. M., Ed., Springer-Verlag, New York, 1971, 75.
16. Vaschicle, N., L'etat de la sensibilite olfactive dans la vielillesse, *Bull. Laryngol.*, 7, 323, 1904.

Table 4
MEAN OLFACTORY THRESHOLDS FOR YOUNG AND ELDERLY SUBJECTS FOR SEVERAL FOODS[a]

	Cherry	Grape	Lemon	Orange	Tomato
Young	1.3	1.0	1.0	1.0	1.0
Elderly	4.3	3.4	4.9	3.5	2.9

	Bacon	Cheddar cheese	Chocolate	Mushroom
Young	1.0	1.5	1.0	1.0
Elderly	3.3	2.9	4.7	4.3

[a] Stimuli were presented through an olfactometer in six different concentrations on a scale of 1 to 6. Each successive unit of the scale represented a 3-times increase in concentration.

From Schiffman, S. S., Moss, J., and Erickson, R. P., *Exp. Aging Res.*, 2(5), 389, 1976. With permission of the authors and EAR, Inc. (now Beech Hill Enterprises Inc., Mt. Desert, Maine).

Table 5
AGE RELATED CHANGES IN VISUAL FUNCTION

I. Structural and Functional Characteristics of the Aging Eye[a]

	Ref.
External eye apparatus	
The drooping of the upper eyelid that occurs with age (senile ptosis) is due to loss of tone in the levator muscle.	81
The loss of orbital fat and decrease in elasticity and tone of the orbital tissue contribute to the development of lower lid inversion with age (senile entropion).	81
The conjunctiva assumes a yellow tinge with age as a result of subcutaneous fat deposits and loses its elasticity with progressive keratinization.	7
Tearing appears to increase with age because the decrease in lacrimal reabsorption exceeds the decrease in lacrimal secretions.	91
The extent of upper gaze changes from 40° in 10 year olds to 20° at 70 years of age and is correlated with disuse and atrophy of the extraocular muscles with age.	17
Cornea	
There is an increase in corneal thickness and a shift of maximal corneal curvature from the horizontal plane to the vertical plane with age.	56,85,93
The astigmatism that occurs with aging changes in corneal curvature results in a greater refraction in the horizontal than in the vertical meridian.	45
The increase in cornea guttata (deposits on the corneal endothelium) with age is associated with increased light scatter in the aging eye.	2
A decrease in the metabolically controlled water content and possibly collagen spacings in the corneal stroma may contribute to the decrease in corneal transparency with age.	77
Critical touch threshold for the cornea increases with age in agreement with early measures of decreased corneal sensitivity.	43,61
The development of arcus senilis, a dense white ring at the scleral iris border which is associated with lipid infiltration, may have different etiologies in young blacks and older whites.	13,55
Sclera	
The sclera becomes yellow in areas of local fat deposition and increases in rigidity with age.	91

Table 5 (continued)
AGE-RELATED CHANGES IN VISUAL FUNCTION

I. Structural and Functional Characteristics of the Aging Eye*

	Ref.
Aqueous humor	
The depth of the anterior chamber declines from about 3.6 to 3.1 mm between the ages of 25 and 86.	68
The ciliary epithelium covering the ciliary processes which extend into the posterior chamber secrete the aqueous humor. There is an increase in the length and volume of the processes and a hyperplasia of the ciliary epithelium with age.	91
Aqueous flow as measured by fluorescein clearance from the eye decreases with age.	39
Both an increase and no change in the outflow resistance of the aqueous humor have been reported.	4,9
Reports of a slight increase and of no change in intraocular pressure with age have also been made.	52—54,95
Changes in eye rigidity with age may obscure the real values for intraocular pressure and aqueous resistance.	83
Glaucoma, a condition of increased intraocular pressure as the result of blockage of aqueous flow, is *not* intrinsic to aging.	2
Iris	
The decrease in pupillary aperture with age, senile miosis, is correlated with a decrease in contraction rate and tension of the dilator muscle with age relative to the sphincter muscle.	60,72
The pupillary latency contraction time in response to light stimulation increases with age.	28
Structural changes associated with aging in the iris include depigmentation, a thinning of the stroma, and an increase in its rigidity.	91
Ciliary muscle	
Hypertrophy of the ciliary muscle parallels the decrease in lens elasticity and is followed by atrophy in later years at a time when the lens is relatively immobile. There is also an increase in interstitial connective tissue between muscle fibers which later atrophies with the muscle.	91
The amplitude of electrical potentials recorded from the ciliary muscle during accommodation decreases with age.	40
Choroid	
Senile alterations in the choroid include hyperplasic changes in Bruch's membrane and the pigment epithelium (functional choroid) localized at the ora serrata. There is also a thickening and yellowing of the membrane. Vessel walls in the choriocapillaries and throughout the vascular layer appear to become more rigid.	91
Lens	
The primary factors in accounting for refractive loss in presbyopia are the decrease in the elastic modulus of the lens capsule, increase in elastic modulus of the lens matrix, and the flattening of the lens with age.	29—32
The increase in light scatter of the lens with age is correlated with an increase in the fraction of insoluble protein.	86,101
Accumulation of macromolecules, possible precursors of insoluble protein, has recently been demonstrated in vivo and theoretically could account for the increase in lens opacification with age.	6,78
Progressive yellowing of the lens is associated with increased light scatter or absorption of shorter wavelengths in the aged lens.	63,70,71
Age-dependent fluorogens which contribute to the yellow color of the lens have been isolated from the insoluble protein fraction.	49,79,82
Increase in at least one fluorogen is correlated with decrease in the high levels of lens glutathione with age.	46,51
Decreases in glycolysis and in the concentration of high energy phosphates are other notable metabolic aging effects.	36,75
Differences in protein metabolism have been found in the normal aging and senile cataractous lenses.	16

Table 5 (continued)
AGE-RELATED CHANGES IN VISUAL FUNCTION

I. Structural and Functional Characteristics of the Aging Eye[a]

	Ref.
Vitreous body	
There is a progressive liquefaction of the vitreous in the human eye, the onset of which coincides with the appearance of aging effects on the lens.	3
The appearance of nonpathological opacities in the retina with age reduces the amount of light reaching the retina.	91
Retina	
The structural organization of receptor elements in the peripheral retina is disrupted with age and is sometimes accompanied by localized retinal detachment.	65
Central visual pathways	
There is a positive correlation between increasing age and decreasing fiber number in the optic nerve.	12
There is a significant decrease in cell count in area striata accompanied by a 20% loss in layer 3.	41,74

II. Tests of Visual Sensitivity[b]

Absolute luminance thresholds are the same in young and old subjects when light limiting factors of the aged eye are compensated.	93
Decreases in static and dynamic acuity with age are partially compensated for by increases in retinal illumination.	14,67
Differential sensitivity, i.e., just noticeable differences of light seen against backgrounds of varying intensities, may not be solely due to increased light scatter in the aging lens.	1
Glare sensitivity (decreased visual acuity in bright light) increases rapidly after 40 and reaches a maximum value after 65 years of age. The primary reason for increase in glare sensitivity is thought to be the increase in light scatter.	14,100,101
Stereopsis thresholds for depth perception requiring accommodation and convergence have been reported to increase between 40 and 50 years of age. Others report no change in threshold through the mid 40s.	5,44,42
Spectral discrimination scores decrease by 25% in the 60s and by 50% in the 80s. Color vision loss with age may differ for each eye.	23,38
Hue discrimination and mixed color matching tests show that, in general, the eye becomes less sensitive to blue wavelengths in the early 40s and less sensitive to red wavelengths after 60.	38,64,84
Aging effects on color vision have been attributed to the decrease in the spectral transmission of the ocular media with age.	69,70
There is a decrease in chromatic aberration with age which may be a consequence of an increase in the index of refraction of the vitreous humor.	62
The visual field begins to decrease in size and sensitivity in the early 40s and reaches a minimum after 60 years of age. Wolf has correlated the early visual field shrinkage with age changes in the eye and the later changes with a decrease in retinal oxygen metabolism.	15,99
Dark adaptation thresholds increase with age. The similarity of dark adaptation aging effects to anoxic effects in young subjects is considered as evidence that the supply of oxygen, particularly to rod cells, is decreased with age.	24,25,58,59
Age-correlated changes in the rate of dark adaptation are ambiguous.	22
Senile miosis and yellowing of the lens also contribute to dark adaptation effects in the aged.	76,92
The frequency at which square pulses of light are perceived as a steady luminance is called the critical flicker frequency (CFF). Age differences in CFF measured at different retinal loci are similar to anoxic effects. The age differences become more pronounced as the light-dark flicker fraction is reduced; however, threshold differences between young and old subjects were only reduced by half when their pupils were dilated.	57,94,102

Table 5 (continued)
AGE-RELATED CHANGES IN VISUAL FUNCTION

III. Perceptual Changes[c]

	Ref.
Increased information extraction time, higher sensitivity to unconventional stimulus contexts, and higher judgment criteria in decision making have generally been associated with aging changes in perception.	27,33,34
A deterioration in the performance of older subjects in target identification is seen as the number or rate of stimuli increased or when stimulus duration decreases.	66,80
The increase in response times for form identification by older subjects is associated with a decrease in the decay of the reciprocal time-intensity relation for the stimulus which could reflect a slower central scanning process.	27
Visual persistence of stored information is about 40 msec longer in younger adults than for older ones.	89
Visual masking studies show that the time over which the mask is effective increases with age.	47,97
The age-related increase in visual mask potency is present but decreased under dichoptic conditions. It is concluded that aging effects on both central and peripheral processes increase perceptual latency in the aged.	88
The longer response times of older subjects in the Stroop color word test and its variants is correlated with a higher sensitivity to disruptive contexts.	8,21,73
An increased susceptibility of the aged to the perceptual components of the Müller-Lyer geometrical illusion has been consistently shown in all studies done.	19,20,26,90
Increased contextual effects have also been shown in verticality judgements of older subjects.	18,20
Aging effects on perceptual closure judgements were strongest for familiar stimuli. Older subjects required more information to make a decision.	87
Results of perceptual flexibility studies in the aged depend on the stimulus series used. Decision times are increased with uncertainty.	10,48

[a] The standard optical demarcation between young and old age is the appearance of presbyopia, a loss in the accommodative power of the eye, which occurs between the ages of 40 and 50. Underlying changes in eye structure affect its decrease in refractive power and changes in the level of retinal illumination. A second decline in visual function is marked by a decrease in visual field size beginning in the early 60s. These changes appear to be limited to the retina and may be affected by its oxygen supply.[99] The combination of senile changes affecting the quantity and distribution of light in the eye and affecting central visual function are realized in the slowing of perceptual processes of the aged.

[b] The effects of senile miosis, presbyopia, and yellowing of the ocular media have generally been considered adequate to account for the decrease in light sensitivity and visual contrast with age. However, the results of visual field, critical flicker frequency, and dark adaptation studies suggest the view that "age strikes light not sight"[93] should be modified.

[c] Aging effects on the perceptual aspects of information processing are consistent with the hypothesis that the formation of a perception takes a longer time in older persons.[27] Non-neural (eye) or peripheral changes are generally not believed to be the primary factors involved in the aging of the perceptual process,[11,50] neural and central factors are. A review of the theories of central changes postulated to account for perceptual slowing with age has been done by Shock.[76]

Table 5 (continued)
AGE-RELATED CHANGES IN VISUAL FUNCTION

REFERENCES

1. Allen, M. J. and Vos, J. J., Ocular scattered light and visual performance as a function of age, *Am. J. Optom.*, 44, 717, 1967.
2. Anderson, B. and Palmore, E., Longitudinal evaluation of ocular function, in *Normal Aging: Reports from Longitudinal Study, 1970-1973*, Palmore, E., Ed., Duke University Press, Durham, N.C., 1974, 24.
3. Balazs, E. A., Intracellular matrix of connective tissue, in *Handbook of the Biology of Aging*, Finch, C. and Hayflick L., Eds., Van Nostrand Reinhold, New York, 1977, 227.
4. Becker, B. and Ley, A. P., Epinephrine and acetazolamide in the therapy of chronic glaucoma, *Am. J. Ophthalmol.*, 45, 639, 1958.
5. Bell, B., Wolf, E., and Bernholz, C. D., Depth perception as a function of age, *Aging Hum. Dev.*, 3(1), 77, 1972.
6. Benedek, G. B., Theory of transparency of the eye, *Appl. Phys.*, 10, 459, 1971.
7. Berens, C., Aging process in eye and adnexa, *Arch. Ophthalmol.*, 29, 171, 1943.
8. Bettner, L. G., Jarvik, L. F., and Blum, J. E., Stroop color word test, nonpsychotic brain syndrome and chromosome loss in aged twins, *J. Gerontol.*, 26, 458, 1971.
9. Boles-Carenini, B. and Cambiaggi, A., Are aqueous humour dynamics influenced by ageing? *Am. J. Ophthalmol.*, 44, 395, 1957.
10. Botwinick, J., A research note on the problem of perceptual modification in relation to age, *J. Gerontol.*, 17, 190, 1962.
11. Botwinick, J., Ed., *Aging and Behavior*, Springer-Verlag, New York, 1973.
12. Bruesch, S. R. and Arey, L. B., The number of myelinated and unmyelinated fibers in the optic nerves of vertebrates, *J. Comp. Neurol.*, 77, 631, 1942.
13. Burch, P. R. J., Murray, J. J., and Jackson, D., The age prevalence of arcus senilis, greying of hair, and baldness: etiological considerations, *J. Gerontol.*, 26, 364, 1971.
14. Burg, A., Light sensitivity as related to age and sex, *Percept. Mot. Skills*, 24, 1279, 1967.
15. Burg, A., Lateral visual field as related to age and sex, *J. Appl. Psychol.*, 52, 10, 1968.
16. Charlton, J. M. and van Heyningen, R., An investigation into the loss of proteins of low molecular size from the lens in senile cataract, *Exp. Eye Res.*, 7, 47, 1968.
17. Chamberlain, W., Restriction in upward gaze with advancing age, *Trans. Am. Opthalmol. Soc.*, 68, 235, 1970.
18. Comalli, P. E., Jr., Wapner, S., and Werner, H., Perception of verticality in middle and old age, *J. Psychol.*, 47, 259, 1959.
19. Comalli, P. E., Jr., Cognitive functioning in 80-90 year-old men, *J. Gerontol.*, 20, 14, 1965.
20. Comalli, P. E., Jr., Krus, M., and Wapner, S., Cognitive functioning in two groups of aged: one institutionalized, the other living in the community, *J. Gerontol.*, 20, 9, 1965.
21. Comalli, P. E., Jr., Wapner, S., and Werner, H., Interference effects of Stroop-color word test in childhood, adulthood and aging, *J. Genet. Psychol.*, 100, 47, 1962.
22. Corso, J. F., Sensory processes and age effects in normal adults, *J. Gerontol.*, 26, 90, 1971.
23. Dalderup, L. M. and Fredericks, M. L. C., Colour sensitivity in old age, *J. Am. Geriatr. Soc.*, 17, 388, 1969.
24. Domey, R. G., McFarland, R. A., and Chadwick, E., Dark adaptation as a function of age and time. II. A derivation, *J. Gerontol.*, 15, 267, 1960.
25. Domey, R. G., McFarland, R. A., and Chadwick, E., Threshold and rate of dark adaptation as functions of age and time, *Hum. Factors*, 2, 109, 1960.
26. Eisner, D. A. and Schaie, K. W., Age change in response to visual illusions from middle to old age, *J. Gerontol.*, 26, 146, 1971.
27. Ericksen, C. W., Hamlin, R. M., and Breitmeyer, R. G., Temporal factors in visual perception as related to aging, *Percept. Psychophys.*, 7, 354, 1970.
28. Feinberg, B. and Podolac, E., Latency of pupillary reflex to light and its relationship to aging, in *Behavior, Aging and the Nervous System*, Welford, A. T. and Birren, J. E., Eds., Charles C Thomas, Springfield, Ill., 1965, 326.
29. Fisher, R. F., Elastic constants of human lens capsule, *J. Physiol. (London)*, 201, 1, 1969.
30. Fisher, R. F., The significance of the shape of the lens and capsular energy in accommodation, *J. Physiol. (London)*, 201, 21, 1969.
31. Fisher, R. F., The elastic constants of the human lens, *J. Physiol. (London)*, 212, 147, 1971.
32. Fisher, R. F., Presbyopia and changes with age in the human crystalline lens, *J. Physiol. (London)*, 228, 765, 1973.
33. Fozard, J. L. and Thomas, J. C., Psychology of aging: basic findings and their psychiatric applications, in *Modern Perspectives in the Psychiatry of Old Age*, Howells, J. G., Ed., Brunner-Mazel, New York, 1975, 107.

Table 5 (continued)
AGE-RELATED CHANGES IN VISUAL FUNCTION

34. Fozard, J. L., Wolf, E., Bell, B., McFarland, R. A., and Podolsky, S., Visual perception and communication, in *Handbook of Psychology of Aging*, Birren, J. E. and Schaie, K. W., Eds., Van Nostrand Reinhold, New York, 1977, 497.
35. Frankhauser, F. and Schmidt, T., Die Untersuchung der Funktionen der dunkcladaptierten Auges mit dem Adoptometer Goldman-Weekers, *Opthalmologica*, 133, 264, 1957.
36. Frohman, C. E. and Kinsey, V. E., Studies on the crystalline lens. I. Distribution of various phosphate containing compounds and its significance with respect to energetics, *AMA Arch. Ophthal.*, 48, 12, 1952.
37. Gajo, F. D., Visual Illusions, Doctoral dissertation, Washington University, St. Louis, Mo., 1966.
38. Gilbert, J. G., Age changes color matching, *J. Gerontol.*, 12, 210, 1957.
39. Goldmann, H., Abflussdruck, minutenvolumen und Widerstand der Kammerwasserstrümung das Menschen, *Doc. Ophthalmol.*, 5-6, 278, 1951.
40. Hagiawara, H. and Ishikawa, S., The action potential of the ciliary muscle, *Ophthalmologica*, 144, 323, 1962.
41. Hanley, T., "Neuronal fall-out" in aging brain: a critical review of the quantitative data, *Age and Ageing*, 3, 133, 1974.
42. Hofstetter, H. W. and Bertsch, J. D., Does stereopsis change with age? *Am. J. Optom. Physiol. Opt.*, 53(10), 664, 1976.
43. Jalavisto, E., Orma, E., and Tawast, M., Aging and relationship between stimulus intensity and duration in corneal sensitivity, *Acta Physiol. Scand.*, 23, 224, 1951.
44. Jani, S. N., The age factor in stereopsis screening, *Am. J. Optom.*, 43, 653, 1966.
45. Kapoor, P. M., Total astigmatism and its components: its changes with age, *Indian J. Med. Res.*, 53, 10, 1965.
46. Kleifeld, O. and Hockwin, O., Über den Glutathionegehalt der Linse, *Ber. Dtsch. Ophthalmol. Gesamte*, 59, 188, 1956.
47. Kline, D. W. and Szafrun, J., Age differences in backward monoptic visual noise making, *J. Gerontol.*, 30, 307, 1957.
48. Korchin, S. J. and Basowitz, H., The judgement of ambiguous stimuli as an index of cognitive functioning in aging, *J. Pers.*, 25, 81, 1956.
49. Lerman, S., Borkman, R., and Saker, E., Induction acceleration and prevention of an aging parameter in the ocular lens, *Ophthalmic Res.*, 8, 213, 1976.
50. Layton, B., Perceptual noise and aging, *Psychol. Bull.*, 82, 875, 1975.
51. Lerman, S., Kuck, J. F., Borkman, R., and Emalina, S., Acceleration of an aging parameter (fluorogen) in the ocular lens, *Ann. Ophthalmol.*, 8 (5), 558, 1976.
52. Levene, B. Z., Tonometry and tonography in a group health population, *Arch. Ophthalmol.*, 66, 42, 1961.
53. Leydhecker, W., Akiyama, K., and Neumann, H. G., Der itraokulare Druck gesunder menschlicher Augen, *Klin. Monatsbl. Augenheilkd.*, 133, 662, 1958.
54. Linnér, E., Adrenocortical steroids and aqueous humor dynamics, *Doc. Ophthalmol.*, 13, 210, 1959.
55. Macsarey, P. V. J., Jr., Lasagna, L., and Synder, B., Arcus not so senilis, *Ann. Intern. Med.*, 68, 345, 1968.
56. Marin-Amat, M., The physiological variations of corneal curvature during life; their significance in ocular refraction, *Bull. Soc. Belge Ophthalmol.*, 113, 25, 1956.
57. McFarland, R. A., Warren, A. B., and Karis, C., Alterations in critical flicker frequency as a function of age and light:dark ratio, *J. Exp. Psychol.*, 56, 529, 1958.
58. McFarland, R. A., Domey, R. G., Warren, A. B. and Ward, D. C., Dark adaptation and age. I. A statistical analysis, *J. Gerontol.*, 15, 149, 1960.
59. McFarland, R. A., Experimental evidence of the relationship between ageing and oxygen want: in search of a theory of aging, *Ergonomics*, 6, 339, 1963.
60. Meyer, N. E., Ogle, K. N., Hollenhorst, R. W., and Moyer, N. J., Derivative curve in evaluation of pupillary response to light, *Exp. Eye Res.*, 8, 355, 1969.
61. Millodot, M., The influence of age on sensitivity of the cornea, *Invest. Ophthalmol. Visual Sci.*, 16(3), 240, 1977.
62. Millodot, M., The influence of age on chromatic aberration of the eye, *Albrecht von Graefes Arch. Klin. Exp. Ophthalmol.*, 198, 235, 1976.
63. Prestrude, A. M., Levenick, K., and Woody, K., The effect of age upon the detection of short wavelength of light, *J. Life Sci.*, 3(1), 101, 1973.
64. Ohta, Y. and Kato, H., Color perception changes with age, *Mod. Probl. Ophthalmol.*, 17, 345, 1976.
65. Prince, J. H., Ed., *Introduction to Aging and Pathology of the Retina*, Charles C Thomas, Springfield, Ill., 1965.
66. Rabbitt, P., An age-decrement in the ability to ignore irrelevant information, *J. Gerontol.*, 20, 233, 1965.

Table 5 (continued)
AGE-RELATED CHANGES IN VISUAL FUNCTION

67. **Reading, V. M.,** Visual resolution as measured by dynamic and static tests, *Pfluegers Arch.,* 333, 17, 1972.
68. **Rosengren, B.,** Studies in the depth of the anterior chamber of the eye in primary glaucoma, *Arch. Ophthalmol.,* 44, 523, 1950.
69. **Ruddock, K. H.,** The effect of age upon color vision. I. Response in the receptoral system of the human eye, *Vision Res.,* 5, 37, 1965.
70. **Ruddock, K. H.,** The effect of age upon color vision. II. Changes with age in light transmission of the ocular media, *Vision Res.,* 5, 48, 1965.
71. **Said, F. S. and Weale, R. A.,** The variation with age of the spectral transmissivity of the living human crystalline lens, *Gerontologia,* 3, 213, 1959.
72. **Schäfer, W. D. and Weale, R. A.,** The influence of age and retinal illumination on the pupillary near reflex, *Vision Res.,* 10, 179, 1970.
73. **Schonfield, D. and Trueman, V.,** Variations on the Stroop theme. *Gerontologist,* 2(14), 59, 1974.
74. **Schefer, V. F.,** Absolute number of neurons and thickness of cerebral cortex during aging, senile and vascular dementia and Pick and Alzheimer's disease, *Neurosci. Behav. Physiol.,* 6, 319, 1973.
75. **Sippel, T. O.,** Energy metabolism in the lens during ageing, *Invest. Ophthalmol.,* 4, 502, 1965.
76. **Shock, N. W.,** Biological theories of aging, in *Handbook of Psychology of Aging,* Birren, J. E. and Schaie, K. W., Eds., Van Nostrand Reinhold, New York, 1977, 103.
77. **Spector, A.,** An outline of progress in ophthalmic biochemistry, *ARVO Suppl. Invest. Ophthalmol. Visual Sci.,* 17(2), 33, 1978.
78. **Spector, A., Li, S., and Sigelman, J.,** Age dependent changes in the molecular size of human lens proteins and their relationship to light scatter, *Invest. Ophthalmol.,* 13, 795, 1974.
79. **Spector, A., Roy, D., and Stauffer, J.,** Isolation and characterization of an age-dependent polypeptide from human lens with non-tryptophan fluorescence, *Exp. Eye Res.,* 21, 9, 1975.
80. **Talland, A.,** Visual signal detection, as a function of age, input rate and signal frequency, *J. Psychol.,* 63, 105, 1966.
81. **Theodore, F. H.,** External eye problems in the elderly, *Geriatrics,* 30(1), 69, 1975.
82. **Van Heyningen, R.,** Photo-oxidation of lens proteins by sunlight in the presence of fluorescent derivatives of Kynurenine isolated from human lens, *Exp. Eye Res.,* 17, 137, 1973.
83. **Venturi, G. and Artifoni, E.,** La tensione endoculare normativa, *Ann. Ottalmol. Clin. Ocul.,* 91, 123, 1965.
84. **Verreist, G.,** Further studies on acquired deficiency of color discrimination, *J. Opt. Soc. Am.,* 53, 185, 1963.
85. **Von Bahr, G.,** Corneal thickness, its measurement and changes, *Am. J. Ophthalmol.,* 42, 251, 1956.
86. **Waley, S. G.,** The lens: function and composition, in *Eye,* Vol 1., Davson, H., Ed., Academic Press, New York, 1969, 302.
87. **Wallace, J. G.,** Some studies on perception in relation to age, *Br. J. Psychol.,* 47, 283, 1956.
88. **Walsh, D. A.,** Age differences in central perceptual processing: a dichoptic backward masking investigation, *J. Gerontol.,* 31, 178, 1976.
89. **Walsh, D. A. and Thompson, L. W.,** Age differences in visual sensory memory. III, *Gerontologist,* 33, 383, 1978.
90. **Wapner, S., Werner, H., and Comalli, P. E.,** Perception of part-whole relationships in middle and old age, *J. Gerontol.,* 15, 412, 1960.
91. **Weale, R. A.,** *The Ageing Eye,* Harper and Row, London, 1963.
92. **Weale, R. A.,** On the eye, *Behavior, Aging and the Nervous System,* Welford, A. T. and Birren, J. E., Eds., Charles C Thomas, Springfield, Ill., 1965, 307.
93. **Weale, R. A.,** The ageing eye, *Sci. Basis Med. Annu. Rev.,* 244, 1971.
94. **Weekers, R. and Roussel, F.,** Introduction on a l'etude de la frequence de fusion en clinique, *Ophthalmologica,* 117, 305, 1946.
95. **Weekers, R., Delmarcelle, Y., and Gusting, J.,** Treatment of ocular hypertension by adrenalin and diverse sympathomimetic amines, *Am. J. Ophthalmol.,* 40, 666, 1955.
96. **Weekers, R., Watillon, M., and de Rudder, M.,** Experimental and clinical investigations into the resistance to outflow of the aqueous humor, *Br. J. Ophthalmol.,* 40, 225, 1956.
97. **Welsandt, R. F., Zupnick, J. J. and Meyer, P. A.,** Age effects in backward visual masking, *J. Exp. Child Psychol.,* 15, 454, 1973.
98. **Witmer, R.,** Altersveränderungen von Iris und Ziliarkörper, *Fortschr. Augenheilkd.,* 17, 131, 1966.
99. **Wolf, E.,** Studies on the shrinkage of the visual field with age, *Highw. Res., Res.,* 167, 1, 1967.
100. **Wolf, E.,** Glare and age, *Arch. Ophthalmol.,* 64, 502, 1960.
101. **Wolf, E. and Gardiner, J. S.,** Studies on the scatter of light in the dioptric media of the eye as a basis of visual glare, *Arch. Ophthalmol.,* 74, 338, 1965.
102. **Wolf, E. and Schraffa, A. M.,** Relation between critical flicker frequency and age in flicker perimetry, *Arch. Ophthalmol.,* 72, 832, 1964.

Table 6
AGE-RELATED CHANGES IN HEARING

	Ref.
In the U.S., hearing loss constitutes one of the major medical problems. In aging adults, the major manifestation is *presbycusis* which is characterized by a progressive bilateral loss of hearing associated with physiological degeneration in the auditory system. The problem is complicated by loss of hearing from external causes, such as noise or pathological disorders. Hearing loss now affects millions of persons and the percentage of population having hearing loss is steadily increasing. Several publications have reviewed the general problem of progressive hearing impairment with age.	3,13,15—17, 29,131,33,34, 53,54,62,69, 73,74,80,87

I. Physiological Changes in the Auditory System

Several kinds of physiological changes in hearing can be anticipated in the aging population; these changes and their consequences may be organized into four categories: (1) sensory presbycusis involves degeneration of the sensory and support cells at the basal end of the organ of Corti and is manifested in a decrease of sensitivity for high frequency tones; (2) neural presbycusis is related to neuronal degeneration in the auditory pathways and is associated with difficulties in speech perception; (3) metabolic presbycusis is due primarily to atrophic alterations in the stria vascularis of the scala media and involves an increase in threshold for most pure tones; and (4) mechanical presbycusis is related to complicated inner ear changes which probably affect the motion mechanics of the basilar membrane, primarily resulting in a high frequency hearing deficiency. In addition, vascular insufficiencies in several locations may contribute to malfunction of the auditory apparatus. These degenerative physiological changes may occur in any combination.	16,29,30,75

Anatomical changes closely correlated with loss of hearing include

Tissue degeneration and cellular loss in all parts of the auditory pathway from receptor cell of the cochlea to the temporal (auditory) cortex.	8,27,38,43,44, 45,46,49,50, 58,71,76,78, 84
Atrophy of the spiral ligament.	43,89
Degenerative changes in blood vessels.	3,7,26,42,43,84
Structural changes of the middle ear, including accumulation of fluids, stiffening of the tympanic membrane, and changes in the ossicles and other bony structures.	3,22,37,44,69, 70
Increased impedance of the middle ear after middle age.	1,2,6,41,64,65
Changes in the muscles and cartilagenous tissues of the ear.	3,22,59,70

II. Tests of Auditory Sensitivity

Threshold intensity for pure tones increases with age with the greatest loss of sensitivity in the high frequency range.	4,12,14,20,32, 33,35,40,51, 52,72,77,81
Ability to discriminate between different pitches decreases with age.	48
The ability to detect and discriminate among speech sounds declines with age.	5,9,24,55,56, 63,67,82,83, 88
Impairment of speech discrimination in the aged under a variety of conditions suggests that information processing may be slowed down in the central nervous system or that memory may be impaired.	4,9,23,24,25, 28,36,39,47, 63,68,76,79, 86,88
Problems of the aged with processing of auditory information may be due to a variety of central and/or peripheral physiological causes. New testing and diagnostic techniques may be able to discriminate among these causes.	10,11,13,15,18, 21,61
The decision criteria used by the elderly in hearing tests may differ from the young and be unrelated to any physiological impairment.	19,85
Presbycusis must be distinguished from deafness caused by noise, especially in industrial situations. The two may be additive in some cases.	7,28,31,51,52, 57,60,66,74

Table 6 (continued)
AGE-RELATED CHANGES IN HEARING

REFERENCES

1. **Alberti, P. and Kristensen, R.**, The compliance of the middle ear: its accuracy in routine clinical practice, in Mayo Foundation Impedance Symp., Rose, D. and Keating, L., Eds., Mayo Clinic Foundation, Rochester, Minn., 1972.
2. **Beattie, R. C. and Leamy, D. P.**, Otoadmittance: normative values, procedural variables, and reliability, *J. Am. Aud. Soc.*, 1, 21, 1975.
3. **Belal, A., Jr.**, Presbycusis: physiological or pathological, *J. Laryngol. Otol.*, 89(10), 1011, 1975.
4. **Bergman, M.**, Hearing and aging, *Audiology (Basel)*, 10, 164, 1971.
5. **Bergman, M., Blumefeld, V. G., Cascardo, D., Dash, B., Levitt, H., and Margulies, M. K.**, Age-related decrement in hearing for speech. Sampling and longitudinal studies, *J. Gerontol.*, 31(5), 533, 1976.
6. **Blood, I. and Greenberg, H. J.**, Acoustic admittance of the ear in the geriatric person, *J. Am. Aud. Soc.*, 2(5), 185, 1977.
7. **Bochenek, Z. and Jachowska, A.**, Atherosclerosis, accelerated presbycusis, and acoustic trauma, *Int. Aud.*, 8, 312, 1969.
8. **Bredberg, G.**, Cellular pattern and nerve supply of the human organ of Corti, *Acta Oto-Laryngol. Suppl.*, 236, 1, 1968.
9. **Calearo, D. and Lazzaroni, A.**, Speech intelligibility in relation to the message, *Laryngology*, 67, 410, 1957.
10. **Carhart, R.**, Updating special hearing tests in otological diagnosis, *Arch. Otolaryngol.*, 97, 88, 1973.
11. **Clark, L. E. and Knowles, J. B.**, Age differences in dichotic listening, *J. Gerontol.*, 28, 173, 1973.
12. **Corso, J. F.**, Age and sex differences in pure tone thresholds, *Arch. Otolaryngol.*, 77, 385, 1963.
13. **Corso, J. F.**, Auditory perception and communication, in *The Handbook of the Psychology of Aging*, Birren, J. E. and Schaie, K. W., Eds., Van Nostrand Reinhold, New York, 1976, 535.
14. **Corso, J. F.**, Hearing, in *Handbook of General Psychology*, Wolman, B. B., Ed., Prentice-Hall, Englewood Cliffs, N.J., 1973, 348.
15. **Corso, J. F.**, Presbycusis as a complicating factor in evaluating noise-induced hearing loss, in *Effects of Noise on Hearing*, Henderson, D., Hamernik, R. P., Dosanjh, D. S., and Mills, J. H., Eds., Raven Press, New York, 1976, 497.
16. **Corso, J. F.**, Presbycusis, hearing aids and aging, *Audiology (Basel)*, 16, 146, 1977.
17. **Corso, J. F.**, The sensory effects of aging in man, *Scientia: Int. Rev. Sci. Synthesis*, 103, 362, 1968.
18. **Corso, J. F., Wright, H. N., and Valerio, M.**, Auditory temporal summation in presbycusis and noise exposure, *J. Gerontol.*, 31(1), 58, 1976.
19. **Craik, F. N.**, Affects of ageing on the detection of faint signals, in Proc. 7th Int. Congr. Gerontol., Vienna, 1966, 6.
20. **Eisdorfer, C. and Wilkie, F.**, Auditory changes in the aged: a follow-up study, *J. Am. Geriatr. Soc.*, 20, 377, 1972.
21. **Elias, J. W. and Elias, M. F.**, Matching of successive auditory stimuli as a function of age and ear of presentation, *J. Gerontol.*, 31(2), 164, 1976.
22. **Etholm, B. and Belal, A., Jr.**, Senile changes in the middle ear joints, *Ann. Otol. Rhinol. Laryngol.*, 83, 49, 1974.
23. **Farrimond, T.**, Prediction of speech hearing loss in older workers, *Gerontologia*, 5, 65, 1961.
24. **Feldman, R. M. and Reger, S. N.**, Relations among hearing, reaction time, and age, *J. Speech Hear. Res.*, 10, 479, 1967.
25. **Findlay, R. C. and Schuchman, G. I.**, Masking level difference for speech: effects of ear dominance and age, *Audiology (Basel)*, 15(3), 232, 1976.
26. **Fitsch, V., Dobozi, M., and Greig, G.**, Degenerative changes of the arterial vessels of the internal auditory meatus during the process of aging, *Acta Oto-Laryngol.*, 73, 259, 1972.
27. **Fleischer, K.**, Der Altersbedingte Ganglienzellenschwund im Innenohr, in *Experimentelle Altersforschung*, Suppl. 4, Versár, F., Ed., Birkhäuser, Basel, 1956, 1.
28. **Fournier, J. E.**, L'analyse et l'identification der message sonore, *J. Fr. Oto. Rhino-Laryngol.*, 3, 257, 1954.
29. **Gacek, R. R.**, Degenerative hearing loss in aging, in *Neurological and Sensory Disorders in the Elderly*, Fields, W. S., Ed., Stratton, New York, 1975, 219.
30. **Gacek, R. R. and Schuknecht, H. F.**, Pathology of presbycusis, *Int. Aud.*, 8, 199, 1969.
31. **Gentile, A.**, Persons with impaired hearing United States, 1971, *Vital Health Stat. Ser.*, 10(101), 1, 1975.
32. **Glorig, A. and Davis, H.**, Age, noise, and hearing loss, *Ann. Otol. Rhinol. Laryngol.*, 70, 556, 1961.

Table 6 (continued)
AGE-RELATED CHANGES IN HEARING

33. **Glorig, A. and Nixon, J.,** Hearing loss as a function of age, *Laryngoscope,* 72, 1596, 1962.
34. **Glorig, A., Wheeler, D., Quiggle, R., Grings, W., and Summerfield, A.,** 1954 Wisconsin State Fair Hearing Survey, Subcommittee on Noise in Industry of the American Academy of Ophthalmology and Otolaryngology, Los Angeles, 1957.
35. **Gonzalez, M. and Cobo, J.,** Bekesy's automatic audiometry in patients of advanced age, *Ann. Otol. Rinol. Laryngol. Ibero Am.,* 2(4), 67, 1975.
36. **Granick, S., Kleban, M. H., and Weiss, A. D.,** Relationships between hearing loss and cognition in normally hearing aged persons, *J. Gerontol.,* 31(4), 434, 1976.
37. **Gross, C. W.,** Sensori-neural hearing loss in clinical and histologic otosclerosis, *Laryngoscope,* 79, 104, 1969.
38. **Hansen, C. C. and Reske-Nielsen, E.,** Pathological studies in presbycusis, *Arch. Otolaryngol.,* 82, 115, 1965.
39. **Hinchcliffe, R.,** The anatomical locus of presbycusis, *J. Speech Dis.,* 27, 301, 1962.
40. **Hinchcliffe, R.,** The threshold of hearing as a function of age, *Acustica,* 9, 303, 1959.
41. **Jerger, J., Jerger, S., and Mauldin, L.,** Studies in impedance audiometry. I. Normal and sensori-neural ears, *Arch. Otolaryngol.,* 96, 513, 1972.
42. **Johnsson, L. G.,** Degenerative Veränderungen in alternder Innerohr, mit besonderer Berücksichtigung der vasculären Veränderungen, in Flächenpräparaten der menschlichen Cochlea dargestellt, *Arch. Klin. Exp. Ohren-Nasen Kehlkopfheilkd.,* 200, 318, 1971.
43. **Johnsson, L. G. and Hawkins, J. E., Jr.,** Sensory and neural degeneration with aging, as seen in microdissections of the human inner ear., *Ann. Otol. Rhinol. Laryngol.,* 81, 179, 1972.
44. **Jorgenson, M. B.,** Changes of ageing in the inner ear, *Arch. Otolaryngol.,* 74, 164, 1961.
45. **Kirikae, K., Sato, T., and Shitara, T.,** A study of hearing in advanced age, *Laryngoscope,* 74, 205, 1964.
46. **Konigsmark, B. W. and Murphy, E. A.,** Volume of the ventral cochlear nucleus in man: its relationship to neuronal population and age, *J. Neuropathol. Exp. Neurol.,* 31, 304, 1970.
47. **Konkle, D. F., Beasley, D. S., and Bess, F. H.,** Intelligibility of time-altered speech in relation to chronological aging, *J. Speech Hear. Res.,* 20(1), 108, 1977.
48. **Konig, E.,** Pitch discrimination and age, *Acta Oto-Laryngol.,* 48, 475, 1957.
49. **Krmpotic-Nemanic, J.,** Presbycusis and retrocochlear structures, *Int. Aud.,* 8, 210, 1969.
50. **Krmpotic-Nemanic, J., Simuni, C. V., Nemani, C. G., and Braun, K.,** Changes due to age in the inner ear, *Verh. Anat. Ges.,* 68, 459, 1974.
51. **Kudo, Y., Okumura, A., Shomoto, M., and Takeda, S.,** Hearing and aging. I. Evaluation of maximum auditory threshold, *Jpn. J. Hyg.,* 30(1), 201, 1975.
52. **Lebo, C. P. and Reddell, R. C.,** The presbycusis component in occupational hearing loss, *Laryngoscope,* 82, 1399, 1972.
53. **Lehman, R. H. and Miller, A. L.,** Presbycusis, *J. Am. Geriatr. Soc.,* 18(6), 486, 1970.
54. **Liden, G.,** The geriatric-audiological problems of modern society, in *Geriatric Audiology,* Liden, G., Ed., Almqvist & Wiksell, Stockholm, 1968, 9.
55. **Lopotko, A. I.,** Auditory function in persons of different age groups according to the data of sonant and whispering speech audiometry, *Vestn. Otorinolaringol.,* 4, 23, 1975.
56. **Lopotko, A. I.,** Hearing function in persons of advanced-age groups according to data of speech audiometry with limited frequency ranges, *Zh. Ushn. Nos. Gorl. Bolezn.,* 2, 46, 1975.
57. **Macrae, J. H.,** Noise-induced hearing loss and presbycusis, *Audiology (Basel),* 10, 323, 1971.
58. **Makishima, K.,** Clinicopathological studies in presbycusis, *Otol. Fukuoka Jibi Inkoka,* 13 (Suppl. 3), 333, 1967.
59. **Magladery, J.,** Neurophysiology of aging, in *Handbook of Aging and the Individual,* Birren, J., Ed., University of Chicago Press, Chicago, 1959, 173.
60. **Mollica, A.,** Acoustic trauma and presbycusis, *Int. Aud.,* 8, 305, 1969.
61. **Mysak, E. D.,** Pitch and duration characteristics of older males, *J. Speech Hear. Res.,* 2, 46, 1959.
62. **Parker, W.,** Hearing and age, *Geriatrics,* 24(4), 151, 1969.
63. **Pestalozza, G. and Shore, I.,** Clinical evaluation of presbycusis on basis of different tests of auditory function, *Laryngoscope,* 65, 1136, 1955.
64. **Philion, Y. and Lescouflair, G.,** Stapedial reflexes in presbycusis and occupational deafness, *Audiology (Basel),* 16(1), 38, 1977.
65. **Porter, T. A.,** Normative otoadmittance values for three populations, *J. Aud. Res.,* 12, 53, 1972.
66. **Price, G. R.,** Age as a factor in susceptibility to hearing loss: young versus adult ears, *J. Acoust. Soc. Am.,* 60(4), 886, 1976.

Table 6 (continued)
AGE-RELATED CHANGES IN HEARING

67. Punch, J. L. and McConnell, F., The speech discrimination function for elderly adults, *J. Aud. Res.*, 9, 159, 1969.
68. Rees, J. N. and Botwinich, J., Detection and decision factors in auditory behavior of the elderly, *J. Gerontol.*, 26, 133, 1971.
69. Richards, S., Deafness in the elderly, *Gerontol. Clin.*, 13, 350, 1971.
70. Rosenwasser, H., Otitic problems in the aged, *Geriatrics*, 19, 11, 1964.
71. Sataloff, J., Otolaryngologic problems, in *Clinical Features of the Older Patient*, Freeman, J. T., Ed., Charles C Thomas, Springfield, Ill., 1965, 428.
72. Schaie, K. W., Baltes, P., and Strother, C. R., A study of auditory sensitivity in advanced age, *J. Gerontol.*, 19, 453, 1964.
73. Schein, J. D., Deafness in the United States: 1970, *Highlights*, 53, 9, 1974.
74. Schmidt, P. H., Presbycusis and noise, *Int. Aud.*, 8, 278, 1969.
75. Schuknecht, H. F., Further observations on the pathology of presbycusis, *Arch. Otolaryngol.*, 80, 369, 1964.
76. Schuknecht, H. G. and Igarashi, M., Pathology of slowly progressive sensori-neural deafness, *Trans. Am. Acad. Ophthalmol. Otolaryngol.*, 68, 222, 1964.
77. Seibert, W. M., Hearing and the ear, in *Engineering Principles in Physiology*, Brown, J. H. U. and Gann, D. S., Eds., Academic Press, New York, 1973, 139.
78. Sercer, A. and Krmpotic-Nemanic, J., Über die ursache der progressiven altersschwerhörgkeit (presbycusis), *Acta Oto-Laryngol. Suppl.*, 143, 1, 1958.
79. Smith, R. and Prather, W. F., Phoneme discrimination in older persons under varying signal to noise conditions, *J. Speech Hear. Res.*, 14, 630, 1971.
80. Spoor, A., Presbycusis values in relation to noise induced hearing loss, *Int. Aud.*, 6, 48, 1967.
81. Spoor, A. and Passchier-Vermeer, W., Spread in hearing-levels of non-noise exposed people at various ages, *Int. Aud.*, 8, 328, 1969.
82. Stevenson, P. W., Responses to speech audiometry and phonemic discrimination patterns in the elderly, *Audiology (Basel)*, 14(3), 185, 1975.
83. Stevenson, P. W. and Martin, M. C., Adaptive speech audiometry and speech discrimination space in hearing-impaired subjects, *Audiology (Basel)*, 16(2), 110, 1977.
84. Suga, F. and Lindsay, J. R., Histopathological observations of presbycusis, *Ann. Otol. Rhinol. Laryngol.*, 85(2 Part 1), 169, 1976.
85. Szafram, J., Psychological studies of aging in pilots, in *Human Aging and Behavior*, Vol. 1, Talland, G. H., Ed., Academic Press, New York, 1968, 37.
86. Warren, R. M. and Warren, R. P., Some age differences in auditory perception, *Bull. N.Y. Acad. Med.*, 47, 1365, 1971.
87. Weiss, A. D., Sensory functions, in *Handbook of Aging and the Individual*, Birren, J. E., Ed., University of Chicago Press, Chicago, 1959, 503.
88. Welsh, O. L., Luterman, D. M., and Bell, B., The effect of aging on responses to filtered speech, *J. Gerontol.*, 24, 189, 1969.
89. Wright, J. L. and Schuknecht, H. F., Atrophy of the spiral ligament, *Arch. Otolaryngol.*, 96, 16, 1972.

Table 7
AGE-RELATED CHANGES IN VESTIBULAR FUNCTION

Ref.

I. Physiological Changes in the Vestibular System

Vestibular degeneration with age has been considered to be moderate in comparison with the auditory system. Recent technological advances such as in electromicroscopy have revealed more extensive changes in the vestibular apparatus.	16,24,25,27
The chronaxie of the 8th nerve is not significantly affected by age.	4
Degeneration of the 8th nerve is found with aging. Fiber diameter is reduced and the number of fibers is less in specimens aged 45 and older in comparison to younger age groups.	3,21
Cochleo-saccular tissues degenerate with aging.	14,26
Cellular degeneration is moderate in the maculae, more evident in the christae. Receptor cell populations decrease in both structures.	22
Otoconia are markedly reduced in number in the macular saculli, less affected in the macula utriculi.	15
Receptor cells show reduced number of cilia, increased number of osmiophilic and laminated inclusions, and reduced volume. The nerve chalices contacting the receptor cells degenerate.	8,10,12,13, 23
Degenerative changes in the monkey vestibular apparatus are parallel to those found in aging man.	8
No changes with age are apparent in the vestibular ganglia.	9

II. Tests of Vestibular Function

Vertigo is a frequent complaint of the elderly.	7,20
Nystagmic responses to caloric stimulation indicate a hyporeactivity in persons over approximately 50 years of age.	2,5,6,18,19, 28,29
Post-rotatory nystagmic responses also reveal a hyporeactivity in aged individuals.	1,2,6,11,17, 18,19,28

REFERENCES

1. Allard, A., Contribution l'étude de la sensibilité de l'appareil semi-circulaire, par la méthode des petites stimulations premaires, post-rotatoires, réalisees au moyen du fauteuil Buys-Rylat, *Ann. Oto-Laryngol.,* 1, 417, 1938.
2. Arslan, M., The senescence of the vestibular apparatus, *Pract. Oto-Rhino-Laryngol.,* 19, 475, 1957.
3. Bergström, B., Morphology of the vestibular nerve. II. The number of myelinated vestibular nerve fibers in man at various ages, *Acta Otolaryngol.* 76, 1, 1973.
4. Bourlière, F., Excitability and aging, *J. Gerontol.,* 3, 191, 1948.
5. Bruner, A. and Norris, T. W., Age-related changes in caloric nystagmus, *Acta Otolaryngol. Suppl.,* 282, 1, 1971.
6. Clement, P. A. R., van der Laan, F. L., and Oosterveld, J., L'Influence de l'age sur la fonction vestibulaire, *Acta Oto-Rhino-Laryngol. Belg.,* 29, 163, 1975.
7. Droller, H. and Pemberton, J., Vertigo in a random sample of elderly people living in their homes, *J. Laryngol.,* 67, 689, 1953.
8. Engström, H., Ades, H. W., Engström, B., Gilchrist, D., and Bourne, G., Structural changes in the vestibular epithelia in elderly monkeys and humans, *Adv. Oto-Rhino-Laryngol.,* 22, 93, 1977.
9. Fleischer, K., Morphological aspects of the aging ear, *HNO,* 20(4), 103, 1973.
10. Friedmann, I., Electron microscopic studies of the diseased macula of the utricle of the human inner ear with particular reference to Menièeres disease, in *Submicroscopic Structure of the Inner Ear,* Iurato, S., Ed., Pergamon Press, New York, 1963, 261.

Table 7 (continued)
AGE-RELATED CHANGES IN VESTIBULAR FUNCTION

11. Guedry, F. E., Jr., Age as a Variable in Post Rotational Phenomena, Project Rep. NM-001-063. 01. 19, U.S. Naval School of Aviation Medicine, Naval Air Station, Pensacola, Florida, 1950, 1.
12. Hilding, D. A. and House, W. F., An evaluation of the ultrastructural finds in the utricle in Meniere's disease, *Laryngoscope,* 74, 1135, 1964.
13. Iurato, S., Submicroscopic changes in the vestibular labrynth in animals, due to aging, in *Submicroscopic Structure of the Inner Ear,* Iurato, S., Ed., Pergamon Press, New York, 1967, 252.
14. Johnsson, L. G., Degenerative changes and anomalies of the vestibular system in man, *Laryngoscope,* 81, 1682, 1971.
15. Johnsson, L. G. and Hawkins, J. E., Sensory and neural degeneration with aging as seen in microdissections of the human inner ear, *Ann. Otol.,* 8(2), 179, 1972.
16. Jorgensen, B. M., Changes of aging in the inner ear, *Arch. Otolaryngol.,* 74(2), 164, 1961.
17. Koskenoja, M. and Orma, E. J., Positional nystagmus in elderly patients with postural dizziness, *Ann. Otol. Rhinol. Laryngol.,* 65, 707, 1956.
18. Kotyza, F., Vestibular reaction at various ages, *Čas. Lék. Česk.,* 78, 755, 1939; *Psychol. Abstr.,* 16(1428), 1942.
19. Okano, H., Klinisch-statistische Untersuchungen der Japanischen Greise in dem oto-rhino-laryngologischen Gebiete, *Z. Oto-Rhino-U. Laryngol. (Tokyo),* 44, 1, 1938.
20. Orma, E. J. and Koskenoja, M., Postural dizziness in the aged, *Geriatrics,* 12, 49, 1957.
21. Rasmussen, A. T., Studies of the VIIIth cranial nerve of man, *Laryngoscope,* 50, 67, 1940.
22. Rosenhall, U., Degenerative patterns in the aging human vestibular neuro-epithelia, *Acta Oto-Laryngol.,* 76, 208, 1973.
23. Rosenhall, U. and Rubin, W., Degenerative changes in the human vestibular sensory epithelia, *Acta Oto-Laryngol.,* 79, 67, 1974.
24. Saxén, A., Pathologie und Klinik der Altersschwerhörigkeit, *Acta Oto-Laryngol. Suppl.,* 23, 1, 1937.
25. Saxén, A. and Fieandt, H., Pathologie und Klinik der Alterschiverhoerigkeit, *Acta Oto-Laryngol. Suppl.,* 23, 1, 1937.
26. Schuknecht, H. F., Igarashi, M., and Gacek, R. R., The pathological types of cochleo-saccular degeneration, *Acta Oto-Laryngol.,* 59, 154, 1964.
27. van der Laan, F. L., *Age and Vestibular Function,* Mur, Aalsmeer, 1972.
28. van der Laan, F. L. and Oosterveld, W. J., Age and vestibular function, *Aerosp. Med.,* 45, 540, 1974.
29. Virolainen, E. S. and Aantaa, E., The nystagmus threshold in turning test in different age groups and in patients suffering from otosclerosis, *Acta Oto-Laryngol.,* 81, 127, 1976.

CENTRAL NERVOUS SYSTEM INTEGRATIVE FUNCTIONS

Terry Mikiten

Table 1
AGING AND THE INTEGRATIVE FUNCTIONS OF THE NERVOUS SYSTEM

		Ref.
1.	Old (600 days) and young rats (30 days) show greater facilitation of learning with D-amphetamine than do 120-day adult rats.	2
2.	Electroconvulsive shock disrupts retention in young rats to a greater degree than in older rats.	3
3.	In humans, the capacity of short-term memory declines with age.	1,6,7
4.	Old mice (360 days) learn a maze more quickly than young (30 days) mice.	4
5.	Older subjects require longer time to recall items from primary memory than younger subjects	5,13
6.	Recall of memory from long-term storage (tertiary memory) is slower with advancing age.	8
7.	Elderly subjects experience greater difficulty in solving problems, making more errors than younger subjects.	9,13
8.	Interpretation of differences between aged and young individuals in memory or learning capacity may be obscured by many variables including recency of practice and anxiety.	10
9.	Old rats (24 months) exhibit significantly greater loss of retention in single trial avoidance tests, the effect becoming apparent within a few hours after training.	11,15
10.	It is conjectured that age-related changes in the human central nervous system biogenic amine systems are correlated with changes in memory storage in senescence.	11
11.	Many neurotransmitters and their related enzymes show age-related decline in senescent human individuals.	12,14,17
12.	It is suggested that dopaminergic neural systems are especially vulnerable to aging.	14
13.	As a memory aid, imagery is less effective in elderly individuals.	16
14.	It is suggested that declining function of the reticular activating system is related to decreased intellecutal capacity in advanced age.	18

REFERENCES

1. Gold, P. E., VanBuskirk, R., and McGaugh, J. L., Age-related changes in learning and memory, in *Survey Report on the Aging Nervous System,* Maletta, G. J., Ed., DHEW Publ. No. NIH 74-296, National Institutes of Health, Public Health Service, U.S. Department of Health, Education and Welfare, Washington, D.C., 1975.
2. Doty, B. A. and Doty, L. A., Facilitation effects of amphetamine on avoidance conditioning in relation to age and problem difficulty, *Psychopharmacologia,* 9, 234, 1966.
3. Thompson, R., The effects of ECS on retention in young and adult rats, *J. Comp. Physiol. Psychol.,* 50, 644, 1957.
4. Olivero, A. and Bovet, D., Effects of age on maze learning and avoidance conditioning of mice, *Life Sci.,* 5, 1317, 1966.
5. Waugh, N. C., Recalling norms from primary and secondary memory, *Gerontologist,* 12, 54, 1972.
6. Fozard, J. L., Predicting age in the adult years for psychological assessment of abilities and personality, *Aging Hum. Dev.,* 3, 175, 1972.
7. Botwinick, J., Geropsychology, *Annu. Rev. Psychol.,* 11, 239, 1970.
8. Thomas, J. C. and Marsh, G. R., Remembering the names of pictured objects, *Gerontologist,* 12, 54, 1972.
9. Welford, A. T., Ed., *Aging and Human Skill,* Oxford University Press, New York, 1958.
10. Fozard, J. L. and Thomas, J. C., Jr., Psychology of aging: basic findings and some psychiatric applications, in *Modern Perspective in the Psychiatry of Old Age,* Howells, J. G., Ed., Brunner-Mazel, New York, 1975, 107.

Table 1 (continued)
AGING AND THE INTEGRATIVE FUNCTIONS OF THE NERVOUS SYSTEM

11. Gold, P. E. and McGaugh, J. L., Changes in learning and memory during aging, *Adv. Behav. Biol.*, 16, 145, 1975.
12. Ordy, J. M., The nervous system, behavior and aging: an interdisciplinary lifespan approach, *Adv. Behav. Biol.*, 16, 85, 1975.
13. Birren, J. E., Ed., *Handbook of Aging and the Individual*, University of Chicago Press, Chicago, 1959.
14. McGeer, E. G. and McGeer, P. L., Age changes in the human for some enzymes associated with metabolism of catecholamine, GABA and acetylcholine, *Adv. Behav. Biol.*, 16, 287, 1975.
15. McNamara, M. C., Benignus, V. A., Benignus, G., and Miller, A. T., Jr., Active and passive avoidance in rats as a function of age, *Exp. Aging Res.*, 3, 3, 1977.
16. Mason, S. E. and Smith, A. D., Imagery in the aged, *Exp. Aging Res.*, 3, 17, 1977.
17. Roberts, J., Goldberg, P. B., and Baskin, S. I., Biochemical changes in the central nervous system with age in the rat, *Exp. Aging Res.*, 3, 61, 1977.
18. Schumacher, S. S., Psychological evidence for primary aging in the brain, *Interdiscip. Top. Gerontol.*, 7, 46, 1970.

Table 2
AGE-RELATED CHANGES IN SLEEP AND IN EEG PATTERNS

		Ref.
1.	Stage IV, slow-wave sleep is reduced by 50% in elderly humans (average age 77 years).	1—3
2.	Elderly normal individuals exhibit abrupt changes in EEG pattern, changing from a sleep pattern to wakefulness. Suggest it may be associated with nocturnal confusion and wandering seen in aged individuals.	3
3.	Aged normal individuals spend a progressively higher percentage of the night with an alert EEG pattern (this may or may not be associated with behavioral arousal).	3
4.	Changes in sleep spindle amplitude and morphology can sometimes be detected in elderly individuals.	4
5.	Dream recall following REM sleep is reduced in elderly individuals.	5
6.	Elderly individuals awaken from sleep more frequently with increase in age from 65—95 years.	3
7.	The incidence of sleep apnea increases with age.	6
8.	Since the locus ceruleus undergoes a decrease in number of cells, and is considered to play a role in sleep, it is suggested that this cell loss may be related to altered sleep patterns with age.	7
9.	Elderly normal individuals show a decrease in mean alpha frequency.	8,9
10.	Diffuse slow activity (delta: 1—4 Hz and theta: 5—7 Hz) is seen with increasing incidence after the 7th decade.	8
11.	Episodic bursts of high-voltage slow waves in the delta and theta range are seen in some elderly individuals (30—50%) in the absence of obvious clinical abnormalities.	10—12
12.	Generalized alpha-slowing can be shown to be correlated with decrease in verbal/performance ratio, as judged by the Wechsler adult intelligence scale.	13
13.	Decreases in cerebral blood flow and oxygen utilization correlate well with both degree of EEG slowing and with decrease in intellectual performance.	8
14.	Averaged evoked responses to visual and somaesthetic stimuli as measured with EEG techniques in humans show age-related progressive increase in latency and amplitude, especially for the late, or secondary components. The change is progressive from adolescence to the 8th decade.	14
15.	Averaged evoked responses to auditory stimuli fail to show significant changes peculiar to aging.	7

REFERENCES

1. **Feinberg, I., Koresko, R., and Hesler, N.,** EEG patterns as a function of normal and pathological aging in man, *J. Psychiatr. Res.,* 5, 107, 1969.
2. **Feinberg, I.,** Change in sleep cycle patterns with age, *J. Psychiatr. Res.,* 10, 283, 1974.
3. **Feinberg, I.,** Functional implications of changes in sleep physiology with aging, in *Neurobiology of Aging,* Terry, R. D. and Gershon, S., Eds., Raven Press, New York, 1976.
4. **Gibbs, F. A. and Gibbs, E. L.,** Eds., *Atlas of Electroencephalography,* Vol. 1, 2nd ed., Addison-Wesley, Reading, Mass., 1974.
5. **Kahn, E., Fisher, C., and Lieberman, L.,** Dream recall in the normal aged, *J. Am. Geriatr. Soc.,* 17, 1121, 1969.
6. **Church, M. W., March, J. D., Hibi, S., Benson, K., Caveness, C., and Feinberg, I.,** Change in frequency and amplitude of delta activity during sleep, *Electroencephalogr. Clin. Neurophysiol.,* 39, 1, 1975.
7. **Brody, H.,** An examination of cerebral cortex and brainstem aging, in *Neurobiology of Aging,* Terry, R. D. and Gershon, S., Eds., Raven Press, New York, 1976, 117.
8. **Obrist, W. D. and Busse, E. W.,** The electroencephalogram in old age, in *Applications of Electroencephalography in Psychiatry,* Wilson, W. P., Ed., Duke University Press, Durham, N.C., 1965.
9. **Thompson, L. W.,** Cerebral blood flow, EEG and behavior in aging, in *Neurobiology of Aging,* Terry, R. D. and Gershon, S., Eds., Raven Press, New York, 1976.

Table 2 (continued)
AGE-RELATED CHANGES IN SLEEP AND IN EEG PATTERNS

10. **Busse, E. W., Barnes, R. H., Silverman, A. J., Shy, G. M., Thaler, M., and Frost, L. L.,** Studies of the process of aging: factors that influence the psyche of elderly persons, *Am. J. Psychiatry,* 110, 897, 1954.
11. **Busse, E. W., Barnes, R. H., Friedman, E. L., and Kelty, E. J.,** Psychological functionary of aged individual, with normal and abnormal electroencephalograms. I. A study of non-hospitalized community volunteers, *J. Nerv. Ment. Dis.,* 124, 135, 1956.
12. **Busse, E. W. and Obrist, W. D.,** Significance of focal electroencephalographic changes in the elderly, *Postgrad. Med.,* 34, 179, 1963.
13. **Wang, H. S., Obrist, W. D., and Busse, E. W.,** Neurophysiological correlates of intellectual function of elderly persons living in the community, *Am. J. Psychiatry,* 126, 1205, 1970.
14. **Beck, E. D., Dustman, R. E. and Schenkenberg, T.,** Life span changes in the electrical activity of the human brain as reflected in the cerebral evoked response, *Adv. Behav. Biol.,* 16, 175, 1975.
15. **Timiras, P. S.,** in *Methods of Animal Experimentation,* Vol. 2, Gay, W. I., Ed., Academic Press, New York, 1965.
16. **Timiras, P. S.,** *Physiology of Development and Aging,* Macmillan, New York, 1972.

NON-NEURONAL ELEMENTS OF THE CENTRAL NERVOUS SYSTEM*

Antonia Vernadakis and Ellen Bragg Arnold

Table 1
DEGENERATION OF ENDOTHELIAL ELEMENTS OF CENTRAL NERVOUS SYSTEM

	Ref.
The aging brain, in a general sense, can be viewed as hypoxic as a result of lowered oxygen delivered to the organ. Certain adaptive cellular responses to this state as well as others, such as gliosis and phagocytosis which occur in response to brain injury, have been suggested as models for the study of aging-related cellular changes. Therefore, this chapter contains a number of references to cellular processes which are characteristic of various degenerative conditions of nervous tissue.	1,2

REFERENCES

1. **Timiras, P. S.**, in *Methods of Animal Experimentation,* Vol. 2, Gay, W. I., Ed., Academic Press, New York, 1965.
2. **Timiras, P. S.**, *Physiology of Development and Aging,* Macmillan, New York, 1972.

---

* Material was co-authored by Dr. Arnold when she was a postdoctoral Fellow at the University of Colorado Medical Center, Department of Pharmacology, Denver, Colorado.

Table 2
ENDOTHELIAL ELEMENTS—DEGENERATION

	Ref.
Stab wounds produce a dramatic infiltration of leukocytes into the damaged region where such cells become phagocytic.	1,2
The body's main cellular defense against brain injury appears to be migration of mononuclear leukocytes into the wound area.	3
Experimental allergic encephalomyelitis (EAE) produces an infiltration of substantial numbers of circulating leukocytes into the CNS. A similar phenomenon has been observed in experimental allergic neuritis.	4,5
Pericytes develop the characteristics of phagocytes in rat cerebral cortex irradiated with alpha particles.	6
Several studies have indicated that certain of the vascular adventitial cells of the CNS may become phagocytic.	7
The leptomeninges of older brains are thicker than those of young persons.	8

REFERENCES

1. **Koniosmark, B. W., and Sidman, R. L.,** Origin of brain macrophages in the mouse, *J. Neuropathol. Exp. Neurol.,* 22, 643, 1963.
2. **Schultz, R. L. and Pease, D. C.,** Cicatrix formation in rat cerebral cortex as revealed by electron microscopy, *Am. J. Pathol.,* 35, 1017, 1959.
3. **Murray, H. M. and Walker, B. E.,** Comparative study of astrocytes and mononuclear leukocytes reacting to brain trauma in mice, *Exp. Neurol.,* 41, 290, 1973.
4. **Lampert, P. W. and Carpenter, S.,** Electron microscopic studies on the vascular permeability and the mechanism of demyelination in experimental allergic encephalomyelitis, *J. Neuropathol. Exp. Neurol.,* 24, 11, 1965.
5. **Astrom, K. E., Webster, H. de F., and Arnason, B. G.,** The initial lesion in experimental allergic neuritis, *J. Exp. Med.,* 128, 469, 1968.
6. **Maxwell, D. S. and Kruger, L.,** Small blood vessels and the origin of phagocytes in the rat cerebral cortex following heavy particle irradiation, *Exp. Neurol.,* 12, 33, 1965.
7. **Vaughn, J. E. and Skoff, R. P.,** Neuroglia in experimentally altered central nervous system, in *Structure and Function of Nervous Tissue,* Vol. 5, Bourne, G. H., Ed., Academic Press, New York, 1972, 39.
8. **Schade, J. P. and Ford, D. H., Eds.,** *Basic Neurology,* Elsevier, New York, 1965, 1.

Table 3
CHANGES IN BRAIN VASCULATURE

	Ref.
Aging of brain arteries is manifested chiefly by the reduction of the force required to bring 50% of the collagen fibers to their unstretched length, i.e., in the degree of "slackness". This is 30% stretch for younger (<16 years of age) vessels, 20% for the older (>48 years of age).	1
The major brain arteries are less distensible than are peripheral arteries of comparable diameter, particularly during early life. Distensibility decreases with age, mainly because the degree of slackness of the collagen fibers is reduced.	1
Unlike peripheral arteries, brain arteries show no significant age-related increase in maximal stiffness (a parameter related to total collagen content). No significant change in thickness of the wall or lumen diameter is found with age.	1
No appreciable differences exist between the histogenesis of cerebral and coronary atherosclerotic plaques.	2
From the available information on overall cerebral blood flow and oxygen consumption in man, there appears to be a rapid fall in the circulation and oxygen utilization of the brain from childhood through adolescence, followed by a more gradual but progressive reduction throughout the remaining life span.	3
A coarsening effect of the intracerebral microvascular network, with small knob-like formations and sinusoidal enlargements along the course of draining cerebral venules, has been observed in specimens of advanced age.	4
Areas of decreased local vascularity correspond to areas where there is definite neuronal loss in the deeper laminae of cerebral cortex.	4
An increasing degree of opaqueness of vessel walls correlates well with advancing age. Another parallel exists between aging and the tubular contour and the degree of resiliency of vessel walls.	4
There is a significant increase in the extent of "coiling", "looping", "winding", or "coursing" effects of perforating intracerebral arteries, arterioles, and venules. This occurs throughout the full thickness of the cerebral cortical laminae of neurons and in cerebral white matter as well. It is assumed that the "cell dropout" and subsequent glial replacement probably play an insignificant role in this genesis.	4
The presence of calcium salt in the vessel walls correlates poorly with advancing age.	4
The presence of either patchy or diffuse atheromatosis has some correlation with advancing age.	4
The infiltration of glial fibers around the vessels of the globus pallidus seems to parallel changes in the vessels, which are prone to a regeneration of the elastic layers with deposition of calcium and iron.	5
Stab wounds constitute an inflammatory type of neural lesion, causing extensive damage to blood vessel walls and provoking the movement of a large number of different blood elements into the wound area.	6
During aging, retinal and choroidal vessels undergo atherosclerosis, usually of a mild and insignificant nature, but vision can be impaired if this condition progresses sufficiently.	7
Sclerosed choroidal vessels are visible ophthalmoscopically as broad, flat, white lines lying deep behind the vessels of the retina.	7
Alterations in the retinal pigment epithelium may occur secondary to changes in aging choroidal vessels. The epithelial cells show fatty infiltration followed by disintegration and visible scattering of pigment.	7

Table 3 (continued)
CHANGES IN BRAIN VASCULATURE

REFERENCES

1. **Busby, D. E. and Burton, A. C.**, The effect of age on the elasticity of the major brain arteries, *Can. J. Physiol. Pharmacol.,* 43, 185, 1965.
2. **Brunnet, M.**, Changes in cerebral arteries with aging, *Arch. Pathol.,* 88, 314, 1969.
3. **Kety, S. S.**, Changes in cerebral circulation and oxygen consumption which accompany maturation and aging, in *Biochemistry of the Developing Nervous System,* Waelsch, H., Ed., Academic Press, New York, 1955, 208.
4. **Fang, H. C. H.**, Observations on aging characteristics of cerebral blood vessels, macroscopic, and microscopic features, in *Neurobiology of Aging,* Terry, R. D. and Gershon, S., Eds., Raven Press, New York, 1976, 155.
5. **Schade, J. P. and Ford, D. H. Eds.**, *Basic Neurology,* Elsevier, New York, 1965, 1.
6. **Schultz, R. L. and Pease, D. C.**, Cicatrix formation in rat cerebral cortex as revealed by electron microscopy, *Am. J. Pathol.,* 35, 1017, 1959.
7. **Timiras, P. S. and Vernadakis, A.**, Structural, biochemical and functional aging of the nervous system, in *Developmental Physiology and Aging,* Timiras, P. S., Ed., Macmillan, New York, 1972, 502.

Table 4
CHANGES IN GLIAL CELLS

	Ref.
There is a general increase in the abundance of glial fibers in the striatum and globus pallidus with advancing years.	1
Glial fibers increase in the subpial zone, spreading deeper into the cortex, particularly along perforating vessels.	1
Oligodendroglia and microglia appear to undergo few changes with age. It has been proposed, although with little proof, that microglia respond less rapidly than do oligodendroglia as phagocytes in older brains.	1
In contrast to neurons, glial cells increase in number with age by a process of amitotic division.	2—4
After birth many astrocytic mitochondria enlarge, with an increase in the amount of material and its crystallization into a fibramentous array, forming "gliosomes".	5
The presence of a small number of labeled cells in the brain of aged mice following injection of ^{3}H-thymidine indicates that some cells continue to proliferate, even at an advanced age.	6
In aged cerebral cortices the increase in glial cell density is greatest in the internal granular and outer half of the internal pyramidal layer.	7
There is an increased number of glial cells in the cerebral cortex and other discrete CNS areas of both hypoxic and aged animals.	8—11
Cell counts of astrocytes within degenerating optic nerves suggest that the population of fibrous astrocytes remains rather constant. This indicates that scarring is carried out mainly by the hypertrophy of existing astrocytes.	12
The Gordon phenomenon, a syndrome produced by injected foreign eosinophils, is characterized by progressive and profound ataxia related to destruction of Purkinje cells. It is used for the study of protoplasmic astrocytosis and for the investigation of the role of Bergman astrocytes in Purkinje cell degeneration.	13
In addition to scar production, typical fibrous astrocytes probably are involved in phagocytosis of some degenerating optic nerve fibers and myelin fragments. Evidence in favor of this statement is (1) a striking increase of lysosomes within fibrous astrocytes; (2) myelin fragments located in membrane-bounded vacuoles, apparently within astrocytic cytoplasm; and (3) the appearance of lipid droplets and dense laminar inclusions in astrocytic cytoplasm, both during and following removal of debris.	14
In an experiment of provoked proliferation of neuroglia cells, the findings suggest that astrocytes, microglia cells, and oligodendrocytes proliferate. Astrocytes and microglia proliferate in directly affected regions, while oligodendrocytes proliferate in pathways and gray matter connected with the lateral geniculate body.	15
Experimentally induced neuronal degeneration shows that chloride and sodium in neuroglia, relative to concentrations in neurons, are high, but that the potassium concentration is roughly equivalent to that in neurons.	16
In degeneration, multipotential glial cells develop very irregular shapes, acquiring many processes and complex folds that intermingle with the degenerating nerve fibers.	17
Reactive oligodendrocytes phagocytose myelinated axons, and astrocytes engulf degenerating nerve boutons.	18
Oligodendrocytes seem to be the glial cell type least involved in phagocytosis, according to numerous recent investigations of damaged CNS tissue.	19—21
Cell proliferation appears to be essential to replace destroyed oligodendroglia and thus permit successful remyelination in CNS tissue.	22
Electron microscopic autoradiographic studies with ^{3}H-labeled thymidine demonstrate that the cells associated with remyelination are newly generated oligodendroglia.	22
Microglial cells are significantly involved with the phagocytosis of debris in degenerating optic nerves. The first changes which appear to take place in a microglial cell are substantial increases in both the amount of perikaryal cytoplasm and the number of cytoplasmic processes.	14
Oligodendrocytes do not develop into phagocytes in substantial numbers.	14
Unlike astrocytes and microglia, oligodendrocytes generally do not show dramatic morphological changes in response to degenerating nerve fibers, although there appears to be an increase in the number of lysosomes within this neuroglial type.	14
The debris-containing vacuoles are phagolysosomes, instead of single indentations of the microglial cell surface produced by degenerating nerve fibers and myelin located in the intracellular spaces. Similar membrane-bound phagocytic vacuoles and phagolysosomes are contained by macrophages in other tissues.	23—25

Table 4 (continued)
CHANGES IN GLIAL CELLS

	Ref.
There is a glial cell type present in late fetal and early postnatal periods of development with a morphological appearance distinct from both astrocytes and oligodendrocytes. This cell type is found to persist in young adult rat optic nerves and is subsequently found in fully mature, adult rat optic nerves.	26
In the facial nucleus of the adult rat, neuroglial cells have been described and designated as microglia. These microglia are found to proliferate following facial nerve transection.	28

REFERENCES

1. Schade, J. P. and Ford, D. H., Eds., *Basic Neurology,* Elsevier, New York, 1965, 146.
2. Andrew, W., Phagocytic activity of the oligodendroglia and amphicytes in the brain, spinal cord, and semilunar ganglion of the mouse during inanition, *Am. J. Pathol.,* 17, 421, 1941.
3. Andrew, W., Cytological changes in senility in trigeminal ganglion, spinal cord and brain of mouse, *J. Anat.,* 75, 406, 1941.
4. Brizzee, K. R., Sherwood, N., and Timiras, P. S., A comparison of cell populations at various depth levels in cerebral cortex of young adult and aged Long-Evans rats, *J. Gerontol.,* 23, 289, 1968.
5. Hashimoto, P. H., Electron microscopic study on gliosome formation in postnatal development of spinal cord in the cat, *J. Comp. Neurol.,* 137, 251, 1969.
6. Dalton, M. M., Hommes, O. R., and Leblond, C. P., Correlation of glial proliferation with age in the mouse brain, *J. Comp. Neurol.,* 134, 397, 1969.
7. Brizzee, K. R., Sherwood, N., and Timiras, P. S., A comparison of cell populations at various depth levels in cerebral cortex of young adult and aged Long-Evans rats, *J. Gerontol.,* 23, 289, 1968.
8. Timiras, P. S., High altitude studies, in *Methods of Animal Experimentation,* Vol. 2, Gay, W. I., Ed., Academic Press, New York, 1965, chap. 7.
9. Timiras, P. S. and Wooley, D., Functional and morphologic development of brain and other organs of rats at high altitude, *Fed. Proc. Fed. Am. Soc. Exp. Biol.,* 25, 1312, 1966.
10. Petropoulos, E. A., Vernadakis, A., and Timiras, P. S., Nucleic acid content in developing rat brain after prenatal and/or neonatal exposure to high altitude, *Fed. Proc. Fed. Am. Soc. Exp. Biol.,* 28, 1001, 1969.
11. Petropoulos, E. A., Vernadakis, A., and Timiras, P. S., Neurochemical changes in rats subjected neonatally to high altitude and electroshock, *Am. J. Physiol.,* 218, 1351, 1970.
12. Vaughn, J. E. and Pease, D. C., Electron microscopic studies of Wallerian degeneration in rat optic nerves. II. Astrocytes, oligodendrocytes and adventitial cells, *J. Comp. Neurol.,* 140, 207, 1970.
13. Schwartz, A. M., Lapham, L. W., and Van Den Noort, S., Cytologic and cytochemical studies of neuroglia, *Neurology,* 16, 1118, 1966.
14. Vaughn, J. E. and Skoff, R. P., Neuroglia in experimentally altered Central Nervous System, in *The Structure and Function of Nervous Tissue,* Vol. 5, Bourne, G. H., Ed., Academic Press, New York, 1972, chap. 2.
15. Altman, J., Autoradiographic study of degenerative and regenerative proliferation of neuroglia cells with tritiated thymidine, *Exp. Neurol.,* 5, 302, 1962.
16. Koch, A., Ranck, J. B., Jr., and Newman, B. L., Ionic content of the neuroglia, *Exp. Neurol.,* 6, 186, 1962.
17. Vaughn, J. E., Hinds, P. L., and Skoff, R. P., Electron microscopic studies of Wallerian degeneration in rat optic nerves. I. The multipotential glia, *J. Comp. Neurol.,* 140, 175, 1970.
18. Westrum, L. E., Electron microscopy of degeneration in the lateral olfactory tract and plexiform layer of the prepyriform cortex of the rat, *Z. Zellforsch. Mikrosk. Anat.,* 98, 157, 1969.
19. Lampert, P. W. and Cressman, M. R., Fine-structural changes in myelin sheaths after axonal degeneration in the spinal cord of rats, *Am. J. Pathol.,* 49, 1139, 1966.
20. Lampert, P. W. and Schochet, S. S., Electron microscopic observations on experimental spongy degeneration of the cerebellar white matter, *J. Neuropathol. Exp. Neurol.,* 27, 210, 1968.
21. Pecci Saavedra, J., Vaccarezza, O. L., and Mascitti, T. A., Degeneration in the parvocellular portion of the lateral geniculate nucleus of the Cebus monkey, *Z. Zellforsch. Mikrosk. Anat.,* 93, 164, 1969.

**Table 4 (continued)
CHANGES IN GLIAL CELLS**

22. Herndon, R. M., Price, D. L., and Weiner, L. P., Regeneration of oligodendroglia during recovery from demyelinating disease, *Science,* 195, 693, 1977.
23. Parakkal, P. F., Involvement of macrophages in collagen resorption, *J. Cell Biol.,* 41, 345, 1969.
24. Collet, A. J., Fine structure of the alveolar macrophage of the cat and modifications of its cytoplasmic components during phagocytosis, *Anat. Rec.,* 167, 277, 1970.
25. Brandes, D. and Anton, E., An electron microscopic cytochemical study of macrophages during uterine involution, *J. Cell Biol.,* 41, 450, 1969.
26. Vaughn, J. E., Undifferentiated neuroglial cells in adult rat optic nerve, *J. Cell Biol.,* 35, 136, 1967.
27. Vaughn, J. E. and Peters, A., A third neuroglial cell type, *J. Comp. Neurol.,* 133, 269, 1968.
28. Blinzinger, K. and Kreutzberg, G., Displacement of synaptic terminals from regenerating motorneurons by microglial cells, *Z. Zellforsch. Mikrosk. Anat.,* 85, 145, 1968.

Neuromuscular System

MOTOR UNIT

Terry Mikiten

Table 1
AGING AND THE MOTOR UNIT

	Ref.
Aged rats (2 years old) show reduction in innervation ratio (number of muscle fibers innervated per motor axon) with no significant change in numbers of alpha motor-neurons.	1, 2
The rate of axoplasmic transport in motor neurons of aging animals is reduced.	2
No significant changes are seen in numbers of axons in the ventral roots of old (900 day) rats or old (13—18 year) cats. Old mice (110 weeks) show reduced numbers of large cells in spinal cord ventral horn.	3
Senile rats show decrease in rate of spontaneous transmitter release, accompanied by alterations of nerve terminals at the neuromuscular junction.	4, 5, 7, 13, 19
Neuromuscular junctions of senile rats exhibit changes in postjunctional membrane morphology, with little evidence of changes generally observed following denervation.	4
It is suggested that aging impairs replacement of deteriorated motor nerve terminals by neurons.	5, 11, 13
Acetylcholinesterase and choline acetyltransferase levels decrease with progressive age in rats.	6, 16
Old age is accompanied by decreased spontaneous activity in animals and man: part of the change may be due to changes in the properties of the motor unit.	4, 8, 9
Motor nerve terminals in senile rat skeletal muscle contain increased numbers of synaptic vesicles, mitochondria, neurotubules, and neurofilaments.	14
During aging, the mixture of fast and slow motor units characteristic of skeletal muscle is often lost, with the development of a homogenous population (rat).	15
The rat diaphragm fails to exhibit significant changes in motor unit distribution with aging.	15, 17
Senescent rat muscle shows decreased membrane resistance, increased threshold for critical depolarization at the endplate, increased absolute and relative refractory periods, and increased negative after-potential.	16
Aging rat muscle shows decreased quantal content of the endplate potential and raised sensitivity to curare.	16, 19
In aging humans, endplates show reduction in number of subsynaptic folds, with thickening of the remaining ones.	18
In aged humans, decreased performance of fast skeletal muscles is associated with a decrease in the number of motor units. The cross-sectional area of the surviving unit is enlarged.	20
In humans, the number of functional motor units of the slow soleus muscle declines with advanced age, while the size of the units remains constant.	21

REFERENCES

1. **Gutmann, E., Hanzlikova, V., and Jakoubek, B.,** Changes in the neuromuscular system during old age, *Exp. Gerontol.,* 3, 141, 1968.
2. **Gutmann, E. and Hanzlikova, V.,** Motor unit in old age, *Nature (London),* 209, 921, 1966.
3. **Brizzee, K. R.,** Gross morphometric analyses and quantitative histology of the aging brain, *Adv. Behav. Biol.,* 16, 401, 1975.
4. **Gutmann, E. Hanzlikova, E. V., and Vyskocil, F. J.,** Age changes in cross-striated muscle of the rat, *J. Physiol. (London),* 216, 331, 1971.
5. **Roberts, J., Baskin, S. I., and Goldberg, P. B.,** Age changes in the neuromuscular system of rats, *Exp. Aging Res.,* 3, 75, 1976.
6. **Frolkis, V. V., Bezrukov, V., Duplinko, Y. K., Schchegoleva, J. V., Shertchuk, V. G., and Verkhratsky, N. S.,** Acetylcholine metabolism and cholinergic regulation of functions in aging, *Gerontologia,* 19, 45, 1973.

Table 1 (continued)
AGING AND THE MOTOR UNIT

7. **Vyskocil, F. and Gutmann, E.,** Spontaneous transmitter release from motor nerve endings in muscle fibers of castrated and old animals, *Experientia,* 25, 945, 1969.
8. **Gutmann, E. and Hanzlikova, V.,** Basic mechanisms of aging in the neuromuscular system, *Mech. Ageing Dev.,* 1, 327, 1972/1973.
9. **Smith, L. C. and Dugal, L. P.,** Age and spontaneous running of male rats, *Can. J. Physiol. Pharmacol.,* 43, 852, 1965.
10. **Gutmann, E., Jakoubek, B., Fischer, J., and Babicky, A.,** Autoradiographic study of protein metabolism in old and adolescent neurons, *Life Sci.,* 6, 2143, 1967.
11. **Hanzlikova, V. and Gutmann, E.,** Retardation of development and involution of the pudendal nerve in female rat, *J. Ultrastruc. Res.,* 38, 302, 1972.
12. **Tauchi, H., Yoshioka, T., and Kobayashi, H.,** Age change of skeletal muscle of rats, *Gerontologia,* 17, 219, 1971.
13. **Fujisawa, K.,** Some observations on the skeletal musculature of aged rats. III. Abnormalities of terminal axons found in motor endplates, *Exp. Gerontol.,* 11, 43, 1976.
14. **Hanzlikova, V. and Gutmann, E.,** Ultrastructural changes in senile muscle, *Adv. Exp. Biol. Med.* 53, 421, 1975.
15. **Gutmann, E. and Hanzlikova, V.,** Denervation, reinnervation and regeneration of senile muscle, *Adv. Exp. Med. Biol.,* 53, 431, 1975.
16. **Frolkis, V. V., Martynenko, O. A., and Zamostyan, V. P.,** Aging of the neuromuscular apparatus, *Gerontology,* 22, 244, 1976.
17. **Gutmann, E. and Hanzlikova, V.,** Fast and slow motor unit in aging, *Gerontology,* 22, 280, 1976.
18. **Tomonaga, M.,** Histochemical and ultrastructural changes in senile human skeletal muscle, *J. Am. Geriatr. Soc.,* 25, 125, 1977.
19. **Kelly, S.,** The effect of age on neuromuscular transmission, *J. Physiol. (London),* 274, 51, 1978.
20. **Campbell, M. J., McComas, A. J., and Petito, F.,** Physiological changes in ageing muscles, *J. Neurol. Nuerosurg. Psychiatry,* 36, 174, 1973.
21. **Sica, R. E., Sanz, O. P., and Columbi, A.,** The effects of ageing upon the human soleus muscle. An electrophysiological study, *Medicina (Buenos Aires),* 36, 443, 1976.

SKELETAL MUSCLE

R. J. M. McCarter

Table 1
AGE-RELATED CHANGES IN SKELETAL MUSCLE

	Ref.
General	
In humans and rats, changes of structure and function of skeletal muscles associated with aging are similar to changes in skeletal muscles associated with many other factors, such as denervation and inactivity.	1—3
The observed age-related changes in skeletal muscle of humans and of rats are highly variable. They depend upon the location of the muscle and the fiber type involved.	4—7
Compositional changes	
The onset and severity of senile muscular atrophy in rats is age-related. In humans and rats the degree of atrophy is more pronounced in the lower (caudal) half than in the upper (rostral) half of the body.	4, 7
The proportion of fast-twitch (Type II) and slow-twitch (Type I) fibers present in a given human muscle varies with age and this variation is different for different muscles.	6
The decrease in mass of fast skeletal muscles of old (24 months of age) rats is due to a decrease in the *volume* of "white" fibers and to a decrease in the *number* of "red" fibers present in the muscles.	8
Atrophy of Type II fibers has been observed more frequently than that of Type I fibers in the skeletal musculature of aged humans (65—98 years of age), particularly in subjects who have been unable to exercise. However, in the diaphragm and intercostal muscles of aged humans, atrophy of Type I fibers is more prominent than atrophy of Type II fibers.	5
There is a decrease in the number of muscle fibers, with no associated decrease in the number of α-motor nerve fibers, in the soleus muscle of rats with advanced age.	9
In the human rectus abdominis muscle there is a decrease in the number and average size of muscle fibers with advanced age. At the same time there is an increase in the amounts of connective tissue and fat cells present.	10
Atrophic muscles of aged rats exhibit scattered hypertrophic fibers containing degenerative changes.	7
Atrophic fibers of aged rat skeletal muscles exhibit ultrastructural degeneration nonuniformly distributed along the length of the fibers. These degenerative changes include streaming of the Z lines, dilatation of the sarcoplasmic reticulum, proliferation of the transverse tubular system, coagulation of the myofibrils, and the formation of contracture bands.	2, 11
Functional changes	
There is a marked reduction in the frequency of miniature endplate potentials in the skeletal muscles of 30-month-old rats as compared with 2-month-old rats.	11
There is no change in the resting membrane potential of skeletal muscles of 30-month-old rats, compared with that of 2-month-old rats.	11
In man, average isometric muscle tension declines after 30 years of age.	19
The rates of tension development and of relaxation are slower in fast muscles of aged rats, compared with young rats.	11
Slow muscles of the rat contract more quickly with advanced age.	20
The muscles of aged humans require less stretch for the development of maximum isometric tension than do the muscles of young adults.	18
Ultrastructural degeneration is evident in fibers of aged human extraocular muscles, but this degeneration is not always associated with functional deficit.	12, 13
The diet of houseflies has a significant effect upon the proportion of mitochondria showing degenerative changes in 15-day-old flies.	14
The glycogen content of skeletal muscles of rats declines with age.	15, 16
Glycogen concentration decreases with age in flight muscles of insects.	17
There is an increase in the intracellular and extracellular concentration of sodium ions in the gastrocnemius muscles of aged rats when compared with adult rats.	15

Table 1 (continued)
AGE-RELATED CHANGES IN SKELETAL MUSCLE

	Ref.
There is a decrease in the intracellular and total potassium concentrations of the gastrocnemius muscles of aged rats compared with adult rats, but an increase in the extracellular concentration of potassium ions in these muscles.	15
There is a movement of water from the intracellular to the extracellular space in the gastrocnemius muscles of aged rats as compared with adult rats.	15
In rats, the rate of calcium transport by isolated vesicles of skeletal muscle sarcoplasmic reticulum increases with age.	21
The oxygen consumption of slices of rat quadriceps femoris muscle declines with age.	23
The mitochondria of aged insects exhibit degenerative changes in which the cristae are disoriented into whorls and cytochrome oxidase activity is decreased.	24, 25
There is a decrease in respiratory activity of mitochondria from aged flies.	26
There is a decline in the specific activity of oxidative enzymes of skeletal muscle with advanced age in rats.	27
There is small decline in the specific activity of the magnesium-activated actomyosin adenosine triphosphatase (ATP-ase) present in muscles of aged (28-month-old) rats compared with that of muscles from adult (6-month-old) rats. There is no change in the specific activity of the calcium-activated myosin ATP-ase of muscles from the same populations of adult and aged rats.	28, 29
Old mosquitoes have less ability to utilize stores of intracellular glycogen in flight muscles than do young mosquitoes.	30
The capacity for sustained flight decreases in aged higher insects (notably in flies).	14

REFERENCES

1. **Skinner, J. S.**, Age and performance, in *Limiting Factors of Physical Performance*, Keul, J., Ed., Thieme, Stuttgart, 1971, 271.
2. **Fujisawa, K.**, Some observations on the skeletal musculature of aged rats. II. Fine morphology of diseased muscle fibers, *J. Neurol. Sci.*, 24, 447, 1974.
3. **McCarter, R. J. M.**, Effects of age on contraction of mammalian skeletal muscle, in *Aging*, Vol. 6, Kaldor, G. and DiBattista, W. J., Eds., Raven Press, New York, 1978, 1.
4. **Tomlinson, B. E., Walton, J. N., and Rebeiz, J. J.**, The effects of ageing and of cachexia upon skeletal muscle. A histopathological study, *J. Neurol. Sci.*, 9, 321, 1969.
5. **Tohgi, H., Shimizu, T., Inoue, K., and Kameyama, M.**, Quantitative histochemical studies on age-dependent changes of human muscles. I. Histograms of fiber diameters, *Clin. Neurol. Tokyo Rinsho Shin Keiga Ku*, 15, 791, 1975.
6. **Tohgi, H., Shimizu, T., Inoue, K., and Kameyama, M.**, Quantitative histochemical studies on age-dependent changes of human muscles. II. Proportion of fiber types and type grouping, *Clin. Neurol. Tokyo Rinsho Shin Keiga Ku*, 15, 798, 1975.
7. **Fujisawa, K.**, Some observations on the skeletal musculature of aged rats. I. Histological aspects, *J. Neurol. Sci.*, 22, 353, 1974.
8. **Tauchi, H., Yoshioka, T., and Kobayashi, H.**, Age changes in skeletal muscle of rats, *Gerontologia*, 17, 219, 1971.
9. **Gutmann, E., Hanzlikova, V., and Jakoubek, B.**, Changes in the neuromuscular system during old age, *Exp. Gerontol.*, 3, 141, 1968.
10. **Inokuchi, S., Ishikwa, H., Iwamoto, S., and Kimura, T.**, Age related changes in the histological composition of the rectus abdominus muscle of the adult human, *Hum. Biol.*, 47(2), 231, 1975.
11. **Gutmann, E., Hanzlikova, V., and Vyskocil, F.**, Age changes in cross-striated muscle of the rat., *J. Physiol. (London)*, 216, 331, 1971.
12. **Rubinstein, L. J.**, Ageing changes in muscle, in *The Structure and Function of the Muscle*, Vol. 3, Bourne, G. H., Ed., Academic Press, New York, 1960, 209.

Table 1 (continued)
AGE-RELATED CHANGES IN SKELETAL MUSCLE

13. Miller, J. E., Aging changes in extraocular muscle, in *Symposium on Basic Mechanisms of Ocular Motility and Their Clinical Implications,* Lennerstrand, G. and Bach-y-Bita, P., Eds., Pergamon Press, Oxford, 1974, 47.
14. Sohal, R. S., Aging changes in insect flight muscle, *Gerontology,* 22, 317, 1976.
15. Friedman, S. M., Streter, F. A., and Friedman, C. L., The distribution of water, sodium, and potassium in the aged rat: a pattern of adrenal preponderance, *Gerontologia,* 7, 44, 1963.
16. Szelenyi, I., Ermini, M., and Moser, P., Glycogen content in young and old rat liver and muscles, *Experientia,* 28, 257, 1972.
17. Williams, C. M., Barness, L. A., and Sawyer, W. H., The utilization of glycogen by flies during flight and some aspects of the physiological ageing of Drosophilia, *Biol. Bull. Woods Hole, Mass.),* 84, 263, 1943.
18. Campbell, M. J., McComas, A. J., and Petito, F., Physiological changes in ageing muscles, *J. Neurol. Neurosurg. Psychiatry,* 36, 174, 1973.
19. Asmussen, E., The neuromuscular system and exercise, in *Exercise Physiology,* Falls, H. B., Academic Press, New York, 1968, 1.
20. Gutmann, E. and Syrovy, I., Contraction properties and myosin-ATPase activity of fast and slow senile muscles of the rat, *Gerontologia,* 20, 239, 1974.
21. Bertrand, H. A., Yu, B. P., and Masoro, E. J., The effect of rat age on the composition and functional activities of skeletal muscle sarcoplasmic reticulum membrane preparations, *Mech. Ageing Dev.,* 4, 7, 1975.
22. Keul, J., Doll, E., and Keppler, D., The oxygen consumption of isolated skeletal muscle mitochondria declines in aged rats, in *Muskelstoffwechsel,* J. A. Barth, Munich, 1969, 1.
23. Angelova-Gateva, P., Tissue respiration and glycolysis in quadriceps femoris and heart of rats of different ages during hypodynamia, *Exp. Gerontol.,* 4, 177, 1969.
24. Webb, S. and Tribe, M. A., Are there major degenerative changes in the flight muscle of ageing diptera?, *Exp. Gerontol.,* 9, 43, 1974.
25. Saktor, B. and Shimada, Y., Degenerative changes in the mitochondria of flight muscle from ageing blowflies, *J. Cell Biol.,* 52, 465, 1972.
26. Tribe, M. A., Changes taking place in the respiratory efficiency of isolated flight muscle sarcosomes associated with the age of the blowfly, *Calliphora erythrocephala, Comp. Biochem. Physiol.,* 23, 607, 1967.
27. Ermini, M., Ageing changes in mammalian skeletal muscle: biochemical studies, *Gerontology,* 22, 301, 1976.
28. Kaldor, G. and Min, B. K., Enzymatic studies on the skeletal myosin A and actomyosin of ageing rats, *Fed. Proc. Fed. Am. Soc. Exp. Biol.,* 34, 191, 1975.
29. Ermini, M., Das Alteren der Skelettmuskulatur, *Gerontologia,* 16, 72, 1970.
30. Rowley, W. A. and Graham, C. L., The effect of age on the flight performance of female *Aedes aegypti* mosquitoes, *J. Insect Physiol.,* 14, 719, 1968.

Blood

PLASMA COMPONENTS

Byung P. Yu

Table 1
SUMMARY OF INFORMATION ON EFFECTS OF AGE ON THE CONCENTRATION IN PLASMA OR SERUM OF SELECTED SUBSTANCES

		Ref.
1.	Some studies show total serum protein of rats and cattle to increase with age; another study shows total protein concentration in the serum of rats to progressively decrease with increasing age.	4,8,10,12
2.	Studies on mice and cattle indicate that the serum albumin concentration does not change with age, but data from the male Fischer 344 rat show decreasing serum albumin levels with increasing age. The concentration of globulins was found to increase with age in rats and cattle.	4,5,7,8,10,12
3.	There are no significant age-associated changes in serum concentrations of Na^+, K^+, Cl^- in rats, mice, and cattle.	4,5,13
4.	Evidence for the age-dependent decreases in the serum concentration of calcium and phosphate has been reported for humans and cattle.	9,13
5.	In elderly human subjects the levels of some amino acids are lower than in the young adults; this is particularly true of the essential amino acids, valine, methionine, isoleucine, leucine, phenylalanine, and lysine.	1
6.	The elevation of the plasma concentration of triglycerides and cholesterol begins at an early age and continues steadily with advancing age.	3,4,6,11
7.	A steady rise after 4 months of age in plasma phospholipid levels of the rat has been reported.	3
8.	There is no consistent change with age in serum free fatty acid concentrations of rats.	3

REFERENCES

1. Ackermann, P. G. and Kheim, T., Plasma amino acids in young and older adult human subjects, *Clin. Chem.* 10, 32, 1964.
2. Brody, S. and Carlson, L. A., Plasma lipid concentrations in the newborn with special reference to the distribution of the different lipid fractions, *Clin. Chim. Acta*, 7, 694, 1962.
3. Carlson, L. A., Fröberg, S. O., and Nye, E. R., Effect of age on blood and tissue lipid levels in the male rat, *Gerontologia*, 14, 65, 1968.
4. Coleman, G. L., Barthold, S. W., Osbaldiston, G. W., Forster, S. J., and Jonas, A. M., Pathological changes during aging in barrier-reared Fischer 344 male rats, *J. Gerontol.*, 32, 258, 1977.
5. Finch, C. E. and Foster, J. R., Hematologic and serum electrolyte values of the C57BL/GJ male mouse in maturity and senescence, *Lab. Anim. Sci.*, 23, 339, 1973.
6. Keys, A., Mickelsen, O., Miller, E., Hayes, E. R., and Todd, R. L., The concentration of cholesterol in the blood serum of normal man and its relation to age, *J. Clin. Invest.*, 29, 1347, 1950.
7. Larson, B. L. and Touchberry, R. W., Blood serum protein level as a function of age, *J. Anim. Sci.*, 18, 983, 1959.
8. Riegle, G. D. and Nellor, J. F., Changes in blood cellular and protein components during aging, *J. Gerontol.*, 21, 435, 1966.
9. Roof, B. S., Piel, C. F., Hansen, J., and Fundenberg, H. H., Serum parathyroid hormone levels and serum calcium levels from birth to senescence, *Mech. Ageing Dev.*, 5, 289, 1976.
10. Salatka, K., Kresge, D., Harris, L., Jr., Edelstein, D., and Ove, P., Rat serum protein changes with age, *Exp. Gerontol.*, 6, 25, 1971.
11. Schilling, F. J., Christakis, G., Orbach, A., and Becker, W. H., Serum cholesterol and triglyceride. An epidemiological and pathogenetic interpretation, *Am. J. Clin. Nutr.*, 22, 133, 1969.
12. Tumbleson, M. E., Burks, M. F., and Wingfield, W. E., Serum protein concentrations as a function of age in female dairy cattle, *Cornell Vet.*, 63, 65, 1973.
13. Tumbleson, M. E., Wingfield, W. E., Johnson, H. D., Campbell, J. R., and Middleton, C. C., Serum electrolyte concentrations, as a function of age, in female dairy cattle, *Cornell Vet.*, 63, 58, 1973.

Table 2
AGE-RELATED CHANGES IN THE CONCENTRATION OF AMINO ACIDS IN HUMAN PLASMA (μM/ℓ)

	Young subjects		Old subjects	
	Men[a]	Women[b]	Men[c]	Women[d]
Taurine	62.0±13.2	55.2± 7.6	56.5±10.8	55.0± 9.3
Aspartic acid	19.2± 4.5	19.5± 3.6	20.2± 3.9	20.5± 4.9
Threonine	146.2±25.2	147.2±24.7	138.8±22.4	145.5±17.0
Serine	105.5±20.7	113.1±22.4	88.7±15.5	90.8±12.4
Proline	202.8±28.5	203.7±23.2	192.9±24.9	199.2±29.1
Glutamic acid	71.5±11.8	77.5±13.2	68.4±13.6	68.6± 8.5
Glycine	224.8±36.0	239.8±42.6	205.1±29.1	208.2±25.5
Alanine	325.1±44.0	328.1±32.1	287.2±31.0	296.2±24.0
Valine	258.8±37.7	247.2±37.9	224.2±31.1	216.4±27.7
Cystine	70.9±13.7	71.7±12.2	71.4± 9.7	74.1±10.5
Methionine	26.0± 7.2	27.3± 4.5	24.0± 4.3	23.2± 3.5
Isoleucine	80.8±10.4	78.7±10.6	69.3± 8.5	68.5±11.2
Leucine	130.9±17.0	128.0±17.5	111.7±24.3	117.4±19.1
Tyrosine	70.3± 9.0	66.9± 9.1	59.6± 9.5	58.9± 9.4
Phenylalanine	67.2± 9.1	66.2± 8.9	58.5± 8.1	55.4± 7.2
Ornithine	67.3±12.7	71.3±14.3	61.5±10.0	63.2±11.8
Lysine	156.5±23.4	153.0±18.3	132.6±19.3	123.7±19.3
Histidine	91.8±12.0	97.8±12.7	89.1±10.1	89.5± 7.9
Arginine	81.5±15.1	83.3±14.1	72.2±10.5	70.5±14.4

[a] Average age 30 years; n = 16.
[b] Average age 32 years; n = 17.
[c] Average age 67 years; n = 17.
[d] Average age 69 years; n = 17.

From Ackermann, P. G. and Kheim, T., *Clin. Chem.*, 10, 32, 1964. With permission.

Table 3
AGE-RELATED CHANGES IN THE CONCENTRATION OF PLASMA LIPIDS AND GLYCEROL IN RAT PLASMA

Age (months)	Plasma FFA (mmol/l)	Plasma glycerol (mmol/l)	Plasma cholesterol (mg/100 mℓ)	Plasma phospholipids (mg/100 mℓ)	Plasma triglycerides (mmol/l)
1	0.45±0.03	0.150±0.004	95±6	130±5	0.51±0.06
n	12	8	12	12	12
4	0.55±0.05	0.174±0.010	94±8	142±12	0.83±0.07
n	12	10	12	12	12
9	0.44±0.02	0.159±0.012	213±33	271±30	2.50±0.38
n	12	12	12	12	12
18	0.57±0.09	0.193±0.011	307±18	353±19	2.55±0.34
n	12	12	12	12	12

Note: n = number of rats.

From Carlson, L. A., Fröberg, S. O., and Nye, E. R., *Gerontologia*, 14, 65, 1968. With permission.

RED BLOOD CELLS AND ERYTHROPOIESIS

Byung P. Yu

Table 1
SUMMARY OF INFORMATION ON EFFECTS OF AGE ON RED BLOOD CELLS AND ERYTHROPOIESIS

	Ref.
1. Data on the red cell population are conflicting; some studies indicate that the number of erythrocytes per milliliter blood decreases with increasing age in the mouse and man; another study indicates that this age-related decrease in erythrocytes occurs only in men who smoke, while other studies failed to show such a change.	3,4,5,16,17
2. A number of studies show that the Hb level in humans is not influenced by age; however, one study reported that after the age of 50 years the Hb level of nonsmoking men increases and that of smoking men decreases. A decrease in Hb concentration was observed with increasing age in the mouse.	4,10,15—17
3. No age-related change in hematocrit was reported in human subjects, but a slight fall was observed with increasing age in the mouse.	4,10,14,16,17
4. Mean corpuscular hemoglobin concentration (MCHC) does not change with age in humans.	10,18
5. A slight but statistically significant increase in mean corpuscular hemoglobin (MCH) was reported for men and women, but not for dairy cattle.	10, 19
6. Mean corpuscular volume (MCV) increases slightly with age in both sexes of human subjects, but not in animals.	10,17,19
7. The concentration of 2,3-diphosphoglycerate (DPG) in human red blood cells in one study was shown to change little with age and in another study was shown to decrease with age.	15,18
8. The P50 (oxygen tension and 50% saturation of hemoglobin with O_2) increases in blood with increasing age in men and women.	2,18
9. In one study the Na⁺ concentration in erythrocytes was reported not to change with age in men and women, but in another study the Na⁺ concentration was increased with age in women, but not in men.	1,13
10. K⁺ concentration in the erythrocyte does not show any age-related changes.	1,13
11. Erythrocyte sedimentation rate (ESR) increases linearly with age.	8,9,16
12. Cholesterol level of erythrocytes increases with age in the rat and in man, but the concentration and profile of phospholipids show no change with age.	11,12
13. The erythropoietic system has been shown not to be age-influenced.	6,7

REFERENCES

1. Beilin, L. J., Knight, G. J., Munro-Faure, A. D., and Anderson, J., The sodium, potassium, and water contents of red blood cells in healthy human adults, *J. Clin. Invest.,* 45, 1817, 1966.
2. Brinstimgle, M., Col, P., and Hawkins, L., Variations in oxyhaemoglobin dissociation with age, smoking, and Buerger's disease, *Br. J. Surg.,* 54, 615, 1967.
3. Das, B. C., Linear and curvilinear functional relationships between human blood components and age, *Gerontology,* 13, 227, 1967.
4. Earney, W. W. and Earney, A. J., Geriatric hematology, *J. Am. Geriatr. Soc.,* 20, 174, 1972.
5. Garcia, J. F., Changes in blood, plasma and red cell volume in the male rat, as a function of age, *Am. J. Physiol.,* 190, 19, 1957.
6. Garcia, J. F., Erythropoietic response to hypoxia as a function of age in the normal male rat, *Am. J. Physiol.,* 190, 25, 1957.
7. Grant, W. C. and LeGrande, C. M., The influence of age on erythropoiesis in the rat, *J. Gerontol.,* 19, 505, 1964.

Table 1 (continued)
SUMMARY OF INFORMATION ON EFFECTS OF AGE ON RED BLOOD CELLS AND ERYTHROPOIESIS

8. **Hamilton, P. J., Dawson, A. A., Ogston, D., and Douglas, S.**, The effect of age on the fribrinlytic enzyme system, *J. Clin. Pathol.*, 27, 326, 1974.
9. **Hayes, G. S. and Stinson, I. V.**, Erythrocyte sedimentation rate and age, *Arch. Opthalmol.*, 94, 939, 1976.
10. **Helman, N. and Rubenstein, L. S.**, The effects of age, sex and smoking on erythrocytes and leukocytes, *Am. J. Pathol.*, 63, 35, 1975.
11. **Iacono, J. M., Zellner, D., Paoletti, R., Ishikawa, T., Frigeni, V., and Fumagalli, R.**, Comparison of blood platelet and erythrocyte lipids in man in three age groups from three regions: Milan, Cincinnati and Sicily, *Haemostasis*, 2, 141, 1974.
12. **Malhotra, S. and Kritchevsky, D.**, Cholesterol exchange between the red blood cells and plasma of young and old rats, *Mech. Ageing Dev.*, 4, 137, 1975.
13. **Nagaki, J. and Teraoka, M.**, Age and sex differences of sodium and potassium concetration in red blood cells, *Clin. Chim. Acta*, 66, 453, 1976.
14. **Olbrich, O.**, Blood changes in the aged, *Edinburgh Med. J.*, 54, 306, 1947.
15. **Purcell, Y. and Brozovic, B.**, Red cell 2,3-diphosphoglycerate concentration in man decreases with age, *Nature (London)*, 251, 511, 1974.
16. **Shapleigh, J. B., Mayes, S., and Moore, C. V.**, Hematologic values in the aged, *J. Gerontol.*, 7, 207, 1952.
17. **Silini, G. and Andreozzi, U.**, Hematological changes in the aging mouse, *Exp. Gerontol.*, 9, 99, 1974.
18. **Tweeddale, P. M., Leggett, R. J. E., and Flenley, D. C.**, Effect of age on oxygen-binding in normal human subjects, *Clin. Sci. Mol. Med.*, 51, 185, 1976.
19. **Wingfield, W. E. and Tumbleson, M. E.**, Hematologic parameters, as a function of age, in female dairy cattle, *Cornell Vet.*, 63, 72, 1973.

Table 2
THE RED BLOOD CELL COUNT[a] IN MEN AND WOMEN OF DIFFERENT AGES

Age (years)	Men n[b]	Nonsmokers	n[b]	Smokers	Women n[b]	Nonsmokers	n[b]	Smokers
20—29	56	5.25±0.4	26	5.14±0.4	74	4.62±0.3	39	4.66±0.3
30—39	62	5.40±0.3	34	5.10±0.3	74	4.51±0.4	31	4.62±0.3
40—49	44	5.10±0.4	29	5.07±0.4	55	4.53±0.3	48	4.62±0.4
50—59	44	5.10±0.4	17	4.90±0.4	59	5.60±0.3	38	4.38±0.4
60—69	25	5.10±0.4	10	4.80±0.4	30	4.70±0.4	5	5.65±0.5

[a] Expressed in × 10^6 cells/μl.
[b] n = number of subjects.

From Helman, N. and Rubenstein, L. S., *Am. J. Clin. Pathol.*, 63, 35, 1975. With permission.

Table 3
THE HEMOGLOBIN CONCENTRATION IN BLOOD[a] OF MEN AND WOMEN OF DIFFERENT AGES

Age (years)	Men n[b]	Nonsmokers	n[b]	Smokers	Women n[b]	Nonsmokers	n[b]	Smokers
20—29	56	15.5±0.9	26	15.8±0.9	74	13.7±0.9	39	14.4±0.8
30—39	62	15.6±0.6	34	16.0±1.2	74	13.6±1.0	31	14.5±1.1
40—49	44	15.3±0.9	29	16.0±1.1	55	13.7±1.0	48	14.5±0.9
50—59	44	15.5±1.0	17	15.2±0.9	59	13.8±0.7	38	14.3±1.1
60—69	25	15.8±0.8	10	15.2±0.6	30	14.2±1.1	5	14.5±1.5

[a] Expressed in g/100 ml.
[b] n = number of subjects.

From Helman, N. and Rubenstein, L. S., *Am. J. Clin. Pathol.*, 63, 35, 1975. With permission.

Table 4
THE HEMATOCRIT[a] IN MEN AND WOMEN OF DIFFERENT AGES

Age (years)	Men n[b]	Nonsmokers	n[b]	Smokers	Women n[b]	Nonsmokers	n[b]	Smokers
20—29	56	46.5±2.3	26	46.9±2.5	74	41.5±2.4	39	43.3±2.2
30—39	62	46.7±2.2	34	48.3±3.2	74	41.2±2.8	31	43.0±2.8
40—49	44	46.6±3.0	29	48.0±3.0	55	41.2±2.4	48	44.2±2.5
50—59	44	46.0±2.6	17	56.2±2.5	59	41.9±2.0	38	43.4±3.1
60—69	25	46.6±2.6	10	46.1±1.9	30	43.0±2.3	5	43.7±2.7

[a] Expressed as percentage (%).
[b] n = number of subjects.

From Helman, N. and Rubenstein, L. S., *Am. J. Clin. Pathol.*, 63, 35, 1975. With permission.

Table 5
CONCENTRATIONS OF 2,3-DIPHOSPHOGLYCERATE (2,3-DPG) IN RED BLOOD CELLS OF HUMANS OF DIFFERENT AGES

	2,3-DPG[a]	
Age (years)	n[b]	Mean±SD
18—24	26	14.9±1.6
25—34	35	14.4±1.3
35—44	17	14.3±1.5
45—54	17	14.2±1.5
55—64	11	14.9±1.8
65—74	56	13.8±1.9
75—84	104	13.9±2.4
85 and over	16	12.8±2.0

[a] Expressed in μmol/g hemoglobin.
[b] n = number of subjects.

From Purcell, Y. and Brozovic, B., *Nature (London)*, 251, 511, 1974. With permission.

Table 6
CONCENTRATION OF NA⁺ AND K⁺ IN RED BLOOD CELLS OF MEN AND WOMEN OF DIFFERENT AGES

Age (years)	Sex	n	Sodium Mean	Sex effect	Potassium Mean	Sex effect
2—9	M	27	9.15±1.24	ns	98.83±2.34	ns
	F	13	9.61±1.18		99.62±2.51	
10—14	M	75	10.52±1.03	ns	97.90±1.83	$p < 0.01$
	F	54	10.23±1.03		99.54±1.46	
15—19	M	17	10.78±1.67	ns	98.71±2.69	ns
	F	17	10.15±1.06		98.74±1.84	
20—44	M	102	9.86±1.25	$p < 0.01$	98.56±2.73	ns
	F	102	9.38±0.94		98.85±2.24	
45—49	M	18	9.97±1.36	ns	98.46±3.08	ns
	F	17	9.46±1.15		98.94±1.84	
50—59	M	29	9.71±1.50	$p < 0.05$	99.80±2.27	$p < 0.05$
	F	24	10.50±1.12		98.30±2.14	
60—90	M	37	10.54±1.30	ns	99.01±2.86	ns
	F	38	10.62±1.39		99.82±2.23	

Note: n = number of subjects; ns = not significant ($p > 0.05$); and the concentrations are expressed as meq/ℓ red blood cells.

From Nagaki, J. and Teraoka, M., *Clin. Chim. Acta*, 66, 453, 1976. With permission.

Table 7
ERYTHROCYTE SEDIMENTATION RATES (ESR) IN HUMANS OF DIFFERENT AGES

Age (years)	n[a]	Mean ESR[b]
<30	23	8.8± 6.2
30—39	26	11.7± 7.8
40—49	24	14.8± 8.2
50—59	25	15.0±11.6
60—69	32	19.3± 8.7
70—79	22	22.7±13.2
80—89	17	26.8±13.8

[a] n = number of subjects.
[b] Expressed in mm/hr.

From Hayes, G. S. and Stinson, I. V., *Arch. Ophthalmol.*, 94, 939, 1976. Copyright 1976, American Medical Association.

Table 8
CHOLESTEROL AND LIPID PHOSPHORUS CONTENT OF RED BLOOD CELLS OF MALE RATS OF DIFFERENT AGES

	1½-month-old rats RBC	12—24-month-old rats RBC
Free cholesterol	0.334±0.020	0.598±0.038[a]
Lipid phosphorus	0.077±0.004	0.077±0.004
Cholesterol:lipid p mass ratio	4.34	7.72

[a] $P < 0.001$.

From Malhotra, S. and Kritchevsky, D., *Mech. Ageing Dev.*, 4, 137, 1975. With permission.

Table 9
PHOSPHOLIPID COMPOSITION OF RED BLOOD CELLS OF MALE RATS OF DIFFERENT AGES

Phospholipid class	1½-month-old rats RBC	12—24-month-old rats RBC
Phosphatidylinositol	7.89±1.0	8.80±2.0
Lysophosphatidylcholine + phosphatidylserine	8.86±1.0	11.37±0.8
Sphingomyelin	13.64±2.0	12.00±0.7
Phosphatidylcholine	36.50±2.0	36.51±2.0
Phosphatidylethanolamine	8.48±2.0	7.46±2.0
Phosphoglycerol phosphate + phosphatidic acid	1.31±0.2	1.30±0.3

From Malhotra, S. and Kritchevsky, D., *Mech. Ageing Dev.*, 4, 137, 1975. With permission.

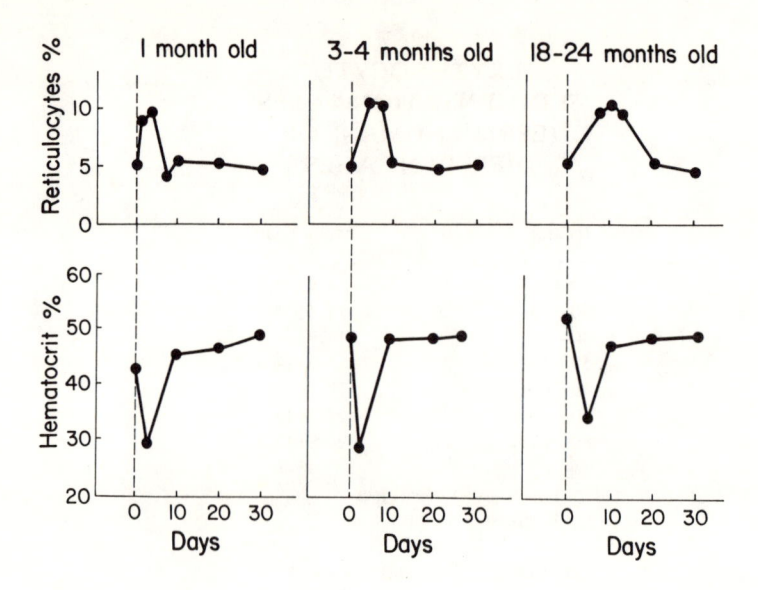

FIGURE 1. The erythropoietic response of male Fischer 344 rats of different ages to the acute loss of blood amounting to a 2% loss of body weight. (From Grant, W. C. and LeGrande, M. C., *J. Gerontol.*, 19, 515, 1964. With permission.)

LEUKOCYTES AND LYMPHOCYTES

Byung P. Yu

Table 1
SUMMARY OF INFORMATION ON EFFECTS OF AGE ON LEUKOCYTES
AND LYMPHOCYTES

		Ref.
1.	There is no set pattern of age-associated changes in distribution and differential counts of leukocyte population.	1,3,6
2.	The total number of leukocytes per milliliter of blood does not change with age in humans and rats.	2—5
3.	The quantitative distribution of leukocytes among the subclasses (e.g., monocytes, polymorphonuclear leukocytes, etc.) is not influenced by age in man and mouse.	1,3,6
4.	There is an age-related decline in the absolute lymphocyte count in barrier-maintained mice with age, while the number of lymphocytes found in the blood of germ-free mice appears to increase with age.	7
5.	In man, a significant increase in the B lymphocytes was observed with advancing age.	8
6.	In rats, the absolute number of lymphocytes decreases sharply until 20 weeks of age and falls slowly until 40 weeks of age; after 70 weeks of age, it rises slowly until death.	9

REFERENCES

1. Earney, W. W. and Earney, A. J., Geriatric hematology, *J. Geriatr. Soc.*, 20, 174, 1972.
2. Everitt, A. V. and Cavanah, L. M., The aging process in the hypophysectomized rat, *Gerontologia*, 11, 198, 1965.
3. Helman, N. and Rubenstein, L. S., The effects of age, sex, and smoking on erythrocytes and leukocytes, *Am. J. Clin. Pathol.*, 63, 35, 1975.
4. Olbrich, O., Blood changes in the age, *Edinburg Med. J.*, 54, 306, 1947.
5. Shapleigh, J. B., Mayes, S., and Moore, C. V., Hematologic values in the aged, *J. Gerontol.*, 7, 207, 1952.
6. Silini, G. and Andreozzi, U., Hematological changes in the aging mouse, *Exp. Gerontol.*, 9, 99, 1974.
7. Anderson, R. E., Scaletti, J. V., and Howarth, J. L., Radiation-induced life shortening in germ-free mice, *Exp. Gerontol.*, 7, 289, 1972.
8. Del Pozo Perez, M. A., Valtuena, J. P., Gonzales Guilabert, M. I., and Velaso Alanso, R., Effects of age and sex on T and B lymphocyte populations in man, *Biomedicine*, 19, 340, 1973.
9. Wagner, M. M. F., Changes with age in the hematopoietic system in a Cesarean-derived, barrier-maintained colony of Wistar rats, *J. Nat. Cancer Inst.*, 57, 501, 1976.

Table 2
DIFFERENTIAL LEUKOCYTE COUNTS IN THE CIRCULATING BLOOD
OF FEMALE HYBRID MICE OF DIFFERENT AGES

Age (days)	n	Cell counted	Neutrophylic (%)	Eosinophylic (%)	Lymphocytes (%)	Monocytes (%)	Other (%)
134	10	978	17.6	1.0	79.2	2.2	—
214	6	300	27.0	1.3	61.0	10.7	—
308	10	633	22.4	3.0	61.1	13.4	0.2
472	10	992	32.3	2.4	54.2	11.1	—
518	10	800	27.5	2.4	66.0	4.1	—
622	5	501	31.9	0.2	56.7	11.2	—
649	9	783	31.4	1.7	57.6	9.1	0.2
800	9	798	24.3	2.0	54.0	19.2	0.5
921	9	500	17.6	1.8	74.0	5.0	1.6

Note: n = number of animals.

Reprinted with permission from *Exp. Gerontol.,* 9, Silini, G. and Andreozzi, U., Hematological changes in the aging mouse, Copyright 1974, Pergamon Press, Ltd.

Table 3
B LYMPHOCYTES: % OF TOTAL
LYMPHOCYTE POPULATION IN YOUNG AND
ELDERLY MEN AND WOMEN

	Young (mean %) of total lymphocytes	Aged (mean %) of total lymphocytes	P
Total B population	16.3±6.7	25.2±11.1	< 0.001
IgG lymphocytes	11.5±5.9	17.2± 8.0	< 0.005
IgM lymphocytes	3.4±2.8	4.9± 3.8	ns
IgA lymphocytes	1.3±1.5	3.1± 3.9	ns

Note: ns = not significant ($P > 0.05$); n = 19 aged between 17 to 29 (young); and n = 44 aged between 52 to 92 (aged).

From Del Pozo Perez, M. A., Valtuena, J. P., Gonzalez Guilabert, M. I., and Velasco Alano, R., *Biomedicine,* 19, 340, 1973. With permission.

PLATELETS AND BLOOD CLOTTING

Byung P. Yu

Table 1
SUMMARY OF INFORMATION ON EFFECTS OF AGE ON PLATELETS AND BLOOD CLOTTING

	Ref.
1. There is little change in cholesterol content and total lipid content, but a slight increase in phospholipid content of platelets with advancing age in human subjects.	4
2. No consistent change with age has been found in the number of platelets per milliliter of blood in humans and mice.	2, 5—7
3. Coagulation factors XI, XII, and antithrombin III levels tend to decrease with age in men and to increase in women, while factors X, VII, and V tend to increase in both men and women with advancing ages. No age or sex differences were found in factor VIII.	2
4. In man, plasminogen does not change with age until after 75 years of age at which time its concentration falls with advancing age. Fibrinogen, FR-antigen, α_1-antitrypsin, and α_2-macroglobulin all increase with age in humans.	3, 8
5. There is a steady increase in antihemophilic globulin (AHG) level until the 6th decade in both men and women.	1

REFERENCES

1. **Cooperberg, A. and Teitelbaum, J.,** The concentration of antihaemophilic globulin related to age, *Br. J. Haematol.*, 6, 281, 1960.
2. **Hamilton, P. J., Allardyce, M., Ogston, D., Dawson, A. A., and Douglas, A. S.,** The effect of age upon the coagulation system, *J. Clin. Pathol.*, 27, 980, 1974.
3. **Hamilton, P. J., Dawson, A. A., Ogston, D., and Douglas, A. S.,** The effect of age on the fibrinolytic enzyme system, *J. Clin. Pathol.*, 27, 326, 1974.
4. **Iacono, J. M., Zellner, D. C., Paoletti, R., Ishikawa, T., Frigeni, V., and Fumagalli, R.,** Comparison of blood platelet and erythrocyte lipids in man in three age groups from three regions, *Haemostasis*, 2, 141, 1974.
5. **Josephson, B. and Dahlberg, G.,** Variations in the cell count and chemical composition of the human blood due to age, sex, and season, *Scand. J. Clin. Lab. Invest.*, 4, 216, 1592.
6. **Shapleigh, J. B., Mayes, S., and Moore, C. V.,** Hematologic values in the aged, *J. Gerontol.*, 7, 207, 1952.
7. **Silini, G. and Andreozzi, U.,** Haematological changes in the ageing mouse, *Exp. Gerontol.*, 9, 99, 1974.
8. **Swan, H. T.,** Fibrinolysis related to age in man, *Br. J. Haematol.*, 9, 911, 1963.

Table 2
LIPID COMPOSITION OF HUMAN PLATELETS FROM SUBJECTS OF DIFFERENT AGES

	Age (years)		
	20—29	30—29	40—49
Pro[a]	59.7±0.6	58.4±2.4	55.4±3.5
Tl[a]	20.9±3.6	19.7±1.9	18.4±2.6
Chol[b]	20.7±3.1	22.7±3.3	25.0±1.8
Pl[b]	59.7±3.3	63.1±3.7	68.3±3.2
Pi[c]	8.0±2.0	8.9±2.9	7.1±1.9
Sph	17.1±1.8	16.7±5.8	14.9±1.1
Pc	31.4±1.7	28.0±3.6	31.0±1.6
Ps	10.3±2.6	11.4±2.9	12.0±1.6
Pe	20.2±2.2	19.5±3.7	18.6±3.2
Pa	4.5±0.8	3.5±2.2	4.5±1.5

Note: Pro = protein; Chol = cholesterol; Pi = phosphatidylinositol; Pc = phosphatidylchonine; Pe = phosphatidylethanolamine; Tl = total lipid; Pl = phospholipid; Sph = sphingomyelin; Ps = phosphatidylserine; Pa = phosphatidic acid; Ca = cardiolipin.

[a] Total solids (%).
[b] Total lipids (%).
[c] Total lipid phosphorus (%).

From Iacono, J. M., Zellner, D. C., Paoletti, R., Ishikawa, T., Frigeni, V., and Fumagalli, R., *Haemostasis,* 2, 141, 1974. With permission.

Table 3
COAGULATION FACTORS IN HUMAN BLOOD FROM SUBJECTS OF DIFFERENT AGES

	Age (years)					
	20—40		65—75		Over 75	
	Male (n = 10)	Female (n = 10)	Male (n = 18)	Female (n = 10)	Male (n = 11)	Female (n = 22)
Platelets (× 10⁹/µℓ)	231±8	249±19	224±15	222±25	227±25	220±12
Factor XII	136±19	127±21	128±15	202±29[a]	103±14	189±23[a]
Factor XI	109±10	85±6	83±5	120±13[b]	92±8	101±6
Factor VIII	109±10	118±9	100±7	101±10	104±10	104±8
Factor X	105±7	97±4	119±5	113±4[b]	105±6	114±6
Factor VII	84±5	92±6	117±74	118±6[b]	104±8	121±5[b]
Factor V	118±9	109±5	132±9[c]	135±9	115±9	94±7[a,b]
Antithrombin III	114±5	106±8	105±4	133±11[d]	97±6	121±5[c]

[a] Difference in means with respect to sex is significant for that age subgroup (p > 0.0 5).
[b] Difference in means with respect to 20 to 40-year age group attains significanct (p > 0.05) (p > 0.01).
[c] Difference in means with respect to 20 to 40-year age group attains significance (p > 0.05) (p > 0.01).
[d] p > 0.001.

From Hamilton, P. J., Allardyce, M., Ogston, D., Dawson, A. A., and Douglas, A. S., *J. Clin. Pathol.*, 27, 980, 1974. With permission.

Table 4
FIBRINOLYTIC ENZYME LEVELS IN HUMAN BLOOD FROM SUBJECTS OF DIFFERENT AGES

	Age (years)			
	20—40 (n = 20)	66—75 (n = 28)	76—85 (n = 27)	>86 (n = 6)
Fibrinogen (mg/dℓ)	272.5±43.6	386.0±81.6	403.7±69.4	350.0±15.8
Plasminogen (units/mℓ)	4.02±0.52	4.02±0.46	4.01±0.43	3.50±0.65
α_1-antitrypsin (mg/dℓ)	236.1±74.0	262.3±81.4	298.6±53.3	297.8±52.8
α_2-macroglobulin (mg/dℓ)	276.0±24.9	336.5±113.1	319.4±71.8	354.3±61.1

Note: n = number of subjects.

From Hamilton, P. J., Dawson, A. A., Ogston, D., and Douglas, A. S., *J. Clin. Pathol.*, 27, 326, 1974. With permission.

Cardiovascular System

HEART

Edward G. Lakatta

Table 1
CARDIAC PERFORMANCE IN THE SENESCENT RAT

	Ref.
Heart rate and stroke index are significantly diminished in unanesthetized Wistar rats at 24 months of age compared to 12 months of age.	1
No difference in blood pressure measured via indwelling cathether is observed in unanesthetized Wistar rats (12 vs. 24 months of age).	1
Blood pressure measured indirectly is increased in Sprague-Dawley rats 950 days of age when compared to adult rats.	2
The baroreceptor response to an elevation of 50 mm in blood pressure is greater in 12-month than in 24-month unanesthetized Wistar rats. This difference persists in the presence of sympathetic blockade.	3
There is no difference in heart rate in anesthetized male Wistar rats 12 vs. 24 months of age.	4
Mean arterial pressure and left ventricular and diastolic pressure (LVEDP) are increased in anesthetized Wistar rats at 24 months of age compared to 12 months of age.	4
Under light anesthesia, heart rate is significantly lower in senescent Sprague-Dawley rats when compared to adults.	5
Heart rate declines significantly from 90—300 days of age in the Wistar rat.	6
Fischer 344 rats (Charles River) have no significant diminution in resting heart rate over the range of 6—28 months.	7
Autonomic responses of the cardiovascular system to stimulation of extracardiac nerves are diminished in senescent rats (also true for rabbits and cats).	8,9
The sensitivity of the cardiovascular system to low doses of injected catecholamines is diminished in rats 28—32 months of age compared to those 12 months of age. On the other hand, the maximal responsiveness to large doses of catecholamines is diminished in the senescent animals.	8
There is no age difference (12 vs. 24 months of age) in aortic flow or stroke work index in response to volume loading in the anesthetized Wistar rat.	4
The senescent anesthetized Wistar rat (24 months) responds to a pressure load induced by angiotensin with a diminished stroke index, and aortic flow and a greater rise in LVEPD when compared to the 12-month rat.	4

REFERENCES

1. Rothbaum, D. A., Shaw, D. J., Angell, C. S., and Shock, N. W., Cardiac performance in the unanesthetized senescent male rat, *J. Gerontol.*, 28, 287, 1973.
2. Berg, B. N. and Harmison, C. R., Blood pressure and heart size in aging rats, *J. Geronotol.*, 10, 416, 1955.
3. Rothbaum, D. A., Shaw, D. J., Angell, C. S., and Shock, N. W., Age differences in the baroreceptor response of rats, *J. Gerontol.*, 29, 488, 1974.
4. Lee, J. C., Karpeles, L. M., Downing, S. E., Age-related changes of cardiac performance in male rats, *Am. J. Physiol.*, 222, 432, 1972.
5. Berg, B. N., The electrocardiogram in aging rats, *J. Gerontol.*, 10, 420, 1955.
6. Everitt, A. V., The electrocardiogram of the ageing male rat, *Gerontologia*, 2, 204, 1958.
7. Roberts, J. and Goldberg, P. B., Changes in cardiac membranes as a function of age with particular emphasis on reactivity to drugs, *Adv. Exp. Med. Biol.*, 61, 119, 1975.
8. Frolkis, V. V., Bezrukov, V. V., Bogatskaya, L. N., Verkhratsky, N. S., Zamostian, V. P., Shevtchuk, V. G., and Shtchegoleva, I. V., Catecholamines in the metabolism and functions regulation in aging, *Gerontologia*, 16, 129, 1970.
9. Frolkis, V. V., Bezrukov, V. V. and Shevchuk, V. G., Hemodynamics and its regulation in old age, *Exp. Gerontol.*, 10, 251, 1975.

Table 2
PERFORMANCE IN THE ISOLATED SENESCENT RAT HEART

	Ref.
In the isolated Langendorf preparation, the spontaneous ventricular rate in hearts from animals at 24 months is significantly less than that in hearts from 12-month Fischer 344 rats.	1
The rate of O_2 consumption at both high and low work loads, normalized for heart weight, is decreased in the aged Fischer 344 rat.	2
The QO_2, normalized for work load, in the working isolated preparation is not age-related in 5- and 24-month-old Wistar rats.	2
Nonworking perfused hearts at constant heart rate and perfusion pressure isolated from 24-month male Wistar rats can extract O_2 from the perfusate as well as hearts from 12-month animals.	3
The flow per gram heart weight is reduced in 24-month Wistar rat hearts (Langendorf, nonworking) compared to that in hearts from 12-month animals.	3
The reponse in external work to a volume infusion is not age-related in the Fischer 344 rat between 5 and 27 months of age.	2
The muscle stiffness calculated from pressure-volume measurements in KCl arrested rat heart is not different at 17 months compared to 9 months.	4

REFERENCES

1. **Roberts, J. and Goldberg, P B.,** Changes in cardiac membranes as a function of age with particular emphasis on reactivity to drugs, *Adv. Exp. Med. Biol.*, 61, 119, 1975.
2. **Abu-Erreish, G. M., Neely, J. R., Whitmer, J. T., Whitman, V., and Sanadi, D. R.,** Fatty acid oxidation by isolated perfused working hearts of aged rats, *Am. J. Physiol.*, 232(3), E258, 1977.
3. **Weisfeldt, M. L., Wright, J. R., Shreiner, D. P., Lakatta, E., and Shock, N. W.,** Coronary flow and oxygen extraction in the perfused heart of senescent male rats, *J. Appl. Physiol.*, 30, 44, 1971.
4. **Janz, R. F., Kubert, B. R., Mirsky, I., Korecky, B., and Taichman, G. C.,** Effect of age on passive elastic stiffness of rat heart muscle, *Biophys. J.*, 16, 281, 1976.

Table 3
PERFORMANCE OF MUSCLE ISOLATED FROM SENESCENT MYOCARDIUM

	Ref.
Developed tension or maximum rate of tension development in the isometric twitch in trabeculae carneae from left ventricle of Wistar rats 6—25 months of age is not age-related	1—5
The time to peak tension, half relaxation time, relaxation time, or contraction duration is significantly prolonged in left ventricular cardiac muscle from rats 25 months of age compared to that from rats 6 or 12 months of age.	1—5
Time to peak tension and half relaxation time are not age-related in right ventricular papillary muscles.	6
The prolongation of the twitch duration is not related to age differences in catecholamine content.	2
The velocity of shortening progressively diminishes from age 3 months to 3 years in Simonsen strain rats.	1
The length-active tension relation is not significantly different in trabeculae carneae from 12- and 25-month-old Wistar rats.	3
Resting tension at the length of optimal tension development is increased or unaltered with age, depending upon experimental design.	2,3,5
Stress relaxation (decline in resting force with time at constant muscle length) is diminished in muscles isolated from the senescent Wistar rat heart when compared to those isolated from 12-month animals.	3
The dynamic stiffness at rest and at all levels of developed force is increased in trabeculae carneae from 24-month Wistar rats compared to that in muscles from 6-month animals.	5
There is no age difference in the potentiation in tension or the maximum rate of tension development response to paired pacing in trabeculae carneae from rats 6—24 months of age.	2
Trabeculae carneae from 25-month-old rats when compared to those from 6- to 12-month-old rats fail to generate a mechanical response to very early premature beats.	2
There is no difference in the transmembrane action potential duration at 80% repolarization or in the effective electrical refractory period in left ventricular muscle from Wistar rats 6 and 2 months of age.	2
The transmembrane action potential in atria from Fischer rats driven at a constant rate is not age-related over the age 6—24 months (phase O, plateau level, and time to 95% of repolarization).	7
The inotropic response to catecholamines in trabeculae carneae isolated from Wistar rats 25 months of age is diminished when compared to that in muscles from 6- or 12-month aged rats. There is no age difference in the dose response to Ca^{++}.	4
The response of developed tension, maximum rate of tension development, and total tension to ouabain is significantly less in trabeculae carneae from 24-month as compared to that of muscles from 6- to 8-month rats.	8
There is no difference in isometric tension during hypoxia or during recovery from hypoxia in trabeculae carneae from rats aged 6—25 months.	2

REFERENCES

1. **Alpert, N. R., Gale, H. H., and Taylor, N.,** The effect of age on contractile protein ATPase activity and the velocity of shortening, in *Factors Influencing Myocardial Contractility*, Tanz, R. D., Kavaler, F., and Roberts, J., Eds., Academic Press, New York, 1967, 127.
2. **Lakatta, E. G., Gerstenblith, G., Angell, C. S., Shock, N. W., and Weisfeldt, M. L.,** Prolonged contraction duration in aged myocardium, *J. Clin. Invest.*, 55, 61, 1975.
3. **Weisfeldt, M. L., Loeven, W. A., and Shock, N. W.,** Resting and active mechanical properties of traveculae carneae from aged male rats, *Am. J. Physiol.*, 220, 1921, 1971.
4. **Lakatta, E. G., Gerstenblith, G., Angell, C. S., Shock, N. W., and Weisfeldt, M. L.,** Diminished inotropic response of aged myocardium to catecholamines, *Circ. Res.*, 36, 262, 1975.
5. **Spurgeon, H. A., Thorne, P. R., Yin, F. C. P., Shock, N. W., and Weisfeldt, M. L.,** Increased dynamic stiffness of trabeculae carneae from senescent rats, *Am. J. Physiol.*, 232(4), H373, 1977.
6. **Grodner, A. S., Pool, P. E., and Braunwald, E.,** Influence of age on the mechanics of rat cardiac muscle, *Circulation Suppl.*, 3, 41/42, III-115, 1970.
7. **Cavoto, F. V., Kelliher, G. J., and Roberts, J.,** Electrophysiological changes in the rat atrium with age, *Am. J. Physiol.*, 226, 293, 1974.
8. **Gerstenblith, G., Lakatta, E. G., Spurgeon, H., Shock, N. W., and Weisfeldt, M. L.,** Diminished ouabain sensitivity in aged myocardium, *Fed. Proc. Fed. Am. Soc. Exp. Biol.*, 34, 365, 1975.

Table 4
THE SENESCENT RAT HEART: ANATOMY AND MORPHOLOGY

	Ref.
Left ventricular weight and left ventricular weight:body weight is increased in the senescent male Wistar rat (24 months), when compared to the adult rat (6 or 24 months).	1—6
Sprague-Dawley rats 950 days of age have an increased heart weight and an increased heart weight:body weight.	7,8
The heart weight:tibial length is increased in senescent male Wistar rats (24—28 months) compared to 6- or 12-month-old rats. Tibial length is constant during senescence. The right ventricle weight:tibial length is not altered in the senescent rat.	4
Heart weight increases with age in senescence.	9
Heart weight increases 15% in the Fischer rat from age 5 months to age 30 months.	10
No change in heart weight:body weight in Fischer (Charles River) rat in senescence.	11
The increase in ventricular mass in the senescent Wistar rat results in an increase in ventricular volume, with estimated wall thickness unchanged.	1,3
The fiber size is increased in the 26-month rat heart and the number of capillaries is diminished compared to the adult heart.	12
The capillary muscle fiber ratio is diminished in hearts from Sprague-Dawley strain at 22 months, compared to those of 5 months of age. The fiber size is unchanged in the senescent vs. the adult animal. However, this depressed ratio in the senescent rat can increase significantly with physical conditioning.	13
Content of collagen increases with age in Sprague-Dawley and Wistar rats.	8,14—16
The collagen content increases at a rate greater than the increases in heart weight in Wistar rats aged 6—40 months.	15,17
The stiffness of collagen increases with age.	18
Lipofuscin pigment accumulates in the senescent rat heart.	19,20
In 1000-day-old Dublin and Charles River rats, greater mitochondrial degeneration and myofibrillar swelling occurred during chronic hypoxia (28 days when PO_2 was 5%) when compared to 600- or 90-day-old rats.	21

REFERENCES

1. Shreiner, D. P., Weisfeldt, M. L., and Shock, N. W., Effects of age, sex, and breeding status on the rat heart, *Am. J. Physiol.*, 217, 179, 1969.
2. Lakatta, E. G., Gerstenblith, G., Angell, C. S., Shock, N. W., and Weisfeldt, M. L., Prolonged contraction duration in aged myocardium, *J. Clin. Invest.*, 55, 61, 1975.
3. Lee, J. C., Karpeles, L. M., and Downing, S. E., Age-related changes of cardiac performance in male rats, *Am. J. Physiol.*, 222, 432, 1972.
4. Yin, F. C. P., Spurgeon, H. A., Lakatta, E. G., Guarnieri, T., Weisfeldt, M. L., and Shock, N. W., Cardiac hypertrophy indexed by tibial length: application in the aging rat, *Gerontologist*, 17, 135, 1977.
5. Froehlich, J. P., Lakatta, E. G., Beard, E., Spurgeon, H. A., Weisfeldt, M. L., and Gerstenblith, G., Studies of sarcoplasmic reticulum function and contraction duration in young adult and aged rat myocardium., *J. Mol. Cell. Cardiol.*, 10, 427, 1978.
6. Framer, B. B., Harris, R. A., Jolly, W. W., and Vail, W. J., Studies on the cardiomegaly of the spontaneously hypertensive rat, *Circ. Res.*, 25, 102, 1974.
7. Berg, B. N. and Harmison, C. R., Blood pressure and heart size in aging rats, *J. Gerontol.*, 10, 416, 1955.
8. Tomanek, R. J., Taunton, C. A., and Liskop, K. S., Relationship between age, chronic exercise, and connectve tissue of heart, *J. Gerontol.*, 27, 33, 1972.
9. Wilens, S. L. and Sproul, E. E., Spontaneous cardiovascular disease in the rat, *Am. J. Pathol.*, 14, 177, 1938.
10. Aub-Erreish, G. M., Neely, J. R., Whitmer, J. T., Whitman, V., and Sanadi, D. R., Fatty acid oxidation by isolated perfused working hearts of aged rats, *Am. J. Physiol.*, 232(3), E258, 1977.
11. Roberts, J. and Goldberg, P. B., Changes in cardiac membranes as a function of age with particular emphasis on reactivity to drugs, *Adv. Exp. Med. Biol.*, 61, 119, 1975.

Table 4 (continued)
THE SENESCENT RAT HEART: ANATOMY AND MORPHOLOGY

12. **Rakušan, K. and Poupa, O.**, Capillaries and muscle fibers in the heart of old rats, *Gerontologia,* 9, 107, 1964.
13. **Tomanek, R. J.**, Effects of age and exercise on the extent of myocardial capillary bed, *Anat. Rec.,* 167, 55, 1970.
14. **Simms, H. S. and Berg, B. N.**, Longevity and the onset of lesions in male rats, *J. Gerontol.,* 12, 244, 1957.
15. **Schaub, M. C.**, The aging of collagen in the heart muscle, *Gerontologia,* 10, 38, 1964/65.
16. **Weisfeldt, M. L., Loeven, W. A., and Shock, N. W.**, Resting and active mechanical properties of trabeculae carneae from aged male rats, *Am. J. Physiol.,* 220, 1921, 1971.
17. **Lowry, O. H., Hastings, A. B., Hull, T. Z., and Brown, A. N.**, Histochemical changes associated with aging. II. Skeletal and cardiac muscle in the rat, *J. Biol. Chem.,* 143, 271, 1942.
18. **Verzar, F.**, The stages and consequences of ageing of collagen, *Gerontologia,* 15, 233, 1969.
19. **Travis, D. F. and Travis, A.**, Ultrastructural changes in the left ventricular rat myocardial cells with age, *J. Ultrastruct. Res.,* 39, 124, 1972.
20. **Tomanek, R. J. and Karlsson, U. L.**, Myocardial ultrastructure of young and senescent rats, *J. Ultrastruct. Res.,* 42, 201, 1973.
21. **Sulkin, N. M. and Sulkin, D. F.**, Age differences in response to chronic hypoxia on the fine structure of cardiac muscle and autonomic ganglion cells, *J. Gerontol.,* 22, 485, 1967.

Table 5
THE SENESCENT RAT HEART: BIOCHEMICAL PARAMETERS APPARENTLY RELATED TO PERFORMANCE

	Ref.
Glycerol extracted myofibrillar ATPase diminished with age from 3 months to 3 years in Simonsen strain rats.	1
The cardiac Ca^{2+} and Mg^{2+} myofibrillar ATPase, as well as the mitochondrial ATPase is not different in rats aged 4—6 months when compared to that in animals greater than 20 months.	2
The velocity of calcium transport in sarcoplasmic reticulum isolated from the 24-month Wistar rat heart is diminished significantly when compared to that isolated from hearts from animals 6 months of age.	3
The total catecholamine content per gram heart weight is diminished by 25% in hearts from senescent (25 months of age) Wistar rats, when compared to that in hearts from 6- or 12-month animals.	4—6
The age decrement in norephinephrine content in the aged Wistar rat can be attributed in part to a diminished synthesis due to a decline in β-hydroxylase, since there is no age difference in the uptake or hydroxylation of tyrosine.	4,7
The uptake of catecholamines in rat heart aged 28—32 months is diminished, compared to that in hearts from 8- to 12-month animals.	5
Total catecholamine per gram heart weight in the left ventricle of Fischer 344 rats is decreased between 6 and 28 months.	8
Acetylcholine synthesis is diminished in atria from senescent rats (28 months) when compared to adult (10 months) counterparts. This decrement may be related to an age-associated decrement in choline acetylase.	9
In hearts from "white" rats aged 28—32 months the ATP and phosphocreatine are diminished, glycogen and lactate are increased, phosphofructokinase and aldolase are increased, and hexokinase is decreased, compared to hearts isolated from 8—12-month rats.	10
There is no age difference in ATP or CP (phosphocreatine) in Fischer 344 rats ages 5 and 24 months.	11
Both the K_m and the amount of LDH are diminished in Wistar rat hearts from 91-week-old animals, compared to 30-week animals.	12
There is no age change in myoglobin in the hearts of Wistar rats from 4 months to 2 years.	13
The number of mitochondria and respiratory activity per gram mitochondrial protein is diminished in hearts of 28- to 32-month "white" rats compared to those 8—12 months of age.	10
Mitochondrial protein per gram heart weight is decreased in 17-month-old Wistar rats.	14
Mitochondrial respiration is unaltered in the senescent Wistar rat.	15
Mitochondrial respiration (state 3) is significantly depressed in the senescent Fischer 344 rat.	16
The protein content per gram wet weight in the supernatant fraction of heart homogenates is diminished in advanced age in the Wistar rat. No change is observed in total H_2O content.	12
In Fischer 344 (Charles River) rats, no age differences between 12—28 months in cardiac water content was found.	17
In female senescent (34 months of age) Sprague-Dawley rats, the intracellular electrolyte content (K^+, Mg^{++}, Ca^{++}, Cl^-) of cardiac muscle was significantly diminished, compared to that measured in the adult (10—12 month) hearts. There was no significant change in H_2O content.	18
In Fischer 344 (Charles River) rats, no age differences between 12—28 months were measured in atrial intracellular Na^+ or K^+ content, Na^+ or K^+ influx, or K^+ efflux.	17
The rate of cardiac protein synthesis in response to thyroid hormone is less in senescent mice than in adult mice, but there is no age difference in the maximum increase in myocardial protein.	19

Table 5 (continued)
THE SENESCENT RAT HEART: BIOCHEMICAL PARAMETERS APPARENTLY RELATED TO PERFORMANCE

REFERENCES

1. Alpert, N. R., Gale, H. F., and Taylor, N., The effect of age on contractile protein ATPase activity and the velocity of shortening, in *Factors Influencing Myocardial Contractility*, Tanz, R. D., Kavaler, F., and Roerts, J., Eds., Academic Press, New York, 1967, 127.
2. Honorati, M. C. and Ermini, M., Myofibrillar and mitochondrial ATPase activity of red, white, diaphragmatic and cardiac muscle of young and old rats, *Experientia*, 30, 215, 1974.
3. Froelich, J. P., Lakatta, E. G., Beard, E., Spurgeon, H. A., Weisfeldt, M. L., and Gerstenblith, G., Studies of sarcoplasmic reticulum funtion and contraction duration in young adult and aged rat myocardium., *J. Mol. Cell. Cardiol.*, 10, 427, 1978.
4. Gey, K. F., Burkard, W. P., and Pletscher, A., Variation of norepinephrine metabolism of the rat heart with age, *Gerontologia*, 11, 1, 1965.
5. Frolkis, V. V., Berzukov, V. V., Bogatskaya, L. N., Verkhratsky, N. S., Zamostian, V. P., Shevtchuk, V. G., and Shtchegoleva, I. V., Catecholamines in the metabolism and functions regulation in aging, *Gerontologia*, 16, 129, 1970.
6. Lakatta, E. G., Gerstenblith, G., Angell, C. S., Shock, N. W., and Weisfeldt, M. L., Prolonged contraction duration in aged myocardium, *J. Clin. Invest.*, 55, 61, 1975.
7. Burkard, W. P., Gey, K. F., and Pletscher, A., Alteration of the catecholamine metabolism of the rat heart in old age, in *Structure and Chemistry of the Aging Heart*, Gey, K. F., et al., Eds., Mss Information Corporation, New York, 1974, 20.
8. Roberts, J. and Goldberg, P. B., Changes in basic cardiovascular activities during the lifetime of the rat, *Exp. Aging Res.*, 2, 487, 1976.
9. Verkhratsky, N. W., Acetylcholine metabolism peculiarities in aging, *Exp. Gerontol.*, 5, 49, 1970.
10. Frolkis, V. V. and Bogatskaya, L. N., The energy metabolism of myocardium and its regulation in animals of various age, *Exp. Gerontol.*, 3, 199, 1968.
11. Abu-Erreish, G. M., Neely, J. R., Whitmer, J. T., Whitman, V., and Sanadi, D. R., Fatty acid oxidation by isolated perfused working hearts of aged rats, *Am. J. Physiol.*, 232(3), E258, 1977.
12. Singh, S. N. and Kanungo, M. S., Alteration in lactate dehydrogenase of the brain, heart, skeletal muscle, and liver of rats of various ages, *J. Biol. Chem.*, 213, 4526, 1968.
13. Rakušan, K., Rádl, J. and Poupa, O., The distribution and content of myoglobin in the heart of rat during postnatal development, *Physiol. Bohemoslov.*, 14, 317, 1965.
14. Farmer, B. B., Harris, R. A., Jolly, W. W., and Vail, W. J., Studies on the cardiomegaly of the spontaneously hypertensive rat, *Circ. Res.*, 35, 102, 1974.
15. Gold, P. H., Gee, M. V., and Strehler, B. L., Effect of age on oxidative phosphorylation in the rat, *J. Gerontol.*, 23, 509, 1968.
16. Chen, J. C., Warshaw, J. B., and Sanadi, D. R., Regulation of mitochondrial respiration in senescence, *J. Cell. Physiol.*, 80, 141, 1972.
17. Goldberg, P. B., Baskin, S. I., and Roberts, J., Effects of aging on ionic movements of atrial muscle, *Fed. Proc. Fed. Am. Soc. Exp. Biol.*, 34, 188, 1975.
18. Mori, K. and Duruisseau, J. -P., Water and electrolyte changes in aging process with special reference to calcium and magnesium in cardiac muscle, *Can. J. Biochem. Physiol.*, 38, 919, 1960.
19. Florini, J. R., Saito, Y., and Manowitz, E. J., The effect of age on thyroxin-induced cardiac hypertrophy in mice, *J. Gerontol.*, 28, 293, 1973.

Table 6
CARDIAC PERFORMANCE IN SENESCENT ANIMALS: SPECIES OTHER THAN THE RAT

	Ref.
No age difference in resting unanesthetized heart rate in beagles 2—12 years of age.	1
Isometric contraction duration is greater in 11-year-old beagles when compared to 2-year-old beagles.	2
In beagles 12 years of age, blood flow, velocity, and arterial wall distensibility are diminished when compared to measurements made in 2- or 5-year-old dogs. Pulse wave velocity increases and blood pressure remains constant with age.	3
The maximal chronotropic response to isoproterenol is significantly diminished in unanesthetized beagles 12 years of age, when compared to adult dogs at 2 years of age. Both adult and senescent dogs can be electrically paced (atrial) at rates nearly twice those elicited by maximal doses of isoproterenol.	1
The left ventricular dynamic stiffness (measured during the contraction by inducing small changes in volume) is increased in the intact senescent beagle.	2
Ventricular muscle from guinea pigs 36—40 months of age has a longer action potential duration than that isolated from animals aged 3—4 months. This difference is observed at pacing rates over the range of 30—420 beats/min.	4
Time to peak tension and half relaxation time are prolonged in ventricular muscle from guinea pigs aged 36—40 months, when compared to that from 3—4-month animals. There is no age difference in the maximum rate of force development in these muscles.	4
The isometric contraction duration in 4-year-old rabbits is prolonged compared to the young adult.	5
Left ventricular ejection time is also increased in the aged rabbit.	5
Cardiac output, heart rate, stroke, and shape volume are diminished, and peripheral vascular resistance is increased in the anesthetized rabbit at 4 years of age when compared to the young adult animal.	5
The left ventricular wall thickness of the rabbit aged 4 years is increased in normotensive rabbits when compared to young adult rabbits.	5
The sensitivity of cardiovascular performance in rabbits aged 48—54 months to small doses of exogenous catecholamines is enhanced, whereas the response to larger doses is diminished, compared to the response of 10- to 14-month rabbits.	5
The heart weight, volume, and compliance of the LSH-SS LAK Syrian hamster increased from 1—8 months and then decreased at 10 and 11 months of age. The calculated elastic modulus as a function of wall stress ($E = K\alpha$) is linear and not age related.	6
Myosin ATPase activity (lithium-chloride ammonium sulfate method) is unchanged from 2 months to 10 years in the dog (breed unspecified).	7
The mitochondrial density decreases 15% from age 8— 44 months in C57BL/6J mice.	8

REFERENCES

1. **Yin, F. C., Spurgeon, H. A., Raizes, C. S., Greene, H. L., Weisfeldt, M. L., and Shock, N. W.,** Age-associated decrease in chronotropic response to isoproterenol, *Circulation,* 54, II-167, 1976.
2. **Templeton, G. H., Willerson, J. T., Platt, M. R., and Weisfeldt, M.,** Contraction duration and diastolic stiffness in the aged canine left ventricle, *Recent Adv. Stud. Card. Struct. Metab.* 11, 169, 1978.
3. **Miller, C. W., Nealeigh, R. C., and Crowder, M. E.,** Evaluation of the cardiovascular changes associated with aging in a colony of dogs, *Biomed. Sci. Instrum.,* 12, 107, 1976.
4. **Rumberger, E. and Timmerman, J.,** Age-changes of the force-frequency-relationship and the duration of action potential of isolated papillary muscles of guinea pig, *Eur. J. Appl. Physiol. Occup. Physiol.,* 35, 277, 1976.
5. **Frolkis, V. V., Bezrukov, V. V., and Shevchuk, V. G.,** Hemodynamics and its regulation in old age, *Exp. Gerontol.,* 10, 251, 1975.
6. **Kane, R. L., McMahon, T. A., Wagner, R. L., and Abelmann, W. H.,** Ventricular elastic modulus as a function of age in the Syrian golden hamster, *Circ. Res.,* 38, 74, 1976.
7. **Luchi, R. J., Kritcher, E. M., and Thyrum, P. T.,** Reduced cardiac myosin adenosinetriphosphatase activity in dogs with spontaneously occurring heart failure, *Circ. Res.,* 24, 513, 1969.
8. **Herbener, G. H.,** A morphometric study of age-dependent changes in mitochondiral populations of mouse liver and heart, *J. Gerontol.,* 31, 8, 1976.

Table 7
CARDIAC FUNCTION IN HUMANS AT REST

	Ref.
Resting heart rate is unaltered with age in normal man.	1,2
There is no age-associated change in cardiac volume from adulthood to senescence as estimated from X-ray or echocardiography.	3,4
Echocardiographic assessment of the left ventricle in normal man indicates a significant increase in diastolic and systolic wall thickness.	5,6
Resting cardiac output and stroke volume decrease with age from 20—90 years in normal men in the supine position.	7—12
Resting cardiac output diminished with age as assessed by precordial counting of ^{131}I or the acetylene rebreathing methods.	13,14
In the sitting position, no change in resting cardiac output with age is observed.	9
The interval from onset of electrical activity to the first heart sound (Q-S$_1$) increases in normal man from the 2nd to 8th decades.	15
The interval from the onset of electrical activity to the carotid upstroke increases from the 2nd to 8th decades.	15
The preejection time (includes electromechanical delay plus isovolumic contraction period) increases significantly with age.	15—19
Left ventricular ejection time increases or is unaltered with age in adult man.	6,20,21
Isovolumic relaxation time (kinetocardiogram) in man is increased with advancing age in normal man.	17
The interval from the second heart sound to the opening of the mitral valve (a correlate of isometric relaxation time) is prolonged in healthy aged man.	22
The left ventricular filling rate, as measured by the E-F slope of the mitral vale on echocardiography is significantly diminished in normal man.	6
The velocity of shortening and fractional shortening of the minor semi axis (correlate of ejection fraction) is not age-related in normal man.	6
The amplitude of the J wave in the ultra-low frequency ballistocardiogram diminishes with advancing age in adult man.	11, 23
Pulse wave velocity increases with advancing age in normal man.	17,24—26
Baroreceptor sensitivity is diminished with age in normal man.	27
The electrocardiogram of healthy males show small but significant increases in the P-R, QRS, and Q-T intervals, and a leftward shift in QRS axis with increased age.	28—32

REFERENCES

1. **Strandell, T.,** Heart rate, arterial lactate concentration, and oxygen uptake during exercise in old men compared with young men, *Acta Physiol. Scand.*, 60, 197, 1964.
2. **Yin, F. C., Spurgeon, H. A., Raizes, G. S., Greene, H. L., Weisfeldt, M. L., and Shock, N. W.,** Age-associated decrease in chronotropic response to isoproterenol, *Circulation*, 54, II-167, 1976.
3. **Strandell, T.,** Heart volume and its relation to anthropometric data in old men compared with young men, *Acta Med. Scand.*, 176, 205, 1964.
4. **Maurea, N. G. and Sollberger, A.,** Normal heart volume, *Acta Cardiol.*, 10, 336, 1955.
5. **Sjorgren, A. L.,** Left ventricular wall thickness determined by ultrasound. In 100 subjects without heart disease, *Chest*, 60, 341, 1971.
6. **Gerstenblith, G., Frederiksen, J., Yin, F. C. P., Fortuin, N. J., Lakatta, E. G., and Weisfeldt, M. L.,** Echocardiographic assessment of a normal adult aging population, *Circulation*, 56, 273, 1977.
7. **Brandfonbrender, M., Landowne, M., and Shock, N. W.,** Changes in cardiac output with age, *Circulation*, 12, 557, 1955.
8. **Julius, S., Antoon, A., Whitlock, L. S., and Conway, J.,** Influence of age on the hemodynamic response to exercise, *Circulation*, 36, 222, 1967.
9. **Strandell, T.,** Circulatory studies on healthy old men, *Acta Med. Scand. Suppl.*, 414, 175, 1, 1964.
10. **Conway, J. Wheeler, R., and Sannerstedt, R.,** Sympathetic nervous activity during exercise in relation to age, *Cardiovasc. Res.*, 5, 577, 1971.

Table 7 (continued)
CARDIAC FUNCTION IN HUMANS AT REST

11. **Knoop, A. A.,** Physiological aspects of circulatory dynamics especially related to ageing as studied by displacement ballistocardiography and other cardiovascular methods, *Bibl. Cardiol.*, 30, 87, 1973.
12. **Cournand, A., Riley, R. L., Breed, E. S., Baldwin, E. De F., and Richards, D. W.,** Measurements of cardiac output in man using the technique of catherization of the right auricle of ventricle, *J. Clin. Invest.*, 24, 106, 1945.
13. **Lammerant, J., Veall, N., and De Visscher, M.,** Observations of cardiac output and "pulmonary blood volume" in normal man by external recording of the intracardiac flow of ^{131}I labelled albumin, *Nucl. Med.*, 1, 353, 1961.
14. **Lewis, W. H., Jr.,** Changes with age in the cardiac output in adult men, *Am. J. Physiol.*, 121, 517, 1938.
15. **Friedman, S. A. and Davison, E. T.,** The phonocardiographic assessment of myocardial function in the aged, *Am. Heart J.*, 78, 752, 1969.
16. **Montoye, H. J., Willis, P. W., Howard, G. E., and Keller, J. B.,** Cardiac preejection period: age and sex comparisons, *J. Gerontol.*, 26, 208, 1971.
17. **Harrison, T. R., Dixon, K., Russell, R. O., Jr., Bidwai, P. S., and Coleman, H. N.,** The relation of age to the duration of contraction, ejection, and relaxation of the normal human heart, *Am. Heart J.*, 67, 189, 1964.
18. **Shaw, D. J., Rothbaum, D. A., Angell, C. S., and Shock, N. W.,** The effects of age and blood pressure upon the systolic time intervals in males aged 20—89 years, *J. Gerontol.*, 28, 133, 1973.
19. **Slodki, S. J., Hussian, A. T., and Luisada, A. A.,** The Q-II interval. III. A study of the second heart sound in old age, *J. Am. Geriatr. Soc.*, 17, 673, 1969.
20. **Willens, J. L., Roelandt, J., De Geest, H., Kesteloot, H., and Joossens, J. V.,** The left ventricular ejection time in elderly subjects, *Circulation*, 42, 37, 1970.
21. **Strandell, T.,** Mechanical systole at rest, during and after exercise in supine and sitting position in young and old men, *Acta Physiol. Scand.*, 64, 297, 1964.
22. **Luisada, A. A., Watanabe, K., Bhat, P. K., and Rao, D. B.,** Correlates of the echocardiographic waves of the mitral valve in normal subjects of various ages, *J. Am. Geriatr. Soc.*, 23, 216, 1975.
23. **Onodera, K., Kato, A., Fukushima, A., Mori, Y., and Oike, Y.,** A study on the relation between cardiac ejection force and aging, using the dye dilution method and ballistocardiography, *Bibl. Cardiol.*, 35, 221, 1976.
24. **Yakovlev, V. M.,** Some data on the functional state of the arterial system in aged persons, *Kardiologiya*, 11, 99, 1971.
25. **Hallock, P. and Benson, I. C.,** Studies on the elastic properties of human isolated aorta, *J. Clin. Invest.*, 16, 595, 1937.
26. **Bramwell, J. C. and Hill, A. V.,** The velocity of the pulse wave in man, *Proc. R. Soc. London Ser. B*, 93, 298, 1922.
27. **Gribbin, B., Pickering, T. G., Sleight, P., and Peto, R.,** Effect of age and high blood pressure on baroreflex sensitivity in man, *Circ. Res.*, 29, 424, 1971.
28. **Simonson, E.,** The effect of age on the electrocardiogram, *Am. J. Cardiol.*, 29, 64, 1972.
29. **Mihalick, M. J. and Fisch, C.,** Electrocardiographic findings in the aged, *Am. Heart J.*, 87, 117, 1974.
30. **Eliaser, M. and Kondo, B. O.,** The electrocardiogram in later life, *Arch. Intern. Med.*, 67, 637, 1941.
31. **Simonson, E.,** *Differentiation Between Normal and Abnormal in Electrocardiography*, C. V. Mosby, St. Louis, 1961, 82.
32. **Simonson, E., Cady, L., and Woodbury, M.,** The normal Q-T interval, *Am. Heart J.*, 63, 747, 1962.

Table 8
HUMAN CARDIAC FUNCTION — RESPONSE TO STRESS

	Ref.
The work load performed on a two-step Master's test is diminished in normal aged man.	1
Peripheral vascular resistance at rest and comparable work loads increases with age.	2—8
Maximum heart rate in exercise is diminished with age (30—83 years) in normal man.	1,3,9
Maximal stroke volume and cardiac output diminish with advancing age in normal man.	3,5,7
The pulmonary artery wedge pressure is increased with exercise in normal aged man when compared with young adults.	4,10
With maximal exercise, (A-V) O_2 difference is diminished with advancing age in normal man.	3,7
The maximum oxygen consumption is diminished in both men and women with advancing age.	3,11—15
The age difference in maximum oxygen consumption persists after physical conditioning.	16
At a given work load, there is no age difference in oxygen consumption and therefore no age difference in work efficiency.	15
Age-associated difference in cardiac output during exercise is diminished in the presence of beta-blockade.	7
The chronotropic response to isoproterenol infusion is diminished in normal healthy men aged 65—80 years when compared to the response in men 20—35 years of age.	17
Aged man responds to atropine with less of an increase in heart rate.	18
The heart rate increase in response to a 45° tilt is diminished in normal aged man. The systolic blood pressure dropped lower and returned slower in the old men, compared to that in the young men.	19
Diminished heart rate and ventilatory rate in response to hypercapnia and hypoxia in normal aging man.	20

REFERENCES

1. Master, A. M. and Oppenheimer, E. T., A simple exercise tolerance test for circulatory efficiency with standard tables for normal individuals, *Am. J. Med. Sci.*, 177, 223, 1929.
2. Brandfonbrener, M., Landowne, M., and Shock, N. W., Changes in cardiac output with age, *Circulation*, 12, 557, 1955.
3. Julius, S., Antoon, A., Whitlock, L. S., and Conway, J., Influence of age on the hemodynamic response to exercise, *Circulation*, 36, 222, 1967.
4. Granath, A., Jonsson, B., and Strandell, T., Circulation in healthy old men studied by right heart catherization at rest and during exercise in supine and sitting position, *Acta Med. Scand.*, 176, 425, 1964.
5. Tsuchiya, M., Kawasaki, S., Masuya, K., Matsui, S., Ishise, S., Hara, S., Funatsu, T., Takeuchi, N., Maeda, M., Onoe, T., Kin, T., Takekoshi, N., Nurakami, E., Milune, J., and Murakami, M., The effect of age on the hemodynamics, *Jpn. J. Geriatr. Nihon Ronen Igakkai Zasshi*, 9, 364, 1972.
6. Strandell, T., Circulatory studies on healthy old men, *Acta Med. Scand. Suppl.*, 414, 175, 1, 1964.
7. Conway, J., Wheeler, R., and Sannerstedt, R., Sympathetic nervous activity during exercise in relation to age, *Cardiovasc. Res.*, 5, 577, 1971.
8. Luisada, A. A., Watanabe, K., Bhat, P. K., and Rao, D. B., Correlates of the echocardiographic waves of the mitral valve in normal subjects of various ages, *J. Am. Geriatr. Soc.*, 23, 216, 1975.
9. Strandell, T., Heart rate, arterial lactate concentration, and oxygen uptake during exercise in old men compared with young men, *Acta Physiol. Scand.*, 60, 197, 1964.
10. Tartülier, M., Bourret, M., and Deyrieux, F., Pulmonary arterial pressures in normal subjects, effects of age and exercise, *Bull. Physio-Pathol. Respir.*, 8, 1295, 1972.
11. Robinson, S., Experimental studies of physical fitness in relation to age, *Arbeitsphysiologie.*, 10, 251, 1938.
12. Mitchell, J. H., Sproule, B. J., and Chapman, C. B., The physiological meaning of the maximal oxygen intake test, *J. Clin. Invest.*, 37, 538, 1958.
13. Dill, D. B., Horvath, S. M., and Craig, F. N., Response to exercise as related to age, *J. Appl. Physiol.*, 12, 195, 1958.

Table 8 (continued)
HUMAN CARDIAC FUNCTION — RESPONSE TO STRESS

14. **Astrand, I.**, Aerobic work capacity in men and women with special reference to age, *Acta Physiol. Scand. Suppl.*, 169, 49, 1, 1960.
15. **Åstrand, I., Åstrand, P. -O., Hallbäck, I., and Kilbom, A.**, Reduction in maximal oxygen uptake with age, *J. Appl. Physiol.*, 35, 649, 1973.
16. **Robinson, S., Dill, D. B., Ross, J. C., Robinson, R. D., Wagner, J. A., and Tzankoff, S. P.**, Training and physiological aging in man, *Fed. Proc. Fed. Am. Soc. Exp. Biol.*, 32, 1628, 1973.
17. **Yin, F. C., Spurgeon, H. A., Raizes, G. S., Greene H. L., Weisfeldt, M. L., and Shock, N. W.**, Age-associated decrease in chronotropic response to isoproterenol, *Circulation*, 54, II-167, 1976.
18. **Dauchot, P. and Gravenstein, J. S.**, Effects of atropine on the electrocardiogram in different age groups, *Clin. Pharmacol. Ther.*, 12, 274, 1971.
19. **Norris, A. H., Shock, N. W., and Yiengst, M. J.**, Age changes in heart rate and blood pressure responses to tilting and standardized exercise, *Circulation*, 8, 521, 1953.
20. **Kronenberg, R. S. and Drage, C. W.**, Attenuation of the ventilatory and heart rate responses to hypoxia and hypercapnia with aging in normal man, *J. Clin. Invest.*, 52, 182, 1973.

Table 9
HUMAN CARDIAC ANATOMY, MORPHOLOGY, AND BIOCHEMISTRY

	Ref.
The muscle mass is diminished and the fibrous tissue is increased in the SA node and internodal tracts in hearts of aged men free of heart disease.	1—3
The right and left atrial volume is increased in autopsy specimens from men free of heart disease.	1
Autopsy study indicates that in the absence of cardiac disease, heart mass increases in aged man.	4
In 7000 human hearts at necropsy, there is no evidence that the heart atrophies with advancing age.	5
Idiopathic cardiac amyloid is found at autopsy in only 1.5% of 1150 hearts from humans older than 70 years of age.	6
The anterior mitral valve leaflet thickens with age.	7
Degenerative calcification of the aortic valve in the absence of additional pathology occurs in advanced age in man.	8
Aortic size is increased from adulthood to senescence in both autopsy specimens and by echocardiogram assessment.	9,10
The Ca^{++}, Mg^{++}, and K^+-EDTA myosin ATPase is unaltered in hearts from a small number of normal men, 6—90 years of age.	11

REFERENCES

1. **Davies, M. J., and Pomerance, A.**, Quantitative study of ageing changes in the human sinoatrial node and internodal tracts, *Br. Heart J.*, 34, 150, 1972.
2. **Lev, M.**, Aging changes in the human sinoatrial node, *J. Gerontol.*, 9, 1, 1954.
3. **Lev, M.**, The conduction system, in *Pathology of the Heart and Blood Vessels*, 3rd ed., Gould, S. E., Ed., Charles C Thomas, Springfield, Ill., 1968, 182.
4. **Strandell, T.**, Heart volume and its relation to anthropometric data in old men compared with young men, *Acta Med. Scand.*, 176, 205, 1964.
5. **Linzbach, A. J. and Akuamoa-Boateng, E.**, Die Alternsveränderungen des menschlichen Herzens. I. Das Herzgewicht im Alter, *Klin. Wochesnchr.*, 51, 156, 1973.
6. **Mulligan, R. M.**, Amyloidosis of the heart, in *Structure and Chemistry of the Aging Heart*, Gey, K. F., et al., Eds., Mss Information Corporation, New York, 1974, 96.
7. **McMillan, J. B. and Lev, M.**, The aging heart. II. The valves, *J. Gerontol.*, 19, 1, 1964.
8. **Pomerance, A.**, The pathogenesis of aortic stenosis in the elderly, *Gerontol. Clin.*, 14, 1, 1972.
9. **Korvetz, L. J.**, Age-related changes in size of the aortic valve annulus in man, *Am. Heart J.*, 90, 569, 1975.
10. **Gerstenblith, G., Frederiksen, J., Yin, F. C. P., Fortuin, N. J., Lakatta, E. G., and Weisfeldt, M. L.**, Echocardiographic assessment of a normal adult aging population, *Circulation*, 56, 273, 1977.
11. **Malhotra, A., Bhan, S., and Scheuer, J.**, Biochemical characteristics of human cardiac myosin, *J. Mol. Cell. Cardiol.*, 9, 73, 1977.

Table 10
RECENT REVIEWS OF CHANGES IN THE CARDIOVASCULAR SYSTEM WITH ADVANCED AGE

	Ref.
A compendium on the rat as an animal model for aging research in cardiovascular physiology, biochemistry, and structure	1
An overview of the effects of aging on cardiovascular responsiveness to drugs used in geriatric patients and in experimental research on mechanism of drug action	2
A synthesis of cardiovascular physiology in aging man both at rest and in response to stress and experimental studies of stressful interventions in the rat myocardium	3
A composite report of research done in the U.S.S.R. over the past decade relating to age changes in metabolism and hormonal and neuronal responsiveness of the cardiovascular system in the aged rat, cat, and rabbit	4

REFERENCES

1. **Roberts, J. and Goldberg, P. B.**, Changes in basic cardiovascular activities during the lifetime of the rat, *Exp. Aging Res.*, 2, 487, 1976; **Goldberg, P. B. and Roberts, J.**, Changes in the biochemistry of the rat heart with increasing age, *Exp. Aging Res.*, 2, 519, 1976.
2. **Goldberg, P. B. and Roberts, J.**, Influence of age on the pharmacology and physiology of the cardiovascular system, in *Special Review of Experimental Aging Research, Progress in Biology*, Elias, M. F., Eleftheriou, B. E., and Elias, P. K., Eds., EAR, Bar Harbor, 1976, 71.
3. **Gerstenblith, G., Lakatta, E. G., and Weisfeldt, M. L.**, Age changes in myocardial function and exercise response, *Prog. Cardiovasc. Dis.*, 19, 1, 1976.
4. **Frolkis, V. V., Berzukov, V. V. and Shevchuk, V. G.**, Hemodynamics and its relation in old age, *Exp. Gerontol.*, 10, 251, 1975.

BLOOD VESSELS

Herman Bader

Table 1
GENERAL STATMENTS ON AGE CHANGES OF THE HUMAN AORTA

	Ref.
The distensibility increases from birth to adulthood and decreases from there on	1,2
The wall stress of the thoracic aorta increases from 0.5 kg · cm^{-2} at birth to 2.5 kg · cm^{-2} in the 3rd decade and decreases from there on to 1 kg · cm^{-2} in the 9th decade of life	3,4
The hysteresis loop between extension and release of the pressure-volume diagram decreases gradually from 15—70 years	5
The volume elastic modulus of the abdominal aorta at physiological pressures of men below 30 years is about twice that of the thoracic aorta, but above 70 years the two are equal	6
The slope of the volume elastic modulus with pressure of the abdominal aorta is flatter than that of the thoracic aorta below 30 years and steeper above 70 years	6
Highly purified elastin from aortas shows almost identical amino acid composition at all ages from 11—90 years, but contains increasing amounts of a fluorescent substance with increasing age	7—9
Transmedial collagen and elastin gradients in the aorta change with age: up to 12 years medial elastin decreases while collagen increases from intima to adventitia, from 14—40 years no definite gradient exists, from 50—80 years elastin increases and collagen decreases from intima to adventitia	10
During growth the number of elastic lamellae increase from 30—55 with no further change with increasing age	4,11
Those humans who become older than 75 years have aortas which retain a relatively good distensibility	12

REFERENCES

1. Saxton, J. A., Jr., Elastic properties of the rabbit aorta in relation to age, *Arch. Pathol.*, 34, 262, 1942.
2. Simon, E. and Meyer, W. W., Das Volumen, die Volumendehnbarkeit und die Drucklängen-Beziehungen des gesamten aortalen Windkessels, *Klin. Wochenschr.*, 36, 424, 1958.
3. Bader, H., Dependence of wall stress in the human thoracic aorta on age and pressure, *Circ. Res.*, 20, 354, 1967.
4. Wolinsky, H., Comparison of medial growth of human thoracic and abdominal aortas, *Circ. Res.*, 27, 531, 1970.
5. Wagner, R. and Kapal, E., The nature of aortal pressure. II. Studies of the human thoracic aorta in different age groups. *Z. Biol. (Munich)*, 105, 263, 1952.
6. Bader, H., Comparison of characteristics of abdominal and thoracic aortas, *Z. Biol. (Munich)*, 108, 321, 1956.
7. La Bella, F. S. and Lindsay, W. G., The structure of human aortic elastin as influenced by age, *J. Gerontol.*, 18, 111, 1963.
8. La Bella, F. S., Vivian, S., and Thornhill, D. P., Amino acid composition of human aortic elastin as influenced by age, *J. Gerontol.*, 21, 550, 1966.
9. John, R. and Thomas, J., Chemical compositions of elastins isolated from aortas and pulmonary tissues of humans of different ages, *Biochem. J.*, 127, 261, 1972.
10. Feldmann, S. A. and Glagov, S., Transmedial collagen and elastin gradients in human aortas: reversal with age, *Atherosclerosis*, 13, 385, 1971.
11. Kobayashi, Y., Veränderungen der Struktur der Brustaorta des Menchen während der prä- und postnatalen Entwicklung und im Senium, *Arch. Histol. Jpn. Niigata Jpn* 13, 503, 1957.
12. Schimmler, W., Untersuchungen zu Elastizitätsproblemen der Aorta. (Statistische Korrelation der Pulswellengeschwindigkeit zu Alter, Geschlecht und Blutdruck), *Arch. Kreislaufforsch.*, 47, 189, 1965.

Table 2
DIMENSIONS OF THE HUMAN AORTA

Dimensions	Birth	1—2	10—15	16—19	20—29	30—39	40—49	50—59	60—69	70—79	80—89	90—100	Ref.
Weight (g) whole ♂	—	—	—	—	25.8	34.6	43.1	47.6	63.1	75.3	—	—	1
aorta (n = 400) ♀	—	—	—	—	22.1	33.6	42.7	47.5	54.7	60.7	—	—	
Volume (mℓ) Whole aorta (n = 37)													
100 mm Hg	3	7	19	44	—	59	—	94	123	159	—	—	2
100 mm Hg	8	15	56	147	—	179	—	204	236	250	—	—	
200 mm Hg	9	18	80	188	—	215	—	231	259	265	—	—	
Storage volume (mℓ) between diastolic and systolic pressure, whole aorta (n = 37)	1.2	3.0	19.5	38.0	—	31.6	—	25.1	21.9	18.6	—	—	3
Length increase in % of length at 0 mm Hg, whole aorta (n = 37)													
0—100 mm Hg	—	—	—	—	—	26.8	—	17.1	16.6	9.0	—	—	2
100—200 mm Hg	—	—	—	—	—	6.6	—	3.6	4.0	3.2	—	—	
Retraction in % of *in situ* length (n = 100) whole aorta	—	18	23	25	20	15	10	6	2.5	1.5	—	—	4
Thickness of media of ascending aorta (mm)													
Sea level (n = 100)	—	0.65	—	—	1.0	—	1.09	—	1.13	—	—	—	5
4000 m altitude (n = 100)	—	0.6	—	—	1.1	—	1.24	—	1.45	—	—	—	
Cross-sectional area of the media of the aorta at the left common carotid (mm²) (n = 335)	—	27.1	—	56.6	62.0	80.9	96.8	108.3	114.8	118.9	133.5	121.5	6
Inner circumference of aorta at left common carotid (cm) (n = 335)	—	—	—	4.3	4.5	5.1	5.8	6.4	7.8	8.1	8.5	—	6
Outer circumference (n = 500) (cm)													
Ascending aorta ♂	—	—	—	5.8	6.2	6.7	7.6	8.1	8.6	9.2	9.5	—	4
♀	—	—	—	5.6	5.7	6.2	6.8	7.5	7.9	8.5	8.3	—	

Descending aorta ♂	—	—	—	—	4.5	4.8	5.2	5.7	6.3	6.7	7.2	7.6	—
♀	—	—	—	—	4.1	4.4	4.9	5.3	5.6	6.4	6.9	7.2	—
Abdominal aorta ♂	—	—	—	—	3.7	4.2	4.6	5.0	5.5	6	6.3	6.7	—
♀	—	—	—	—	3.6	3.7	4.2	4.6	5.1	5.5	6.0	6.3	—
Outer circumference (n = 220) (cm)													
Ascending aorta ♂	—	—	—	—	5.2	5.9	5.7	7.3	7.8	8.3	8.2	8.8	—
♀	—	—	—	—	5.3	5.5	6.0	6.8	7.3	7.7	7.7	7.5	—
Descending aorta ♂	—	—	—	—	4.3	4.7	5.0	5.4	6.0	6.6	6.7	6.7	—
♀	—	—	—	—	4.1	4.4	4.6	5.1	5.4	5.7	6.1	6.2	—
Aorta at diaphragm ♂	—	—	—	—	4.0	4.3	4.6	5.3	5.7	6.0	5.9	6.4	—
♀	—	—	—	—	3.8	4.1	4.2	4.6	5.2	5.3	5.8	—	—
Aorta at bifurcation ♂	—	—	—	—	2.9	3.3	3.5	4.1	4.5	4.7	4.7	5.0	—
♀	—	—	—	—	2.8	3.0	3.3	3.5	3.9	4.2	4.4	4.5	—
Wall thickness of media (mm) at left common carotid (n = 335)	—	—	—	—	1.34	1.3	1.56	1.67	1.65	1.65	1.55	1.63	6
Wall thickness (mm) (n = 220)													
Ascending aorta ♂	—	—	—	—	1.64	1.65	1.72	1.71	1.84	1.83	1.95	1.67	7
♀	—	—	—	—	1.51	1.53	1.72	1.8	1.88	1.57	1.73	2.46	—
Descending aorta ♂	—	—	—	—	1.25	1.34	1.43	1.62	1.66	1.78	1.82	1.7	—
♀	—	—	—	—	1.12	1.25	1.36	1.52	1.59	1.58	1.7	1.94	—
At diaphragm ♂	—	—	—	—	1.23	1.25	1.32	1.49	1.57	1.58	1.53	1.57	—
♀	—	—	—	—	1.03	1.14	1.33	1.39	1.49	1.41	1.56	—	—
At bifurcation ♂	—	—	—	—	1.17	1.17	1.15	1.25	1.24	1.27	1.07	1.42	7
♀	—	—	—	—	1.14	1.09	1.18	1.27	1.29	1.16	1.35	—	8
Outer circumference of ascending aorta (cm) (n = 194)	—	—	—	—	5.8	6.2	7.1	7.5	7.8	8.1	8.4	—	—

85

Table 2 (continued)
DIMENSIONS OF THE HUMAN AORTA

REFERENCES

1. **Meyer, W. W.**, *Bull. Schweiz. Akad. Med. Wiss.*, 13, 115, 1957.
2. **Simon, E. and Meyer, W. W.**, Das Volumen, Die Volumendehnbarkeit und die Drucklangen-Beziehungen des gesamten aortalen Windkessels, *Klin. Wochenschr.*, 36, 424, 1958.
3. **Meyer, W. W.**, Die Lebenswandlungen der Struktur der Arterien und Venen, *Verh. Dtsch. Ges. Kreislaufforsch.*, 24, 15, 1958.
4. **Scheel, O.**, Gefassmessungen und Arteriosklerose, *Virchows Arch. Pathol. Anat. Physiol.*, 191, 135, 1908.
5. **Saldana, M. and Arias-Stella, J.**, Studies on the structure of the pulmonary trunk. III. The thickness of the media of the pulmonary trunk and ascending aorta in high altitude natives, *Circulation*, 27, 1101, 1963.
6. **Wellman, W. E. and Edwards, J. E.**, Thickness of the media of the thoracic aorta in relation to age, *Arch. Pathol.*, 50, 183, 1950.
7. **Kani, I.**, Systematische Lichtungs- und Dickenmessungen der grossen Arterien und ihre Bedeutung fur die Pathologie der Gefasse, *Virchows Arch. Pathol. Anat. Physiol.*, 201, 45, 1910.
8. **Meyer, W. W. and Richter, H.**, Das Gewicht der Lungenschlagader als Gradmesser der Pulmonalarteriensklerose und als morphologisches Kriterium der pulmonalen Hypertonie. Eine quantitativ-anatomische und feingewebliche Untersuchung, *Virchows Arch. Pathol. Anat. Physiol.*, 328, 121, 1956.

Table 3
PERCENT CHANGE WITH PRESSURE OF CIRCUMFERENCE AND LENGTH OF HUMAN AORTA

Pressure (mm Hg)	Measurements	Age (years) 10—30	31—40	41—50	51—65	66—85
0—50	a	9.4	20.8	19.8	12.8	18.1
	b	10.4	21.8	21.9	19.1	12.2
	c	11.1	23.0	23.0	20.5	12.7
	d	11.8	27.1	23.8	20.7	8.4
	e	12.2	11.5	9.9	8.2	6.4
50—100	a	16.7	10.7	7.5	6.3	2.2
	b	17.4	13.1	6.5	6.2	3.9
	c	17.3	13.0	9.1	5.6	2.1
	d	17.7	9.5	5.9	3.0	1.4
	e	17.0	14.0	6.2	4.1	3.1
100—150	a	8.7	3.5	3.0	1.0	0.9
	b	10.5	2.4	3.3	1.9	1.5
	c	11.4	2.5	3.7	1.7	1.1
	d	10.7	2.6	2.8	1.6	1.1
	e	7.0	7.6	3.5	2.1	1.2
150—200	a	2.8	1.5	1.6	0.8	0.8
	b	4.3	1.3	2.0	0.9	1.0
	c	4.5	1.0	0.9	0.8	0.9
	d	4.1	0.8	0.9	0.2	—
	e	3.4	2.8	1.3	0.9	0.8
200—250	a	1.6	1.1	0.6	0.1	0.3
	b	1.7	0.8	0.8	0.2	0.7
	c	1.1	0.5	0.8	0.2	0.2
	d	1.9	—	0.9	0.2	—
	e	2.2	1.3	0.9	0.5	0.5
0—250	a	43.5	41.5	35.1	22.3	23.2
	b	51.4	44.2	38.3	30.3	20.5
	c	52.1	44.6	41.6	30.9	18.4
	d	56.5	43.7	37.2	26.5	11.1
	e	49.0	42.7	23.7	16.8	12.6

Note: a = circumference of ascending aorta; b = circumference of aorta at 3rd intercostal artery; c = circumference of aorta at diaphragm; d = circumference at end of aorta; and e = length of aorta from valves to bifurcation. All measurements post-mortem, n = 20.

From Karnbaum, S., Innendruckabhängige Umfangmessungen bei Alters- und Hochdruckaorten, *Z. Gesamte Exp. Med.,* 128, 510, 1957. With permission.

Table 4
ELASTIC MODULI OF BLOOD VESSELS

		Ref.
Force related tangential elastic modulus, E_f	$E_f = \dfrac{dF}{dr} \cdot \dfrac{r}{9}$	1,2
Stress related tangential elastic modulus, E_s	$E_s = \dfrac{d\sigma}{dr} \cdot r$	1,2,4
Pressure related tangential elastic modulus, E_p	$E_p = \dfrac{dp}{dr} \cdot r$	1,3
Incremental tangential elastic modulus, E_{inc}	$E_{inc} = \dfrac{dp}{dr_o} \cdot \dfrac{2(1-\mu^2)\, r_i^2 \cdot r_o}{r_o - r_i^2}$	5
Volume elastic modulus, κ	$\kappa = \dfrac{dp}{dV} \cdot V$	1,2
	$\kappa = \rho c^2$	1,7
Dynamic elastic modulus, E_d	$E_d = E_c \cdot \cos\phi$	2,6
Viscous retarding force	$\eta\omega = E_c \cdot \sin\phi$	2,6
Conversions of elastic moduli when the vessel is fixed in length	$E_s = E_f - \dfrac{dq}{dr} \cdot \dfrac{\sigma \cdot r}{q}$	2
	$\kappa = 2 \cdot E_p$	2
	$E_f = (2\kappa + p)\dfrac{r}{h} \cdot (1 - \mu^2)$	2
	$E_f = E_{inc} + \sigma \cdot (1 - \mu^2)$	2
Conversion of elastic moduli when vessel is free to lengthen	$E_s = (2.16\kappa + 1.2p)\dfrac{r}{h}$	4

Note: Symbols — r = radius, r_i = inside radius, and r_o = outside radius; h = wall thickness; q = cross-section perpendicular to applied force; F = force; σ = tangential wall stress = $p \cdot r/h$; μ = Poisson's ratio; V = volume; E_c = complex elasticity modulus (apparant elastic modulus at dynamic measurements); η = viscosity of wall; ω = angular frequency; ϱ = density of blood; and c = pulse wave velocity.

Table 4 (continued)
ELASTIC MODULI OF BLOOD VESSELS

REFERENCES

1. **Frank, O.**, *Z. Biol. (Munich),* 71, 255, 1920.
2. **Wetterer, E. and Kenner, Th.**, *Grundlagen der Dynamik des Arterienpulses,* Springer-Verlag, Berlin, 1968.
3. **Gozna, E. R., Marble, A. E., Shaw, A., and Holland, J. G.**, Age-related changes in the mechanics of the aorta and pulmonary artery of man, *J. Appl. Physiol.,* 36, 407, 1974.
4. **Bader, H.**, Dependence of wall stress in the human thoracic aorta on age and pressure, *Circ. Res.,* 20, 354, 1967.
5. **Bergel, D. H.**, The static elastic properties of the arterial wall, *J. Physiol. (London),* 156, 445, 1961.
6. **Learoyd, B. M. and Taylor, M. G.**, Alterations with age in the viscoelastic properties of human arterial wall, *Circ. Res.,* 18, 278, 1966.
7. **Bramwell, J. C. and Hill, A. V.**, *Proc. R. Soc. London,* 93, 298, 1922.

Table 5
ELASTIC BEHAVIOR OF THE HUMAN AORTA

	Birth	1—10	10—20	20—30	30—40	40—50	50—60	60—70	70—80	80—90	Ref.
Volume elastic modulus of the thoracic aorta at 100 mm Hg (n = 18)	—	0.174	—	0.314	0.506	0.792	0.814	1.032	1.252	1.54	1
Volume elastic modulus of the thoracic aorta at 85 mm Hg (n = 18)	—	—	—	0.195	0.239	0.355	0.443	—	0.948	—	2
Volume elastic modulus of the whole aorta between 80 and 120 mm Hg (n = 41)	0.595	0.32	0.174	—	0.266	—	0.55	0.731	1.15	—	3
Volume elastic modulus of the whole aorta at 100 mm Hg (n = 14)	—	—	—	—	—	0.674	1.051	—	1.304	—	4
Volume elastic modulus of the thoracic aorta between 100 and 110 mm Hg (n = 20)	—	—	0.18	0.27	0.36	0.56	0.72	0.93	—	—	5
Stress of isolated elastic network of the thoracic aorta (n = 21)	—	4.95	—	4.94	—	4.36	3.33	2.38	2.81	—	6
Volume elastic modulus of the thoracic aorta (n = 41)											7
50 mm Hg	—	—	0.112	0.1	0.106	0.145	0.25	0.425	0.63	—	
100 mm Hg	—	—	0.202	0.202	0.275	0.446	0.725	1.12	1.5	—	
150 mm Hg	—	—	0.541	0.578	0.77	1.03	1.43	1.92	2.23	—	

Note: Measurements post-mortem in kg · cm^{-2}.

REFERENCES

1. **Frank, O.**, *S. ber. Ges. Morph. Munchen*, 37, 23, 1926.
2. **Hallock, P. and Benson, I. C.**, Studies on the elastic properties of human isolated aorta, *J. Clin. Invest.*, 16, 595, 1937.
3. **Simon, E. and Meyer, W. W.**, Das Volumen, die Volumendehnbarkeit und die Drucklangen-Beziehungen des gesamten aortalen Windkessels, *Klin. Wochenschr.*, 36, 424, 1958.
4. **Karnbaum, S. and Sperling, M.**, Die elastischen Eigenschaften ganzer menschlicher Hochdruckaorten, *Z. Gesamte Exp. Med.*, 128, 498, 1957.
5. **Wagner, R. and Kapal, E.**, The nature of aortal pressure. II. Studies of the human thoracic aorta in different age groups, *Z. Biol. (Munich)*, 105, 263, 1952.
6. **Hass, G. M.**, Elastic tissue. III. Relations between the structure of the aging aorta and the properties of the isolated aortic elastic tissue, *Arch. Pathol.*, 35, 29, 1943.
7. **Moret, P. R.**, *Bibl. Cardiol.*, 15, 40, 1964.

Table 6
ELASTIC PROPERTIES OF HUMAN THORACIC AORTAS

Age (years)	Measurements	\multicolumn{8}{c}{Blood pressure (mm Hg)}	Ref.
		0	20	40	60	80	100	120	150	200	
13—15 (n = 3)	a	6.1	7.27	8.88	10.8	12.88	14.76	16.13	17.37	18.55	4
	b	0.0	0.194	0.474	0.864	1.375	1.976	2.582	3.475	4.954	2
	c	0.135	0.246	0.313	0.372	0.368	0.302	0.195	0.114	0.057	2,3
	d	0.158	0.144	0.138	0.141	0.173	0.257	0.444	0.811	1.477	1—3
	e	2.10	2.43	3.14	4.23	6.34	10.43	18.3	33.83	63.6	4
26—35 (n = 4)	a	6.55	8.47	10.93	13.57	16.33	18.22	19.37	20.39	21.26	4
	b	0.0	0.227	0.583	1.096	1.743	2.432	3.1	4.075	5.67	2
	c	0.306	0.42	0.511	0.569	0.445	0.272	0.164	0.094	0.056	2,3
	d	0.111	0.103	0.11	0.126	0.199	0.373	0.653	1.196	2.064	1—3
	e	1.55	2.11	3.21	4.84	8.97	17.22	30.54	56.27	99.02	4
36—45 (n = 4)	a	6.34	8.22	10.71	13.03	14.82	15.75	16.33	16.91	17.48	4
	b	0.0	0.219	0.572	1.043	1.584	2.105	2.615	3.36	4.678	2
	c	0.577	0.773	0.851	0.753	0.406	0.246	0.161	0.107	0.068	2,3
	d	0.105	0.102	0.12	0.158	0.337	0.597	0.956	1.486	2.435	1—3
	e	1.42	2.06	3.38	5.56	12.36	21.94	35.85	56.57	94.75	4
46—55 (n = 5)	a	6.01	7.93	10.17	12.12	13.3	14.0	14.38	14.79	15.24	4
	b	0.0	0.212	0.544	0.969	1.421	1.865	2.302	2.959	4.069	2
	c	0.7	0.97	1.039	0.722	0.4	0.236	0.158	0.106	0.07	2,3
	d	0.111	0.103	0.127	0.215	0.457	0.797	1.212	1.849	2.876	1—3
	e	1.4	1.94	3.33	6.58	14.21	25.44	39.18	60.61	95.94	4
56—65 (n = 3)	a	6.28	8.22	10.04	11.14	11.8	12.2	12.48	12.78	13.08	4
	b	0.0	0.22	0.536	0.891	1.26	1.629	2.001	2.538	3.49	2
	c	1.12	1.251	1.062	0.609	0.324	0.203	0.149	0.105	0.07	2,3
	d	0.093	0.112	0.176	0.36	0.694	1.107	1.539	2.19	3.308	1—3
	e	1.16	2.19	4.387	9.54	18.72	30.23	42.46	61.6	94.67	4

66—75 (n = 3)	a	6.07	7.95	9.14	9.77	10.1	10.33	10.49	10.66	10.88	4
	b	0.0	0.212	0.489	0.782	1.082	1.38	1.682	2.132	2.9	2
	c	1.9	1.398	0.588	0.342	0.215	0.149	0.112	0.083	0.061	2,3
	d	0.083	0.148	0.365	0.712	1.147	1.687	2.274	3.108	4.277	1—3
	e	1.05	2.67	7.21	14.74	24.62	36.93	49.17	70.0	98.97	4

Note: a = ratio of internal radius to wall thickness r/h; b = tangential wall stress σ (kg · cm^{-2}); c = compliance C (ml · mm H$_g^{-1}$); d = volume elastic modulus K (kg · cm^{-2}); and e = tangential stress-related elastic modulus E, (kg · cm^{-2}). Measurements on human thoracic aortas from a. brachiocephalica to diaphragm post-mortem, free to lengthen.

REFERENCES

1. **Bader, H.**, Comparison of characteristics of abdominal and thoracic aortas, *Z. Biol. (Munich)*, 108, 321, 1956.
2. **Kapal, E. and Bader, H.**, Uber die elastischen Eigenschaften des Aortenwindkessels. Untersuchungen an ganzen menschlichen Aorten, *Z. Kreislaufforsch.*, 47, 66, 1958.
3. **Bader, H. and Kapal, E.**, Altersveranderungen der Aortenelastizitat, *Gerontologia*, 2, 253, 1958.
4. **Bader, H.**, Dependence of wall stress in the human thoracic aorta on age and pressure, *Circ. Res.*, 20, 354, 1967.

Table 7
PULSE WAVE VELOCITY AND VOLUME ELASTIC MODULUS OF THE HUMAN AORTA — ILIAC ARTERY

Age (years)	Measurements	Blood pressure (mm Hg)							
		80	100	120	140	160	180	200	220
25	a	5.75	6.4	7.1	7.75	8.4	9.0	9.7	10.3
	b	0.35	0.43	0.53	0.64	0.75	0.86	1.0	1.12
35	a	6.0	6.8	7.6	8.4	9.25	10.1	10.9	11.75
	b	0.38	0.49	0.61	0.75	0.91	1.08	1.26	1.46
45	a	6.25	7.25	8.25	9.25	10.25	11.25	12.25	13.0
	b	0.41	0.56	0.72	0.91	1.11	1.34	1.59	1.87
55	a	6.5	7.75	9.0	10.2	11.4	12.6	13.86	15.1
	b	0.48	0.64	0.86	1.1	1.38	1.68	2.03	2.42
65	a	7.35	8.6	9.85	11.05	12.3	13.55	14.8	16.0
	b	0.57	0.78	1.03	1.29	1.6	1.94	2.32	2.71
75	a	9.25	10.15	11.0	11.9	12.75	13.65	14.55	15.4
	b	0.91	1.09	1.28	1.5	1.72	1.97	2.25	2.51

Note: Normalized values for age and pressure, in vivo measurements (n = 1326). a = pulse wave velocity c (m · cm^{-1}) and b = volume elastic modulus K (kg · cm^{-2}).

From Schimmler, W., Untersuchungen zu Elastizitätsproblemen der Aorta, (Statistische Korrelation der Pulswellengeschwindigkeit zu Alter, Geschlecht und Blutdruck), *Arch. Kreislaufforsch.*, 47, 189, 1965. With permission of Dr. Dietrich Steinkopff Verlag, Darmstadt, West Germany.

Table 8
REGRESSION EQUATIONS OF AGE CHANGES OF HUMAN AORTA

Condititions	Regression equations	Ref.
Radius at diaphragm at zero pressure in mm (25—85 years) (n = 27)	$R = 5 + 0.064\,A$	1
% vol increase from 0—100 mm Hg (25—85 years) (n = 27)	$V\,\% = 234 - 2.27\,A$	1
Pressure at inflexion point of the pressure-volume-relationship in mm Hg (25—85 years) (n = 27)	$p = 106 - 1.32\,A$	1
Tangential wall stress at different pressures (mm Hg) between 80 and 220 mm Hg 25—85 years in kg/cm² (n = 27)	$\sigma = 0.04p - 0.00035\,Ap + 0.01\,A - 0.9$	1
Stress related tangential elastic modulus at 100 mm Hg (n = 27)	$E_s = 0.5\,A$	1
Volume elastic modulus between 100—250 mm Hg and 25—85 years in kg/cm² (n = 27)	$x = 0.0095p + 0.0002\,Ap + 0.0092\,A - 1.467$	1
Pressure related tangential elastic modulus of the ascending aorta between 20 and 50 years a physiological pressures (in vivo) in g/cm² (n = 22)	$E_p = 90 + 16\,A$	2
Shrinking temperature (Ts) for isotonic thermocontraction of the thoracic aorta in centigrade	$Ts = 56.23 + 0.123\,A$	3
Shrinking temperature (Ts) for isotonic thermocontraction of the abdominal aorta in centigrade	$Ts = 56.68 + 0.131\,A$	3
Elastin in % of dry weight during growth from birth to 20 years (n = 16)	$\text{Elastin}\,\% = 17.5 + 1.65\,A$	4
Elastin in % of dry weight from 20—80 years (n = 19)	$\text{Elastin}\,\% = 36.1 - 0.198\,A$	5
Collagen in % of dry weight from 20—80 years (n = 26)	$\text{Collagen}\,\% = 17.8 + 182\,A$	5

Note: A = age in years.

Table 8 (continued)
REGRESSION EQUATIONS OF AGE CHANGES OF HUMAN AORTA

REFERENCES

1. **Bader, H.**, Dependence of wall stress in the human thoracic aorta on age and pressure, *Circ. Res.*, 20, 354, 1967.
2. **Gozna, E. R., Marble, A. E., Shaw, A., and Holland, J. G.**, Age-related changes in the mechanics of the aorta and pulmonary artery of man, *J. Appl. Physiol.*, 36, 407, 1974.
3. **Krug, H.**, The effect of ageing on the thermoelastic contraction of the human aorta, *Exp. Gerontol.*, 3, 197, 1968.
4. **Scarselli, V.**, Increase in elastin content of the human aorta during growth, *Nature (London)*, 191, 710, 1961.
5. **Faber, M. and Møller-Hou, G.**, The human aorta. V. Collagen and elastin in the normal and hypertensive aorta, *Acta Pathol. Microbiol. Scand.*, 31, 377, 1952.

Table 9
PHYSICAL PROPERTIES OF THE HUMAN PULMONARY TRUNK

Age

	Birth	2—10 (month)	10—19 (years)	20—29 (years)	30—39 (years)	40—49 (years)	50—59 (years)	60—69 (years)	70—79 (years)	80—95 (years)	Ref.
Media thickness (mm)											
Sea level (n = 100)	—	0.412	—	0.652	—	0.68	—	0.76	—	—	1
4000 m altitude (n = 100)	—	0.566	—	0.731	—	0.84	—	0.98	—	—	1
% vol increase from 2—40 mm Hg (n = 50)	—	—	—	187.4	155.0	127.4	113.7	90.6	74.1	59.4	2
% vol increase from 10—50 mm Hg (n = 31)	158.0	78.0	142.0	97.0	—	—	—	43.5	—	—	3
Compliance between 10—20 mm Hg (n = 50) (mℓ · mm Hg^{-1})	—	—	—	1.03	1.5	1.01	1.2	1.06	0.93	0.67	2
Volume elastic modulus between 10—20 mm Hg (kg · cm^{-2}) (n = 50)	—	—	—	0.051	0.053	0.078	0.064	0.084	0.095	0.127	2
Volume elastic modulus between 10—25 mm Hg (kg · cm^{-2}) (n = 31)	0.031	0.039	0.023	0.027	—	—	—	0.076	—	—	3
Circumference of pulmonary trunk (cm)											
(n = 500) ♂	—	—	6.3	6.8	6.9	7.3	7.4	7.7	8.2	7.7	4
♀	—	—	6.0	6.4	6.8	7.1	7.3	7.6	7.7	8.2	4
(n = 220) ♂	—	—	5.6	6.6	6.8	7.8	7.9	7.9	7.9	8.1	5
♀	—	—	6.0	6.2	6.5	7.3	7.2	7.5	7.8	7.0	5

97

Table 9 (continued)
PHYSICAL PROPERTIES OF THE HUMAN PULMONARY TRUNK

	Birth	2—10 (month)	10—19 (years)	20—29 (years)	30—39 (years)	40—49 (years)	50—59 (years)	60—69 (years)	70—79 (years)	80—95 (years)	Ref.
Wall thickness (mm) (n = 220)											
♂	—	—	1.24	1.12	1.05	1.31	1.27	1.29	1.24	1.34	5
♀	—	—	0.99	1.04	1.06	1.12	1.27	1.28	1.31	1.8	5
Circumference of the pulmonary trunk (cm) (n = 205)	—	—	—	6.1	6.5	7.2	7.6	7.7	8.2	—	6

Note: All measurements post-mortem from individuals at low altitude except where indicated.

REFERENCES

1. **Saldana, M. and Arias-Stella, J.**, Studies on the structure of the pulmonary trunk. III. The thickness of the media of the pulmonary trunk and ascending aorta in high altitude natives, *Circulation*, 27, 1101, 1963.
2. **Hagele, U.**, Das Volumen und die Volumelastizitat der Pulmonalisgabel und ihre Beziehung zu Lebensalter, Korperlange und Herzgewicht, *Z. Biol. (Munich)*, 115, 372, 1967.
3. **Meyer, W. W. and Simon, E.**, The phase-like variation of the pulmonalis volume flexibility in the life course in relation to the structure of the arterial wall, *Arch. Kreislaufforsch.*, 31, 95, 1959.
4. **Scheel, O.**, Gefassmessungen und Arteriosklerose, *Virchows Arch. Pathol. Anat. Physiol.*, 191, 135, 1908.
5. **Kani, I.**, Systematische Lichtungs- und Dickenmessungen der grossen Arterien und ihre Bedeutung fur die Pathologie der Gefasse, *Virchows Arch. Pathol. Anat. Physiol.*, 201, 45, 1910.
6. **Meyer, W. W. and Richter, H.**, Das Gewicht der Lungenschlagader als Gradmesser der Pulmonalarteriensklerose und als morphologisches Kriterium der pulmonalen Hypertonie. Eine quantitativ-anatomische und feingewebliche Untersuchung, *Virchows Arch. Pathol. Anat. Physiol.*, 328, 121, 1956.

Table 10
REGRESSION EQUATIONS OF THE
HUMAN PULMONARY ARTERY

Conditions	Regression equation	Ref.
Weight of pulmonary trunk between 20—80 years post mortem (g) (n = 205)	W = 2.4 + 0.095 A	1
Volume of pulmonary trunk between 16—80 years at 2mm Hg postmortem (mℓ) (n = 50)	V = 13.1 + 0.415 A	2
Volume increase of pulmonary trunk from 2—120 mm Hg between 16—80 years post-mortem (mℓ) (n = 50)	V = 59.1 − 0.25 A	2
Pressure related elastic modulus of the right pulmonary artery in vivo between 1—60 years (n = 22)	E_p = 105 + 2.6 A	3

Note: A = age in years.

REFERENCES

1. **Meyer, W. W. and Richter, H.**, Das Gewicht der Lungenschlagader als Gradmesser der Pulmonalarteriensklerose und als morphologisches Kriterium der pulmonalen Hypertonie. Eine quantitativ-anatomische und feingewebliche Untersuchung, *Virchows Arch. Pathol. Anat. Physiol.,* 328, 121, 1956.
2. **Hägele, U.**, Das Volumen und die Volumelastizität der Pulmonalisgabel und ihre beziehung zu Lebensalter, Körperlänge und Herzgewicht, *Z. Biol. (Munich),* 115, 372, 1967.
3. **Gozna, E. R., Marble, A. E., Shaw, A., and Holland, J. G.**, Age-related changes in the mechanics of the aorta and pulmonary artery of man, *J. Appl. Physiol.,* 36, 407, 1974.

Table 11
AGE CHANGES OF THE HUMAN CAROTID SINUS

	\multicolumn{6}{c}{Age (years)}	
	20	30	40	50	60	70	Ref.
External diameter (mm) (n = 13)							
Common carotid	6.0	—	—	6.4	6.1	7.2	1
Carotid sinus	6.0	—	—	6.4	6.1	7.0	1
Internal carotid	3.7	—	—	4.0	3.8	4.3	1
External carotid	4.7	—	—	4.7	—	4.4	1
Media in % of external diameter (n = 13)							
Common carotid	14.6	—	—	11.2	12.8	10.3	1
Carotid sinus	8.2	—	—	5.4	4.8	4.0	1
Internal carotid	13.5	—	—	13.6	12.3	11.4	1
External carotid	12.6	—	—	8.4	—	12.6	1
Intima in % of external diameter (n = 13)							
Common carotid	1.5	—	—	6.1	3.6	6.2	1
Carotid sinus	5.6	—	—	9.9	15.0	8.7	1
Internal carotid	0.5	—	—	1.4	1.1	1.5	1
External carotid	1.4	—	—	8.8	—	3.2	1
Circumference of common carotid (cm) (n = 220)							
Male	1.9	1.9	1.8	2.1	2.1	2.1	3
Female	1.7	1.7	1.7	1.7	1.9	1.7	3
Wall thickness of common carotid (mm) (n = 220)							
Male	0.91	0.87	0.88	1.04	1.06	1.18	3
Female	0.81	0.88	0.86	0.97	1.01	1.95	3
Percentage occlusion of carotid sinus by intima proliferation between 20 and 80 years (n = 37)							
Male	\multicolumn{6}{c}{Percentage occlusion = 0.56 A + 9.5}	1
Female	\multicolumn{6}{c}{Percentage occlusion = 0.3 A + 13.6}	1
The human carotid sinus is at all ages less extensible than the common carotid artery (n = 30)							2
The human carotid sinus shows increasing atherosclerosis with age, more severe than in either the common or internal carotid artery (n = 38)							1

Note: A = age in years.

REFERENCES

1. **Heath, D., Smith, P., Harris, P., and Winson, M.,** The atherosclerotic human carotid sinus, *J. Pathol.*, 110, 49, 1973.
2. **Winson, M., Heath, D., and Smith, P.,** Extensibility of the human carotid sinus, *Cardiovasc. Res.*, 8, 58, 1974.
3. **Kani, I.,** Systematische Lichtungs- und Dickenmessungen der grossen Arterien und ihre Bedeutung für die Pathologie der Gefässe, *Virchows Anat. Pathol. Anat. Physiol.*, 201, 45, 1910.

Table 12
PROPERTIES OF HUMAN CORONARY ARTERIES[1]

Properties	Birth—10 ♂	Birth—10 ♀	10—20 ♂	10—20 ♀	20—30 ♂	20—30 ♀	30—40 ♂	30—40 ♀
External diameter (mm) (n = 100)								
Left coronary	1.38	1.33	1.73	1.58	1.98	1.44	2.43	2.03
Anterior descending	1.34	1.0	1.67	1.25	1.97	1.56	2.12	2.02
Right coronary	1.25	1.0	1.51	1.34	1.86	1.35	2.18	2.05
Wall thickness (mm) (n = 100)								
Left coronary	0.215	0.198	0.263	0.257	0.426	0.283	0.592	0.418
Anterior descending	0.2	0.153	0.285	0.215	0.399	0.296	0.576	0.411
Right coronary	0.215	0.151	0.297	0.27	0.42	0.283	0.464	0.374
Ratio of media to wall thickness (n = 100)								
Left coronary	0.88	0.594	0.497	0.514	0.473	0.537	0.468	0.38
Anterior descending	0.604	0.723	0.502	0.559	0.505	0.514	0.309	0.429
Right coronary	0.632	0.78	0.502	0.561	0.5	0.532	0.362	0.502
Ratio of intima to wall thickness (n = 100)								
Left coronary	0.189	0.175	0.177	0.187	0.379	0.272	0.556	0.421
Anterior descending	0.159	0.177	0.225	0.225	0.371	0.332	0.51	0.289
Right coronary	0.211	0.211	0.205	0.214	0.282	0.23	0.261	0.191

Note: The compliance of the coronary arteries remains above 50 mm Hg constant throughout life.[2]

REFERENCES

1. **Neufeld, H. N., Wagenvoort, C. A., and Edwards, J. E.,** Coronary arteries in fetuses, infants, juveniles, and young adults, *Lab. Invest.,* 11, 837, 1962.
2. **Köhler, F. and Köhler, H.,** Über Altersveränderungen der elastischen Wandeigenschaften menschlicher Coronararterien, *Verh. Dtsch. Ges. Pathol.,* 59, 344, 1975.

Table 13
DIMENSIONAL CHANGES OF HUMAN ARTERIES AND VEINS WITH AGE

Age (years)	Measure-ments	Aorta at diaphragm	A. carotis communis	A. hepatica	A. lienalia	A. mesenterica superior	A. renalis	A. femoralis	A. coronaris sinistra descendens	A. thyreoidea superior	A. basilaris cerebri	Vena cava caudalis
1—4 (n = 24)	a	1.94	2.73	9.03	8.45	6.51	8.75	6.57	6.70	10.62	13.16	
	b	2.8	1.34	0.6	0.533	1.18	0.685	0.82	0.576	0.45	0.67	3.36
	c	0.49	0.33	0.105	0.112	0.12	0.098	0.173	0.092	0.086	0.072	
	d	0.036	0.02	0.014	0.008	0.03	0.012	0.021	0.061	0.012	0.009	0.36
5—10 (n = 12)	a	1.51	2.28	5.4	4.85	3.52	5.75	2.73	3.79	4.51	9.34	
	b	4.34	1.82	0.42	0.85	1.6	1.09	1.32	0.75	0.57	0.94	6.02
	c	0.662	0.542	0.201	0.182	0.26	0.177	0.32	0.17	0.166	0.088	
	d	0.033	0.021	0.018	0.01	0.032	0.018	0.033	0.061	0.015	0.012	0.38
16—20 (n = 19)	a	1.20	1.72	3.54	3.09	2.42	3.54	1.85	2.79	3.54	8.10	
	b	5.54	1.95	1.06	1.241	1.91	1.3	1.94	1.01	0.64	1.04	8.75
	c	0.83	0.58	0.26	0.266	0.327	0.245	0.467	0.214	0.194	0.091	
	d	0.062	0.059	0.035	0.031	0.041	0.017	0.051	0.145	0.031	0.018	0.53
21—30 (n = 15)	a	1.17	1.57	3.18	2.48	2.28	3.12	1.52	2.52	3.54	7.82	
	b	6.25	1.98	1.14	1.37	2.05	1.51	2.22	1.1	0.65	1.08	8.9
	c	1.0	0.59	0.276	0.377	0.381	0.312	0.613	0.231	0.212	0.121	
	d	0.081	0.074	0.027	0.036	0.042	0.022	0.062	0.143	0.037	0.027	0.53
31—40 (n = 15)	a	1.11	1.54	2.91	2.18	2.40	2.97	1.52	2.15	3.54	7.57	
	b	6.54	2.31	1.15	1.57	2.27	1.6	2.4	1.13	0.66	1.09	9.0
	c	1.06	0.59	0.311	0.405	0.406	0.32	0.6	0.231	0.218	0.126	
	d	0.129	0.084	0.042	0.05	0.046	0.025	0.073	0.162	0.036	0.028	0.53
41—50 (n = 16)	a	1.11	1.51	2.76	2.09	2.34	2.76	1.52	2.09	3.54	7.27	
	b	6.73	2.36	1.2	1.73	2.28	1.72	2.49	1.16	0.7	1.13	9.1
	c	1.07	0.597	0.317	0.445	0.378	0.36	0.621	0.169	0.227	0.124	
	d	0.152	0.1	0.054	0.054	0.051	0.028	0.12	0.201	0.042	0.028	0.54

51—60	a	1.08	1.48	2.7	2.03	2.18	2.73	1.46	2.09	3.33	7.06
(n = 16)	b	7.21	2.4	1.24	1.69	2.45	1.75	2.6	1.18	0.73	1.18	9.2
	c	1.41	0.628	0.325	0.445	0.376	0.371	0.652	0.165	0.233	0.126
	d	0.212	0.094	0.057	0.054	0.08	0.03	0.113	0.22	0.036	0.034	0.6
61—70	a	1.02	1.26	2.64	1.85	2.12	2.58	1.45	2.06	3.27	6.70
(n = 15)	b	7.5	2.44	1.4	1.89	2.5	1.85	3.2	1.35	0.82	1.29	9.3
	c	1.67	0.715	0.33	0.46	0.416	0.386	0.654	0.148	0.281	0.121
	d	0.234	0.112	0.06	0.093	0.09	0.047	0.124	0.254	0.043	0.036	0.61

Note: The ratio internal radius to mean wall thickness remains constant for each artery throughout life. A. = arteria; a = ratio of inner wall surface to wall volume; b = internal radius (mm); c = media (mm); and d = intima (mm). Measurements at 0 mm Hg post-mortem.

REFERENCES

1. **Hieronymi, G.**, *Sitzungsber. Heidelb. Akad. Wis.*, 221, 1956.
2. **Hieronymi, G.**, Angiometric examination of veins and arteries in various age groups, *Frankf. Z. Pathol.*, 69, 18, 1958.

Table 14
PROPERTIES OF HUMAN MUSCULAR ARTERIES

	\multicolumn{7}{c}{Age (years)}	
	20	30	40	50	60	70	80	Ref.
Pressure related elastic modulus of the femoral artery in vivo (n = 68) (kg·cm^{-2})	—	—	2.6	3.9	—	6.4	—	1
% Vol change/mm Hg of leg arteries in vivo (n = 27)								2
50 mm Hg	0.347	—	0.2	—	0.153	0.108	—	
150 mm Hg	0.097	—	0.063	—	0.062	0.047	—	
Small pulmonary arteries, measurements in % of wall (n = 27)								3
Circular muscles	—	—	73	75	65	49	50	
Longitudinal muscles	—	—	19	16	20	26	24	
Collagen	—	—	7	8	12	24	24	
Circumference of iliaca communis (cm) (n = 220)								6
♂	2.2	2.2	2.3	2.8	2.9	3.3	3.0	
♀	1.9	2.0	2.0	2.1	2.3	2.6	2.7	
Wall thickness of iliaca communis (mm) (n = 220)								
♂	0.93	0.96	0.94	1.11	1.04	1.27	1.13	
♀	0.9	0.88	0.93	1.03	1.09	1.06	1.07	
Circumference of a. renalis (cm) (n = 220)								6
♂	1.3	1.4	1.4	1.5	1.6	1.6	1.5	
♀	1.2	1.2	1.3	1.3	1.3	1.3	1.3	
Wall thickness of a. renalis (mm) (n = 220)								
♂	0.54	0.54	0.58	0.71	0.8	0.84	0.79	
♀	0.54	0.49	0.62	0.65	0.74	0.73	0.85	
Longitudinal "elastance" $E_s \cdot h$ of the iliac artery post-mortem between 30 and 90 years (n = 19)	\multicolumn{7}{l}{Elastance (kg·cm^{-1}) = 0.0435 A − 0.1}	4
Collapse pressure of the iliac artery post-mortem between 10 and 90 years (n = 63)	\multicolumn{7}{l}{Collapse pressure (mm Hg) = 29.6 + 0.36 A}	4
The tangential elastance ($E_s \cdot h$) of the iliac artery is at all ages about 2.5 times lower than the longitudinal elastance								4
In brain arteries, half of the collagen fibers are stretched, when the circumferencial stretch reaches 30% in young humans and 20% in old humans (n = 30)								5

Note: A = age in years.

REFERENCES

1. **Mozersky, D. J., Sumner, D. S., Hokanson, D. E., and Strandness, D. E., Jr.,** Transcutaneous measurement of arterial wall properties as a potential method of estimating aging, *J. Am. Geriatr. Soc.,* 21, 18, 1973.
2. **Carter, S. A.,** *Can. J. Physiol. Pharmacol.,* 42, 399, 1964.
3. **Naeye, R. L. and Dellinger, W. S.,** Pulmonary arterial changes with age and smoking, *Arch. Pathol.,* 92, 284, 1971.
4. **Roach, M. R. and Burton, A. C.,** The effect of age on the elasticity of human iliac arteries, *Can. J. Biochem. Physiol.,* 37, 557, 1959.
5. **Busby, D. E. and Burton, A. C.,** *Can. J. Physiol. Pharmacol.,* 43, 185, 1965.
6. **Kani, I.,** Systematische Lichtungs- und Dickenmessungen der grossen Arterien und ihre Bedeutung für die Pathologie der Gefässe, *Virchows Arch. Pathol. Anat. Physiol.,* 201, 45, 1910.

Table 15
VISCOELASTIC PROPERTIES OF HUMAN ARTERIES

Arteries	Years	Retraction (%)	r/h	E_{inc}	E_d	$\eta\omega$	C
Thoracic	Y	22.9	16.1	7.5	12.5	2.0	5.9
aorta	O	13.6	11.4	16.6	25.8	3.2	8.8
Abdominal	Y	30.0	13.5	10.2	13.9	1.7	6.3
aorta	O	18.2	8.0	11.9	16.0	2.0	8.3
Iliac	Y	32.7	15.6	30.0	44.5	5.2	8.1
	O	20.0	5.9	7.8	15.4	1.9	9.4
Femoral	Y	38.9	8.8	30.1	62.1	13.6	—
	O	24.3	5.2	14.5	35.3	5.0	—
Carotid	Y	25.0	10.6	8.6	12.7	2.9	—
	O	18.0	6.9	10.0	16.1	1.5	—

Note: Retraction in % of *in situ* length: r/h = ratio of radius to wall thickness at 100 mm Hg; E_{inc} = static tangential incremental elastic modulus at 100 mm Hg (kg·cm^{-2}); E_d = dynamic tangential incremental elastic modulus at 100 mm Hg(kg·cm^{-2}); $\eta\omega$ = viscous retarding force of the complex dynamic elastic modulus at 100 mm Hg and 4 cycles/min (kg·cm^{-2}); C = pulse wave velocity at physiological pressures (m·sec^{-1}); Y = 10 to 20 years (n = 6); and O = 36 to 52 years (n = 6). Pulse wave velocities measured in vivo, all other measurements post-mortem, smooth muscles dead.

From Learoyd, B. M. and Taylor, M. G., Alterations with age in the viscoelastic properties of human arterial wall, *Circ. Res.*, 18, 278, 1966. By permission of the American Heart Association, Inc.

Table 16
PULSE WAVE VELOCITY IN HUMAN ARTERIES

Author	Arteries	0—10	11—20	21—30	31—40	41—50	51—60	61—70	71—80	81—90	91—100	Ref.
Fulton and McSwiney (n = 103)	b_1	—	4.2	4.7	5.0	5.5	5.6	5.6	6.0	—	—	1
	b_2	—	6.0	8.3	8.9	10.4	11.4	11.0	11.0	—	—	1
Hallock (n = 474)	a	4.0	4.3	5.4	6.0	7.0	8.0	9.0	10.5	—	—	2
	b	5.0	5.8	6.1	7.3	8.1	8.8	9.3	9.6	—	—	2
Wezler and Standl (n = 45)	a	4.5	4.2	5.5	6.3	9.4	—	10.1	—	—	—	3,4
	b	6.9	6.8	7.7	8.1	9.7	—	9.8	—	—	—	3,4
	c	8.8	7.3	9.0	10.3	11.7	—	11.6	—	—	—	3,4
Ludwig (n = 173)	a	—	5.1	5.7	6.4	6.8	8.3	8.8	9.8	—	—	5
	b	—	6.1	6.8	7.1	7.4	—	9.3	—	—	—	5
Landowne (n = 94)	b	—	6.1	8.3	8.7	10.3	10.8	10.5	9.5	8.7	9.0	6
Karnbaum (n = 75)	a	—	—	6.82	6.4	7.67	8.55	11.53	12.95	—	—	7
Schimmler (n = 1326)	a ♂	—	—	6.55	6.92	7.55	8.33	9.23	10.93	—	—	8
	a ♀	—	—	5.84	6.8	7.04	8.0	8.47	9.85	—	—	8
Nikolaev (n = 100)	a ♂	—	—	—	6.07	6.86	8.1	9.45	—	—	—	9
	a ♀	—	—	—	6.52	6.8	7.73	8.14	—	—	—	9
	b ♂	—	—	—	7.76	8.51	9.3	9.9	—	—	—	9
	b ♀	—	—	—	8.19	8.32	8.93	8.55	—	—	—	9

Note: Measurements in vivo at physiological pressures in m·sec⁻¹: a = aorta-iliac artery; b = brachio-radial artery, b_1 = brachial artery; b_2 = radial artery; and c = femoral artery.

REFERENCES

1. **Fulton, J. S. and McSwiney, B. A.**, The pulse wave velocity and extensibility of the brachial and radial artery in man, *J. Physiol. (London)*, 69, 386, 1930.
2. **Hallock, P.**, Arterial elasticity in man in relation to age as evaluated by the pulse wave velocity method, *Arch. Int. Med. Exp.*, 54, 770, 1934.
3. **Wezler, K.**, *Z. Kreislaufforsch.*, 27, 721, 1935.
4. **Wezler, K. and Standl, R.**, Die normalen Alterskurven der Pulswellengeschwindigkeit in elastischen und muskelaren Arterien des Menschen, *Z. Biol. (Munich)*, 97, 265, 1936.
5. **Ludwig, H.**, Experimentelles zur Hydromechanik und Hamodynamik; die Pulswellengeschwindigkeit bei Gesunden und Kranken, *Z. Gesamte Exp. Med.*, 99, 352, 1936.
6. **Landowne, M.**, The relation between intra-arterial pressure and impact pulse wave velocity with regard to age and arteriosclerosis, *J. Gerontol.*, 13, 153, 1958.
7. **Karnbaum, S.**, Kreislaufanalytische Untersuchungen bei Normotonikern, *Z. Kreislaufforsch.*, 46, 709, 1957.
8. **Schimmler, W.**, Untersuchungen zu Elastizitatsproblemen der Aorta. (Statistische Korrelation der Pulswellengeschwindigkeit zu Alter, Geschlecht und Blutdruck). *Arch. Kreislaufforsch.*, 47, 189, 1965.
9. **Nikolaev, E. I.**, O Polovykh Razlichiiakh v vozrastnoi Dinamike Nekotorykh Pokazatelei uprugo-viazkogo sostoianii arterii, *Probl. Endokrinol.*, 16, 45, 1970.

Table 17
REGRESSION EQUATIONS FOR PULSE WAVE PROPERTIES OF HUMAN ARTERIES

Conditions	Regression equations	Ref.
Pulse wave velocity of ascending aorta (m/sec) (n = 21)	C = 3.0 + 0.1 A	1
Pulse wave velocity of pulmonary artery (m/sec) (n = 22)	C = 2.2 + 0.02 A	1
Amplification of pressure wave between aortic arch and iliac artery in % of pulse pressure amplitude at aortic arch (n = 39)	Amplification = 58.9 − 0.9 A	2
Transmission time of pulse wave from aortic arch to diaphragm (msec) (n = 39)	Transmission time = 30 − 0.043 A	2
Transmission time of pulse wave from diaphragm to end of common iliac artery (msec) (n = 39)	Transmission time = 63.5 − 0.616 A	2

Note: Measurements in vivo at physiological presures. A = age in years.

REFERENCES

1. Gozna, E. R., Marble, A. E., Shaw, A., and Holland, J. G., Age-related changes in the mechanics of the aorta and pulmonary artery of man, *J. Appl. Physiol.*, 36, 407, 1974.
2. O'Rourke, M. F., Blazek, J. V., Morreels, C. L., and Krovetz, L. J., Pressure wave transmission along the human aorta. Changes with age and in arterial degenerative disease, *Circ. Res.*, 23, 567, 1968.

Table 18
ELASTIN, COLLAGEN, AND MUSCLE CONTENT OF HUMAN ARTERIES

	\multicolumn{9}{c}{Age (years)}	
	0—1	1—10	10—20	20—30	30—40	40—50	50—60	60—70	70—80	80—90	Ref.
Elastin											
% of dry fat-free weight of thoracic aorta (n = 21)	—	—	35.7	40.6	36.8	—	38.5	—	37.2	—	1
% of dry weight of thoracic arota (n = 83)	—	—	—	37.4	37.4	—	28.8	26.8	26.6	—	2
% of dry fat-free weight of thoracic aorta (n = 110)	—	48.5	48.2	43.3	41.4	44.1	41.4	43.8	43.8	41.1	3
% of dry fat-free weight of pulmonary artery (n = 94)	—	—	31.0	31.0	32.0	32.5	33.0	35.0	38.0	—	4
% of wall (n = 52)											
Thoracic aorta											
♂	27.0	38.0	25.5	42.8	29.6	—	20.8	16.0	—	—	6
♀	15.6	23.0	19.5	22.3	26.0	—	21.3	21.5	15.0	—	6
Abdominal aorta											
♂	19.0	—	24.5	29.0	21.6	—	15.1	10.7	—	—	6
♀	17.5	19.2	16.5	17.5	19.0	—	15.0	12.5	8.0	—	6
% of dry fat-free weight (n = 15)											
Thoracic aorta	—	—	41.4	50.0	34.0	—	51.2	—	49.5	—	7
Abdominal aorta	—	—	40.8	34.0	35.5	—	33.2	—	35.5	—	7
% solubilization of elastin by elastase of thoracic aorta (n = 60)	98	96	—	95	—	84	79	65	56	45	8

109

Table 18 (continued)
ELASTIN, COLLAGEN, AND MUSCLE CONTENT OF HUMAN ARTERIES

	Age (years)									Ref.
	0—1	1—10	10—20	20—30	30—40	40—50	50—60	60—70	70—80	80—90	
% dialyzable of solubilized elastin of thoracic aorta (n = 60)	37	40	—	30	—	29	31	27	21	14	8
Collagen											
% of dry weight of thoracic aorta (n = 83)	—	—	—	15.4	15.5	—	17.4	18.1	19.1	—	2
% of dry fat-free weight of aorta (n = 1)	31.8	25.3	20.5	19.9	18.5	20.3	22.0	21.7	21.7	—	5
% of wall (n = 52)											
Thoracic aorta											
♂	16.2	16.0	37.0	34.4	47.3	—	50.3	49.5	—	—	6
♀	26.2	29.5	22.5	41.3	44.0	—	42.0	41.0	—	—	6
Abdominal aorta											
♂	17.7	22.0	33.5	37.4	54.3	—	57.4	55.2	—	—	6
♀	19.6	23.5	30.0	35.3	49.0	—	35.6	30.5	—	—	6
% of dry fat-free weight (n = 15)											
Thoracic aorta	—	—	28.4	18.0	24.5	—	20.25	—	20.5	—	7
Abdominal aorta	—	—	26.2	28.0	27.5	—	34.25	—	27.5	—	7
% hydroxyproline of dry fat-free weight of aorta	—	—	0.42	—	0.49	—	0.67	0.99	1.21	—	9

Smooth muscles % of wall (n = 52)										
Thoracic aorta										
♂	56.8	47.0	37.5	22.8	23.0	—	29.1	34.5	—	6
♀	58.3	47.7	58.0	36.3	30.0	—	36.3	37.0	—	6
Abdominal aorta	60.2	48.0	42.0	33.8	24.3	—	27.7	33.7	—	6
♂	62.8	57.0	53.5	27.0	31.0	—	49.3	57.0	—	6
♀	—	1.28	—	0.82	0.76	0.59	0.57	0.52	0.43	9
DNA in mg/g wet weight of aorta	—	1.223	1.16	1.27	1.095	1.168	0.781	1.271	0.886	10
DNA in mg/g wet weight of thoracic aorta	1.57	1.29	1.18	1.1	0.91	0.85	0.63	0.78	0.68	11
DNA in μmol/g wet weight of thoracic aorta	—	1.27	1.31	1.08	1.055	0.802	0.752	0.649	0.565	10
Creatine in μmol/g wet weight of thoracic aorta	—	—	—	90	83	—	76	74	54	2
Creatine in mg % of wet weight of aorta (n = 83)										

Table 18 (continued)
ELASTIN, COLLAGEN, AND MUSCLE CONTENT OF HUMAN ARTERIES

REFERENCES

1. **Hass, G. M.**, Elastic tissue. III. Relations between the structure of the aging aorta and the properties of the isolated aortic elastic tissue, *Arch. Pathol.*, 35, 29, 1943.
2. **Myers, V. C. and Lang, W. W.**, Some chemical changes in the human thoracic aorta accompanying the aging process, *J. Gerontol.*, 1, 441, 1946.
3. **Lansing, A. I., Alex, M., and Rosenthal, T. B.**, Atheromatosis as sequel to senescent changes in arterial wall, *J. Gerontol.*, 5, 112, 1950.
4. **Lansing, A. I.**, *Ciba Found. Colloq. Ageing*, 1, 88, 1954.
5. **Kanabrocki, E. L., Fels, I. G., and Kaplan, E.**, Calcium, cholesterol, and collagen levels in human aortas, *J. Gerontol.*, 15, 383, 1960.
6. **Ahmed, M. M.**, Age and sex differences in the structure of the tunica media of the human aorta, *Acta Anat.*, 66, 45, 1967.
7. **Feldmann, S. A. and Glagov, S.**, Transmedial collagen and elastin gradients in human aortas: reversal with age, *Atherosclerosis*, 13, 385, 1971.
8. **La Bella, F. S. and Lindsay, W. G.**, The structure of human aortic elastin as influenced by age, *J. Gerontol.*, 18, 111, 1963.
9. **Lindner, J.**, Gefasswand und Gelenkknorpel, *Verh. Dtsch. Ges. Pathol.*, 59, 181, 1975.
10. **Kirk, J. E.**, *Coenzyme Contents of Arterial Tissue*, S. Karger, Basel, 1974.
11. **Kresse, H., Friese, W., and Buddecke, E.**, *Altern*, Platt, D., Ed., Schattauer Verlag, Stuttgart, 1974, 205.

Table 19
MUCOPOLYSACCHARIDES OF HUMAN BLOOD VESSELS

	Age (years)									
	0—10	10—20	20—30	30—40	40—50	50—60	60—70	70—80	80—90	Ref.
% hexosamine of wet aorta (n = 124)	0.29	0.31	0.3	0.33	0.29	0.3	0.29	0.29	0.3	1
% hexosamine of wet pulmonary artery (n = 91)	0.26	0.28	0.3	0.27	0.25	0.28	0.28	0.29	0.27	1
% hyaluronate of total mucopolysaccharide of aorta (n = 33)	—	20	24	18	14	15	12	—	—	2
% chondroitin-sulfate of total mucopolysaccharide of aorta (n = 33)	—	66	61	65	64	55	53	—	—	2
% dermatansulfate of total mucopolysaccharide of aorta (n = 33)	—	8	8	9	10	15	15	—	—	2
% heparitinsulfate of total mucopolysaccharide of aorta (n = 33)	—	6	7	8	12	15	21	—	—	2
% glucosamine of dry aorta (n = 21)	—	—	0.146	0.173	0.239	0.23	0.238	0.216	—	3
% galactosamine of dry aorta (n = 21)	—	—	0.124	0.11	0.167	0.172	0.184	0.138	—	3
% acid mucopolysaccharide of dry aorta (n = 17)	—	0.4	0.446	0.482	—	0.526	0.521	—	—	4
% hyaluronic acid of dry aorta (n = 17)	—	0.028	0.026	0.035	—	0.028	0.03	—	—	4

Table 19 (continued)
MUCOPOLYSACCHARIDES OF HUMAN BLOOD VESSELS

	\multicolumn{8}{c	}{Age (years)}	
	0—10	10—20	20—30	30—40	40—50	50—60	60—70	70—80	80—90	Ref.
% keratansulfate of dry aorta (n = 17)	—	0.053	0.067	0.066	—	0.074	0.073	—	—	4
% heparitinsulfate of dry aorta (n = 17)	—	0.072	0.06	0.056	—	0.066	0.063	—	—	4
% dermatansulfate of dry aorta (n = 17)	—	0.052	0.068	0.072	—	0.09	0.073	—	—	4
% chondroitin-4-sulfate of dry aorta (n = 17)	—	0.09	0.103	0.122	—	0.155	0.165	—	—	4
% chondroitin-6-sulfate of dry aorta (n = 17)	—	0.084	0.093	0.102	—	0.09	0.09	—	—	4
% heparin of dry aorta (n = 17)	—	0.021	0.029	0.029	—	0.028	0.027	—	—	4
% hexosamine of acid mucopolysaccharide of dry fat-free aorta	0.3	—	—	—	0.55	—	0.625	—	—	5
% hexosamine of neutral mucopolysaccharides of dry fat-free aorta	0.132	—	—	—	0.56	—	0.176	—	—	5
% chondroitin-6-sulfate of total mucopolysaccharide of aorta	—	65	—	57	—	58	—	54	—	8
% dermatansulfate of total mucopolysaccharide of aorta	—	10	—	10	—	7	—	15	—	8
% heparitinsulfate of total mucopolysaccharide of aorta	—	6	—	7	—	11	—	19	—	8

% hyaluronate of total mucopolysaccharide of aorta	—	21	—	21	—	15	—	10	—	8
35S incorporation in aorta (cpm/mg acid mucopolysaccharide) (n = 68)	60,000	10,000	390	210	160	85	41	—	—	9
35S incorporation in aorta (imp/min/g) Intima	—	—	7400	6000	4500	4000	3800	—	—	7
Media	—	—	3300	2800	2300	2200	2100	—	—	7
% hexosamine of dry fat-free aorta (n = 71) (between birth and 70 years)					Hexosamine % = 0.485 + 0.004 A					6

REFERENCES

1. **Kirk, J. E. and Dyrbye, M.**, Hexosamine and acid-hydrolyzable sulfate concentrations of the aorta and pulmonary artery in individuals of various ages, *J. Gerontol.*, 11, 273, 1956.
2. **Kaplan, D. and Meyer, K.**, Mucopolysaccharides of aorta at various ages (26015), *Proc. Soc. Exp. Biol. Med.*, 105, 78, 1960.
3. **Buddecke, E.**, Untersuchungen zur Chemie der Arterienwand. II. Arteriosklerotische Veranderungen am Aortenbindegewebe des Menschen, *Hoppe-Seyler's Z. Physiol. Chem.*, 310, 182, 1958.
4. **Tomaszewski, J., Hanzlik, J., Lopatynski, J., and Gilatowska, B.**, Badania nad skladem chemicznym sciany naczyniowej. XI. Glikozoaminoglikany sciany ludykiej tetnicy glownej w procesie finzjologicznego starzenia, *Pol. Arch. Med. Wewn.*, 47, 51, 1971.
5. **Bertelsen, S.**, Presence of neutral carbohydrates in human aortic tissue, *Nature (London)*, 187, 411, 1960.
6. **Kanabrocki, E. L., Fels, I. G., Decker, C. F., and Kaplan, E.**, Total hexosamine sulfur, and nitrogen levels in human aorta, *J. Gerontol.*, 18, 18, 1963.
7. **Lindner, J. and Johannes, G.**, Contribution on the aging of arterial connective tissue, *Connective Tissue and Aging*, Vogel, H. G., Ed., Excerpta Medica, Amsterdam, 1973, 68.
8. **Kresse, H., Friese, W., and Buddecke, E.**, *Altern*, Platt, D., Ed., Schattauer Verlag, Stuttgart 1974, 205.
9. **Hauss, W. H., Junge-Hulsing, G., and Gerlach, U.**, *Die Unspezifische Mesenchymreaktion*, Georg Thieme, Stuttgart, 1968.

Table 20
NONFIBROUS ELEMENTS OF HUMAN BLOOD VESSELS

	Age (years)									
	0—10	10—20	20—30	30—40	40—50	50—60	60—70	70—80	80—90	Ref.
% acid hydrolyzable, sulfate										
Of wet aorta (n = 124)	0.072	0.071	0.087	0.084	0.072	0.077	0.06	0.079	0.075	1
Of wet pulmonary artery (n = 91)	0.064	0.048	0.066	0.056	0.06	0.075	0.08	0.081	0.07	1
% nitrogen										
Of wet aorta (n = 124)	4.41	4.22	4.13	3.75	3.39	3.37	3.29	3.2	3.53	1
Of wet pulmonary artery (n = 91)	3.15	3.87	3.98	3.34	3.34	3.24	3.51	2.98	3.36	1
% sulfur										
Of dry aorta (n = 32)	0.24	0.34	0.32	0.67	—	0.83	—	—	—	2
% nitrogen										
Of dry aorta (n = 32)	13.6	13.5	13.4	12.4	—	12.1	—	—	—	2
% phosphate										
Of dry aorta (n = 32)	0.06	0.15	0.25	0.3	—	0.56	—	—	—	2
% nitrogen										
Of dry a. femoralis (n = 176)	14.9	14.7	14.1	13.9	13.8	13.2	12.7	12.8	—	3
% sulfur										
Of dry a. femoralis (n = 130) ♂	—	0.352	0.378	0.448	0.5	0.508	0.51	0.51	0.539	3
♀	—	0.325	0.344	0.419	0.456	0.477	0.484	0.492	0.487	3
% nitrogen										
Of dry vena femoralis (n = 96)	—	14.91	14.53	14.08	13.8	13.48	13.74	13.15	12.88	4
% phosphate										
Of dry aorta	—	—	0.227	0.436	—	0.6	—	0.77	—	5

% sulfur								
Of dry fat free aorta (n = 71) (between birth and 70 years)	—	0.23	—	—	—	—	—	6
% potassium								
Of dry aorta (n = 149)	—	—	0.139	0.134	0.145	0.131	0.142	0.11	3
Of pulmonary artery	—	0.14	0.115	0.117	0.114	0.091	0.108	0.08	3
Of vena cava	—	0.26	0.287	0.218	—	0.213	0.229	0.195	3
Metals in mg % of Wet weight of aorta								
Zinc	—	—	3.0	2.5	—	1.5	—	—	7
Chromium	—	—	1.4	1.8	—	2.1	—	—	7
Strontium	—	—	0.7	0.7	—	0.6	—	—	7
Nickel	—	—	0.6	0.3	—	0.3	—	—	7
Copper	—	—	0.2	0.2	—	0.2	—	—	7
Lead	—	—	0.07	0.08	—	0.11	—	—	7
Lithium	—	—	0.1	0.1	—	0.1	—	—	7
Manganese	—	—	0.01	0.06	—	0.05	—	—	7
Cadmium	—	—	0.06	0.03	—	0.02	—	—	7
Silver	—	—	0.008	0.01	—	0.004	—	—	7
Tin	—	—	0.008	0.005	—	0.005	—	—	7
Glyceraldehyde-3-phosphate dehydrogenese (mmol of substrate metabolized/gm wet tissue/hr)								
Aorta (n = 3—21)	0.65	0.175	0.179	0.176	0.196	0.142	0.165	—	8
Pulmonary artery (n = 4—12)	0.56	0.153	0.183	0.179	0.214	0.183	0.204	—	8
Coronary artery (n = 3—9)	0.004	0.064	0.029	0.093	0.082	0.08	0.129	—	8
Vena cava inferior (n = 2—8)	0.008	0.017	0.022	0.055	0.098	0.091	0.075	—	8

Sulfur % = 0.485 + 0.001 A

Table 20 (continued)
NONFIBROUS ELEMENTS OF HUMAN BLOOD VESSELS

	\multicolumn{8}{c}{Age (years)}	
	0—10	10—20	20—30	30—40	40—50	50—60	60—70	70—80	80—90	Ref.
Glycero phosphate dehydrogenese (mmol of substrate metabolized/gm wet tissue/hr										
Aorta (n = 5—19)	0.0087	0.0138	0.0242	0.0218	0.0167	0.0133	0.0085	0.0122	—	8
Pulmonary artery (n = 3—17)	0.0226	0.0546	0.0328	0.0738	0.0625	0.0630	0.0420	0.0517	—	8
Coronary artery (n = 3—12)	0.0934	0.121	0.061	0.1356	0.1332	0.1084	0.081	0.0824	—	8
Vena cava inferior (n = 3—8)	0.0254	0.025	0.0307	0.0394	0.0362	0.0348	0.0487	0.0503	—	8

Note: A = age in years.

REFERENCES

1. **Kirk, D. E. and Dyrbye, M.**, *J. Gerontol.*, 11, 273, 1956.
2. **Hevelke, G.**, *Dtsch. Arch. Klin. Med.*, 203, 528, 1956.
3. **Hevelke, G.**, *Verh. Dtsch. Ges. Kreislaufforsch.*, 24, 131, 1958.
4. **Hevelke, G.**, *Z. Alternsforsch.*, 13, 337, 1959.
5. **Bürger, M.**, *Z. Gesamte Neurol. Psychiatr.*, 167, 273, 1939.
6. **Kanabrocki, E. L., Fels, I. G., Decket, C. F., and Kaplan, E.**, *J. Gerontol.*, 18, 18, 1963.
7. **Avtandilov, G. G.**, *Arch. Pathol.* 29, 40, 1967.
8. **Kirk, J. E. and Ritz, E.**, *J. Gerontol.*, 22, 427, 1967.

Table 21
LIPID CONTENT OF HUMAN ARTERIES

	\multicolumn{9}{c	}{Age (years)}	
	10	20	30	40	50	60	70	80	90	Ref.
% cholesterol of dry aorta (n = 50)	0.35	—	1.06	—	1.55	—	2.23	—	—	1
% total lipid of dry aorta (n = 50)	3.75	—	5.85	—	6.8	—	6.42	—	—	1
% total lipid of dry aortic media (n = 25)	5.94	6.0	6.3	8.5	8.1	10.0	10.7	13.0	—	2
% free cholesterol of dry aortic media (n = 25)	0.66	1.11	1.01	1.33	1.39	1.82	1.91	1.98	—	2
% cholesterol ester of dry aortic media (n = 25)	0.47	1.71	—	1.35	1.81	2.68	4.06	—	—	2
% total phospholipid of dry aortic media (n = 25)	1.64	2.27	2.28	2.6	2.71	2.77	2.93	3.36	—	2
% total lipid of dry aorta (n = 32)	1.87	2.59	3.27	3.19	4.96	7.4	11.4	—	—	3
% total cholesterol of dry aorta (n = 101) ♂ ♀	0.4 0.35	0.56 0.41	1.15 0.51	1.1 —	2.34 —	2.0 1.62	5.0 6.3	3.81 6.9	— —	4 4
% cholesterol of wet aorta (n = 124)	0.45	0.62	0.87	1.16	1.64	2.08	2.66	2.17	2.77	5
% cholesterol of wet pulmonary artery (n = 91)	0.58	0.42	0.54	0.53	0.91	0.85	1.15	0.95	1.1	5
% total lipid of dry aorta (n = 42)	—	—	7.7	—	9.2	—	11.1	—	—	6

Table 21 (continued)
LIPID CONTENT OF HUMAN ARTERIES

	Age (years)									Ref.
	10	20	30	40	50	60	70	80	90	
% free cholesterol of dry aorta (n = 42)	—	—	0.89	—	1.14	—	1.47	—	—	6
% cholesterol ester of dry aorta (n = 42)	—	—	0.35	—	0.67	—	1.21	—	—	6
% plasmalogen of dry aorta (n = 42)	—	—	0.099	—	0.092	—	0.083	—	—	6
% total lipid of dry aorta	—	5.6	—	—	10.8	—	—	16.0	—	7
% cholesterol ester of total lipid	—	26.6	—	—	42.3	—	—	57.2	—	7
% free cholesterol of total lipid	—	19.9	—	—	13.0	—	—	10.5	—	7
% phospholipid of total lipid	—	42.6	—	—	29.3	—	—	17.2	—	7
% triglyceride of total lipid	—	10.9	—	—	15.4	—	—	15.1	—	7
% total lipid of dry pulmonary artery (n = 98)	7.14	7.97	8.51	10.75	10.12	12.05	13.47	13.8	15.87	8
% phospholipid of dry pulmonary artery (n = 98)	1.08	1.18	1.29	1.43	1.28	1.51	1.64	1.63	1.81	8
% sphingomyelin of dry pulmonary artery (n = 98)	0.373	0.428	0.495	0.542	0.524	0.638	0.765	0.803	0.95	8
% total lipid of dry aorta (n = 32)	6.63	—	6.42	—	8.31	—	9.76	—	—	9

% phospholipid of dry aorta (n = 32)	2.45	—	2.15	—	2.01	—	2.25	—	—	9
% cholesterol of dry weight										
Aorta	0.13	0.39	0.46	1.1	1.12	2.11	2.19	2.69	2.9	10
Pulmonary artery	0.17	0.35	0.55	0.47	0.67	0.64	0.82	0.93	1.26	10
Vena cava	0.36	0.35	0.26	0.39	0.35	0.51	0.4	0.45	0.31	10
Vena femoralis	0.186	0.235	0.269	0.275	0.255	0.394	0.385	0.382	—	11
% cholesterol of wet weight										
A. brachialis	0.126	0.14	0.181	0.227	0.217	0.218	0.269	0.256	—	12
A. femoralis	0.124	0.142	0.201	0.249	0.246	0.273	0.373	0.648	—	13
Total cholesterol in % of wet weight	Cholesterol % = 0.1 + 0.0076 A									13
Total phospholipid in % of wet weight	Phospholipid % = 0.36 + 0.0065 A									13
Total sphingomyelin in % of wet weight	Sphingomyelin % = 0.06 + 0.0047 A									13
Other phospholipids in % of wet weight	Cephalin % = 0.24 (no age changes) Lecithin % = 0.15 (no age changes)									13

Note: A = age in years.

Table 21 (continued)
LIPID CONTENT OF HUMAN ARTERIES

REFERENCES

1. **Burger, M.**, Stoffliche und funktionelle Altersserscheinungen beim Menschen, *Z. Gesamte Neurol. Psychiatr.*, 167, 273, 1939.
2. **Weinhouse, S. and Hirsch, E. F.**, Chemistry of atherosclerosis. I. Lipid and calcium content of the intima and of the media of the aorta with and without atherosclerosis, *Arch. Pathol.*, 29, 31, 1940.
3. **Kanabrocki, E. L., Fels, I.G., Decker, C. F., and Kaplan, E.**, Total hexosamine, sulfur, and nitrogen levels in human aortae, *J. Gerontol.*, 18, 18, 1963.
4. **Kanabrocki, E. L., Fels, I. G., and Kaplan, E.**, *J. Gerontol.*, 15, 383, 1960.
5. **Kirk, J. E. and Dyrbye, M.**, Hexosamine and acid-hydrolyzable sulfate concentrations of the aorta and pulmonary artery in individuals of various ages, *J. Gerontol.*, 11, 273, 1956.
6. **Buddecke, E. and Andresen, G.**, Untersuchungen zur Chemie der Arterienwand. IV. Quantitative Bestimmung der Acetalphosphatide (Plasmalogen) in der Aorta des Menschen unter Berucksichtingung der Arteriosklerose, *Hoppe-Seyler's Z. Physiol. Chem.*, 314, 38, 1959.
7. **Smith, E. B. and Slater, R. S.**, Lipids and lipoproteins in ageing aortic intima, *Proc. R. Soc. Med.*, 65, 675, 1972.
8. **Hevelke, G.**, Alternswandlungen der menschlichen Lungenschlagader, dargestellt am Phospholipidgehalt, *Muench. Med. Wochenschr.*, 107, 2309, 1965.
9. **Hevelke, G.**, Angiochemical studies of the aorta in physiosclerosis, arteriosclerosis, and diabetic angiopathy, *Dtsch. Arch. Klin. Med.*, 203, 528, 1956.
10. **Helvelke, G.**, The chemistry of blood vessels and their physiological change in aging, *Verh. Dtsch. Ges. Kreislaufforsch.*, 24, 131, 1958.
11. **Hevelke, G.**, On the problem of physiosclerosis. Studies on human veins, *Z. Alternsforsch.*, 13, 337, 1959.
12. **Hevelke, G.**, Beitrage zur Funktion und Struktur der Gefasse; vergleichende angiochemische Untersuchungen der Arteria branchialis und Arteria femoralis, *Z. Alternsforsch.*, 8, 219, 1954.
13. **Buck, R. C. and Rossiter, R. J.**, Lipids of normal and atherosclerotic aortas. A chemical study, *Arch. Pathol.*, 51, 224, 1951.

Table 22
CALCIUM CONTENT OF HUMAN ARTERIES AND VEINS

	Birth—20	20—30	30—40	40—50	50—60	60—70	70—80	80—100	Ref.
% of dry weight of aorta (n = 25)									
Media	—	0.27	—	0.97	1.14	2.35	2.77	—	1
Intima	—	—	—	0.26	0.33	0.18	—	—	1
% of dry elastin of aorta (n = 110)	0.5	1.2	1.9	4.7	6.6	5.1	6.9	5.5	2
% of dry weight of aorta (n = 50)	0.045	0.26	—	0.54	—	—	1.0	—	3
Relative intensity of calcification of arteries									
Aorta (n = 110)	0	0.3	0.7	1.2	1.6	1.6	1.7	1.9	4
Iliac (n = 131)	1.3	2.1	1.8	2.5	3.2	3.5	3.6	3.5	4
Coronary (n = 140)	0.3	0.9	0.6	1.8	2.5	2.7	3.0	3.9	4
Renal (n = 140)	0.6	1.1	1.0	1.7	2.3	2.6	2.8	3.9	4
Hepatic (n = 128)	0.7	0.7	0.8	1.2	1.4	1.8	2.0	2.5	4
% of dry weight of media									
Ascending aorta (n = 65)	0.14	—	0.57	—	1.17	—	2.25	3.39	5
Thoracic aorta (n = 56)	0.14	—	0.78	—	1.32	—	1.94	2.58	5
Abdominal aorta (n = 56)	0.13	—	0.81	—	1.32	—	1.73	2.59	5
Pulmonary artery (n = 53)	0.13	—	0.19	—	0.35	—	0.42	0.46	5
% of dry fat free weight (n = 122)									
Male	0.07	0.19	0.32	0.48	0.56	0.77	0.51	—	6
Female	0.07	0.12	—	—	0.37	0.98	1.3	—	6
% calcium binding in vitro of elastic tissue of the aorta	0.2	0.4	—	0.55	—	0.65	0.65	—	7

Table 22 (continued)
CALCIUM CONTENT OF HUMAN ARTERIES AND VEINS

	Birth—20	20—30	30—40	40—50	50—60	60—70	70—80	80—100	Ref.
% of wet weight of ascending aorta									
Male (n = 18)	—	0.13	0.67	1.0	1.8	2.32	2.96	2.36	8
Female (n = 22)	—	0.02	0.24	1.05	0.36	0.78	3.02	1.77	8
% of dry aorta (n = 149)	0.08	0.12	0.31	0.59	0.64	1.26	2.44	3.1	9
% of dry a. pulmonalis (n = 149)	0.07	0.08	0.12	0.09	0.12	0.22	0.24	0.27	9
% of dry v. cava (n = 149)	0.03	0.04	0.04	0.04	0.04	0.06	0.06	0.07	9
% of dry v. femoralis (n = 96)	0.211	0.191	0.226	0.261	0.279	0.317	0.371	—	10
% of wet a. brachialis (n = 96)	0.094	0.105	0.182	0.22	0.288	0.286	0.266	—	11
% of wet a. femoralis (n = 96)	0.095	0.104	0.189	0.221	0.512	0.625	1.588	—	11

REFERENCES

1. **Weinhouse, S. and Hirsch, E. F.**, Chemistry of atherosclerosis. I. Lipid and calcium content of the intima and of the media of the aorta with and without atherosclerosis, *Arch. Pathol.*, 29, 31, 1940.
2. **Lansing, A. I., Alex, M., and Rosenthal, T. B.**, *J. Gerontol.*, 5, 112, 1950.
3. **Burger, M.**, Stoffliche und funktionelle Alternserscheinungen beim Menschen, *Z. Gesamte Neurol. Psychiatr.*, 167, 273, 1939.
4. **Blumenthal, H. T., Lansing, A. I., and Gray, S. H.**, The interrelation of elastic tissue and calcium in the genesis of arteriosclerosis, *Am. J. Pathol.*, 26, 989, 1950.
5. **Gray, S. H., Handler, F. P., Blache, J. O., Zuckner, J., and Blumenthal, H. T.**, Aging process of aorta and pulmonary artery in negro and white races, *Arch. Pathol.*, 56, 238, 1953.
6. **Kanabrocki, E. L., Fels, I. G., and Kaplan, E.**, *J. Gerontol.*, 15, 383, 1960.
7. **Eisenstein, R., Ayer, J. P., Papajiannis, S., Hass, G. M., and Ellig, H.**, Mineral binding by human arterial elastic tissue, *Lab. Invest.*, 13, 1198, 1964.
8. **Blankenhorn, D. H.**, The relation of age and sex to diffuse aortic calcification in man, *J. Gerontol.*, 19, 72, 1964.
9. **Hevelke, G.**, The chemistry of blood vessels and their physiological change in aging, *Verh. Dtsch. Ges. Kreislaufforsch.*, 24, 131, 1958.
10. **Hevelke, G.**, On the problem of physiosclerosis. Studies on human veins, *Z. Alternsforsch.*, 13, 337, 1959.
11. **Hevelke, G.**, Beitrage zur Funktion und Struktur der Gefasse; vergleichende angiochemische Untersuchungen der Arteria brachialis und Arteria femorais, *Z. Alternsforsch.*, 8, 219, 1954.

Table 23
AGE CHANGES OF THE HUMAN VASCULAR SYSTEM

	Ref.
Baroreceptor sensitivity decreases with age	1
The capacity of the whole arterial system increases linearly from 9.6 ml/kg body weight at 20 years to 13.3 ml/kg body weight at 75 years	2
The number of fully functioning valves in the veins of the leg decreases with age while the partially functioning valves increase	3—5
The radii of arteries and veins increase with age; the ratio of the radius of the veins to corresponding arteries remains the same throughout life	6
The ratio of radius to wall thickness differs in different arteries; it remains in each artery at 0 mm Hg the same throughout life	7
The pulmonary artery changes during growth from an elastic type vessel to a muscular type vessel (adult form)	8,9
The most basic aging processes in vascular collagen and elastin are altered properties rather than concentration changes	10
Aging of collagen is characterized by progressive insolubility, chemical stabilization, and increased stiffness probably caused by increasing crosslinking of subunits	10
Aging of elastin is characterized by fragmentation, increased calcium binding, and close association with nonelastin protein, finally causing decreasing strength of the fibers	10—13
The involvement of collagen fibers, which is indicated by the inflexion point of the pressure-volume diagram, moves with age to continually lower pressures	14,15
Collagen accumulates, smooth muscle decreases, lipids and minerals increase in blood vessels with age	10,13
As the intima thickens, it is invaded by smooth muscles from the media, collagen accumulates	16—20
There is no conclusive evidence if the water content of blood vessels increases, doesn't change or decreases with age	19,21,22
The fragmentation and separation of elastic fibers is accompanied by accumulation of mucopolysaccharides. The lipid accumulation is independent of this process.	23—25
The thickening of the intima and the accumulation of lipid and calcium seem to be primary aging processes which may lead to atherogenesis	24,26,27
The viscosity of arterial mucopolysaccharides decreases with age	28
Langhans cells (myogenic foam cells) of the intima triple from 10—40 years and decrease after 70 years	29
Giant cells with polymorphic nuclei appear in the endothelium between 30 and 60 years	30,31
Arterioles develop with age characteristic arteriosclerosis (hyalinosis)	32—34
A marked decrease with age of enzyme activities in blood vessels is found for glycogen phosphorylase, phosphoglucomutase, fumarase, and creatine phosphokinase	35
A rise with age of enzyme activities in blood vessels is found for glucuronidase and 5'-nucleotidase	35

REFERENCES

1. **Gribbin, B., Pickering, T. G., Sleight, P., and Peto, R.,** Effect of age and high blood pressure on baroreflex sensitivity in man, *Circ. Res.,* 29, 424, 1971.
2. **Meyer, W. W. and Ströker, W.,** The capacity of the arterial system in man, *Z. Kreislaufforsch.,* 51, 900, 1962.
3. **Bardeleben, K.,** Das Klappen-Distanz-Gesetz, *Jena. Z. Naturwiss.,* 14, 467, 1880.
4. **Klotz, K.,** Untersuchungen über die Vena saphena magna beim Menschen, besonders rücksichtlich ihrer Klappenverhältnisse, *Arch. Anat. Entwicklungsmech.,* 159, 1887.
5. **Marinov, G.,** Vuzrastovi izmeneiia na klapniia aparat v povurkhnostnite i dulbokite veni na podbedritsata, *Eksp. Med. Morfol.,* 12, 86, 1973.
6. **Hieronymi, G.,** Angiometric examination of veins and arteries in various age groups, *Frankf. Z. Pathol.,* 69, 18, 1958.

Table 23 (continued)
AGE CHANGES OF THE HUMAN VASCULAR SYSTEM

7. **Hieronymi, G.,** *Sitzungsber. Heidelb. Akad. Wiss.,* 221, 1956.
8. **Meyer, W. W. and Simon, E.,** The phase-like variation of the pulmonalis volume flexibility in the life course in relation to the structure of the arterial wall, *Arch. Kreislaufforsch.,* 31, 95, 1959.
9. **Saldana, M. and Arias-Stella, J.,** Studies on the structure of the pulmonary trunk. II. The evolution of the elastic configuration of the pulmonary trunk in people native to high altitudes, *Circulation,* 27, 1094, 1963.
10. **Kohn, R. R.,** *Handbook of the Biology of Aging,* Finch, C. E. and Hayflick, L., Eds., Van Nostrand Reinhold, New York, 1977, 281.
11. **Hass, G. M.,** Elastic tissue. III. Relations between the structure of the aging aorta and the properties of the isolated aortic elastic tissue, *Arch. Pathol.,* 35, 29, 1943.
12. **Patridge, S. M. and Keeley, F. W.,** Age-related and atherosclerotic changes in aortic elastin, *Adv. Exp. Med. Biol.,* 43, 173, 1974.
13. **Schlatmann, T. J. M. and Becker, A. E.,** Histologic changes in the normal aging aorta: implications for dissecting aortic aneurysm, *Am. J. Cardiol.,* 39, 13, 1977.
14. **Bader, H. and Kapal, E.,** Altersveränderungen der Aortenelastizität, *Gerontologia,* 2, 253, 1958.
15. **Roach, M. R. and Burton, A. C.,** The effect of age on the elasticity of human iliac arteries, *Can. J. Biochem. Physiol.,* 37, 557, 1959.
16. **Gross, L., Epstein, E. Z., and Kugel, M. A.,** Histology of the coronary arteries and their branches in the human heart, *Am. J. Pathol.,* 10, 253, 1934.
17. **Lindner, J.,** Gefässwand und Gelenkknorpel, *Verh. Dtsch. Ges. Pathol.,* 59, 181, 1975.
18. **Parker, F., Healey, L. A., Wilske, K. R., and Odland, G. F.,** Light and electron microscopic studies on human temporal arteries with special reference to alterations related to senescence, atherosclerosis, and giant cell arteritis, *Am. J. Pathol.,* 79, 57, 1975.
19. **Geer, J. C. and Webster, S.,** Morphology of mesenchymal elements of normal artery, fatty streaks, and plaques, *Adv. Exp. Med. Biol.,* 43, 9, 1974.
20. **Buck, R. C.,** *Atherosclerosis and its Origin,* Sandler, M. and Bourne, G. H., Eds., Academic Press, New York, 1963, 1.
21. **Hevelke, G.,** On the problem of physiosclerosis. Studies on the behavior of dry residue of venous and arterial blood vessels in the various age groups, *Z. Alternsforsch.,* 13, 280, 1959.
22. **Kanabrocki, E. L., Fels, I. G., Decker, C. F., and Kaplan, E.,** Total hexosamine sulfur, and nitrogen levels in human aortae, *J. Gerontol.,* 18, 18, 1963.
23. **Lindner, J.,** Gefasswand und Gelenkknorpel, *Verh. Dtsch. Ges. Pathol.,* 59, 181, 1975.
24. **Bertelsen, S. and Jensen, C. E.,** Histochemical studies on human aortic tissue, *Acta Pathol. Microbiol. Scand.,* 48, 305, 1960.
25. **Bertelsen, S.,** Alterations in human aorta and pulmonary aorta with age, *Acta Pathol. Microbiol. Scand.,* 51, 206, 1961.
26. **Khominskaya, M. B.,** Sravnitel'noe gistokhimicheskoe issledovanie vozrastnykh izmenenii krupnykh arterii cheloveka, *Arkh. Pathol.,* 35, 33, 1973.
27. **Smith, E. B. and Slater, R. S.,** Lipids and lipoproteins in ageing aortic intima, *Proc. R. Soc. Med.,* 65, 675, 1972.
28. **Bertelsen, S. and Jensen, C. E.,** Physio-chemical investigations on acid mucopolysaccharides in human aortic tissue, *Acta Pharmacol. Toxicol.,* 16, 250, 1960.
29. **Schönfelder, M.,** Orthologie und Pathologie der Langhans-Zellen der Aortenintima des Menschen, *Pathol. Microbiol.,* 33, 129, 1969.
30. **Sinapius, D.,** Über das Aortenondothel, *Virchows Arch. Pathol. Anat. Physiol.,* 322, 662, 1952.
31. **Lautsch, E. V., McMillan, G. C., and Duff, G. L.,** Technics for the study of the normal and atherosclerotic arterial intima from its endothelial surface, *Lab. Invest.,* 2, 397, 1953.
32. **Moritz, A. R. and Oldt, M. R.,** Arteriolar sclerosis in hypertensive and nonhypertensive individuals, *Am. J. Pathol.,* 13, 679, 1937.
33. **McKinney, B.,** Hyaline arteriolosclerosis in the spleen. I. Methods of study and data from Europeans, *Exp. Mol. Pathol.,* 1, 275, 1962.
34. **Ball, M. J. and Silver, M. D.,** Influence of age and hypertension on splenic hyaline arteriolosclerosis, *Can. Med. Assoc. J.,* 99, 1239, 1968.
35. **Kirk, J. E.,** *Enzymes of the Arterial Wall,* Academic Press, New York, 1969.

Table 24
AGE CHANGES OF BLOOD VESSELS OF THE RAT

	Ref.
Baroreceptor reactivity is significantly lower in 24-month-old rats than in 12-month-old rats	1
The elastic modulus of the thoracic aorta at a specific stress decreases threefold from 90—600 days of age	2
The elastic modulus and the tangential stress of the thoracic aorta at a specific strain increases from 2—24 months of age	3
The elastic modulus of the thoracic aorta at a given pressure remains the same from 2—24 months of age	3
The maximum active stress response to smooth muscle contraction of the thoracic aorta decreases from 2—24 months of age	3
The threshold of the abdominal aorta to norepinephrine stimulation moves from 10^{-9} M at 1 year to $5 \cdot 10^{-7}$ M at 2 years of age	4
The maximum tension developed to norepinephrine stimulation of the abdominal aorta is 200 mg/mg wet weight at 1 year and decreases to 30 mg/mg wet weight at 2 years of age	4
There seems to be no turnover of elastin of the aorta from 4—31 months of age	5
The intracellular membrane population of the aortic smooth muscle decreases while the ratio of plasma membrane to intracellular membranes increases with age	6
The elastic laminae become thinner with age and become distributed as a network through the media	7
Collagen fibers, which are bundled at 6 months of age, are distributed uniformly through the musculoelastic network of the media at 2 years of age	7
Intimal thickening of the aorta occurs with age in the absence of appreciable extracellular lipid	8
As the intima thickens, cells derived from the media and from the blood are found in it	8
Relaxation of aorta and pulmonary artery by isoproterenol decreases with increasing age, whereas such response caused by nitroglycerine or sodium nitrite is not age dependent, suggesting a loss in β-receptor activity in arteries with age	9
Aging does not influence relaxation of portal vein to isoproterenol or nitroglycerine	9
Exogenous cAMP relaxes aortas from young rats markedly but has minimal effects on aortas from older animals suggesting reduced activity of older vessels toward the relaxing effect of cAMP	10
Relaxation of mesenteric arteries caused by cAMP is less in old rats than in young rats	12
In older rat aortas, adenyl cyclase activity is increased and phosphodiesterase activity is decreased	10
^{35}S incorporation into the aorta decreases exponentially up to 4 months and remains from there on at the same low value throughout life	11

REFERENCES

1. **Rothbaum, D. A., Shaw, D. J., Angell, C. S., and Shock, N. W.,** Age differences in the baroreceptor response of rats, *J. Gerontol.,* 29, 488, 1974.
2. **Hume, J. F.,** Tensility of rat's aorta as influenced by age environmental temperature and certain toxic substances, *Am. J. Hyg.,* 29, 11, 1939.
3. **Cox, R. H.,** Effects of age on the mechanical properties of rat carotid artery, *Am. J. Physiol.,* 233, 263, 1977.
4. **Tuttle, R. S.,** Age-related changes in the sensitivity of rat aortic strips to norepinephrine and associated chemical and structural alterations, *J. Gerontol.,* 21, 510, 1966.
5. **Walford, R. L., Carter, P. K., and Schneider, R. B.,** Stability of labeled aortic elastic tissue with age and pregnancy in the rat, *Arch. Pathol.,* 78, 43, 1964.
6. **Stein, O., Eisenberg, S., and Stein, Y.,** Aging of aortic smooth muscle cells in rats and rabbits. A morphologic and biochemical study, *Lab. Invest.,* 21, 386, 1969.

Table 24 (continued)
AGE CHANGES OF BLOOD VESSELS OF THE RAT

7. **Cliff, W. J.,** The aortic tunica media in aging rats, *Exp. Mol. Pathol.*, 13, 172, 1970.
8. **Gerrity, R. G. and Cliff, W. J.,** The aortic tunica intima in young and ageing rats, *Exp. Mol. Pathol.*, 16, 382, 1972.
9. **Fleisch, J. H. and Hooker, C. S.,** The relationship between age and relaxation of vascular smooth muscle in the rabbit and rat, *Circ. Res.*, 38, 243, 1976.
10. **Ericsson, E. and Lundholm, L.,** Adrenergic β-receptor activity and cyclic AMP metabolism in vascular smooth muscle; variations with age, *Mech. Ageing Dev.*, 4, 1, 1975.
11. **Lindner, J. and Johannes, G.,** Connective Tissue and Aging, Vogel, H. G., Ed., Excerpta Medica, Amsterdam, 1973, 68.
12. **Cohen, M. L. and Berkwitz, B. A.,** Age-related changes in vasular responsiveness to cyclic nucleotides and contractile agonists, *J. Pharmacol. Exp. Ther.*, 191, 147, 1974.

Table 25
MECHANICAL AND CHEMICAL PROPERTIES OF RAT THORACIC AORTA

		Age (months)			Ref.
		4.5	6	18	
Measurements at 115 mm Hg (n = 30)					
Diameter (mm)		2.3	2.45	2.74	1
Wall thickness (mm)		0.1	0.092	0.118	
Number of elastic lamellae		8.12	7.92	8.0	
Tension/lamellar unit (dyn·cm^{-1})		1950	2430	2650	
% elastin of dry weight		42.0	43.8	40.9	
% collagen of dry weight		15.8	19.0	24.6	
% alkali soluble protein of dry weight		19.2	17.1	16.1	
Measurements in longitudinal direction (n = 20)		a	b	a	b
Dynamic elastic modulus (force related) (kg·cm^{-2})	0.9 Hz	1.1	5.8	0.9	11.3	2
	4.8 Hz	1.3	6.5	1.4	12.2	
Viscous retarding force (kg·cm^{-2})	0.9 Hz	0.2	1.6	0.6	4.4	
	4.8 Hz	0.5	3.4	1.0	4.4	
Retraction %			22.5		18.0	

Note: a = natural length of the aorta and b = 1.2 × natural length of the aorta.

REFERENCES

1. **Wolinsky, H.,** Effects of hypertension and its reversal on the thoracic aorta of male and female rats. Morphological and chemical studies, *Circ. Res.*, 28, 622, 1971; **Wolinsky, H.,** Long-term effects of hypertension on the rat aortic wall and their relation to concurrent aging changes. Morphological and chemical studies, *Circ. Res.*, 30, 301, 1972.
2. **Band, W., Goedhard, W. J. A., and Knoop, A. A.,** Effects of aging on dynamic viscoelastic properties of the rat's thoracic aorta, *Pfluegers Arch.*, 331, 357, 1972.

Table 26
COMPOSITION OF THE BLOOD VESSELS OF RATS

	\multicolumn{9}{c	}{Age (days)}	
	30	45	100	182	365	547	600	730	1100	Ref.
% protein of dry aorta (n = 48)	—	—	44	—	30	—	—	34	—	1
% total lipid of dry aorta (n = 48)	—	—	9.5	—	8.9	—	—	10.1	—	1
% DNA of dry aorta (n = 48)	—	—	0.57	—	0.6	—	—	1.3	—	1
% H$_2$O of wet aorta (n = 48)	—	—	67.6	—	68.1	—	—	73.2	—	1
Nuclei/mm^2 of aorta (n = 48)	—	—	66.4	—	—	—	—	38.8	—	1
% DNA of wet aorta (n = 25)	0.31	0.22	0.18	—	0.18	—	0.17	—	—	2
Ratio of phospholipid phosphorus to DNA of aorta (µg/mg) (n = 25)	50	68	68	—	76	—	81	—	—	2
Wall thickness of aorta (µm) (n = 32)	61	—	65	79	101	99	—	112	119	2
Nuclei per unit area of aorta (n = 32)	21	—	15	12	10	9	—	8	8	3
% collagen of dry carotid artery (n = 36)	—	38.7	—	—	39.0	—	—	46.1	—	4
% elastin of dry carotid artery (n = 36)	—	33.8	—	—	25.4	—	—	24.9	—	4

% collagen of dry fat-free aorta (n = 16)	—	—	30.2	29.7	27.4	31.9	—	—	5
% elastin of dry fat-free aorta (n = 16)	—	—	43.9	39.3	39.7	33.6	—	—	5
% calcium of dry aorta (n = 50) ♂ ♀	— —	0.031 0.032	0.041 0.046	— —	0.046 0.055	— —	0.056 0.071	0.061 0.07	6 6
% elastin of dry fat-free aorta (n = 412)	47	44	43	40	37	—	—	32	7
% collagen of dry fat-free aorta (n = 412)	30	34	39	40	39	—	—	39	7
Cells/mg dry fat-free aorta (n = 196)	3160	2070	1580	1350	1250	—	—	1250	7
% DNA of dry fat-free aorta (n = 196)	1.45	1.25	0.97	0.81	0.6	—	—	—	7

Table 26 (continued)
COMPOSITION OF THE BLOOD VESSELS OF RATS

REFERENCES

1. **Tuttle, R. S.**, Age-related changes in the sensitivity of rat aortic strips to norepinephrine and associated chemical and structural alterations, *J. Gerontol.*, 21, 510, 1966.
2. **Stein, O., Eisenberg, S., and Stein, Y.**, Aging of aortic smooth muscle cells in rats and rabbits. A morphologic and biochemical study, *Lab. Invest.*, 21, 386, 1969.
3. **Cliff, W. J.**, The aortic tunica media in aging rats, *Exp. Mol. Pathol.*, 13, 172, 1970.
4. **Cox, R. H.**, Effects of age on the mechanical properties of rat carotid artery, *Am. J. Physiol.*, 233, 263, 1977.
5. **Fischer, G. M.**, Effects of spontaneous hypertension and age on arterial connective tissue in the rat, *Exp. Gerontol.*, 11, 209, 1976.
6. **Morgan, A. J. and Bellamy, D.**, Influence of age and sex on the calcification of rat aorta in relation to bone mineralization, *Age Ageing*, 4, 73, 1975.
7. **Looker, T. and Berry, C. L.**, The growth and development of the rat aorta. II. Changes in nucleic acid and scleroprotein content, *J. Anat.*, 113, 17, 1972.

Table 27
AGE CHANGES OF THE AORTA OF CATTLE AND HORSES

	Age (years)							
	0—1	1—5	6—10	11—15	16—20	21—25	26—36	Ref.
Cattle								
Wall thickness of aorta (mm)								
Ascendens	3.0	7.0	7.9	7.5	—	—	—	1
Arcus	3.1	7.9	10.8	11.2	—	—	—	1
Diaphragm	1.5	2.0	1.9	1.8	—	—	—	1
% nitrogen of dry weight (n = 73)	0.0147	0.0157	0.0152	0.0151	—	—	—	1
% cholesterol of dry weight (n = 73)	0.442	0.369	0.416	0.432	—	—	—	1
% calcium of dry weight (n = 73)	0.039	0.045	0.048	0.056	—	—	—	1
Horses								
Wall thickness of aorta (mm)								
Ascendens	—	4.4	—	—	4.75	—	5.6	2
Arcus	—	4.75	—	—	5.5	—	6.0	2
Diaphragm	—	3.5	—	—	3.7	—	4.9	2
% nitrogen of dry weight (n = 69)	—	0.0174	0.0176	0.017	0.0157	0.0146	0.0155	2
% cholesterol of dry weight (n = 69)	—	0.575	0.753	0.797	0.817	0.85	0.976	2
% calcium of dry weight (n = 69)	—	0.048	0.07	0.08	0.084	0.091	0.114	2
% sulfur of dry weight	0.658	—	—	—	0.893	—	0.919	3

REFERENCES

1. **Gerritzen, P.,** Beiträge zur physiologischen Chemie des Alterns der Gewebe; Untersuchungen an Rinderaorten, *Z. Gesamte Exp. Med.*, 85, 700, 1932.
2. **Keuenhof, W. and Kohl, H.,** Beiträge zur Physiologie des Alterns; chemische und histologische Untersuchungen an Pferdeaorten, *Z. Gesamte Exp. Med.*, 99, 645, 1936.
3. **Bürger, M.,** Stoffliche und funktionelle Alternserscheinungen beim Menschen, *Z. Ges. Neurol. Psychiatr.*, 167, 273, 1939.

Table 28
AGE CHANGES OF ARTERIES OF RHESUS MONKEYS

	Birth	1	1—5	6—10	11—15	16—26	Ref.
Thickness of intima (μm) (n = 116)							
Aorta	—	—	12.9	22.9	22.6	32.8	1
Coronary artery	—	—	7.1	11.4	13.4	16.7	1
Lipid in intima of aorta (mg/g dry weight) (n = 116)							
Total lipid	—	—	37.2	47.5	50.7	53.1	1
Total cholesterol	—	—	6.71	10.43	12.57	13.19	1
Cholesterol ester	—	—	2.29	4.04	4.62	4.65	1
Lipid in intima and inner media of aorta (mg/g wet weight) (n = 54)							
Free cholesterol	1.21	1.11	1.54	—	—	—	2
Cholesterol ester	0.061	0.18	0.28	—	—	—	2
Sphingomyelin	0.47	0.58	1.38	—	—	—	2
Prominent change with aging of the vessel wall is proliferation of plasma membranes							2

REFERENCES

1. Atherosclerosis Research Group, Serum lipids, intimal total lipids and morphologic changes of the aorta and coronary arteries in rhesus monkeys, *Chin. Med. J.*, 1, 34, 1975.
2. **Portman, O. W. and Alexander, M.**, Changes in arterial subfractions with aging and atherosclerosis, *Biochim. Biophys. Acta*, 260, 460, 1972.

Table 29
AGE CHANGES OF BLOOD VESSELS OF ANIMALS

	Ref.
Rabbit	
Baroreceptor sensitivity does not change during development up to 4 months of age, but is in 50-month-old rabbits considerably lower than in 12-month-old rabbits	1,2
Rings of the rabbit aorta are more extensible at 4—5 years than at 1—2 years of age	3
Relaxation of aorta and pulmonary artery by isoproterenol decreases with age, suggesting a loss of β-receptor activity in arteries with age	4
The dose response curve for relaxation of the aorta by nitroglycerine shifts to the right with age, but the maximal relaxation remains the same	4
Aging does not influence relaxation of portal vein to isoproterenol or nitroglycerine	4
The rate of endoplasmic reticulum membrane lipid formation per cell in the aorta increases with age while the rate of triglyceride formation decreases	5
The DNA concentration of the aorta decreases from 3 mg DNA per g wet weight at 1 month to 1.7 mg DNA per g wet weight at 24 months of age	6
The ratio of phospholipid to DNA of the aorta increases with age	6
The intracellular membrane population of the aortic smooth muscle decreases while the ratio of plasma membrane to intracellular membranes increases	6
The mean life span of the endothelial cell of the rabbit aorta increases with age from about 1 month in the 1.5-month-old rabbit to about 4.6 months in the 12-month-old rabbit	7
Guinea pig	
The aorta of the guinea pig shows the following changes from 8 weeks to 3 years:	
The intima becomes thicker, endothelial cells with two and more nuclei appear; the elastica interna becomes thinner from 3—1μm; the thickness of the media increases; the number of the elastic lamellae remains constant at 14 to 17, but they split with age; smooth muscles become longer and thinner; and collagen increases	8
Dog and sheep	
Dog and sheep aortas show in contrast to human aortas no change of the volume elastic modulus between 1 and 10 years of age at specific transmural pressures	9
The inflexion point of the pressure-volume relationship, which is caused by the involvement of collagen fibers, stays in dog and sheep aortas at 100 mm Hg from 1—10 years of age	9
Cattle	
The activity relative to the DNA content of N-acetyl-β-D-glucosaminidase, β-D-glucuronidase, cathepsin D, and acid carboxypeptidase of the aorta increases from birth to 13 years of age while hyaluronidase decreases	10
^{35}S incorporation into mucopolysaccharides decreases fast in the first year and slower from 1—13 years of life	10
^{14}C incorporation into chondroitinsulfate, heparitinsulfate, and dermatansulfate shows a similar decrease with age as the ^{35}S incorporation	10
^{14}C incorporation into hyaluronic acid increases threefold from birth to 7 years of age and decreases from there on	10
The pattern of acid mucopolysaccharides of the aorta in respect to chondroitinsulfate, dermatansulfate, heparitinsulfate, and hyaluronic acid does not change from birth to 13 years of age	11

Table 29 (continued)
AGE CHANGES OF BLOOD VESSELS OF ANIMALS

REFERENCES

1. **Bloor, C. M.,** Aortic baroreceptor threshold and sensitivity in rabbits at different ages, *J. Physiol. (London),* 174, 136, 1964.
2. **Frolkis, V. V., Bezrukov, V. V., and Shevchuk, V. G.,** Hemodynamics and its regulation in old age, *Exp. Gerontol.,* 10, 251, 1975.
3. **Saxton, J. A., Jr.,** Elastic properties of the rabbit aorta in relation to age, *Arch. Pathol.,* 34, 262, 1942.
4. **Fleisch, J. H. and Hooker, C. S.,** The relationship between age and relaxation of vascular smooth muscle in the rabbit and rat, *Circ. Res.,* 38, 243, 1976.
5. **Björkerud, S.,** Influence of animal and tissue age on arterial smooth muscle synthesis of membrane and storage lipids, *Scand. J. Clin. Lab. Invest. Suppl.,* 34, 141, 65, 1974.
6. **Stein, O., Eisenberg, S., and Stein, Y.,** Aging of aortic smooth muscle cells in rats and rabbits. A morphologic and biochemical study, *Lab. Invest.,* 21, 386, 1969.
7. **Kunz, J. and Keim, U.,** On the regeneration of aortic endothelium at different ages, *Mech. Ageing Dev.,* 4, 361, 1975.
8. **Städeli, H.,** Der Einfluss des Lebensalters auf die Wandstruktur der isolierten, ungedehnten Aorta thoracalis des Meerschweinchens, *Angiologica,* 3, 40, 1966; **Städeli, H.,** Der Einfluss des Lebensalters auf die Wandstruktur der isolierten, künstlich gedehnen Aorta thoracalis des Meerschweinchens, *Angiologica,* 3, 213, 1966.
9. **Bader, H. and Kapal E.,** Vergleichende Untersuchungen über die Elastizität der Aorten verschiedener Tierarten und des Menschen, *Z. Biol. (Munich),* 114, 89, 1963.
10. **Kresse, H., Friese, W., and Buddecke, E.,** *Altern,* Platt, D., Ed., Schattauer Verlag, Stuttgart, 1974, 205.
11. **Buddecke, E., Segeth, G., and Kresse, H.,** *Connective Tissue and Aging,* Vogel, H. G., Ed., Elsevier, Amsterdam, 1973, 62.

HEMODYNAMICS

Charles W. Miller

Table 1
EFFECT OF AGE UPON ARTERIAL BLOOD PRESSURE IN WHITE HUMANS

Age (years)	Blood pressure (mm Hg) Systolic	Diastolic
Female[a]		
25—34	117.3	72.1
35—44	125.0	78.8
45—54	138.2	83.8
55—64	149.3	85.5
65—74	159.0	83.8
Male[b]		
25—34	126.4	75.9
35—44	130.4	82.2
45—54	137.7	86.8
55—64	147.6	86.0
65—74	157.8	85.1

Note: Casual systolic blood pressure rose with age, whereas the diastolic blood pressure rose approximately to age 50 and either remained constant or decreased slightly thereafter. Included in this study were individuals currently receiving drug treatment for hypertension. Blood pressure determinations were made using the sphygmomanometer method.

[a] Total females in survey = 1360.
[b] Total males in survey = 1175.

REFERENCE

1. Christmas, B. W., Blood pressure levels of an urban adult New Zealand population: Napier, 1973, *N. Z. Med. J.*, 86, 369, 1977.

Table 2
EFFECT OF AGE UPON ARTERIAL BLOOD PRESSURE IN OLD WHITE HUMANS

Age (years)	Systolic Blood pressure (mm Hg) ($\bar{X} \pm SD$)	Diastolic	No.
Female			
60—64	157.3 ± 19.6	85.5 ± 8.2	68
65—69	164.1 ± 21.5	86.3 ± 7.5	55
70—74	170.1 ± 19.4	86.7 ± 7.8	64
75—79	174.5 ± 20.2	86.1 ± 8.9	37
80—84	181.9 ± 20.0	87.2 ± 9.8	25
85—89	168.5 ± 21.4	93.0 ± 8.8	8
Male			
60—64	153.1 ± 17.8	85.8 ± 8.0	69
65—69	153.4 ± 22.5	85.6 ± 7.4	85
70—74	161.5 ± 20.0	85.4 ± 7.9	93
75—79	165.9 ± 22.4	85.9 ± 9.7	73
80—84	168.9 ± 23.0	87.9 ± 7.9	45
85—89	165.1 ± 27.2	87.1 ± 13.9	9

Note: Within the age range of 60 to 89 years of age, systolic blood pressure increased with age for both sexes and at all age levels the systolic blood pressure was higher in women than the corresponding means for men. Diastolic blood pressure is not significantly influenced by age for either sex. Blood pressure determinations were made using the sphygmomanometer method.

REFERENCE

1. Anderson, W. F. and Cowan, N. R., Arterial blood pressure in healthy older people, *Gerontol. Clin.*, 14, 129, 1972.

Table 3
EFFECT OF AGE UPON ARTERIAL BLOOD PRESSURE IN WHITE HUMANS 7—74 YEARS OF AGE[a]

Age (years)	Blood pressure (mm Hg) ($\bar{X} \pm SD$) Systolic	Diastolic
Female		
7—11	103.3 ± 12.3	64.3 ± 10.0
12—17	111.9 ± 13.4	69.0 ± 9.7
18—24	114.8 ± 13.1	71.5 ± 10.2
25—34	116.7 ± 14.1	74.9 ± 10.6
35—55	123.6 ± 19.2	80.2 ± 12.5
45—54	132.9 ± 24.4	83.6 ± 13.7
55—64	144.0 ± 25.6	86.6 ± 12.7
65—74	152.5 ± 25.2	85.9 ± 12.9
Male		
7—11	103.3 ± 12.0	65.1 ± 9.6
12—17	114.9 ± 13.8	70.5 ± 10.0
18—24	123.5 ± 13.0	76.3 ± 10.0
25—34	125.5 ± 13.9	81.1 ± 10.3
35—44	127.7 ± 15.4	84.8 ± 11.5
45—54	135.3 ± 20.7	87.9 ± 13.1
55—64	139.7 ± 20.8	86.8 ± 12.3
65—74	146.9 ± 24.7	85.4 ± 13.2

[a] 17,796 persons were included in this entire study.

Note: The mean systolic blood pressure of the white U.S. population increases with age from 103.3 mm Hg among children ages 7 to 11 years to 150.1 mm Hg among the oldest adults in the study (65 to 74 years of age). From 12 through 54 years of age the mean levels of systolic blood pressure among males exceed those for females, but from 55 through 74 years, the mean levels of women are higher. The mean diastolic blood pressure increased to approximately 55 years of age and declined or remained constant thereafter. Blood pressure determinations were made using the sphygmomanometer.

REFERENCE

1. National Center for Health Statistics, Advance Data: Blood Pressure of Persons 6—74 Years of Age in the United States, Vital and Health Statistics, No. 1, U.S. Public Health Service, Washington, D. C., October 18, 1976.

Table 4
EFFECT OF AGE UPON ARTERIAL BLOOD PRESSURE IN NEGRO HUMANS 7—74 YEARS OF AGE[a]

Age (years)	Blood pressure (mm Hg) ($\bar{X} \pm SE$) Systolic	Diastolic
Female		
7—11	104.2 ± 1.34	64.8 ± 0.89
12—17	111.6 ± 1.22	69.3 ± 1.02
18—24	113.2 ± 1.11	72.7 ± 1.02
25—34	121.5 ± 0.96	78.0 ± 0.95
35—44	130.5 ± 1.52	86.9 ± 1.29
45—54	150.8 ± 5.69	93.5 ± 2.20
55—64	153.4 ± 4.44	90.6 ± 2.23
65—74	161.3 ± 2.88	90.4 ± 1.31
Male		
7—11	102.1 ± 1.32	63.8 ± 1.20
12—17	112.5 ± 1.46	71.1 ± 0.95
18—24	122.9 ± 2.20	76.2 ± 1.03
25—34	129.3 ± 1.61	84.3 ± 1.60
35—44	136.7 ± 2.29	91.2 ± 1.43
45—54	141.7 ± 4.23	91.9 ± 2.45
55—64	144.2 ± 3.57	93.4 ± 2.23
65—74	156.6 ± 3.57	90.9 ± 1.20

[a] 17,796 persons were included in this entire study.

Note: The mean systolic blood pressure of the negro U.S. population increases with age from 103.2 mm Hg among children ages 7 to 11 years to 159.3 mm Hg among the oldest adults in the study (65 to 74 years of age). From 12 through 44 years of age the mean levels of systolic blood pressure among males exceed those of females, but from 45 through 74 years, the mean levels of women are higher. The diastolic blood pressure increased with age to approximately 50 years of age in both sexes and then declined or remained constant thereafter. Blood pressure determinations were made using the sphygmomanometer.

REFERENCE

1. National Center for Health Statistics, Advance Data: Blood Pressure of Persons 6—74 Years of Age in the United States, Vital and Health Statistics, No. 1, U.S. Public Health Service, Washington, D.C., October 18, 1976.

Table 5
EFFECT OF AGE UPON ARTERIAL BLOOD PRESSURE IN MAN

Age (years)	Blood pressure (mm Hg) Systolic	Diastolic	Method	No.
23.6	115.3 ± 2.4	65.1 ± 2.1	Direct via	9
34.1	119.2 ± 4.2	63.7 ± 2.0	brachial	10
43.3	124.8 ± 3.6	68.7 ± 2.7	artery (no	11
54.8	132.3 ± 8.5	70.0 ± 3.5	anesthesia)	11
65.4	137.4 ± 3.9	61.0 ± 2.6		10
73.3	134.0 ± 5.8	62.1 ± 3.0		9
82.0	144.1 ± 6.3	59.3 ± 1.7		7

Note: The systolic blood pressure rose with age whereas the diastolic blood pressure increased to approximately age 55 and declined or remained constant thereafter.

From Landowne, M., Brandfonbrener, M., and Shock, N., The relation of age to certain measures of performance of the heart and the circulation, *Circulation*, 12, 567, 1955. By permission of the American Heart Association, Inc.

Table 6
THE EFFECT OF AGE UPON ARTERIAL BLOOD PRESSURE IN !KUNG BUSHMAN IN NORTHERN BOTSWANA

Age (years)	Blood pressure (mm Hg) Systolic	Diastolic	No.
Female			
15—19	114	72	5
20—29	114	73	17
30—39	113	73	13
40—49	116	74	17
50—59	123	76	9
60—69	130	72	8
70—83	123	68	4
Male			
15—19	120	75	3
20—29	124	75	16
30—39	120	75	19
40—49	116	75	17
50—59	118	72	14
60—69	113	67	6
70—83	117	66	4

Note: Systolic blood pressure rose slightly in women after menopause but their diastolic blood pressure decreased slightly with age. In men, the systolic and diastolic blood pressure declined with increasing age. Blood pressure determinations were made using the sphygmomanometer method.

From Truswell, A. S., Kennelly, B. M., Hansen, J. D. L., and Lee, R. B., Blood pressures of !Kung Bushmen in Northern Botswana, *Am. Heart J.*, 84, 5, 1972. With permission.

Table 7
COMMUNITIES IN WHICH ARTERIAL BLOOD PRESURE DOES NOT INCREASE WITH AGE

Ethnic or socioeconomic group	Geographical location	Ref.
Africans	Kavirondo, Kenya	1
Africans	Eastern Providence, Uganda	2,3
Ponape Islanders	East Caroline Islands, Micronesia	4
Pukapuka Islanders	North Cook Islands, Polynesia	5—7
Ethiopians	Ethiopia	8
Various communities	Papua, and East New Guinea	9,10
Lower socioeconomic group men — industrial and rural	Delhi, India	11
Bushmen	Central Kalahari, Botswana	12
Abaiang Islanders	Gilbert Islands, Micronesia	13
Carajas Indians	Amazon Basin, Northern Brazil	14
Samburu Nomads	Northern Frontier Province, Kenya	15
Rendille Nomads	Northern Frontier Province, Kenya	15
Turkana Nomads	Northern Frontier Province, Kenya	15
Masai Tribesmen	Tanzania	16
Orang Asli	West Malaysia	17

REFERENCES

1. **From Truswell, A. S., Kennelly, B. M., Hansen, J. D. L., and Lee, R. B.,** Blood pressures of !Kung Bushmen in Northern Botswana, *Am. Heart J.,* 84, 5, 1972.
2. **Donnison, C. P.,** Blood pressure in the African native, *Lancet,* 1, 6, 1929.
3. **Williams, A. W.,** The blood pressure of Africans, *East Afr. Med. J.,* 18, 109, 1941.
4. **Murrill, R. I.,** A blood pressure study of the natives of Ponape Island, Eastern Carolines, *Hum. Biol.,* 21, 47, 1949.
5. **Murphy, W.,** Some observations on blood pressures in humid tropics, *N. Z. Med. J.,* 54, 64, 1955.
6. **Hunter, J. D.,** Diet, body build, blood pressure and serum cholesterol levels in coconut-eating, *Fed. Proc. Fed. Am. Soc. Exp. Biol.,* 21, 36, 1962.
7. **Prior, I. A. M., Evans, J. G., Harvey, H. P. B., Davidson, F., and Lindsey, M.,** Sodium intake and blood pressure in two Polynesian populations, *N. Engl. J. Med.,* 279, 515, 1968.
8. Ethiopia, 1958. Nutrition survey, A Report by the Interdepartmental Committee on Nutrition for National Defense (ICNND), U.S. Government Printing Office, Washington, D.C., September 1959.
9. **Whyte, H. M.,** Body fat and blood pressure of natives in New Guinea: reflections on essential hypertension, *Australas. Ann. Med.,* 7, 36, 1958.
10. **Maddocks, I.,** Blood pressure in Melanesians, *Med. J. Aust.,* 1, 1123, 1967.
11. **Padmavati, S. and Gupta, S.,** Blood pressure studies in rural and urban groups in Delhi, *Circulation,* 19, 395, 1959.
12. **Kaminer, B. and Lutz, W. P. W.,** Blood pressure in Bushmen of the Kalahari Desert, *Circulation,* 22, 289, 1960.
13. **Maddocks, I.,** Possible absence of essential hypertension in two complete Pacific Island populations, *Lancet,* 2, 396, 1961.
14. **Lowenstein, F. W.,** Blood pressure in relation to age and sex in the tropics and an investigation in two tribes of Brazil Indians, *Lancet,* 1, 389, 1961.
15. **Shaper, A. G.,** Blood pressure studies in East Africa, in *The Epidemiology of Hypertension,* Stamler, J., Stamler, R., and Pullman, T. N., Eds., Grune & Stratton, New York, 1967, 139.
16. **Mann, G. V., Shaffer, R. D., Anderson, R. S., and Sandstead, H. H.,** Cardiovascular disease in the Masai, *J. Atheroscler. Res.,* 4, 289, 1964.
17. **Burns-Cox, C. J., and Maclean, J. D.,** Splenomegaly and blood pressure in an Orang Asli community in West Malaysia, *Am. Heart J.,* 80, 718, 1970.

Table 8
EFFECT OF AGE UPON ARTERIAL BLOOD PRESSURE IN VERTEBRATES OTHER THAN MAN

Species	Subjects (age, sex, number)	Blood pressure (mm Hg), Systolic	Method	Ref.
Mus musculus (mouse)	2—4 months	121 (109—132)	Plethysmograph (no anesthesia)	1
	10—16 months	123 (110—136)		
	24—30 months	127 (115—139)		
Ratus norvegicus (rat)				
Wistar	340d (68 males)	121 (100—150)	Indirect optical method, caudal artery (ether)	2
	675d (34 males)	114 (60—155)		
Sprague-Dawley	219d (18 males)	122	Photoelectric (no anesthesia)	3
	528d (35 males)	120		
	528d (1 male)	144		
	582d (36 males)	121		
	677d (14 males)	128		
	677d (4 males)	145		
	762d (18 males)	125		
	762d (6 males)	156		
	850d (20 males)	125		
	850d (17 males)	160		
	937d (26 males)	116		
	937d (8 males)	159		
	338d (9 females)	114		
	442d (17 females)	115		
	583d (10 females)	110		
	633d (29 females)	118		
	633d (1 female)	161		
	747d (20 females)	120		
	747d (3 females)	149		
	869d (8 females)	118		
	869d (4 females)	155		
	1022d (15 females)	114		
	1022d (9 females)	154		
Gallus domesticus (chicken)	14 months (28 males)	207	Dynograph (no anesthesia)	4
	24 months (28 males)	200		
	36 months (28 males)	213		
	40 months (28 males)	234		
	14 months (28 females)	149		
	24 months (28 females)	144		
	36 months (28 females)	125		
	40 months (28 females)	137		
White Leghorn	10—14 months (35 males)	164 (160—168)	Cuff, proximal to hock (no anesthesia)	5
	22—30 months (20 males)	189 (150—228)		
	34—54 months (22 males)	188 (159—217)		
	10—14 months (60 females)	131 (112—150)		
	19—26 months (62 females)	139 (120—158)		
	30—38 months (54 females)	155 (133—177)		
	42—54 months (21 females)	160 (131—189)		
White Leghorn	131—147d (527 females)	142 (80—217)	Indirect (no anesthesia)	6
	221—230d (286 females)	152 (67—251)		
	384—391d (129 females)	151 (93—209)		

Note: A small age-related increase in blood pressure may have been evident in the mouse. No consistent age increase in blood pressure existed in the rat. In the chicken, the males exhibited a substantially higher blood pressure than females, but an age-related trend was not obvious.

Table 8 (continued)
EFFECT OF AGE UPON ARTERIAL BLOOD PRESSURE IN VERTEBRATES OTHER THAN MAN

REFERENCES

1. Henry, J. P., Meehan, J. P., Stephens, P., and Santisteban, G. A., Arterial pressure in CBA mice as related to age, *J. Gerontol.*, 20, 239, 1965.
2. Everitt, A. V., Systolic blood pressure and heart rate in relation to lung disease and life duration in male rats, *J. Gerontol.*, 12, 378, 1957.
3. Berg, B. N. and Harmison, C. R., Blood pressure and heart size in aging rats, *J. Gerontol.*, 10, 416, 1955.
4. Muller, H. D. and Carroll, M. E., The relationships of blood pressure, heart rate and body weight to aging in the domestic fowl, *Poult. Sci.*, 45, 1195, 1966.
5. Sturkie, P. D., Weiss, H. S., and Ringer, R. K., Effects of age on blood pressure in the chicken, *Am. J. Physiol.*, 174, 405, 1953.
6. Hollands, K. G., Gorve, R. S., and Morse, P. M., Effects of food restriction on blood pressure, heart rate, and certain organ weights of chickens, *Br. Poult. Sci.*, 6, 297, 1965.

Table 9
EFFECT OF AGE UPON ARTERIAL BLOOD PRESSURE IN THE DOG

Sex	Age (months)	Systolic	Diastolic	Method	No.	Ref.
Male and female	2—8	98 ± 28^a	46 ± 16^a	Direct at	5	1
	7—10	121 ± 40^a	65 ± 27^a	level of	7	
	23—59	130 ± 29^a	67 ± 8^a	femoral artery (sodium pentabarbital anesthesia)	7	
	12	108.0 ± 5.9^b	57.3 ± 2.7^b	Direct at	6	2
	24	98.7 ± 5.2^b	61.3 ± 4.4^b	level of	7	
	60	119.3 ± 4.2^b	66.3 ± 4.0^b	femoral artery	18	
	144	97.8 ± 7.4^b	53.5 ± 4.4^b	(methoxyflurane anesthesia)	6	

Blood pressure (mm Hg)

Note: No age-related change in systolic or diastolic blood pressure was apparent in dogs from 2 months to 12 years of age studied while anesthetized with methoxyflurane.

[a] $\overline{X} \pm SD$.
[b] $\overline{X} \pm SE$.

REFERENCES

1. Miller, C. W., Tietz, W. J., and Smith, G. E., Cardiovascular system, in *The Beagle as an Experimental Dog,* Anderson, A. C., Ed., Iowa State University Press, Ames, 1970, 44.
2. Miller, C. W. and Nealeigh, R. C., Cardiovascular Changes with Aging, Annual Report for 1977, Collaborative Radiological Health Laboratory, U.S. Public Health Service, Federal Drug Administration, Fort Collins, Colo., 1978.

Table 10
EFFECT OF AGE UPON CARDIAC OUTPUT IN MAN

Age (years)	Cardiac output (ℓ/min)[a]	Cardiac index (ℓ/min/m²)[a]	Stroke volume (mℓ/beat)[a]	No.
23.6	6.49 ± 0.51	3.72 ± 0.28	85.6 ± 6.1	9
34.1	6.57 ± 0.56	3.54 ± 0.30	91.8 ± 7.1	10
43.3	5.34 ± 0.32	2.96 ± 0.17	78.3 ± 4.7	11
54.8	4.63 ± 0.21	2.78 ± 0.13	67.2 ± 3.1	11
65.4	4.29 ± 0.28	2.58 ± 0.15	69.5 ± 4.9	10
73.3	4.05 ± 0.25	2.54 ± 0.18	63.0 ± 4.7	9
82.0	3.87 ± 0.39	2.36 ± 0.23	60.1 ± 5.1	7

Note: The cardiac output decreased at a rate of approximately 1% per year of age in 67 male subjects. Cardiac output determinations were made using indicator dye methods.

[a] $\overline{X} \pm SE$.

From Brandfonbrener, M., Landowne, M., and Shock, N. W., Changes in cardiac output with age, *Circulation*, 12, 557, 1955. By permission of the American Heart Association, Inc.

Table 11
THE EFFECT OF AGE UPON PERIPHERAL RESISTANCE IN MAN

Age (years)	Resistance (mm Hg min/ℓ)[a]	Method	No.
23.6	13.7 ± 0.9	Direct arterial blood	9
34.1	14.0 ± 0.9	pressure catheter and	10
43.3	18.0 ± 1.1	dye dilution for cardiac	11
54.8	21.3 ± 1.3	output	11
65.4	21.5 ± 0.9		10
73.3	22.9 ± 1.8		9
82.0	25.5 ± 3.3		7

Note: The peripheral resistance showed a rapid increase until approximately age 50 and then the rate of increase slowed thereafter. The increase with age in peripheral resistance in the 67 male subjects was attributed to a reduction in cardiac output.

[a] $\overline{X} \pm SE$.

From Landowne, M., Brandfonbrener, M., and Shock, N. W., The relation of age to certain measures of performance of the heart and the circulation, *Circulation*, 12, 567, 1955. By permission of the American Heart Association, Inc.

Table 12
THE EFFECT OF AGE UPON CARDIAC OUTPUT DURING EXERCISE IN WOMEN

Age (years)	Work load (kg-m/min)	Cardiac output (l/min)[a]
20	150	9.2 ± 1.6
30	150	11.2 ± 1.4
40	150	10.3 ± 2.0
50	150	11.8 ± 3.2
60	150	9.6 ± 1.6
20	350	11.8 ± 1.6
30	350	14.3 ± 3.9
40	350	13.1 ± 2.7
50	350	17.1 ± 3.3
60	350	14.1 ± 2.2
20	550	16.6 ± 1.6
30	550	18.1 ± 0.8
40	550	16.2 ± 5.3
50	550	17.1[b]

Note: For a given work load, cardiac output increased with age in 46 women. Cardiac output determinations were made by using the indirect Fick method.

[a] $\bar{X}$ ± SD.
[b] Only two subjects in group.

From Becklake, M. R., Frank, H., Dagenais, G. R., Ostiguy, G. L., and Gyzman, C. A., *J. Appl. Physiol.*, 20, 938, 1965. With permission.

Table 13
THE EFFECT OF AGE UPON CARDIAC OUTPUT DURING EXERCISE IN MEN

Age (years)	Work load (kg-m/min)	Cardiac output (l/min)[a]
20	150	9.7 ± 1.6
30	150	10.3 ± 3.8
40	150	11.4 ± 1.6
50	150	10.5 ± 3.0
60	150	12.8 ± 3.0
70	150	9.6 ± 1.4
20	350	10.7 ± 2.0
30	350	12.0 ± 2.3
40	350	14.1 ± 1.5
50	350	14.4 ± 2.7
60	350	15.8 ± 5.3
70	350	15.9 ± 6.5
20	550	14.3 ± 3.7
30	550	15.1 ± 3.6
40	550	18.4 ± 4.8
50	550	18.1 ± 4.2
60	550	20.6 ± 3.9

[a] $\bar{X}$ ± SD.

Note: For a given work load, cardiac output increased with age in 48 males. Exercise cardiac output was higher in women at the younger ages than in men. No such differences were apparent in subsequent years. Cardiac output determinations were made using the indirect Fick method.

From Becklake, M. R., Frank, H., Dagenais, G. R., Ostiguy, G. L., and Gyzman, C. A., *J. Appl. Physiol.,* 20, 938, 1965. With permission.

Table 14
THE EFFECT OF AGE UPON FLOW CHARACTERISTICS IN THE BEAGLE DOG

Age (years)	Peak arterial blood flow (ml/sec/kg)[a] Thoracic aorta	Peak arterial blood flow (ml/sec/kg)[a] Abdominal aorta	Max reverse blood velocity (cm/sec)[a] Thoracic aorta	Max reverse blood velocity (cm/sec)[a] Abdominal aorta	Average blood flow (ml/sec/kg)[a] Thoracic aorta	Average blood flow (ml/sec/kg)[a] Abdominal aorta
1	3.79 ± 0.41 (15)	2.41 ± 0.25 (15)	29.1 ± 2.6 (15)	27.6 ± 2.5 (15)	1.02 ± 0.13 (15)	0.43 ± 0.04 (14)
2	3.71 ± 0.26 (19)	1.86 ± 0.17 (20)	25.8 ± 1.5 (19)	27.4 ± 2.3 (20)	0.99 ± 0.09 (19)	0.43 ± 0.04 (19)
5	2.89 ± 0.18 (29)	1.64 ± 0.10 (14)	17.6 ± 1.8 (30)	19.5 ± 2.0 (14)	0.91 ± 0.06 (28)	0.42 ± 0.05 (14)
8	2.88 ± 0.30 (11)	1.41 ± 0.17 (11)	16.6 ± 2.6 (11)	20.2 ± 2.1 (11)	0.99 ± 0.10 (11)	0.39 ± 0.04 (10)
12	2.60 ± 0.28 (14)	0.85 ± 0.08 (14)	17.5 ± 2.3 (14)	15.8 ± 1.5 (14)	0.82 ± 0.08 (13)	0.19 ± 0.03 (14)

Note: A general decline in the peak arterial blood flow in the thoracic aorta and abdominal aorta occurred with age. The maximum reverse blood velocity tended to be less in the older dogs than in younger ones and the average blood flow tended to rmain relatively constant with advancing age. Measurements were made with a pulsed ultrasonic Doppler velocity detector in dogs anesthetized with methoxyflurane gas anesthetic.

[a] $\overline{X}$ ± SE.

REFERENCE

1. **Miller, C. W. and Nealeigh, R. C.**, Cardiovascular Changes with Aging, Annual Report for 1977, Collaborative Radiological Health Laboratory, U.S. Public Health Service, Federal Drug Administration, Fort Collins, Colo., 1978.

NEURAL AND HUMORAL REGULATION OF CARDIOVASCULAR SYSTEM

Thomas G. Pickering

Table 1
REGULATION OF HEART RATE

	Ref.
Resting heart rate changes little between ages 20 and 60, but may decrease over 60	1
Intrinsic heart rate (IHR), i.e., the heart rate after combined sympathetic and parasympathetic blockade — decreases with age; IHR = 118 − 0.6 × age 2 with age; IHR = 118 − 0.6 × age	2
In the rat there are similar changes of resting heart rate and intrinsic heart rate; the decline in the latter is partially compensated by the sympathetic, for chemical sympathectomy using 6-hydroxydopamine produces more cardiac slowing in older rats	3
Vagal cardiac restraint decreases with age, as shown by a smaller response to atropine	4,5
Sympathetic effects on resting heart rate vary little with age, as shown by a similar effect of propranolol on heart rate in young and old	6
Maximum heart rate during exercise decreases with age; Max HR = 204 − 0.6 × age; this is probably due to impaired sympathetic drive or cardiac responsiveness	6,7
Heart rate changes in response to stimuli are generally diminished in the elderly; these include:	
Sinus arrhythmia — mainly vagally mediated	8
Tachycardia during the strain of Valsalva maneuver	9
Tachycardia during tilting	10
Tachycardia during hypoxia	5
Bradycardia before, and tachycardia after, presentation of a reaction time task	11
After exercise there is a delayed return of heart rate to resting levels in the elderly	1

REFERENCES

1. **Montoye, J. H., Willis, P. W., and Cunningham, D. A.**, Heart rate response to submaximal exercise: relation to age and sex, *J. Gerontol.*, 23, 127, 1968.
2. **Jose, A. D. and Collison, D.**, The normal range and determinants of the intrinsic heart rate in man, *Cardiovasc. Res.*, 4, 160, 1970.
3. **Weisfeldt, M. L.**, Function of cardiac muscle in aging rat, *Adv. Exp. Med. Biol.*, 61, 95, 1974.
4. **Nalefski, L. A. and Brown, C. F. G.**, Action of atropine on the cardiovascular system in normal persons, *Arch. Intern. Med.*, 86, 898, 1950.
5. **Simonson, E.**, Effect on age on the cardiovascular system in recent Russian research, *J. Gerontol.*, 19, 121, 1964.
6. **Conway, J.**, Effect of age on the response to propranolol, *Int. J. Clin. Pharmacol. Ther. Toxicol.*, 4, 148, 1970.
7. **Wolthuis, R. A., Froelicher, V. F., Fischer, J., and Triebwasser, J. H.**, The response of healthy men to treadmill exercise, *Circulation*, 55, 153, 1977.
8. **Jennett, S. and McKillop, J. H.**, Observations on the incidence and mechanism of sinus arrhythmia in man at rest, *J. Physiol. (London)*, 213, 58P, 1971.
9. **Gross, M.**, Circulatory reflexes in cerebral ischaemia involving different vascular territories, *Clin. Sci.*, 38, 491, 1970.
10. **Norris, A. H., Shock, N. W., and Yiengst, M. J.**, Age changes in heart rate and blood pressure responses to tilting and standardized exercise, *Circulation*, 8, 521, 1953.
11. **Morris, J. D. and Thompson, L. W.**, Heart rate changes in a reaction time experimnt with young and aged subjects, *J. Gerontol.*, 24, 269, 1969.

Table 2
REGULATION OF CARDIAC OUTPUT

	Ref.
The reasons for the fall of cardiac output with increasing age are not clear; possible causes include:	
A. Decreased metabolic requirements of the tissues, although the fall in cardiac output exceeds the fall of oxygen consumption	1
B. Changes in intrinsic cardiac function, which resemble those of ventricular hypertrophy	2
C. Decreased sympathetic drive: propranolol causes a greater reduction of cardiac output in young than in old subjects	3
D. Decreased content of catecholamines has been reported in rat hearts and a diminished inotropic response to catecholamines	4,5

REFERENCES

1. **Landowne, M. Brandfonbrener, M., and Shock, N. W.,** The relation of age to certain measures of performance of the heart and circulation, *Circulation,* 12, 567, 1955.
2. **Simonson, E.,** Effect of age on the cardiovascular system in recent Russian research, *J. Gerontol.,* 19, 121, 1964.
3. **Conway, J., Effect of age on the response to propranolol,** Int. J. Clin. Pharmacol. Ther. Toxicol.,
4. **Weisfeldt, M. L.,** Function of cardiac muscle in aging rat, *Adv. Exp. Med. Biol.,* 61, 95, 1974.
5. **Lakatta, E. G., Gerstenblith, G., Angell, C. S., Shock, N. W., and Weisfeldt, M. L.,** Diminished inotropic response to catecholamines in the aged, *Adv. Exp. Biol. Med.,* 61, 272, 1974.

Table 3
HUMORAL REGULATION OF CARDIOVASCULAR SYSTEM

	Ref.
Plasma norepinephrine increases with age and shows a bigger increment with standing in older people, but not in hypertensives	1—3
Sensitivity to alpha agonists (norepinephrine) of rat aorta decreases with age	4
Sensitivity to beta agonists (isoproterenol) of rat aorta, measured as relaxation, decreases with age	5
Plasma adrenaline decreases with age; dopamine does not change	6
Plasma dopamine β-hydroxylase (sometimes regarded as a measure of sympathetic tone) does not change with age	7
Plasma volume does not change with age	8

REFERENCES

1. Ziegler, M. G., Lake, C. R., and Kopin, I. J., Plasma noradrenaline increases with age, *Nature (London)*, 261, 333, 1976.
2. Lake, C. R., Ziegler, M. G., Coleman, M. D., and Kopin, I. J., Age-adjusted plasma norepinephrine levels are similar in normotensive and hypertensive subjects, *N. Engl. J. Med.*, 296, 208, 1977.
3. Sever, P. S., Birch, M., Osikowska, B., and Tunbridge, R. D. G., Plasma-noradrenaline in essential hypertension, *Lancet*, 1, 1078, 1977.
4. Tuttle, R. S., Age-related changes in the sensitivity of rat aortic strips to norepinephrine and associated chemical and structural alterations, *J. Gerontol.*, 21, 510, 1966.
5. Fleisch, J. H., Maling, H. M., and Brodie, B. B., Beta-receptor activity in aorta. Variations with age and species, *Circ. Res.*, 26, 151, 1970.
6. Franco-Morselli, R., Elghozi, J. L., Joly, E., Di Giuilio, S., and Meyer, P., Increased plasma adrenaline concentrations in benign essential hypertension, *Br. Med. J.*, 2, 1251, 1977.
7. Horwitz, D., Alexander, R. W., Lovenberg, W., and Keiser, H. R., Human serum dopamine-β-hydroxylase relationship to hypertension and sympathetic activity, *Circ. Res.*, 32, 594, 1973.
8. Chien, S. S., Usami, S., McAllister, F. F., and Gregersen, M.I., Blood volume and age: repeated measurements on normal men after 17 years, *J. Appl. Physiol.*, 21, 83, 1966.

Table 4
CARDIOVASCULAR REFLEXES

	Ref.
Aortic and carotid sinus baroreflexes show a diminished sensitivity with increasing age	1
Reflex increase of diastolic pressure during the strain of a Valsalva maneuver is diminished with age	2
Older people show a bigger fall of blood pressure and less reflex tachyardia during head-up tilting	3
Incidence of postural hypotension increases with age: 30% of people over 75 years show a fall of systolic pressure of 20 mm Hg or more on standing	4
Carotid sinus hypersensitivity to external compression is more common in the elderly, particularly men	5
Mecholyl produces more sustained hypotension in old people	6

REFERENCES

1. **Gribbin, B., Pickering, T. G., Sleight, P., and Peto, R.,** Effect of age and high blood pressure on baroflex sensitivity in man, *Circ. Res.,* 29, 424, 1971.
2. **Gross, M.,** Circulatory reflexes in cerebral ischaemia involving different vascular territories, *Clin. Sci.,* 38, 491, 1970.
3. **Norris, A. H., Shock, N. W., and Yiengst, M. J.,** Age changes in heart rate and blood pressure responses to tilting and standardized exercise, *Circulation,* 8, 521, 1953.
4. **Caird, F. I., Andrews, G. R., and Kennedy, R. D.,** Effect of posture on blood pressure in the elderly, *Br. Heart J.,* 35, 527, 1973.
5. **Sigler, L. H.,** Hyperactive cardio-inhibitory carotid sinus reflex. A possible aid in the diagnosis of coronary disease, *Arch. Intern. Med.,* 67, 177, 1941.
6. **Nelson, R. and Gellhorn, E.,** The influence of age and functional neurophychiatric disorders on sympathetic and parasympathetic functions, *J. Psychosom. Res.,* 3, 12, 1958.

MICROCIRCULATION AND LYMPHATICS

Sanford M. Rosenthal

Table 1
STRUCTURAL CHANGES IN CAPILLARIES

	Ref.
Decrease in ration of capillaries to tissue mass with age	
Muscle, rat	1
Heart, rat	2
Heart, man	3
Subcutaneous, man	4,5
Muscle, man	6
Deformities in capillaries with age	
Ear, man	7
Eye, man	8,9
Kidney, man	10
Various tissues, man	11
Heart, brain, dog, hog	12
Kidney, dog	23
Thickening of capillary endothelium with age	
Various tissues, mouse, rat	13
Muscle, man	14—16
Eye, rodents	17
Eye, man	18,19
Diminished capillary pore size with age	
Eye, man	18
Lung, rabbit	20
Lung, sheep	21
Diminished extracellular space with age	
Brain, rat	22

REFERENCES

1. **Rakusan, K. and Poupa, O.**, Capillaries and muscle fibers in the heart of old rats, *Gerontologia,* 9, 107, 1964.
2. **Tomanek, R. J.**, Effects of age and exercise on the extent of the myocardial capillary bed, *Anat. Rec.,* 167, 55, 1970.
3. **Samoteikin, M. A. and Irkin, I. V.**, Mikrotsirkuliasiia parenkhimatoznostromal'nye vzaimootnosheniia serdtsa cheloveka v vozrastnom aspekte i pri gipertonicheskof bolezni, *Arkh. Patol.,* 26, 39, 1974.
4. **Ryan, T. J.**, Pathophysiology of skin capillaries, *Int. J. Dermatol.,* 14, 708, 1975.
5. **Korkushko, O. V. and Sarkisov, K. G.**, Age-specific characteristics of microcirculation in middle and old age, *Kardiologiya,* 16, 19, 1976.

Table 1 (continued)
STRUCTURAL CHANGES IN CAPILLARIES

6. Parizkova, J., Eislet, E., Sprynarova, S., and Wachtlova M., Body composition, aerobic capacity, and density of muscle capillaries in young and old men, *J. Appl. Physiol.*, 31, 323, 1971.
7. Johnsson, L. and Hawkins, J. E., Jr., Vascular changes in the human inner ear associated with aging, *Ann. Otol. Rhinol. Laryngol.*, 81, 364, 1972.
8. Curri, S., Senile involution of the conjunctival and hypothalamic small blood vessels, 8th Conf. Eur. Soc. Microcirc. Le Touquet, 1974.
9. Massoni, G. and Piovella, C., Sulla riduzione del flusso ematico distrettuale nell'eta senile, *G. Gerontol. Suppl.*, 38, 1968.
10. Darmady, E. M., Offer, J., and Woodhouse, M. A., The parameters of the ageing kidney, *J. Pathol.*, 109, 195, 1973.
11. Hassler, O., A senile vascular change resulting from excessive spialing of arteries, *J. Gerontol.*, 24, 37, 1969.
12. Getty, R., Histomorphological studies in the dog and hog as related to aging, in *Radiation and Ageing*, Sacher, G. and Lindop, P., Eds., Taylor and Francis, London, 1966, 245.
13. Gersh, I., and Catchpole, H. R., The organization of ground substance and basement membrane and its significance in tissue injury, disease, and growth, *Am. J. Anat.*, 85, 457, 1949.
14. Tomonaga, M. and Mori, Y., Thickening of the capillary basement membrane of the muscle in various neuromuscular diseases and in the aged, *Jpn. J. Geriatr. Nihon Ronen Igakkai Zasshi*, 10, 161, 1973.
15. Kilo, C., Vogler, N., and Williamson, J. R., Muscle capillary basement membrane changes related to aging and to diabetes mellitus, *Diabetes*, 21, 881, 1972.
16. Jordan, S. W. and Perley, M. J., Microangiopathy in diabetes mellitus and aging, *Arch. Pathol.*, 93, 261, 1972.
17. Levenberger, P. M., Ultrastructure of the ageing retinal vascular system, with special reference to quantitative and qualitative changes of capillary basement membranes, *Gerontologia*, 19, 1, 1973.
18. Brancato, R. and Pellegrini, M. S., Etude ultramicroscopique sur le vieillissement des cappillaires de la conjonctive, *Opthalmologica*, 166, 105, 1973.
19. Regnault, F. and Kern, P., Age-related changes of capillary basement-membrane, *Path. Biol.*, 22, 737, 1974.
20. Matalon, S. V. and Wangensteen, O. D., Pulmonary capillary filtration and reflection coefficients in the newborn rabbit, *Microvasc. Res.*, 14, 99, 1977.
21. Boyd, R. D. H., Hill, J. R., Humphreys, P. W., Normand, I. C. S., Reynolds, E. O. R., and Strang, L. B., Permeability of lung capillaries to macromolecules in foetal and new-born lambs and sheep, *J. Physiol. (London)*, 201, 567, 1969.
22. Bondareff, W. and Narotzky, R., Age changes in the neuronal microenvironment, *Science*, 176, 1135, 1972.
23. Ashworth, C. T., Erdmann, R. R., and Arnold, N. J., Age changes in the renal basement membrane in rats, *Am. J. Pathol.*, 36, 165, 1960.

Table 2
FUNCTIONAL CHANGES IN MICROCIRCULATION WITH AGE

	Ref.
Decreased capillary permeability with age	
Macromolecules	
Lung, dog	1
Lung, sheep	2
Mesentery, rabbit	3
Lung, rabbit	4,5
Micromolecules	
Lung, rabbit	4,5
Lung, dog	6
Brain, rat	7
Subcutaneous, rat	8
Muscle, man	9,11
Man	10
Uterus, rabbit	12
Decreased blood flow with age	
Subcutaneous, visceral, muscle, renal, man	9—11
Uterus, rabbit	12
Decreased transvasscular fluid movement with age	
Peripheral, mouse	13
Decreased reactivity of skin vessels to permeability factors, rabbit	14
Decreased response to acetylcholine and sodium load	
Kidney, man	15

REFERENCES

1. Taylor, P. M., Boonyaprakob, U., Watson, D., and Lopata, E., Clearances of plasma proteins from pulmonary vascular beds of adult dogs and pups, *Am. J. Physiol.*, 213, 441, 1967.
2. Boyd, R. D. H., Hill, J. R., Humphreys, P. W., Normand, I. C. S., Reynolds, E. O. R., and Strang, L. B., Permeability of lung capillaries to macromolecules in foetal and new-born lambs and sheep, *J. Physiol. (London)*, 201, 567, 1969.
3. Hauck, G., and Schroer, H., Change of capillary protein permeability in rabbits in dependence on age, *Angiologica*, 10, 248, 1973.
4. Wangensteen, O. D., Lysaker, E., and Savaryn, P., Pulmonary capillary filtration and reflection coefficients in the adult rabbit, *Microvasc. Res.*, 14, 81, 1977.
5. Matalon, S. V. and Wngensteen, O. D., Pulmonary capillary filtration and reflection coefficients in the newborn rabbit, *Microvasc. Res.*, 14, 99, 1977.
6. Levine, O. R., Rodriguez-Martinez, F., and Mellins, R. B., Fluid filtration in the lung of the intact puppy, *J. Appl. Physiol.*, 34, 683, 1973.
7. Bondareff, W. and Lin-Liu, S., Age-related change in the neuronal micro-environment: penetration of ruthenium red into extracellular space of brain in young adult and senescent rats, *Am. J. Anat.*, 148, 57, 1977.
8. Robert, J., Marignac, T., Hottier, D., and Bertrand, A., Variations du debit capillaire specifique du muscle et du tissue cellulaire sous-cutane de la souris et du rat en fonction de l'age et due poids, *C. R. Soc. Biol.*, 164, 1324, 1970.

Table 2 (continued)
FUNCTIONAL CHANGES IN MICROCIRCULATION WITH AGE

9. **Bender, A. D.,** The effect of increasing age on the distribution of peripheral blood flow in man, *J. Am. Geriatr. Soc.,* 13, 192, 1965.
10. **Hruza, Z.,** Connective tissue, in *Microcirculation,* Vol. 1, Kaley, G. and Altura, B. M., Eds., University Park, Baltimore, 1977, 1977.
11. **Kuchar, O., Kuba, J., and Tomsu, M.,** Messung der Muskeldurchblutung in den unteren Exremitaten nach der Lokalen Xenon 133-clearance Methode. I. Normalwerte und ihre Abhangigkeit vom Lebensalter, *Radiol. Diagn.,* 13, 217, 1972.
12. **Larson, L. L., and Foote, R. H.,** Uterine blood flow in young and aged rabbits, *Proc. Soc. Exp. Biol. Med.,* 141, 67, 1972.
13. **Rosenthal, S. M. and LaJohn, L. A.,** Effect of age on transvascular fluid movement, *Am. J. Physiol.,* 228, 134, 1975.
14. **Little, R. A.,** Changes in the reactivity of the skin blood vessels of the rabbit with age, *J. Pathol.,* 99, 131, 1969.
15. **Hollenberg, N. K., Adams, D. F., Solomon, H. S., Rashid, A., Abrams, H. L., and Merrill, J. P.,** Sensecence and the renal vasculature in normal man, *Circ. Res.,* 34, 309, 1974.

Table 3
PHYSIOLOGICAL CHANGES IN LYMPHATICS WITH AGE

	Ref.
Thickening of thoracic duct wall with age	
Man	1
Decrease of lymph tissue with age	
Man	2
Decreased efferent lymph flow with age	
Dog, subcutaneous	3
Sheep, thoracic duct	4

REFERENCES

1. **Borchard, F., Borchard, H., and Huth, F.,** Lymphangiosclerosis of the thoracic duct. Morphometric investigations in 88 cases, *Beitr. Pathol.,* 146, 145, 1972.
2. **Yoffey, J. M. and Courtice, F. C.,** *Lymphatics, Lympy and Lymphoid Tissues,* 2nd ed., Edward Arnold, London, 1956.
3. **Holman, R.,** Flow and protein content of subcutaneous lymph in dogs of different ages, *Am. J. Physiol.,* 118, 354, 1937.
4. **Humphreys, P. W., Normand, I. C. S., Reynolds, E. O. R., and Strang, L. B.,** Pulmonary lymph flow and the uptake of liquid from the lungs of the lamb at the start of breathing, *J. Physiol. (London),* 193, 1, 1967.

CORONARY CIRCULATION

M. L. Weisfeldt

Table 1
AGE CHANGES IN CORONARY VASCULATURE IN MAN

	Ref.
Decreased coronary flow capacity	1, 2
No age changes in fiber/capillary ratio except an increase in hearts with atrophy	1, 2

REFERENCES

1. **Dock, W.**, The decrease in vascularity of human hearts and kidneys between the third and sixth decades, *Science,* 93, 349, 1941.
2. **Roberts, J. T. and Wearn, J. T.**, Quantitative changes in capillary muscle relationships in human hearts during normal growth and hypertrophy, *Am. Heart J.,* 21, 617, 1941.

Table 2
AGE CHANGES IN CORONARY ANATOMY AND FUNCTION IN ANIMAL MODELS

	Ref.
Frequent major age-associated arterial lesions of the rat	1,2
Few lesions in major coronary arteries of the rat	3—6
Atherosclerotic lesions mainly in repeatedly bred rats	5
Increased fiber/capillary ratio in aging rat	7—9
Some decrease in functional capacity of coronary bed during early adulthood of rabbit	10
Little age change in maximal coronary vascular bed capacity with age in rat (slight decrease in proportion to hypertrophy)	4
No age change in maximal oxygen extraction ability in rat (functional coronary capacity)	4
Exercise induces increase in coronary bed and cross-sectional area of major coronary arteries (young>old, but some increase in senescent animals)	9,11

REFERENCES

1. **Humphreys, E. M.,** The occurrence of atheromatous lesions in the coronary arteries of rats, *Q. J. Exp. Physiol.*, 42, 96, 1957.
2. **Wilens, S. L. and Sproul, E. E.,** Spontaneous cardiovascular disease in the rat. I. Lesions of the heart, *Am. J. Pathol.*, 14, 177, 1938.
3. **Berg, B. N.,** *Pathology of Laboratory Rats and Mice,* Cotchin, E. and Rose, F. J., Eds., Blackwell Scientific, Oxford, 1967, 226.
4. **Weisfeldt, M. L., Wright, J. R., Shreiner, D. P., Lakatta, E., and Shock, N. W.,** Coronary flow and oxygen extraction in the perfused heart of senescent male rats, *J. Appl. Physiol.*, 30, 44, 1971.
5. **Wexler, B. C.,** Spontaneous coronary arteriosclerosis in repeatedly bred male and female rats, *Circ. Res.*, 14, 32, 1964.
6. **Hartroft, W. S., Ridout, J. H., Sellars, E. A., and Best, C. H.,** *Proc. Exp. Biol.*, 81, 384, 1952.
7. **Rakusan, K. and Poupa, O.,** Capillaries and muscle fibers in the heart of the old rats, *Gerontologia,* 9, 107, 1964.
8. **Gautier, D., Martini, J., and Coraboeuf, E.,** Etude comparative de la densite capillaire coronaire chez le rat et le cobaye, *J. Physiol. (Paris)*, 56, 356, 1964.
9. **Tomanek, R. J.,** Effects of age and exercise on the extent of the myocardial capillary bed, *Anat. Rec.,* 167, 55, 1970.
10. **Rakusan, K., Rochemont, W. M., Braasch, W., Tschopp, H., and Bing, R. J.,** Capacity of the terminal vascular bed during normal growth in cardiomegaly and in cardiac atrophy, *Circ. Res.,* 21, 209, 1967.
11. **Bloor, C. M., Pasyk, S., and Leon, A. S.,** Interaction of age and exercise on organ and cellular development, *Am. J. Pathol.,* 58, 185, 1970.

OTHER SPECIAL CIRCULATIONS

John M. Johnson

Table 1
RENAL CIRCULATION IN MAN

							Ref.
Renal blood flow							
RBF[a]	1247 ± 357	1203 ± 69	1185 ± 78	1069 ± 56	1011 ± 187	1026 ± 143	—	1
(ml/min/1.73 m²)								
Age range	(17—18)	(22—29)	(30—39)	(40—49)	(50—54)	(62—68)	—	
RBF[a]	—	1077 ± 53	1181 ± 80	1008 ± 69	849 ± 39	775 ± 46	589 ± 47	2
(ml/min/1.73 m²)								
Age range	—	(20—29)	(30—39)	(40—49)	50—59	(60—69)	(70—79)	
RBF[b] = 0.628 − 0.00361 (age) ml/min/m² p < 0.001								3
RBF[c] = 4.39 − 0.026 (age) ml/g/min p < 0.001								4
Cortical RBF = 5.84 − 0.030 (age) ml/g/min p < 0.001								
Renal plasma flow								
RPF[a]	755 ± 36	724 ± 52	654 ± 39	570 ± 48	597 ± 62	—	—	1
(ml/min/1.73 m²)								
Age range	(17—29)	(30—39)	(40—49)	(50—59)	(60—69, n = 2)			
RPF[a]	614 ± 26	649 ± 41	574 ± 37	500 ± 28	442 ± 27	354 ± 30	289 ± 27	2
(ml/min/1.73 m²)								
Age range	(20—29)	(30—39)	(40—49)	(50—59)	(60—69)	(70—79)	(80—89)	
RPF[a]	—	—	—	—	—	489 ± 35	—	5
(ml/min/1.73 m²)								
Age range	—	—	—	—	—	(65—80)	—	
RPF[b]	612	—	529	512	439	386	—	6
(ml/min/1.73 m²)								
Age range	(20—29)	—	(40—49)	(50—59)	(60—69)	(70—79)	—	
RPF[a]	674 ± 72	—	—	—	352 ± 56	272 ± 29	—	7
(ml/min/1.73 m²)								
Age range	(16—41)	—	—	—	(60—69)	(70—80)	—	

Table 1 (continued)
RENAL CIRCULATION IN MAN

						Ref.
Renal blood flow RPF[b] (mℓ/min/1.73 m²)	603	—	449	—	277	8
Age range	(20—49)	—	(50—69)	—	(70—84)	
RPF[b] (mℓ/min)	681 ± 27	—	414 ± 44	—	283 ± 27	9
Age range	(17—40)	—	(54—64)	—	(77—88)	
RPF[b] (mℓ/min)	583 ± 29	—	366 ± 33	—	—	3
Age range	(19—34)	—	(47—82)	—	—	
Significant linear decrease in RPF[b] with age, beginning at age 20, of 35 mℓ/min/1.73 m²/decade						10
Renal vasomotor responses						
45° head up tilt — renal response (C$_{PAH}$) of young (23.9) 583—445 mℓ/min old (63.6) 366—291 mℓ/min						3
Renal vasodilator response to pyrogen exists at all ages						
RPF[b]/RPF with pyrogen (mℓ/min/1.73 m²)	603/1019		449/817		277/517	8
Age range	(20—49)		(50—69)		(70—84)	
Maximal renal vasodilation with acetylcholine (100 µg/min intra-arterial) falls with age						4
Max RBF[c] = 8.50 − 0.050 (age) mℓ/min/g p < 0.001						
Fall in renal blood flow with 30 ng/min angiotensin (intra-arterial) is unchanged by age						4
RBF[c] = 3.88 − 0.023 (age) control						
RBF[c] = 3.29 − 0.022 (age) angiotensin						
Renal extraction of para-aminohippurate unaltered by age						6
Extraction (%)	90.7	93.0	92.5	89.6	91.2	
Age range	(20—29)	(40—49)	(50—59)	(60—69)	(70—79)	
Incidence of aglomerular cortical and juxtamedullary arterioles, and other arterial-arteriolar abnormalities increases with advancing age						11—13

Note: Renal circulation and advancing age. Renal blood flow (RBF) or renal plasma flow (RPF) ± SEM. All studies (References 1 to 10) found a statistically significant reduction in renal blood flow or renal plasma flow with age.

[a] Diodrast clearance.
[b] PAH clearance.
[c] ¹³³Xenon clearance with external monitoring, cortical flow estimated from rapid component.
[d] No statistical difference in % fall in RPF, absolute values of the older group are lower p < 0.01 at rest or during tilt.

REFERENCES

1. Goldring, W., Chasis, H., Ranges, H. A., and Smith, H. W., Relations of effective renal blood flow and glomerular filtration to tubular excretory mass in normal man, *J. Clin. Invest.*, 19, 739, 1940.
2. Davies, D. F. and Shock, N. W., Age changes in glomerular filtration rate, effective renal plasma flow, and tubular excretory capacity in adult males, *J. Clin. Invest.*, 29, 496, 1950.
3. Lee, T. D., Lindeman, R. D., Yiengst, M. J., and Shock, N. W., Influence of age on the cardiovascular and renal responses to tilting, *J. Appl. Physiol.*, 21, 55, 1966.
4. Hollenberg, N. K., Adams, D. F., Solomon, H. S., Rashid, A., Abram, L. A., and Merrill, J. P., Senescence and the renal vasculature in normal man, *Circ. Res.*, 34, 309, 1974.
5. Olbrich, O., Ferguson, M. H., Robson, J. S., and Stewart, C. P., Renal function in aged subjects, *Edinburgh Med. J.*, 57, 117, 1950.
6. Miller, J. H., McDonald, R. K., and Shock, N. W., The renal extraction of p-aminohippurate in the aged individual, *J. Gerontol.*, 6, 213, 1951.
7. Shock, N.W., Kidney function tests in aged males, *Geriatrics*, 1, 232, 1968.
8. McDonald, R. K., Solomon, D. H., and Shock, N. W., Aging as a factor in the renal hemodynamic changes induced by a standardized pyrogen, *J. Clin. Invest.*, 30, 457, 1951.
9. Lindeman, R. D., Lee, T. D., Jr., Yiengst, M. J., and Shock, N. W., Influence of age, renal disease, hypertension, diuretics and calcium on the antidiuretic responses to suboptimal infusions of vasopressin, *J. Lab. Clin. Med.*, 68, 206, 1966.
10. Slack, T. K. and Wilson, D. M., Normal renal function. C_{in} and C_{PAH} in healthy donors before and after nephrectomy, *Mayo Clin. Proc.*, 51, 296, 1976.
11. Ljungqvist, A. and Lagergren, C., Normal intrarenal arterial pattern in adult and aging human kidney. A microangiographic and histological study, *J. Anat.*, 96, 285, 1962.
12. Davidson, A. J., Talner, L. B., and Downs, W. M., A study of the angiographic appearance of the kidney in an aging normotensive population, *Radiology*, 92, 975, 1969.
13. Takasakura, E., Sawabu, N., Handa, A., Takada, A., Shinoda, A., and Takeuchi, J., Intrarenal vascular changes with age and disease, *Kidney Int.*, 2, 224, 1972.

Table 2
CEREBRAL CIRCULATION IN MAN

Cerebral blood flow							Ref.
CBF[a]	54 ± 3.3						1
Age	23 (av)[b]						2
CBF[a]	54.2 ± 2.5					42.5 ± 2.1[c]	
Age range	(23—42)					(50—91)	
CBF[a]	62 ± 3.18	57 ± 3.79				55 ± 3.40	3
Age range	(21—35)	(35—45)				(50—76)	
CBF[a]	65.3	60.5 ± 1.7				50.6 ± 3.0[c]	4
Age range	(18—36)	(38—55)				(56—79)	
CBF[a]	52	46[c]					5
Age range	(20—44)	(45—75)					
CBF[a]						39.3 ± 1.7[c]	6
Age range						(90—102)	
CBF[a,d]	56	50	57	47	50	49	44	47
Age range	(13—19)	(20—24)	(25—29)	(30—34)	(35—39)	(40—44)	(45—49)	(50—54)	(55—59)	(60—91)
CBF[a]		79.3	57.5				47.7[c]	7
Age range		(17—18)	(18—47)				(57—99)	
CBF[a]		52.6 ± 5.1					34.2 ± 4.2[c]	8
Age range		(24—47)					(59—96)	
CBF[a]	50.35 ± 4.91					50.16 ± 10.86		9
Age range	(22-29)					(66—79)		
CBF[a]						57.8 ± 10.4		10
Age range						(65—81)		
CBF[a]	62.1 ± 2.9					57.9 ± 2.1		11
Age range	(20.8 ± 0.4)					(65—81)		
CBF[a]						56.9 ± 3.5		12
Age range						(> 65, av 71.3)		13

Mean transit time (MTT) of indicator through the cerebral vasculature

MTT (sec)	10.5 ± 1.91		13.1 ± 1.92[c]	15
Age range	<50		>50	
MTT (left)[e]	9 ± 0.71	10 ± 0.92	10.1 ± 0.67	13 ± 0.67[c]	16
(right)	9.8 ± 0.78	11.1 ± 0.88	11.6 ± 0.64	13 ± 0.92	

Cerebral blood flow

	(10—20)	(20—30)	(30—50)	(>50)	
Age range					
MTT			9.6 ± 0.2	10.3 ± 0.2[c]	17
Age range			(27—40)	(40—72)	

Response of CBF to hypercapnia — man

CBF[a] (control)	62 ± 3	57 ± 4	55 ± 4		3
CBF ($5\% CO_2$)	105 ± 6	86 ± 5	77 ± 10		
CBF ($7\% CO_2$)	139 ± 4	120 ± 7	119 ± 10		
Age range	(21—35)	(35—45)	(50—76)		

Response of CBF to hypercapnia and hypoxia — rats (Fischer 344)

CBF[f] (control)	82.3 ± 5.0	62.8 ± 3.0[c,g]	18
CBF[f] (hypoxia)	310.6 ± 13.6	242.2 ± 27.5[c]	
CBF[f] (control)	79.2 ± 4.5	64.4 ± 4.9	
CBF[f] (hypercapnia)	414.8 ± 24.3	351.4 ± 20.5	
CBF[h] (control)	68.9 ± 5.0	46.8 ± 3.0[c,g]	
CBF[h] (hypoxia)	125.7 ± 3.4	78.8 ± 13.1[c]	
CBF[h] (control)	63.5 ± 4.3	52.4 ± 4.8	
CBF[h] (hypercapnia)	190.3 ± 22.6	158.0 ± 11.8	
Age	6 months	24 months	

Note: Cerebral blood flow (CBF) and aging. Average values and ages shown in table. There appears to be little change in cerebral blood flow with age in some studies, but a significant fall in others (References 2, 4, 5, 6, 8, and 9). The discrepancy may be due to the manner of subject selection or exclusion with respect to subtle cerebrovascular disease.[14,19] Constant CBF[a] at around 58 mℓ/min from age 20 through the mid 50s, after which there is a steady fall to an average of around 40/100 mℓ/min at age 65. The fall is felt by the author to be a manifestation of an increased incidence of cerebrovascular disease in the older population.[14]

[a] Measured by nitrous oxide technique (Reference 1), flow in mℓ/100 mℓ brain per min.
[b] Age from Reference 20.
[c] Group shows a statistically significant reduction in cerebral blood flow (or an increased mean transit time) with respect to younger group or groups.
[d] Calculated from published data from total CBF and brain weight.
[e] Left and right hemispheres.
[f] Hydrogen clearance from frontal cortex.
[g] Selected groups showed significant control differences with respect to age; however, there was no overall age-related reduction in cortical or cerebellar blood flow.

Table 2 (continued)
CEREBRAL CIRCULATION IN MAN

REFERENCES

1. **Kety, S. S. and Schmidt, C. F.**, The nitrous oxide method for the quantitative determination of cerebral blood flow in man: theory, procedure and normal values, *J. Clin. Invest.*, 27, 476, 1948.
2. **Fazekas, J. F., Walman, R., and Bessman, A. N.**, Cerebral physiology of the aged, *Am. J. Med. Sci.*, 223, 245, 1952.
3. **Schieve, J. F. and Wilson, W. P.**, The influence of age, anesthesia, and cerebral arteriosclerosis on cerebral vascular activity to CO$_2$, *Am. J. Med.*, 15, 171, 1953.
4. **Scheinberg, P., Blackburn, I., Rich, M., and Saslow, M.**, Effects of aging on cerebral circulation and metabolism, *Arch. Neurol. Psychiatry*, 70, 77, 1953.
5. **Heyman, A., Patterson, J. L., Jr., Duke, T. W., and Battey, L. L.**, The cerebral circulation and metabolism in arteriosclerotic and hypertensive cerebrovascular disease with observations on the effects of inhalation of different concentrations of oxygen, *N. Engl. J. Med.*, 249, 223, 1953.
6. **Fazekas, J. F., Kleh, J., and Witkin, L.**, Cerebral hemodynamics and metabolism in subjects over 90 years of age, *J. Am. Geriatr. Soc.*, 1, 836, 1953.
8. **Gordon, G. S.**, Influence of steroids on cerebral metabolism in man, *Recent Prog. Horm. Res.*, 12, 153, 1956.
8. **Fazekas, J. F., Kleh, J., and Finnerty, F. A.**, Influence of age and vascular disease on cerebral hemodynamics and metabolism, *Am. J. Med.*, 18, 477, 1955.
9. **Fazekas, J. F., Thomas, A., Johnson, J. V. V., and Young, W. K.**, Effect of arterenol (norepinephrine) and epinephrine on cerebral hemodynamics and metabolism, *AMA Arch. Neurol.*, 2, 435, 1960.
10. **Lassen, N. A., Feinberg, I., and Lane, M. H.**, Bilateral studies of cerebral oxygen uptake in young and aged normal subjects and in patients with organic dementia, *J. Clin. Invest.*, 39, 491, 1960.
11. **Obrist, W. D., Sokoloff, L., Lassen, N. A., Lane, M. H., Butler, R. N., and Feinberg, I.**, Relation of EEG to cerebral blood flow and metabolism in old age, *Electroencephalogr. Clin. Neurophysiol.*, 15, 610, 1963.
12. **Dastur, D. K., Love, M. H., Hansen, D. B., Kety, S. S., Butler, R. N., Perlin, S., and Sokoloff, L.**, Effects of aging on cerebral circulation and metabolism in man, in *Human Aging: A Biological and Behavioral Study*, Birren, J. E., Butler, R. N., Greenhouse, S. W., Sokoloff, L., and Yarrow, M. R., Eds., Publ. Health Services No. 986, National Institute of Mental Health, Washington, D.C., 1963, 59.
13. **Dichiro, G. and Libow, L. S.**, Carotid sinus calcification and cerebral blood flow in the healthy aged male, *Radiology*, 99, 103, 1971.
14. **Bernsmeier, A.**, Probleme der Hirndurchblutung, *Z. Kreislaufforsch.*, 48, 278, 1959.
15. **Burke, G. and Halko, A.**, Cerebral blood flow studies with sodium pertechnetate Tc99m and the scintillation camera, *J. Am. Med. Assoc.*, 204, 319, 1968.

16. **Klanova, J. and Heinis, P.**, The mean transit time determined with the gamma camera as a value of the cerebral blood flow, *Radiol. Clin. Biol.*, 41, 193, 1972.
17. **Oldendorf, W. H. and Kitani, M.**, Radioisotope measurement of brain blood turnover time as a clinical index of brain circulation, *J. Nucl. Med.*, 8, 570, 1967.
18. **Haining, J. L., Turner, M. D., and Pantall, R. M.**, Local cerebral blood flow in young and old rats during hypoxia and hypercapnia, *Am. J. Physiol.*, 218, 1020, 1970.
19. **Libow, L. S., Obrist, W. D., and Sokoloff, L.**, Cerebral circulatory and electroencephalographic changes in elderly men, in *Human Aging II, An Eleven Year Followup Biomedical and Behavioral Study*, Granick, S. and Patterson, R. D., Eds., U.S. Government Printing Office, Washington, D.C., 1971.
20. **Kety, S. S.**, Changes in cerebral circulation and oxygen consumption which accompany maturation and aging, in *Biochemistry of the Developing Nervous System*, Waelsch, H., Ed., Academic Press, New York, 1955, 208.

Table 3
SPLANCHNIC AND HEPATIC CIRCULATION

					Ref.
Splanchnic circulation — man					
SBF[a]	1550 ± 78	1608 ± 88	1390 ± 92	1251 ± 66[b]	1219 ± 89[b]	1—3
Age	19—20	30—39	40—49	50—59	60—75	
Liver blood flow — rats (Hebrew U. strain)					4
Flow[c]	1.90 ± 0.16		0.92 ± 0.16[b]	0.99 ± 0.13[b]	
Flow[d]	8.52 ± 0.73		6.62 ± 0.19[b]	3.49 ± 0.49[b]	
Weight[e] (g)	80—150		200—300	300—450	

Note: Reductions in splanchnic blood flow (SBF) with age.

[a] Data compiled from References 1, 2, and 3; blood flow measured by bromsulphalein clearance; flow in mℓ/min ± SEM.
[b] Statistically significant reduction in blood flow as compared to youngest group.
[c] Flow in mℓ/min/g of liver (measured by colloid removal).
[d] Flow in mℓ/min/100 g body weight.
[e] Rat ages not given.

REFERENCES

1. **Bradley, S. E., Ingelfinger, F. J., Bradley, G. P., and Curry, J. J.**, The estimation of hepatic blood flow in man, *J. Clin. Invest.*, 24, 890, 1945.
2. **Myers, J. D.**, The hepatic blood flow and splanchnic oxygen consumption of man — their estimation from urea production on bromsulphalein excretion during catheterization of the hepatic veins, *J. Clin. Invest.*, 26, 1130, 1947.
3. **Sherlock, S., Beam, A. G., Billing, B. H., and Patterson, J. C. S.**, Splanchnic blood flow in man by the bromsulphalein method: the relation of peripheral plasma bromsulphalein level to the calculated flow, *J. Lab. Clin. Med.*, 35, 923, 1950.
4. **Wiener, E. and Rabinovici, N.**, Liver haemodynamics and age, *Proc. Soc. Exp. Biol. Med.*, 108, 752, 1961.

Table 4
SKELETAL MUSCLE CIRCULATION IN MAN

				Ref.
Resting skeletal muscle				
MBF[a]	2.20 ± 0.13	1.96 ± 0.12		1
Age range	< 50	> 50		
MBF[a]	3.36 ± 0.22	3.22 ± 0.22	3.15 ± 0.14	2
Age range	(17—34)	(35—49)	(50—75)	
Muscle blood flow following ischemic exercise				
MBF[a]	54.9 ± 11.6	51.8 ± 11.5		1
Age range	< 50	> 50		
MBF[a]	64.8 ± 3.0	52.1 ± 3.19[b]		3
Age range	< 50	> 50		
Maximal leg blood flow following exhaustive ischemic exercise fell significantly with age				
MBF[a] = 72.9 − 0.038 age	($p < 0.001$)[b]			2
Histological changes with age				
No significant change in the number of capillaries per mm² in quadriceps muscle biopsies with age				
Capillaries/mm²	270.1 ± 99.2	362.4 ± 134.9	314.7 ± 99.2	4
Average age	20.7	73.9 (active)	72.5 (sedentary)	

Note: Muscle blood flow (MBF) at rest and following ischemic exercise in young and old subjects. No difference noted in resting values or number of capillaries/mm². Two of three studies found a fall in maximal muscle blood flow following exhaustive ischemic exercise (References 2 and 3).

[a] Measured by ^{133}Xenon clearance from anterior tibialis muscle, flow in mℓ/min/100 mℓ of muscle.
[b] Statistically significant reduction in blood flow as compared to younger subjects.

REFERENCES

1. Lassen, N. A., Lindbjerg, I. F., and Munck, O., Measurement of blood flow through skeletal muscle by intramuscular injection of Xenon^{133}, *Lancet*, 1, 686, 1964.
2. Amery, A., Bossaert, H., and Verstraete, M., Muscle blood flow in normal and hypertensive subjects, *Am. Heart J.*, 78, 211, 1969.
3. Lindbjerg, I. F., Diagnostic application of the ^{133}Xenon method in peripheral arterial disease, *Scand. J. Clin. Lab. Invest.*, 17, 589, 1965.
4. Parizkova, J., Eiselt, E., Sprynarova, S., and Wachtlova, M., Body composition, aerobic capacity, and density of muscle capillaries in young and old men, *J. Appl. Physiol.*, 31, 323, 1971.

Table 5
LIMB AND CUTANEOUS CIRCULATION IN MAN

			Ref.
Finger blood flow[b]	47.7 ± 6.2	27.6 ± 1.9[c]	1
Age range	< 40 (av 26)	> 50 (av 59)	
Finger blood flow[b]	10.2 ± 7.2	23.6 ± 9.7[d]	2
Age range (women)	(19—39)	(51—67)	
No apparent relation of hand blood flow[b] to age			3
No age trend in hand or foot blood flow after 30 min at a local temperature of 43°C			4
Foot blood flow[b]	3.5 (1.6—5.7)	2.5 (1.0—5.7)	5
Age range	(18—24)	(70—82)	
Calf blood flow[b]	2.1 (0.8—4.9)	1.7 (0.7—3.1)	5
Age range	(18—24)	(70—82)	
Forearm blood flow[b]	1.5 (1.0—2.5)	1.8 (1.0—3.6)	6
Age range	(19—31)	(39—45)	
Forearm blood flow[b,e]	2.36 ± 0.12	4.01 ± 0.35[d]	7
Age range	(18—37)	(38—73)	
Forearm blood flow[b,f]	1.90 ± 0.14	4.17 ± 0.44[d]	7
Age range	(18—37)	(38—73)	
Skin blood flow[g]	3.4 ± 1.65	25.6 ± 5.05[d]	7
Muscle blood flow[g]	2.7 ± 0.18	2.8 ± 0.48	
Age range	(18—37)	(38—73)	
Forearm blood flow[b]	2.66 ± 0.35 5.36 ± 1.15 5.58 ± 0.46[d]		8
Age range	(23—29) (37—46) (55—72)		
Forearm vascular response to systemic hypoxia changes from a vasodilator response in subjects less than 40 years old to a vasoconstrictor response in subjects greater than 45 years old ($p < 0.01$)			8
Only after 90 min in a hot, humid environment is forearm blood flow greater in older (41—57 years) than in younger (17—26 years) subjects			9
Leg blood flow[h]	0.42 ± 0.04		10
Age range	(25—30)		
Leg blood flow[h]		0.53 ± 0.04[d]	11
Age range		(52—59)	
Leg blood flow response to leg exercise is less at a given level of whole body oxygen consumption in middle age (52—59) than younger (25—30) men			11
Slight downward trend in capillary density of scalp skin with age ($0.05 < p < 0.1$)			12,12
Decreased rate of clearance of intradermally injected ^{22}Na from older (av age 76) than younger (av age 23) subjects ($p < 0.01$); may be due to decreased blood flow or connective tissue changes with age			14

Note: Alterations of limb and cutaneous circulations with age. Differences in finger blood flow changes may be endocrine related. There is no apparent change in hand or calf blood flow, but there is an increased forearm blood flow (per 100 mℓ of forearm) with age, possibly confined to skin (Reference 7). Total leg blood flow during exercise is reduced with age (References 10 and 11).

[a] The limbs are mixed vascular beds, largely representing muscle and cutaneous blood flows, some responses reflect changes in skin blood flow, others reflect changes in muscle blood flow.
[b] Measured by venous occlusion plethysmography, flow in mℓ/100 mℓ of limb per minute.
[c] Indicates a statistically significant fall in blood flow per 100 mℓ of tissue as compared to the younger group.
[d] Indicates a statistically significant rise in blood flow per 100 mℓ of tissue as compared to the younger group.
[e] Measured 6 cm proximal to midpoint of forearm.
[f] Measured 6 cm distal to midpoint of forearm.
[g] Estimated from fraction of skin and muscle at two sites on the forearm, flow in mℓ/min/100 mℓ of skin or muscle.
[h] Dye infusion technique, flow in ℓ/min.

Table 5 (continued)
LIMB AND CUTANEOUS CIRCULATION IN MAN

REFERENCES

1. **Ring, G. C., Kurbatov, T., and Shannon, G. J.,** Changes in central pulse and finger plethysmography during aging, *J. Gerontol.,* 14, 189, 1959.
2. **Bollinger, A. and Schlumpf, M.,** Finger blood flow in healthy subjects of different age and sex and in patients with primary Raynaud's disease, *Acta Chir. Scand. Suppl.,* 465, 42, 1976.
3. **Duff, R. S.,** Circulation in the hands in hypertension, *Br. Med. J.,* 2, 974, 1956.
4. **Kunkel, P. and Stead, E. A., Jr.,** Blood flow and vasomotor reactions in the foot in health, in arteriosclerosis and in thromboangiitis obliterans, *J. Clin. Invest.,* 17, 715, 1968.
5. **Allwood, M. J.,** Blood flow in the foot and calf in the elderly: a comparison with that in healthy young adults, *Clin. Sci.,* 17, 331, 1958.
6. **Hellon, R., Lind, A., and Weiner, J.,** The physiological reactions of men of two age groups to a hot environment, *J. Physiol. (London),* 133, 118, 1956.
7. **Hellon, R. and Clarke, R. S. J.,** Changes in forearm blood flow with age, *Clin. Sci.,* 18, 1, 1959.
8. **Kravec, T. F., Eggers, G. W. N., Jr., and Kettel, L. J.,** Influence of patient age on forearm and systemic vascular response to hypoxia, *Clin. Sci.,* 42, 555, 1972.
9. **Hellon, R. F. and Lind, A. R.,** The influence of age on peripheral vasodilatation in a hot environment, *J. Physiol. (London),* 141, 262, 1958.
10. **Jorfeldt, L. and Wahren, J.,** Leg blood flow during exercise in man, *Clin. Sci.,* 41, 459, 1971.
11. **Wahren, J., Saltin, B., Jorfeldt, L., and Pernow, B.,** Influence of age on the local circulatory adaptation to leg exercise, *Scand. J. Clin. Lab. Invest.,* 33, 79, 1975.
12. **Giacometti, L.,** The anatomy of the human scalp, *Adv. Biol. Skin,* 6, 97, 1965.
13. **Ellis, R. A.,** Vascular patterns of the skin, *Adv. Biol. Skin,* 2, 20, 1961.
14. **Christophers, E. and Klingman, A. M.,** Percutaneous absorption in aged skin, *Adv. Biol. Skin,* 6, 163, 1965.

Table 6
MISCELLANEOUS SPECIAL CIRCULATIONS

					Ref.
Uterus (rabbits)					
Flow[a]	37.7	43.9	40.1	29.6	18.6[b]	1
Age (months)	3	6	6	30	45
	(Prepubertal)	(Postpubertal; nulliparous)	(Uniparous)	(Multiparous)	(Polyparous)
Conjunctiva (man)					
With age, there is an increased tortuosity of venules and increased venous sacculation in microscopic observation of conjunctival vessels					2—4

Note: Changes in uterine and conjunctival circulations with age.

[a] mℓ/min/100 g uterus, measured by ^{85}Kr washout.
[b] Statistically significant reduction in blood flow per 100 g as compared to younger groups.

REFERENCES

1. **Larson, L. L. and Foote, R. H.**, Uterine blood flow in young and aged rabbits, *Proc. Soc. Exp. Biol. Med.*, 141, 67, 1972.
2. **Ditzel, J.**, Angioscopic changes in the smaller blood vessels in diabetes mellitus and their relationship to aging, *Circulation*, 14, 386, 1956.
3. **Labram, C. and Lestradet, H.**, La auto aglomeration des globules rouges observee in vivo. Interet de l'examen biomicroscopique des vaisseaux de la conjunctive bulbaire, *Presse Med.*, 69, 187, 1961.
4. **Frayser, R., Knisely, W. H., Barnes, R., and Satterwhite, W. M., Jr.**, In vivo observations on the conjunctival circulation in elderly subjects, *J. Gerontol.*, 19, 494, 1964.

Kidney and Body Fluids

KIDNEY

Robert D. Lindeman

Table 1
CHANGES IN RENAL MORPHOLOGY AND COMPOSITION WITH AGE

Species	Age		Ref.
Human	30—90 years	The weight and volume of the kidney decrease 20—30% during adult life; the cortex decreases more than the medulla	1—3
	0—80 years	The number of glomeruli remains constant from birth to maturity; a 30—50% decrease in the number of glomeruli occurs during late adult life	2,5
	40—90 years	The number of abnormal glomeruli increases with age, e.g., 5% at age less than 40 years vs. 37% at age 90 years	6
	30—90 years	Of the remaining identifiable glomeruli, more than 10% are sclerosed in 80-year-olds compared to only 1% in young adults	7
	Adult	Mesangial volume in glomeruli increases from 6.2—10.4% with age	8
	Adult	Reduplication and focal thickening of both glomerular and tubular basement membranes occur with age	9,10
Rat	0—500 days	A 3-fold increase in the number of glomeruli occurs from birth to 100 days; the number of glomeruli remains constant to 350 days, then declines by 30% to 500 days	4
Human	40—80 years	A decrease in proximal tubule volume and length occurs with age	3,10
	0—90 years	The number of distal tubular diverticuli increases with age	10
	Adult	Muscular arteries show deposition of collagen between intima and internal elastic lamina; fraying, splitting, reduplication, and calcification of elastic lamina; and replacement of muscular cells with collagen; there is no decrease in luminal size of arteries unless hypertension is present; the arteriolar lesion associated with aging is mild hyalinization; again there is no increase in arteriolar wall thickness or decrease in lumen size unless hypertension is present	10—12
	Adult	Ischemic obsolescence of glomeruli is characterized by collapse of glomerular tufts, wrinkling of basement membranes, simplification and reduction in vascular channels, hyaline deposition in residual glomerular tufts and Bowman's capsule; the obsolete glomerulus may be reabsorbed and disappear entirely with scanty cellular response and residual scar	13,14
	Adult	Angiographic studies show presence and development of shunts in juxtamedullary glomeruli; cortical glomeruli atrophy with abrupt termination of the arteriole (see Figure 1)	15—17
	Adult	There is a slight but insignificant increase in the volume of interstitial tissue with age	2

Table 1 (continued)
CHANGES IN RENAL MORPHOLOGY AND COMPOSITION WITH AGE

Species	Age		Ref.
Rat	1—24 months	There is no change in the renal content of soluble or insoluble collagen or elastin with age	18
	0—18 months	The collagen content of the kidney, measured as hydroxyproline content, increases with age ($2\frac{1}{2}\times$); acid mucopolysaccharide (AMPS) increased to 12 months, then decreased 30%	19
Human	1—84 years	AMPS did not change in cortex; increased ($3\times$) to age 40 years, then declined thereafter	20

REFERENCES

1. Roessle, R. and Roulet, F., *Mass und Zahl in der Pathologie*, J. Springer, Berlin, 1932.
2. Dunnill, M. S. and Halley, W., Some observations of the quantitative anatomy of the kidney, *J. Pathol.*, 110, 113, 1973.
3. Tauchi, H., Tsuboi, K., and Sato, K., Histology and experimental pathology of senile atrophy of the kidney, *Nagoya Med. J.*, 4, 71, 1958.
4. Arataki, M., On the post natal growth of the kidney, with special reference to the number and size of the glomeruli (albino rat), *Am. J. Anat.*, 36, 399, 1926.
5. Moore, R. A., Total number of glomeruli in the normal human kidney, *Anat. Rec.*, 48, 153, 1931.
6. Sworn, M. J. and Fox, M., Donor kidney selection for transplantation, *Br. J. Urol.*, 44, 377, 1972.
7. Kaplan, C., Pasternack, B., Shaw, H., et al., Age-related incidence of sclerotic glomeruli in human kidneys, *Am. J. Pathol.*, 80, 227, 1975.
8. Wehner, H., Stereologische Untersuchungen am Mesangium normaler menschlicher Nieren, *Virchows Arch. A*, 344, 286, 1968.
9. Farquhar, M. G., Vernier, R. L., and Good, R. A., The application of electron microscopy in pathology. Study of renal biopsy tissues, *Schweiz. Med. Wochenschr.*, 87, 501, 1957.
10. Darmady, E. M., Offer, J., and Woodhouse, M. A., The parameters of the aging kidney, *J. Pathol.*, 109, 195, 1973.
11. Williams, R. H. and Harrison, T. R., A study of the renal arteries in relation to age and to hypertension, *Am. Heart J.*, 14, 645, 1937.
12. Yamaguchi, T., Omae, T., and Katsuki, S., Quantitative determination of renal vascular changes related to age and hypertension, *Jpn. Heart J.*, 10, 248, 1969.
13. MacCallum, D. B., The bearing of degenerating glomeruli on the problem of the vascular supply of the mammalian kidney, *Am. J. Anat.*, 65, 69, 1939.
14. McManus, J. F. A. and Lupton, C. H., Jr., Ischemic obsolescence of renal glomeruli, *Lab. Invest.*, 9, 413, 1960.
15. Ljungqvist, A. and Lagergren, C., Normal intrarenal arterial pattern in adult and aging human kidney. A microangiographical and histologic study, *J. Anat.*, 96, 285, 1962.
16. Ljungqvist, A., Structure of the arteriole-glomerular units in different zones of the kidney, *Nephron*, 1, 329, 1964.
17. Takazakura, E., Wasabu, N., Handa, A., et al., Intrarenal vascular changes with age and disease, *Kidney Int.*, 2, 224, 1972.
18. McGavack, T. and Kao, K. T., The influence of age and sex on the soluble collagen, insoluble collagen, and elastin of rat tissues, *Exp. Med. Surg.*, 18, 104, 1960.
19. Ber, A., Allalouf, D., Wasserman, L., et al., Age-related changes in renal connective tissue of rats, *Gerontologia*, 15, 252, 1969.
20. Inoue, G., Sawada, T., Fukunaga, Y., et al., Levels of acid mucopolysaccharides in aging human kidneys, *Gerontologia*, 16, 261, 1970.

Table 2
CHANGES IN RENAL FUNCTION WITH AGE

Species	Age		Ref.
		Glomerular filtration rate	
Human	20—90 years	An accelerating decline in glomerular filtration rate (GFR) occurs after age 40 years at the rate of approximately 1% per year (see Figures 2 and 3)	1—6
		Renal plasma and blood flow, filtration fraction	
	1—88 years	An accelerating decrease in effective renal plasma (ERPF) (PAH clearance) occurs with age which is slightly greater than the decrease in GFR	2,4
	23—75 years	Extraction ratios of low arterial PAH concentrations were approximately 92% and were not influenced by age indicating that PAH clearances can be used to estimate renal plasma and blood flows throughout life	7,8
	20—85 years	An increase in the filtration fraction (GFR/ERPF) occurs with age	2,4,9,10
	20—90 years	There is a decrease in the fraction of the total cardiac output received by the kidney with age	11—13
	20—85 years	Administration of pyrogen produces a greater vasodilatation in the arteriolar system of the older subject than the younger subject suggesting a greater resting vasoconstriction in older subjects	9
	17—76 years	Perfusion of outer cortical nephrons fell more with age than did perfusion of corticomedullary nephrons; acetylcholine increased renal blood flow more in young than old subjects, but the vasoconstrictor response to angiotensin was similar in young and old subjects	14
		Maximum tubular transport capacity	
	20—90 years	The tubular maximum for diodrast or PAH (Tm_D or Tm_{PAH}) decreases with age at a rate paralleling the decrease in GFR	2,7
	24—86 years	The tubular maximum for glucose reabsorption decreases with age at a rate paralleling the decrease in GFR	15
Rat	12—28 months	Fewer energy-producing mitochondria, lower enzyme concentrations, low concentrations of sodium-potassium activated ATPase activity, and decreased tubular transport capacity are found in tubular cells of old compared to young kidneys; the decrease in maximum transport capacity in man with age parallels the decrease in GFR suggesting surviving nephrons function normally; these data indicate a change in the basic biochemistry of the aging tubular cell	16,17

Table 2 (continued)
CHANGES IN RENAL FUNCTION WITH AGE

REFERENCES

1. **Lewis, W. H., Jr. and Alving, A. S.,** Changes with age in the renal function in adult men. I. Clearance of urea. II. Amount of urea nitrogen in the blood. III. Concentrating ability of the kidneys, *Am. J. Physiol.,* 123, 500, 1938.
2. **Davies, D. F. and Shock, N. W.,** Age changes in glomerular filtration rate, effective renal plasma flow, and tubular excretory capacity in adult males, *J. Clin. Invest.,* 29, 496, 1950.
3. **Pelz, K. S., Gottfried, S. P., and Paz, E.,** Kidney function in old men and women, *Geriatrics,* 20, 145, 1965.
4. **Wesson, L. G., Jr.,** Renal hemodynamics in physiological states, in *Physiology of the Human Kidney,* Wesson, L. G., Jr., Ed., Grune & Stratton, New York, 1969, 98.
5. **Rowe, J. W., Andres, R., Tobin, J. D., et al.,** The effect of age on creatinine clearance in men: a cross-sectional and longitudinal study, *J. Gerontol.,* 31, 155, 1976.
6. **Muether, R. O., Schuessler, W. P., and Sommer, A. J.,** Laboratory studies on the aging kidney, *J. Am. Geriatr. Soc.,* 15, 260, 1967.
7. **Miller, J. H., McDonald, R. K., and Shock, N. W.,** The renal extraction of p-aminohippurate in the aged individual, *J. Gerontol.,* 6, 213, 1951.
8. **Bradley, S. E.,** Trans. 1st Conf. Factors Regulating Blood Pressure, Josiah Macy Jr. Foundation, New York, 1947, 118.
9. **McDonald, R. F., Solomon, D. H., and Shock, N. W.,** Aging as a factor in the renal hemodynamic changes induced by a standardized pyrogen, *J. Clin. Invest.,* 30, 457, 1951.
10. **Lindeman, R. D., Lee, T. D., Jr., Yiengst, M. J., et al.,** Influence of age, renal disease, hypertension, diuretics, and calcium on the antidiuretic responses to suboptimal infusions of vasopressin, *J. Lab. Clin. Med.,* 68, 206, 1966.
11. **Landowne, M. and Stanley, J.,** Aging of the cardiovascular system, in *Aging—Some Social and Biological Aspects,* Shock, N. W., Jr., American Association for the Advancement of Science, 1960, 159.
12. **Bender, A. D.,** The effect of increasing age on the distribution of peripheral blood flow in man, *J. Am. Geriatr. Soc.,* 13, 192, 1965.
13. **Lee, T. D., Jr., Lindeman, R. D., Yiengst, M. J., et al.,** Influence of age on the cardiovascular and renal responses to tilting, *J. Appl. Physiol.,* 21, 55, 1966.
14. **Hollenberg, N. K., Adams, D. F., Solomon, H. S., et al.,** Senescence and the renal vasculature in normal man, *Circ. Res.,* 34, 309, 1974.
15. **Miller, J. H., McDonald, R. K., and Shock, N. W.,** Age changes in the maximal rate of renal tubular reabsorption of glucose, *J. Gerontol.,* 7, 196, 1952.
16. **Barrows, C. H., Jr., Falzone, J. A., Jr., and Shock, N. W.,** Age differences in the succinoxidase activity of homogenates and mitochondria from the livers and kidneys of rats, *J. Gerontol.,* 15, 130, 1960.
17. **Beauchene, R. E., Fanestil, D. D., and Barrows, C. H., Jr.,** The effect of age on active transport and sodium-potassium-activated ATPase activity in renal tissues of rats, *J. Gerontol.,* 20, 306, 1965.

Table 3
CONCENTRATING AND DILUTING ABILITY AND REGULATION OF SERUM OSMOLALITY WITH AGE

Species	Age		Ref.
Human	17—88 years	A progressive decrease in maximum urine concentrating ability is observed with age	1—6
	17—88 years	A progressive decrease in maximum urine diluting ability is observed with age; free water clearance (CH_2O) decreases at the same rate as GFR	2
	17—88 years	Elderly hydrated persons respond normally to graded doses of antidiuretic hormone (Pitressin®) insufficient to maximally concentrate the urine	2
	20—90 years	Maximum urine osmolality following high dose Pitressin® infusion was significantly decreased in elderly hydrated subjects	4
	21—92 years	Elderly patients appear to be more prone to stress-induced hyponatremia; older subjects increased their serum arginine vasopressin (ADH) levels more after a standardized hypertonic saline infusion (increasing serum osmolality from 290—306 mOgm/kg H_2O) above comparable basal levels (4½ vs. 2½-fold increases) than did young subjects; ethanol infusions, known to inhibit ADH secretions, produced a more prolonged decrease in serum ADH concentrations in young than in old subjects	7
Rats	<6 months vs. >20 months	Intracarotid injection of hypertonic saline has little effect on urine concentration in old compared to young rats; interpreted as a decline in neurohypophyseal function with age	8
	<6 months vs. >20 months	Extracellular fluid volumes and sodiums increased in old rats similar to changes seen in young rats with diabetes insipidus; daily urine volume and sodium excretion greater in old rats, even in presence of severe water deprivation; daily Pitressin® injections tended to restore values observed in old rats toward those observed in young rats; old rats show good response to Pitressin® ruling out renal cause; and findings suggest old rats have relative posterior pituitary failure	9

Table 3 (continued)
CONCENTRATING AND DILUTING ABILITY AND REGULATION OF SERUM OSMOLALITY WITH AGE

REFERENCES

1. Lewis, W. H., Jr. and Alving, A. S., Changes with age in the renal function in adult men. I. Clearance of urea. II. Amount of urea nitrogen in the blood. III. Concentrating ability of the kidneys, *Am. J. Physiol.,* 123, 500, 1938.
2. Lindeman, R. D., Lee, T. D., Jr., Yiengst, M. J., et al., Influence of age, renal disease, hypertension, diuretics, and calcium on the antidiuretic responses to suboptimal infusions of vasopressin, *J. Lab. Clin. Med.,* 68, 206, 1966.
3. Lindeman, R. D., VanBuren, H. C., and Raisz, L. G., Osmolar renal concentrating ability in healthy young men and hospitalized patients without renal disease, *N. Engl. J. Med.,* 262, 1306, 1960.
4. Miller, J. H. and Shock, N. W., Age differences in the renal tubular response to antidiuretic hormone, *J. Gerontol.,* 8, 446, 1953.
5. Dontas, A. S., Marketos, S., and Papanayiotou, P., Mechanisms of renal tubular defects in old age, *Postgrad. Med. J.,* 48, 295, 1972.
6. Rowe, J. W., Shock, N. W., and DeFronzo, R. A., The influence of age on the renal response to water deprivation in man, *Nephron,* 17, 270, 1976.
7. Helderman, J. H., Vestal, R. E., Rowe, J. W., et al., The response of arginine vasopressin to intravenous ethanol and hypertonic saline in man: the impact of aging, *J. Gerontol.,* 33, 39, 1978.
8. Friedman, S. M., Hinke, J. A. M., and Friedman, C. L., Neurohypophyseal responsiveness in the normal and senescent rat, *J. Gerontol.,* 11, 286, 1956.
9. Friedman, S. M., Friedman, C. L., and Nakashima, M., Effect of pitressin on old-age changes of salt and water metabolism in the rat, *Am. J. Physiol.,* 199, 35, 1960.

Table 4
CHANGES IN GLOMERULAR PERMEABILITY WITH AGE

Species	Age		Ref.
Human	65 + years	There is an increasing incidence of proteinuria after age 65 years; still, by age 55 years, only 32% had detectable proteinuria	1
	20—90 years	Glomerular permeability to free hemoglobin, i.e., free hemoglobin/inulin clearance, does not change with age	2
	15—79 years	No difference in glomerular permeability to a spectrum of different molecular weight dextrans exists between young and old subjects	3
	<1—61 years	Filtration characteristics of intact glomeruli show no changes in glomerular pore size with increasing age	4
Rats, mice, hamsters	All ages	Aging rodents, in contrast to humans, spontaneously develop morphologic alterations in renal glomeruli (glomerular sclerosis) with an increase in permeability of the glomerular basement membrane and with proteinuria	5,6

REFERENCES

1. **VanZonneveld, R. J.,** Some data on the genito-urinary system as found in old age surveys in the Netherlands, *Gerontol. Clin.,* 1, 167, 1959.
2. **Lowenstein, J., Faulstick, D. A., and Yiengst, M. J.,** The glomerular clearance and renal transport of hemoglobin in adult males, *J. Clin. Invest.,* 40, 1172, 1961.
3. **Faulstick, D., Yiengst, M. J., Ourster, D. A., et al.,** Glomerular permeability in young and old subjects, *J. Gerontol.,* 17, 40, 1962.
4. **Arturson, G., Groth, T., and Grotte, G.,** Human glomerular membrane porosity and filtration pressure: dextran clearance data analyzed by theoretical models, *Clin. Sci.,* 40, 137, 1971.
5. **Guttman, P. H. and Kohn, H. I.,** Progressive intercapillary glomerulosclerosis in the mouse, rat, and Chinese hamster, associated with aging and X-ray exposure, *Am. J. Pathol.,* 37, 293, 1960.
6. **Berg, B. N.,** Spontaneous nephrosis with proteinuria, hyperglobulinemia, and hypercholesterolemia in the rat, *Proc. Soc. Exp. Biol. Med.,* 119, 417, 1965.

Table 5
CHANGES WITH AGE IN THE RENAL RESPONSE TO ALTERATIONS IN SODIUM INTAKE AND OTHER CHANGES IN THE ENVIRONMENT

Species	Age (years)		Ref.
Human	18—76	Older subjects do not conserve sodium as rapidly and efficiently as do younger subjects when salt is restricted	1
	<1—76	Elderly subjects have lower plasma renin activities and urinary aldosterone excretions, both on unrestricted and restricted sodium intake; serum cortisol and renin substrate concentrations were not different in young and old subjects	2—5
	22—63	Elderly males are more likely to develop an exaggerated natriuresis after administration of a water or saline load than are younger male subjects; older hypertensive patients developed a more marked natriuresis with saline loading than did young hypertensive patients	6,7
	18—88	The diurnal variations in electrolyte excretion (sodium, potassium, chloride) and GFR are blunted in older subjects compared to young subjects	8
	19—82	There is little difference in the percent decrease in sodium excretion and GFR in response to 1 hr of 45° tilt in young vs. old subjects	9

REFERENCES

1. **Epstein, M. and Hollenberg, N. K.**, Age as a determinant of renal sodium conservation in normal man, *J. Lab. Clin. Med.*, 87, 411, 1976.
2. **Weidmann, P., DeMyttenaeu-Bursztein, S., Maxwell, M. H., et al.**, Effect of aging on plasma renin and aldosterone in normal man, *Kidney Int.*, 8, 325, 1975.
3. **Crane, M. G. and Harris, J. J.**, Effect of aging on renin activity and aldosterone excretion, *J.Lab. Clin. Med.*, 87, 947, 1976.
4. **Hayduk, K., Krause, D. K., Kaufmann, W., et al.**, Age-dependent changes of plasma renin concentrations in humans, *Clin. Sci. Mol. Med.*, 45, 2735, 1973.
5. **Flood, C., Gherondache, C., Pincus, G., et al.**, The metabolism and secretion of aldosterone in elderly subjects, *J. Clin. Invest.*, 46, 960, 1967.
6. **Lindeman, R. D., Adler, S., Yiengst, M. J., et al.**, Natriuresis and carbohydrate-induced antinatriuresis after overnight fast and hydration, *Nephron*, 7, 289, 1970.
7. **Schalekamp, M. A. D. H., Krauss, X. H., Schalekamp-Kuyken, M. P. A., et al.**, Studies on the mechanism of hypernatriuresis in essential hypertension in relation to measurements of plasma, renin concentration, body fluid compartments, and renal function, *Clin. Sci.*, 41, 219, 1971.
8. **Lobban, M. C. and Tredie, B. E.**, Diurnal rythyms of renal excretion and of body temperature in aged subjcts, *J. Physiol. (London)*, 188, 48, 1967.
9. **Lee, T. D., Jr., Lindeman, R. D., Yiengst, M. J., et al.**, Influence of age on the cardiovascular and renal responses to tilting, *J. Appl. Physiol.*, 21, 55, 1966.

Table 6
PATHOPHYSIOLOGY OF THE DECREASE IN RENAL FUNCTION WITH AGE

Species	Age		Ref.
Evidence that renal changes with age are due to a progressive involutional change			
Human	—	Normal diploid human fibroblasts have a finite life span; the population-doubling potential of these cells is inversely related to the age of the donor	1,2
Rat	12—28 months	Renal tubular cells have fewer energy producing mitochondria, lower enzyme concentrations, lower concentrations of sodium-potassium-activated ATPase activity, and diminished tubular transport in older animals than in younger animals	3,4
Evidence that renal changes with age are due to superimposed pathology			
Human	60—93 years	Abnormal renal scars were found in 70% of elderly patients; 46% showed focal areas of diminished uptake felt to represent ischemic lesions; findings consistent with focal lesions due to vascular occlusions and/or interstial infection	5
	40—80 years	Sclerotic and fibrotic changes in the renal vasculature paralleled a generalized atherosclerotic process and appeared to be responsible for the senile changes observed in the kidney; atherosclerotic changes occurred earlier and were more severe in the kidneys of Japanese than Caucasians	6
	21—90 years	The incidence of persistent bacteriuria increased steadily after age 60 years, reaching 42% in individuals over age 80 years; mean GFR was lower in subjects with persistent bacteriuria than in age-controlled nonbacteriuric subjects	7,8
Rats, mice	3—24 months	Accumulations of fluorescent staining antibodies and complement in the kidney increase with age	9,10

REFERENCES

1. **Hayflick, L.**, Current theories of biologic aging, *Fed. Proc. Fed. Am. Soc. Exp. Biol.*, 34, 9, 1975.
2. **Hayflick, L.**, The cell biology of human aging, *N. Engl. J. Med.*, 295, 1302, 1976.
3. **Barrows, C. H., Jr., Falzone, J. A., Jr., and Shock, N. W.**, Age differences in the succinoxidase activity of homogenates and mitochondria from the livers and kidneys of rats, *J. Gerontol.*, 15, 130, 1960.
4. **Beauchene, R. E., Fanestil, D. D., and Barrows, C. H., Jr.**, The effect of age on active transport and sodium-potassium-activated ATPase activity in renal tissues of rats, *J. Gerontol.*, 20, 306, 1965.
5. **Friedman, S. A., Raizner, A. E., Rosen, H., et al.**, Functional defects in the aging kidney, *Ann. Int. Med.*, 76, 41, 1972.
6. **Tauchi, H., Tsuboi, K., and Okutomi, J.**, Age changes in the human kidney of the different races, *Gerontologia*, 17, 87, 1971.
7. **Dontas, A. S., Papanayiotou, P., Marketos, S. G., et al.**, The effects of bacteriuria on renal functional patterns in old age, *Clin. Sci.*, 34, 73, 1968.
8. **Wolfson, S. A., Kalmanson, G. M., Rubini, M. E., et al.**, Epidemiology of bacteriuria in a predominately geriatric male population, *Am. J. Med. Sci.*, 250, 168, 1965.
9. **Couser, W. G. and Stilmant, M. M.**, Immunopathology of the aging rat kidney, *J. Gerontol.*, 31, 13, 1976.
10. **Shiminzu, F., Abe, F., and Ito, K., et al.**, Age-associated presence of immunoglobulin and complement in renal glomeruli in mice, *Contrib. Nephrol.*, 6, 79, 1977.

Table 7
CHANGES IN COMPENSATORY RENAL HYPERTROPHY WITH AGE

Species	Age		Ref.
Rat	<1—18 months	The magnitude of the compensatory hypertrophy observed after unilateral nephrectomy decreases with age	1—11
Human	All ages		
Rat	<1—18 months	Compensatory hypertrophy is directly related to protein intake after unilateral nephrectomy, but age differences persist when this variable is controlled	1,5
	<1—18 months	The number of glomeruli do not increase after birth so that the compensatory hypertrophy is not due to an increase in the number of nephrons; the remaining glomeruli increase in volume and the tubules enlarge (primarily the proximal convoluted segments) after unilateral nephrectomy; one contradictory study in rats shows an increase in the number of nephrons in the remaining kidney up to 50 days of age after unilateral nephrectomy	10—13
	<1—18 months	The predominant cause of renal enlargement in young animals is cellular hyperplasia (increased DNA); in older animals, cellular hypertrophy accounts for most of the renal enlargement (increased RNA)	6—8
Human	All ages	Renal compensatory hypertrophy is important in kidney transplant donors; there is an inverse relationship between the age at nephrectomy and increase in renal function; the greatest increase occurs in the first 3 weeks but some increase continues up to 4 weeks post-nephrectomy	11,14—17

REFERENCES

1. MacKay, L. L., MacKay, E. M., and Addis, T., Influence of age on degree of renal hypertrophy produced by high protein diets, *Proc. Soc. Exp. Biol. Med.,* 24, 335, 1926.
2. MacKay, E. M., MacKay, L. L., and Addis, T., The degree of compensatory hypertrophy following unilateral nephrectomy. I. The influence of age, *J. Exp. Med.,* 56, 255, 1932.
3. Verzar, F., Compensatory hypertrophy of kidney and adrenal in the life span of rats, in *Old Age in the Modern World,* Report 3rd Congr. Int. Assoc. Gerontology, Churchill Livingstone, Edinburgh, 1954, 139.
4. Barrows, C. H., Jr., Roeder, L. M., and Olewine, D. A., Effect of age on renal compensatory hypertrophy following unilateral nephrectomy in the rat, *J. Gerontol.,* 17, 148, 1962.
5. Konishi, F., Renal hyperplasia in young and old rats fed a high protein diet following unilateral nephrectomy, *J. Gerontol.,* 17, 151, 1962.
6. Reiter, R. J., McCreight, C. E., and Sulkin, N. M., Age differences in cellular proliferation in rat kidneys, *J. Gerontol.,* 19, 485, 1964.
7. Phillips, T. L. and Leong, G. F., Kidney cell proliferation after unilateral nephrectomy as related to age, *Cancer Res.,* 2, 286, 1967.
8. Dicker, S. and Shirley, D. G., Compensatory renal growth after unilateral nephrectomy in the newborn rat, *J. Physiol. (London),* 228, 193, 1973.
9. Galla, J. H., Klein-Robbenhear, T., and Hayslett, J. P., Influence of age on the compensatory response in growth and function to unilateral nephrectomy, *Yale J. Biol. Med.,* 47, 218, 1974.
10. Kaufman, J. M., Hardy, R., and Hayslett, J. P., Age-dependent characteristics of compensatory renal growth, *Kidney Int.,* 8, 21, 1975.
11. Bonavalet, J. P., Champion, M., Wonstock, F., et al., Compensatory renal hypertrophy in young rats. Increase in the number of nephrons, *Kidney Int.,* 1, 391, 1972.
12. Dunnill, M. S. and Halley, W., Some observations of the quantitative anatomy of the kidney, *J. Pathol.,* 110, 113, 1973.
13. Moore, R. A., Total number of glomeruli in the normal human kidney, *Anat. Rec.,* 48, 153, 1931.

Table 7 (continued)
CHANGES IN COMPENSATORY RENAL HYPERTROPHY WITH AGE

14. Ogden, D. A., Donor and recipient function 2 to 4 years after renal homotransplantation, *Ann. Intern. Med.,* 67, 998, 1967.
15. Boner, G., Shelp, W. D., Neton, M., et al., Factors influencing the increase in glomerular filtration rate in the remaining kidney of transplant donors, *Am. J. Med.,* 55, 169, 1973.
16. Pabico, R. C., McKenna, B. A., and Freeman, R. B., Renal function before and after unilateral nephrectomy in renal donors, *Kidney Int.,* 8, 166, 1975.
17. Flanigan, W. J., Burns, R. O., Takaco, F. J., and Merrill, J. P., Serial studies of glomerular filtration rate and renal plasma flow in kidney transplant donors, identical twins, and allograft recipients, *Am. J. Surg.,* 116, 788, 1968.

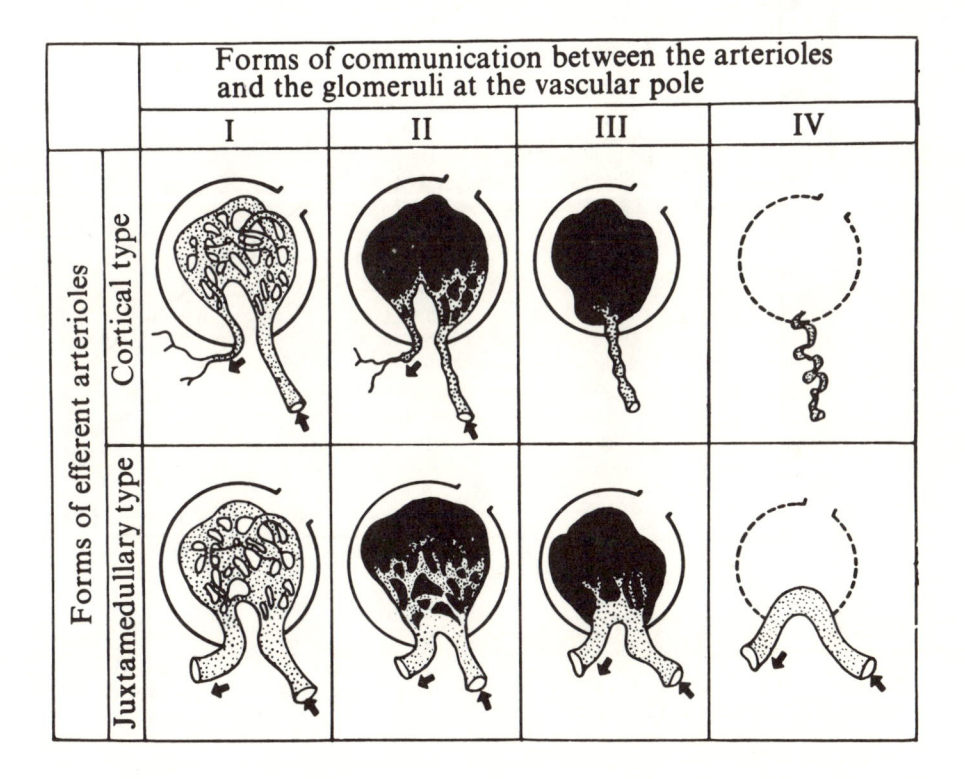

FIGURE 1. Diagram of the degenerative process in the cortical and juxtamedullary nephrons. (Reprinted from *Kidney International,* 2, 224, 1972. With permission.)

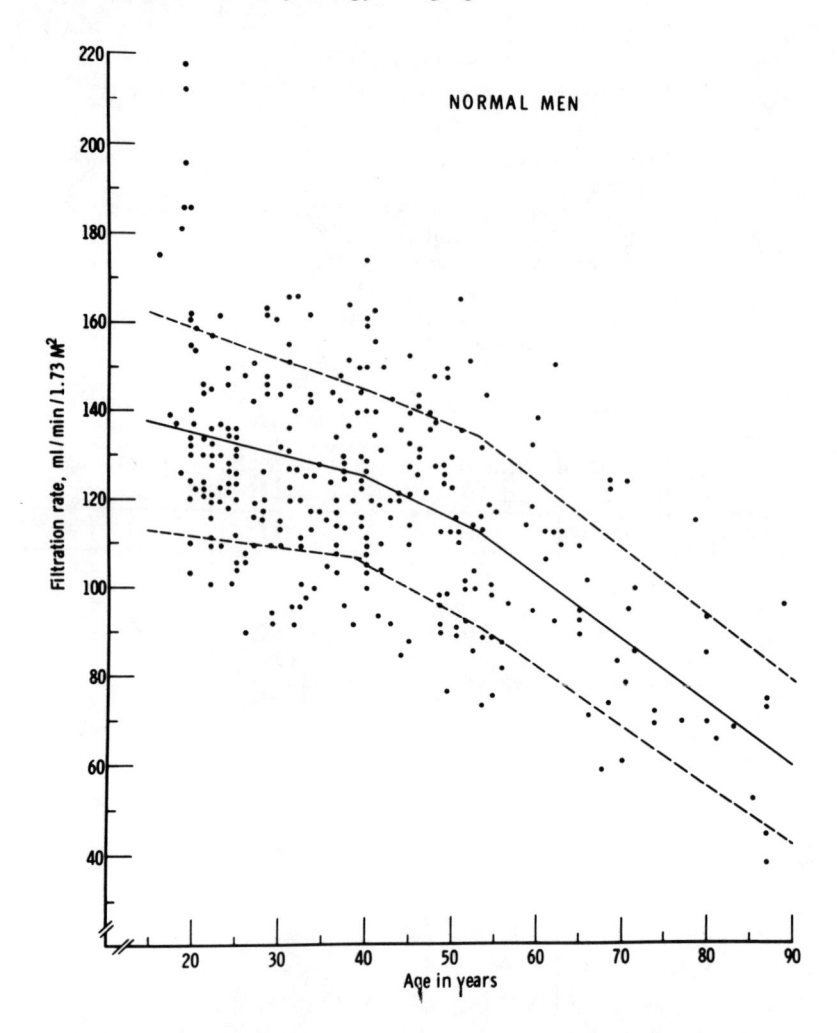

FIGURE 2. Glomerular filtration rates (inulin clearances) per 1.73 m² in normal men of various ages. The solid and broken lines represent mean ± one standard deviation, respectively. Data from 38 studies reported by L. C. Wesson, Jr. (From Wesson, L. G., Jr., in *Physiology of Human Kidney,* Wesson, L. G., Jr., Ed., Grune & Stratton, New York, 1969, 99. By permission.)

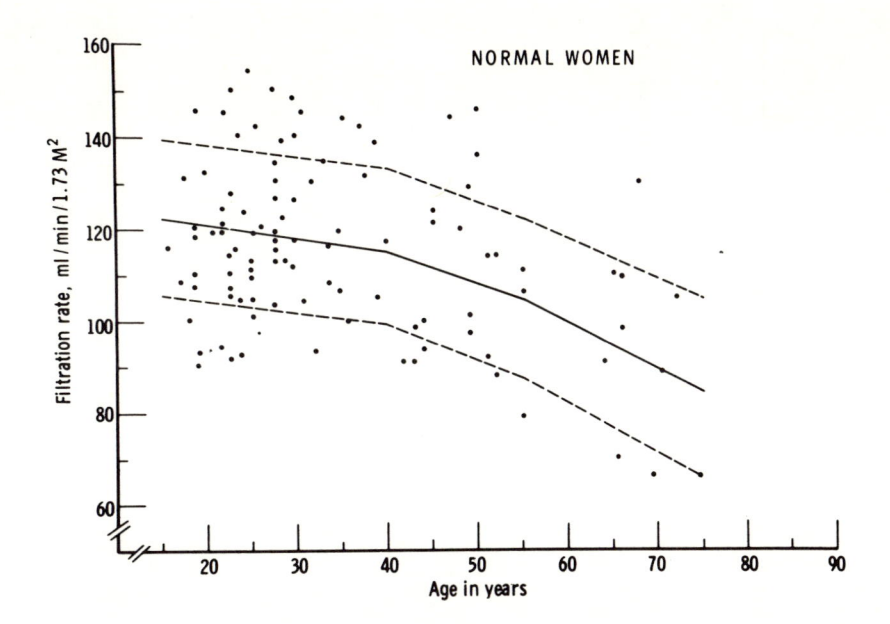

FIGURE 3. Glomerular filtration rates (inulin clearance) per 1.73 m² in normal women of various ages. The solid and broken lines represent mean ± one standard deviation. Data from 38 studies reported by L. G. Wesson, Jr. (From Wesson, L. G., Jr., in *Physiology of Human Kidney,* Wesson, L. G., Jr., Ed., Grune & Stratton, New York, 1969, 99. By permission.)

BODY FLUIDS

Robert D. Lindeman

Table 1
CHANGES IN COMPARTMENTAL FLUID VOLUMES AND ELECTROLYTE CONCENTRATIONS WITH AGE

Species	Age		Ref.
Human	20—90 years	No change in total blood, plasma, or extracellular fluid volumes occurs with age; intracellular volume decreases with age	1
	20—90 years	Mean plasma and total blood volumes do not change with age	1
	21—95 years	Extracellular water volume (thiocyanate space) does not change with age; there is a significant decrease in body surface area, total body water (antipyrine space), and intracellular water volumes with age	2
	All ages	Serum sodium, potassium, chloride, calcium, and magnesium concentrations do not vary significantly with age	3—5
	20—84 years	There is a small but significant decrease in serum zinc concentration with age	6
	20—89 years	There is a small but significant increase in serum copper concentration with age	7
	18—80 years	Total body and exchangeable potassium decrease with age	8,9

REFERENCES

1. **Cohn, J. E. and Shock, N. W.**, Blood volume studies in middle-aged and elderly males, *Am. J. Med. Sci.*, 217, 388, 1949.
2. **Shock, N. W., Watkin, D. M., Yiengst, M. J., et al.**, Age differences in the water content of the body as related to basal oxygen consumption in males, *J. Gerontol.*, 18, 1, 1963.
3. **Elkinton, J. R. and Danowski, T. S.**, *The Body Fluids, Basic Physiology and Practical Therapeutics*, Williams & Wilkins, Baltimore, 1955.
4. **Shock, N. W.**, Physiologic aspects of aging in man, *Annu. Rev. Physiol.*, 23, 97, 1961.
5. **Korenchevsky, V.**, *Physiological and Pathological Aging*, Bourne, G. H., Ed., Hafner, New York, 1961, 129.
6. **Lindeman, R. D., Clark, M. L., and Colmore, J. P.**, Influence of age and sex on plasma and red-cell zinc concentrations, *J. Gerontol.*, 26, 358, 1971.
7. **Yunice, A. A., Lindeman, R. D., Czerwinski, A. W., et al.**, Influence of age and sex on serum copper and ceruloplasmin levels, *J. Gerontol.*, 29, 277, 1974.
8. **Sagild, V.**, Total exchangeable potassium in normal subjects with special reference to changes with age, *Scand. J. Clin. Lab. Invest.*, 8, 44, 1956.
9. **Allen, T. H., Anderson, E. C., and Langham, W. H.**, Total body potassium and gross body composition in relation to age, *J. Gerontol.*, 15, 348, 1960.

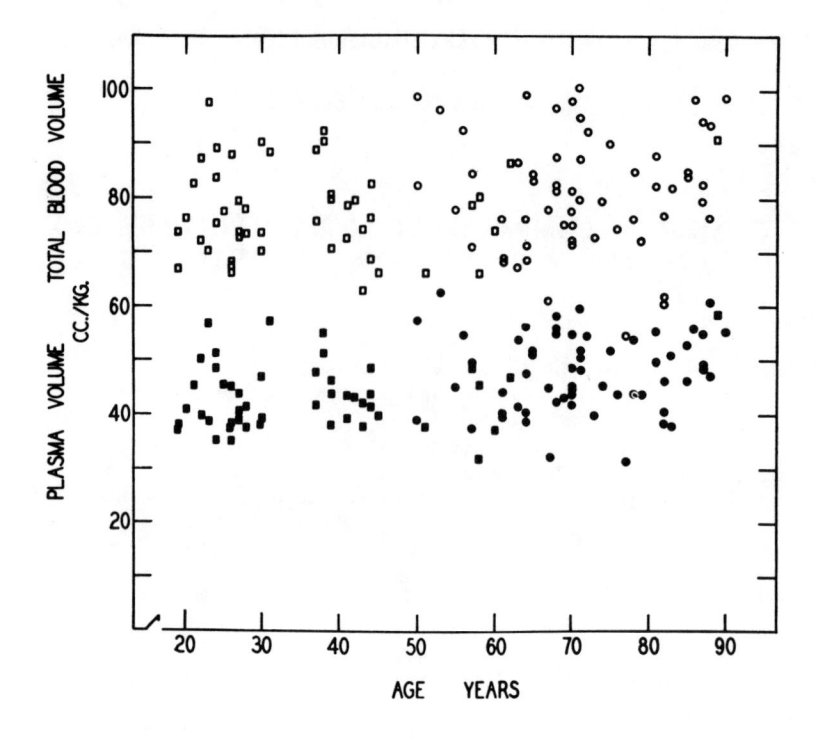

FIGURE 1. Plasma and blood volume of normal men of various ages. Open squares and circles refer to blood volume and filled circles and squares refer to plasma volume. (From Cohn, J. E. and Shock, N. W., *Am. J. Med. Sci.*, 217, 388, 1949. With permission.)

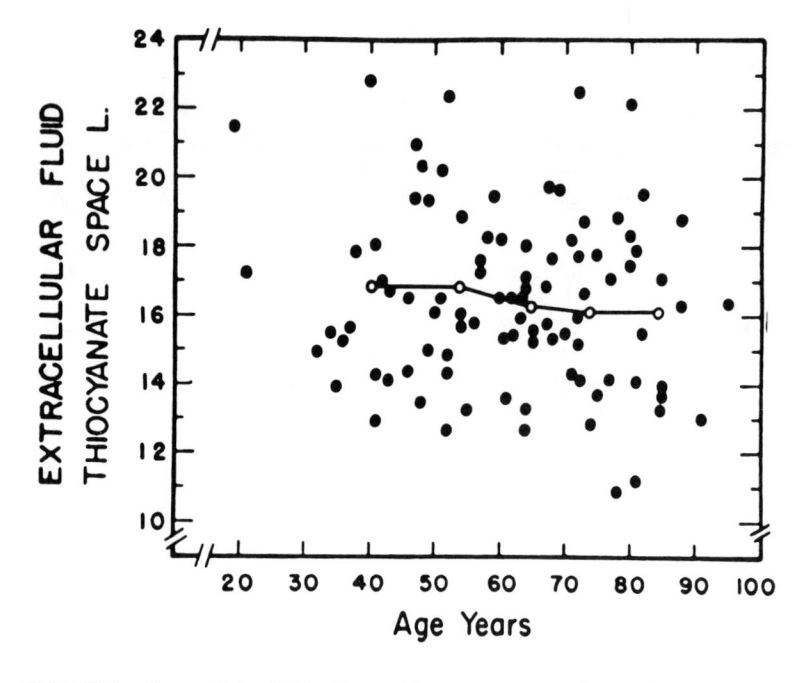

FIGURE 2. Extracellular fluid volume (thiocyanate space) of normal men of various ages. (From Shock, N. W., *Bull. N.Y. Acad. Med.*, 32, 268, 1956. With permission.)

ACID-BASE REGULATION

Robert D. Lindeman

Table 1
MAINTENANCE OF ACID-BASE BALANCE WITH AGE

Species	Age (years)		Ref.
Human	17—93	The blood pH, pCO$_2$ and bicarbonate concentrations of aged persons without renal disease do not differ from the values observed in young subjects under basal conditions	1,2
	17—93	The decrease in blood pH and bicarbonate concentrations are prolonged in elderly subjects after ingestion of an acid load; the minimum urine pH achieved after an acid load is similar in young and old subjects; total acid excretion (ammonia plus tetratable acid minus bicarbonate) decreases at a rate paralleling the decrease in GFR (see Figure 1)	2—4

REFERENCES

1. **Shock, N. W. and Yiengst, M. J.**, Age changes in the acid-base equilibrium of the blood of males, *J. Gerontol.*, 5, 1, 1950.
2. **Adler, S., Lindeman, R. D., Yiengst, M. J., et al.**, Effect of acute acid loading on urinary acid excretion by the aging human kidney, *J. Lab. Clin. Med.*, 72, 278, 968.
3. **Shock, N. W. and Yiengst, M. J.**, Experimental displacement of the acid-base equilibrium of the blood in aged males, *Fed. Proc. Fed. Am. Soc. Exp. Biol.*, 7, 114, 1948.
4. **Hilton, J. G., Goodbody, M. F., Jr., and Kruesi, O. R.**, The effect of prolonged administration of NH$_4$Cl on the blood acid-base equilibria of geriatric subjects, *J. Am. Geriatr. Soc.*, 3, 697, 1955.

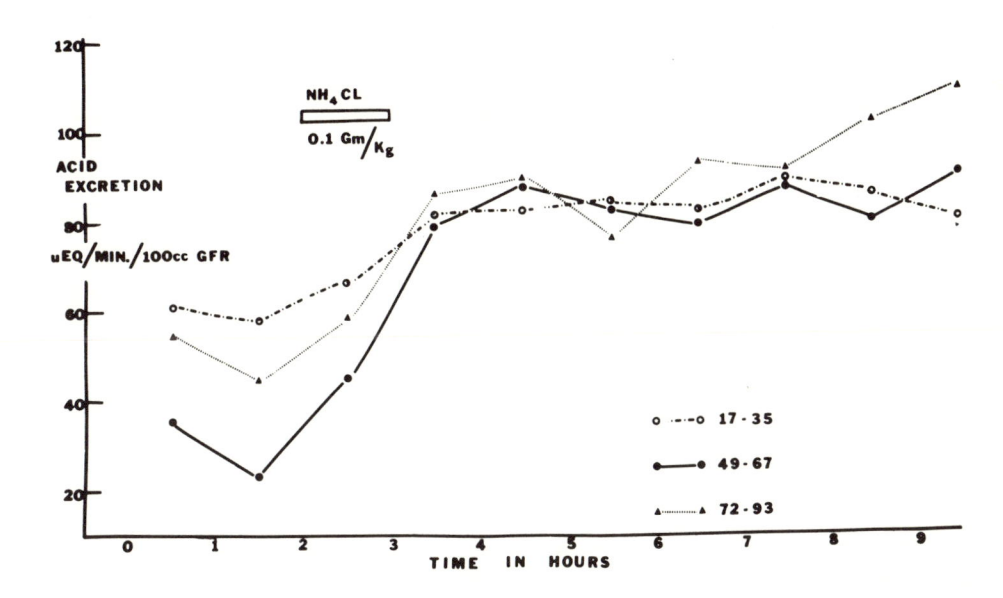

FIGURE 1. Mean total acid excretion in men of various ages before and after ingestion of 0.1 g/k of NH$_4$Cl. (From Adler, Sheldon, Lindeman, Robert D., Yiengst, Marvin J., Beard, Elsie, and Shock, Nathan W., Effect of acute acid loading on urinary acid excretion by the aging human kidney, *J. Lab. Clin. Med.*, 72, 278, 1968. With permission.)

MICTURITION

J. T. Herlihy and R. J. M. McCarter

Table 1
AGE-RELATED CHANGES IN MICTURITION SYSTEM

	Ref.
1. Anatomical and tissue changes of the bladder in old age have received little attention and virtually no work has been done on species other than man	1
2. Changes in human female bladder function with age include	2—5
1. Lower bladder capacity	
2. Higher volume of residual urine	
3. Greater occurrence of uninhibited contractions	
4. Increased occurrence of incontinence associated with abnormal cystometrograms	
3. Urinary incontinence in aged humans is frequently associated with age-related clinical abnormalities such as disorders of the CNS and surgical removal of the prostate	6—9
4. Cytological changes occur with age in the female urethra; these changes are associated with variations in estrogen activity	10

REFERENCES

1. **Brocklehurst, J. C.**, Aging of the human bladder, *Geriatrics,* 27, 154, 1972.
2. **Brocklehurst, J. C. and Dillane, J. B.**, Studies of the female bladder in old age. I. Cystometrograms in non-incontinent women, *Gerontol. Clin.*, 8, 285, 1966.
3. **Brocklehurst, J. C. and Dillane, J. B.**, Studies on the female bladder in old age. II. Cystometrograms in 100 incontinent women, *Gerontol. Clin.*, 8, 306, 1966.
4. **Brocklehurst, J. C. and Dillane, J. B.**, Studies of the female bladder in old age. III. Micturating cystograms in incontinent women, *Gerontol. Clin.*, 9, 47, 1967.
5. **Brocklehurst, J. C. and Dillane, J. B.**, Studies of the female bladder in old age. IV. Drug effects in urinary incontinence, *Gerontol. Clin.*, 9, 182, 1967.
6. **Brocklehurst, J. C.**, The causes and management of incontinence in the elderly, *Nurs. Mirror,* 144(15), 11, 1977.
7. **Helps, E. P. W.**, Diseases of the urinary system. Urinary incontinence in the elderly, *Br. Med. J.*, 2(6089), 754, 1977.
8. **Rudd, T. N.**, Urinary incontinence in old age, *Gerontol. Clin.*, 10, 304, 1968.
9. **Willington, F. L., Ed.**, *Incontinence in the Elderly,* Academic Press, London, 1976, 3.
10. **Smith, P.**, Age changes in the female urethra, *Br. J. Urol.*, 44, 667, 1972.

Respiration

LUNG-THORAX SYSTEM

J. L. Mauderly

Table 1
CHANGES IN LUNG-THORAX STRUCTURE OF
MAN DURING GROWTH AND THROUGHOUT
ADULT LIFE

	Ref.
Changes during growth	
The number of alveoli increases exponentially from approximately 24×10^6 at birth to 300×10^6 at 8 years, then remains constant through young adulthood	1,2
Alveolar diameter and lung volume per unit lung weight increase from birth to 8 years and then remain constant	2,3
Alveolar surface area increases exponentially from 20—30 m^2 at birth until 8 years, then increases at a slower rate until the adult value of 70—80 m^2 is reached	2,4
The number of conducting airways is complete at birth, but the number of respiratory airways increases from approximately 1.5×10^6 at birth to 14×10^6 in the adult	2,5
Conducting airways grow in length and diameter from birth to adulthood in proportion to body size	6,7
Before 5 months of age, conducting and respiratory airways grow at approximately the same rate, but after 1 year, the respiratory airways grow faster than the conducting airways and increase in length at a greater rate than diameter	8
The adult number of pulmonary capillary segments is reached by 8 years of age	9
Lung connective tissue density increases through late adolescence and an increase in lung elastic tissue fibers from birth to young adulthood has been reported	10,11
Changes in adults	
Alveolar duct volume increases at the expense of alveolar volume, becoming evident after 40 years of age	12—14
Alveoli are dilated with concurrent losses of alveolar septal tissue and alveolar surface area with advancing age	4,14—16
The number and size of interalveolar fenestrae increase with age and there is a degeneration of elastic fibers adjacent to enlarged fenestrae	17
A progressive reduction in the number and thickness of elastic fibers in walls of alveoli and alveolar ducts becomes evident at approximately 50 years of age	18
The total lung elastin content increases with age due to increases in the pleura, septae, bronchi, and vessels, but the elastin content of lung parenchyma remains relatively constant with age	19,20

Table 1 (continued)
CHANGES IN LUNG-THORAX STRUCTURE OF MAN DURING GROWTH AND THROUGHOUT ADULT LIFE

	Ref.
There is a decrease in the cross-linking of elastic tissue in the lung with age, which may be partially responsible for the age-related decrease in elastic recoil of the lung	21
There is a decrease in the distensibility of strips of alveolar tissue with age, primarily due to an increased degree of distension in the resting state	22
There is an increase in thickness of pulmonary arterial walls with age, primarily due to a thickening of intimal and medial layers, and the vascular thickness becomes more variable with age	15,23—25
The bronchial mucous gland layer of subjects approximately 80 years of age was reported to be thicker than that of 59-year-old subjects	26
An increased calcification of bronchial cartilage was found in lungs from subjects over 90 years of age as compared to subjects ranging from 40—50 years old	15
The thorax becomes shorter and the anterior-posterior diameter increases with age	27,28

REFERENCES

1. **Weibel, E. R.**, Morphometrische bestimmung von zahl volumen und Oberfläche der alveolen und kapillaren der menschlichen lunge, *Z. Zellforsch. Mikrosk. Anat.*, 57, 648, 1962.
2. **Dunnill, M. S.**, Postnatal growth of the lung, *Thorax*, 17, 329, 1962.
3. **Stigol, L. C., Vawter, G. F., and Mead, J.**, Studies on elastic recoil of the lung in a pediatric population, *Am. Rev. Respir. Dis.*, 105, 552, 1972.
4. **Thurlbeck, W. M.**, Internal surface area and other measurements in emphysema, *Thorax*, 22, 483, 1967.
5. **Hogg, J. C., Williams, J., Richardson, J. B., Macklem, P. T., and Thurlbeck, W. M.**, Age as a factor in the distribution of lower airway conductance and in the pathologic anatomy of obstructive lung disease, *N. Engl. J. Med.*, 282, 1283, 1970.
6. **Hislop, A., Muir, D. C. F., Jacobsen, M., Simon, G., and Reid, L.**, Postnatal growth and function of the pre-acinar airways, *Thorax*, 27, 265, 1972.
7. **Cudmore, R. E., Emery, J. L., and Mithal, A.**, Postnatal growth of the bronchi and bronchioles, *Arch. Dis. Child.*, 37, 481, 1962.
8. **Hieronymi, G.**, Uber den durch das alter bedingten formwandel meschlicher lungen, *Ergeb. Allg. Pathol. Pathol. Anat.*, 41, 1, 1961.
9. **Weibel, E. R. and Gomez, D. M.**, Architecture of the human lung, *Science*, 137, 577, 1962.
10. **Ingram, R. H. and O'Cain, C. P.**, Frequency dependence of compliance in apparently healthy smokers versus nonsmokers, *Bull. Physio-Pathol. Respir.*, 7, 195, 1971.
11. **Loosli, C. G. and Potter, E. I.**, Pre- and postnatal development of the respiratory portion of the human lung, with special reference to the elastic fibers, *Am. Rev. Respir. Dis.*, Suppl. 1, 80, 1959.
12. **Weibel, E. R.**, Morphometrics of the lung, in *Handbook of Physiology, Section 3*, Vol. 1, Fenn, W. O. and Rahn, H., Eds., American Physiological Society, Washington, D.C., 1964, 285.
13. **Ryan, S. F., Vincent, T. N., Mitchell, R. S., Filley, G. F., and Dart, G.**, Ductectasia; an assymptomatic pulmonary change related to age, *Med. Thorac.*, 22, 181, 1965.
14. **Yamanaka, A.**, Pulmonary emphysema in Japan, *Pathol. Microbiol.*, 35, 161, 1970.

Table 1 (continued)
CHANGES IN LUNG-THORAX STRUCTURE OF MAN DURING GROWTH AND THROUGHOUT ADULT LIFE

15. Liebow, A. A., Biochemical and structural changes in the aging lung. Summary, in *Aging of the Lung,* Cander, L. and Moyer, J. H., Eds., Grune and Stratton, New York, 1964, 97.
16. Pump, K. K., The aged lung, *Chest,* 60, 571, 1971.
17. Pump, K. K., Fenestrae in the alveolar membrane of the human lung, *Chest,* 65, 431, 1974.
18. Wright, R. R., Elastic tissue of normal and emphysematous lungs, *Am. J. Pathol.,* 39, 355, 1961.
19. Pierce, J. A., Biochemistry of aging in the lung, in *Aging of the Lung,* Cander, L. and Moyer, J. H., Eds., Grune and Stratton, New York, 1964, 61.
20. Pierce, J. A. and Ebert, R. V., Fibrous network of the lungs and its change with age, *Thorax,* 20, 469, 1965.
21. John, R. and Thomas, J., Chemical compositions of elastins isolated from aortas and pulmonary tissues of humans of different ages, *Biochem. J.,* 127, 261, 1972.
22. Sugihara, T., Martin, C. J., and Hildebrandt, J., Length-tension properties of alveolar wall in man, *J. Appl. Physiol.,* 30, 874, 1971.
23. Welch, K. J. and Kinney, T. D., The effect of patent ductus arteriosus and of interauricular and interventricular septal defects on the development of pulmonary vascular lesions, *Am. J. Pathol.,* 29, 727, 1948.
24. Simmons, P. and Reid, L., Muscularity of pulmonary artery branches in the upper and lower lobes of the normal and aged lung, *Br. J. Dis. Chest,* 63, 38, 1969.
25. Semmens, M., The pulmonary artery in the normal aged lung, *Br. J. Dis. Chest,* 64, 65, 1970.
26. Hernandez, J. A., Anderson, A. E., Holmes, W. L., Morrone, N., and Foraker, A. G., The bronchial glands in aging, *J. Am. Geriatr. Soc.,* 13, 799, 1965.
27. Kaltreider, N. L., Fray, W. W., and Hyde, H. V. E., The effect of age on the total pulmonary capacity and its subdivisions, *Am. Rev. Tuberc.,* 37, 662, 1938.
28. Pierce, J. A. and Ebert, R. V., The barrel deformity of the chest, the senile lung and obstructive pulmonary emphysema, *Am. J. Med.,* 25, 13, 1958.

Table 2
CHANGES IN LUNG-THORAX STRUCTURE IN ANIMALS DURING GROWTH AND THROUGHOUT ADULT LIFE

	Ref.
Changes during growth	
Alveolar sizes of newborn mammals ranging from mice to calves are nearly constant, but alveolar size among adults varies as a function of body size and metabolic rate	1—3
The ratio of alveolar surface area to oxygen consumption of small mammals increases during maturation, but that of larger mammals (over 1.0 kg adult body weight) decreases	1
The lung weight of Syrian hamsters and miniature swine constitutes approximately 2.2% of the body weight at birth and 1.3—1.5% at weanling age; at maturity, the lungs of miniature swine constitute 0.8% of the body weight	4,5
The conducting airways of the dog grow in length and width in proportion to the cube root of body weight	6
The peripheral airways of dogs, including respiratory bronchioles, grow at a faster rate than proximal airways	7
Changes in mature animals	
The fraction of body weight contributed by lung weight in the miniature swine is reduced from 0.8% at maturity to 0.5% at 1—2.6 years and then remains constant	5
The alveolar duct volume in dogs increases with age and is associated with reductions in parenchymal tissue volume, total alveolar volume and alveolar surface area	8,9
There is an increase in the size of mucous glands, an increased calcification of cartilage, and a decrease in the percent of smooth muscle in walls of bronchi of the dog with increasing age	8,10
No significant increase was found in the number or size of interalveolar fenestrae in dogs over 1 year old	11
Lung parenchymal strips of monkeys were decreasingly distensible with age, but no change was found in tissue from rat, rabbit, or horse lungs	12
The fraction of red muscle fibers in the guinea pig diaphragm decreases approximately 24% from 6—40 weeks of age and diaphragm muscle fibers enlarge with age	13

Table 2 (continued)
CHANGES IN LUNG-THORAX STRUCTURE IN ANIMALS DURING GROWTH AND THROUGHOUT ADULT LIFE

REFERENCES

1. **Bartlett, D. and Areson, J. G.**, Quantitative lung morphology in newborn mammals, *Respir. Physiol.*, 29, 193, 1977.
2. **Tenney, S. M. and Remmers, J. E.**, Comparative quantitative morphology of the mammalian lung: diffusing area, *Nature (London)*, 197, 54, 1963.
3. **Johanson, W. G. and Pierce, A. K.**, Lung structure and function with age in normal rats and rats with papain emphysema, *J. Clin. Invet.*, 52, 2921, 1973.
4. **Robinson, P. F.**, The body weight-organ weight relationships of the immature hamster *Mesocricetus auratus*, from birth to weanling, *Growth*, 35, 253, 1971.
5. **Thomas, J. M. and Beamer, J. L.**, Age-weight relationships of selected organs and body weight for miniature swine, *Growth*, 35, 259, 1971.
6. **Horsefield, K.**, Postnatal growth of the dog's bronchial tree, *Respir. Physiol.*, 29, 185, 1977.
7. **Boyden, E. A. and Tompsett, D. H.**, The postnatal growth of the lung in the dog, *Acta Anat.*, 47, 185, 1961.
8. **Robinson, N. E. and Gillespie, J. R.**, Morphologic features of the lungs of aging Beagle dogs, *Am. Rev. Respir. Dis.*, 108, 1192, 1973.
9. **Hyde, D. M., Robinson, N. E., Gillespie, J. R., and Tyler, W. S.**, Morphometry of the distal air spaces in lungs of aging dogs, *J. Appl. Physiol.*, 43, 86, 1977.
10. **Fukuchi, Y.**, Aging of the bronchial tree and bronchial vascular system, *Jpn. J. Geriatr.*, 9, 19, 1972.
11. **Martin, H. B.**, The effect of aging on the alveolar pores of Kohn in the dog, *Am. Rev. Respir. Dis.*, 88, 773, 1963.
12. **Martin, C. J., Chihara, S., and Chang, D. B.**, A comparative study of the mechanical properties in aging alveolar wall, *Am. Rev. Respir. Dis.*, 115, 981, 1977.
13. **Lieberman, D. A., Maxwell, L. C., and Faulkner, J. A.**, Adaptation of guinea pig diaphragm muscle to aging and endurance training, *Am. J. Physiol.*, 222, 556, 1972.

Table 3
AGE-RELATED CHANGES IN THE LUNG VOLUMES OF MAN

	Ref.
Total lung capacity	
The total lung capacity of children and adolescents increases in proportion to body growth	1—3
There are reports of both increases and decreases of total lung capacity with age in adults and it is generally agreed that changes are more closely related to height than to age	4,5
Vital capacity	
Vital capacity increases with age until young adulthood, then decreases throughout the lifespan	3,5—11
The vital capacity of children is linearly related to body size and is closely correlated to height and body surface area	2,12
Vital capacity increases most rapidly during adolescence, and the increase is more rapid in males than in females, beginning at 12—14 years	13—16
The vital capacity is generally reported to reach maximal values at 14—20 years in females and 18—25 years in males, although there are reported maxima as late as 35 years	7,9,12,17,18
The reduction of vital capacity with age is evident even if data are adjusted for height, weight, and sex differences	5,19
The reduction in vital capacity with age is thought to be largely related to a loss of chest wall mobility	20
Vital capacity is smaller in adult females than males, but the rate of reduction with age is more rapid in males	5,10
The reduction of vital capacity with age becomes more rapid after 45 years	3
Functional residual capacity	
The functional residual capacity of children increases proportionately faster than height or weight from 2 months to 6 years of age	21
The functional residual capacity of older children and adolescents increases in proportion to body growth	1,2,22
Reports of age-related changes in functional residual capacity of adults are conflicting, but the majority favor a slight increase with age	4,5,11,20
Residual volume	
The residual volume of children and adolescents increases in proportion to body growth	2
The residual volume/total lung capacity ratio remains nearly constant until young adulthood	1—3,23
The residual volume continues to increase with age throughout adulthood	5,11,24,25
The residual volume/total lung capacity ratio also continues to increase with age in adults	1,2,5,11,26

Table 3 (continued)
AGE-RELATED CHANGES IN THE LUNG VOLUMES OF MAN

	Ref.
Reports of sex differences in the rate of increase of the residual volume/total lung capacity ratio with age are conflicting, but the most recent data indicate no statistically significant sex difference	23
Deadspace	
Anatomic deadspace volume has been found to increase with age in adults	26
The physiologic deadspace/tidal volume ratio increases with age in adults	27—30
The deadspace/tidal volume ratio is higher in the newborn than in adults, but the adult value is reached by 24 hr of age	31,32
Other lung volumes	
The inspiratory and expiratory reserve volumes both decrease with age in the adult	24
The inspiratory capacity decreases with age in the adult	33

REFERENCES

1. **Needham, C. D., Rogan, M. C., and McDonald, I.,** Normal standards for lung volumes, intrapulmonary gas mixing, and maximum breathing capacity, *Thorax,* 9, 313, 1954.
2. **Helliesen, P. J., Cook, C. D., Friedlander, L., and Agathon, S.,** Studies of respiratory physiology in children. I. Mechanics of respiration and lung volumes in 85 normal children 5 to 17 years of age, *Pediatrics,* 22, 80, 1958.
3. **Drinkwater, B. L., Horvath, S. M., and Wells, C. L.,** Aerobic power of females, ages 10 to 68, *J. Gerontol.,* 30, 385, 1975.
4. **Turner, J. M., Mead, J., and Wohl, M. E.,** Elasticity of human lungs in relation to age, *J. Appl. Physiol.,* 25, 664, 1968.
5. **Muieson, G., Sorbini, C. A., and Grassi, V.,** Respiratory function in the aged, *Bull. Physio-Pathol. Respir.,* 7, 973, 1971.
6. **Bafitis, H. and Sargent, F.,** Human physiological adaptability through the life sequence, *J. Gerontol.,* 32, 402, 1977.
7. **Berglund, E., Birath, G., Bjure, J., Gramby, G., Kjellmer, I., Sandarist, L., and Soderholm, B.,** Spirometric studies in normal subjects. I. Forced expirograms in subjects between 7 and 70 years of age, *Acta Med. Scand.,* 173, 185, 1963.
8. **Donevan, R. E., Palmer, W. H., Varvis, C. J., and Bates, D. V.,** Influence of age on pulmonary diffusing capacity, *J. Appl. Physiol.,* 14, 483, 1959.
9. **Englert, M.,** *Le Resean Capillaire Pulmonaire chez l'homme; Etude Physiopathologie,* Masson, Paris, 1967.
10. **Goldman, H. I. and Becklake, M. R.,** Respiratory function tests: normal values at median altitudes and the prediction of normal results, *Am. Rev. Tuberc.,* 79, 459, 1959.
11. **Shephard, R. J.,** Prediction formulas and normal values for lung volumes: man. I. Standard volumes and capacities, in *Respiration and Circulation,* Altman, P. L. and Dittmer, D. S., Eds., Federation of American Societies for Experimental Biology, Bethesda, 1971, 36.
12. **Emerson, P. W. and Green, H.,** Vital capacity of the lungs of children, *Am. J. Dis. Child.,* 22, 202, 1921.
13. **Stewart, C. A.,** The vital capacity of the lungs of children in health and disease, *Am. J. Dis. Child.,* 24, 451, 1922.

Table 3 (continued)
AGE-RELATED CHANGES IN THE LUNG VOLUMES OF MAN

14. Ferris, B. G., Whittenberger, J. L., and Gallagher, J. R., Maximum breathing capacity and vital capacity of male children and adolescents, *Pediatrics*, 9, 659, 1952.
15. Lyons, H. A., Tanner, R. W., and Picco, T., Pulmonary function studies in children, *Am. J. Dis. Child.*, 100, 196, 1960.
16. Moore, R. E. and Gibson-Williams, M. G., The vital capacity and maximum breathing capacity of adolescent boys, *Great Armond Street Journal*, 1, 137, 1951.
17. Krumholz, R. A., Pulmonary membrane diffusing capacity and pulmonary capillary blood volume: an appraisal of their clinical usefulness, *Am. Rev. Respir. Dis.*, 94, 195, 1966.
18. Seely, J. E., Guzman, C. A., and Becklake, M. R., Heart and lung function at rest and during exercise in adolescence, *J. Appl. Physiol.*, 36, 34, 1974.
19. Cole, T. J., The influence of height on the decline in ventilatory function, *Int. J. Epidemiol.*, 3, 145, 1974.
20. Bates, D. V. and Christie, R. V., Effects of aging on respiratory function in man, *Ciba Found. Colloq. Ageing*, 1, 56, 1955.
21. Taussig, L. M., Harris, T. R., and Lebowitz, M. D., Lung function in infants ad young children, *Am. Rev. Respir. Dis.*, 116, 233, 1977.
22. DeMuth, G. R., Howatt, W. F., and Hill, B., Lung volumes, *Pediatrics*, 35, 162, 1965.
23. Brody, A. W., Johnson, J. R., Townley, R. G., Herrera, H. R., Snider, D., and Campbell, J. C., The residual volume, *Am. Rev. Respir. Dis.*, 109, 98, 1974.
24. Chebotarev, D. F., Korkusko, O. V., and Ivanov, L. A., Mechanisms of hypoxemia in the elderly, *J. Gerontol.*, 29, 393, 1974.
25. Pride, N. B., Pulmonary distensibility in age and disease, *Bull. Physio-Pathol. Respir.*, 10, 103, 1974.
26. Tenney, S. M. and Miller, R. M., Deadspace ventilation in old age, *J. Appl. Physiol.*, 9, 321, 1956.
27. Serrano, S., The pulmonary system in the aged, *Minerva Med.*, 47, 1534, 1956.
28. Cole, R. B. and Bishop, J. M., Effect of varying O_2 tension on alveolar-arterial O_2 tension difference in man, *J. Appl. Physiol.*, 18, 1043, 1963.
29. Raine, J. M. and Bishop, J. M., A-a difference in O_2 tension and physiological deadspace in man, *J. Appl. Physiol.*, 18, 284, 1963.
30. Mellemgaard, K., The alveolar-arterial oxygen difference: its size and components in normal man, *Acta Physiol. Scand.*, 67, 10, 1966.
31. Strang, L. B., Alveolar gas and anatomic deadspace measurements in normal newborn infants, *Clin. Sci.*, 21, 107, 1961.
32. Koch, G., Alveolar ventilation, diffusing capacity, and the A-a $^PO_2$ difference in the newborn infant, *Respir. Physiol.*, 4, 168, 1968.
33. Cohn, J. E. and Donoso, H. D., Mechanical properties of lung in normal men over 60 years old, *J. Clin. Invest.*, 42, 1406, 1963.

Table 4
AGE-RELATED CHANGES IN THE LUNG VOLUMES OF ANIMALS

	Ref.
Total lung capacity	
No significant correlation was found between age and total lung capacity of 22 dogs from 0.8—10.6 years old	1
Vital capacity	
The vital capacity of 22 adult dogs from 0.8—10.6 years was reduced with increasing age	1
The vital capacity of young adult rabbits was larger than that of immature rabbits, but the vital capacity per unit body weight decreased during maturation	2
Functional residual capacity	
No significant relationship was found between functional residual capacity and age in 22 anesthetized dogs from 0.8—10.6 years, but functional residual capacity was significanty larger in 36 dogs 8—10.6 years old than in 50 1-year-old dogs measured without anesthesia	1,3
The functional residual capacity was significantly larger in anesthetized rabbits over 36 months of age than in rabbits from 6—12 months old	4
The functional residual capacity of anesthetized rats has been reported to increase with age between 4 and 18 months and to be higher in rats over 12 months of age than in those younger than 12 months	5,6
Residual volume	
Both residual volume and the residual volume/total lung capacity ratio were found to increase with age in 22 dogs from 0.8—10.6 years old	1
Deadspace	
Alveolar deadspace ventilation as a percent of minute volume was significantly higher in 36 dogs from 8.0—10.5 years of age than in 50 dogs at 1.0 year	3
Other lung volumes	
The inspiratory capacity of adult rabbits was larger than that of immature rabbits, but the inspiratory capacity per unit body weight decreased during maturation	2
The inspiratory capacity and expiratory reserve volume were both decreased with age in 22 dogs from 0.8—10.6 years of age	1

Table 4 (continued)
AGE-RELATED CHANGES IN THE LUNG VOLUMES OF ANIMALS

REFERENCES

1. **Robinson, N. E. and Gillespie, J. R.**, Lung volumes in aging Beagle dogs, *J. Appl. Physiol.*, 35, 317, 1973.
2. **Caldwell, E. J. and Fry, D. L.**, Pulmonary mechanics in the rabbit, *J. Appl. Physiol.*, 27, 280, 1969.
3. **Mauderly, J. L.**, Influence of sex and age on the pulmonary function of the unanesthetized Beagle dog, *J. Gerontol.*, 29, 282, 1974.
4. **Davidson, J. T., Wasserman, K., Lillington, G. A., and Schmidt, W.**, Effect of aging on respiratory mechanics and gas exchange of rabbits, *J. Appl. Physiol.*, 21, 837, 1966.
5. **King, T. K. C.**, Measurements of functional residual capacity in the rat, *J. Appl. Physiol.*, 21, 233, 1966.
6. **Johanson, K. G. and Pierce, A. K.**, Lung structure and function with age in normal rats and rats with papain emphysema, *J. Clin. Invest.*, 52, 2921, 1973.

Table 5
AGE-RELATED CHANGES IN LUNG AND CHEST WALL MECHANICS OF MAN

	Ref.
Pressure-volume relationships	
Both static and dynamic lung compliance increase in proportion to height and lung volume during growth from 5—17 years of age	1—4
The deflation pressure-volume curve of the lung shifts to the right with growth from 6—17 years of age	4
The lung pressure-volume curve of adults shifts to the left with age and the lung elastic recoil pressure becomes less with age at lung volumes above functional residual capacity	3,5—9
The fraction of the total work of breathing related to overcoming lung elastic forces decreases with age	10
Dynamic lung compliance decreases and the difference between static and dynamic lung compliance increases with age in adults	7,11,12
Dynamic lung compliance becomes more frequency-dependent with age in adults	13,14
The chest wall becomes less mobile and chest wall compliance is reduced with age in adults	15,16
Pressure-flow relationships	
Resistance to airflow decreases with age during growth, but the decrease is primarily related to an increase in lung volume with age rather than to age itself	1,2,17
Airway conductance increases with lung volume during growth and rises sharply at about 5 years of age	18,19
Specific airway conductance decreases with age during growth because lung volume increases faster than conductance	19
There are conflicting reports of increasing and decreasing resistance with age in adults and thus there appears to be no clear age-related trend	7
Forced expiration	
The forced expiratory volume and percent of vital capacity expired in 1 sec and maximal midexpiratory flow rates all increase with growth during childhood and adolescence; females reach peak adult values at 14—20 years and males at 18—27 years of age	20—23
The timed forced expiratory volumes and midexpiratory flow indices are all reduced with age in adults after peak values are reached	7,24—26
The rate of decline of the forced expiratory indices with age is more rapid in males than females	27
The rate of decline of the forced expiratory indices becomes more rapid after the age of 60 years	28
Airway closure	
The closing volume as a percent of vital capacity is reduced during growth to a minimal value at approximately 18 years of age	29

Table 5 (continued)
AGE-RELATED CHANGES IN LUNG AND CHEST WALL MECHANICS OF MAN

	Ref.
The single-breath alveolar plateau (Phase III) of subjects between 7 and 16 years of age is much flatter and the cardiogenic oscillations are more damped than those of adults	30
Closing volume, closing capacity, and closing voume as a fraction of the vital capacity or functional residual capacity all increase with age in adults due to loss of lung elastic recoil, changes in the small airways, and changes in vertical pleural pressure gradients	29—36
The slope of the single-breath alveolar plateau (Phase III) of adults becomes steeper with age	30
Airway closure occurs at or above the functional residual capacity at 65—66 years of age in seated subjects	6,33,37,38
In older adults, the closing volume or closing capacity as a percent of vital capacity is higher in the supine position than when standing and the closing volume when supine exceeds the functional residual capacity at 44—45 years of age	32,36,38

REFERENCES

1. **Cook, C. D., Hellisen, P. J., and Agathon, S.,** Relation between mechanics of respiration, lung size, and body size from birth to young adulthood, *J. Appl. Physiol.*, 13, 349, 1958.
2. **Hellisen, P. J., Cook, C. D., Friedlander, L., and Agathon, S.,** Studies of respiratory physiology in children. I. Mechanics of respiration and lung volumes in 85 normal children 5 to 17 years of age, *Pediatrics*, 22, 80, 1958.
3. **Frank, R. and McIlroy, M. B.,** Pulmonary compliance. I. In relation to age and size: man, in *Respiration and Circulation*, Altman, P. L. and Dittmer, D. S., Eds., Federation of American Societies for Experimental Biology, Bethesda, 1971, 93.
4. **Zapletal, A., Paul, T., and Samanek, M.,** Pulmonary elasticity in children and adolescents, *J. Appl. Physiol.*, 40, 953, 1976.
5. **Hartung, W.,** Die altersveranderungen der lungenelastizitat nach messungen an isolierten leichenluungen, *Beitr. Pathol. Anat. Allg. Pathol.*, 118, 368, 1957.
6. **Holland, J., Milic-Emili, J., Macklem, P. T., and Bates, D. J.,** Regional distribution of pulmonary ventilation and perfusion in elderly subjects, *J. Clin. Invest.*, 47, 81, 1968.
7. **Muiesan, G., Sorbini, C. A., and Grassi, V.,** Respiratory function in the aged, *Bull. Physio-Pathol. Respir.*, 7, 973, 1971.
8. **Pride, N.B.,** Pulmonary distensibility in age and disease, *Bull. Physio-Pathol. Respir.*, 10, 103, 1974.
9. **Gibson, G. J. and Pride, N. B.,** Lung distensibility, the static pressure-volume curve of the lungs and its use in clinical assessment, *Br. J. Dis. Chest*, 70, 143, 1976.
10. **Bates, D. V. and Christie, R. V.,** Effects of aging on respiratory function in man, *Ciba Found. Colloq. Ageing*, 1, 56, 1955.
11. **Butler, J., Caro, C. G., Alcala, R., and DuBois, A. B.,** Physiological factors affecting airway resistance in normal subjects and in patients with obstructive respiratory disease, *J. Clin. Invest.*, 39, 584, 1960.
12. **Grandillo, F., Cicala, V., Rambald , ., and Imparato, B.,** Studio della meccania polmonare in soggetti aduli e vecchi normali e in soggetti con disordini volumetrici di tripo restrittiva e obsruttivo, *Gerontology*, 13, 1051, 1965.
13. **Cohn, J. E. and Donoso, H. D.,** Mechanical properties of lung in normal men over 60 years old, *J. Clin. Invest.*, 42, 1406, 1963.

Table 5 (continued)
AGE-RELATED CHANGES IN LUNG AND CHEST WALL MECHANICS OF MAN

14. **DuBois, A. B. and Alcala, R.**, Airway resistance and mechanics of breathing in normal subjects 75 to 90 years of age, in *Aging of the Lung*, Cander, L. and Moyer, J. H., Eds., Grune and Stratton, New York, 1964, 156.
15. **Mittman, C., Edelman, N. H., Norris, A. H., and Shock, N. W.**, Relationship between chest wall and pulmonary compliance, *J. Appl. Physiol.*, 20, 1211, 1965.
16. **Rizzato, G. and Marazzini, L.**, Thoracoabdominal mechanics in elderly men, *J. Appl. Physiol.*, 28, 457, 1970.
17. **Briscoe, W. A. and DuBois, A. B.**, The relationship between airway resistance, airway conductance, and lung volume in subjects of different age and body size, *J. Clin. Invest.*, 37, 1279, 1958.
18. **Hogg, J. C., Williams, J., Richardson, J. B., Macklem, P. T., and Thurlbeck, M. B.**, Age as a factor in the distribution of lower airway conductance and in the pathologic anatomy of obstructive lung disease, *N. Engl. J. Med.*, 282, 1283, 1970.
19. **Stocks, J. and Godfrey, S.**, Specific airway conductance in relation to postconceptual age during infancy, *J. Appl. Physiol.*, 43, 144, 1977.
20. **Berglund, E., Birath, G., Bjure, J., Gramby, G., Kjellmer, I., Sandarist, L., and Soderholm, B.**, Spirometric studies in normal subjects. I. Forced expirograms in subjects between 7 and 70 years of age, *Acta Med. Scand.*, 173, 185, 1963.
21. **Lawther, P. J., Brooks, A. G. F., and Waller, R. E.**, Respiratory function measurements in a cohort of medical students, *Thorax*, 25, 172, 1970.
22. **Dickman, M. L., Schmidt, C. D., and Gardner, R. M.**, Spirometric standards for normal children and adolescents, ages 5 through 18 years, *Am. Rev. Respir. Dis.*, 104, 680, 1971.
23. **Knudson, R. J., Slatin, R. C., Lebowitz, M. D., and Burrows, B.**, The maximal expiratory flow-volume curve, *Am. Rev. Respir. Dis.*, 113, 587, 1976.
24. **Michie, I.**, Lung function in the elderly, *Gerontol. Clin.*, 13, 125, 1971.
25. **Chebotarev, D. F., Korkuskc, O. V., and Ivanov, L. A.**, Mechanisms of hypoxemia in the elderly, *J. Gerontol.*, 29, 393, 1974.
26. **Gelb, A. F. and Zamel, N.**, Effect of aging on lung mechanics of healthy nonsmokers, *Chest*, 68, 538, 1975.
27. **Ashley, F., Kannel, W. B., Sorlie, P. D., and Masson, R.**, Pulmonary function: relation to aging, cigarette habit and mortality, *Ann. Intern. Med.*, 82, 739, 1975.
28. **Pollock, M. L., Miller, H. S., and Wilmore, J.**, Physiological characteristics of champion American track athletes 40 to 75 years of age, *J. Gerontol.*, 29, 645, 1974.
29. **Mansell, A., Bryan, C., and Levison, H.**, Airway closure in children, *J. Appl. Physiol.*, 33, 711, 1972.
30. **Anthonisen, N. R., Danson, J., Robertson, P. C., and Ross, W. R. D.**, Airway closure as a function of age, *Respir. Physiol.*, 8, 58, 1969/70.
31. **McCarthy, D. S., Spencer, R., Greene, R., and Milic-Emili, J.**, Measurement of closing volume as a simple and sensitive test for early detection of small airway disease, *Am. J. Med.*, 52, 747, 1972.
32. **Nishida, O., Sewake, N., Takano, M., Yoshimi, T., Kuraoka, T., and Nishimoto, Y.**, Effects of age an body position on argon closing volume, *Hiroshima J. Med. Sci.*, 23, 255, 1974.
33. **Ruff, F.**, Effects of age and posture on closing volume, *Scand. J. Respir. Dis. Suppl.*, 85, 190, 1974.
34. **Collins, J. V., Clark, T. J. H., and Brown, D. J.**, Airway function in healthy subjects and patients with left heart disease, *Clin. Sci. Mol. Med.*, 49, 217, 1975.
35. **Bode, F. R., Dosman, J., Martin, R., Ghezzo, H., and Macklem, P. T.**, Age and sex differences in lung elasticity and in closing capacity in nonsmokers, *J. Appl. Physiol.*, 41, 129, 1976.
36. **Ohtsuka, H., Soma, K., Takahashi, T., and Tomita, T.**, Pulmonary gas exchange function of supine elderly subjects in relation to closing volumes, *Respir. Circ.*, 24, 329, 1976.
37. **Bates, D. V., Macklem, P. T., and Christie, R. V.**, Regional distribution of pulmonary ventilation and perfusion in elderly subjects, *J. Clin. Invest.*, 47, 81, 1968.
38. **Leblanc, P., Ruff, F., and Milic-Emili, J.**, Effect of age and body position on airway closure in man, *J. Appl. Physiol.*, 28, 448, 1970.

Table 6
AGE-RELATED CHANGES IN LUNG AND CHEST WALL MECHANICS OF ANIMALS

	Ref.
Pressure-volume relationships	
The static compliance of excised rat lungs increases with age from 4—18 months, but dynamic lung compliance is lower in rats over 12 months old than in rats under 12 months	1,2
Both lung and chest wall compliance of rabbits increase with growth to maturity and the static lung compliance of rabbits 3—5 years old is higher than that of 6—12-month-old rabbits	3,4
There is a decrease in elastic recoil pressure and a shift to the left of the pressure-volume curve in dogs over 8 years of age compared to dogs aged from 4—8 years, and chest wall compliance of dogs is increased with age; dynamic lung compliance; however, is significantly lower in dogs over 8 years of age than in 1-year-old dogs	5,6
Pressure-flow relationships	
No significant difference was found in airway resistance of rats over 12 months old as compared to that of rats under 12 months of age	2
Airway resistance of 3—5-year-old rabbits was higher than that of 6—12-month-old rabbits	4
Airway resistance of dogs over 8 years of age was found to be higher than that of 1-year-old dogs	6

REFERENCES

1. **Johanson, W. G. and Pierce, A. K.,** Lung structure and function with age in normal rats and rats with papain emphysema, *J. Clin. Invest.,* 52, 2921, 1973.
2. **King, T. K. C.,** Mechanical properties of the lungs in the rat, *J. Appl. Physiol.,* 21, 259, 1966.
3. **Caldwell, E. J. and Fry, D. L.,** Pulmonary mechanics in the rabbit, *J. Appl. Physiol.,* 27, 280, 1969.
4. **Davidson, J. T., Wasserman, K., Lillington, G. A., and Schmidt, W.,** Effect of aging on respiratory mechanics and gas exchange of rabbits, *J. Appl. Physiol.,* 21, 837, 1966.
5. **Robinson, N. E. and Gillespie, J. R.,** Lung volumes in aging Beagle dogs, *J. Appl. Physiol.,* 35, 317, 1973.
6. **Mauderly, J. L.,** Influence of sex and age on the pulmonary function of the unanesthetized Beagle dog, *J. Gerontol.,* 29, 282, 1974.

Table 7
AGE-RELATED CHANGES IN VENTILATION AND VENTILATION-PERFUSION RELATIONSHIPS IN MAN

	Ref.
Breathing patterns	
Tidal and minute volume increase and respiratory frequency and minute volume per unit body surface area decrease with age until late adolescence	1
There are conflicting reports on changes in respiratory frequency with age in adults and it appears that there is little, if any, significant age effect in normal subjects at rest	1—3
The literature appears to indicate a trend toward increasing minute volume with age in adults, although the effect is neither marked nor consistent	1,2,4,5
The minute volume during exercise is increased with age in adults	6—8
Maximal ventilatory effort	
The maximum breathing capacity increases linearly with increasing lung volume during growth through childhood and adolescence	9—11
The maximum breathing capacity and maximum voluntary ventilation decrease with age in adults	3,11—18
The maximum breathing capacity and maximum voluntary ventilation of males decreases at more rapid rate with age than that of females	13,14,16,17
Intrapulmonary gas mixing	
Intrapulmonary gas mixing becomes less efficient and the distribution of inspired gas becomes less uniform with age in adults, whether measured by single or multiple breath techniques	3,19—22
Ventilation-perfusion balance	
Two authors, using alveolar-arterial nitrogen gradients and radioisotopic scanning, reported finding no significant age-related changes in ventilation-perfusion balance in adults	23,24
Three authors, using analysis of expired gas, radioisotopic scanning, and alveolar arterial nitrogen gradients have reported finding ventilation-perfusion imbalances in older adults	25—27
Pulmonary blood flow in the upper lung regions has been reported to be increased in subjects over 65 years of age	26
Control of ventilation	
The magnitude of ventilatory responses to hypoxia and hypercapnia is reduced in older adults	28,29

REFERENCES

1. **Robinson, S.,** Experimental studies of physical fitness in relation to age, *Arbeitsphysiologie,* 10, 251, 1938.
2. **deVries, H. A. and Adams, G. M.,** Comparison of exercise responses in old and young men. II. Ventilatory mechanics, *J. Gerontol.,* 27, 349, 1972.

Table 7 (continued)
AGE-RELATED CHANGES IN VENTILATION AND VENTILATION-PERFUSION RELATIONSHIPS IN MAN

3. **Chebotarev, D. F., Korkusko, O. V., and Ivanov, L. A.,** Mechanisms of hypoxemia in the elderly, *J. Gerontol.*, 29, 393, 1974.
4. **Tenney, S. M. and Miller, R. M.,** Dead space ventilation in old age, *J. Appl. Physiol.*, 9, 321, 1956.
5. **Robinson, S., Dill, D. B., Tzankoff, S. P., Wagner, J. A., and Robinson, R. D.,** Longtudinal studies of aging in 37 men, *J. Appl. Physiol.*, 38, 263, 1975.
6. **Norris, A. H., Shock, N. W., and Wiengst, M. J.,** Age differences in ventilatory and gas exchange responses to graded exercise in males, *J. Gerontol.*, 10, 145, 1955.
7. **Durnin, J. V. G. A. and Mikulicic, V.,** The influence of graded exercises on the oxygen consumption, pulmonary ventilation, and heart rate of young and elderly men, *Q. J. Exp. Physiol.*, 41, 442, 1956.
8. **Gibelli, A., Morpurgo, M., Giarola, P., Beulcke, G., Casaccia, M., Petrini, C., and Rampulla, C.,** Comparative study of coagulation, fibrinolysis and cardiorespiratory function in elderly and young subjects after exercise, *J. Am. Geriatr. Soc.*, 20, 59, 1972.
9. **Moore, R. E. and Gibson-Williams, M. G.,** The vital capacity and maximum breathing capacity of adolescent boys, *Great Armond Street J.*, 1, 137, 1951.
10. **Ferris, B. G., Whittenberger, J. L., and Gallagher, J. R.,** Maximum breathing capacity and vital capacity of male children and adolescents, *Pediatrics*, 9, 659, 1952.
11. **Bafitis, H. and Sargent, F.,** Human physiological adaptability through the life sequence, *J. Gerontol.*, 32, 402, 1977.
12. **Goldman, H. I. and Becklake, M. R.,** Respiratory function tests, normal values at median altitudes and the prediction of normal results, *Am. Rev. Tuberc.*, 79, 457, 1959.
13. **Birath, G., Kjellmer, I., and Sandquist, L.,** Spirometric studies in normal subjects. II. Ventilatory capacity tests in adults, *Acta Med. Scand.*, 173, 193, 1963.
14. **Grimby, G. and Soderholm, B.,** Spirometric studies in normal subjects. III. Static lung volumes and maximum voluntary ventilation in adults with a note on physical fitness, *Acta Med. Scand.*, 173, 199, 1963.
15. **Anderson, T. W., Brown, J. R., Hall, J. W., and Shephard, J. T.,** The limitations of linear regressions for the prediction of vital capacity and forced expiratory volume, *Respiration*, 25, 140, 1968.
16. **Ericsson, P. and Irnell, L.,** Effect of five years aging in ventilatory capacity and physical work capacity in elderly people, *Acta Med. Scand.*, 185, 193, 1969.
17. **Akgun, N. and Ozgonul, H.,** Spirometric studies on normal turkish subjects aged 21 to 40 years, *Respiration*, 28, 54, 1972.
18. **Shephard, R. J.,** Prediction formulas and normal values for maximal ventilation: man, in *Respiration and Circulation*, Altman, P. L. and Dittmer, D. S., Eds., Federation of American Societies for Experimental Biology, Bethesda, 1971, 46.
19. **Sandquist, L. and Kjellmer, I.,** Normal values for the single breath nitrogen elimination test in different age groups, *Scand. J. Clin. Lab. Invest.*, 12, 131, 1960.
20. **Edelman, N. H., Mittman, C., Norris, A. H., and Shock, N. W.,** Effects of respiratory pattern on age differences in ventilation uniformity, *J. Appl. Physiol.*, 24, 49, 1968.
21. **Shephard, R. J.,** Indexes of gas mixing efficiency in pulmonary respiration: man, in *Respiration and Circulation*, Altman, P. L.O and Dittmer, D. S., Eds., Federation of American Societies for Experimental Biology, Bethesda, 1971, 49.
22. **Muiesan, G., Sorbini, C. A., and Grassi, V.,** Respiratory function in the aged, *Bull. Physio-Pathol. Respir.*, 7, 973, 1971.
23. **Bachofen, H., Hobi, H. J., and Scherrer, M.,** Alveolar-arterial N_2 gradients at rest and during exercise in healthy men of different ages, *J. Appl. Physiol.*, 34, 137, 1973.
24. **Kronenberg, R. S., Drage, C. W., Ponto, R. A., and Williams, L. E.,** The effect of age on the distribution of ventilation and perfusion in the lung, *Am. Rev. Respir. Dis.*, 108, 576, 1973.
25. **Read, J.,** Pulmonary ventilation and perfusion in normal subjects and in patients with emphysema, *Clin. Sci.*, 18, 465, 1959.
26. **Holland, J., Milic-Emili, J., Macklem, P. T., and Bates, D. V.,** Regional distribution of pulmonary ventilation and perfusion in elderly subjects, *J. Clin. Invest.*, 47, 81, 1968.
27. **Corbet, A. J. S., Ross, J. A., and Beaudry, P. H.,** The effect of age on arterial-alveolar nitrogen difference in normal adults, *Can. J. Physiol. Pharmacol.*, 53, 63, 1975.
28. **Patrick, J. M. and Howard, A.,** The influence of age, sex, body size, and lung size on the control and pattern of breathing during CO_2 inhalation in caucasians, *Respir. Physiol.*, 16, 337, 1972.
29. **Kronenberg, R. S. and Drage, C. W.,** Attenuation of the ventilatory and heart rate responses to hypoxia and hypercapnia with aging in normal men, *J. Clin. Invest.*, 52, 1812, 1973.

Table 8
AGE-RELATED CHANGES IN VENTILATION IN ANIMALS

	Ref.
Breathing patterns	
The tidal volume of rabbits increases with age during growth to maturity, but the tidal volume per unit body weight decreases	1
The respiratory frequency of rats decreases during growth until maturity, then remains constant; tidal and minute volume increase with age in both immature and mature rats; the minute volume per unit body weight decreases throughout life	2
The respiratory frequency of adult dogs increases with age while the tidal and minute volume decrease, but only the change in tidal volume was significant	3
Intrapulmonary gas mixing	
The multiple breath nitrogen washout efficiency of 10-year-old dogs is significantly less than that of 1-year-old dogs	3,4
Control of ventilation	
The degree of bronchoconstriction resulting from injection of acetylcholine into the bronchial artery is less in dogs over 4 years old than in dogs under 4 years	5

REFERENCES

1. **Caldwell, E. J. and Fry, D. L.**, Pulmonary mechanics in the rabbit, *J. Appl. Physiol.*, 27, 280, 1969.
2. **Leong, K. J., Dowd, G. F., and MacFarland, H. N.**, A new technique for tidal volume measurement in unanesthetized small animals, *Can. J. Physiol. Pharmacol.*, 42, 189, 1964.
3. **Mauderly, J. L.**, Influence of sex and age on the pulmonary function of the unanesthetized beagle dog, *J. Gerontol.*, 29, 282, 1974.
4. **Mauderly, J. L.**, A new technique for evaluating nitrogen washout efficiency, *Am. J. Vet. Res.*, 38, 69, 1977.
5. **Fukuchi, Y.**, Aging of the bronchial tree and bronchial vascular system. III. Effect of aging on intrinsic regulatory mechanism of the bronchial tree, *Jpn. J. Geriatr.*, 9, 19, 1972.

Table 9
AGE-RELATED CHANGES IN GAS EXCHANGE IN MAN

	Ref.
Pulmonary diffusing capacity	
The carbon monoxide diffusing capacity per unit lung volume increases from birth to 24 hr and then remains constant until adulthood	1
Both the oxygen and carbon monoxide diffusing capacity at rest and during exercise are reduced with age in adults	2—5
The membrane factor (Dm) in carbon monoxide diffusing capacity is reduced with age in adults	6,7
The rate of decline in diffusing capacity with age is more rapid in males than in females	5
Alveolar-capillary oxygen and carbon dioxide transfer	
The alveolar-arterial oxygen tension difference of adults increases with age, but the alveolar oxygen tension remains relatively constant	5,8—10
The alveolar-arterial carbon dioxide tension difference has also been reported to increase with age in adults	11
Arterial oxygen tension	
The arterial oxygen tension decreases with age in adults	5,10
The decrease in oxygen tension with age is evident during either air or oxygen breathing	12
The arterial oxygen content and oxygen saturation of hemoglobin have also been found to be lower in older adults	10
The arterial oxygen tension of older subjects is more markedly reduced by going from the standing to the supine position than in younger adults	13
Oxygen consumption	
The basal oxygen consumption decreases with age in adults	14,15
Maximal oxygen consumption increases from birth until 16—18 years of age	16
Maximal oxygen consumption decreases with age during adulthood	5,16,17
The rate of oxygen consumption at a given work or exercise level is increased in older adults	10
The ratio of oxygen consumption to minute volume is decreased both at rest and during exercise in older adults	5,14,15,17

Table 9 (continued)
AGE-RELATED CHANGES IN GAS EXCHANGE IN MAN

REFERENCES

1. **Koch, G.,** Lung function and acid-base balance in the newborn infant, *Acta Paediatr. Scand. Suppl.,* 81, 1968.
2. **Cohn, J. E., Carroll, D. G., Armstrong, B. W., Shepard, R. N., and Riley, R. L.,** Maximal diffusing capacity of the lung in normal male subjects of different ages, *J. Appl. Physiol.,* 6, 558, 1954.
3. **Donevan, R. E., Palmer, W. H., Varvis, C. J., and Bates, D. V.,** Influence of age on pulmonary diffusing capacity, *J. Appl. Physiol.,* 14, 483, 1959.
4. **Sherrer, M. and Birchler, A.,** Altersabhangigkeit des alveolo-arteriellen O_2 partialdruckgradienten bei schewarbeit in normoxie, hypoxie und hyperoxie, *Med. Thorac.,* 24, 99, 1967.
5. **Muiesan, G., Sorbini, C. A., and Grassi, V.,** Respiratory function in the aged, *Bull. Physio-Pathol. Respir.,* 7, 973, 1971.
6. **Hamer, N. A. J.,** The effect of age on the components of the pulmonary diffusing capacity, *Clin. Sci.,* 23, 85, 1962.
7. **Frans, A. and Brasseur, L.,** La mesure de la capacite de diffusion de la membrane alveola-capillaire (Dm) et du volume capillaire pulmonaire (Vc) Chez 65 volontaires normaux du sexe masculin, *Bull. Physio-Pathol. Respir.,* 4, 635, 1968.
8. **Terman, J. W. and Newton, J. L.,** Changes in alveolar and arterial gas tensions as related to altitude and age, *J. Appl. Physiol.,* 19, 21, 1964.
9. **Mellemgaard, K.,** The alveolar-arterial oxygen difference: it's size and components in normal man, *Acta Physiol. Scand.,* 67, 10, 1966.
10. **Chebotarev, D. F., Korkusko, O. V., and Ivanov, L. A.,** Mechanisms of hypoxemia in the elderly, *J. Gerontol.,* 29, 393, 1974.
11. **Bachofen, H., Hobi, H. J., and Scherrer, M.,** Alveolar-arterial N_2 gradients at rest and during exercise in healthy men of different ages, *J. Appl. Physiol.,* 34, 137, 1973.
12. **Kitamura, H., Sawa, T., and Ikezono, E.,** Postoperative hypoxemia: the contribution of age to the maldistribution of ventilation, *Anesthesiology,* 36, 244, 1972.
13. **Ostsuka, H., Soma, K., Takahashi, T., and Tomita, T.,** Pulmonary gas exchange function of supine elderly subjects in relation to closing volumes, *Respir. Circ.,* 24, 329, 1976.
14. **Baldwin, E. Cournand, D., and Richards, D. W.,** Pulmonary insufficiency, physiological classification, clinical methods of analysis, and standard volumes in normal subjects, *Medicine,* 27, 243, 1948.
15. **Gibelli, A., Morpurgo, M., Giarola, P., Beulcke, G., Casaccia, M., Petrini, C., and Rampulla, C.,** Comparative study of coagulation, fibrinolysis and cardiorespiratory function in elderly and young subjects after exercise, *J. Am. Geriatr. Soc.,* 20, 59, 1972.
16. **Astrand, P. O.,** Physical performance as a function of age, *J. Am. Med. Assoc.,* 205, 729, 1968.
17. **Robinson, S., Dill, D. B., Tzankoff, S. P., Wagner, J. A., and Robinson, R. D.,** Longitudinal studies of aging in 37 men, *J. Appl. Physiol.,* 38, 263, 1975.

Table 10
AGE-RELATED CHANGES IN GAS EXCHANGE IN ANIMALS

	Ref.
The carbon monoxide diffusing capacity of rats increased from 4 to 18 months of age	1
The carbon monoxide diffusing capacity of 8- to 10.5-year-old dogs was significantly lower than in 1-year-old dogs	2
The alveolar-arterial oxygen and carbon dioxide tension differences of 8- to 10.5-year-old dogs were larger than those of 1-year-old dogs	2
No significant age-related differences were found in arterial oxygen and carbon dioxide tensions of rabbits aged 6 to 12 months and 3 to 5 years	3
The arterial oxygen tension and pH were slightly decreased and arterial carbon dioxide tension was slightly increased in 8- to 10.5-year-old dogs as compared to 1-year-old dogs	2
There was a progressive increase in resting oxygen consumption with age among groups of dogs at 1 year, 3 to 4 years, and 8 to 10.5 years of age	2

REFERENCES

1. **Johanson, W. G. and Pierce, A. K.**, Lung structure and functions with age in normal rats and rats with papain emphysema, *J. Clin. Invest.*, 52, 2921, 1973.
2. **Mauderly, J. L.**, Influence of sex and age on the pulmonary function of the unanesthetized Beagle dog, *J. Gerontol.*, 29, 282, 1974.
3. **Davidson, J. T., Wasserman, K., Lillington, G. A., and Schmidt, W.**, Effect of aging on respiratory mechanics and gas exchange of rabbits, *J. Appl. Physiol.*, 21, 837, 1966.

GAS TRANSPORT

R. D. Woodson

Table 1
EFFECT OF AGE ON ARTERIAL PO₂ AND PCO₂

Species	Age	Sex	N	PaO₂ (mm Hg, $\overline{X}\pm SD$)	PaCO₂ (mm Hg, $\overline{X}\pm SD$)	PaO₂ — Age regression	Remarks	Ref.
Man	18—30 years	M,F	38	94.2±3.3	39.0±1.8	PaO₂ = 109.0—0.43 (age) (r = −0.91; p<0.001)	Healthy, nonsmoking subjects; arterial blood	1
	31—40 years	M,F	30	87.2±3.5	38.5±2.0			
	41—50 years	M,F	30	83.9±4.1	39.6±2.4			
	51—60 years	M,F	30	81.2±3.7	39.0±1.9			
	>60 years	M,F	24	74.3±4.4	39.8±2.1			
Man	18—30 years	M,F	117	93.7±6.6		Not linear	Basically healthy subjects; presumably includes smokers and mild emphysema in older groups; capillary blood	2
	31—40 years	M,F	79	84.5±8.7				
	41—50 years	M,F	99	80.1±7.6				
	51—60 years	M,F	66	76.9±5.6				
	>60 years	M,F	29	70.0—				
Man	43±17 years	F	65			PaO₂ = 109.5—0.31 (age) (r = −0.47; p<0.001)	Pre-operative patients; FEV₁ >70%; includes smokers; arterial blood	3
	45±16 years	M	86			PaO₂ = 114.8—0.41 (age) (r = −0.53; p<0.001)		
Dog (beagle)	12—14 months	M	50	75±5	41±3		Healthy, unanesthetized, restrained; arterial blood	4
		F	50	76±5	40±3			
	3—4 years	M	10	77±3	37±2			
		F	10	77±6	37±4			
	8—10.5 years	F	36	73±7	41±3			
Rabbit	6—12 years	?	19	88	33.5		Healthy, unanesthetized; arterial blood	5
	3—5 years	?	29	99	29.5			

Table 1 (continued)
EFFECT OF AGE ON ARTERIAL PO₂ AND PCO₂

REFERENCES

1. Sorbini, C. A., Grassi, V., Solinas, E., and Muiesan, G., Arterial oxygen tension in relation to age in healthy subjects, *Respiration* 25, 3, 1968.
2. Loew, P. G. and Thews, G., Die Altersabhangigkeit des arteriellen Sauerstoffdruckes bei der berufstatigen Bevolkerung, *Klin. Wochenschr.*, 21, 1093, 1962.
3. Diament, M. L. and Palmer, K. N. V., An analysis of pre-operative PaO₂ in a general surgical population, *Thorax*, 24, 126, 1969.
4. Mauderly, J. L., Influence of sex and age on the pulmonary function of the unanesthetized beagle dog, *J. Gerontol.*, 29, 282, 1974.
5. Davidson, J. T., Wasserman, K., Lillington, G., and Schmidt, R. W., Effect of aging on respiratory mechanics and gas exchange in rabbits, *J. Appl. Physiol.*, 21, 837, 1966.

Table 2
EFFECT OF AGE ON 2,3-DIPHOSPHOGLYCERATE AND BLOOD OXYGEN AFFINITY

Species	Age	Sex	N	Hemoglobin (g/l, $\bar{X}\pm SD$)	DPG (M/M Hb, $\bar{X}\pm SD$)	$P_{50}{}^a$ (mm Hg, $\bar{X}\pm SD$)	Smokers included	Ref.
Man	18—39 years	M,F	27	141±12	0.94±0.12	27.4±1.1	?	1
	40—59 years	M,F	10	148±8	0.87±0.10	27.9±0.7		
	60—89 years	M,F	25	137±11	0.93±0.10	29.3±1.1		
Man	1—10 years	M,F	37	155±10 (20)	1.11±0.23		?	2
	11—20 years	M,F	62	152±12 (29)	0.99±0.21			
	21—30 years	M,F	139	149±20 (70)	0.91±0.30			
	31—40 years	M,F	91	143±16 (42)	0.88±0.26			
	41—50 years	M,F	78	153±16 (41)	0.90±0.27			
	51—60 years	M,F	100	147±19 (61)	0.91±0.29			
	61—70 years	M,F	97	149±18 (44)	0.84±0.21			
	71—80 years	M,F	98	147±15 (43)	0.83±0.28			
	81—86 years	M,F	43	146±11 (19)	0.84±0.22			
Man	18—24 years	M,F	53	150±10 (36)	0.46±0.10		Yes	3
	25—34 years	M,F	44	154±6 (36)	0.93±0.08			
	35—44 years	M,F	21	156±6 (14)	0.92±0.10			
	45—54 years	M,F	17	146±3 (8)	0.92±0.10			
	55—64 years	M,F	11	151±3 (6)	0.96±0.12			

	65—74 years	M,F	56	153±13 (26)	139±8 (30)	0.89±0.12
	75—84 years	M,F	104	148±9 (46)	139±8 (58)	0.90±0.15
	≥85 years	M,F	16	151±8 (4)	141±11 (12)	0.83±0.13
Rat	2 months	M	14	151±26		1.16±0.11
	12 months	M	10	149±6		1.19±0.16
	24 months	M	11	141±13		1.09±0.14
	40 months	M	9	135±27	—	1.70±0.33 [4]

Note: The position of the blood oxyhemoglobin dissociation curve is expressed as the P_{50}, which is the PO_2 at which 50% of hemoglobin is O_2 saturated. Information on changes in 2,3-diphosphoglycerate and P_{50} with aging is relatively limited. Major variables which affect both, some of which may change with aging, are generally not given.

[a] At pH 7.4, 37°C.

REFERENCES

1. **Tweeddale, P. M., Leggett, R. J. E., and Flenley, D. C.**, Effect of age on oxygen-binding in normal human subjects, *Clin. Sci. Mol. Med.*, 51, 185, 1976.
2. **Kalofoutis, A., Paterakis, S., Koutselinis, A., and Spanos, V.**, Relationship between erythrocyte 2,3-diphosphoglycerate and age in a normal population, *Clin. Chem.*, 22, 918, 1976.
3. **Purcell, Y. and Broxovic, B.**, Red cell 2,3-diphosphoglycerate concentration in man decreases with age, *Nature (London)*, 251, 511, 1974.
4. **Martin, G., Connors, J. M., McGrath, James J., and Freeman, J.**, Altitude-induced erythrocytic 2,3-DPG and hemoglobin changes in rats of various ages, *J. Appl. Physiol.*, 39, 258, 1975.

UTILIZATION OF O₂ BY TISSUES

H. Wohlrab

Table 1
AGE-RELATED CHANGES IN O₂ UTILIZATION BY ORGANISMS, ORGANS, AND TISSUES

	Ref.
Whole body	
From age 10 throughout life, there is a linear decrease of maximal oxygen intake of 0.40 mℓ/kg·min/year of life in human males	1
It is highly probable that the apparent reduction in basal metabolism is only a reflection of tissue loss with advancing age	2
There is evidence that aging is associated with a progressive decrease in the relative weight of those organs that have the highest metabolic rate; thus in the Sprague-Dawley rat, the decline in liver, brain, heart, and kidney per body weight between 30 and 120 days account for 50% of the decline in basal metabolic rate (BMR)	3
Among male Sprague-Dawley rats (58 days vs. 700 days), there is a significantly greater mortality among young rats after exposure to acute hypoxia	4
Eighteen hormones were considered; only changes in age, T_3, and T_4 affect the minimal oxygen consumption (MOC) among the approximate 70 experimental variables studied in this paper (Zivic-Miller rats)	5
The MOC of the female Zivic-Miller rat declines from 2.45 (3 weeks old) to 1.14 (75 weeks old) (mℓ O₂ per 100 g body weight per min)	6,7
Feeding female C_{57} BL/6J mice a lower protein diet, increases the oxygen consumption in aged animals from 2.50—2.85 (12 months) and 2.54—3.17 (27 months) (mℓ O₂ per g), respectively, at 26 and 4% casein	8
Steady decline in oxygen consumption (minimal stress and activity) from 365—780 days of age in the C_{57} BL/6 mouse	9
Heart	
In working heart preparation (Fisher 344 rats) the oxygen consumption decreases in proportion to tissue mass by about 15% between 5 and 24 months	10
With reduction of perfusate PaO₂, oxygen consumption per g dry weight was lower in hearts of 24—27 months compared to 12-month-old Wistar nonbreeder rats	11
The endogenous respiration of heart slices decreases from 4.4—2.3 $\mu\ell$ O₂ per hr/mg dry weight in Wistar rats from 6—8 to 24—25 months old	12
Muscles (other than heart)	
The cellular respiration in skeletal muscle is reduced with age	13
The endogenous tissue respiration in quadriceps femoris decreases in Wistar rats between 6—8 to 24—25 months old	12
There occurs a decrease in aerobic oxidative enzymes in the slow soleus muscle and no change in the diaphragm or the fast extensor digitorum longus muscle during aging of the Wistar strain rat	14
The percent of red muscle fibers (oxidative enzymes) decreases in the diaphragm muscle of the guinea pig with age, i.e., a decline from 86—65% from 6—40 weeks of age	15
Kidney	
The endogenous oxygen consumption per wet weight tissue of kidney slices from unmated McCollum strain rats decreases by 11% (females) and 6% (males) from 12—14 to 24—27 months of age; the decrease is parallel to a decrease of tissue DNA	16
The tissue (kidney) concentration of malate dehydrogenase (representative of aerobic metabolism) decreases by 55% between 120- and 700-day-old male C_{57}BL/6 mice	17
Liver	
The endogenous oxygen consumption per wet weight of liver slices does not change significantly between 12—14 and 24—27 months old unmated McCollum strain rats	16
There is no correlation between age and endogenous oxygen consumption of rat liver homogenates	18
No age-related decline in endogenous respiration of intact hepatocytes of female WAG/Rij rats	19

Table 1 (continued)
AGE-RELATED CHANGES IN O₂ UTILIZATION BY ORGANISMS, ORGANS, AND TISSUES

	Ref.
Whole body	
with age (3, 12, and 36 months) has been found; also no change in the ratio of respiration in the presence of uncouplers of oxidative phosphorylation to that in the presence of atractyloside or oligomycin	
The tissue (liver) concentration of malate dehydrogenase (representative of aerobic metabolism) decreases between 120 and 500 days, remains constant between 600 and 700 days, and increases after 800 days to the 400 day level	20
Testes	
The tissue (testes) malate dehydrogenase (aerobic metabolism) activity decreases with age in $C_{57}BL/6$ mice	20
Brain	
The cerebral metabolic rate in elderly adults over 66 years was lower than in young adults	21
The brain oxygen consumption ($CMRO_2$) decreases with age in man by about 50% between 1 and 80 years; 50% of this decline has occurred by 10 years	22
The endogenous respiration of rat brain homogenate is 30% lower in 24-month-old rats than young ones	18
The succinate respiration catalyzed by brain homogenate from Sprague-Dawley rats does not decrease with age	23
There was no significant difference in the endogenous respiration of homogenized ventromedial and lateral hypothalamus of Sprague-Dawley rats with age (50 days vs. 180 days)	24
No decline in the respiration rate of fortified rat (Sprague-Dawley) brain homogenates with age has been found	25
The endogenous respiration of the hippocampus and the amygdala decreases from 21 days to 4 months and does not change further until 27 months in Long-Evans rats; the endogenous respiration also decreases from 21 days to 4 months and then from 12—27 months in the hypothalamus; no change was observed in the endogenous respiration of the cerebral cortex between 21 days and 12 months; low oxidative activity of the hypothalamus and amygdala in old age was observed in castrated/hypophysectomized rats; respiration rates were determined in the homogenized tissues	26
The oxidation rate of 3-hydroxybutyrate decreased by 35% in cerebral cortex slices of 3-month vs. 2-year-old Charles River CD male rats	27
The rate of in vivo high energy phosphate utilization decreased in the frontal and parietal cortex, the cerebellum, and the striatum between 4 an 29 months $C_{57}BL/6J$ mice; no change was observed in the hippocampus; the largest decline was by 48% in the striatum	28
The endogenous respiration of brain slices of Syrian hamsters did not change with age (8 months vs. 18 months)	29
The cerebral metabolic rate ($CMRO_2$) (ml O_2 per 100 g · min) in dogs decreases with age: 5.27 (0.5—1.5 years), 4.85 (2.5—3.0 years), and 4.22 (older than 3.0 years)	30

REFERENCES

1. **Dehn, M. M. and Bruce, R. A.,** Longitudinal variations in maximal oxygen intake with age and activity, *J. Appl. Physiol.*, 33, 805, 1972.
2. **Shock, N. W.,** Physiological aspects of aging in man, *Annu. Rev. Physiol.*, 23, 97, 1961.
3. **Conrad, M. C. and Miller, A. T. Jr.,** Age changes in body size, body composition, and basal metabolism, *Am. J. Physiol.*, 186, 207, 1956.
4. **Stupfel, M., Moutet, J. P., and Magnier, M.,** An apparently paradoxical action of aging: decrease of acute hypoxic mortality in male aged rats, *J. Gerontol.*, 30, 154, 1975.
5. **Denckla, W. D. and Marcum, E.,** Minimal oxygen consumption as an index of thyroid status: standardization method, *Endocrinology*, 93, 61, 1973.
6. **Denckla, W. D.,** Minimal oxygen consumption in the female rat, some new definitions and measurements, *J. Appl. Physiol.*, 29, 263, 1970.

Table 1 (continued)
AGE-RELATED CHANGES IN O_2 UTILIZATION BY ORGANISMS, ORGANS, AND TISSUES

7. Denckla, W. D., Role of the pituitary and thyroid glands in the decline of minimal oxygen consumption with age, *J. Clin. Invest.*, 53, 572, 1974.
8. Leto, S., Kokkonen, G. C., and Barrows, C. H., Dietary protein, life-span, and physiological variables in female mice, *J. Gerontol.*, 31, 149, 1976.
9. Pettegrew, R. R. and Ewing, K. L., Life history study of oxygen utilizaton in the $C_{57}BL/6$ mouse, *J. Gerontol.*, 26, 381, 1971.
10. Abu-Erreish, G. M., Neeley, J. R., Whitmer, J. T., Whitman, V., and Sanadi, D. R., Fatty acid oxidation by isolated perfused working hearts of aged rats, *Am. J. Physiol.*, 232, E258, 1977.
11. Weisfeldt, M. L., Wright, J. R., Shreiner, D. P., Lakatta, E., and Shock, N. W., Coronary flow and oxygen extraction in the perfused heart of senescent male rats, *J. Appl. Physiol.*, 30, 44, 1971.
12. Angelova-Gateva, P., Tissue respiration and glycolysis in quadriceps femoris and heart of rats of different ages during hypodynamia, *Exp. Gerontol.*, 4, 177, 1969.
13. Ermini, M., Ageing changes in mammalian skeletal muscle, *Gerontologia*, 22, 301, 1976.
14. Bass, A., Gutmann, E., and Hanzlikova, V., Biochemical and histological changes in energy supply-enzyme pattern of muscles of the rat during old age, *Gerontologia*, 21, 31, 1975.
15. Liebermann, D. A., Maxwell, L. C., and Faulkner, J. A., Adaptation of guinea pig diaphragm muscle to aging and endurance training, *Am. J. Physiol.*, 222, 556, 1972.
16. Barrows, C. H. Jr., Yiengst, M. J., and Shock, N. W., Senescence and the metabolism of various tissues of rats, *J. Gerontol.*, 13, 351, 1958.
17. Burich, R. L., Effects of age on renal function and enzyme activity in male $C_{57}BL/6$ mice, *J. Gerontol.*, 30, 539, 1975.
18. Reiner, J. M., The effect of age on the carbohydrate metabolism of tissue homogenate, *J. Gerontol.*, 2, 315, 1947.
19. Brouwer, A., von Bezooijen, C. F. A., and Knook, D. L., Respiratory activities of hepatocytes isolated from rats of various ages. A brief note, *Mech. Ageing Dev.*, 6, 265, 1977.
20. Burich, R. L., The activity of lactate and malate dehydrogenases in the liver and testes of senescent $C_{57}BL/6$ mice, *J. Gerontol.*, 29, 389, 1974.
21. Lassen, N. A., Feinberg, I., and Lane, M. H., Bilateral studies of cerebral oxygen uptake in young and aged normal subjects and in patients with organic dementia, *J. Clin. Invest.*, 39, 491, 1960.
22. Feinberg, I. and Carlson, V. R., Sleep variables as a function of age in man, *Arch. Gen. Psychiatry*, 18, 239, 1968.
23. Weinbach, E. C. and Garbus, J., Age and oxidatie phosphorylation in rat liver and brain, *Nature (London)*, 178, 1225, 1956.
24. Panksepp, J. and Reilly, P., Medial and lateral hypothalamic oxygen consumption as a function of age, starvation, and glucose administration in rats, *Brain Res.*, 94, 133, 1975.
25. Garbus, J., Respiration of brain homogenates of old and young rats, *Am. J. Physiol.*, 183, 618, 1955.
26. Peng, M. T., Peng, Y. I., and Chen, F. N., Age-dependent changes in the oxygen consumption of the cerebral cortex, hypothalamus, hippocampus, and amygdaloid in rats, *J. Gerontol.*, 32, 517, 1977.
27. Patel, M. S., Age-dependent changes in the oxidative metabolism of rat brain. *J. Gerontol.*, 32, 643, 1977.
28. Ferrendelli, J. A., Sedgwick, W. G., and Suntzeff, V., Regional energy metabolism and lipofuscin accumulation in mouse brain during aging, *J. Neuropathol. Exp. Neurol.*, 30, 638, 1971.
29. Fox, J. H., Parmacek, M. S., and Patel-Mandlik, K., Effect of aging on brain respiration and carbohydrate metabolism in Syrian hamsters, *Gerontologia*, 21, 224, 1975.
30. Michenfelder, J. D. and Theye, R. A., The relationship of age to canine cerebral metabolic rate (CMR), *J. Surg. Res.*, 9, 645, 1969.

CHEMICAL REGULATION OF VENTILATION

R. S. Kronenberg

Table 1
EFFECT OF AGING ON VENTILATORY RESPONSES TO HYPERCAPNIA AND HYPOXIA IN NORMAL HUMANS[a]

Age (years)	Subjects (n)[b]	Body surface area (m²)	Response to hypercapnia, slope (l/min× mm Hg⁻¹)[c]	Response to hypoxia ΔV40 (l/min)[d]	Ref.
34 ± 1	17	—	2.7 ± 0.3	—	1
63 ± 2	9	—	1.8 ± 0.2	—	1
9—10	6M 7F	1.14 ± 0.02	1.2 ± 0.1	14.0 ± 1.2	2
23 ± 0.9	6	1.9 ± 0.1	2.8 ± 0.5	—	3
21 ± 1	5M	1.90 ± 0.1	—	18.0 ± 3.9	4
32 ± 1	40M 4F	1.90 ± 0.0	2.7 ± 1.2	20.3 ± 1.4	5
26 ± 1	8M	1.88 ± 0.1	3.4 ± 0.5	40.1 ± 4.7	6
70 ± 1	8M	2.00 ± 0.0	2.0 ± 0.2	10.2 ± 1.2	6
26 ± 1	9M	1.87 ± 0.0	—	19.4 ± 0.5	7
27 ± 2	6M 5F	1.79 ± 0.1	1.9 ± 0.1	15.8 ± 2.7	8
14 ± 4	8M	—	1.8 ± 0.2	—	9
14 ± 2	11F	—	2.0 ± 0.3	—	9
26 ± 9	23	—	—	10.9 ± 2.4[e]	10
26 ± 10	9M	—	—	9.6 ± 2.4[e]	11
29 ± 2	10M	2.0 ± 0.1	—	24.8 ± 2.0	12
29 ± 2	10M[f]	2.0 ± 0.1	2.5 ± 0.3	—	13
24—40	8M	—	2.5 ± 0.2	17.7 ± 2.0	14
26—36	10M	—	3.2 ± 0.1	—	15

[a] Unless a range is given, all numbers are $\overline{X}$ ± SEM.
[b] M = male; F = female.
[c] Hypercapnic response is given as the slope of the hyperoxic rebreathing CO_2 response line in l/min/torr body temperature and pressure saturated (BTPS).
[d] ΔV40 is the incremental ventilation in (BTPS) between hyperoxia ($PO_2 \geq 100$ torr) and $PO_2 = 40$ torr.
[e] Given as l/min/m² body surface area.
[f] Same subjects as in Reference 12.

REFERENCES

1. Altose, M. D., McCauley, W. C., Kelsen, S. G., and Cherniack, N. S., Effects of hypercapnia and inspiratory flow-resistive loading on respiratory activity in chronic airways obstruction, *J. Clin. Invest.*, 59, 500, 1977.
2. Byrne-Quinn, E., Sodal, I. E., and Weil, J. V., Hypoxic and hypercapnic drives in children native to high altitude, *J. Appl. Physiol.*, 32, 44, 1972.
3. Freedman, S., Dalton, K. J., Holland, D., and Patton, J. M. S., The effects of added elastic loads on the respiratory response to CO_2 in man, *Respir. Physiol.*, 14, 237, 1972.
4. Gabel, R. A. and Weiskopf, R. B., Ventilatory interaction between hypoxia and [H⁺] at chemoreceptors of man, *J. Appl. Physiol.*, 39, 292, 1975.
5. Hirshman, C. A., McCullough, R. E., and Weil, J. V., Normal values for hypoxic and hypercapnic ventilatory drives in man, *J. Appl. Physiol.*, 38, 1095, 1975.

Table 1 (continued)
EFFECT OF AGING ON VENTILATORY RESPONSES TO HYPERCAPNIA AND HYPOXIA IN NORMAL HUMANS

6. Kronenberg, R. S. and Drage, C. W., Attenuation of the ventilatory and heart rate responses to hypoxia and hypercapnia with aging in normal men, *J. Clin. Invest.*, 52, 1812, 1973.
7. Kronenberg, R., Hamilton, F. N., Gabel, R., Hickey, R., Read, D. J. C., and Severinghaus, J., Comparison of three methods for quantitating respiratory response to hypoxia in man, *Respir. Physiol.*, 16, 109, 1972.
8. Rebuck, A. S., Kangalee, M., Pengelly, L. D., and Campbell, E. J. M., Correlation of ventilatory responses to hypoxia and hypercapnia, *J. Appl. Physiol.*, 35, 173, 1973.
9. Saunders, N. A., Leeder, S. R., and Rebuck, A. S., Ventilatory response to carbon dioxide in young athletes: a family study, *Am. Rev. Respir. Dis.*, 113, 497, 1976.
10. Sorensen, S. C. and Severinghaus, J. W., Respiratory sensitivity to acute hypoxia in man born at sea level living at high altitude, *J. Appl. Physiol.*, 25, 211, 1968.
11. Sorensen, S. C. and Severinghaus, J. W., Irreversible respiratory insensitivity to acute hypoxia in man born at altitude, *J. Appl. Physiol.*, 25, 217, 1968.
12. Weil, J. V., Byrne-Quinn, E., Sodal, I. E., Friesen, W. O., Underhill, B., Filley, G. F., and Grover, R. F., Hypoxic ventilatory drive in normal man, *J. Clin. Invest.*, 49, 1061, 1970.
13. Weil, J. V., Byrne-Quinn, E., Sodal, I. E., Filley, G. F., and Grover, R. F. Acquired attenuation of chemoreceptor function in chronically hypoxic man at altitude, *J. Clin. Invest.*, 50, 186, 1971.
14. Weil, J. V., Byrne-Quinn, E., Sodal, I. E., Kline, J. S., McCullough, R. E., and Filley, G. F., Augmentation of chemosensitivity during mild exercise in normal man, *J. Appl. Physiol.*, 33, 813, 1972.
15. Zackon, H., Despas, P. J., and Anthonisen, N. R., Occlusion pressure responses in asthma and chronic obstructive pulmonary disease, *Am. Rev. Respir. Dis.*, 114, 917, 1976.

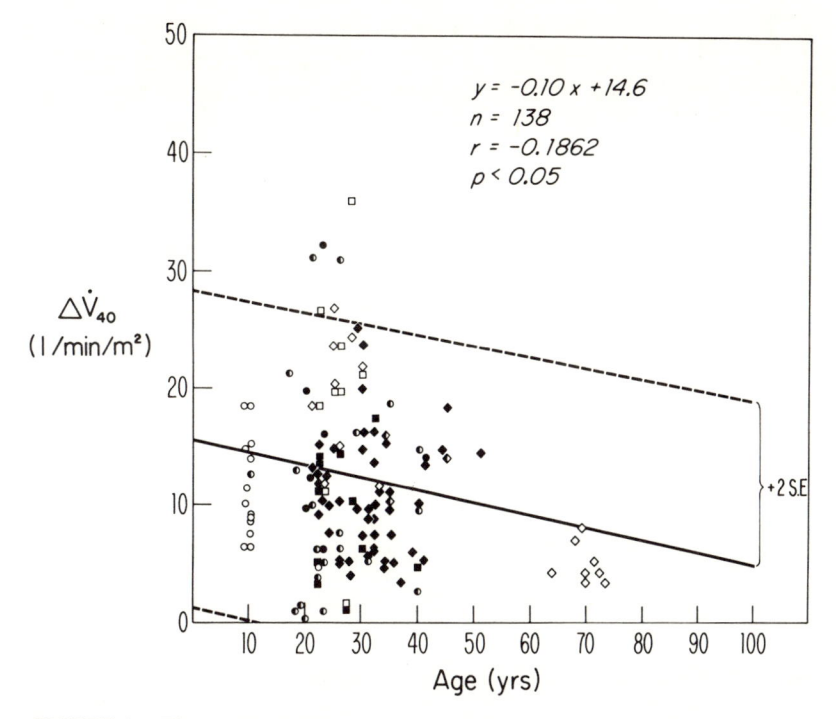

FIGURE 1. The correlation between hypoxic ventilatory drive and aging in normal people. Hypoxic ventilatory drive ($\Delta V40$) is defined as the incremental ventilation normalized for body surface area between high PO_2 (≥ 100 torr) and a PO_2 of 40 torr. The symbols refer to the references cited below and numbers are as follows: ○ — Reference 1, ● — Reference 2; □ — Reference 3; ◇ — Reference 4; ⌑ — Reference 5; ■ — Reference 6; ◉ — Reference 7; ◆ — Reference 8.

REFERENCES

1. **Byrne-Quinn, E., Sodal, I. E., and Weil, J. V.**, Hypoxic and hypercapnic drives in children native to high altitude, *J. Appl. Physiol.*, 32, 44, 1972.
2. **Gabel, R. A. and Weiskopf, R. B.**, Ventilatory interactions between hypoxia and [H⁺] at chemoreceptors of man, *J. Appl. Physiol.*, 39, 292, 1975.
3. **Hirshman, C. A., McCullough, R. E., and Weil, J. V.**, Normal values for hypoxic and hypercapnic ventilatory drives in man, *J. Appl. Physiol.*, 38, 1095, 1974.
4. **Kronenberg, R. S. and Drage, C. W.**, Attenuation of the ventilatory and heart rate responses to hypoxia and hypercapnia with aging in normal men, *J. Clin. Invest.*, 52, 1812, 1973.
5. **Kronenberg, R. S., Hamilton, F. N., Gabel, R., Hickey, R., Read, D. J. C., and Severinghaus, J.**, Comparison of three methods for quantitating respiratory response to hypoxia in man, *Respir. Physiol.*, 16, 109, 1972.
6. **Rebuck, A. S., Kangalee, M., Pengaly, L. D., and Campbell, E. J. M.**, Correlation of ventilatory responses to hypoxia and hypercapnia, *J. Appl. Physiol.*, 35, 173, 1973.
7. **Sørensen, S. C. and Severinghaus, J. W.**, Respiratory sensitivity to acute hypoxia in man born at sea level living at high altitude, *J. Appl. Physiol.*, 25, 211, 1968.
8. **Weil, J. V., Byrne-Quinn, E., Sodal, I. E., Friesen, W. O., Underhill, B., Filley, G. F., and Grover, R. F.**, Hypoxic ventilatory drive in normal man, *J. Clin. Invest.*, 49, 1061, 1970.

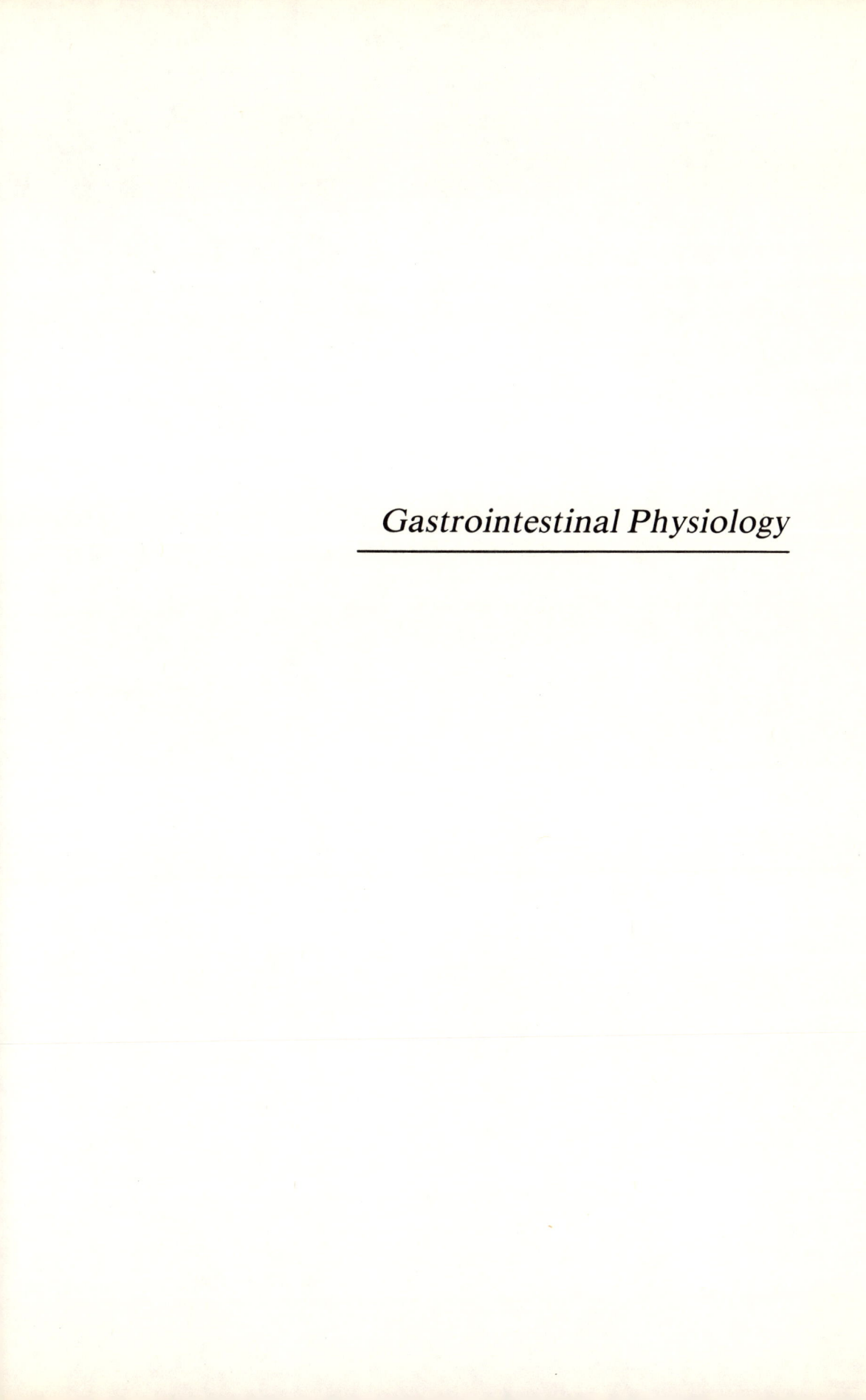

Gastrointestinal Physiology

MOTILITY

M. D. Kaye

Table 1
ASPECTS OF GASTROINTESTINAL MOTILITY FOR WHICH RELIABLE DATA CONCERNING THE EFFECTS OF AGING ARE UNAVAILABLE OR INCOMPLETE

Basic mechanisms	
Muscle	
Structure	Upper esophageal sphincter, esophageal body, lower esophageal sphincter, stomach, small intestine, colon, rectum, anal sphincters, gallbladder, sphincter of Oddi
Physical properties	
Biochemistry	
Response to pharmacological aspects	
Contractile properties	
Innervation	Upper esophageal sphincter (cricopharyngeus), esophageal body, lower esophageal sphincter, stomach, small intestine, colon, rectum, anal sphincters, gallbladder, sphincter of Oddi
Electrical control activity	Stomach, small intestine, colon
Functions	
Sphincters	
Maintenance of tone	Upper esophageal, lower esophageal, Oddi's, anal
Relaxation responses	Upper esophageal, anal
Prevention of prograde flow	Anal
Prevention of retrograde flow	Lower esophageal, pyloric, Oddi's, ileo-cecal
Mixing	Stomach, small intestine, colon
Emptying	Stomach, gallbladder, rectum
Transport (propulsion, transit time)	Small intestine, colon

Note: There is a distressing paucity of studies which address the effects of aging upon gastrointestinal motility, either in man or in experimental animals. Indeed, there are no longitudinal studies, and very few cross-sectional studies, in which observations pertinent to a given aspect of gastrointestinal motility encompass the entire life-span of the species. Comparisons between infants and young adults in respect to a variety of facets of gastrointestinal motor function are relatively abundant; but these data have not been tabulated, since they do not relate specifically to the effects of aging.

Table 2
CHANGES IN MOTILITY OF THE GASTROINTESTINAL TRACT WITH AGE

	Ref.
Esophagus	
Esophageal ganglion cells of Auerbach's plexus are reduced in number in elderly individuals	1
The incidence of non-peristaltic esophageal contractions increases after the age of 70 in man	2—4
Esophageal emptying time (of barium) increases after the age of 70 in man	2—4
Amplitude of esophageal contractions is diminished in men aged over 70	5
The incidence of impaired relaxation, in response to swallowing of the lower esophageal sphincter is increased in human nonagenarians	3
Stomach	
Periods of gastric quiescence are shorter, and periods of hunger activity longer, in young than in old dogs	6
Interval between feeding and onset of hunger activity increases with age in dogs	7
[a]With advancing age, the volume aspirated from the human stomach at a fixed interval after ingestion of a Ewald test meal diminishes	8
Colon	
Colonic diverticula develop in aged rats fed low roughage diets	9
Diverticula can be produced at autopsy by distension of senile, but not young, human colons	10

[a] This might be due to reduction in volume of gastric secretion rather than to alteration in motility per se.

REFERENCES

1. **Eckardt, V. F. and LeCompte, P. M.**, Histology of esophageal smooth muscle and Auerbach's plexus in elderly persons, *Gastroenterology*, 72, 1055, 1977.
2. **Mandelstam, P. and Lieber, A.**, Cinderadiographic evaluation of the esophagus in normal adults: a study of 146 subjects ranging in age from 21 to 90 years, *Gastroenterology*, 58, 32, 1970.
3. **Soergel, K. H., Zboralske, F. F., and Amberg, J. R.**, Presbyesophagus: esophageal motility in nonagenarians, *J. Clin. Invest.*, 43, 1472, 1964.
4. **Zboralske, F. F., Amberg, J. R., and Soergel, K. H.** Presbyesophagus: cineradiographic manifestations, *Radiology*, 82, 463, 1964.
5. **Hollis, J. B. and Castell, D. O.**, Esophageal function in elderly men. A new look at presbyesophagus, *Ann. Intern. Med.*, 80, 371, 1974.
6. **Carlson, A. J.** *The Control of Hunger in Health and Disease,* University of Chicago Press, Chicago, 1916.
7. **Ivy, A. C.**, Unpublished observations quoted in *Cowdry's Problems of Ageing,* Lansing, A. I., Ed., Williams and Wilkins, Baltimore, 1952, 497.
8. **Vanzant, F. R., Alvares, W. C., Eusterman, G. B., Dunn, H. L., and Berkson, J.**, The normal range of gastric acidity from youth to old age, *Arch. Intern. Med.*, 49, 345, 1932.
9. **Carlson, A. J. and Hoelzel, F.**, Relation of diet to diverticulosis of the colon in rats, *Gastroenterology*, 12, 108, 1949.
10. **Hausemann, D.**, Über die Enstehung Falscher Darmdivertikel, *Virchows Arch.*, 144, 400, 1896.

Table 3
HUMAN DISORDERS RELATED TO ALTERED MOTILITY AND INCREASING WITH AGE

	Ref.
Pharyngo-esophageal diverticula[a]	1
Diffuse esophageal spasm[a]	2—6
Diverticulosis coli[a]	7—11
Duodenal and jejunal diverticula[b]	12—14
Gallstones[b]	15

[a] "Abnormal" motility documented (References 3 to 6 and 16 to 20).
[b] "Abnormal" motility possibly contributory.

REFERENCES

1. **MacMillan, A. S.**, Pouches of the pharynx and esophagus, *J. Am. Med. Assoc.*, 98, 964, 1932.
2. **Moersch, H. J. and Camp, J. D.**, Diffuse spasm of the lower part of the esophagus, *Ann. Otol.*, 43, 1165, 1934.
3. **Creamer, B., Donoghue, F. E., and Code, C. F.**, Pattern of esophageal motility in diffuse spasm, *Gastroenterology*, 34, 782, 1958.
4. **Roth, H. P. and Fleshler, B.**, Diffuse esophageal spasm. Clinical, radiological and manometric observations, *Ann. Intern. Med.*, 61, 914, 1964.
5. **Craddock, D. R., Logan, A., and Walbaum, P. R.**, Diffuse esophageal spasm, *Thorax*, 21, 511, 1966.
6. **Gillies, M., Nicks, R., and Skyring, A.**, Clinical, manometric, and pathological studies in diffuse esophageal spasm, *Br. Med. J.*, 2, 527, 1967.
7. **Kocour, E. J.**, Diverticulosis of the colon, *Am. J. Surg.*, 37, 433, 1937.
8. **Hughes, L. E.**, Postmortem survey of diverticular disease of the colon. I. Diverticulosis and Diverticulitis. II. The Muscular Abnormality in the Sigmoid Colon, *Gut*, 10, 336, 344, 1969.
9. **Manousos, O. N., Truelove, S. C., and Lumsden, K.**, Prevalence of diverticulosis in general population of Oxford area, *Br. Med. J.*, 3, 762, 1967.
10. **Parks, T. G.**, Natural history of diverticular disease of the colon: a review of 521 cases, *Br. Med. J.*, 4, 639, 1969.
11. **Slack, W. W.**, The anatomy, pathology, and some clinical features of diverticulitis of the colon, *Br. J. Surg.*, 50, 185, 1962.
12. **Grant, J. C. B.**, On the frequency and age incidence of duodenal diverticula, *Can. Med. Assoc. J.*, 33, 258, 1935.
13. **Horton, B. T. and Mueller, S.C.**, Duodenal diverticula: an anatomic study, with notes on the etiologic role played by dystopia of pancreatic tissue, *Proc. Staff Meet. Mayo Clin.*, 7, 185, 1932.
14. **King, E. S. J.**, Diverticula of the small intestine, *Aust. N. Z. J. Surg.*, 19, 301, 1950.
15. **Friedman, G. D., Kannel, W. B., and Dawber, T. R.**, The epidemiology of gallbladder disease: observations in the Framingham study, *J. Chronic Dis.*, 19, 273, 1966.
16. **Ardran, G. M., Kemp, F. H., and Lund, W. S.**, The etiology of the posterior pharyngeal diverticulum: a cineradiographic study, *J. Laryngol. Otol.*, 78, 333, 1964.
17. **Ellis, F. H., Jr., Schlegel, J. F., Lynch, V. P., and Payne, W. S.**, Cricopharyngeal myotomy for pharyngo-esophageal diverticulum, *Ann. Surg.*, 170, 340, 1969.
18. **Arfwidsson, F.**, Pathogenesis of multiple diverticula of the sigmoid colon in diverticular disease, *Acta Chir. Scand. Suppl.*, 342, 1, 1964.
19. **Painter, N. S.**, The aetiology of diverticulosis of the colon with special reference to the action of certain drugs on behaviour of the colon, *Ann. R. Coll. Surg. Engl.*, 34, 98, 1964.
20. **Painter, N. S. and Truelove, S. C.** Potential dangers of morphine in acute diverticulitis of the colon, *Br. Med. J.*, 2, 33, 1963.

ORAL CAVITY

D. L. Schmucker and R. K. J. Wang

Table 1
AGE-RELATED CHANGES IN THE STRUCTURE AND COMPOSITION OF THE TEETH

Species	Changes	Ref.
Human	Tooth enamel becomes increasingly impermeable with advancing age	1, 2
	The formation of reparative dentin increases with age	3—5
	The teeth increase in translucency from the root apex to the crown with age	3—5
	The number of odontoblasts is reduced with increasing age	3—5
	The fluoride content of the dentin increases with age and reaches maximal levels by approximately 55 years	6
	The water content of dentin decreases with age	7
Human, rat	The number of cells in tooth pulp decreases with age; declining approximately 50% by 70 years in humans, whereas the tooth pulp of senescent rats contains only 25% of the original number of cells	8
Human	The degree of fibrosis and the amount of reticular fibers in the pulp increase with advancing age	2
	The number and size of pulpstones or denticles (calcification of the pulp) increases with age; approximately 90% of the pulp is calcified in old humans	9
	The D/L aspartic acid ratio in dentinal protein increases with age	10
	The functional period of dentition decreases with age primarily due to a reduction in the volume of saliva secretion	11

REFERENCES

1. **Blake, G.,** An experimental investigation into the permeability of enamel and dentine with reference to its relation to dental caries, *Proc. R. Soc. Med.,* 51, 678, 1958.
2. **Tonna, E.,** Aging of skeletal-dental systems and supporting tissues, in *Handbook of the Biology of Aging,* Finch, C. and Hayflick, L., eds., Van Nostrand Reinhold, New York, 1977, 470.
3. **Philippas, G. and Applebaum, E.,** Age factor in secondary dentin formation, *J. Dent. Res.,* 45, 778, 1966.
4. **Philippas, G. and Applebaum, E.,** Age changes in the permanent upper lateral incisor, *J. Dent. Res.,* 46, 1002, 1967.
5. **Philippas, G. and Applebaum, E.,** Age change in the permanent upper canine teeth, *J. Dent. Res.,* 47, 411, 1968.
6. **Jackson, D. and Wedmann, S.,** The relationship between age and the fluorine content of human dentine and enamel: a regional survey, *Br. Dent. J.,* 107, 303, 1959.
7. **Toto, P., Kastelic, E., Duyvejonck, K., and Rapp, G.,** Effect of age on water content in human teeth, *J. Dent. Res.,* 50, 1284, 1971.
8. **Pinzon, R., Kozlov, M., and Burch, W.,** Histology of rat molar pulp at different ages, *J. Dent. Res.,* 46, 202, 1967.
9. **Bernick, S.,** Effect of aging on the nerve supply to human teeth, *J. Dent. Res.,* 46, 694, 1967.
10. **Helfman, P. and Bada, J.,** Aspartic acid racemisation in dentine as a measure of aging, *Nature (London),* 262, 279, 1976.
11. **Langer, A.,** Oral signs of aging and their clinical significance, *Geriatrics,* 31, 63, 1976.

Table 2
AGE-RELATED CHANGES IN THE STRUCTURE OF THE ORAL MUCOSA

Species	Age	Changes	Ref.
Human		The surface epithelium of the oral mucosa atrophies and the underlying connective tissue degenerates with age	1
		The number of Fordyce spots (sebaceous glands) increases with age	2
		The polysaccharide content of the mucosal epithelium increases with age as does the number of mast cells in the connective tissue comprising the lamina	3
Rat (Sprague-Dawley)	2—27 months	The number of stem or progenitor cells in the palate and tongue decreases while the synthetic index (% stem cell population incorporating ^{3}H-Thymidine) increases between maturity (9 months) and senescence (27 months); the two changes compensate each other and a constant rate of tissue turnover is maintained[a]	4
Human	?—85 years	The number of taste buds on both circumvallate and filiform papillae and the number of taste bud nerve endings decrease with age	5,6

[a] See Figure 1.

REFERENCES

1. **McCarthy, P. and Shklar, G.**, *Normal Anatomy, Histology and Histochemistry of the Oral Mucosa*, McGraw-Hill, New York, 1961, 1.
2. **Miles, A.**, Aging in the teeth and oral tissues, in *Structural Aspects of Ageing*, Bourne, G. H., Ed., Hafner, New York, 1961, 351.
3. **Shklar, G.**, The effects of aging upon oral mucosa, *J. Invest. Dermatol.*, 47, 115, 1956.
4. **Sharav, Y. and Massler, M.**, Age changes in oral epithelia. Progenitor populations, synthesis index and tissue turnover, *Exp. Cell Res.*, 47, 132, 1967.
5. **Arey, L., Tremain, M., and Monzingo, F.**, The numerical and topographical relation of taste buds to human circumvallate papillae throughout the life-span, *Anat. Rec.*, 64, 9, 1935.
6. **Rollin, H.**, Elektrische Geschmacksschwell en der Zunge und des weichen Gaumens. II. Einfluss von Lebensalter, Geschlecht und Rauchgewohnheiten, *Arch. Klin. Exp. Ohren-Nasen-Kehlkopfheikd.*, 204, 81, 1973.

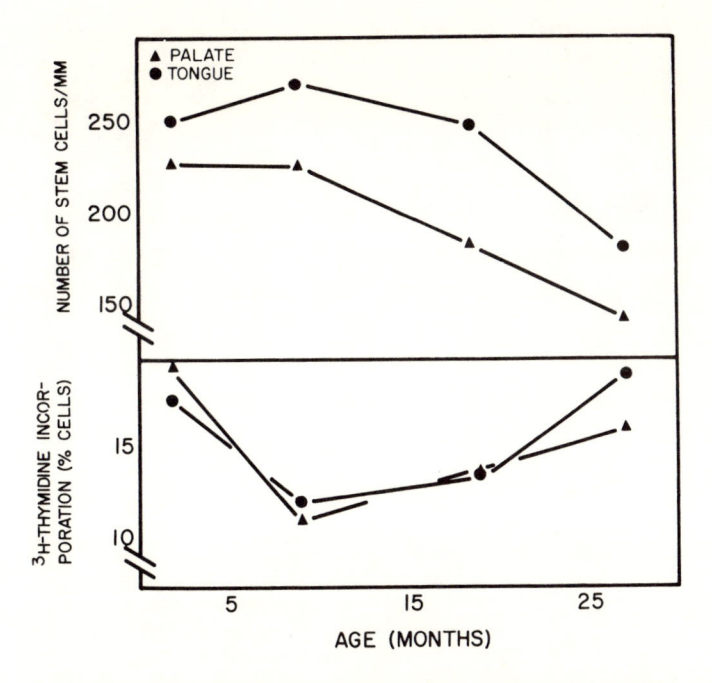

FIGURE 1. The effect of aging on the oral mucosa stem cell population and the synthetic index in the Sprague-Dawley rat. The top panel demonstrates the age-related loss of stem or proliferator cells on the tongue and palate. The bottom panel shows the increased rate of ^{3}H-thymidine uptake (synthetic index) in both cell populations as a function of animal age. (Drawn from data presented by Sharavi, Y. and Massler, M., *Exp. Cell Res.*, 47, 132, 1967.)

ESOPHAGUS

D. L. Schmucker and R. K. J. Wang

Table 1
AGE-RELATED CHANGES IN ESOPHAGEAL STRUCTURE AND FUNCTION

Species	Age		Ref.
Mouse, Swiss (male)	3—20 months	There is an age-dependant decline in the rate of proliferation of the esophageal epithelium as determined by ^{3}H-thymidine uptake; this results in a slower rate of cell turnover rather than a reduction in cell number	1
		The length of the cell cycle of esophageal epithelium approximately doubles in mice between the ages of 10 and 638 days[a]	2
Human (male, female)	90—92 years	Aging results in increased tertiary contractions, delayed esophageal emptying, and dilation of the esophagus[b]	3, 4
		The incidence of reduced motor control of the esophagus and lower esophageal sphincter is higher in old individuals, i.e., "Presbyesophagus" (abnormal esophageal motility caused by aging)[c]	3, 5
Human (male)	19—27 years; 70—87 years	There is no age-related increase in spontaneous abnormal esophageal motility (Presbyesophagus), suggesting a lower amplitude of contraction due to weakened esophageal smooth musculature rather than reduced motor control[c]	6
Human (male, female)	90—97 years	Aging results in the decreased ability to initiate relaxation of the lower esophageal sphincter and primary peristaltic contractions; 44% in the young, 95—100% in the aged	3
Human		The normal esophagus (no manifest disease) of old men responds differently than that of young individuals; including increased nonperistaltic response, delayed transit time and failure of the lower sphincter to relax after swallowing	7
		The incidence of hiatal hernia increases with age; <10% under 30 years, up to 60% beyond 60 years of age	4
		The resting lower esophageal sphincter pressure decreases in elderly patients with symptomatic gastro-esophageal reflux, suggesting that a deficiency in gastrin secretion may be responsible	4, 7, 8

[a] See Figure 1.
[b] See Table 4.
[c] Conflicting results obtained in two separate studies.

REFERENCES

1. **Cameron, I.**, Cell proliferation and renewal in aging mice, *J. Gerontol.*, 27, 162, 1972.
2. **Thrasher, J.**, Age and the cell cycle of the mouse esophageal epithelium, *Exp. Gerontol.*, 6, 19, 1971.
3. **Soergel, L., Zboralske, F., and Amberg, J.**, Presbyesophagus: esophageal motility in nonagenarians, *J. Clin. Invest.*, 43, 1472, 1964.
4. **Bhanthumnavin, K. and Schuster, M.**, Aging and gastrointestinal function, in *Handbook of the Biology of Aging*, Finch, C. and Hayflick, L., Eds., Van Nostrand Reinhold, New York, 1977, 209.
5. **Zboralske, F., Amberg, J., and Soergel, K.**, Presbyesophagus: cineradiographic manifestations, *Radiology*, 82, 463, 1964.
6. **Hollis, J. and Castell, D.**, Esophageal function in elderly men, a new look at "Presbyesophagus", *Ann. Intern. Med.*, 80, 371, 1974.
7. **Farrell, R., Castell, D., and McGugan, J.**, Measurements and comparisons of lower esophageal sphincter pressures and serum gastrin levels in patients with gastro-esophageal reflux, *Gastroenterology*, 67, 415, 1974.
8. **Cohen, S. and Harris, L.**, The lower esophageal sphincter, *Gastroenterology*, 63, 166, 1972.

Table 2
EFFECT OF AGING ON ESOPHAGEAL RESPONSE IN HUMANS

Parameter	Response in the elderly (% test population)
Incidence of normal peristalsis after swallowing	Decreased ∼ 50%
Incidence of tertiery contractions after swallowing	Increased ∼ 35%
Incidence of lower esophageal sphincter failure to relax after swallowing	Increased > 50%
Incidence of delay in esophageal emptying	Increased > 50%

Adapted from data presented by Bhanthamnavin, K. and Schuster, M., Aging and gastrointestinal function, in *Handbook of the Biology of Aging,* Finch, C. and Haflick, L., Eds., Van Nostrand Reinhold, New York, 1977, 209.

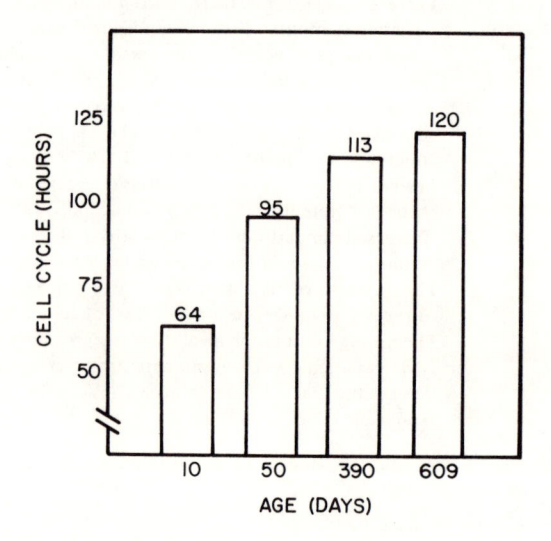

FIGURE 1. The effect of age on the cell cycle of the esophageal mucosal epithelium. The length of time required for the cell cycle nearly doubles in mice between 10 and ∼ 600 days of age. (Drawn from data presented by Thrasher, J., *Exp. Gerontol.,* 6, 19, 1971.)

STOMACH

D. L. Schmucker and R. K. J. Wang

Table 1
AGE-RELATED CHANGES IN THE STOMACH

Species	Changes	Ref.
Human	The effect of age on the rate of gastric emptying has not been studied definitively, although the available evidence suggests that this process is delayed in elderly patients with atrophic gastritis	1, 2
	Aging results in an increased incidence of chronic atrophic gastritis characterized by diffuse lesions, thinning of the gastric glands, loss of parietal cells, and goblet cell metaplasia in individuals free of manifest gastric disease; this condition results in decreased absorption of iron and vitamin B_{12}[a]	1—5
	There is a direct correlation between the incidence of parietal cell and intrinsic factor auto-antibodies and (1) the severity of the gastric mucosal lesions and (2) age (2% in subjects < 20 years; 16% in subjects > 60 years)	6—9

[a] See Figure 1.

REFERENCES

1. **Bhanthumnavin, K. and Schuster, M.,** Aging and gastrointestinal function, in *Handbook of the Biology of Aging,* Finch, C. and Hayflick, L., Eds., Van Nostrand Reinhold, New York, 1977, 209.
2. **Isokoski, M., Krohn, K., Varis, K., and Siurala, M.,** Parietal cell and intrinsic factor antibodies in a Finnish rural population sample, *Scand. J. Gastroenterol.,* 4, 521, 1969.
3. **Hebbel, R.,** The topography of chronic gastritis in otherwise normal stomachs, *Am. J. Pathol.,* 25, 125, 1949.
4. **Andrews, G., Haneman, B., Arnold, B., Booth, J., and Taylor, K.,** Atrophic gastritis in the aged, *Australas. Ann. Med.,* 16, 230, 1967.
5. **Hradsky, M., Groh, J., Langr, F., and Herout, V.,** Chronische Gastitis bei jungen und atten Personen Histolische and histochemische Untersuchung, *Gerontol. Clin.,* 8, 164, 1966.
6. **Adams, J., Glen, A., Kennedy, E., Mackenzie, I., Morrow, J., Anderson, J., Gray, K., and Middleton, D.,** The histological and secretory changes in the stomach in patients with autoimmunity to gastric parietal cells, *Lancet,* 1, 401, 1964.
7. **Coghill, N., Doniach, D., Roitt, I., Mollin, D., and Wynn, A.,** Auto-antibodies in simple atrophic gastritis, *Gut,* 6, 48, 1965.
8. **Doniach, D. and Roitt, I.,** An evaluation of gastric and thyroid auto-immunity in relation to hematologic disorders, *Semin. Hematol.,* 1, 313, 1964.
9. **Roitt, I., Doniach, D., and Shapland, C.,** Autoimmunity in pernicious anemia and atrophic gastritis, *Ann. N.Y. Acad. Sci.,* 124, 644, 1965.

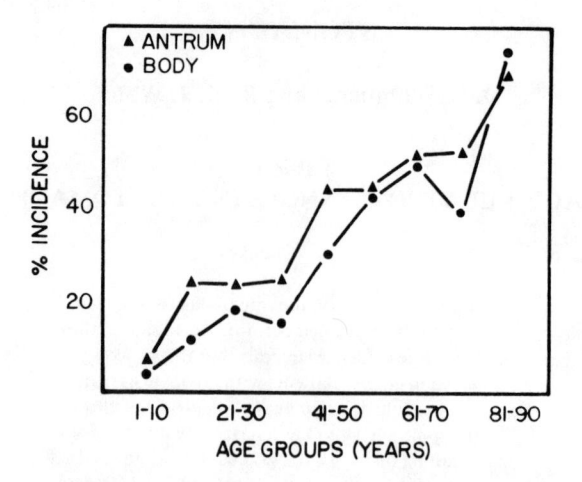

FIGURE 1. The effect of age on the incidence of all types of gastric lesions in humans. (Drawn from data of Hebbel, R., *Am. J. Pathol.*, 25, 125, 1949.)

LIVER

D. L. Schmucker and R. K. J. Wang

Table 1
EFFECTS OF AGING ON SEVERAL LIVER PARAMETERS

Species	Age		Ref.
Human	25—92 years	Average liver weight and liver weight as percent body weight decline in individuals beyond 60 years of age[a,b]	1
		Livers from 85% of a sample population over 75 years of age did not show a weight loss at the time of necropsy[b]	2
Human (male)	29—70 years	Plasma retention of BSP (Sulfobromophthalein) increased and BSP clearance rates decreased as a function of age[b]	3
Human		In a longitudinal study, no obvious relationship was observed between plasma BSP retention and age[b]	4
	> 50 years	Serum bilirubin concentration, alkaline phosphatase and GOT activities, and BSP and rose bengal retention were unaffected by increasing age[b]	5
		Total hepatic blood flow (portal vein and hepatic artery) decreases as a function of age; approximately 0.3—1.5% per year	3
Rat (Sprague-Dawley, male)	1—18 months	The cholesterol concentration in the liver increases continuously from 1—18 months, whereas the phospholipids decline and there is no net change in the triglyceride content	6

[a] See Figure 1.
[b] Conflicting results obtained in two different studies.

REFERENCES

1. **Calloway, N., Foley, C., and Lagerbloom, P.,** Uncertainties in geriatric data. II. Organ size, *J. Am. Geriatr. Soc.*, 13, 20, 196.
2. **Morgan, Z. and Feldman, M.,** The liver, biliary tract and pancreas in the aged: an anatomic and laboratory evaluation, *J. Am. Geriatr. Soc.*, 5, 59, 1957.
3. **Bhanthumnavin, K. and Schuster, M.,** Aging and gastrointestinal function, in *Handbook of the Biology of Aging,* Finch, C. and Hayflick, L., Eds., Van Nostrand Reinhold, New York, 1977, 209.
4. **Koff, R., Garvey, A., Burney, S., and Bell, B.,** Absence of an age effect on sulfobromophthalein retention in healthy men, *Gastroenterology,* 65, 300, 1973.
5. **Kampmann, J., Sinding, J., and Moller-Jorgensen, I.,** Effect of age on liver function, *Geriatrics,* 30, 91, 1975.
6. **Carlson, L., Froberg, S., and Nye, E.,** Effect of age on the blood and tissue lipid levels in the male rat, *Gerontologia,* 14, 65, 1968.

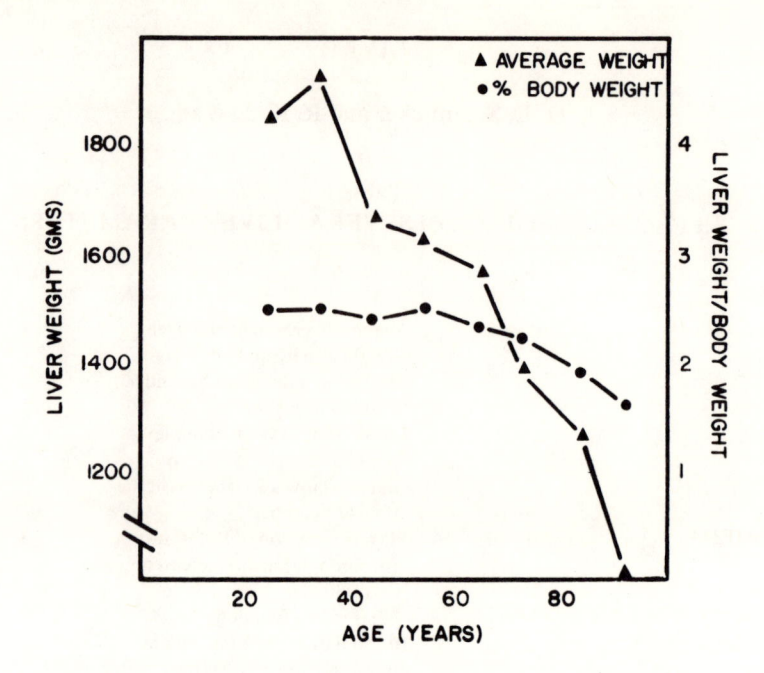

FIGURE 1. The effect of age on liver weight in humans. Both the average liver weight and the liver weight/body weight ratio decline, although the latter parameter only during the 7th and 8th decades. (Drawn from data presented by Calloway, N., Foley, C., and Lagerbloom, P., *J. Am. Geriatr. Soc.*, 13, 20, 1965.)

Table 2
EFFECT OF AGING ON LIVER STRUCTURE

Species	Age		Ref.
Rat (Wag/Rij, female)	2 weeks	The volume of individual hepatocytes increases with age[a]	1—4
Mouse (male)	36 months	The volume of individual hepatocytes increases with age[a]	1—4
Rat (F344, Wistar, male, female)	1—30 months	The volume of individual hepatocytes decreases with age, i.e., between adult and senescent animals[a]	5—7
Human (male)	36—97 years	The volume of individual hepatocytes is not affected by aging[a]	8
Human (male)	36—97 years	The number of hepatocytes per volume of liver tissue declines with age	7,8
Rat (F344, male)	1—3 months	The number of hepatocytes per volume of liver tissue declines with age	7,8
Mouse (C57BL/ICRF/a, male)	6—30 months	Aging results in a net increase in the volume density (vol/vol of liver tissue) of hepatocyte mitochondria[a]	9
Mouse (C57BL/6j, male, female)	8—44 months	The volume density of hepatocyte mitochondria undergoes a net decrease with age[a]	7,10,11
Rat (Wistar, female)	1—27 months	There is no significant change in the volume density of rat liver mitochondria as a function of animal age[a]	6
Human (male, female)	30—90 years	The number of hepatocyte mitochondria per volume of liver tissue decreases with age	6,8,12
Rat (male, female)	3—32 months	The number of hepatocyte mitochondria per volume of liver tissue decreases with age	6,8,12
Mouse (SM, female)	70 days—24 months	The number of microbodies (peroxisomes) per volume of liver tissue increases with age	13
Rat (F344, male)	1—30 months	The volume density of hepatocyte microbodies does not change as a function of animal age	7
Rat (Wistar, female)	1—20 months	The volume density of hepatocyte microbodies and dense bodies (lysosomes) collectively does not change, whereas the number of these organelles decreases with age	6
Rat (Sprague-Dawley, F344, BN/BiRij, male, female)	1—35 months	The volume of hepatocyte dense bodies (per volume of liver tissue and per average parenchymal cell) undergoes a net increase with age	7,14,15
Rat (BN/BiRij, female)	3—35 months	The number of dense bodies per volume of liver tissue increases with age	15
Rat (F344, male)	1—30 months	There is no net age-related change in the amount of rough surfaced endoplasmic reticulum membrane in hepatocytes[a,c]	7

Table 2 (continued)
EFFECT OF AGING ON LIVER STRUCTURE

Species	Age		Ref.
Rat (Wistar, female)	1—27 months	The amount of hepatocyte rough surfaced endoplasmic reticulum membrane undergoes a marked reduction as a function of animal age[a]	6
Rat (F344, male)	1—30 months	The amount of hepatocyte smooth surfaced endoplasmic reticulum declines significantly with age[a,c]	7
Rat (Wistar, female)	1—27 months	The amount of hepatocyte smooth surface endoplasmic reticulum does not change with increasing age[a]	6
Rat (F334, male)	1—30 months	There are no apparent age-related changes in the amount of hepatocyte Golgi membrane	7
Rat (F344, male)	1—30 months	Quantitative age-related changes in hepatocyte ultrastructure occur regardless of the sublobular location of the cells, i.e., centrolobular or periportal	7
Rat (F344, WAG/Rij, male, female)	2 weeks; 36 months	Most hepatocyte fine structural parameters, both qualitative and quantitative, are similar in very young and senescent rats; real age-dependant losses in the volumes or surface areas of organelles occur only between maturity (10—16 months) and senescence (> 25 months)	4,7

[a]   Conflicting results obtained in separate studies.
[b]   See Figure 2.
[c]   See Figure 3.

Table 2 (continued)
EFFECT OF AGING ON LIVER STRUCTURE

REFERENCES

1. **Andrew, W.,** Changes in the nucleus with advancing age of the organism, *Adv. Gerontol. Res.,* 1, 87, 1964.
2. **Andrew, W.,** The fine structural and histochemical changes in aging, in *The Biological Basis of Medicine,* Bittar, E., Ed., Academic Press, New York, 1968, 461.
3. **van Bezooijen, C., Grell, T., and Knook, D.,** On the role of hepatic cell ploidy changes in liver function with age following partial hepatectomy, *Mech. Ageing Dev.,* 1, 351, 1972.
4. **van Bezooijen, C., van Noord, M., and Knook, D.,** The viability of parenchymal liver cells isolated from young and old rats, *Mech. Aging Dev.,* 3, 107, 1974.
5. **Ross, M.,** Aging, nutrition, and hepatic enzyme activity patterns in the rat. II, *J. Nutr.,* 97 (Suppl. 1), 563, 1969.
6. **Pieri, C., Nagy, Zs., Muzzufferi, G., and Giuli, G.,** The aging of rat liver as revealed by electron microscopic morphometry. I. Basic parameters, *Exp. Gerontol.,* 10, 291, 1975.
7. **Schmucker, D., Mooney, J., and Jones, A.,** Age-related changes in the hepatic endoplasmic reticulum: a quantitative analysis, *Science,* 197, 1005, 1977.
8. **Tauchi, H. and Sato, T.,** Effect of environmental conditions upon age changes in the human liver, *Mech. Ageing Dev.,* 4, 71, 1975.
9. **Wilson, P. and Franks, L.,** The effect of age on mitochondrial ultrastructure, *Gerontologia,* 21, 81, 1975.
10. **Herbener, G.,** A morphometric study of age-dependent changes in mitochondrial populations of mouse liver and heart, *J. Gerontol.,* 31, 8, 1976.
11. **Tate, M. and Herbener, G.,** A morphometric study of the density of mitochondrial cristae in heart and liver of ageing mice, *J. Gerontol.,* 31, 129, 1976.
12. **Tauchi, H. and Sato., T.** Age changes in size and number of mitochondria of human hepatic cells, *J. Gerontol.,* 23, 454, 1968.
13. **Tauchi, H., Sato, T., and Kobayashi, H.,** Effect of age on ultrastructural changes of cortisone treated mouse hepatic cells, *Mech. Ageing Dev.,* 3, 279, 1974.
14. **Schmucker, D.,** Age-related changes in hepatic fine structure: a quantitative analysis, *J. Gerontol.,* 31, 135, 1976.
15. **Knook, D., Sleyster, E., and van Noord, M.,** Changes in lysosomes during aging of parenchymal and non-parenchymal liver cells, in *Cell Impairment in Aging and Development,* Cristofalo, V. and Holeckova, E., Eds., Plenum Press, New York, 1975, 155.

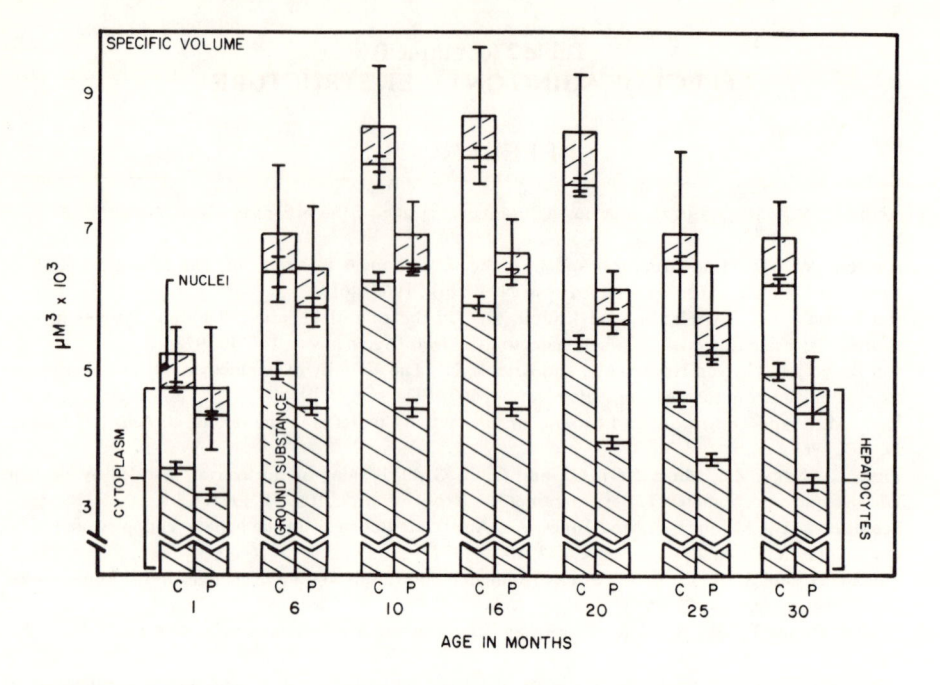

FIGURE 2. The effect of aging on average rat hepatocyte volume. During development and maturation, cell volume increases, followed by a significant decline between maturation and senescence. This age-related change occurs regardless of the sublobular location of the parenchymal cells. (Drawn from data presented by Schmucker, D., Mooney, J., and Jones, A., *Science,* 197, 1005, 1977; **Schmucker, D., Mooney, J., and Jones, A.,** unpublished data.)

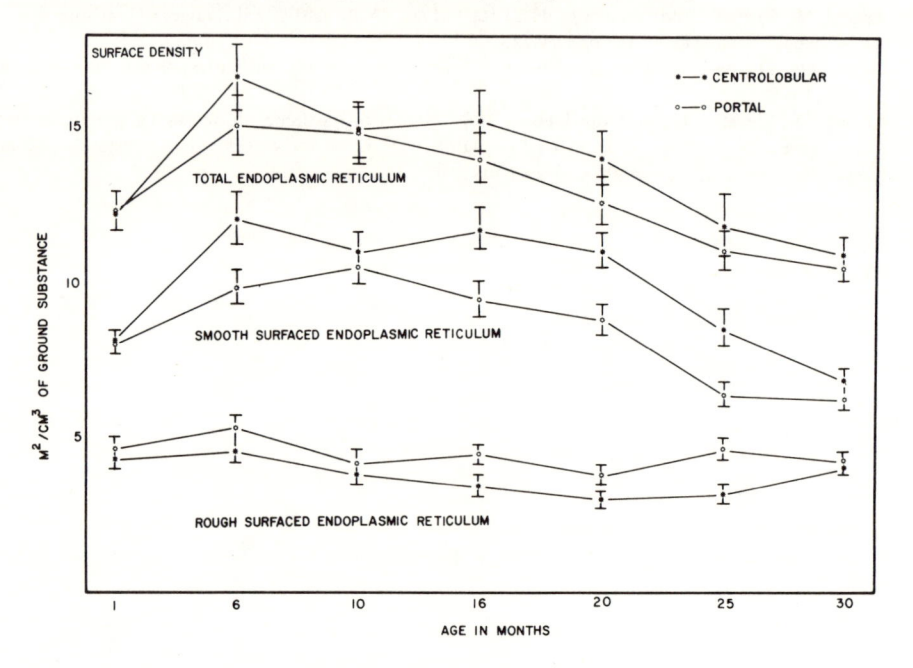

FIGURE 3. The effect of aging on the amount (surface area) of endoplasmic reticulum membrane per volume of hepatocyte ground substance (surface density). The surface area of the total endoplasmic reticulum undergoes a significant decline between maturation and senescence and this overall loss of membrane is entirely attributable to a concomitant reduction in the amount of smooth surfaced endoplasmic reticulum. (Drawn from data presented by Schmucker, D., Mooney, J., and Jones, A., *Science,* 197, 1005, 1977; **Schmucker, D., Mooney, J., and Jones, A.,** Unpublished data.)

Table 3
EFFECT OF AGE ON HEPATIC METABOLISM AND ENZYMES

Species	Age		Ref.
Various strains of rats		The livers of old animals exhibit a reduced capacity to respond to a number of stimuli, such as drugs and hormones (a reduced adaptive responsiveness or hypofunction)	1—5,6,7
Various strains of rats and mice	$\sim$1—30 months	In vivo and in vitro studies reported that total hepatic protein synthesis, especially albumin declines with age[a]	8—13
	$\sim$1—30 months	In vivo and in vitro studies reported that total hepatic protein synthesis either (1) remains unchanged or (2) increases with animal age[a]	14—18
Rat (Fisher, female)	4 weeks—20 months	The hepatic capacity to synthesize proteins, especially albumin, in newly regenerated livers is similar to that in the normal (resting) livers of young animals for up to 12 weeks posthepatectomy	19
Rat		There is a decline in the protein synthesizing capacity of hepatic microsomal preparations from animals between 1 and 9 months of age and no subsequent change in this parameter between 9 and 18 months of age	20
		The reported age-dependant decrease in hepatic protein synthesis may be the result of a defect at the translational level	12,13,21
Rat (Sprague-Dawley, Wistar, F344, male)	1—24 months	The hepatic cholesterol level rises with age in the rat, but the increase in variable (9—28%)	22,24
Rat (F344, male)	1—24 months	The hepatic triglyceride concentration increases by approximately 54% between 2 and 24 months of age, but the level declines in animals between 12 and 24 months, i.e., there is an 88% increase between 2 and 18 months	22,24
Rat (Wistar, F344, male)	1—24 months	Hepatic cholesterol synthesis declines with age: (1) the incorporation of ^{14}C-acetate into cholesterol decreases (63%) and (2) the activity of hepatic 3-hydroxy-3-methylglutaryl CoA reductase decreases by approximately 52% between 2 months and the remaining time points measured, i.e., 9, 12, and 24 months	22,23

Table 3 (continued)
EFFECT OF AGE ON HEPATIC METABOLISM AND ENZYMES

Species	Age		Ref.
Rat (F344, male)	1—24 months	The hepatic capacity to synthesize fatty acids from acetate increases in animals between 2 and 24 months of age (56%)	22,23
Rat (Sprague-Dawley, male)	2—16 months	The rates of hepatic cholesterol turnover and excretion decline with age	25,27
Rat (Wistar, male)	1—18 months	Liver mitochondrial side chain cleavage of cholesterol, i.e., the oxidation of [26-^{14}C] cholesterol to [^{14}CO$_2$], declines 70% between 2 and 18 months of age	22
Rat (Wistar, F344)	1—24 months	The activity of the primary enzyme in bile acid synthesis, microsomal cholesterol -7α-hydroxylase, declines 47% in Wistar rats between 2 and 18 months of age, but this decrease is not significant in F344 rats (9%) between 2 and 24 months	22,23
Human	15—60 years	The lithogenic index of bile increases significantly with age	29
Rat		The activity of certain hepatic microsomal drug-metabolizing enzymes (NADPH cytochrome-C reductase), the amount of hepatic microsomal cytochrome P-450 and the overall hepatic capacity to metabolize drugs (aminopyrene N-demethylation) are markedly reduced in old animals[a]	30,32
Rat	3—29 months	A number of hepatic microsomal enzymes, including NADPH cytochrome-C reductase, in young and old rats respond similarly to phenobarbital stimulation[a]	33,34
Rat (Sprague-Dawley)	2—24 months	The livers of old rats demonstrated a significant reduction in their ability to incorporate leucine into NADPH-cytochrome-C reductase in response to phenobarbital stimulation when compared to those of young animals	35
Mouse (mostly C57BL/6J), rat (male, female)	1—>30 months	There is no definitive pattern to age-dependant changes in hepatic enzyme activities; the activities of some diminish with age, others remain unchanged, and still others increase	36—40
Mouse (C57BL/6J, male, female)	18—30 months	Aging results in a general decline in the activities of hepatic mitochondrial respiratory enzymes[c]	39

Table 3 (continued)
EFFECT OF AGE ON HEPATIC METABOLISM AND ENZYMES

Species	Age		Ref.
Mouse (C57Bl/ICRF, male)	3—32 months	No changes in the levels of cytochrome oxidase or malate dehydrogenase, the overall respiratory capacity or the functional integrity of hepatic mitochondria occur as a function of age[a]	41—43
Rat (WAG/Rij, female)	3—36 months	No changes in the levels of cytochrome oxidase or malate dehydrogenase, the overall respiratory capacity or the functional integrity of hepatic mitochondria occur as a function of age[a]	41—43
Rat (Sprague-Dawley, F344, male)	3—24 months	Age-related changes in hepatic enzyme activities may vary greatly depending on animal strain: hepatic glucose-6-phosphate dehydrogenase decreases ($\sim$50%) between 3 and 24 months of age in Sprague-Dawley rats; whereas the activity of this enzyme doubles in Fischer 344 rats during the same age span	44
Rat (various strains)		The activities of several hepatic lysosomal enzymes have been reported to: (1) increase, (2) decrease, or (3) remain unchanged, i.e., conflicting results	39,40,45—47
Rat (BN/BiRij, female)	3—35 months	The age-related changes in the specific activities of lysosomal enzymes vary depending on their cellular origin, i.e., from parenchymal (hepatocytes) or nonparenchymal (endothelial and Kupffer) cells	48

[a] Conflicting results obtained in separate studies.

REFERENCES

1. **Adelman, R.,** An age-dependent modification of enzyme regulation, *J. Biol. Chem.*, 245, 1032, 1970.
2. **Adelman, R.,** Age-dependent effects in enzyme induction — a biochemical expression of aging, *Exp. Gerontol.*, 6, 75, 1971.
3. **Kanungo, M. and Gandhi, B.,** Induction of malate dehydrogenase isoenzymes in livers of young and old rats, *Proc. Natl. Acad. Sci. USA*, 69, 2035, 1972.
4. **Adelman, R. and Freeman, C.,** Age-dependent regulation of glucokinase and tyrosine aminotransferase activities of rat liver in vivo by adrenal, pancreatic, and pituitary hormones, *Endocrinology*, 90, 1551, 1972.
5. **Rahman, Y. and Peraino, C.,** Effects of age on patterns of enzyme adaptation in male and female rats, *Exp. Gerontol.*, 8, 93, 1973.

Table 3 (continued)
EFFECT OF AGE ON HEPATIC METABOLISM AND ENZYMES

6. **Adelman, R.,** Impaired hormonal regulation of enzyme activity during aging, *Fed. Proc. Fed. Am. Soc. Exp. Biol.*, 34, 179, 1975.
7. **Adelman, R.,** Age-dependent control of enzyme adaptation, *Adv. Gerontol. Res.*, 2, 1, 1972.
8. **Mainwaring, W.,** The effect of age on protein synthesis in mouse liver, *Biochem. J.*, 113, 869, 1969.
9. **Hrachovec, J.,** The effect of age on tissue protein synthesis, *Gerontologia*, 17, 75, 1971.
10. **Mainwaring, W.,** Changes in the ribonucleic acid metabolism of aging mouse tissues with particular reference to the prostate gland, *Biochem. J.*, 110, 79, 1968.
11. **Buetow, D. and Gandhi, P.,** Decreased protein synthesis by microsomes isolated from senescent rat liver, *Exp. Gerontol.*, 8, 243, 1973.
12. **Britton, G. and Sherman, F.,** Altered regulation of protein synthesis during aging as determined by in vitro ribosomal assays, *Exp. Gerontol.*, 10, 67, 1975.
13. **Beauchene, R., Roeder, L., and Barrows, C.,** The interrelationships of age, tissue protein synthesis and proteinuria, *J. Gerontol.*, 25, 359, 1970.
14. **Ove, P., Obenrader, M., and Lansing, A.,** Synthesis and degradation of liver proteins in young and old rats, *Biochim. Biophys. Acta*, 227, 211, 1972.
15. **Chen, J., Ove, P., and Lansing, A.,** In vitro synthesis of microsomal protein and albumin in young and old rats, *Biochim. Biophys. Acta*, 312, 598, 1973.
16. **Blok, L., Krasnitskaya, A., Anokhina, G., and Nikitan, V.,** Protein synthesis in a cell-free system by microsomes and ribosomes of the liver of rats of different ages, *Dokl. Biochem.*, 217, 340, 1974.
17. **van Bezooijen, C., Grell, T., and Knook, D.,** The effect of age on protein synthesis by isolated liver parenchymal cells, *Mech. Ageing Dev.*, 6, 293, 1977.
18. **van Bezooijen, C., Grell, T. and Knook, D.,** Albumin synthesis by liver parenchymal cells isolated from young, adult and old rats, *Biochem. Biophys. Res. Commun.*, 71, 513, 1976.
19. **Obenrader, M., Chen, J., Ove, P., and Lansing, A.,** Functional regeneration in liver of old rats after partial hepatectomy, *Exp. Gerontol.*, 9, 181, 1974.
20. **Layman, D., Ricca, G., and Richardson, A.,** The effect of age on protein synthesis and ribosome aggregation to messenger RNA in rat liver, *Arch. Biochem. Biophys.*, 173, 246, 1976.
21. **Kurtz, D.,** The effect of aging on in vitro fidelity of translation in mouse liver, *Biochem. Biophys. Acta*, 407, 479, 1975.
22. **Story, J., Tepper, S., and Kritchevsky, D.,** Lipid metabolism in aging rats, *Adv. Exp. Med. Biol.*, 61, 281, 1975.
23. **Story, J., Tepper, S., and Kritchevsky, D.,** Age-related changes in the lipid metabolism of Fisher 344 rats, *Lipids*, 11, 623, 1976.
24. **Kritchevsky, D.,** Lipid metabolism in aging, *Mech. Ageing Dev.*, 1, 275, 1972.
25. **Hruza, Z.,** Effect of endocrine factors on cholesterol turnover in young and old rats, *Exp. Gerontol.*, 6, 199, 1971.
26. **Hruza, Z. and Zbuzkova, V.,** Decrease of excretion of cholesterol during aging, *Exp. Gerontol.*, 8, 29, 1973.
27. **Hruza, Z. and Wachtlova, M.,** Decrease of cholesterol turnover in young and old rats, *Exp. Gerontol.*, 4, 245, 1969.
28. **Story, J. and Kritchevsky, D.,** Cholesterol oxidation by rat liver preparation: effect of age, *Experientia*, 30, 242, 1974.
29. **Trash, D., Ross, P., Murison, J., and Boucher, I.,** The influence of age on cholesterol saturation of bile, *Gut*, 17, 394, 1976.
30. **Kato, R. and Takanaka, A.,** Metabolism of drugs in old rats. I. Activities of NADPH-linked electron transport and drug metabolizing enzyme systems in liver microsomes of old rats, *J. Biochem.*, 63, 406, 1968.
31. **Conney, A.,** Pharmacological implications of microsomal enzyme induction, *Pharmacol. Rev.*, 19, 317, 1967.
32. **Schlede, E.,** Varying effect of phenobarbital on hepatic drug metabolism in rats of different ages, *Naunyn Schmiedebergs Arch. Pharmakol.*, 282, 311, 1974.
33. **Gold, G. and Widnell, C.,** Reversal of age-related changes in microsomal enzyme activities following the administration of triamcindone, triiodothyronine and phenobarbitol, *Biochim. Biophys. Acta*, 334, 75, 1974.
34. **Baird, M., Nicolosi, R., Massie, H., and Samis, H.,** Microsomal mixed-function oxidase activity and senescence. I. Hexobarbital sleeptime and induction of components of the hepatic microsomal enzyme system in rats of different ages, *Exp. Gerontol.*, 10, 89, 1975.
35. **Adelman, R., Freeman, C. and Cohen, B.,** Enzyme adaptation as a biochemical probe of development and aging, *Adv. Enzyme Regul.*, 10, 365, 1972.

Table 3 (continued)
EFFECT OF AGE ON HEPATIC METABOLISM AND ENZYMES

36. **Ross, M.,** Aging, nutrition, and hepatic enzyme activity patterns in the rat. II. *J. Nutr.,* 97 (Suppl. 1), 563, 1969.
37. **Wilson, P.,** Enzyme patterns in young and old mouse liver and lungs, *Gerontologia,* 18, 36, 1972.
38. **Florini, J.,** Differences in enzyme levels and physiological processes in mice of different ages, *Exp. Aging Res.,* 1, 137, 1975.
39. **Wilson, P.,** Enzyme changes in aging mammals, *Gerontologia,* 19, 79, 1973.
40. **Finch, C.,** Enzyme activities, gene function and aging in mammals (Review), *Exp. Gerontol.,* 7, 53, 1972.
41. **Wilson, P., Hill, B., and Franks, L.,** The effect of age on mitochondrial enzymes and respiration, *Gerontologia,* 21, 95, 1975.
42. **Brouwer, A., van Bezooijen, C., and Knook, D.,** Respiratory activities of hepatocytes isolated from rats of various ages. A brief note, *Mech. Ageing Dev.,* 6, 265, 1977.
43. **Gold, P., Gee, M. and Strehler, B.,** Effect of age on oxidation phos-phorylation in the rat, *J. Gerontol.,* 23, 509, 1968.
44. **Wang, R. and Mays, L.,** Opposite changes in rat liver glucose-6-phosphate dehydrogenase during aging in Sprague-Dawley and Fischer 344 male rats, *Exp. Gerontol.,* 12, 177, 1977.
45. **Zorzoli, A.,** The influence of age on phosphatase activity in the liver of the mouse, *J. Gerontol.,* 10, 156, 1955.
46. **Elens, A. and Wattiaux, R.,** Age-correlated changes in lysosomal enzyme activities: an index of agingμ, *Exp. Gerontol.,* 4, 131, 1969.
47. **Comolli, R.,** Hydrolase activity and intracellular pH in liver, heart, and diaphragm of aging rats, *Exp. Gerontol.,* 6, 219, 1971.
48. **Knook, D. and Sleyster, E.,** Lysosomal enzyme activities in parenchymal and nonparenchymal liver cells isolated from young, adult and old rats, *Mech. Ageing Dev.,* 5, 389, 1976.

SMALL INTESTINE

D. L. Schmucker and R. K. J. Wang

Table 1
AGE-RELATED CHANGES IN SMALL INTESTINAL MORPHOLOGY

Species	Age		Ref.
Mouse (CE, 129, Swiss, male, female)	3—27 months	The small intestine undergoes an age-related involution characterized by a proliferation of connective tissue and the formation of fibrous sclerotic tissue in the tunica	1—3
Rat (female)	6—28 months	Both the wet and dry weight of the small intestine increase with age	3
Mouse (C57)		Age-related changes in small intestine morphology include atrophic and widely separated crypts, an increased amyloid content (less in the jejunum than in the rest of the tract), and an increased variation in the cell population of the lamina propria	4—6
Mouse		The morphological changes that occur in the epithelial cells from the crypt to the villus tip are similar in adult and senescent mice; however, older animals have a less dense basal lamina near the villus tip and the epithelial cells contain enlarged mitochondria	7
Rat		The number of enterocytes declines beginning at 3 months of age and continuing through senescense; the height of the enterocytes increases between 1 and 9 months and subsequently decreases through 18 months of age: the microvilli are longer in enterocytes of old animals	8
		Enterocyte RNA, water and protein content, and the rate of uptake and incorporation of amino acids decrease with age	9
Mouse (C57 BL)	<18—<35 months	The incidence of epithelial tumors and carcinomas in the gut increases with age in mice (∼ 2% between 27—32 months of age) and demonstrates a predilection for the small bowel rather than the colon as in man	6

255

Table 1 (continued)
AGE-RELATED CHANGES IN SMALL INTESTINAL MORPHOLOGY

Species	Age		Ref.
Mouse (CE, 129, Swiss, male, female)	3—27 months	The histochemical activity of enterocyte alkaline phosphatase declines with age, although there is no age-related effect on the distribution of brush border alkaline phosphatase activity throughout the entire small intestine[a]	1
Rat		The intensity of the histochemical staining of mucopolysaccharides, protein and RNA in the apical cytoplasm of enterocytes diminished in animals beyond 9 months of age	9
		Histochemical demonstration of cell surface enzyme activities: (1) alkaline phosphatase increases up to 6 months and remains constant; (2) α-glucosidase decreases after 9 months of age; (3) β-glucosidase decreases during the first month and remains constant thereafter[a]	10
Human, cow, pig, rat		Peyer's patches are most obvious and largest in young individuals; become less distinct during middle age; and are generally smallest, indistinct or absent in senescent subjects; this age-related reduction occurs equally throughout all parts of the small intestine[a]	11—17
Rat		There is no pronounced age-related atrophy of the Peyer's patches in the rat small intestine[a]	19
Human		The number of lymphoid follicles per Peyer's patch decreases with age	16, 17
Mouse	?—15 months	Most of the age-related fine structural changes in the Peyer's patches appear to occur in the stroma and the reticular cells rather than in the lymphoid elements	18

[a] Conflicting results obtained in two different studies.

REFERENCES

1. **Suntzeff, V.** and **Angelletti, P.**, Histological and histochemical changes in intestines of mice with aging, *J. Gerontol.*, 16, 226, 1961.
2. **Lascalea, M.**, The digestive system in old age, *Excerpts Med.*, 2, 419, 1959.

3. Pénzes, L., Intestinal absorption of glycine, L-alanine and L-leucine in the old rat, *Exp. Gerontol.*, 9, 245, 1974.
4. Andrew, W. and Andrew, N., An age involution in the small intestine of the mouse, *J. Gerontol.*, 12, 136, 1957.
5. Rowlatt, C., Franks, L., Sheriff, M., and Chesterman, F., Naturally occurring tumors and other lesions of the digestive tract in untreated C57BL mice, *J. Natl. Cancer Inst.*, 43, 1353, 1969.
6. Andrew, W., Behnke, R., and Shimizu, Y., Variations in cell population of intestinal lamina propria in relation to age, *Gerontologia*, 12, 129, 1966.
7. Rowlatt, C., Cell aging in the intestinal tract, in *Cell Impairment in Aging and Development*, Cristofalo, V. and Holečková, E., Eds., Plenum Press, New York, 1974, 215.
8. Leutert, G., Rotzsch, W., and Beier, W., On the aging of intermitotic cells — investigations on enterocytes and hepatocytes, in *Cell Impairment in Aging and Development*, Cristofalo, V. and Holečková, E., Eds., Plenum Press, New York, 1974, 235.
9. Tews, K., Jahn, K., and Leutert, G., Bausteinhistochemische Studien an Dunndarmepithel von Ratten verschiedenen Alters, *Z. Mickrosk. Anat. Forsch.*, 83, 423, 1971.
10. Leutert, G., Jahn, K., and Weise, K., Altersabhängige Veränderungen der Enzymaktivität von Enterozytenhistochemische Untersuchungen, *Z. Alternsforsch.*, 26, 375, 1973.
11. Gray, H., *Gray's Anatomy, Descriptive and Applied*, 33rd ed., Davies, D. and Davies, F., Eds., Longmans, London, 1962, 1456.
12. Drennan, M., in *Cunningham's Textbook of Anatomy*, 9th ed., Brash, J., Ed., Oxford University Press, London, 1951, 627.
13. Ham, A. and Leeson, T., *Histology*, 4th ed., Pitman Medical Publishing Company, London, 1961, 628.
14. Carlens, O., Studien über das lymphatische Gewebe des Darmkanals bei einiger. Haustieren, mit besonderer Berücksichtingung der embryöonalen Entwicklung, der Mengenverhaltnisse und der Altersinvolution dieses Gewebes in Dünndarm des Rindes, *Z. Anat. Entwicklungsgesch.*, 86, 393, 1928.
15. Dukes, C. and Bussey, H., The number of lymphoid follicles in the human large intestine, *J. Pathol. Bacteriol.*, 29, 111, 1926.
16. Cornes, J., Number, size, and distribution of Peyer's patches in the human small intestine. II. The effect of aging on Peyer's patches, *Gut*, 6, 230, 1965.
17. Bhanthumnavin, K. and Schuster, M., Aging and gastrointestinal function, in *Handbook of the Biology of Aging*, Finch, C. and Hayflick, L., Eds., Van Nostrand Reinhold, New York, 1977, 209.
18. Chin, K., Ultrastructure of Peyer's patches in the aged mouse, *Acta Anat.*, 84, 523, 1973.
19. Andreasen, E., Studies on the thryrolymphatic system. Quantitative investigations on the thyrolymphatic system in normal rats at different ages under normal conditions and during inanition and restitution after starvation, *Acta Pathol. Microbiol. Scand. Suppl.*, 49, 81, 1943.

Table 2
EFFECTS OF AGING ON INTESTINAL EPITHELIAL CELLS

Species	Age			Ref.
Mouse (CAF₁)	12—30 months		There is no apparent age-related difference in the transit time of jejunal epithelial cells rom the crypt to the villus tip (~50 hr in 12- and 30-month-old mice)[a]	1
Mouse (CAF₁)	89—945 days		There is a marked age-dependent increase in the crypt to villus transit time of duodenal and jejunal epithelial cells[a,b]	2, 3
Mouse (CAF₁, male, female)	93—940 days		There is no apparent age-related change in crypt to villus transit time of epithelial cells in the ileum	4
Mouse (Swiss, BCF, CAF₁)	10—1050 days		The cell cycle of the duodenal, jejunal, and dial epithelium increases with age in the mouse intestine[c]	2-5, 9-11
Mouse (BDF, CDF)	93—940 days		Aging results in a decrease in the population of proliferation or stem cells in the crypts of the small intestine, i.e., a decrease in the percent of crypt cells labeled with ³H-thymidine/unit time.	5, 9, 12
	Age (days)	Number cells/crypt		
	100	126		
	825	89		
Rat			The amounts of certain intestinal intracellular oxidoreductase enzymes (succinodehydrogenase, NADH-diaphorase, isocitrate dehydrogenase) decrease in animals beyond 6 months of age, whereas others (lactate dehydrogenase) increase up to 6 months and remain constant thereafter	6
Mouse (female)	11—34 months		The V_{max} of intestinal phosphomonoesterase decreases while there is no change in the K_m as a function of animal age, suggesting that the enzyme concentration decreases but the activity remains constant	7
Mouse			Epithelial cell fumerase activity in the proximal 2/3rds of the small intestine does not change with increasing animal age	8

a   Conflicting results from two different studies.
b   See Figure 1.
c   See Figures 1 and 2.

REFERENCES

1. **Fry, F., Lesher, S., and Kohn, H.**, Age effect on cell transit time in mouse jejunal epithelium, *Am. J. Physiol.*, 201, 213, 1961.
2. **Baserga, R.**, Cell division and the cell cycle, in *Handbook of the Biology of Aging*, Finch, C. and Hayflick, L., Eds., Van Nostrand Reinhold, New York, 1977, 101.
3. **Lesher, S., Fry, R., and Kohn, H.**, Influence of age on the transit time of cells of the mouse intestinal epithelium. I. Duodenun, *Lab. Invest.*, 11, 289, 1962.
4. **Fry, R., Lesher, S., and Kohn, H.**, Influence of age on the transit time of cells of the mouse intestinal epithelium. II. Ileum, *Lab. Invest.*, 11, 289, 1962.
5. **Lesher, S.**, Chronic irradiation and ageing in mice and rats, in *Radiation and Aging*, Lindopp, P. and Sacher, G., Eds., Taylor and Francis, London, 1966, 183.
6. **Leutert, G., Rotzsch, W., and Beier, W.**, On the aging of intermitotic cells — investigations on enterocytes and hepatocytes, in *Cell Impairment in Aging and Development*, Cristofalo, V. and Holeckova, E., Eds., Plenum Press, New York, 1974, 235.
7. **Sayeed, M.**, Age-related changes in intestinal phosphomonoesterases, *Fed. Proc. Fed. Am. Soc. Exp. Biol.*, 26, 259, 1967.
8. **Bakerman, S.**, Ed., *Aging Life Processes*, Charles C. Thomas, Springfield, Ill., 1969.
9. **Lesher, S., Fry, R., and Kohn, H.**, Age and the generation time of the mouse duodenal epithelial cell, *Exp. Cell Res.*, 24, 334, 1961.
10. **Lesher, S., Fry, R., and Kohn, H.**, Aging and the generation cycle of intestinal epithelial cells in the mouse, *Gerontologia*, 5, 176, 1961.
11. **Thrasher, J. and Greulic, R.**, The duodenal progenitor population. I. Age-related increase in the duration of the cryptal progentor cycle, *J. Exp. Zool.*, 159, 39, 1965.
12. **Thrasher, J. and Greulich, R.**, The duodenal progenitor population. II. Age-related changes in size and distribution, *J. Exp. Zool.*, 159, 385, 1965.

260 *CRC Handbook of Physiology in Aging*

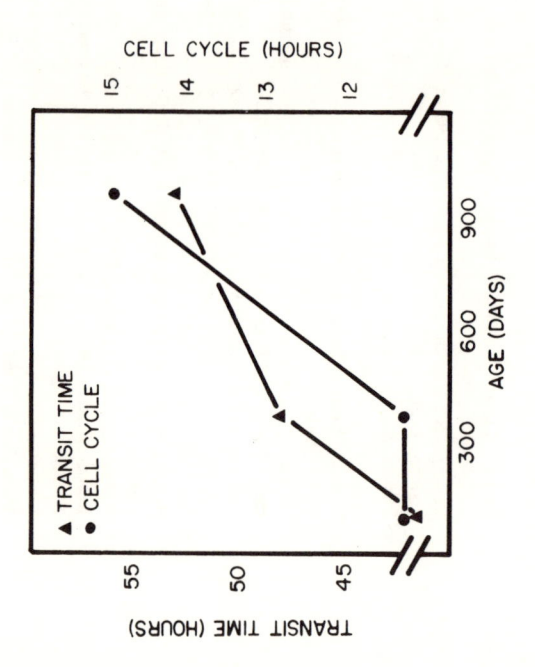

FIGURE 1. The effect of age on the transit time and cell cycle of the duodenal mucosal epithelium in the mouse. Both the cell transit time and the cell cycle increase markedly with age. (Drawn from data presented in Baserga, R., *Handbook of the Biology of Aging*, Finch, C. and Hayflick, L., Eds., Plenum Press, New York, 1977, 101.)

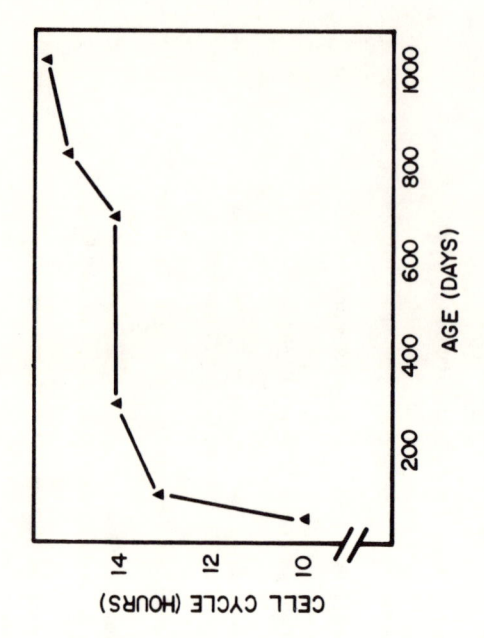

FIGURE 2. The effect of age on the cell cycle of the intestinal epithelium of the mouse. The average length of the cell cycle in all three segments of the small intestine increases much more rapidly (50-100 days of age) in comparison to that measured in the duodenal epithelium alone (∼350 days of age) (See Figure 1). (Drawn from data presented by Lesher, S., *Radiation and Aging*, Lindopp, P. and Sacher, G., Eds., Taylor and Francis, London, 1966, 183.)

Table 3
EFFECT OF AGING ON SEVERAL SMALL INTESTINAL FUNCTIONAL PARAMETERS

Species	Age		Ref.
Human	34—71 years	There is an age-related impairment in the general digestive capacity of individuals without manifest gastrointestinal disorders	1
	34—71 years	The capacity to digest and/or absorb large amounts of dietary protein (>1.5 gm/kg body weight) is reduced in the elderly as a function of age and results in a negative nitrogen balance[a]	2
		Protein digestion and absorption (I^{131}-labeled gelatin) is similar in young and old individuals[a]	3
Rat (Wistar)	19 days—20 months	The transit or passage time of a food bolus through the small intestine is unaffected by aging	4
Rat (Wistar, female)	2—27 months	There is no age-related change in the carbon or nitrogen contents of the small intestinal wall, although the amounts of several amino acids decline in older animals	5

[a] Conflicting results obtained in two different studies.

REFERENCES

1. Kountz, W., Ackerman, P., Kheim, J., and Toro, G., Effects of increased protein intake in older people, *Geriatrics*, 8, 63, 1953.
2. Werner, I. and Hambreaus, L., The digestive capacity of elderly people, *Acta Soc. Med. (Ups.)* 76, 239, 1971.
3. Chinn, A., Lavik, P., and Cameron, D., Measurement of protein digestion and absorption of aged persons by test meal of I^{131}-labelled protein, *J. Gerontol.*, 11, 151, 1956.
4. Varga, F., Transit time changes with age in the gastrointestinal tract of the rat, *Digestion*, 14, 319, 1976.
5. Penzes, L., Data of the chemical composition of the aging intestine, *Digestion*, 3, 174, 1970.

LARGE INTESTINE

D. L. Schmucker and R. K. J. Wang

Table 1
EFFECTS OF AGING ON THE LARGE INTESTINE (COLON)

Species	Age		Ref.
Rat (Wistar)	19 days—20 months	The length of transit time of fecal material increases with age in the rat	1
Human		The incidence of constipation increases with advancing age due to decreased muscle tone and motor function in the colon	2—7
Human		The incidence of diverticular disease increases markedly with age (9% in subjects < 50 years; > 50% in subjects > 70 years)[a]	8—10, 15
Mouse (Swiss, male)	3—20 months	The renewal or transit time of the epithelial cells of the descending colon is prolonged in aged mice (3 months = 40 hr; 20 months = 54 hr)	11
Mouse (CE, 129, Swiss, male, female)	3—27 months	Alkaline phosphatase activity in the tunica of the large intestine increases with age	12
Human		The colon and fecal material of individuals 70—100 years of age contain fewer anaerobic lactobacilli and greater numbers of fungi and coliforms than those of younger subjects (20—70 years)	13, 14

[a] See Figure 1.

Table 1 (continued)
EFFECTS OF AGING ON THE LARGE INTESTINE (COLON)

REFERENCES

1. **Varga, F.**, Transit time changes with age in the gastrointestinal tract of the rat, *Digestion*, 14, 319, 1976.
2. **Bhanthumnavin, K. and Schuster, M.**, Aging and gastrointestinal function in *Handbook of the Biology of Aging*, Finch, C. and Hayflick, L., Eds., Plenum Press, New York, 1977, 209.
3. **Shklar, M.**, Functional bowel distress and constipation in the aged, *Geriatrics*, 27, 79, 1972.
4. **Portis, S. and King, J.**, The gastrointestinal tract in old age, *J. Am. Med. Assoc.*, 148, 1073, 1952.
5. **Busse, E., Barnes, R., and Silverman, A.**, Studies in the processes of aging, *Dis. Nerv. Syst.*, 15, 22, 954.
6. **Berry, T.**, Gastrointestinal disorders with aging, *Med. Times*, 89, 704, 1961.
7. **Meyer, J. and Necheles, H.**, Studies in old age. IV. The clinical significance of salivary, gastric and pancreatic secretion in the aged, *J. Am. Med. Assoc.*, 115, 2050, 1940.
8. **Hughes, L.**, Postmortem survey of diverticular disease of the colon, *Gut*, 10, 336, 1969.
9. **Bumm, R.**, Die Divertikelder Dickdarms und Ihre Komplikationem, *Longenbecks Arch. Klin. Chir.*, 174, 14, 1933.
10. **Parks, T.**, Natural history of diverticular disease of the colon. A review of 521 cases, *Br. Med. J.*, 4, 639, 1969.
11. **Cameron, I.**, Cell proliferation and renewal in aging mice, *J. Gerontol*, 27, 162, 1972.
12. **Suntzeff, V. and Angelletti, P.**, Histological and histochemical changes in intestines of mice with aging, *J. Gerontol.*, 16, 225, 1961.
13. **Gorbach, S., Nahas, L., Lerner, P., and Weinstein, L.**, Studies of intestinal microflora. I. Effects of diet, age, and periodic sampling on number of fecal microorganisms in man, *Gastroenterology*, 53, 845, 1967.
14. **Ketyi, I. and Barna, K.**, Studies on the human intestinal flora. I. The normal intestinal flora and the stability of its constituents, *Acta Microbiol. Acad. Sci. Hung.*, 11, 173, 1964.
15. **Manousos, O., Truelove, S., and Lumsden, K.**, Prevalence of colonic diverticulosis in the general population of the Oxford area, *Br. Med. J.*, 2, 762, 1967.

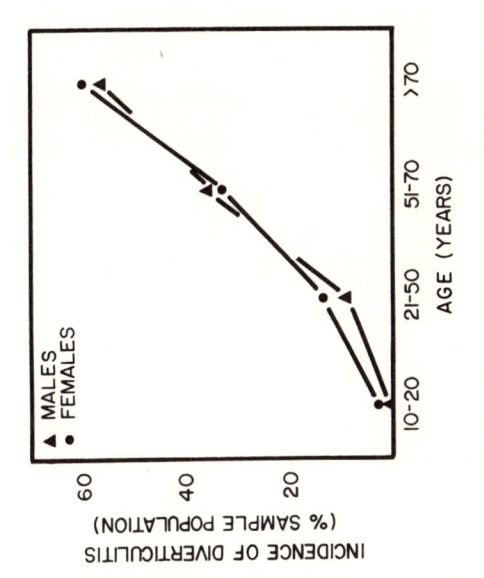

FIGURE 1. The effect of age and sex on the incidence of diverticulitis in humans. The percentage of a given population demonstrating diverticular disease at necropsy increases linearly with age. (Drawn from data presented by Hughes, L., *Gut*, 10, 336, 1969.)

GASTROINTESTINAL SECRETION

D. L. Schmucker and R. K. J. Wang

Table 1
AGE RELATED CHANGES IN THE STRUCTURE AND COMPOSITION OF THE SALIVARY GLANDS

Species	Age		Ref.
Rat (Wistar), human, dog, sheep	21—1100 days	The acinar and duct cells of the salivary glands, particularly the parotid, undergo a marked fatty degeneration with age; the number of "oncocytes" increases	1—9
Rat (Wistar), human, cow, sheep, goat, guinea pig	21—700 days	Aging results in lymphocyte and mast cell infiltration into salivary gland parenchyma and connective tissue and the lumina of the glands are obscured	1,4,10
Rat (Wistar)	65—700 days	The number of pyknotic duct cell nuclei in the salivary glands increases with age	4
Rat (Wistar male, female)	12—30 months	Histochemical analyses revealed: (1) Age-related decreases in the activities of succinic dehydrogenase, cholinesterase, esterase, and alkaline phosphatase; (2) an age-related increase in acid phosphatase activity; (3) age-related decreases in acid mucopolysaccharide and RNA contents, and (4) no age-related change in the DNA content of the secretory cells of the submandibular gland	11
Rat (Wistar)	65—700 days	The glycoprotein bound hexose/protein nitrogen ratio decreases slightly with age	4
Human	-70 years	The amount of endoplasmic reticulum membrane in salivary gland acinar cells is decreased in individuals beyond 60—70 years of age	12
Rat (Wistar)	100—997 days	The mitochondria and the Golgi membranes (complex) in salivary gland secretory cells undergo age-related changes[a]	13
Rat (Wistar, male)	4—24 months	The general fine structure of submandibular gland acinar cells in young and old rats is similar[a]	14

[a] Conflicting results obtained in two separate studies.

REFERENCES

1. **Andrew, W.**, Age changes in the parotid glands of Wistar Institute rats with special reference to the occurance of oncocytes in senility, *Am. J. Anat.*, 85, 157, 1949.
2. **Alberherdt, F.**, Beitrage zur Histologie and Histogenese der Unterkilferdruse (Ge. Mandibuloris) von Hund und Katze, *Z. Mikrosk. Anat. Forsch.*, 40, 558, 1936.
3. **Hamperl, H.**, Beiträge zur normalen und pathologischen Histologie menschlischer Speicheldrüsen, *Z. Mikrosk. Anat. Forsch.*, 27, 1, 1931.
4. **Church, L.**, Age changes in the nuclei of salivary glands of Wistar Institute rats, *Oral Surg., Oral Med. and Oral Pathol.*, 8, 301, 1955.
5. **Hauser, H.**, über Bau and Funktion der Wiederkänerparotes Zugleich ein Beitragzur Mastzellenfrage, *Z. Mikrosk. Anat. Forsch.*, 41, 177, 1937.
6. **Garrett, J.**, Some observation on human submandibular salivary glands, *Proc. R. Soc. Med.*, 55, 448, 1962.
7. **Waterhouse, J.**, Focal adenities in salivary and lacrimal glands, *Proc. R. Soc. Med.*, 56, 911, 1963.
8. **Seifert, G.**, über spontuneränderungen der grössen Kopfspeicheldrüsen bei Laboratoriumstieren, *Beitr. Pathol. Anat.*, 123, 299, 1960.

Table 1 (continued)
AGE RELATED CHANGES IN THE STRUCTURE AND COMPOSITION OF THE SALIVARY GLANDS

9. **Andrew, W.**, Age changes in the salivary glands of Wistar Institute rats with particular reference to the submandibular gland, *J. Gerontol.*, 4, 95, 1949.
10. **Burzynski, N.**, Aging in guinea pig salivary gland, *J. Gerontol.*, 26, 204, 1971.
11. **Bogart, B.**, The effect of age on the histochemistry of the rat submandibular gland, *J. Gerontol.*, 22, 372, 1967.
12. **Rauch, S.**, *Die Speicheldrüsen des Menschen*, Stuttgart, Thieme, 1959.
13. **Kurtz, S.**, Cytologic studies of the salivary glands of the rat in reference to the aging process, *J. Gerontol.*, 9, 421, 1954.
14. **Myśliwski, A.**, Age-related changes in course of restitution of secretory material in rat submandibular gland stimulated with isoproterenol, *Exp. Gerontol.*, 12, 81, 1977.

Table 2
AGE-RELATED CHANGES IN SALIVARY GLAND FUNCTION AND IN THE COMPOSITION OF SALIVA

Species	Age (years)		Ref.
Human		The flow rate of salivary secretion (volume of saliva/unit time) decreases with age, particularly in the parotid gland, and may result from a loss of functional tissue	1—4
	12—96	The concentration of carbohydrate-splitting enzymes in saliva (salivary α-amylase or pytalin) declines with age (30—60% in individuals >60 years of age)	1
		The potassium ion concentration in saliva is unaffected by age[a]	2,5
	40—92	The sodium ion concentration of total resting saliva undergoes a significant increase in men between 40 and 92 years of age, but no age-related difference was observed in the saliva of women in the same age group	6
		The calcium concentration in unstimulated total saliva increases with age	7
	40—92	The salivary concentration of potassium is slightly increased in males and females >40 years of age[a]	6
		The concentration of inorganic phosphorous in resting total saliva tends to increase with age	8
		There is no age-related change in the pH of saliva	9
Rat (Wistar, male)		There is a marked age-related decrease in the response of rat salivary glands to isoproterenol stimulation, both in the time required to initiate and in the magnitude of increased DNA synthesis	10

[a] Conflicting results obtained in two separate studies.

REFERENCES

1. **Meyer, J., Spier, E., and Neuwelt, F.,** Basal secretion of digestive enzymes in old age, *Arch. Intern. Med.*, 65, 171, 1940.
2. **Schneyer, L. and Schneyer, C.,** Inorganic composition of saliva, in *Handbook of Physiology*, Section 6, Vol. 3, Code, C. F. and Heidel, W., Eds., American Physiological Society, Washington, D.C., 1967, 497.
3. **Lourie, R.,** Rate of secretion of parotid glands in normal children, *Am. J. Dis. Child.*, 65, 455, 1943.
4. **Becks, H. and Wainwright, W.,** Human saliva. XIII. Rate of flow of resting saliva of healthy individuals, *J. Dent. Res.*, 22, 291, 1943.
5. **Meyer, J., Golden, J., Steiner, N., and Necheles, H.,** The pytalin content of human saliva in old age, *Am. J. Physiol.*, 119, 600, 1937.
6. **Grad, B.,** Diurnal, age, and sex changes in the sodium and potassium concentrations of human saliva, *J. Gerontol.*, 9, 276, 1954.
7. **Becks, H.,** Human saliva. XIV. Total calcium content of resting saliva of 650 healthy individuals, *J. Dent. Res.*, 22, 397, 1943.
8. **Wainwright, W.,** Human saliva. XV. Inorganic phosphorous content of resting saliva of 650 healthy individuals, *J. Dent. Res.*, 22, 403, 1943.
9. **Brawley, R.,** Studies on the pH of normal resting saliva. I. Variations with age and sex. *J. Dent. Res.*, 15, 55, 1935.
10. **Adelman, R., Stein, G., Roth, G., and Englander, D.,** Age-dependent regulation of mammalian DNA synthesis and cell proliferation in vivo, *Mech. Ageing Dev.*, 1, 49, 1972.

Table 3
EFFECTS OF AGING ON GASTRIC GLAND SECRETION

Species	Age (years)		Ref.
Human (male, female)	19—66	Aging results in reduced basal gastric HCl secretion (achlorohydria) in individuals beyond 50 years of age; the rate of secretion is greater in males than in females; and this decrease is usually associated with an increased incidence of atrophic gastritis	1—5,12
	19—65	Histamine-stimulated gastric acid secretion decreases with age in males and females, but the decline is more marked in females	3,6
Human		The acidity and the volume of gastric acid secreted following a submaximal dose of histamine (0.01 μgm/kg), decline with age	7,8
Human (male)	—87	The secretion of gastric intrinsic factor is reduced with age and this decline is associated with: (1) a loss of parietal cells and (2) sometimes the appearance of parietal cell autoantibodies	1,9
Human	12—96	Gastric secretion of pepsin declines with age (>70 years)	10,11,13
	12—90	Aging results in incomplete digestion of carbohydrates in the mouth and stomach of old individuals	10
	18—62	The free acidity of psychologically induced gastric secretion declines within 10 min after the stimulation in old individuals, whereas it remains at a high level in younger subjects	14
		There is no age-related decrease in gastric acid secretion if the data are expressed against the exchangeable potassium ion pool rather than body weight	15
Human (male, female)	19—66	The age-related decline in gastric juice secretion is almost entirely attributable to a concomitant decrease in the parietal component rather than the nonparietal component[a]	3

[a] See Table 4.

REFERENCES

1. **Andrews, G., Haneman, B., Arnold, B., Booth, J., and Taylor, K.,** Atrophic gastritis in the aged, *Australas. Ann. Med.,* 16, 230, 1967.
2. **Hradsky, M.,** Chronische Gastritis bei jungen and alten Personen Histologische und histochemische Untersuchung, *Gerontol. Clin.* 8, 164, 1966.
3. **Baron, J.,** Studies of basal and peak acid output with an augmented histamine test, *Gut,* 4, 136, 1963.
4. **Levin, E., Kirsner, J., and Palmer, W.,** A simple measure of gastric secretion in man: comparison of one hour basal secretion, histamine secretion, and 12 hour nocturnal gastric secretion, *Gastroenterology,* 19, 88, 1951.
5. **Pollard, W.,** Histamine test meals. An analysis of 988 consecutive tests, *Arch Intern. Med.,* 51, 903, 1933.
6. **Grossman, M., Kirsner, J., and Gillespie, I.,** Basal and histolog-stimulated gastric secretion in control subjects and in patients with peptic ulcer or gastric cancer, *Gastroenterology,* 45, 14, 1963.
7. **Bloomfield, A. and Keefer, C.,** Gastric acidity: relation to various factors such as age and physical fitness, *J. Clin. Invest.,* 5, 205, 1928.
8. **Bloomfield, A. and Keefer, C.,** Gastric motility and the volume of gastric secretion in man, *J. Clin. Invest.,* 5, 295, 1928.
9. **Coghill, N., Doniach, D., Roitt, I., Mollin, D., and Wynn, A.,** Autoantibodies in simple atrophic gastritis, *Gut,* 6, 48, 1965.

Table 3 (continued)
EFFECTS OF AGING ON GASTRIC GLAND SECRETION

10. **Meyer, J., Spier, E., and Neuwelt, F.,** Basal secretion of digestive enzymes in old age, *Arch. Intern. Med.*, 65, 171, 1940.
11. **Osterberg, A., Vanzant, F., Alvarez, W., and Rivers, A.,** Studies of pepsin in human gastric juice, *Am. J. Dig. Dis. Nutr.*, 3, 35, 1936.
12. **Davies, D. and Jones, J.,** Investigation into gastric secretion of 100 normal persons over age of 60, *Q. J. Med.*, 23, 1, 1930.
13. **Meyer, J. and Necheles, H.,** Studies in old age. IV. The clinical significance of salivary, gastric, and pancreatic secretion in the aged, *J. Am. Med. Assoc.*, 115, 2050, 1940.
14. **Necheles, H. and Maskin, H.,** Studies on constitution and peptic ulcer. I. Appetite secretion in normal persons and in ulcer patients, *Am. J. Dig. Dis. Nutr.*, 3, 90, 1936.
15. **Bernier, J., Vidon, N., and Mignon, M.,** The value of a cooperative multicenter study for establishing a table of normal values for gastric acid secretion as a function of sex, age and weight, *Biol. Gastroenterol.*, 6, 287, 1973.

Table 4
AGE-RELATED CHANGES IN THE PARIETAL AND NONPARIETAL COMPONENTS OF BASAL AND HISTAMINE-STIMULATED GASTRIC SECRETION IN HUMANS

Components	Basal, age (years) <30	Basal, age (years) >30		Histimine-stimulated, age (years) <30	Histimine-stimulated, age (years) >30
Parietal (mℓ/hr)	23	8	(mℓ/hr peak)	192	98
Nonparietal (mℓ/hr)	20	12	(mℓ/hr peak)	39	41

Note: The age-related decreases in both the basal and stimulated levels are largely attributable to concomitant decreases in the parietal component.

Table 5
EFFECTS OF AGING ON THE STRUCTURE AND FUNCTION OF THE EXOCRINE PANCREAS

Species	Age (years)		Ref.
Rat (Gray-Norway), human		Aging results in the proliferation of undifferentiated intralobular duct epithelial cells and the degeneration of the acini in the Gray-Norway rat, but not in several other strains	1
Human		The epithelium of the pancreatic ducts undergoes a metaplastic change in senile individuals	2
	12—90	The secretion of pancreatic amylase is only slightly decreased and pancreatic lipase concentration is unchanged with age[a]	3
	12—96	There is a 20% decrease in the pancreatic lipase concentration of (1) fasting duodenal content and (2) stimulated pancreatic secretion[a]	4
	12—96	The concentration of trypsin in stimulated pancreatic juice is similar in young and old individuals	4
	22—82	There is little or no age or sex-related decline in the peak volume and bicarbonate responses of the pancreas to secretin stimulation	5

[a] Conflicting results obtained in two separate studies.

REFERENCES

1. **Andrew, W.**, Senile changes in the pancreas of Wistar Institute rats and of man with special regard to the similarity of locule and cavity formation, *Am. J. Anat.*, 74, 97, 1944.
2. **Kurtz, S.**, Aging changes in the salivary glands and pancreas, in *Structural Aspects of Aging,* Bourne, G., Ed., Hafner, New York, 1961, 71.
3. **Meyer, J., Spier, E., and Neuwelt, F.**, Basal secretion of digestive enzymes in old age, *Arch. Intern. Med.*, 65, 171, 1940.
4. **Meyer, J. and Necheles, H.**, Studies in old age. IV. The clinical significance of salivary, gastric, and pancreatic secretion in the aged, *J. Am. Med. Assoc.*, 115, 2050, 1940.
5. **Rosenberg, I., Friedland, N., Janowitz, H., and Dreiling, D.**, The effect of age and sex upon human pancreatic secretion of fluid and bicarbonate, *Gastroenterology,* 50, 191, 1966.

ABSORPTION

H. A. Bertrand

Table 1
THE EFFECT OF AGE ON THE ABSORPTION OF IONS

Ion	Organism	Observation	Preparation	Ref.
Calcium	Man	The amount of dietary calcium required to achieve calcium balance was greater in 8 elderly subjects (69—88 years) than in the young even when the elderly subjects were in positive nitrogen balance		1
		When measured by blood radiocalcium levels, the rate of calcium absorption decreases beyond the age of 55—60 years in females and 65—70 years in males		2
		Comparing the calcium absorption of 12 elderly patients (60—80 years) with what is known about younger subjects, it was found that the elderly subjects absorbed less calcium more slowly than the younger subjects		3
		Ingestion of 10 g CaCO$_3$ produced a much lower maximum serum calcium concentration in 6 elderly subjects (70—90 years) than in 6 young subjects (23—33 years)		4
		Comparing the jejunal absorption of calcium (as gluconate) at 1.0, 2.5, 5, and 10 mM in 7 young adults (22—31 years) and 6 elderly adults (61—75 years) after they had been on a low (300mg/day) or high (2000 mg/day) calcium diet for 4—8 weeks prior to the jejunal perfusion experiment, it was found that calcium absorption was greater in the young than in the elderly adults	Triple-lumen intestinal perfusion system	5
	Rat (Sprague-Dawley)	Calcium absorption is greater in 6—8 week old rats (100—150 g) than in 16—20 week-old rats (200—330 g)		6
	Rat (Wistar)	Calcium absorption decreases from 1.5—106 weeks of age when animals are maintained on a diet containing 0.5% calcium		7
		Fecal calcium increased between 1 month and 2 years of age: on a diet with 0.129% calcium and 0.229% phosphorus, calcium balance decreased from a positive 96.4% at 1 month of age to a negative 6.7% at 2 years of age		8

Table 1 (continued)
THE EFFECT OF AGE ON THE ABSORPTION OF IONS

Ion	Organism	Observation	Preparation	Ref.
	Rat (male, Wistar)	Using 2 and 12 month-old rats, it was calculated the calcium absorption of the older rats was less than that of the younger rats by studying calcium turnover when ^{45}Ca was injected into animals on a balanced diet containing 4 mg each calcium and phosphorus per g diet		9
	Rat (male, Sherman)	The ability of the duodenum to take up calcium from 4×10^{-5} M CaCl$_2$ decreased between rats of 1—1.5 months of age (50—90 g) and rats of more than 12 months of age (400—500 g)	Everted duodenal sac	10
	Rat (male)	Intestinal absorption is greater in 2 month-old rats (70 g mean body mass) than in 22—28 month-old rats (250 g mean body mass) at low calcium concentrations (2.5 and 10 mM)	Intestine *in situ*	11
	Rat	The ability to absorb calcium falls markedly from 1—4 months of age in females and from 2—4 months in males at which age males and females absorb the same amount of calcium; absorption continues to decrease at least until 18 months of age		12
	Rat (Wistar)	Younger rats (1—6.5 months old) absorb more ^{45}Ca than did older rats (16 months old)		13
	Rat (male)	When challenged by a low calcium diet, older rats (18, 21, and 24 months old) cannot stay in calcium balance, whereas younger rats (less than 18 months old) maintain calcium balance with the same challenge; also the higher the calcium content of the diet prior to the low calcium challenge, the greater the magnitude of the negative calcium balance for the older rats		14
	Rat (male)	Although the K$_t$ of calcium transport did not change between 6 and 38 weeks, calcium influx decreased and the permeability to calcium decreased	Intestinal sacs	15
	Rat (Sprague-Dawley)	Combining the use of ^{45}Ca and balance studies to evaluate calcium absorption, there was no marked difference in the amount of calcium consumed or excreted between old rats (22—32 months old) and mature rats (10—12 months old) although the amount of endogenous calcium as fecal calcium was greater in old than in mature rats		16

Calcium	Rat (male, Wistar)	Membranes prepared from the basal-lateral portion of the proximal 14 cm of the intestine from 3.5 and 6.5 week-old rats were studied to assess the activity of the (Na$^+$ + Ca^{++})-ATPase believed to move calcium from the intestinal epithelial cells to the fluid bathing the serosal surface of these cells and the activity was found to be greater in membranes prepared from the younger than from the older rats	17
	Dog	Comparing older dogs (7—14 years) of various breeds with young beagles (up to 34 weeks of age), it was found that the older dogs did not stay in calcium balance unless their diet was rich in the element	18
	Cattle (Hereford)	The percent of oral ^{45}Ca retained decreased with increasing age from 95% at 0.3 months of age to 17% at 144—190 months of age, whereas retention of ^{45}Ca administered intravenously decreased from 98—75% over the same age span	19
Phosphorus	Man	No evidence was found that dietary phosphorus requirements are greater in 8 elderly subjects (69—88 years) than in young subjects	1
Iron	Rat (McCollum)	The absorption of iron measured as percent of oral dose retained decreased with age between 1 and 12 months in males and between 1.5 and 12 months in females with the amount being absorbed by females being lower than that absorbed by males at all ages; when males were subjected to 48 hr of reduced atmospheric pressure prior to the iron absorption test, increased iron absorption occurred at both 1 and 12 months of age	20
	Rat	Absorption is virtually complete in the neonate and decreases with increasing animal weight until 21—23 days of age at which age the adult iron absorption level (less than 25% presented) is reached	21
Strontium	Rat	Absorption is virtually complete in the neonate and decreases with increasing animal weight until 21—23 days of age at which the adult strontium absorption level is reached	21
Lead	Monkey (Rhesus)	Older monkeys (years) show lead toxicity more rapidly than young monkeys (days or months) possibly because they absorb more of the lead if the difference in fecal lead between days old and months old monkeys can be extended to monkeys at several years of age	22	Lead presented as lead paint mixed in a vitamin D supplement spread on bread
	Rat	Absorption is virtually complete in the neonate and decreases with increasing animal weight until 21—23 days of age at which age the adult lead absorption level is reached	21

Table 1 (continued)
THE EFFECT OF AGE ON THE ABSORPTION OF IONS

REFERENCES

1. **Ackermann, P. G. and Toro, G.**, Calcium and phosphorus balance in elderly men, *J. Gerontol.*, 8, 289, 1953.
2. **Bullamore, J. R., Gallagher, J. C., Wilkinson, R., Nordin, B. E. C., and Marshall, D. H.**, Effect of age on calcium absorption, *Lancet*, 535, 1970.
3. **Lender, M., Verner, E., Stankiewicz, H., and Menczel, J.**, Intestinal absorption of ^{47}Ca in elderly patients with osteoporosis, Paget's disease, and osteomalacia. Effects of calcitonin, oestrogen and vitamin D$_2$ *Gerontology*, 23, 31, 1977.
4. **Epstein, S., Van Mieghem, W., Sagel, J., and Jackson, W. P. U.**, Effect of single large doses of oral calcium on serum calcium levels in the young and the elderly, *Metabolism*, 22, 1163, 1973.
5. **Ireland, P. and Fordtran, J. S.**, Effect of dietary calcium and age on jejunal calcium absorption in humans studied by intestinal perfusion, *J. Clin. Invest.*, 52, 2672, 1973.
6. **Harrison, H. E. and Harrison, H. C.**, Studies with radiocalcium: the intestinal absorption of calcium, *J. Biol. Chem.*, 188, 83, 1951.
7. **Hansard, S. L. and Crowder, H. M.**, The physiological behavior of calcium in the rat, *J. Nutr.*, 62, 325, 1957.
8. **Henry, K. M. and Kon, S. K.**, The effect of age and of supply of phosphorus on the assimilation of calcium by the rat, *Biochem. J.*, 41, 169, 1947.
9. **Milhaud, G., Cherian, A. G., and Mouktar, M. S.**, Calcium metabolism in the rat studied with calcium^{45}: effect of age, *Proc. Soc. Exp. Biol. Med.*, 114, 382, 1963.
10. **Schachter, D., Dowdle, E. B., and Schenker, H.**, Active transport of calcium by the small intestine of the rat, *Am. J. Physiol.*, 198, 263, 1960.
11. **Winter, D., Dobre, V., and Oeriu, S.**, Calcium transport through the duodenal wall of rats, *Experientia*, 31, 198, 1975.
13. **Hansard, S. L., Comar, C. L. and Plumlee, M. P.**, Effect of calcium status, mass of calcium administered, and age on Ca^{45} metabolism in the rat, *Proc. Soc. Exp. Biol. Med.*, 78, 455, 1951.
14. **Henry, K. M. and Kon, S. K.**, The relationship between calcium retention and body stores of calcium in the rat: effect of age and vitamin D, *Br. J. Nutr.*, 7, 147, 1953.
15. **Papworth, D. G. and Patrick, G.**, The kinetics of influx of calcium and strontium into rat intestine in vitro, *J. Physiol. (London)*, 210, 999, 1970.
16. **Hironaka, R., Draper, H. H., and Kastelic, J.**, Physiological aspects of aging. III. The influence of aging on calcium metabolism in rats, *J. Nutr.*, 71, 356, 1960.
17. **Birge, S. J. and Gilbert, H. R.**, Identification of an intestinal sodium and calcium-dependent phosphatase stimulated by parathyroid hormone, *J. Clin. Invest.*, 54, 710, 1974.
18. **Liu, C. H. and McCay, C. M.**, Studies of calcium metabolism in dogs, *J. Gerontol.*, 8, 264, 1953.
19. **Hansard, S. L., Comar, C. L., and Davis, G. K.**, Effects of age upon the physiologic behavior of calcium in cattle, *Am. J. Physiol.*, 177, 383, 1954.
20. **Yeh, S. D. J., Stoltz, W., and Chow, B. F.**, The effect of age on iron absorption in rats, *J. Gerontol.*, 20, 177, 1965.
21. **Forbes, G. B. and Reina, J. G.**, Effect of age on gastrointestinal absorption (Fe, Sr, Pb) in the rat, *J. Nutr.*, 102, 647, 1972.
22. **Zook, B. C., London, W. T., Sever, J. L., and Sauer, R. M.**, Experimental lead paint poisoning in nonhuman primates. I. Clinical signs and course, *J. Med. Primatol.*, 5, 23, 1976.

Table 2
THE EFFECT OF AGE ON THE ABSORPTION OF CARBOHYDRATE

Carbohydrate	Organism	Observation	Preparation	Ref.
Glucose	Man	In some elderly people (72—88 years), the rate of glucose absorption is slow from a test meal containing 1 g glucose/kg body mass		1
	Rat (male, Wistar)	The amount of glucose absorbed from the stomach and intestine in 3 hr after a 24 hr fast decreased with increasing body mass between 100 g and 350—400 g animals	0.6 g glucose/100 g body mass presented in a 30% solution by stomach tube	2
		Studying the glucose absorption of 2, 5, 10, 15, 20, 26, and 32 month-old rats it was found that glucose absorption either increased significantly during the first 10 months when expressed as mg/hr or mg/cm of intestine or decreased significantly during the first 10 months when expressed as mg/100 g body weight/hr; after 10 months there was no change in glucose absorption	Intestinal loop *in situ*	3
3-Methyl-glucose	Man	The 5 hr urinary excretion of 3-methyl-glucose decreased with age while renal function was normal suggesting absorption is the cause of the decreased urinary excretion		4
6-Deoxy-D-glucose	Mouse (C57Bl/6)	The ability of intestinal tissue to concentrate 0.6 mM 6-Deoxy-D-glucose increases until animal reaches 21 days of age after which there is no significant decrease in this ability between 21 days and 24 months of age; ability of intestinal tissue to concentrate 0.6 mM 6-deoxy-D-glucose is greater in females between 4 and 14 months of age than it is in males of the same age, but by 24 months of age there is no sex difference in the ability of intestinal tissue to concentrate this sugar	Everted sac of first two-thirds of small intestine	5
Galactose	Man	Rate of absorption after a 40 g galactose meal was slower in 35 elderly subjects (43—108 years) than in 30 young subjects (13—40 years), when measured by blood galactose 30, 60, and 90 min after the meal		6

Table 2 (continued)
THE EFFECT OF AGE ON THE ABSORPTION OF CARBOHYDRATE

Carbohydrate	Organism	Observation	Preparation	Ref.
Xylose	Man	Although decreasing with age the decrease may partially be an artifact resulting from reduced renal clearance since absorption is measured by urinary output; nevertheless, there is either a gradual decline in xylose absorption occurring over many decades or a marked decline in xylose absorption only above 80 years of age		7—13
		Moreover, by correcting xylose absorption for decreased renal clearance and slower gastric emptying it has been observed that only 26% of 85 patients in the hospital for cerebrovascular disease between the ages of 63 and 95 years had a lower xylose absorption than 20 primary orthopedic patients between the ages of 18 and 35 years	25 g oral xylose, 5 g intravenous xylose	14

REFERENCES

1. Chinn, A. B., Lavik, P. S., and Cameron, D. B., Measurement of protein digestion and absorption in aged persons by a test meal of ^{131}I-labeled protein, *J. Gerontol.*, 11, 151, 1956.
2. Phillips, R. A. and Gilder, H., Metabolism studies in the albino rat: the relation of age, nutrition, and hypophysectomy on the absorption of dextrose from the gastrointestinal tract, *Endocrinology*, 27, 601, 1940.
3. Klimas, J. E., Intestinal glucose absorption during the lifespan of a colony of rats, *J. Gerontol.*, 23, 529, 1968.
4. Sapp, O. L., Sessions, J. T., and Rose, J. W., Effect of aging on intestinal absorption of sugars, *Clin. Res.*, 12, 31, 1964.
5. Calingaert, A. and Zorzoli, A., The influence of age on 6-deoxy-D-glucose accumulation by mouse intestine, *J. Gerontol.*, 20, 211, 1965.
6. Meyer, J., Sorber, H., Oliver, J., and Necheles, H., Studies in old age. VII. Intestinal absorption in old age, *Gastroenterology*, 1, 876, 1943.
7. Fowler, D. and Cooke, W. T., Diagnostic significance of D-xylose tolerance test, *Gut*, 1, 67, 1960.
8. Finlay, J. M., Hogarth, J., and Wrightman, K. J. R., A clinical evaluation of the D-xylose tolerance test, *Ann. Intern. Med.*, 61, 411, 1964.
9. Texter, E. C., Cooper, J. A. D., Vidinli, M. and Finlay, J. M., Laboratory procedures in the diagnosis of malabsorption, *Med. Clin. North Am.*, 48, 117, 1964.
10. Fikry, M. E. and Aboul-Wafa, M. H., Intestinal absorption in the old, *Gerontol. Clin.*, 7, 171, 1965.
11. Kendall, M. J., The influence of age on the xylose absorption test, *Gut*, 11, 498, 1970.
12. Pelz, K. S., Gottfried, S. P., and Soos, E., Intestinal absorption studies in the aged, *Geriatrics*, 23, 149, 1968.
13. Guth, P. H., Physiologic alterations in small bowel function with age, *Am. J. Dig. Dis.*, 13, 565, 1968.
14. Webster, S. G. P. and Leeming, J. T., Assessment of bowel function in the elderly using a modified xylose tolerance test, *Gut*, 16, 109, 1975.

Table 3
THE EFFECT OF AGE ON THE ABSORPTION OF PROTEIN AND AMINO ACIDS

Substance studied	Organism	Observation	Preparation	Ref.
Protein	Man	There was no marked decrease with age in the absorption of ^{131}I into blood from an ^{131}I-albumin test meal when elderly subjects (72—88 years) were compared with young subjects (16—61 years)		1
	Man	A larger protein nitrogen intake is required for elderly subjects to achieve nitrogen balance than is required in young adults, and the time required to respond to changes in protein nitrogen intake is greater in the elderly than in the young adult subjects		2
Amino acids	Man	Ingestion of 7.5 g amino acid from a protein hydrolysate causes a rise in serum amino acid reaching a peak of 2 mg/l in 1 hr in adult subjects, whereas the same intake caused no increase in serum amino acid in aged subjects; moreover, ingestion of 15 g amino acid caused a 40—50 mg/l rise in serum amino acid in 1 hr in adults but a lower increase in serum amino acid was observed in aged subjects		3
Glycine	Rat (female, Wistar)	Expressed on a wet intestinal weight basis, there was no marked difference in glycine absorption between 6-month (216 g mean body mass), 12-month (257 g mean body mass), and 25—28-month (267 g mean body mass) animals at luminal glycine concentrations ranging from 10—80 mM	Small intestinal perfusion *in situ*	4
Alanine	Rat (female, Wistar)	Expressed on an intestinal wet weight basis, there was no marked difference in alanine absorption between 6-month (216 g mean body mass), 12-month (257g mean body mass), and 25—58-month (267 g mean body mass) animals at luminal alanine concentrations ranging from 10—40 mM	Small intestinal perfusion *in situ*	4
Leucine	Rat (female, Wistar)	Expressed on an intestinal wet weight basis, there was no marked difference in leucine absorption between 6-month (216 g mean body mass), 12-month (257 mean body mass), and 25—58-month (267 g mean body mass) animals at luminal leucine concentrations ranging from 10—80 mM	Small intestinal perfusion *in situ*	4

Table 3 (continued)
THE EFFECT OF AGE ON THE ABSORPTION OF PROTEIN AND AMINO ACIDS

Substance studied	Organism	Observation	Preparation	Ref.
Lysine	Rat (female, Wistar)	The Michaelis constant of lysine absorption is not influenced by age when 6-month (205 g mean body mass), 12 month (242 g mean body mass), and 25—26-month (278 g mean body mass) animals were studied using luminal lysine concentrations varying from 1—20 mM	Small intestinal perfusion *in situ*	10
Arginine	Rat (female, Wistar)	The Michaelis constant of arginine absorption is lower in 11-week-old rats than in 9- or 27.5-month-old rats with the Michaelis constant of arginine absorption being greatest in 9-month-old animals	Small intestinal perfusion *in situ*	11
		The Michaelis constant of arginine absorption is not influenced by age when 6-month (221 g mean body mass), 12-month (248 g mean body mass), and 25—26-month (255 g mean body mass) animals were studied using luminal arginine concentrations varying from 1—20 mM	Small intestinal perfusion *in situ*	10
Methionine	Man	Nitrogen balance in elderly men is achieved only at double the methionine intake required to keep younger men in nitrogen balance		12
	Rat (female, Wistar)	There is an increase in the amount of ^{35}S-methionine removed from the duodenal lumen with age when 6-month-old rats (235 g mean body mass) are compared with 26-month-old rats (255 g mean body mass)	Duodenum *in situ*	13
Cysteine	Rat (male)	The rate at which orally or intraluminally administered cysteine appeared in blood is greater in 18-month-old rats than in 2-month-old rats but the maximal blood values were the same at both ages; however, since the treatment of the 18-month-old rats with folcysteine for 3 weeks before the experiment eliminated the greater rate of cysteine transport in this group, it was suggested that the age effect on cysteine absorption was a consequence of nutritional deficiency in the older animals		14

Valine	Rat (male, Wistar)	Transport of 3 mM valine decreased between 4 and 18 weeks of age with no further significant decrease between 18 and 40 weeks of age when the ability of intestinal tissue to concentrate valine is one-sixth what it was at 8 weeks of age	Everted sac of mid small intestine	5
	Rat (Wistar)	By comparing the kinetic characteristics of valine transport at valine concentrations of 0.5—5 mM in 2-day-old rats with those of adult rats (180—260 g), it was found that the Michaelis constants for valine accumulation were not statistically different between 2 day old and adult rats but that the maximum valine accumulation of the 2-day-old rat was statistically greater than that of adult rats	Intestinal segments	6
Tryptophan	Rat	On a diet containing 0—0.33% tryptophan, postprandial plasma, tryptophan levels were greater in old rats than in young rats, whereas there was little difference in this measurement between ages when the rats were postabsorptive		7
	Rat (female, Wistar)	Tryptophan absorption is similar in 6-month (233 g mean body mass) and 27-month (243 g mean body mass) animals at luminal tryptophan concentrations ranging from 2—20 mM	Small intestinal perfusion *in situ*	8
Phenylalanine	Rat (female, Wistar)	The Michaelis constant for phenylalanine absorption decreases with age between 6-month (233 g mean body mass), 12-month (279 g mean body mass), and 27-month (243 g mean body mass) animals when luminal phenylalanine concentrations vary from 5—30 mM	Small intestinal perfusion *in situ*	8
Proline	Rat (female, Wistar)	The Michaelis constant for proline absorption decreases with age between 6-month (233 g mean body mass), 12-month (279 g mean body mass), and 27-month (243 g mean body mass) animals when luminal proline concentrations vary from 10—80 mM	Small intestinal perfusion *in situ*	8
Lysine	Rat (female, Wistar)	The Michaelis constant of lysine absorption is greater at 8 and 27.5 months than at 2.5 months but the Michaelis constant of lysine absorption is not affected by age between 8 and 27.5 months	Small intestinal perfusion *in situ*	9

Table 3 (continued)
THE EFFECT OF AGE ON THE ABSORPTION OF PROTEIN AND AMINO ACIDS

REFERENCES

1. Chinn, A. B., Lavi, P. S., and Cameron, D. B., Measurement of protein digestion and absorption in aged persons by a test meal of ^{131}I-labeled protein, *J. Gerontol.*, 11, 151, 1956.
2. Kountz, W. B., Hofstatter, L., and Ackermann, P. G., Nitrogen balance studies in four elderly men, *J. Gerontol.*, 6, 20, 1951.
3. Oeriu, S., Proteins in development and senescence, in *Advances in Gerontological Research*, Strehler, B. L., Ed., Academic Press, New York, 1964, 44.
4. Penzes, L., Intestinal absorption of glycine, L-alanine, and L-leucine in the old rat, *Exp. Gerontol.*, 9, 245, 1974.
5. Ning, M., Reiser, S., and Christiansen, P. A., Variation in intestinal transport of L-valine in relation to age, *Proc. Soc. Exp. Biol. Med.*, 129, 799, 1968.
6. Reiser, S., Fitzgerald, J. F., and Christiansen, P. A., Kinetics of the accelerated intestinal valine transport in 2-day-old rats, *Biochim. Biophys. Acta*, 203, 351, 1970.
7. Munro, H. N., Basic concepts in the use of amino acids and protein hydrolysates for parenteral nutrition, *Drug Intell. Chem. Pharm.*, 6, 216, 1972.
8. Penzes, L. and Boross, M., Intestinal absorption of some heterocyclic and aromatic amino acids from the ageing gut, *Exp. Gerontol.*, 9, 253, 1974.
9. Penzes, L., The effect of concentration on the intestinal absorption of L-lysine in ageing rats, *Exp. Gerontol.*, 4, 223, 1969.
10. Penzes, L., Further data on the age-dependent intestinal absorption of dibasic amino acids, *Exp. Gerontol.*, 9, 259, 1974.
11. Penzes, L., Intestinal transfer of L-arginine in relation to age, *Exp. Gerontol.*, 5, 193, 1970.
12. Tuttle, S. G., Swendseid, M. E., and Bassett, S. H., Methionine requirements of men over sixty, *Fed. Proc. Fed. Am. Soc. Exp. Biol.*, 19, 11, 1960.
13. Penzes, L., Simon, G., and Winter, M., Intestinal absorption and utilization of radiomethionine in old age, *Exp. Gerontol.*, 3, 257, 1968.
14. Winter, D., Dobre, V., and Oeriu, S., Cystein-S^{35} absorption in old rats, *Exp. Gerontol.*, 6, 367, 1971.

Table 4
THE EFFECT OF AGE ON THE ABSORPTION OF WATER-SOLUBLE VITAMINS

Vitamin	Organism	Observation	Preparation	Ref.
Thiamine	Man	A thiamine deficient diet followed by a thiamine repletion diet had the same effect on urinary thiamine levels in 5 young subjects (28—44 years) and 6 elderly subjects (62—81 years)		1
	Man	Examining absorption by the urinary excretion of ^{35}S from orally administered ^{35}S-thiamine, no difference was found in the thiamine absorption of the young (21 subjects aged 28—56 years) and the old (24 subjects aged 76—90 years)	Flush with 200 mg nonradioactive thiamine i.v.	2
	Rat (Sprague-Dawley)	Fecal recovery of ^{14}C from ^{14}C-thiamine administered to anesthetized, fasted rats increased from 4.8% of the administered dose in 1—2-month-old rats to 23.4% of the administered dose in 22—24-month-old rats and almost doubled from 12.9% of the administered dose in 19—20-month-old rats to that found in 22—24-month-old rats		3
	Rat (male, Wistar)	By comparing the absorption of thiamine in 3.5-month-old rats (160—175 g) with that of 26-month-old rats (400—490 g), it was found that the intestine of the young rats absorbed more than 76% of the thiamine introduced into the intestine, whereas the intestine of the old rats absorbed only 15% of the same amount of thiamine (200 μg) and, although almost all forms of thiamine were lower in the liver and intestine of the old rats, the intestinal thiamine pyrophosphate of the old rats was almost double the level found in the intestine of the young rats	Intestine *in situ*	4
Riboflavin	Man	A riboflavin deficient diet followed by a riboflavin repletion diet had the same effect on urinary riboflavin levels in 5 young subjects (28—44 years) and in 6 elderly subjects (62—81 years)		1
Niacin	Man	No difference was observed in the dietary niacin requirement of 5 young subjects (28—44 years) and in 6 elderly subjects (62—81 years)		1
	Rat (male, Wistar)	When luminal folic acid is in the nanomolar concentration range, absorption decreases to 15 weeks of age with no further decrease in absorption at 31 weeks of age; a protein-free diet from 11—14 weeks of age resulted in greater duodenal absorption at 14 weeks of age; distal jejunal absorption of folic acid was lost by 15 weeks of age	Isolated everted sac	5

Table 4 (continued)
THE EFFECT OF AGE ON THE ABSORPTION OF WATER-SOLUBLE VITAMINS

Vitamin	Organism	Observation	Preparation	Ref.
	Rat	When luminal folic acid is in the micromolar concentration range duodenal absorption does not change between 1.5 and 24 months of age	Isolated everted sac	6
B_{12}	Man	Elderly subjects appear to have no impairment in their ability to absorb this vitamin when presented at a rate of 20 μg orally/day or 0.7 μg/test although, when blood vitamin levels were studied in 201 subjects between 37 and 92 years of age, there was a significant decline in plasma B_{12} with age equal to 5.21 pg/mℓ plasma/year		7—9
Ascorbic acid		Raising the vitamin C intake of 13 subjects (65—91 years) had little effect on fecal levels of the vitamin		10

REFERENCES

1. **Horwitt, M. K.**, Dietary requirements of the aged, *J. Am. Diet. Assoc.*, 29, 443, 1953.
2. **Thomson, A. D.**, Thiamine absorption in old age, *Gerontol. Clin.*, 8, 354, 1966.
3. **Draper, H. H.**, Physiological aspects of ageing. I. Efficiency of absorption and phosphorylation of radiothiamine, *Proc. Soc. Exp. Biol. Med.*, 97, 121, 1958.
4. **Lazarov, J.**, Resorption of vitamin B₁. XII. Changes in the resorption and phosphorylation of thiamine in rats in relation to age, *Exp. Gerontol.*, 12, 75, 1977.
5. **Ziemlanski, S., Wartanowicz, M., and Palaszewska, M.**, Effect of age and various diets on folic acid absorption in the alimentary tract, *Acta Physiol. Pol.*, 22, 219, 1971.
6. **Bhanthumnavin, K., Wright, J. R., and Halstead, J. R.**, Intestinal transport of tritiated folic acid (³H-PGA) in the everted gut sac of different aged rats, *Johns Hopkins Med. J.*, 135, 153, 1974.
7. **Davis, R. L., Lawton, A. H., Prouty, R., and Chow, B. F.**, The absorption of oral vitamin B₁₂ in an aged population, *J. Gerontol.*, 20, 169, 1965.
8. **Hyams, D. E.**, The absorption of vitamin B₁₂ in the elderly, *Gerontol. Clin.*, 6, 193, 1964.
9. **Chernish, S. M., Helmer, O. M., Fouts, P. J., and Kohlstaedt, K. G.**, The effect of intrinsic factor on the absorption of vitamin B₁₂ in older people, *Am. J. Clin. Nutr.*, 5, 651, 1957.
10. **Chieffi, M. and Kirk, J. E.**, The ascorbic acid excretion in the stool in elderly subjects, *J. Nutr.*, 59, 273, 1956.

Table 5
THE EFFECT OF AGE ON THE ABSORPTION OF LIPIDS

Lipid	Organisms	Observation	Ref.
Glycerides	Man	Vascular disease (previous myocardial infarction) produces a decrease in the blood ^{131}I from an ^{131}I-triolein test meal whereas age between 65 and 90 years has no pronounced effect on this measurement	1
		The rate of chylomicron appearance in plasma was essentially the same in 11 young subjects (less than 31 years) and in 6 older subjects (greater than 49 years) studied through 6 hr after a fatty test meal	2
		Total serum chylomicrons and their return to fasting levels was greater in 30 old subjects (50—87 years) than in 30 young subjects (10—34 years) after a fat test meal	3
		Total serum lipids of 11 old subjects (greater than 50 years) was higher 6, 12, and 24 hr after a fat meal than that of 10 young subjects (less than 35 years) but there was no difference in the maximum rise above fasting serum lipids between the two age groups	4
Cholesterol	Rat (male, Wistar)	Both plasma and liver radioactivity decreased with age when examined 12 hr after the administration of 4-^{14}C-cholesterol (0.4 μCi/100 g body mass) when 2-, 4-, and 18-month-old animals were studied	5

REFERENCES

1. Berkowitz, D., Sklaroff, D. M., and Likoff, W., Radioactive fat absorptive patterns in the geriatric patient, *J. Am. Geriatr. Soc.*, 7, 741, 1959.
2. White, S. G., Ralston, W. C., and Carne, H. O., The effects of age and bed rest on plasma fat particle as measured by a fat tolerance test, *Gastroenterology*, 18, 355, 1951.
3. Becker, G. H., Meyer, J., and Necheles, H., Fat absorption in young and old age, *Gastroenterology*, 14, 80, 1950.
4. Herzstein, J., Wang, C., and Adlersberg, D., Fat-loading studies in relation to age, *AMA Arch. Intern. Med.*, 92, 265, 1953.
5. Yamamoto, M. and Yamamura, Y., Changes of cholesterol metabolism in the ageing rat, *Atherosclerosis*, 13, 365, 1971.

Endocrine System

ADENOHYPOPHYSIS

J. A. Severson and G. H. Donahue

Table 1
PLASMA GROWTH HORMONE

Species	Strain	Sex (n)	Age	GH (ng/ml)	Method	Ref.
Mouse	C57BL/6J	M (10)	12 months	27.0 ± 9.1	RIA[a]	1
		M (10)	28 months	29.0 ± 6.4		
	C57BL/St	F		See Figure 1		
	C3H/St	F				
Human		M + F (12)	20—73 years	Sleep peak absent in 80% SS older than 50 years	RIA[a]	2
		M + F (8)	23—42 years	Sleep peak present in all	RIA[a]	3
		M + F (5)	47—62 years	Sleep peak absent in 80% of SS older than 43 years		3
		M (44)	22—81 years	Basal levels, glucose-induced, arginine-induced, no impairment; see Figures 2—5	RIA[a]	4

[a] Radioimmunoassay.

REFERENCES

1. Finch, C. E., Jonec, V., Wisner, J. R., Jr., Sinha, Y. N., De Vellis, J. S., and Swerdloff, R. S., Hormone production by the pituitary and testes of male C57BL/6J mice during aging, *Endocrinology*, 101, 1310, 1977.
2. Carlson, H. E., Gillin, J. C., Gordon, P., and Snyder, F., Absence of sleep-related growth hormone peaks in aged normal subjects and acromegaly, *J. Clin. Endocrinol. Metab.*, 34, 1102, 1972.
3. Finkelstein, J. W., Raffwary, H. P., Boyar, R. M., Kream, J., and Hellman, L., Age-related change in the twenty-four hour spontaneous secretion of growth hormone, *J. Clin. Endocrinol. Metab.*, 35, 665, 1972.
4. Dudl, R. J., Ensinck, J. W., Palmer, H. E., and Williams, R. H., Effect of age on growth hormone secretion in man, *J. Clin. Endocrinol. Metab.*, 37, 11, 1973.

Table 2
THYROID STIMULATING HORMONE (TSH)

Species	Strain	Sex (n)	Age	TSH level (range)	Method	Ref.
Mouse	C57BL/6J	M (7)	12 months	260 ± 28 ng/mℓ	RIA[a]	1
	C57BL/6J	M (7)	28 months	282 ± 46 ng/mℓ	RIA[a]	1
Human		M + F (19)	78.4±9.1 years	4.0 ± 1.63 mµ/ℓ	RIA[a]	2
		F (23)	≤ 39 years	1.6 ± (0.2—4.0)	RIA[a]	3
		F (23)	40—69 years	2.2 ± (0.2—5.8)	RIA[a]	3
		F (35)	≥ 70 years	2.0 ± (0.2—7.3)	RIA[a]	3
		M (39)	≤ 39 years	1.4 ± (0.2—4.5)	RIA[a]	3
		M (19)	40—69 years	1.7 ± (0.2—5.8)	RIA[a]	3
		M (31)	≥ 70 years	1.8 ± (0.2—7.4)	RIA[a]	3

[a] Radioimmunoassay.

REFERENCES

1. **Finch, C. E., Jonec, V., Wisner, J. R., Sinha, Y. N., De Vellis, J. S., and Swerdloff, R. S.**, Hormone production by the pituitary and testes of male C57BL/6J mice during aging, *Endocrinology*, 101, 1310, 1977.
2. **Hesch, R. D., Gatz, J., Pape, J., Schmidt, E., and von zur Mühlen, A.**, Total and free triiodothyronine and thyroid-binding globulin concentration in elderly human persons, *Eur. J. Clin. Invest.*, 6, 139, 1976.
3. **Blichert-Taft, M., Hummer, L., and Dige-Petersen, H.**, Human serum thyrotrophin level and response to thyrotrophin-releasing hormone in the aged, *Gerontol. Clin.*, 17, 191, 1975.

Table 3
RESPONSE OF SERUM THYROID STIMULATING HORMONE (TSH) TO THYROTROPHIN-RELEASING HORMONE (TRH)

Species	Strain	Sex (n)	Method	Age	Basal TSH (mµ/ℓ)	TRH dose	TSH peak after TRH (mµ/ℓ)	Ref.
Mouse	C57BL/6J	M (7)	RIA[a]	9—12 months	260 ± 28[b]	10 µg/100 g BW	580 ± 64[b]	1
	C57BL/6J	M (7)	RIA[a]	28 months	282 ± 46[b]	10 µg/100 g BW	561 ± 41[b]	1
Rat	"Outbred"	M (10)	RIA[a]	1.5—2 months	4.4 ± 0.3			2
		M (12)		8—10 months	6.1 * 0.8			2
		M (12)		18—24 months	8.5 ± 0.9			2
		M (10)		28—32 months	3.3 ± 0.5[c]			2
Human		F (17)	RIA[a]	20—60 years	0.2—3.8[d]	200 mg	13.0 ± (4.8—25.0)[d]	3
		F (12)	RIA[a]	70—86 years	0.2—3.2[d]	200 mg	9.0 ± (0.2—26.0)[d]	3
		M (12)	RIA[a]	18—50 years	0.2—2.3[d]	200 mg	6.5 ± (2.4—13.0)[d]	3
		M (12)	RIA[a]	70—93 years	0.2—7.4[d]	200 mg	6.6 ± (1.3—31.0)[d]	3
		M (5)	RIA[a]	22—37 years	2.6 ± 0.4	50 µg	8.0 ± 0.8(5.9—12.5)[d]	4
		F (5)						
		M (5)	RIA[a]	71—88 years	2.3 ± 0.2	50 µg	8.0 ± 1.7(4.3—15.2)[d]	4
		F (5)						
		F (12)	"	20—39 years	< 2—8[d]	400 µg	16.8 ± 1.6	5
		M (12)	"	20—39 years	< 2—8[d]	400 µg	14.3 ± 1.7	5
		M (12)	"	40—59 years	< 2—8[d]	400 µg	9.1 ± 2.1	5
		M (12)	"	60—79 years	< 2—8[d]	400 µg	6.1 ± 1.2	5

[a] Radioimmunoassay.
[b] Units = ng/mℓ plasma.
[c] Free T₄ was not decreased with age in the blood samples.
[d] Range.
[e] According to Odell, W., Wilber, J., and Utiger, R., *Recent Prog. Horm. Res.*, 23, 47, 1967.

Table 3 (continued)
RESPONSE OF SERUM THYROID STIMULATING HORMONE (TSH) TO THYROTROPHIN-RELEASING HORMONE (TRH)

REFERENCES

1. Finch, C. E., Jonec, V., Wisner, J. R., Sinha, Y. N., de Vellis, J. S., and Swerdloff, R. S., Hormone production by the pituitary and testes of male C57BL/6J mice during aging, *Endocrinology*, 101, 1310, 1977.
2. Valueva, G. V. and Verzhikovskaya, N. V., Thyrotropic activity of hypophysis during aging, *Exp. Gerontol.*, 12, 97, 1977.
3. Blichert-Taft, M., Hummer, L., and Dige-Petersen, H., Human serum thyrotrophin level and response to thyrotrophin-releasing hormone in the aged, *Gerontol. Clin.*, 17, 191, 1975.
4. Otsuki, M., Dakoda, M. and Baba, S., Influence of glucocorticoids on TRF-induced TSH response in man, *J. Clin. Endocrinol. Metab.*, 36, 95, 1973.
5. Snyder, P. J. and Utiger, K. D., Response to thyrotropin releasing hormone (TRH) in normal man, *J. Clin. Endocrinol. Metab.*, 34, 380, 1972.

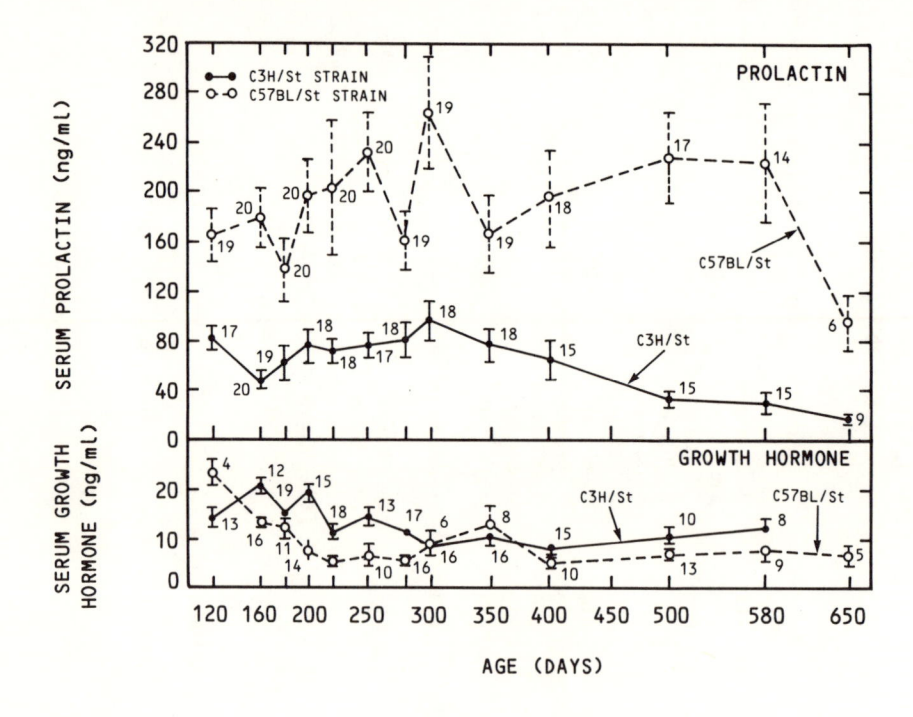

FIGURE 1. Serum prolactin and growth hormone concentrations between 120 and 650 days of age in female mice of the C3H/St and C57BL/St strains. Vertical lines represent standard errors of the means. Numbers on the chart indicate the number of mice in each group. Blood was collected serially from the same mice by orbital puncture. (From Sinha, Y. N., Salocks, C. B., and Vanderlaan, W. P., *J. Toxicol. Environ. Health Suppl.*, 1, 131, 1976. With permission.)

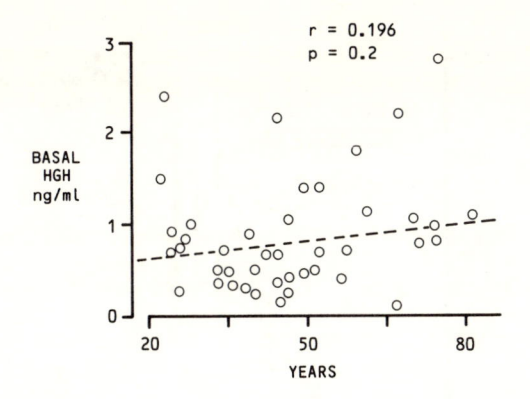

FIGURE 2. Basal human serum growth hormone levels. (From Dudl, R. J., Ensinck, J. W., Palmer, H. E., and Williams, R. H., *J. Clin. Endocrinol. Metab.*, 37, 11, 1973. With permission.)

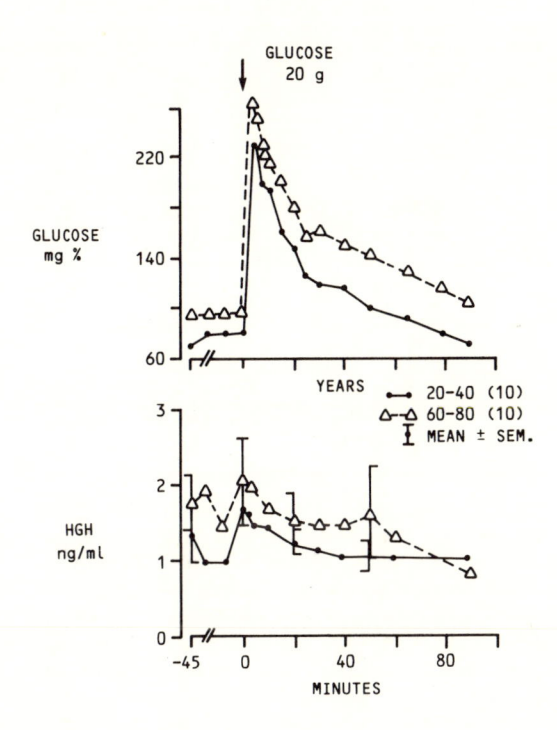

FIGURE 3. Changes in serum growth hormone levels in response to a glucose "pulse". (From Dudl, R. J., Ensinck, J. W., Palmer, H. E., and Williams, R. H., *J. Clin. Endocrinol. Metab.*, 37, 11, 1973. With permission.)

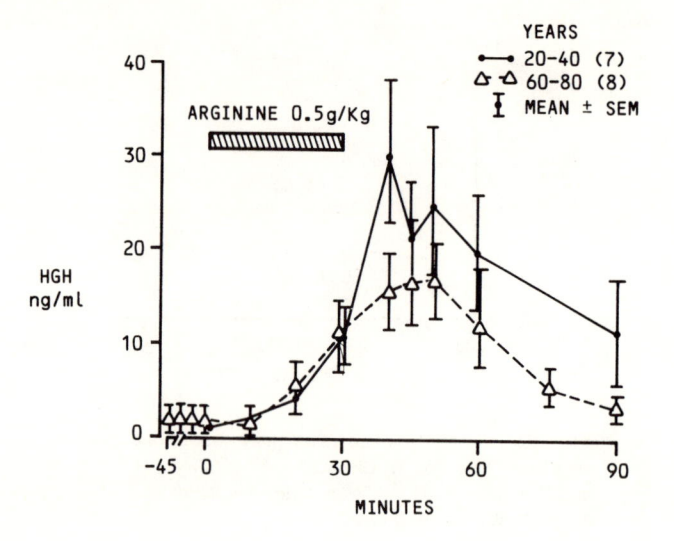

FIGURE 4. Changes in serum growth hormone levels in response to arginine administration. (From Dudl, R. J., Ensinck, J. W., Palmer, H. E., and Williams, R. H., *J. Clin. Endocrinol. Metab.*, 37, 11, 1973. With permission.)

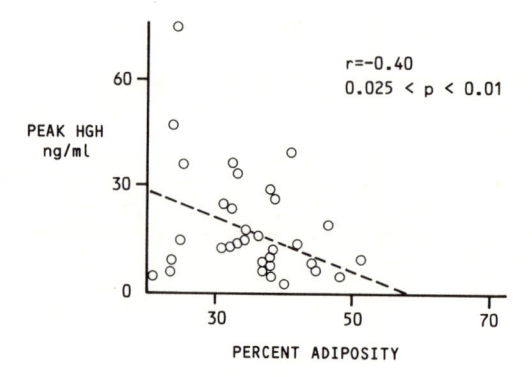

FIGURE 5. Relationship between adipose mass and peak growth hormone levels in response to arginine infusion in men of varying ages. (From Dudl, R. J., Ensinck, J. W., Palmer, H. E., and Williams, R. H., *J. Clin. Endocrinol. Metab.*, 37, 11, 1973. With permission.)

ADRENAL CORTEX

J. A. Severson

Table 1
RESTING PLASMA ADRENOCORTICAL STEROID LEVELS IN HUMANS

Sex	Compound measured	Method of analysis	Age (years)	Plasma steroid levels (μg/100 mℓ, $\overline{X}$ ± SEM)	Ref.
M & F	Cortisol	F[a]	18—34	17.4 ± 1.3	1
			73—88	11.2 ± 0.8	
M	Cortisol		14—59	15.2 ± 0.88	2
			66—92	15.6 ± 0.80	
F	Cortisol		14—59	14.7 ± 0.63	2
			66—94	14.4 ± 0.74	
M	Cortisol	CPB[b]	19—40	10.2 ± 0.69	3
			60—86	11.2 ± 1.0	
M & F	17-OHCS[c]	C[d]	23—55	13.6	4
			66—92	15.6	
	17-OHCS	F	"Young adults"	13.2 ± 0.9	5
			66—92	15.6 ± 1.2	
M	17-OHCS	C	25—40	12.4 ± 1.1	6
			60—69	12.7 ± 1.1	
			70—79	14.8 ± 1.9	
			≥80	14.5 ± 1.8	
	Total corticoids	CPB	25	13.9 ± 1.3	7
			71	14.6 ± 1.1	
F	Total corticoids	CPB	24	12.7 ± 1.1	7
			71	12.4 ± 0.7	
M	Aldosterone	—[e]	18—35	4.7 ± 0.6	8
			67—88	2.6 ± 0.3	
	Estrone	RIA[f]	19—40	2.46 ± 0.13	3
			60—86	3.61 ± 0.21	
	Estradiol	RIA	19—40	1.85 ± 0.10	3
			60—86	2.87 ± 0.14	

Table 1 (continued)
RESTING PLASMA ADRENOCORTICAL STEROID LEVELS IN HUMANS

Sex	Compound measured	Method of analysis	Age (years)	Plasma steroid levels (μg/100 ml, $\overline{X} \pm$ SEM)	Ref.
M	Dehydroepiandrosterone sulfate	GC[g]	3—10	15 ± 3.2	9
			11—15	81 ± 6.0	
			16—20	180 ± 10.1	
			21—30	165 ± 9.4	
			31—40	108 ± 9.1	
			41—50	86 ± 8.3	
			51—60	70 ± 9.7	
			≥60	34 ± 5.1	
F	Dehydroepiandrosterone sulfate	GC	3—10	14 ± 6.7	9
			11—15	95 ± 5.2	
			16—20	148 ± 10.7	
			21—30	109 ± 6.7	
			31—40	89 ± 8.2	
			41—50	71 ± 8.1	
			51—60	62 ± 9.1	
			≥60	30 ± 3.5	

[a] Fluorometric.
[b] Competitive protein binding.
[c] 17-Hydroxycorticosteroids.
[d] Colorimetric.
[e] Calculated from metabolic clearance rate and secretion rate data.
[f] Radioimmunoassay.
[g] Gas chromatography.

REFERENCES

1. **Blichert-Toft, B. and Blichert-Toft, M.**, Adrenocortical function in the aged assessed by the rapid corticotrophin test (synacher), *Acta Endocrinol. (Copenhagen)*, 64, 410, 1970.
2. **Jensen, H. K. and Blichert-Toft, M.**, Serum corticotrophin, plasma cortisol, and urinary excretion of 17-ketogenic steroids, *Acta Endocrinol. (Copenhagen)*, 66, 25, 1971.
3. **Kley, H. K., Nieschlag, E., and Kruskemper, H. L.**, Age dependence of plasma oestrogen response to HCG and ACTH in men, *Acta Endocrinol. (Copenhagen)*, 79, 95, 1975.
4. **Samuels, L. T.**, Factors affecting the metabolism and distribution of cortisol as measured by levels of 17-hydroxycorticosteroids in blood, *Cancer*, 10, 746, 1957.
5. **Tyler, F. H., Eik-Nes, K., Sandberg, A. A., Florentin, A. A., and Samuels, L. T.**, Adrenocortical capacity and the metabolism of cortisol in elderly patients, *J. Am. Geriatr. Soc.*, 3, 79, 1955.
6. **West, C. D., Brown, H., Simons, E. L., Carter, D. B., Kumagai, L. F., and Englert, E., Jr.**, Adrenocortical function and cortisol metabolism in old age, *J. Clin. Endocrinol. Metab.*, 21, 1197, 1961.
7. **Grad, B., Kral, V. A., Payne, R. C., and Berenson, J.**, Plasma and urinary corticoids in young and old persons, *J. Gerontol.*, 22, 66, 1967.
8. **Flood, C., Gherondache, C., Pincus, G., Tait, J. F., Tait, S. A. S., and Willoughby, S.**, The metabolism and secretion of aldosterone in elderly subjects, *J. Clin. Invest.*, 46, 960, 1967.
9. **Yamaji, T. and Ibayashi, H.**, Plasma dehydroepiandrosterone sulfate in normal and pathological conditions, *J. Clin. Endocrinol. Metab.*, 29, 273, 1969.

Table 2
RESTING LEVELS OF PLASMA GLUCOCORTICOIDS IN RATS, MICE, COWS, GOATS, DOGS, AND MONKEYS

Species	Strain	Sex	Compound measured	Method of analysis	Age	Plasma glucocorticoid levels (μg/100 mℓ, $\bar{X}$ ± SEM)	Ref.
Rat	Sprague-Dawley	M	Corticosterone	F[a]	2 months	8.0 ± 0.9	1
					12 months	12.5 ± 1.8	
					24 months	10.3 ± 1.0	
	Sprague-Dawley	M	Corticosterone	F	2 months	8.5 ± 2.1	1
					12 months	10.3 ± 1.0	
					24 months	12.7 ± 1.5	
	Sprague-Dawley	M	Corticosterone	F	3—4 months	16.6 ± 2.7	2
					15—18 months	33.8 ± 4.0	
	Long-Evans	M	Corticosterone	F	5 months	4.9 ± 1.3	3
					21 months	5.6 ± 1.6	
	Long-Evans	F	Corticosterone	F	5 months	9.6 ± 2.0	3
					25 months	11.5 ± 2.2	
	Long-Evans	M	Corticosterone	F	5 months	6.4 ± 0.6	4
					25 months	13.8 ± 1.6	
	Long-Evans	F	Corticosterone	F	5 months	9.6 ± 0.8	4
					25 months	23.0 ± 2.6	
	Fischer	M	Corticosterone	F	3 months	3.5 ± 0.49	5
					11 months	6.7 ± 0.63	
					18 months	7.1 ± 0.85	
					23 months	9.5 ± 1.54	
	Fischer	F	Corticosterone	F	3 months	4.8 ± 0.80	5
					11 months	7.1 ± 0.57	
					18 months	9.0 ± 0.96	
					23 months	8.5 ± 1.49	
	Wistar G	M	Corticosterone	F	3 months	13.62 ± 2.00	6
					13—14 months	15.45 ± 3.23	
					23—24 months	16.55 ± 1.71	

Mouse[b]						
C57BL/6J	M	Corticosterone	F	6 months	6.4[c]	7
				27 months	5.5	
C57BL/6J	M	Corticosterone	RIA[d]	8—12 months	0.56 ± 0.07[e]	8
				28—32 months	0.41 ± 0.04	
C57BL/6J	M	Corticosterone	F	2 months	4.9 ± 0.4	9
				6 months	12.1 ± 0.5	
				9 months	12.3 ± 0.5	
				12 months	6.2 ± 0.5	
				18 months	10.7 ± 0.1	
				24 months	7.5 ± 0.2	
				30 months	4.1 ± 0.2	
C57BL/6J	M	Corticosterone	CPB[f]	2 months	10.7 ± 1.1	10
				4 months	1.2 ± 0.4	
				6 months	3.1 ± 0.6	
				8 months	3.2 ± 0.8	
				12—13 months	3.0 ± 0.5	
				23—24 months	2.6 ± 1.2	
				25—26 months	1.6 ± 0.6	
C57BL/6J	F	Corticosterone	CPB	2 months	7.9 ± 1.4	10
				4 months	3.3 ± 1.0	
				6 months	7.4 ± 3.1	
				8 months	11.1 ± 2.7	
				12—13 months	6.3 ± 0.9	
				23—24 months	7.2 ± 2.4	
				25—26 months	2.6 ± 0.8	
DBA/2J	M	Corticosterone	F	2 months	9.9 ± 0.1	9
				6 months	7.4 ± 0.3	
				9 months	7.1 ± 0.2	
				12 months	6.4 ± 0.2	
				18 months	12.1 ± 0.2	
				24 months	12.4 ± 0.2	
				30 months	9.8 ± 0.2	

299

Table 2 (continued)
RESTING LEVELS OF PLASMA GLUCOCORTICOIDS IN RATS, MICE, COWS, GOATS, DOGS, AND MONKEYS

Species	Strain	Sex	Compound measured	Method of analysis	Age	Plasma glucocorticoid levels (μg/100 mℓ, $\overline{X}$ ± SEM)	Ref.
Cow	Holstein-Freisian	M	Cortisol	C[a]	≤4 years	2.53 ± 0.21	11
	Holstein-Freisian	M	Corticosterone	C	≥8 years	3.07 ± 0.29	11
					≤4 years	0.88 ± 0.06	
					≥8 years	1.03 ± 0.09	
Goat	Toggenburg	F	Cortisol	C	1—5 years	4.08 ± 0.37	12
					6—9 years	4.45 ± 0.57	
	Toggenburg	F	Corticosterone	C	1—5 years	1.29 ± 0.19	12
					6—9 years	1.32 ± 0.05	
Dog	Not specified	M & F	Cortisol	F	1—3 years	1.7 ± 0.34	13
					5—6 years	1.35 ± 0.56	
					8—10 years	1.81 ± 0.63	
Monkey	Rhesus *(Macaca mulatta)*	M & F	Cortisol	C	7.8 months —4.6 years	31.4 ± 7.8	14
					7.1—14.9 years	27.1 ± 7.1	

[a] Fluorometric.
[b] Animals autopsied for lesions that could influence results.
[c] Values derived from graph.
[d] Radioimmunoassay.
[e] Mice handled for 1 week prior to blood sampling to minimize stressful effects of handling prior to sacrifice.
[f] Competitive protein binding radioassay.
[g] Colorimetric.

REFERENCES

1. **Britton, G. W., Rotenberg, S., Freeman, C., Britton, V. J., Karoly, K., Ceci, L., Klug, T. L., Lacko, A. G. and Adelman, R. C.**, Regulation of corticosterone levels and liver enzyme activity in aging rats, *Adv. Exp. Med. Biol.*, 61, 209, 1975.
2. **Lewis, B. K. and Wexler, B. C.**, Serum insulin changes in male rats associated with age and reproductive activity, *J. Gerontol.*, 29, 139, 1974.
3. **Hess, G. D. and Riegle, G. D.**, Adrenocortical responsiveness to stress and ACTH in aging rats, *J. Gerontol.*, 25, 354, 1970.
4. **Riegle, G. D.**, Chronic stress effects on adrenocortical responsiveness in young and aged rats, *Neuroendocrinol.*, 11, 1, 1973.
5. **Senčar-Čupović, I. and Milković, S.**, The development of sex differences in adrenal morphology and responsiveness in stress of rats from birth to end of life, *Mech. Ageing Dev.*, 5, 1, 1976.
6. **Rapaport, P. A., Allaire, Y., Bourlière, F., and Girard, F.**, Réactivité au <<stress>> et capicité d'adaptation à une situation inhabituelle chez le rat jeune, adulte et âgé, *Gerontologia*, 10, 20, 1964.
7. **Finch, C. E. Foster, J. R., and Mirsky, A. E.**, Ageing and the regulation of cell activities during exposure to cold, *J. Gen. Physiol.*, 54, 690, 1969.
8. **Latham, K. R. and Finch, C. E.**, Hepatic glucocorticoid binders in mature and senescent C57BL/6J male mice, *Endocrinology*, 98, 1480, 1976.
9. **Eleftheriou, B. E.**, Changes with age in pituitary-adrenal responsiveness and reactivity to mild stress in mice, *Gerontologia*, 20, 224, 1974.
10. **Grad, B. and Khalid, R.**, Circulating corticosterone levels of young and old, male and female C57BL/6J mice, *J. Gerontol.*, 23, 522, 1968.
11. **Riegle, G. D. and Nellor, J. E.**, Changes in adrenocortical function during aging in cattle, *J. Gerontol.*, 22, 83, 1967.
12. **Riegle, G. D., Przekop, F., and Nellor, J. E.**, Changes in adrenocortical responsiveness to ACTH infusion in aging goats, *J. Gerontol.*, 23, 187, 1968.
13. **Breznock, E. M. and McQueen, R. D.**, Adrenocortical function during aging in the dog, *Am. J. Vet. Res.*, 31, 1269, 1973.
14. **Bowman, R. E. and Wolf, R. C.**, Plasma 17-hydroxycorticosteroid response to ACTH in *M. mulatta*: dose, age, weight, and sex, *Proc. Soc. Exp. Biol. Med.*, 130, 61, 1969.

Table 3
CHANGES IN PLASMA ADRENOCORTICAL STEROID IN THE RESPONSE OF HUMANS TO ACTH

Sex	Compound measured	Method of analysis	Dose of ACTH	Age (years)	Prestimulation level (µg/100 ml, $\overline{X} \pm$ SEM)	Poststimulation level (µg/100 ml, $\overline{X} \pm$ SEM)	% Change (prestim-poststim) prestim × 100%	Ref.
M	Cortisol	CPB[a]	1 mg (i.v.)	19—40	10.2 ± 0.69	35.5 ± 1.9	+248%	1
				60—86	11.2 ± 1.0	38.5 ± 2.3	+244%	
M & F	Cortisol	F[b]	250 µg (i.v.)	18—34	17.4 ± 1.3	37.6 ± 1.8	+116%	2
				73—88	11.2 ± 0.8	35.2 ± 1.8	+214%	
M	17-OHCS[c]	C[d]	25 units (i.v.)	25—40	12.1 ± 1.1	41.0 ± 3.2	+239%	3
				≥60	15.3	44.6	+192%	
	Estrone	RIA[e]	1 mg (i.v.)	19—40	2.46 ± 0.13	5.29 ± 0.23	+115%	1
				60—86	3.61 ± 0.21	6.39 ± 0.29	+77%	
	DHAS[f]	GC[g]	40 units (i.m.)	19—30	156 ± 15	425 ± 38	+172%	4
				51—75	44 ± 5	110 ± 14	+150%	

[a] Competitive protein binding.
[b] Fluorimetric.
[c] 17-Hydroxycorticosteroids.
[d] Colorimetric.
[e] Radioimmunoassay.
[f] Dehydroepiandrosterone sulfate.
[g] Gas chromatography.

REFERENCES

1. **Kley, H. K., Nieschag, E., and Kruskemper, H. L.**, Age dependence of plasma oestrogen response to HCG and ACTH in men, *Acta Endocrinol. (Copenhagen)*, 79, 95, 1975.
2. **Blichert-Toft, B. and Blichert-Toft, M.**, Adrenocortical function in the aged assessed by the rapid corticotrophin test (Synacher), *Acta Endocrinol. (Copenhagen)*, 64, 410, 1970.
3. **West, C. D., Brown, H., Simons, E. L., Carter, D. B., Kumagai, L. F., and Englert, E., Jr.**, Adrenocortical function and cortisol metabolism in old age, *J. Clin. Endocrinol. Metab.*, 21, 1197, 1961.
4. **Yamaji, T. and Ibayashi, H.**, Plasma dehydroepiandrosterone sulfate in normal and pathological conditions, *J. Clin. Endocrinol. Metab.* 29, 273, 1969.

Table 4
SECRETION RATES OF ADRENOCORTICAL STEROID HORMONES IN HUMANS

Sex	Compound measured	Method of analysis	Age (years)	Secretion rate (mg/day)	Ref.
M & F	Cortisol	CPB[a]	⅓—10	5.7 ± 0.9	1
			11—20	16.4 ± 1.5	
			21—30	24.5 ± 2.7	
			31—40	18.5 ± 1.4	
			41—50	20.3 ± 1.1	
M	Cortisol	Isotope dilution	25.3	23.6 ± 1.75	2,3
			74.7	17.7 ± 1.39	
			+ 80 units ACTH i.m.		
			25.3	58.2 ± 7.9 (+ 147% over basal)	3
			74.7	54.5 ± 13.1 (+ 208% over basal)	
M & F	Cortisol	C[b]	23—55	33.6[c]	4
			66—92	23.0	
			+ 25 units ACTH i.v.		
			23—55	258.7 (+ 606% over basal)	
			66—92	201.6 (+ 776% over basal)	
	Cortisol	F[d]	25—35	69.7 ± 11.2[c]	5
			≥70	49.5 ± 4.3	
M	Corticosterone	Isotope dilution	20—35	4.0 ± 0.73	6
			71—88	2.6 ± 0.83	
	Deoxycorticosterone	Isotope dilution	20—35	0.091 ± 0.017	6
			71—88	0.057 ± 0.011	
	Aldosterone	Isotope dilution	18—35	0.077 ± 0.015	7
			67—88	0.034 ± 0.006	

[a] Competitive protein binding.
[b] Colorimetric.
[c] Calculated from data given on basis of 70 kg man.
[d] Fluorimetric.

REFERENCES

1. **Juselius, R. E. and Kenny, F. M.**, Urinary free cortisol excretion during growth and aging: correlation with cortisol production rate and 17-hydroxycorticosteroid excretion, *Metabolism*, 23, 847, 1974.
2. **Romanoff, L. P., Morris, C. W., Welch, P., Rodriguez, R. M., and Pincus, G.**, The metabolism of cortisol-4-C^{14} in young and elderly men. I. Secretion rate of cortisol and daily excretion of tetrahydrocortisol, allotetrahydrocortisol, tetrahydrocortisone and cortalone (20α and 20β), *J. Clin. Endocrinol. Metab.*, 21, 1413, 1961.
3. **Romanoff, L. P., Baxter, M. N., Thomas, A. W., and Ferrechio, G. B.**, Effect of ACTH on the metabolism of pregnenolone-7α-^{3}H and cortisol-4-^{14}C in young and elderly men, *J. Clin. Endocrinol. Metab.*, 29, 819, 1969.
4. **Samuels, L. T.**, Factors affecting the metabolism and distribution of cortisol as measured by levels of 17-hydroxycorticosteroids in blood, *Cancer*, 10, 746, 1957.
5. **Serio, M., Piolanti, P., Cappelli, G., De Magistris, L., Ricchi, F., Anzalone, M., and Gusti, G.**, The miscible pool and turnover rate of cortisol with aged and variations in relation to time of day, *Exp. Gerontol.*, 4, 95, 1969.
6. **Romanoff, L. P. and Baxter, M. N.**, The secretion rates of dioxycorticosterone and corticosterone in young and elderly men, *J. Clin. Endocrinol. Metab.*, 41, 630, 1975.
7. **Flood, C., Gherondache, C., Pincus, G., Tait, J. F., Tait, S. A. S., and Willoughby, S.**, The metabolism and secretion of aldosterone in elderly subjects, *J. Clin. Invest.*, 46, 960, 1967.

Table 5
PLASMA GLUCOCORTICOID RESPONSE TO ADRENOCORTICAL STIMULATION IN RATS, MICE, COWS, GOATS, DOGS, AND MONKEYS

Species	Strain	Sex	Compound measured	Method of analysis	Method of stimulation	Age	Prestimulation levels (μg/100 ml, $\overline{X} \pm$ SEM)	Poststimulation levels	% Change[a]	Ref.
Rat	Sprague-Dawley	M	Corticosterone	F[b]	ACTH (5 units i.p.)	2 months	8.5 ± 2.1	49.9 ± 2.4	+487%	1
						12 months	10.3 ± 1.0	43.2 ± 2.8	+319%	
						24 months	12.7 ± 1.5	41.8 ± 2.6	+229%	
	Wistar G	M	Corticosterone	F	Ether vapor exposure	3 months	13.6 ± 2.6	48.95 ± 1.38	+260%	2
						13—14 months	15.45 ± 3.23	50.74 ± 4.69	+228%	
						23—24 months	16.55 ± 1.71	43.65 ± 3.58	+164%	
	Wistar G	M	Corticosterone	F	Nembutal (7 mg/100 g,i.p.)	3 months	13.6 ± 2.0	37.30 ± 4.35	+174%	2
						13—14 months	15.45 ± 3.23	23.13 ± 2.45	+50%	
						23—24 months	16.55 ± 1.71	28.92 ± 3.69	+75%	
	Fischer	M	Corticosterone	F	Histamine (5 mg, s.c.)	3 months	3.5 ± 0.49	37.1 ± 1.98	+960%	3
						11 months	6.7 ± 0.63	54.7 ± 3.32	+716%	
						18 months	7.1 ± 0.85	47.0 ± 2.69	+562%	
						23 months	9.5 ± 1.54	52.2 ± 2.84	+449%	
	Fischer	F	Corticosterone	F	Histamine (5 mg s.c.)	3 months	4.8 ± 0.80	63.2 ± 2.14	+1217%	3
						11 months	7.1 ± 0.57	82.3 ± 7.46	+1059%	
						18 months	9.0 ± 0.96	69.0 ± 3.74	+667%	
						23 months	8.5 ± 1.49	69.1 ± 3.57	+713%	
	Long-Evans	M	Corticosterone	F	ACTH (4 units, s.c.)	6 months	4.9 ± 1.3	57.8 ± 1.4	+1080%	4
						21 months	5.6 ± 1.6	51.5 ± 1.4	+820%	
	Long-Evans	F	Corticosterone	F	ACTH (1 unit, s.c.)	5 months	9.6 ± 2.0	126.8 ± 3.1	+1221%	4
						25 months	11.5 ± 2.2	87.2 ± 3.0	+658%	
	Long-Evans	M	Corticosterone	F	Ether vapor exposure	6 months	4.9 ± 1.3	68.7 ± 1.2	+1302%	4
						21 months	5.6 ± 1.6	58.9 ± 2.4	+952%	
	Long-Evans	F	Corticosterone	F	Ether vapor exposure	5 months	9.6 ± 2.0	104.4 ± 2.4	+988%	4
						25 months	11.5 ± 2.2	83.8 ± 1.7	+629%	
	Long-Evans	M	Corticosterone	F	ACTH (2 units, s.c.)	4 months	53.2 ± 5.3	91.2 ± 5.7	+71%	5
							54.3 ± 4.3 ACTH[c]	58.3 ± 3.9	0	
						24 months	44.3 ± 2.9	75.4 ± 5.7	+70%	
							53.9 ± 7.6 control	53.6 ± 6.2	0	
	Long-Evans	M	Corticosterone	F	Ether vapor exposure	4 months	60.4 ± 4.8 ACTH[c]	34.2 ± 5.5	−43%	5
							63.2 ± 4.8 control	62.1 ± 1.7	0	
						24 months	45.1 ± 2.7 ACTH[c]	48.5 ± 6.7	0	
							51.7 ± 7.6 control	48.5 ± 6.5	0	

Strain	Sex	Hormone	Treatment	Age		Value	% change	n
Long-Evans	F	Corticosterone	ACTH (2 units, s.c.)	4 months	ACTH^c	70.6 ± 4.6	123.5 ± 6.1	+75%	5
					control	73.8 ± 3.9	95.5 ± 4.6	+29%	
				24 months	ACTH^c	67.4 ± 3.3	96.4 ± 6.6	+43%	
					control	73.9 ± 3.7	77.8 ± 4.2	0	
Long-Evans	F	Corticosterone	Ether vapor exposure	4 months	ACTH^d	86.2 ± 3.7	72.7 ± 5.9	+12%	5
					control	89.2 ± 2.4	99.9 ± 2.9	+35%	
				24 months	ACTH^d	72.9 ± 5.8	98.4 ± 5.5	0	
					control	79.2 ± 2.0	82.8 ± 3.1		
Long-Evans	M	Corticosterone	Ether vapor exposure	5 months		59.0 ± 1.3^c	30.8 ± 3.2^c	−48%	6
				25 months		55.7 ± 2.8^c	50.4 ± 2.4^f	0	6
Long-Evans	F	Corticosterone	Ether vapor exposure	5 months		118.4 ± 4.3^c	45.4 ± 3.7^f	−62%	6
				25 months		90.3 ± 3.7^c	58.0 ± 3.9^g	−36%	6
Long-Evans	M	Corticosterone	Chronic restraint	5 months		79.0 ± 2.6^c	40.5 ± 3.0^c	−49%	6
				25 months		75.9 ± 4.3^c	43.8 ± 2.9^a	−42%	
Long-Evans	F	Corticosterone	Chronic restraint	5 months		154.4 ± 4.6	41.6 ± 3.3	−63%	6
				25 months		104.7 ± 4.4	75.4 ± 6.5	−28%	
Long-Evans	M	Corticosterone	ACTH (2 units, s.c.)	5 months		56.7 ± 1.1^c	67.6 ± 4.1^c	+19%	6
				25 months		49.8 ± 2.1^c	58.9 ± 1.8^c	+18%	
Long-Evans	F	Corticosterone	ACTH (2 units, s.c.)	5 months		106.7 ± 4.8^c	78.4 ± 2.3^c	−27%	6
Long-Evans	M	Corticosterone	Chronic restraint	25 months		75.8 ± 3.3^c	69.9 ± 3.4^c	0	6
				5 months		6.4 ± 0.6^a	12.7 ± 2.1^f	+98%	
Long-Evans	F	Corticosterone	Chronic restraint	25 months		13.8 ± 1.6^a	17.4 ± 2.2^f	0	6
				5 months		9.6 ± 0.8^a	15.9 ± 1.7^f	+66%	
Long-Evans	M	Corticosterone	Ether vapor exposure	25 months		23.0 ± 2.6^a	22.1 ± 2.1^f	0	7
				5 months	Control	46.5 ± 3.6^m	46.9 ± 5.6^a	0	
					dexamethasone	53.9 ± 3.5^m	5.8 ± 1.0^a	−89%	
				25 months	Control dexamethasone	62.8 ± 3.1^m	57.2 ± 3.4^a	0	
Long-Evans	F	Corticosterone	Ether vapor exposure	5 months	Control	62.8 ± 3.3^m	24.1 ± 1.9^a	−62%	7
					dexamethasone	106.7 ± 9.2^m	55.8 ± 11.2^a	−48%	
				27 months	Control	113.1 ± 5.0^m	7.1 ± 0.7^a	−94%	
					dexamethasone	75.9 ± 6.5^m	53.1 ± 11.8^a	0	
Mouse^a C57BL/6J	M	Corticosterone	Cold exposure (45 min at 10°C)	6 months		75.4 ± 5.7^m	7.0 ± 0.7^a	91%	8
				27 months		6.4	37.7	+489%	
						5.5	36.6	+565%	

307

Table 5 (continued)
PLASMA GLUCOCORTICOID RESPONSE TO ADRENOCORTICAL STIMULATION IN RATS, MICE, COWS, GOATS, DOGS, AND MONKEYS

Species	Strain	Sex	Compound measured	Method of analysis	Method of stimulation	Age	Prestimulation levels (μg/100 mℓ, $\overline{X} \pm$ SEM)	Poststimulation levels	% Change[a]	Ref.
	C57BL/6J	M	Corticosterone	F	ACTH (1 unit, i.m.)	2 months	4.4	50.0	+1036%	9
						6 months	12.0	49.4	+312%	
						12 months	5.7	44.6	+682%	
						18 months	10.6	37.5	+254%	
						24 months	11.3	37.8	+235%	
						30 months	4.4	33.8	+668%	
	DBA/2J	M	Corticosterone	F	ACTH (1 unit, i.m.)	2 months	12.0	48.7	+306%	9
						6 months	10.1	46.8	+363%	
						12 months	6.7	36.4	+443%	
						18 months	11.6	30.3	+161%	
						24 months	11.6	29.1	+151%	
						30 months	9.1	21.9	+141%	
Cow	Holstein-Freisian	M	Cortisol	C	ACTH (10 units/100 lb, i.v.)	≤4 years	5.33 ± 1.09	10.63 ± 1.40	+99%	10
	Holstein-Freisian	M	Corticosterone	C	ACTH (10 units/100 lb, i.v.)	≥8 years	3.40 ± 0.37	5.18 ± 0.53	+52%	10
						≤4 years	1.74 ± 0.44	2.8 ± 0.40	0	
						≥8 years	1.06 ± 0.16	1.46 ± 0.15	0	
Goat	Toggenburg	F	Cortisol	C	ACTH (30 units, i.v.)	1—5 years	4.08 ± 0.37	8.37 ± 1.90	+105%	11
						6—9 years	4.45 ± 0.57	5.03 ± 0.40	0	
	Toggenburg	F	Corticosterone	C	ACTH (30 units, i.v.)	1—5 years	1.29 ± 0.19	1.97 ± 0.36	0	11
						6—9 years	1.32 ± 0.05	1.76 ± 0.17	+33%	
Dog	Not specified	M & F	Cortisol	F	ACTH (1 unit, i.m.)	1—3 years	1.70 ± 0.34	9.0 · 0.87	+429%	12
						5—6 years	1.35 ± 0.56	7.32 ± 1.06	+442%	
						8—10 years	1.81 ± 0.63	6.52 ± 0.69	+260%	
Monkey	Rhesus (Macaca mulatta)	M & F	Cortisol	C	ACTH (4 units, i.m.)	7.8 months—4.6 years	31.4 ± 7.8	78.8	+151%	13
						7.2—14.9 years	27.1 ± 7.1	64.4	+138%	

- Stim-Unstim / Unstim × 100%.
- Fluorometric.
- Chronic ACTH: 10 units/day subcutaneously for 6 weeks.
- Chronic ACTH: 6 units/day subcutaneously for 6 weeks.
- Response prior to 2 weeks of restraint stress.
- Response after 2 weeks of restraint stress.
- Plasma levels after 1 day of restraint stress.
- Plasma levels after 20 days of restraint stress.
- Response prior to 19 days of restraint stress.
- Response after 19 days of restraint stress.
- Resting levels prior to 19 days of chronic restraint.
- Resting levels on 1st day after completion of 19 days of chronic restraint.
- Response before 22 days of treatment with 25 μg/100 g body weight dexamethasone sub Q daily.
- Response after.
- Only 10 days of trt (this group only).
- Animals autopsied for lesions that could influence results.
- Colorimetric.

REFERENCES

1. **Britton, G. W., Rotenberg, S., Freeman, C., Britton, V. J., Karoly, K., Ceci, L., Klug, T. L., Lacko, A. G., and Adelman, R. C.,** Regulation of corticosterone levels and liver enzyme activity in aging rats, *Adv. Exp. Med. Biol.*, 61, 209, 1975.
2. **Rapaport, P. A., Allaire, Y., Bourlière, F., and Girard, F.,** Réactivité au <<stress>> capacité d'adoption à une situation inhabituelle chez le rat jeune, adulte et âgé, *Gerontologia*, 10, 20, 1964.
3. **Senčar-Čupović, I. and Milković, S.,** The development of sex differences in adrenal morphology and responsiveness in stress of rats from birth to the end of life, *Mech. Ageing Dev.*, 5, 1, 1976.
4. **Hess, G. D. and Riegle, G. D.,** Adrenocortical responsiveness to stress and ACTH in aging rats, *J. Gerontol.*, 25, 354, 1970.
5. **Hess, G. D. and Riegle, G. D.,** Effects of chronic ACTH stimulation on adrenocortical function in young and aged rats, *Am. J. Physiol.*, 222, 1458, 1972.
6. **Riegle, G. D.,** Chronic stress effects on adrenocortical responsiveness in young and aged rats, *Neuroendocrinology*, 11, 1, 1973.
7. **Riegle, G. D. and Hess, G. D.,** Chronic and acute dexamethasone suppression of stress activation of the adrenal cortex in young and aged rats, *Neuroendocrinology*, 9, 175, 1972.
8. **Finch, C. E., Foster, J. R., and Mirsky, A. E.,** Ageing and the regulation of cell activities during exposure to cold, *J. Gen. Physiol.*, 54, 690, 1969.
9. **Eleftheriou, B. E.,** Changes with age in pituitary-adrenal responsiveness and reactivity to mild stress in mice, *Gerontologia*, 20, 224, 1974.
10. **Riegle, G. D. and Nellor, J. E.,** Changes in adrenocortical function during aging in cattle, *J. Gerontol.*, 22, 83, 1967.
11. **Riegle, G. D., Przekop, F., and Nellor, J. E.,** Changes in adrenocortical responsiveness to ACTH infusion in aging goats, *J. Gerontol.*, 23, 187, 1968.
12. **Breznock, E. M. and McQueen, R. D.,** Adrenocortical function during aging in the dog, *Am. J. Vet. Res.*, 31, 1269, 1973.
13. **Bowman, R. E. and Wolf, R. C.,** Plasma 17-hydroxycorticosteroid response to ACTH in *M. mulatta*: dose, age, weight and sex, *Proc. Soc. Exp. Biol. Med.*, 130, 61, 1969.

Table 6
URINARY ADRENOCORTICOSTEROID EXCRETION IN HUMANS

Sex	Compound measured	Method of analysis	Age (years)	Steroid excretion (mg/day)	Ref.
M	17-KS[a]	GC[b]	29.2	3.71	1
			73.3	2.81	
M & F	17-KS	C[c]	33—39	8.97 ± 1.02	2
			63—89	3.64 ± 0.28	
M	17-KS	GC	3—9	0.54 ± 0.12	3
			10—14	2.67 ± 0.32	
			15—19	12.23 ± 2.22	
			20—29	18.39 ± 1.53	
			30—39	11.34 ± 2.74	
			40—49	13.03 ± 2.96	
			50—59	7.83 ± 1.38	
			≥60	7.57 ± 1.49	
	17-KS	C	20—30	9.88 ± 0.97	4
			40—49	9.14 ± 0.66	
			50—59	6.96 ± 0.59	
			60—83	6.73 ± 0.67	
	17-KS	C	20—29	13.39 ± 0.84	5
			30—39	13.80 ± 1.15	
			40—49	10.03 ± 0.77	
			50—59	8.18 ± 0.50	
			60—69	7.03 ± 0.50	
			70—79	4.39 ± 0.60	
			80—89	3.67 ± 0.60	
F	17-KS	C	20—29	8.50 ± 0.74	5
			30—39	8.35 ± 0.62	
			40—49	5.57 ± 0.48	
			50—59	4.73 ± 0.50	
			60—69	3.53 ± 0.50	
			70—79	2.93 ± 0.26	
			80—89	1.99 ± 0.17	
	17-KS	GC	2—9	0.44 ± 0.17	3
			10—14	3.16 ± 0.44	
			15—19	8.32 ± 0.54	
			20—29	10.58 ± 0.56	
			30—39	6.80 ± 0.50	
			40—49	6.56 ± 0.51	
			50—59	10.90 ± 1.24	
			≥60	4.84 ± 0.50	
M & F	17-OHCS[d]	CPB[e]	1/3—10	1.2 ± 0.24	6
			11—20	3.0 ± 0.3	
			21—30	8.7 ± 0.4	
			31—40	5.3 ± 0.35	
			41—50	6.1 ± 0.23	
M	17-OHCS	C	20—30	5.95 ± 0.40	4
			40—49	4.89 ± 0.41	
			50—59	4.86 ± 0.52	
			60—83	4.40 ± 0.46	
	17-OHCS	C	20—35	7.0 ± 1.13	7
			71—88	4.1 ± 0.45	
	17-OHCS	C	20—29	6.6 ± 0.5	8
			30—39	8.0 ± 0.8	
			40—49	7.1 ± 0.6	
			50—59	7.1 ± 0.6	
			60—69	4.9 ± 0.5	
			70—80	4.0 ± 0.3	

Table 6 (continued)
URINARY ADRENOCORTICOSTEROID EXCRETION IN HUMANS

Sex	Compound measured	Method of analysis	Age (years)	Steroid excretion (mg/day)	Ref.
M & F	17-OHCS	C	25—40	8.5 ± 0.4	9
			60—69	6.1 ± 0.6	
			70—79	5.3 ± 0.6	
			≥80	3.9 ± 1.6	
	Cortisol	CPB[e]	⅓—10	13.3 ± 2.3	6
			11—20	25.8 ± 4.3	
			21—30	49.0 ± 2.9	
			31—40	55.0 ± 5.1	
			41—50	50.4 ± 9.0	
M	Cortisol	C	23—39	5.8	10
			68—80	3.4	
	Cortisol	Isotope dilution	27.5	23.6 ± 1.8	11
			69.8	17.7 ± 1.4	
M & F	Total corticoids	C	33—39	0.742 ± 0.060	2
			64—89	0.648 ± 0.049	
M	Total corticoids	CPB	25	0.580 ± 0.084	12
			71	0.444 ± 0.064	
F	Total corticoids	CPB	24	0.380 ± 0.040	12
			71	0.268 ± 0.024	
M	Progesterone	Isotope dilution	23—39	4.5	10
			68—80	1.8	
	Progesterone	Isotope dilution	23—34	4.5	13
			74—79	1.5	
	Progesterone	Isotope dilution	23—34	15.0	13
			74—79	3.5	
	Pregnanediol	Isotope dilution	23—39	0.60	10
			68—80	0.14	
M & F	Pregnanediol	GC	29.2	0.27	1
			73.3	0.32	
M	Pregnanediol	Isotope dilution	20—29	0.60 ± 0.06	8
			30—39	0.62 ± 0.10	
			40—49	0.34 ± 0.08	
			50—59	0.30 ± 0.05	
			60—69	0.21 ± 0.05	
			70—80	0.17 ± 0.03	

[a] 17-ketosteroids.
[b] Gas chromatography.
[c] Colorimetric.
[d] 17-hydroxycorticosteroids.
[e] Competitive protein binding.

REFERENCES

1. **Antonini, F. M., Porro, A., Serio, M., and Tinti, P.,** Gas chromatographic analyses of urinary 17-ketosteroids response to gonadotropin and ACTH in young and old persons, *Exp. Gerontol.*, 3, 181, 1968.
2. **Friedberg, R.,** ACTH administration, adrenal response and age, *J. Gerontol.*, 9, 429, 1954.
3. **Keutman, H. E. and Mason, W. B.,** Individual urinary 17-ketosteroids of healthy persons determined by gas chromatography: biochemical and clinical considerations, *J. Clin. Endocrinol. Metab.*, 27, 406, 1967.
4. **Moncloa, F., Gómez, R., and Pretell, E.,** Response to corticotrophin and correlation between excretion of creatinine and urinary steroids and between the clearance of creatinine and urinary steroids in ageing, *Steroids*, 1, 437, 1963.

Table 6 (continued)
URINARY ADRENOCORTICOSTEROID EXCRETION IN HUMANS

5. **Pincus, G., Romanoff, L. B., and Carló, J.**, The excretion of urinary steroids by men and women of various ages, *J. Gerontol.*, 9, 113, 1954.
6. **Juselius, R. E. and Kenny, F. M.**, Urinary free cortisol excretion during growth and aging: correlation with cortisol production rate and 17-hydroxycorticosteroid excretion, *Metabolism*, 23, 847, 1974.
7. **Romanoff, L. P. and Baxter, M. N.**, The secretion rates of deoxycorticosterone and corticosterone in young and elderly men, *J. Clin. Endocrinol. Metab.*, 41, 630, 1975.
8. **Romanoff, L. P., Thomas, A. W., and Baxter, N. M.**, Effect of age on pregnanediol excretion by men, *J. Gerontol.*, 25, 98, 1970.
9. **West, C. D., Brown, H., Simons, H. L., Carter, D. B., Kumagai, L. F., and Englert, E., Jr.**, Adrenocortical function and cortisol metabolism in old age, *J. Clin. Endocrinol. Metab.*, 21, 1197, 1961.
10. **Romanoff, L. P., Morris, C. W., Welch, P., Grace, M. P., and Pincus, G.**, Metabolism of progesterone-4-C^{14} in young and elderly men, *J. Clin. Endocrinol. Metab.*, 23, 286, 1963.
11. **Romanoff, L. P., Morris, C. W., Welch, P., Rodriguez, R. M., and Pincus, G.**, The metabolism of cortisol-4-C^{14} in young and elderly men. 1. Secretion rate of cortisol and daily excretion of tetrahydrocortisol, allotetrahydrocortisol, tetrahydrocortisone and cortolone (20α and 20β), *J. Clin. Endocrinol. Metab.*, 21, 1413, 1961.
12. **Grad, B., Kral, V. A., Payne, R. C., and Berenson, J.**, Plasma and urinary corticoids in young and old persons, *J. Gerontol.*, 22, 66, 1967.
13. **Romanoff, L. P., Grace, M. P., Baxter, M. N., and Pincus, G.**, Metabolism of pregnenolone-7α-^{3}H and progesterone-4-^{14}C in young and elderly men, *J. Clin. Endocrinol. Metab.*, 26, 1023, 1966.

Table 7
URINARY ADRENOCORTICAL STEROID EXCRETION IN HUMANS EXPRESSED PER GRAM OF URINARY CREATININE

Sex	Compound measured	Method of analysis	Age (years)	Steroid excretion (mg/day/g creatinine) ($\overline{X} \pm$ SEM)	Ref.
M	17-KS[a]	C[b]	18—35	3.7 ± 0.22	1
			74—87	3.5 ± 0.35	
F	17-KS	C	22—38	3.4 ± 0.36	1
			64—80	4.0 ± 0.23	
M	17-OHCS[c]	C	20—39	4.0 ± 0.19	2
			40—49	3.8 ± 0.23	
			50—59	4.2 ± 0.30	
			60—69	4.1 ± 0.37	
			70—80	3.8 ± 0.27	
	Cortisol	Isotope dilution	27.5	13.8 ± 1.3	3
			69.8	15.0 ± 1.2	
	Cortisol	C	23—39	3.7	4
			68—80	3.4	
M & F	Cortisol	CPB[d]	⅓—10	78.0 ± 16.7	5
			11—20	24.5 ± 3.66	
			21—30	33.1 ± 2.0	
			31—40	36.6 ± 2.4	
			41—50	32.0 ± 7.9	
M	Total corticoids	CPB	25	431 ± 41	6
			71	338 ± 32	
F	Total corticoids	CPB	24	346 ± 36	6
			71	277 ± 25	

Table 7 (continued)
URINARY ADRENOCORTICAL STEROID EXCRETION IN HUMANS EXPRESSED PER GRAM OF URINARY CREATININE

Sex	Compound measured	Method of analysis	Age (years)	Steroid excretion (mg/day/g creatinine) ($\overline{X} \pm$ SEM)	Ref.
M	Progesterone	Isotope dilution	23—39	2.9	4
			68—80	1.7	
	Pregnanediol	Isotope dilution	23—39	0.40	4
			68—80	0.14	
	Pregnanediol	Isotope dilution	20—39	0.35 ± 0.03	2
			40—49	0.20 ± 0.05	
			50—59	0.19 ± 0.04	
			60—69	0.16 ± 0.03	
			70—80	0.18 ± 0.03	

[a] 17-Ketosteroids.
[b] Colorimetric.
[c] 17-Hydroxycorticosteroids.
[d] Competitive protein binding.

REFERENCES

1. **Romanoff, L. P., Rodriguez, R. M., Seelye, J. M., Parent, C., and Pincus, G.**, The urinary excretion of tetrahydrocortisol, 3α-allotetrahydrocortisol and tetrahydrocortisone in young and elderly men and women, *J. Clin. Endocrinol. Metab.*, 18, 1285, 1958.
2. **Romanoff, L. P., Thomas, A. W., and Baxter, M. N.**, Effect of age on pregnanediol excretion, *J. Gerontol.*, 25, 98, 1970.
3. **Romanoff, L. P., Morris, C. W., Welch, P., Rodriguez, R. M., and Pincus, G.**, The metabolism of cortisol-4-C[14] in young and elderly men. I. Secretion rate of cortisol and daily excretion of tetrahydrocortisol, allotetrahydrocortisol, tetrahydrocortisone and cortolone (20α and 20β), *J. Clin. Endocrinol. Metab.*, 21, 1413, 1961.
4. **Romanoff, L. P., Morris, C. W., Welch, P., Grace, M. P., and Pincus, G.**, Metabolism of progesterone-4-C[14] in young and elderly men, *J. Clin. Endocrinol. Metab.*, 23, 286, 1963.
5. **Juselius, R. E. and Kenny, F. M.**, Urinary free cortisol excretion during growth and aging: correlation with cortisol production rate and 17-hydroxycorticosteroid excretion, *Metabolism*, 23, 847, 1974.
6. **Grad, B., Kral, V. A., Payne, R. C., and Berenson, J.**, Plasma and urinary corticoids in young and old persons, *J. Gerontol.*, 22, 66, 1967.

Table 8
URINARY ADRENOCORTICOSTEROID EXCRETION IN HUMANS IN RESPONSE TO ACTH STIMULATION

Sex	Compound measured	Method of analysis	Dose of ACTH	Age (years)	Prestimulation level (mg/day, $\overline{X} \pm$ SEM)	Poststimulation level	% change $\left(\dfrac{\text{Post-Pre}}{\text{Pre}}\right) \times 100\%$	Ref.
M & F	17-KS[a]	C[b]	80 units (i.m.)	33—39	8.97 ± 1.02	10.38 ± 1.73	0	1
				64—89	3.64 ± 0.28	5.29 ± 0.82	0	
M	17-KS	C	40 units (i.v.)	20—30	9.88 ± 0.97	16.48 ± 1.25	+67%	2
				50—69	6.96 ± 0.59	12.17 ± 1.32	+75%	
	17-KS	GC	25 units (i.v.)	29.2	3.71	6.98	+88%	3
				73.3	2.81	3.53	+26%	
	17-OHCS[d]	C	40 units (i.v.)	20—30	5.95 ± 0.40	20.85 ± 1.93	+250%	2
				50—69	4.86 ± 0.52	15.60 ± 0.80	+221%	
M & F	Total corticoids	C	80 units (i.m.)	33—39	0.742 ± 0.600	1.179 ± 0.130	+59%	1
				64—89	0.648 ± 0.049	1.424 ± 0.177	+120%	
M	Pregnanediol	GC	25 units (i.v.)	29.2	0.27	0.48	+77%	3
				73.3	0.32	0.37	+16%	

[a] 17-Ketosteroids.
[b] Colorimetric.
[c] Gas chromatography.
[d] 17-Hydroxycorticosteroids.

REFERENCES

1. **Friedberg, R.**, ACTH administration, adrenal response, and age, *J. Gerontol.*, 9, 429, 1954.
2. **Moncloa, F., Gómez, R., and Pretell, E.**, Response to corticotrophin and correlation between excretion of creatinine and urinary steroids and between the clearance of creatinine and urinary steroids in ageing, *Steroids*, 1, 437, 1963.
3. **Antonini, F. M., Porro, A., Serro, M., and Tinti, P.**, Gas chromatographic analysis of urinary 17-ketosteroid response to gonadotropin and ACTH in young and old persons, *Exp. Gerontol.*, 3, 181, 1968.

Table 9
MISCELLANEOUS PARAMETERS OF ADRENOCORTICAL FUNCTION IN HUMANS

Sex	Parameter measured	Age (years)	Reported values ($\overline{X} \pm$ SEM)	Ref.
M	Binding of cortisol in plasma (% bound)	19—40	84.1 ± 2.1	1
		60—86	84.8 ± 2.5	
	Half-life of cortisol in plasma (min)	25—40	112.0 ± 5.1	2
		60—69	114.0 ± 7.3	
		70—79	154 ± 11.2	
		≥80	169 ± 8.8	
	Apparent distribution volume of cortisol (% of body weight)	25—40	81.0 ± 3.3	2
		60—69	92.0 ± 4.7	
		70—79	94.0 ± 7.3	
		≥80	92.0 ± 6.7	
	Metabolic clearance rate of aldosterone (ℓ plasma/day)	18—35	1631 ± 106	3
		67—88	1288 ± 121	

REFERENCES

1. Kley, H. K., Nieschlag, E., and Krüskemper, H. L., Age dependence of plasma oestrogen response to HCG and ACTH in men, *Acta Endocrinol.*, 79, 95, 1975.
2. West, C. D., Brown, H., Simons, E. L., Carter, D. B., Kumagai, L. F., and Englert, E., Jr., Adrenocortical function and cortisol metabolism in old age, *J. Clin. Endocrinol. Metab.*, 21, 1197, 1961.
3. Flood, C., Gherondache, C., Pincus, G., Tait, J. F., Tait, S. A. S., and Willoughby, S., The metabolism and secretion of aldosterone in elderly subjects, *J. Clin. Invest.*, 46, 960, 1967.

Table 10
MISCELLANEOUS PARAMETERS OF ADRENOCORTICAL FUNCTION IN RATS AND MICE

Species	Strain	Sex	Parameter measured	Age (months)	Level	Ref.
Rat	Sprague-Dawley	M	Blood volume (ml)	2	10.9 ± 0.2	1
				12	18.3 ± 0.6	
				24	22.8 ± 1.2	
	Sprague-Dawley	M	Serum corticosterone binding (%)	2	95.9 ± 0.9	1
				12	98.1 ± 1.6	
				24	98.7 ± 1.0	
	Long-Evans	F	Distribution volume of corticosterone (% of body weight)	5	63.0 ± 3.9	2
				27	61.2 ± 3.8	
	Long-Evans	F	Biological half-life of corticosterone (min)	5	9.3 ± 0.4	2
				27	10.6 ± 0.3	
Mouse[a]	C57BL/6J	M	Plasma corticosterone binding (pmol/mg protein)	10	2.19 ± 0.22	3
				30	1.78 ± 0.16	
Rat	Not specified	F	Urinary 17-ketosteroids (μg/rat/day)	Intact	31.4 ± 1.3	4
				6	34.8 ± 3.3	
				12	35.8 ± 3.3	
				24		
				Ovariectomized		
				6	17.0 ± 1.3	4
				12	13.7 ± 2.5	
				24	22.0 ± 2.6	
	Long-Evans	F	Adrenal Δ⁵-3β-hydroxysteroid dehydrogenase (μg androstenedione formed per min)	1	5.5 ± 0.3	5
				2	13.6 ± 1.2	
				4	19.6 ± 1.6	
				6	16.3 ± 1.7	
				12	14.7 ± 1.0	
				18	13.9 ± 1.2	
				24	13.1 ± 1.1	
	Long-Evans	F	Adrenal Δ⁵-3β-hydroxysteroid dehydrogenase (μg androstenedione formed per mg protein)	1	2.2 ± 0.2	5
				2	6.7 ± 0.2	
				4	7.9 ± 0.4	
				6	6.8 ± 0.6	
				12	8.0 ± 0.6	
				18	7.7 ± 0.6	
				24	7.4 ± 0.8	

[a] Animals autopsied at sacrifice for pathological lesions.

REFERENCES

1. **Britton, G. W., Rotenberg, S., Freeman, C., Britton, V. J., Karoly, K., Ceci, L., Klug, T. L., Lacka, A. G., and Adelman, R. C.,** Regulation of corticosterone levels and liver enzyme activity in aging rats, *Adv. Exp. Med. Biol.*, 61, 209, 1975.
2. **Hess, G. D. and Riegle, G. D.,** Effects of chronic ACTH stimulation on adrenocortical function in young and aged rats, *Am. J. Physiol.*, 222, 1458, 1972.
3. **Latham, K. R. and Finch, C. E.,** Hepatic glucocorticoid binders in mature and senescent C57BL/6J male mice, *Endocrinology*, 98, 1480, 1976.
4. **Kullander, S.,** The level of urinary 17-ketosteroids in female rats, *Acta Endocrinol. (Copenhagen)*, 34, 353, 1960.
5. **Shapiro, B. H. and Leatham, J. H.,** Aging and adrenal Δ⁵-3β-hydroxysteroid dehydrogenase in female rats, *Proc. Soc. Exp. Biol. Med.*, 136, 19, 1971.

THYROID

G. H. Donahue

Table 1
HUMAN SERUM TRIIODOTHYRONINE (T₃) CONCENTRATION

Method	Sex(n)	Age (years)	Free T₃ (ng/ml)	Ref.
RIA[a]	Not specified			
	(34)	19—45	1.15 ± 0.24	1
	(21)	60—95	0.79 ± 0.21	
	M + F (34)	19—45	1.16 ± 0.21	2
	M + F (22)	60—93	0.8 ± 0.24[b]	
[c]	F (24)	20—39	1.10 ± 0.22	3
	F (16)	60—79	0.91 ± 0.32	
	F (5)	80—90	0.85 ± 0.2	
	M (10)	20—39	1.05 ± 0.28	
	M (9)	60—79	0.89 ± 0.27	
	M (5)	80—90	0.61 ± 0.28	
RIA[a,d]	M + F (13)	20—29	1.35 ± 0.08	4
	M + F (22)	30—39	1.25 ± 0.05	
	M + F (9)	60—79	1.15 ± 0.05	
	M + F (13)	80—93	0.92 ± 0.07	
RIA[a]	M (12)	20—39	1.12 ± 0.6	5
	M (12)	40—59	1.02 ± 0.04	
	M (12)	60—79	0.83 ± 0.07	
	F (12)	20—39	1.09 ± 0.06	
[e]	M + F (356)	20—64	1.27 ± 0.36	6
	M + F (91)	65—92	0.62 ± 0.3	

[a] Radioimmunoassay.
[b] Free T₃ values were not correlated with total T₃, thyroid binding globulin, or plasma TSH (Reference 2).
[c] Chromatography procedure of Sterling, K., Bellabarba, D., Newman, E. S., and Brenner, M. A., Determination of triiodothyronine concentration in human serum, *J. Clin. Invest.*, 48, 1150, 1969.
[d] Thyroid hormone binding proteins were denatured (95% ethanol) followed by RIA.
[e] Methodology not specified.

REFERENCES

1. Hesch, R. D., Gatz, J., Juppner, H. and Stubbe, P., TBG-dependency of age related variations of thyroxine and triiodothyronine, *Horm. Metab. Res.*, 9, 141, 1977.
2. Hesch, R. D., Gatz, J., Pape, J., Schmidt, E., and von zur Muhlen, A., Total and free triiodothyronine and thyroid-binding globulin concentration in elderly human persons, *Eur. J. Clin. Invest.*, 6, 139, 1976.
3. Hansen, J. M., Skovsted, L., and Nielsen, K. S., Age dependent changes in iodine metabolism and thyroid function, *Acta Endocrinol. (Copenhagen)*, 79, 60, 1975.
4. Rubenstein, H. A., Butler, V. P., and Werner, S. C., Progressive decrease in serum triiodothyronine concentrations with human aging: radioimmunoassay following extraction of serum, *J. Clin. Endocrinol. Metab.*, 37, 247, 1973.
5. Snyder, P. J. and Utiger, R. D., Response of thyrotropin releasing hormone (TR.H) in normal man, *J. Clin. Endocrinol. Metab.*, 34, 380, 1972.
6. Herrmann, J., Rusche, H. J., Kroll, H. J., Hilger, P., and Kruskemper, H. L., Free triiodothyronine and thyroxine (T₄) serum levels in old age, *Horm. Metab. Res.*, 6, 239, 1974.

Table 2
HUMAN SERUM THYROXINE (T₄)
CONCENTRATION

Method	Sex (n)	Age (years)	T_4 (ng/ml)	Ref.
	Not specified			
RIA[a]	(34)	19—45	72.7 ± 22.6	1
RIA[a]	(21)	60—95	57.9 ± 15.6	
[b]	F (7)	20—39	102.0 ± 14.0	2
	F (23)	60—90	88.0 ± 14.0	
	F (8)	80—90	78.0 ± 17.0	
	M (16)	20—39	78.0 ± 11.0	
	M (22)	60—79	86.0 ± 15.0	
	M (5)	80—90	82.0 ± 1.0	
[c]	M + F (137)	20—64	78.0 ± 22.0	3
	M + F (77)	65—92	64.0 ± 15.0	
[d]	M (12)	20—39	78.0 ± 5.0	4
	M (12)	40—59	73.0 ± 3.0	
	M (12)	60—79	75.0 ± 5.0	
	F (12)	20—39	80.0 ± 3.0	

[a] Radioimmunoassay.
[b] Competitive protein binding assay.
[c] Methodology not specified.
[d] According to Odell, W. D., Wilber, J. F., and Utiger, R. D., Studies of thyrotropin physiology by means of radioimmunoassay, *Recent Prog. Horm. Res.*, 23, 47, 1967.

REFERENCES

1. Hesch, R. D., Gatz, J., Juppner, H., and Stubbe, P., TBG-dependency of age related variations of thyroxine and triiodothyronine, *Horm. Metab. Res.*, 9, 141, 1977.
2. Hansen, J. M., Skovsted, L., and Nielsen, K. S., Age dependent changes in iodine metabolism and thyroid function, *Acta Endocrinol.*, 79, 60, 1975.
3. Herrmann, J., Rusche, H. J., Kroll, H. J., Hilger, P., and Kruskemper, H. L., Free triiodothyronine and thyroxine (T₄) serum levels in old age, *Horm. Metab. Res.*, 6, 239, 1974.
4. Snyder, P. J. and Utiger, R. D., Response to thyrotropin releasing hormone (TRH) in normal man, *J. Clin. Endocrinol. Metabl.*, 34, 380, 1972.

Table 3
SERUM PROTEIN-BOUND IODINE (PBI) IN RATS AND HUMANS

Species	Strain	Sex (n)	Method	Age	Serum PBI (μg/100 ml)	Ref.
Rat	Wistar	F (8)	a	4—5 months	3.36 ± 0.18 (plasma)	1
		F (9)	a	24—25 months	3.60 ± 0.15 (plasma)	
Human	—	F (68)	b	c	4.22 ± 0.92	
		F (69)	b	d	5.73 ± 1.46	2
		F (141)	e	c	5.70 ± 0.4	
		F (145)	e	d	5.06 ± 0.65	
	—	M + F (311)	f	10—39 years	5.34 ± 0.96	3
			f	>50 years	5.09 ± 0.93	
	—	M (12)	g	18—27 years	6.90 ± 1.10	
		M + F (13)	g	65.1 (mean)	6.83 ± 1.07	4
		M + F (13)	g	83.2 (mean)	6.24 ± 0.60	
	—	M (9)	h	25—39 years	5.1 ± 2.3 (SD)	
		M (19)	h	60—69 years	4.6 ± 2.0 (SD)	
		M (16)	h	70—79 years	4.2 ± 1.5 (SD)	
		M (9)	h	>80 years	3.3 ± 1.3 (SD)	5
		F (10)	h	25—39 years	4.5 ± 1.4 (SD)	
		F (15)	h	60—69 years	5.0 ± 2.4 (SD)	
		F (15)	h	70—79 years	4.7 ± 1.9 (SD)	
		F (8)	h	>80 years	3.8 ± 2.2 (SD)	
	—	M + F (124)	b	27—94 years	5.53 ± 0.9	6
		M + F (72)	i	18—91 years	6.55 ± 1.2 (plasma)	
	—	M (1)	b	46 years	5.7 (mean)	
		M (1)	b	51 years	5.1 (mean)	
		M (1)	b	81 years	7.1 (mean)	7
		M (1)	b	88 years	5.9 (mean)	
		M (1)	b	92 years	5.8 (mean)	
	—	M (26)	j	56—90 years	5.94 (mean)	
				60—69 years	5.40 (mean)	8
		F (28)	j	70—79 years	5.85 (mean)	

a According to Zak, B., Willard, H. H., Meyers, G. B., and Boyle, A. J., Chloric acid method for determination of protein-bound iodine, *Anal. Chem.*, 24, 1346, 1952.
b Analysis made by Bioscience Lab, Los Angeles, CA using alkaline-ash method of Barker, S. B., Humphrey, M. J., and Soley, M. H., The clinical determination of protein-bound iodine, *J. Clin. Invest.*, 30, 55, 1951.
c Premenopause.
d Postmenopause.
e Analysis made by University of Arkansas Medical Center according to Barker, H. G. and Clark, J. K., Study of renal oxygen consumption and man: effect of tubular loading (Pah order diuresis)
f According to Barker, H. G. and Clark, J. K., Study of renal oxygen consumption and man: effect of tubular loading (Pah order diuresis) and osmotic (mannitol diuresis), *J. Clin. Invest.*, 30, 55, 1951.
g According to O'Neal, L. W. and Simms, E. S., Determination of protein-bound iodine in plasma or serum, *Am. J. Clin. Pathol.*, 23, 493, 1958; as mdified by Gaffney, G. W., Gregerman, R. I., Yiengst, M. J., and Shock, N. W., *J. Gerontol.*, 15, 234, 1960 (Reference 6).
h According to Chaney, A. L., Improvements in determination of iodine in blood, *Ind. Eng. Chem. Anal. Ed.*, 12, 179, 1940; as modified by Taurog, A. and Chaikoff, I. L., On the determination of plasma iodine, *J. Biol. Chem.*, 163, 313, 1946.
i According to O'Neal, L. W. and Simms, E. S., Determination of protein-bound iodine in plasma or serum: a simple and rapid method, *Am. J. Clin. Pathol.*, 23, 493, 1953.
j Method not specified.

Table 3 (continued)
SERUM PROTEIN-BOUND IODINE (PBI) IN RATS AND HUMANS

REFERENCES

1. **Wilansky, D. L., Newsham, L. G., and Hoffman, M. M.,** The influence of senescence on thyroid function: functional changes evaluated with I^{131}, *Endocrinology*, 61, 327, 1957.
2. **Oddie, T. H., Melby, J. C., and Scoggs, J. E.,** Statistical analyses of radioiodine and protein bound iodine test. Results on Arkansas thyroid patients, *J. Clin. Endocrinol. Metab.*, 22, 1138, 1962.
3. **Radcliff, F. J., Baker, J. M., Croydon, M. J., Hart, M. J., and Hales, I. B.,** Diagnostic value of the estimation of protein bound iodine in thyroid disease: survey of an Australian population group, *J. Clin. Endocrinol. Metab.*, 24, 883, 1964.
4. **Gregerman, R. I., Gaffney, G. W., and Shock, N. W.,** Thyroxine turnover in euthyroid man with special reference to changes with age, *J. Clin. Invest.*, 41, 2065, 1962.
5. **Kountz, W. B., Chieff, M., and Kirk, E.,** Serum protein-bound iodine and age, *J. Gerontol.*, 4, 132, 1949.
6. **Gaffney, G. W., Gregerman, R. I., Yiengst, M. J., and Shock, N. W.,** Serum protein-bound iodine concentration in blood of euthyroid men aged 18 to 94 years, *J. Gerontol.*, 15, 234, 1960.
7. **Baker, S. P., Gaffney, G. W., Shock, N. W., and Landowne, M.,** Physiological responses of five middle-aged and elderly men to repeated administration of TSH, *J. Gerontol.*, 14, 37, 1959.
8. **McGavack, T. H. and Seegers, W.,** Status of the thyroid after age 50, *Metabolism*, 8, 136, 1959.

Table 4
I[131] UPTAKE BY THYROID

Species	Strain	Sex (n)	Age	% Uptake of initial dose of I[131]	Time after initial dose (hr)	Ref.
Rat	Wistar	F (11)	4—5 months	22.5 ± 1.2	24	1
		F (12)	24—25 months	18.8 ± 0.8	24	
Human	—	F (7)	20—39 years	43.0 ± 5.6	24	
		F (23)	60—79 years	37.6 ± 8.0	24	2
		F (8)	80—90 years	34.7 ± 4.7	24	
	—	M (16)	20—39 years	40.8 ± 6.4	24	
		M (22)	60—79 years	41.6 ± 9.4	24	
		M (5)	80—90 years	39.4 ± 4.9	24	
	—	a	25—40 years	31.2 ± 4.3	24	
		M + F (526)	40—101 years	21.2 ± 3.2	24	
		M + F (429)	60—101 years	20.9 (mean)	24	
		M + F (134)	60—69 years	21.0 (mean)	24	3
		M + F (183)	>0—79 years	21.0 (mean)	24	
		M + F (94)	80—89 years	21.6 (mean)	24	
		M + F (18)	90—101 years	21.3 (mean)	24	
	—	M + F (5)	41—49 years	37.1 ± 16.7 (SD)	24	
		M + F (27)	50—59 years	37.1 ± 10.6 (SD)	24	
		M + F (31)	60—69 years	35.3 ± 7.4 (SD)	24	4
		M + F (39)	70—79 years	33.6 ± 10.7 (SD)	24	
		M + F (26)	80—89 years	39.2 ± 9.0 (SD)	24	
		M + F (3)	90—94 years	30.6 ± 2.7 (SD)	24	
	—	M (1)	46 years	44.7 (mean)	24	
		M (1)	51 years	53.2 (mean)	24	
		M (1)	81 years	48.0 (mean)	24	5
		M (1)	88 years	43.2 (mean)	24	
		M (1)	92 years	32.2 (mean)	24	
	—	M (1)	46 years	26.0 (mean)	4	
		M (1)	51 years	30.0 (mean)	4	
		M (1)	81 years	25.5 (mean)	4	5
		M (1)	88 years	23.5 (mean)	4	
		M (1)	92 years	14.8 (mean)	4	
		M + F (27)	50—59 years	13.3 ± 4.5 (SD)	2	
		M + F (26)	80—89 years	12.4 ± 3.0 (SD)	2	4
		M + F (3)	90—94 years	9.0 ± 0.9 (SD)	2	
	—	M + F (27)	50—59 years	22.2 ± 7.8 (SD)	6	
		M + F (26)	80—89 years	20.7 ± 6.3 (SD)	6	4
		M + F (3)	90—94 years	15.9 ± 2.9 (SD)	6	

a Consisting of a rather large but unrecorded number of subjects (Reference 3).

REFERENCES

1. **Wilawsky, D. L., Neusham, L. G., and Hoffman, M. M.**, The influence of senescence on thyroid function: functional change evaluated with I[131], *Endocrinology*, 61, 327, 1957.
2. **Hansen, J. M., Skovsted, L., and Nielsen, K. S.**, Age dependent changes in iodine metabolism and thyroid function, *Acta Endocrinol. (Copenhagen)*, 79, 60, 1975.
3. **McGavack, T. H. and Seegers, W.**, Status of the thyroid after age 50, *Metabolism*, 8, 136, 1959.
4. **Gaffney, G. W., Gregerman, R. I., and Shock, N. W.**, Relationship of age to the thyroidal accumulation, renal excretion and distribution of radioiodide in euthyroid man, *J. Clin. Endocrinol. Metab.*, 22, 784, 1962.
5. **Baker, S. P., Gaffney, G. W., Shock, N. W., and Landowne, M.**, Physiological response of five middle-aged and elderly men to repeated administration of TSH, *J. Gerontol.*, 14, 37, 1959.

Table 5
VARIOUS ASPECTS OF THYROID FUNCTION

Species	Strain	Parameter measured	Sex (n)	Ages	Reported value	Ref.
Human	—	Thyroid iodide clearance	F (7)	20—39 years	21.5 ± 6.1 ml/min	1
			F (10)	40—59 years	20.2 ± 7.2 ml/min	
			F (8)	80—90 years	7.1 ± 5.1 ml/min	
			M (16)	20—39 years	21.8 ± 7.6 ml/min	
			M (5)	80—90 years	13.2 ± 4.2 ml/min	
	—	Thyroid iodide clearance	M + F (4)	41—49 years	21.8 ± 13.8 (SD)	2
			M + F (25)	50—59 years	17.7 ± 10.1 (SD)	
			M + F (21)	80—89 years	15.7 ± 7.8 (SD)	
			M + F (2)	90—94 years	10.3 ± 1.4 (SD)	
	—	Accumulation gradient[a]	F (6)	12—19 years	4.1 ± 0.6	3
			F (35)	20—49 years	4.9 ± 0.47	
			F (49)	> 50 years	2.4 ± 0.22	
			M (11)	12—19 years	4.4 ± 0.95	
			M (27)	>50 years	1.7 ± 0.19	
Rat	Wistar	Thyroxine distribution space	F (14)	1 year	68.2 ± 3.5 ml	4
			F (22)	1 year	64.7 ± 3.0 ml	
			F (41)	2 years	97.1 ± 6.8 ml	
	Wistar	Thyroxine ½ life	F (9)	4—5 months	3.1 days	5
			F (11)	24—25 months	4.0 days	
Human	—	Thyroxine ½ life	M (12)	18—27 years	6.61 ± 0.87 days	6
			M + F (13)	65.1 years (mean)	9.10 ± 1.35 days	
			M + F (13)	83.2 years (mean)	9.25 ± 0.89 days	
	—	Thyroxine binding globulin	F (13)	78.4 ± 9.1 years	1.30 ± 0.18	7
			M (9)	Sex not specified		
	—	Thyroxine binding globulin	(21)	60—95 years	1.28 ± 0.15	8
			(28)	19—29 years	0.95 ± 0.14	
Rat	Wistar	Thyroxine secretion rate[b]	F (33)	4—5 months	3.2 μg/100 g BW/day	9
			F (32)	24—25 months	1.9 μg/100 g BW/day	
	Wistar	Thyroxine secretion rate[c]	F (8)	4—5 months	2.25 μg/100 g BW/day	5
			F (8)	24—25 months	1.75 μg/100 g BW/day	
	Wistar	Thyroxine secretion rate[d]	F (13)	3½ months	1.20 ± 0.09 μg/100 g BW/day	

Human	—	Thyroxine degradation rate	F (13)	12 months	1.20 ± 0.10 μg/100 g BW/day	4
			F (41)	24 months	1.63 ± 0.12 μg/100 g BW/day	
			M (12)	18—27 years	88.65 ± 25 μg thyroxine I/day	6
			M + F (13)	65.1 years (mean)	58.84 ± 17 μg thyroxine I/day	
			M + F (13)	83.2 years (mean)	43.9 ± 6.7 μg thyroxine I/day	

[a] Method according to Stanley, M. M. and Astwood, E. B., Determination of the relative activities of antithyroid compounds in man using radioactive iodine, *Endocrinology*, 41, 66, 1947.
[b] Goiter prevention assay.
[c] Maximal thyroid secretion inhibition with thyroxine administration.
[d] Thyroxine turnover technique.

REFERENCES

1. **Hansen, J. M., Skovsted, L., and Nielsen, K. S.**, Age dependent changes in iodine metabolism and thyroid function, *Acta Endocrinol. (Copenhagen)*, 79, 60, 1975.
2. **Gaffney, G. W., Gregerman, R. I., and Shock, N. W.**, Relationship of age to the thyroidal accumulation, renal excretion and distribution of radioiodidide in euthyroid man, *J. Clin. Endocrinol. Metab.*, 22, 784, 1962.
3. **Perlmutter, M. and Riggs, D.**, Thyroid collection of radioactive iodide and serum protein bound iodine concentration in senescence, in hypothyroidism and in hypopituitarism, *J. Clin. Endocrinol. Metab.*, 9, 430, 1949.
4. **Gregerman, R. I.**, Estimation of thyroxine secretion rate in the rat by the radioactive thyroxine turnover technique: influences of age, sex and exposure to cold, *Endocrinology*, 72, 382, 1963.
5. **Wilansky, D. L., Newsham, L. G., and Hoffman, M. M.**, The influence of senescence on thyroid function: functional changes evaluated with I[131], *Endocrinology*, 61, 327, 1957.
6. **Gregerman, R. I., Gaffney, G. W., and Shock, N. W.**, Thyroxine turnover in euthyroid man with special reference to changes with age, *J. Clin. Invest.*, 41, 2065, 1962.
7. **Hesch, R. D., Gatz, J., Pape, J., Schmidt, E., and von zur Muhlen, A.**, Total and free triiodothyronine and thyroid-binding globulin concentration in elderly human persons, *Eur. J. Clin. Invest.*, 6, 139, 1976.
8. **Hesch, R. D., Gatz, J., Juppner, H., and Stubbe, P.**, TBG-dependency of age-related variations of thyroxine and triiodothyronine, *Horm. Metab. Res.*, 9, 141, 1977.
9. **Grad, B. and Hoffman, M. M.**, Thyroxine secretion rates and plasma cholesterol levels of young and old rats, *Am. J. Physiol.*, 182, 497, 1955.

Table 6
RESPONSES OF RATS AND MICE TO THYROID HORMONES

Parameter studied	Effect of age	Effect of thyroid hormone(s) or thyroidectomy (Tx) (old vs. young)	Species	Ref.
O$_2$ consumption (entire animal)	Increase	Increased response to thyroid hormones	Rat	1
O$_2$ consumption (entire animal)	—	Increased (dose dependent) response to thyroid hormone	Rat	2
O$_2$ consumption (myocardium)	—	Tx decreases it in adult but not in senescent	Rat	2
"Thyroidal minimal oxygen consumption" (entire animal)	Decrease	Decreased response to thyroid hormones	Rat	3
Food intake	—	Increased response to thyroid hormones	Rat	1
Catabolic effect (N excretion)	—	Increased response to thyroid hormones	Rat	2
Heart rate increase	—	Increased response to thyroid hormones	Rat	1
Cardiac hypertrophy	—	Delayed response to thyroid hormones	Mouse	4
Graft rejection; colloidal carbon clearance	—	Decreased (immature vs. adults) response to thyroid hormones	Rat	5
α-Glycerophosphate dehydrogenase	No effect	Same 6-fold increase in response to thyroid hormones at both ages; same decrease after Tx	Rat	6

REFERENCES

1. **Grad, B.**, The metabolic responsiveness of young and old female rats to thyroxine, *J. Gerontol.*, 24, 5, 1969.
2. **Frolkis, V. V., Verzhikovskaya, N. V., and Valueva, G. V.**, The thyroid and age, *Exp. Gerontol.*, 8, 285, 1973.
3. **Denckla, W. D.**, Role of the pituitary and thyroid glands in the decline of minimal oxygen consumption with age, *J. Clin. Invest.*, 53, 572, 1974.
4. **Florini, J. R., Saito, Y., and Manowitz, E. J.**, Effect of age on thyroxine-induced cardiac hypertrophy in mice, *J. Gerontol.*, 28, 293, 1973.
5. **Bilder, G. E. and Denckla, W. D.**, Restoration of ability to reject xenografts and clear carbon after hypophysectomy of adult rats, *Mech. Ageing Develop.*, 6, 153, 1977.
6. **Bulos, B., Sacktor, B., Grossman, I. W., and Altman, N.**, Thyroid control of mitochondrial α-glycerophosphate dehydrogenase in rat liver as a function of age, *J. Gerontol.*, 26, 13, 1971.

NEUROHYPOPHYSIS

J. H. Helderman and R. W. Steger

Table 1
IMPACT OF AGING ON THE ANTIDIURETIC HORMONE

	Ref.
1. Pharmacologic principles — There are no published data on volume of distribution, blood levels, or half times for ADH (arginine vasopressin) in the aged	—
2. Renal responsiveness to ADH	
a. Clinical data — Hyponatremic syndromes are seen exclusively or more frequently in the aged	1—3
b. There is diminished renal response to endogenous ADH observed by urinary composition studies in	
1. Rats	4—6
2. Man	7—12
c. In contrast, submaximal doses of exogenous ADH behave normally in man	10,11
d. Reduced renal forces for establishing concentration gradients in aging exist which explains diminished ADH effects	13—15
3. Secretory function of neurohypophyseal axis related to ADH and age	
a. Morphologic evidence points to increased hypothalamic-pituitary activity in the aged; neuronal number, secretory granule content, or appearance of activity is either unchanged or increased	16—21
b. There is heightened AVP secretory response to stimuli such as ethanol and hypertonic salt	22
c. There also is diminished secretory response of AVP secretion to volume-pressure stimuli in aging; evidence of a defect in afferent reflex pathways	
1. Peripheral afferent pathway	
2. Intracerebral afferent pathways	23
a. Morphologic	24
b. Functional	25

REFERENCES

1. **Deutsch, S., Goldberg, M., and Dripps, R. D.,** postoperative hyponatremia with the inappropriate release of antidiuretic hormone, *Anaesthesia*, 27, 250, 1966.
2. **Weissman, P. N., Shenkman, L., and Gregerman, R. I.,** Chloropropamide hyponatremia: drug-induced inappropriate antidiuretic hormone activity, *N. Engl. J. Med.*, 284, 65, 1971.
3. **Findley, T.,** Role of neurohypophysis in the pathogenesis of hypertension and some allied disorders associated with aging, *Am. J. Med.*, 7, 70, 1949.
4. **Dunihue, F. W.,** Reduced juxtaglomerular cell granularity, pituitary neurosecretory material, and width of the zona glomerulosa in aging rats, *Endocrinology*, 77, 948, 1965.
5. **Friedman, S. M., Friedman, C. L., and Nakashima, M.,** Effect of pitressin on old-age changes of salt and water metabolism in the rat, *Am. J. Physiol.*, 199, 35, 1960.
6. **Friedman, S. M., Hinke, J. A. M., and Friedman, C. L.,** Neurohypophyseal responsiveness in the normal and senescent rat, *J. Gerontol.*, 11, 286, 1956.
7. **Dontas, A. S., Karketos, S., and Papanayioutou, P.,** Mechanisms of renal tubular defects in old age, *Postgrad. Med. J.*, 48, 295, 1972.
8. **Lewis, W. H. and Alving, A. S.,** Changes with age in the renal function of adult men: clearance ability of the kidneys, *Am. J. Physiol.*, 123, 505, 1938.
9. **Lindeman, R. D., Van Buren, H. C., and Raisz, L. G.,** Osmolar renal concentrating ability in healthy young men and hospitalized patients without renal disease, *N. Engl. J. Med.*, 262, 1396, 1960.

Table 1 (continued)
IMPACT OF AGING ON THE ANTIDIURETIC HORMONE

10. **Lindeman, R. D., Lee, T. D., Jr., Yiengst, M. J., and Shock, N. W.**, Influences of age, renal disease, hypertension, diuretics, and calcium on the antidiuretic responses to suboptimal infusions of vasopressin, *J. Lab. Clin. Med.*, 68, 206, 1966.
11. **Miller, J. H. and Shock, N. W.**, Age differences in the renal tubular response to antidiuretic hormone, *J. Gerontol.*, 8, 446, 1953.
12. **Mukherjee, A. P., Coni, N. K., and Davison, W.**, Osmoreceptor function among the elderly, *Gerontol. Clin.*, 15, 227, 1973.
13. **Ljunqvist, A. and Lagergren, C.**, Normal intrarenal arterial pattern in adult an aging human kidney, *J. Anat.*, 96, 285, 1962.
14. **Takazakura, E., Sawabu, N., Handa, A., Takada, A., Shindda, A., and Takeuchi, J.**, Intrarenal vascular changes with age and disease, *Kidney Int.*, 2, 224, 1972.
15. **Hollenberg, N. K., Adams, D. F., Solomon, H. S., Rashid, A., Abrams, H. L., and Merrill, J. P.**, Senescence and the renal vasculature in normal man, *Circ. Res.*, 34, 309, 1974.
16. **Christ, J.**, Zur Anatomie des Tuber cinerum beim erwachsenen Menschen, *Dtsch. Z. Nervenheilkd.*, 165, 340, 1951.
17. **Hommes, O. R.**, Effects of hypophysectomy and age on the infundibular nucleus in man, *J. Endocrinol.*, 63, 479, 1974.
18. **Andrew, W.**, Structural alterations with aging in the nervous system, *J. Chronic Dis.*, 3, 575, 1956.
19. **Buttlar-Brentano, von K.**, Zur Lebensgeschichte des Nucleus basalis, tuberomammillaris, suprapoticus, and paraventricularis unter normalen und pathogenen Bedingungen, *J. Hirnforschung*, 1, 337, 1954.
20. **Frolkis, V. V., Bezrukov, V. V., Duplenko, Y. K., and Genis, E. D.**, The hypothalamus in aging, *Exp. Gerontol.*, 7, 169, 1972.
21. **Hsu, H. K. and Peng, M. T.**, Hypothalamic neuron number of old female rats, *Gerontology*, 24, 6, 434, 1978.
22. **Helderman, J. H., Vestal, R. E., Rowe, J. W., Tobin, J. D., Andrea, R., and Robertson, G. L.**, The response of argintine vasopressin to intravenous ethanol in man: the impact of aging, *J. Gerontol.* 33, 39, 1978.
23. **Rowe, J. W. and Robertson, G. L.**, Age-related failure of volume-pressure mediated vasopressin release in man, *Kidney Int.*, 14, 660, 1978.
24. **Machado-Salas, J., Scheibel, M. E., and Scheibel, A. B.**, Morphologic changes in the hypothalamus of the old mouse, *Exp. Neurol.*, 51, 1, 102, 1977.
25. **Rowe, J. W., Baylis, P. H., and Robertson, G. L.**, Stimulation of vasopressin secretion by pitressin in man: influence of sodium depletion and age, *Clin. Res.*, 26, 494A, 1978.

Table 2
THE EFFECTS OF AGE ON POSTERIOR PITUITARY FUNCTION IN RELATION TO OXYTOCIN SECRETION

	Ref.
Human	
Increase weight of neurohypophysis with age probably due to increases in connective tissue	1, 2
Decreased vascularity	3
Invasion of basophils	4, 5
No apparent relationship between age and oxytocin content	6
Rats	
Neurosecretory material in the neurohypophysis decreases with age	7, 8
Cattle	
Decreased ADH and oxytocin content with advancing age	10

REFERENCES

1. **Turkington, M. R. and Everitt, A. V.**, The neurohypophysis and aging with special reference to the antidiuretic hormone, in *Hypothalamus, Pituitary and Aging,* Everitt, A. V. and Burgess, J. A., Eds., Charles C. Thomas, Springfield, Ill., 1976, 123.
2. **Rasmussen, A. T.**, The proportions of the various subdivisions of the normal human hypophysis cerebri., *Res. Publ. Assoc. Res. Nerv. Ment. Dis.,* 17, 118, 1938.
3. **Xuereb, G. P., Res.** The changes which occur with ageing in the vascular patterns of the infundibular progress of the human hypophysis cerebri, *J. Endocrinol.,* 10, 238, 1954.
4. **Randall, R. V.**, The pituitary body and aging, *J. Am. Geriatr. Soc.,* 10, 6, 1962.
5. **Spark, C.**, The relation between basophilic invasion of the neurohypophysis and hypertensive disorders, *Arch. Pathol.,* 19, 473, 1935.
6. **Currie, A. R., Adamsong, H., and VanDyke, H. B.**, Vasopressin and oxytocin in the posterior lobe of the pituitary of man, *J. Clin. Endocrinol.,* 20, 947, 1960.
7. **Rodeck, H., Lederis, K., and Heller, H.**, The hypothalamo-neurohypophysial system in old rats, *J. Endocrinol.,* 21, 225, 1960.
8. **Dunihue, F. S.**, Reduced juxtaglomerular cell granularity, pituitary neurosecretory material, and width of the zona glomerulosa in aging rats, *Endocrinology,* 77, 948, 1965.
9. **Morrison, A. B. and Staroscik, R. M.**, The neurosecretory substance in the neurohypophysis of the rat during maturation and aging, *Gerontologia,* 9, 65, 1964.
10. **Nikitin, V. N.**, Changes in the endocrine glands due to aging, *Russ. Rev. Biol.,* 50, 180, 1961.

HYPOTHALAMIC-HYPOPHYSIAL SYSTEM

R. W. Steger and C. E. Finch

Table 1
AGE-RELATED CHANGES IN GONADOTROPIN-RELEASING HORMONE (GnRH) AND PROLACTIN-INHIBITING FACTOR (PIF) CONTENT OF THE HYPOTHALAMUS

Rat	Ref.
Medial basal hypothalamic GnRH is decreased below levels seen in young estrus or diestrus rats, in the old anestrus rat, but not in the old constant-estrus or old pseudopregnant rat; anterior hypothalamic LHRH content unchanged	1
FSH releasing activity of the hypothalamus enhanced in old constant-estrus rats (bioassay)	2
LH releasing activity of hypothalamic extracts is less in old male and female rats ($P<0.20$)	3,4
PIF activity unchanged with age (bioassay)	2—4
Stalk-median eminence LH-FSH releasing factor content similar in young estrus and old constant-estrus rats; levels in old anestrus rats similar to those seen in young diestrus rats (bioassay)	5

REFERENCES

1. Steger, R. W., Huang, H. H., and Meites, J., Relation of aging to hypothalamic LHRH content and serum gonadal steroids in female rats, *Proc. Soc. Exp. Biol. Med.*, 161, 261, 1979.
2. Clemens, J. A. and Meites, J., Neuroendocrine status of old constant-estrous rats, *Neuroendocrinology*, 17, 249, 197.
3. Riegle, G. D., Meites, J., Miller, A. E., and Wood, S. M., Effect of aging on hypothalamic LH-releasing and prolactin inhibiting activities and pituitary responsiveness to LHRH in the male laboratory rat, *J. Gerontol.*, 32, 13, 1977.
4. Riegle, G. D. and Miller, A. E., Aging effects on the hypothalamic-hypophyseal-gonadal control system in the rat, in *The Aging Reproductive System,* Schneider, E. L., Ed., Raven Press, New York, 1978, 159.
5. Pi, W. P., Huang, H. H., and Peng, M. T., Pituitary luteinizing hormone and follicle stimulating hormone concentrations and stalk median eminence LH-releasing factor and FSH-RF levels of old female rats, *J. Formosan Med. Assoc.*, 72, 485, 1973.

Table 2
RELATIONSHIPS BETWEEN HYPOTHALAMIC BIOGENIC AMINE METABOLISM AND GONADOTROPIN SECRETION IN OLD RATS

	Ref.
A decreased catecholamine and an increased serotonin in the hypothalamus of old male rats may be related to the observed decrease in gonadotropin and increase in prolactin release	1
Decreased content of dopamine and norepinephrine in old male rats may contribute to changes in endocrine control mechanisms	2
Intact old constant-estrus rats and young proestrus and estrus rats have similar anterior hypothalamic dopamine (DA) concentrations and turnover rates, but old rats show reduced nonepinephrine (NA) turnover; NA and DA content or turnover in the posterior hypothalamus was not affected by age	3, 4
Ovariectomy resulted in an increased anterior hypothalamic norepinephrine turnover in young, but not old rats; reduced NE turnover was associated with reduced serum LH and FSH levels in the old rats	3, 4

REFERENCES

1. Simpkins, J. W., Mueller, G. P., Huang, H. H., and Meites, J., Evidence for depressed catecholamine and enhanced serotonin metabolism in aging male rats: possible relation to gonadotropin secretion, *Endocrinology,* 100, 1672, 1977.
2. Miller, A. E., Shaar, C. J., and Riegle, G. D., Aging effects on hypothalamic dopamine and norepinephrine content in the male rat, *Exp. Aging Res.,* 2, 475, 1976.
3. Huang, H. H., Relation of neuroendocrine system to loss of reproductive function in aging female rats, Ph. D. dissertation, Department of Physiology, Michigan State University, East Lansing, 1977.
4. Huang, H. H., Simpkins, J. W., and Meites, J., Hypothalamic norepinephrine (NE) and dopamine (DA) turnover and relation to LH, FSH, and prolactin release in old female rats, Abstr. 59th Annu. Meeting Endocrine Soc., Miami, Fla., 1977.

Table 3
EFFECTS OF DRUGS MODIFYING HYPOTHALAMIC BIOGENIC AMINE METABOLISM ON REPRODUCTIVE FUNCTION IN OLD RODENTS

	Ref.
Drugs which increase central catecholamine metabolism or decrease serotonin metabolism can reinitiate regular estrous cycles in old constant-estrus or irregular cycling female rats	1—6
L-Dopa prolongs life-span and fertility of the mouse	7
L-Dopa administration results in less reduction of prolactin in old constant-estrus or old persistant-diestrus than in young estrus or diestrus rats	8
L-Dopa increases serum LH in old constant-estrus, but not old pseudopregnant rats, the increase in serum LH occurred later and lasted longer in the old constant-estrus rats than in the young estrus rats	8
Tryptophan deficiency delays growth, development, and maturation, but increases longevity and delays the age at which fertility is lost, possibly by decreasing serotonin	9

Table 3 (continued)
EFFECTS OF DRUGS MODIFYING HYPOTHALAMIC BIOGENIC AMINE METABOLISM ON REPRODUCTIVE FUNCTION IN OLD RODENTS

REFERENCES

1. Clemens, J. A., Amenomori, Y., Jenkins, T., and Meites, J., Effect of hypothalamic stimulation, hormones, and drugs on ovarian function in old female rats, *Proc. Soc. Exp. Biol. Med.*, 132, 561, 1969.
2. Clemens, J. A. and Bennett, D. R., Do aging changes in the preoptic area contribute to loss of cyclic endocrine function, *J. Gerontol.*, 32, 19, 1977.
3. Huang, H. H., Marshall, S., and Meites, J., Induction of estrous cycles in old non-cyclic rats by progesterone, ACTH, ether stress, or L-dopa, *Neuroendocrinology*, 20, 21, 1976.
4. Lehman, J. R., McArthur, D. A., and Hendricks, S. E., Pharmacological induction of ovulation in old and neonatally androgenized rats, *Exp. Gerontol.*, 13 (3—4), 197, 1978.
5. Linnoila, M. and Cooper, R. L., Reinstatement of vaginal cycles in aged female rats, *J. Pharmacol.*, 199, 477, 1976.
6. Quadri, S. K., Kledzik, G, S., and Meites, J., Reinitiation of estrous cycles in old constant-estrous rats by central-acting drugs, *Neuroendocrinology*, 11, 248, 1973.
7. Cotzias, G. C., Miller, S. T., Tang, L. C., Papavasiliou, P. S., and Wang, Y. Y., Levodopa, fertility, and longevity, *Science*, 196, 549, 1977.
8. Watkins, B. E., McKay, D. W., Meites, J., and Riegle, G. D., L-Dopa effects on serum LH and prolactin in old and young female rats, *Neuroendocrinology*, 19, 331, 1975.
9. Segall, P. E. and Timiras, P. S., Patho-physiologic findings after chronic tryptophan deficiency in rats: a model for delayed growth and aging, *Mech. Ageing Develop.*, 5, 109, 1976.

Table 4
PLASMA DOPAMINE β-HYDROXYLASE IN HUMANS OF BOTH SEXES

Age group (years)	Number of subjects	DβH ($\mu M/min/l$ serum) mean ± SD	Range
Birth (umbilical cord blood)	43	5.5 ± 1.8[a]	2.2— 11.0
1—9	23	35.5 ± 29.3	0.2—125.
10—19	8	30.7 ± 22.1	9.7—77.8
20—29	73	45.8 ± 36.0	3.0—188.6
30—39	15	41.7 ± 23.6	13.8—105.3
40—49	14	47.4 ± 12.0	33.0—70.4
50—59	13	39.6 ± 21.2	19.3—85.1
>60	6	29.3 ± 10.7[a]	13.2—43.2

[a] Differs from 40 to 49 year group, P <0.01; samples obtained by venipuncture before breakfast.

REFERENCE

1. Fujita, K., Nagatsu, T., Maruta, K., Teradaira, R., Beppu, H., Tsuji, Y., and Kato, T., Fluorescence assay for dopamine β-hydroxylase activity in human serum by high-performance liquid chromatography, *Anal. Biochem.*, 82, 130, 1977.

REPRODUCTION

R. W. Steger, H. Huang, and J. Meites

Table 1
GENERAL CONSIDERATION OF AGING AND REPRODUCTION

	Ref.
The reproductive axis in man and many other mammals shows an age-related decline or cessation of functional activity well before the end of the normal life-span	1—7
The period of age-related reproductive senescence varies considerably from one species to another and even between strains and individuals of the same species	1—7
Much data still have to be collected to gain an understanding of why the reproductive axis ceases to function in the old animal	

REFERENCES

1. *Biology Data Book*, Vol. 1, Altman, P. and Dittmer, D., Eds., Federation of the American Societies for Experimental Biology, Washington, D.C., 1972, 229.
2. **Leathem, J. H.**, The effects of aging on reproduction, in *The Endocrinology of Reproduction*, Velardo, J. T., Ed., Oxford University Press, London, 1958, 315.
3. **Steger, R. W.**, Aging and the hypothalamo-hypophyseal-gonadalaxis, in *Aging and Reproductive Physiology*, Vol. 2, Hafez, E. S. E., Ed., Ann Arbor Science, Ann Arbor, Mich., 1976, 51.
4. **Talbert, G. B.**, Effect of maternal age on reproductive capacity, *Am. J. Gynecl.*, 102, 451, 1968.
5. **Talbert, G. B.**, Aging of the reproductive system, in *Handbook of the Biology of Aging*, Finch, C. E. and Hayflick, L., Eds., Van Nostrand Reinhold, New York, 1977, 318.
6. **Timiras, P. S.**, *Developmental Physiology and Aging*, Macmillan, New York, 1972, 527.
7. **Krohn, P. L.**, Ageing processes in the female reproductive tract, *Lect. Sci. Basis Med.*, 7, 285, 1958.

Table 2
REPRODUCTIVE LIFE-SPAN IN THE FEMALE OF SELECTED SPECIES

Species	Life-span Av	Life-span Max	Reproductive life-span Av	Reproductive life-span Max	Comments	Ref.
Man	70 years	100+ years	41—48 years[a]	52 years[b]	Average age of the menopause has gradually increased during the last 100 years	1—5
					Reports that parity and age of the menarche affect reproductive life-span have not been substantiated	4, 6
Nonhuman Primates						
Rhesus		29 years	20—25 years	29 years	Data questionable due to small numbers of animals and difficulty of establishing chronological age	1, 7, 8, 33
Chimpanzee	17 years	44 years		44 years	Anovulatory cycles may precede the cessation of menstruation by several years	9
Baboon		>31 years		>24 years	Animals over 35 breed, but often abort or have still births	10
					Report on one animal, cycled to 24 years, with irregular bleeding to 31 years; at autopsy ovarian tumors and uterine polyps found	
Domestic						
Horse	25 years	62 years		>33 years	Fertility at peak between 7 and 14 years; decrease becomes marked at >19 years.	1, 8
Cattle	23 years	30 years	13.5[c]	16 years	Usually slaughtered before fertility declines; breed differences may exist	11
				>21 years	Breeding and maintenance conditions could effect results	1
Buffalo	12 years	>20 years	>15 years			12
Sheep		>20 years		>20 years	Performance optimum between 3—7 years, followed by a variable decline, depending on breed	1, 13, 14
Pigs	16 years	27 years				15, 16
Goats	9 years	18 years		18 years		8

Laboratory animals				
Rat	30 months	>3 years	12 months	Second litter the largest with a reversible decline after that point	8, 17—19, 36, 37
			>20 months[e]	Cycles generally become irregular at 8—12 months at which time rats enter a state of constant estrus or a pseudopregnant-like condition	
Mouse	2—2½ years	>3 years		Some rats cycle regularly at 18 months Great variability depending on strain and degree of imbreeding	8, 20, 1
				Hybrid strains often maintain reproductive capacity to a significantly older age than the inbred strains from which they derived	22—25, 35
Hamster	2 years	4 years	18 months	Litter size in older animal is reduced from 6 or more to 1	26, 27, 8
Guinea pig	2 years	>7 years		Fertility very low after 3 years	28, 29, 8
Rabbit	6 years	>13 years	6 years	Does 3 years in age or greater showed 29.7% fewer pregnancies and 25% more embryonic mortality than young controls	8, 30, 34
Wild animals					
Elephant	40 years	70 years	57 years	Reports that the African elephant can produce and rear young into extreme old age	8, 31
Bear		37 years			32

[a] Average age of menopause in U.S. and Western Europe. An ovulatory cycle may precede the menopause (References 1 to 5).
[b] Reports of pregnancies up to the age of 62 have been reported, but not completely documented (References 2 and 3).
[c] Study of 2000 Hariana cattle in India.
[d] Reports of cows producing calves in U.S. or Great Britain.
[e] Regular cycles and pregnancy can be induced after this age using a variety of experimental procedures.

Table 2 (continued)
REPRODUCTIVE LIFE-SPAN IN THE FEMALE OF SELECTED SPECIES

REFERENCES

1. **Talbert, G. B.**, Effect of maternal age on reproductive capacity, *Am. J. Obstet. Gynecol.*, 102, 451, 1968.
2. **Newell, J. W. and Rock, J.**, Upper age limit of parturition: a review of the literature, *Am. J. Obstet. Gynecol.*, 63, 875, 1952.
3. **Wharton, L. R.**, Normal pregnancy with living children in women past the age of fifty, *Am. J. Obstet. Gynecol.*, 90, 672, 1962.
4. **MacMahon, B. and Worcester, J.**, Age at menopause, Vital Health Stat. Publ. 1000, Ser. 11, No. 19, 1966, 1.
5. **Frommer, D. J.**, Changing age of the menopause, *Br. Med. J.*, 2, 349, 1964.
6. **Hauser, V. G. A., Remen, U., Valaer, M., Erb, H., Muller, T., and Obiri, J.**, Menarche and menopause in Israel, *Gynaecologia*, 155, 39, 1963.
7. **VanWagenen, G.**, Induction of ovulation in *Macaca mulatta*, *Fertil. Steril.*, 19, 15, 1967.
8. *Biology Data Book*, Vol. 1, Altman, P. and Dittmer, D., Ed., Federation of the American Societies for Experimental Biology, Washington, D.C., 1972, 233.
9. **Guilloud, N. B.**, Personal communication, cited in Talbert, G. B., Aging of the reproductive system, in *Biology of Aging*, Finch, C. and Hayflick, L., Van Nostrand Reinhold, New York, 1977, 318.
10. **Zuckerman, S.**, Duration of reproductive life in the baboon, *J. Endocrinol.*, 5, 220, 1947.
11. **Hammond, J. and Marshall, F. H. A.**, The life cycle in *Marshall's Physiology of Reproduction*, Vol. 2, Park, A. S., Ed., Longmans, Green and Co., London, 1952, chap. 23.
12. **Ahmed, I. A. and Tantawy, O. A.**, Breeding efficiency of Egyptian cows and buffaloes, *Emp. J. Exp. Agric.*, 27, 17, 1959.
13. **Terrill, C. E. and Stoehr, J. A.**, Reproduction in range sheep, *32nd Proc. Am. Soc. Animal Prod.*, 1939, 369.
14. **Turner, H. N. and Dolling, C. H. S.**, Vital statistics for an experimental flock of merino sheep. II. The influence of age on reproductive performance, *Aust. J. Agric. Res.*, 16, 699, 1965.
15. **Perry, J. S.**, Fecundity and embryonic mortality in pigs, *J. Embryol. Exp. Morphol.*, 2, 308, 1959.
16. **Bal, H. S. and Getty, R.**, Changes in the histomorphology of the uterus of the domestic pig with advancing age, *J. Gerontol.*, 28, 160, 1973.
17. **Aschheim, P.**, Aging in the hypothalamic-hypophyseal-ovarian-axis in the rat, in *Hypothalamus, Pituitary, and Aging*, Everitt, A. V. and Burgess, J. A., Eds., Charles C Thomas, Springfield, Ill., 1976, 376.
18. **Block, S.**, Untersuchungen uber das genitale Alten des Rattenweibokens, *Gerontologia*, 5, 55, 1961.

19. **Ingram, D. L.**, The vaginal smear of senile laboratory rats, *J. Endocrinol.*, 19, 182, 1959.
20. **Thung, P. L., Booth, L. M. and Muhlbook, O.**, Senile changes in the oestrous cycle and in ovarian structures in some inbred strains of mice, *Acta Endocrinol.*, 23, 8, 1956.
21. **Harman, S. M. and Talbert, G. B.**, The effect of maternal age on ovulation, corpora lutea of pregnancy, and implantation failure in mice, *J. Reprod. Fertil.*, 23, 33, 1970.
22. **Eaton, O. N.**, Heterosis in the performance of mice, *Genetics (USSR)*, 38, 609, 1953.
23. **Jones, E. C.**, The ageing ovary and its influence on reproductive capacity, *J. Reprod. Fertil. Suppl.*, 12, 17, 1979.
24. **Finn, C. A.**, Reproductive capacity and litter size in mice effect of age and environment, *J. Reprod. Fertil.*, 6, 205, 1963.
25. **Hollander, W. F. and Strong, L. C.**, Intrauterine mortality and placental fusions in the mouse, *J. Exp. Zool.*, 115, 131, 1950.
26. **Blaha, G. C.**, Reproductive senescence in the female golden hamster, *Anat. Rec.*, 150, 405, 1964.
27. **Soderwall, A. L., Kent, H. A., Turbyfill, C., and Britenbaker, A. L.**, Variation in gestation length and litter size of the golden hamster, *mesocricetus auratus*, *J. Gerontol.*, 15, 246, 1960.
28. **Rogers, J. B. and Taylor, R. C.**, Age changes in the uterus and ovary of the guinea pig, *Anat. Rec.*, 121(Abstr.), 448, 1955.
29. **Rogers, J. B.**, Reproduction, and longevity in the guinea pig, *Anat. Rec.*, 103, 498, 1949.
30. **Maurer, R. R. and Foote, R. H.**, Maternal ageing and embryonic mortality in the rabbit. II. Hormonal changes in young and ageing females, *J. Reprod. Fertil.*, 31, 15, 1972.
31. **Perry, J. S.**, The reproduction of the African elephant (*Loxodonta Africana*), *Philos. Trans. R. Soc. London Ser. B*, 237, 93, 1953.
32. **Popoff, N.**, L'Oraire D'une Ourse (*Ursus Arctos*) Ser. B, De Quartre ANS, *C. R. Assoc. Anat.*, 29, 471, 1934.
33. **Van Wagenen, G.**, Menopause in a subhuman primate, *Anat. Rec.*, 166, 392, 1970.
34. **Adams, C. E.**, Ageing and reproduction in the female mammal with particular reference to the rabbit, *J. Reprod. Fertil. Suppl.*, 12, 1, 1970.
35. **Biggers, J. D., Finn, C. A., and McLaren, A.**, Long-term reproductive performance of female mice. I. Effect of removing one ovary, *J. Reprod. Fertil.*, 3, 303, 1962.
36. **Huang, H. H.**, Relation of Neuroendocrine System to Loss of Reproductive Function in Aging Female Rats, Ph.D. dissertation, Michigan State University, East Lansing, 1977.
37. **Meites, J., Huang, H. H., and Riegle, G. D.**, Relation of the hypothalamo-pituitary-gonadal system to decline of reproductive functions in aging female rats, in *Hypothalamus and Endocrine Functions*, Labrie, F., Meites, J., and Pelletier, G., Eds., Plenum Press, New York, 1976, 3.

Table 3
GENERAL ASPECTS OF AGE-RELATED CHANGES IN THE FEMALE REPRODUCTIVE TRACT

	Ref.
The decline of reproductive function with aging is characterized in the female of various species by a decline in litter size and/or frequency of birth, and increased incidence of fetal abnormalities and prenatal mortality	1—4
Although the alterations in the hypothalamic-hypophyseal-ovarian axis ultimately terminate the estrous cycles, alterations of the reproductive tract may be responsible for reproductive decline prior to these events	5—9
In laboratory animals, litter size decreases with advancing age even though ovulation rate remains constant	10
During the phase of declining litter size, there are increased numbers of regressing implantations	11
Embryonic mortality may be due to combined effects of abnormalities in the aged ova, blastocyst, and/or a hostile uterine environment	
Young ova transferred into old mice have less chance of survival than young ova transferred into young mice; old ova survived as well in young uteri as did young ova	14
In aging women, a variety of clinical complaints including vaginal prolapse, coital or noncoital injury, and senile vaginitis are commonly seen	15
Age-related changes in the connective tissue and histology of the vagina have been described in the rat, mouse, and hamster	16—19

REFERENCES

1. **Krohn, P. L.,** Ageing processes in the female reproductive tract, *Lect. Sci. Basis Med.,* 7, 285, 1958.
2. **Mariona, F. G.,** Is pregnancy a risk in the elderly woman, in *Aging and Reproductive Physiology,* Vol. 2, Hafez, E. S. E., Ed., Ann Arbor Science, Ann Arbor, Mich., 1976, 67.
3. **Talbert, G. B.,** Effect of maternal age on reproductive capacity, *Am. J. Obstet. Gynecol.,* 102, 451, 1968.
4. **Talbert, G. B.,** Aging of the reproductive system, in *Handbook of the Biology of Aging,* Finch, C. E. and Hayflock, L., Eds., Van Nostrand Reinhold, New York, 1977, 318.
5. **Aschheim, P.,** Aging in the hypothalamic-hypophyseal ovarian axis in the rat, in *Hypothalamus, Pituitary, and Aging,* Everitt, A. V. and Brugess, J. A., Eds., Charles C Thomas, Springfield, Ill., 1976, 376.
6. **Meites, J., Huang, H. H., and Riegle, G. D.,** Relation of the hypothalamo-pituitary-gonadal system to decline of reproductive functions in aging female rats, in *Hypothalamus and Endocrine Functions,* Labrie, F., Meites, J., and Pelletier, G., Eds., Plenum Press, New York, 1976, 3.
7. **Meites, J., Huang, H. H., and Simpkins, J. W.,** Recent studies on neuroendocrine control of reproductive senescence in rats, in *The Aging Reproductive System,* Schneider, E. L., Ed., Raven Press, New York, 1978, 213.
8. **Steger, R. W.,** Aging and the hypothalamo-hypophyseal-gonadal-axis, in *Aging and Reproductive Physiology,* Vol. 2, Hafez, E. S. E., Ed., Ann Arbor Science, Ann Arbor, Mich., 1978, 51.
9. **Finn, C. A.,** The Ageing uterus and its influence on reproductive capacity, *J. Reprod. Fertil. Suppl.,* 12, 1970, 31.
10. **Biggers, J. D.,** Problems concerning the uterine causes of embryonic death, with special reference to the effects of ageing of the uterus, *J. Reprod. Fertil. Suppl.,* 8, 27, 1969.
11. **Finn, C. A.,** Embryonic death in aged mice, *Nature (London),* 194, 499, 1962.
12. **Peluso, J. J.,** Aging of mammalian ova, in *Aging and Reproductive Physiology,* Vol. 2, Hafez, E. S. E., Ed., Ann Arbor Science, Ann Arbor, Mich., 1976, 35.
13. **Butcher, R. L.,** Pre-ovulatory and post-ovulatory overripeness, *Int. J. Gynaecol. Obstet.,* 14, 105, 1976.

Table 3 (continued)
GENERAL ASPECTS OF AGE-RELATED CHANGES IN THE FEMALE REPRODUCTIVE TRACT

14. Talbert, G. B. and Krohn, P. L., Effect of maternal age on viability of ova and uterine support of pregnancy in mice, *J. Reprod. Fertil.,* 11, 399, 1966.
15. Steger, R. W. and Hafez, E. S. E., Age associated changes in the human vagina, in *The Human Vagina,* Hafez, E. S. E. and Evans, T. N., Eds., Elsevier/North-Holland, Amsterdam, 1977, 79.
16. Wolfe, J. M., Buracke, E., Lansing, W., and Wright, A. W., The effects of advancing age on the connective tissue of the uterus, cervix, and vagina of the rat, *Am. J. Anat.,* 70, 135, 1942.
17. Barnett, S. A., Munro, K. M. H., and Stoddart, R. C., Growth and pathology of aged house mice, *Exp. Gerontol.,* 9, 275, 1974.
18. Loeb, L., Suntzeff, V., and Burns, E. L., Changes in the nature of the stroma in vagina, cervix and uterus of the mouse produced by long continuous injections of oestrogen and by advancing age, *Am. J. Cancer,* 35, 159, 1939.
19. Rolle, G. K. and Charipper, H. A., The effect of advancing age upon the histology of the ovary, uterus, and the vagina of female golden hamster *(cricetus auratus), Anat. Rec.,* 105, 281, 1949.

Table 4
AGE-RELATED CHANGES IN THE VULVA OF WOMEN

	Ref.
Diminution of subcutaneous fat and elastic tissue	1, 2
Pubic hair becomes sparser and coarser	
Labia majora shrink more than the labia minora	
Bartholin's gland atrophy	
Vulvar dermis atrophies and epithelium narrows	
Decreased epithelial cell size without a concurrent thickening of the keratin layer	
Kraurosis vulvae associated with hyperkeratosis acanthosis and subepithelial edema or tissue collagenication often seen	3, 4
Skin appears reddened, edematous, and dry	4
Vulvar folds flattened in some places and thickened in others	
Infiltration of lymphocytes and plasma cells in the subepithelial layer	

REFERENCES

1. Schiff, I. and Wilson, E., Clinical aspects of aging of the female reproductive system, in *The Aging Reproductive System,* Schneider, E. L., Ed., Raven Press, New York, 1978, 9.
2. Gardner, H. L. and Kaufman, R. H., Eds., Atrophic vulvovaginitis, in *Benign Diseases of the Vulva and Vagina,* C. V. Mosby, St. Louis, 1969, 216.
3. Lang, W. R. and Aponte, G. E., Gross and microscopic anatomy of the aged female reproductive Organs, *Clin. Obstet. Gynecol.,* 10, 454, 1967.
4. Kuppe, G., Metzger, H., and Ludwig, H., Aging and structural changes in the female reproductive tract, in *Aging and Reproductive Physiology,* Vol. 2, Hafez, E. S. E., Ed., Ann Arbor Science, Ann Arbor, Mich., 1976, 21.

Table 5
STRUCTURAL CHANGES OF THE HUMAN VAGINA WITH ADVANCING AGE

	Ref.
Decrease in depth and caliper	1, 2
Decrease elasticity and expansive ability	1, 2
Regression of rugae	1, 3
Changes in color due to loss of vascularity and/or chronic inflammation	1, 3
Increase in chronic inflammation	1
Increase or decrease in vaginal discharges	3
Vaginal prolapse	3

REFERENCES

1. Lang, W. R. and Aponte, G. E., Gross and microscopic anatomy of the aged female reproductive organs, *Clin. Obstet. Gynecol.,* 10, 454, 1967.
2. Masters, W. H. and Johnson, V. E., *Human Sexual Response,* Little, Brown Boston, 1966, 233.
3. Schiff, I. and Wilson, E., Clinical aspects of aging of the female reproductive system, in *The Aging Reproductive System,* Schneider, E. L., Ed., Raven Press, New York, 1978, 9.

Table 6
CELLULAR CHANGES IN THE HUMAN VAGINA DURING THE REPRODUCTIVE CYCLE AND MENOPAUSE

Phase	Exfoliative cytology	Histology	Histochemistry	Surface ultrastructure
Proliferative	Progressive increase in superficial cell Rise in karyopyknotic index Decrease in leukocytes and bacteria	Well-defined epithelial layer consisting of 4 distinct cell layers (basal, parabasal, intermediate, and superficial)	Glycogen accumulates to a maximum just prior to ovulation	Numerous exfoliating cells especially just prior to menstruation Well-defined microridges and cell borders
Secretory	Dominated by intermediate cells often found in clusters Individual cells folded or have curled edges Low karyopyknotic index	Similar to proliferative phase with possible reduction in superficial cell layer	Glycogen decreases without depletion in intermediate layer	Decreased numbers of exfoliating cells Microridges still well developed
Menopausal	Variable from highly proliferative to atrophic, with mixed patterns of superficial and parabasal cells	Epithelial thickness variable, but generally thinner	Glycogen in variable generally low increased collagen deposition in lamina propria	Decreased number of microridges on some cells Microridges oriented in one direction only
Postmenopausal	Variable, occasionally completely atrophic with a predominance of parabasal cells Abundant intermediate cells with occasional superficial and parabasal cells Low karyopyknotic index	Epithelium becomes markedly thinner, often invaded with leukocytes Areas completely denuded of an epithelial covering are often present	Glycogen is very low or completely absent, restored by estrogen administration Collagen replaces many of elastic fibers in lamina propria Lipofucsin granules in muscle cells	Decrease in numbers of exfoliating cells Surface microridges absent or markedly reduced Cell borders less distinct and nuclear bulges occasionally visible

From Steger, R. W. and Hafez, E. S. E., in *The Human Vagina*, Hafez, E. S. E. and Evans, T. N., Eds., Elsevier/North-Holland, Amsterdam, 1977, 82. With permission.

Table 7
AGE-RELATED CHANGES IN THE CERVIX OF WOMEN

	Ref.
Decrease in size is usually not evident until some years after the menopause	1
The cervix shrinks less than the fundus resulting in a cervix/fundus ratio similar to that seen in adolescence	2
The cervical canal is reduced in size	2
Progressive atrophy of cervical crypts and stenosis of the ducts may lead to formation of retention cysts	2
Decreased height of the endocervical columnar epithlium	3
Thinning of the ectocervical squamous epithelium	4
Decreased glycogen in the squamous epithelium	4
Decreased amount of cervical mucus; the mucus still present becomes thickened and cellular in nature	1
Replacement of columnar epithelium with squamous epithelium	5, 6
Junctional zone between columnar and squamous epithelium moves into the endocervical canal after the menopause	3, 6
Hyalinization of the stroma with age	3

REFERENCES

1. **Rakoff, A. E. and Nowrooz, K.,** The female climacteric, in *Geriatric Endocrinology,* Greenblatt, R. B., Ed., Raven Press, New York, 1978, 165.
2. **Hammond, C. B.,** Menopause, a American view, in *The Management of the Menopause and Postmenopausal Years,* Campbell, S., Ed, University Park Press, Baltimore, 1976, 405.
3. **Kuppe, G., Metzger, H., and Ludwig, H.,** Aging and structural changes in the female reproductive tract, in *Aging and Reproductive Physiology,* Vol. 2, Hafez, E. S. E., Ed., Ann Arbor Science, Ann Arbor, Mich., 1976, 21.
4. **Crompton, A. E.,** Cervical colposcopic changes associated with the menopause, in *The Management of the Menopause and Postmenopausal Years,* Campbell, S., Ed., University Park Press, Baltimore, 1976, 271.
5. **Lang, W. R. and Aponte, G. E.,** Gross and microscopic anatomy of the aged female reproductive organs, *Clin. Obstet. Gynecol.,* 10, 454, 1967.
6. **Fluhman, C. F.,** *The Cervix Uteri and Its Diseases,* W. B. Saunders, Philadelphia, 1961, 79.

Table 8
GROSS UTERINE CHANGES WITH AGE

	Ref.
Human	
Uterine atrophy including 50% weight loss after the menopause if hypertrophy and hyperplasia not present	1—4
Shrinkage of fibroids	
Reduced vascularity	5
Cervical atrophy, the internal OS closing prior to the external OS	
Inward migration of the squamocolumnar junction	6
Scanty cervical mucus	
Ectocervix flattened and no longer protrudes into the vaginal vault	7
Rat	
Uterine atrophy in old anestrous, but not constant estrous or repeat pseudopregnant rats	8, 9
Rabbit	
Dry-weight fraction of the uterus does not change between 34—204 weeks	10
Decreased uterine blood flow	11
Increasing frequency of spontaneous uterine tumors	12
Guinea pig	
Cervix and uterus enlarge and become less pliable	13
Decreased cervical mucus	

REFERENCES

1. **Woessner, J. F.**, Aging of human uterus connective tissue, *J. Gerontol.*, 17 (Abstr.), 453, 1962.
2. **Woessner, J. F.**, Age-related changes of the human uterus and its connective tissue framework, *J. Gerontol.*, 18, 220, 1963.
3. **Lang, W. R.**, Cervical portio from menarche on: a colposcopic study, *Ann. N.Y. Acad. Sci.*, 97, 653, 1962.
4. **Lang, W. R. and Aponte, G. E.** Gross and microscopic anatomy of the aged female reproductive organs, *Clin. Obstet. Gynecol.*, 10, 454, 1967.
5. **Speert, H.**, The endometrium in old age, *Surg. Gynecol. Obstet.*, 89, 551, 1949.
6. **Fluhman, C. F.**, *The Cervic Uteri and Its Diseases*, W. B. Saunders, Philadelphia, 1961, 126.
7. **Kuppe, G., Metzger, H., and Ludwig, H.**, Aging and structural changes in the female reproductive tract, in *Aging and Reproductive Physiology*, Vol. 2, Hafez, E. S. E., Ed., Ann Arbor Science, Ann Arbor, Mich., 1976, 21.
8. **Huang, H. H.**, Relation of neuroendocrine system to loss of reproductive function in aging female rats, Ph.D. dissertation, Michigan State University, East Lansing, 1977.
9. **Huang, H. H. and Meites, J.**, Reproductive capacity of aging female rats, *Neuroendocrinology*, 17, 289, 1975.
10. **Maurer, R. R. and Foote, R. H.**, Uterine collagenase and collagen in young and aging rabbits, *J. Reprod. Fertil.*, 30, 301, 1972.
11. **Larson, L. L. and Foote, R. H.**, Uterine blood flow in young and aged rabbits, *Proc. Soc. Exp. Biol. Med.*, 141, 67, 1972.
12. **Greene, H. S. N.**, Uterine adenomata in the rabbit, *J. Exp. Med.*, 73, 273, 1941.
13. **Rogers, J. B. and Taylor, R. C.**, Age changes in the uterus and ovary of the guinea pig, *Anat. Rec.*, 121, 448, 1955.

Table 9
HISTOLOGY OF THE AGED UTERUS

	Ref.
Human	
Cervix	
Sclerosis of the cervical stroma	1—3
Flattening of the columnar epithelium of the endocervix	1—3
Hyalinization of the stroma	1—3
Endometrium	
Variation in endometrial picture	2—6
Most commonly a thin and atrophic mucosa	3
Mucosa of varying thickness with "Swiss cheese-type" hyperplasic without proliferation	5, 6
Active hyperplasia, either diffuse or in scattered patches, sometimes polypoid	
Cystic atrophy characterized by a low functionalis not clearly demonstrated from basalis; narrow endometrial glands and cuboidal as opposed to columnar epithelial cells; moderate cystic dilation of some glands	
Glandular cystic hyperplasia characterized by epithelial and stromal cell enlargement; great variation in gland size	
Decrease in cilia microvilli, and glandular activity	7
Myometrium	
Fibrous replacement of smooth muscle cells	2
Severe muscular hypertrophy of myometrial vessels with thickening of the subendothelial layers and occasional calcification of the media	3
Rat	
Endometrium	
Decrease microvilli and secretory material	7
Myometrium	
Accumulation of "lipoidal-hemosiderin" deposits	8
Mouse	
Endometrium	
Reduction in density of microvilli	9
Increase in hyalinized material in stroma, especially marked around glands and arteries near myometrium	10
Increased incidence of spontaneous lesions	11
Myometrium	
Tends to thicken with age	10
Pigment (lipofuscin) accumulation in all levels (more prevalent in horns subject to pregnancy)	12
Pig	
Myometrium and endometrium	
Lipofuscin accumulation in the myometrium and in the walls of the large endometrial veins	13
Guinea pig	
Increased muscle mass	14
Increased thickness of blood vessels	
Glands decrease in size or become cystic	

REFERENCES

1. **Fluhman, C. F.**, *The Cervix Uteri and Its Diseases*, W. B. Saunders, Philadelphia, 1961, 79.
2. **Kuppe, G., Metzger, H., and Ludwig, H.**, Aging and structural changes in the female reproductive tract, in *Aging and Reproductive Physiology*, Vol. 2, Hafez, E. S. E., Ed., Ann Arbor Science, Ann Arbor, Mich., 1976, 21.
3. **Lang, W. R. and Aponte, G. E.**, Gross and microscopic anatomy of the aged female reproductive organs, *Clin. Obstet. Gynecol.*, 10, 454, 1967.

Table 9 (continued)
HISTOLOGY OF THE AGED UTERUS

4. McBride, J. M., The normal postmenopausal endometrium, *J. Obstet. Gynaecol. Br. Commonw.*, 61, 691, 1954.
5. Bigelow, B., Comparison of ovarian and endometrial morphology spanning the menopause, *J. Obstet. and Gynecol. Br. Commonw.*, 11, 487, 1958.
6. Speert, H., The endometrium in old age, *Surg. Gynecol. Obstet.*, 89, 551, 1949.
7. Steger, R. W., Huang, H. H., Kuppe, G., Meites, J., Hafez, E. S. E., and Ludwig, H., Effect of age on uterine surface ultrastructure, in *Scanning Electron Microscopy*, Illinois Institute of Technology Research Institute, Chicago, 1976, 359.
8. Warbrick, J. G., A pigment in the rat's uterus, *Q. J. Microsc. Sci.*, 97, 11, 1956.
9. Jones, E. C., The endometrium and effects of aging (mouse), in *Scanning Electron Microscopic Atlas of Mammalian Reproduction*, Hafez, E. S. E., Ed., Igaku Shoin, Tokyo, 1975, 190.
10. Loeb, L., Suntzeff, V., and Burns, E. L., Changes in the nature of the stroma in vagina, cervix and uterus of the mouse produced by long continuous injections of oestrogen and by advancing age, *Am. J. Cancer*, 35, 159, 1939.
11. Malinin, G. E. and Malinin, I. M., Age-related spontaneous uterine lesions in mice, *J. Gerontol.*, 27, 193, 1972.
12. Biggers, J. D., Problems concerning the uterine causes of embryonic death, with special reference to the effects of ageing of the uterus, *J. Reprod. Fertil. Suppl.*, 8, 27, 1969.
13. Bal, H. S. and Getty, R., Changes in the histomorphology of the uterus of the domestic pig with advancing age, *J. Gerontol.*, 28, 160, 1973.
14. Rogers, J. B. and Taylor, R. C., Age changes in the uterus and ovary of the guinea pig, *Anat. Rec.*, 121, 448, 1955.

Table 10
UTERINE COLLAGEN AND ELASTIN WITH AGE

	Ref.
Human	
Increase from age 15—30, constant from age 30—49, 60% loss during menopause involution	1, 2
Decreased thermal shrinkage temperature and increased fluorescent properties of collagen	1, 2
43% loss in elastin with remaining elastin showing an increased hydroxyproline content	1, 2
Increased resistance to collagenase digestion with age	1, 2
Rat	
Progressive deposition of total collagen with age	3—6
Decline in thermolabile collagen	6
Increase in resistance to collagenase	6
Lowered capacity of aged uterus to synthesize collagen	7
Mouse	
Progressive deposition of collagen with age	8—10
Increase in both total collagen content and collagen concentration but no difference between horns which had contained fetuses and others which, as a result of unilateral ovariectomy had not	11
Rabbit	
Decrease in collagen with age (34 vs. 204 weeks)	12
Decrease in uterine collagenase with age	
Uterine acid-soluble collagen higher in old pregnant does (38 vs. 174 weeks)	
Hamster	
Progressive deposition of collagen with age	13

REFERENCES

1. **Woessner, J. F.**, Aging of human uterus connective tissue, *J. Gerontol.,* 17 (Abstr.), 453, 1962.
2. **Woessner, J. F.**, Age-related changes of the human uterus and its connective tissue framework, *J. Gerontol.,* 18, 221, 1963.
3. **Burack, E., Wolfe, J. M., Lansing, W., and Wright, A. W.**, The effect of age upon the connective tissue of the uterus, cervix, and vagina of the rat, *Cancer Res.,* 1, 227, 1941.
4. **Kao, K. and McGarack, T. H.**, Connective tissue. I. Age and sex influence on protein composition of rat tissues, *Proc. Soc. Exp. Biol. Med.,* 101, 153, 1959.
5. **Schaub, M. C.**, Changes in the collagen in the aging and in the pregnant uterus of white rats, *Gerontologia,* 10, 137, 1964.
6. **Wolfe, J. M., Buracke, E., Lansing, W., and Wright, A. W.**, The effects of advancing age on the connective tissue of the uterus, cervix and vagina of the rat, *Am. J. Anat.,* 70, 135, 1942.
7. **Kao, K. T., Lu, S. C., Hitt, W., and McGarack, T. H.**, Connective tissue. VI. Synthesis of collagen by rat uterine slices, *Proc. Soc. Ex. Biol. Med.,* 109, 4, 1962.
8. **Finn, C. A.**, The ageing uterus and its influence on reproductive capacity, *J. Reprod. Fertil. Suppl.,* 12, 31, 1970.
9. **Finn, C. A., Fitch, S. M., and Harkness, R. D.**, Collagen content of barren and previously pregnant uterine horns in old mice, *J. Reprod. Fertil.,* 6, 405, 1963.
10. **Finn, C. A. and Porter, D. G.**, Uterine function in aged animals, in *Uterus* Finn, C. A. and Porter, D. G., Eds., Publishing Sciences Group, Acton, Mass., 1975, 100.
11. **Loeb, L., Suntzeff, V., and Burns, E. L.**, Changes in the nature of the stroma in vagina, cervix and uterus of the mouse produced by long continuous injections of oestrogen and by advancing age, *Am. J. Cancer,* 35, 159, 1939.
12. **Maurer, R. R. and Foote, R. H.**, Uterine collagenase and collagen in young and ageing rabbits, *J. Reprod. Fertil.,* 30, 301, 1972.
13. **Rahima, A. and Sodewall, A. L.**, Uterine collagen content in young and senescent pregnant golden hamsters, *J. Reprod. Fertil.,* 49, 161, 1974.

Table 11
PHYSIOLOGICAL RESPONSE OF THE AGING UTERUS

	Ref.
Mouse	
Stromal and endometrial cells retain the capacity to proliferate in response to estrogen and progesterone	1, 2
Failure of lumen closure in response to estrogen and progesterone; also, irregular lumen orientation	1, 2
Decrease in decidualization reaction	1—7
Increased fetal resorbtions	2, 8—12
Hamster	
Decreased implantation rate with age	13, 14
Decreased decidual reaction	14, 15
Increased fetal resorbtions	16
Failure of luminal closure	17, 18
12-hr delay in time of implantation	18

REFERENCES

1. **Finn, C. A. and Martin, L.**, The cellular response of the uterus of the aged mouse to oestrogen and progesterone, *J. Reprod. Fertil.*, 20, 545, 1969.
2. **Finn, C. A. and Porter, D. G.**, Uterine function in aged animals, in *Uterus* Finn, C. A. and Porter, D. G., Eds., Publishing Sciences Group, Acton, Mass., 1975, 100.
3. **Finn, C. A.**, The initiation of the decidual cell reaction in the uterus of the aged mouse, *J. Reprod. Fertil.*, 11, 423, 1066.
4. **Finn, C. A.**, The ageing uterus and its influence on reproductive capacity, *J. Reprod. Fertil. Suppl.*, 12, 31, 1971.
5. **Holinka, C. F. and Finch, C. E.**, Age related changes in the decidual responses of the C57BL/6J mouse uterus, *Biol. Reprod.*, 16, 385, 1977.
6. **Holinka, C. F., Hetland, M. D., and Finch, C. E.**, The response to a single dose of estradiol in the uterus of ovariectomized C57BL/6J mice during aging, *Biol. Reprod.*, 17, 262, 1977.
7. **Shapiro, M. and Talbert, G. B.**, The effect of maternal age on decidualization in the mouse, *J. Gerontol.*, 29, 145, 1974.
8. **Biggers, J. D.**, Problems concerning the uterine causes of embryonic death, with special reference to the efforts of ageing of the uterus, *J. Reprod. Fertil. Suppl.*, 8, 27, 1969.
9. **Finn, C. A.**, Embryonic death in aged mice, *Nature (London)*, 194, 499, 1962.
10. **Finn, C. A.**, Reproductive capacity and litter size in mice effect of age and environment, *J. Reprod. Fertil.*, 6, 205, 1963.
11. **Hollander, W. F. and Strong, L. C.**, Intrauterine mortality and placental fusions in the mouse, *J. Exp. Zool.*, 115, 131, 1950.
12. **Talbert, G. B.**, Effect of maternal age on postimplantation reproduction failure in mice, *J. Reprod. Fertil.*, 24, 449, 1971.
13. **Connors, T. J., Thorpe, L. W., and Soderwall, A. L.**, An analysis of preimplantation embryonic death in senescent golden hamsters, *Biol. Reprod.*, 6, 131, 1972.
14. **Blaha, G. C.**, Reproductive senescence in the female golden hamster, *Anat. Rec.*, 150, 405, 1964.
15. **Blaha, G. C.**, Effects of age, treatment and method of induction on deciduomata in the golden hamster, *Fertil. Steril.*, 18, 477, 1967.
16. **Thorneycroft, I. H. and Soderwall, A. L.**, The nature of the litter size loss in senescent hamsters, *Anat. Rec.*, 165, 343, 1969.
17. **Thorpe, L. W., Conners, T. J., and Soderwall, A. L.**, Closure of the uterine lumen at implantation in senscent golden hamsters, *J. Reprod. Fertil.*, 39, 29, 1974.
18. **Parkening, T. A. and Soderwall, A. J.**, Delayed embryonic development and implantation in senescent golden hamsters, *Biol. Reprod.*, 8, 427, 1973.

Table 12
BIOCHEMICAL RESPONSES OF THE AGING UTERUS

	Ref.
Mice	
Decreased concentration of RNA in 15 month-old as compared to 4-, 7- and 11-month-old mice	1, 2
RNA synthesis remains responsive to estrogen stimulation but the response is less with age	1, 2
Protein concentration unchanged on a wet weight basis, but decreased by 15 months when expressed on a dry weight basis	1, 2
Small, but nonsignificant decrease in estrogen uptake	3
Significantly less protein and alkaline phosphatase activity in old vs. young ovariectomized steroid primed C57BL/6J mice	4
Significantly less uterine DNA, glycogen, protein, and alkaline phosphatase activity in the old decidualized uterus	4
Rats	
Age related decrease (1 month, prepubertal vs. 24-month-old rats) in uterine phosphofructokinase and phosphohexose isomerase activity after estrogen stimulation	5
Decrease estradiol uptake in old constant-estrus or anestrus, but not old pseudopregnant rats	6
Rabbit	
Decreased uterine progesterone and estradiol uptake with age	7
Hamster	
Depletion of glycogen occurs in old uteri at a time when the embryo is still dependent on uterine glycogen	8

REFERENCES

1. Soriero, A. A., The aging uterus and fallopian tubes, in *The Aging Reproductive System*, Schneider, E. L., Ed., Raven Press, New York, 1978, 85.
2. Soriero, A. A. and Talbert, G. B., The effect of estrogen on protein and RNA concentration and on *de novo* synthesis of RNA in the uterus of aging ovariectomized mice, *J. Gerontol.*, 30, 264, 1976.
3. Gosden, R. G., Uptake and metabolism *in vivo* of tritiated oestradiol-17B in tissue of aging female mice, *J. Endocrinol.*, 68, 153, 1976.
4. Holinka, C. F., Hetland, M. D., and Finch, C. E., The response to a single dose of estradiol in the uterus of ovariectomized C57BL/6J mice during aging, *Biol. Reprod.*, 17, 262, 1977.
5. Singhal, R. L. and Valadares, J. R. E., Influence of age on uterine enzyme induction, *Fed. Proc. Fed. Am. Soc. Exp. Biol.*, 26, 854, 1967.
6. Peng, M. T. and Peng, Y. M., Changes in the uptake of tritiated estradiol in the hypothalamus and adenohypophysis of old female rats, *Fertil. Steril.*, 24, 539, 1973.
7. Lauritzen, C., The hypothalamic anterior pituitary system in the climacteric age period, *Front. Horm. Res.*, 3, 20, 1975.
8. Parkening, T. A. and Soderwall, A. L., Histochemical localization of glycogen in preimplantation and implantation stages of young and senescent golden hamsters, *J. Reprod. Fertil.*, 41, 285, 1974.

Table 13
AGE-RELATED CHANGES IN THE OVIDUCT

	Ref.
Man	
Few histological changes except for the loss of cyclic changes for up to 15 years after the menopause	1
Continued presence of ciliated cells debatable	
Cilia rarely found in postmenopausal women, although microvilli are still present	2, 3
Ciliated cells still present in the infundibula and ampulla at 20 to 30 years postmenopause	4
Marked decline in secretory activity	5, 6
Decreased smooth muscle and an increased collagen content	7
Folds of the tubal mucosa are flattened or absent	7
Mice	
Primary block in ova transport at the ampullary-isthmic junction	8
Hamster	
Retention of oocytes and blastocysts in the oviduct	8
Rats	
No retention (tubal locking) of oocytes in old rats	8

REFERENCES

1. **Soriero, A. A.,** The aging uterus and fallopian tubes, in *The Aging Reproductive System,* Schneider, E. L., Ed., Raven Press, New York, 1978, 85.
2. **Ferenczy, A., Richard, R. M., Agale, F. J., Durkenson, M., and Dempsey, F. W.,** Scanning electron microscopy of the human fallopian tube, *Science,* 175, 783, 1972.
3. **Gaddum-Rosse, P., Rumery, R. E., Blandau, R. J., and Thiersch, J. B.,** Studies on the mucosa of postmenopausal oviducts: surface appearance, ciliary activity and the effect of estrogen treatment, *Fertil. Steril.,* 26, 951, 1975.
4. **Patek, E., Nilsson, L., and Johannisson, E.,** Scanning electron microscopic study of the human fallopian tube, *Fertil. Steril.,* 23, 719, 1972.
5. **Shimoyama, T.,** Electron microscopic studies of the mucous membrane of the human fallopian tube in the embryonal, pregnancy and senile period, *J. Jpn. Obstet. Gynecol. Soc.,* 12, 132, 1965.
6. **Novak, E. and Everett, H. S.,** Cyclic and other variations in the tubal epithelium, *Am. J. Obstet. Gynecol.,* 16, 499, 1928.
7. **Kuppe, G., Metzger, H., and Ludwig, H.,** Aging and structural changes in the female reproductive tract, *Aging and Reproductive Physiology,* Vol. 2, Hafez, E. S. E., Ed., Ann Arbor Science, Ann Arbor, Mich., 1976, 21.
8. **Parkening, T. A.,** Retention of ova in oviducts of senescent mice and hamsters, *J. Exp. Zool.,* 196, 307, 1976.

Table 14
THE EFFECT OF ADVANCING AGE ON IMPLANTATION RATE AND TIMING

	Ref.
Mice	
Implantation failure in old mice possibly due to the failure of lumen closure and other uterine factors	1—4
Progressive decrease in implantation rate despite a constant ovulation rate	5, 6
Uterine factors appear responsible for loss of litters	7
Hamsters	
Few 15-month-old hamsters show implantations despite continuation of regular 4-day cycles and ovulation rate	8, 9
Implantation failure the major cause of embryonic mortality in old animals	10, 11
Implantation delayed in aging animals	12

REFERENCES

1. **Finn, C. A.**, Embryonic death in aged mice, *Nature (London)*, 194, 499, 1962.
2. **Finn, C. A.**, Reproductive capacity and litter size in mice, effect of age and environment, *J. Reprod. Fertil.*, 6, 205, 1963.
3. **Finn, C. A.**, The ageing uterus and its influence on reproductive capacity, *J. Reprod. Fertil. Suppl.*, 12, 31, 1970.
4. **Finn, C. A. and Martin, L.**, The cellular response of the uterus of the aged mouse to oestrogen and progesterone, *J. Reprod. Fertil.*, 20, 545, 1969.
5. **Harman, S. M. and Talbert, G. B.**, The effect of maternal age on ovulation, corpora lutea of pregnancy, and implantation failure in mice, *J. Reprod. Fertil.*, 23, 33, 1970.
6. **Talbert, G. B.**, Effect of maternal age on postimplantation reproduction failure in mice, *J. Reprod. Fertil.*, 24, 449, 1971.
7. **Albrecht, E. D., Koos, R. D., and Wehrenbert, W. B.**, Ovarian Δ^5-3β-hydroxysteroid dehydrogenase and cholesterol in the aged mouse during pregnancy, *Biol. Reprod.*, 13, 158, 1975.
8. **Blaha, G. C.**, Reproductive senescence in the female golden hamster, *Anat. Rec.*, 150, 405, 1964.
9. **Soderwall, A. L., Kent, H. A., Turbyfill, C., and Britenbaker, A. L.**, Variation in gestation length and litter size of the golden hamster, *mesocricetus auratus*, *J. Gerontol.*, 15, 246, 1960.
10. **Connors, T. J., Thorpe, L. W., and Soderwall, A. L.**, An analysis of primplantation embryonic death in senescent golden hamsters, *Biol. Reprod.*, 6, 131, 1972.
11. **Thorneycroft, I. H. and Soderwall, A. L.**, The nature of the litter size loss in senescent hamsters, *Anat. Rec.* 165, 343, 1969.
12. **Parkening, T. A. and Soderwall, A. J.**, Delayed embryonic development and implantation in senescent golden hamsters, *Biol. Reprod.*, 8, 427, 1973.

Table 15
THE EFFECTS OF ADVANCING AGE ON
PRENATAL COMPLICATIONS, INTRAPARTUM
PERFORMANCE, AND MATERNAL MORTALITY

	Ref.
Human	
Steady increase in the incidence of hypertension in gravidas over 45	1
The incidence of toxemia is decreased in the elderly multigravida	1—3
Thromboembolic disease increases with age	4, 5
High incidence of premature delivery in very young and very old gravidas	6
Cesarean section rate increases in elderly gravidas	7, 8
Maternal mortality high in older gravidas	1, 5
Gametes	
The effects of advancing age on gametes have been extensively reviewed in a recent book edited by R. J. Blandau, and will not be covered in this review	9

REFERENCES

1. **Mariona, F. G.,** Is pregnancy a risk in the elderly woman, in *Aging and Reproductive Physiology,* Vol. 2, Hafez, E. S. E., Ed., Ann Arbor Science, Ann Arbor, Mich., 1976, 67.
2. **Young, H. J.,** Age and parturition in primigravidae, *J. Obstet. Gynaecol. Br. Commonw.,* 70, 636, 1963.
3. **Koren, Z., Zudkerman, H., and Brzezinski, A.,** Pregnancy and delivery after forty, *Obstet. Gynaecol.,* 21, 165, 1963.
4. **Alment, E. A. J.,** The early primigravida, *Practitioner,* 204, 371, 1971.
5. **Arthure, H. G.,** Maternal deaths from pulmonary embolism, *J. Obstet. Gynaecol. Br. Commonw.,* 75, 1309, 1968.
6. **Booth, R. T. and Williams, G. L.,** Elderly primigravidae, *J. Obstet. Gynaecol. Br. Commonw.,* 71, 249, 1964.
7. **Crawford, J. S.,** Maternal age as an isolated factor in the incidence of perinata aphyxia, *Am. J. Obstet. Gynecol.,* 95, 569, 1966.
8. **Israel, S. L. and Deutschberger, M. A.,** Relation of the mother's age to obstetric performance, *Obstet. Gynaecol.,* 24, 411, 1964.
9. *Aging Gametes — Their Biology and Pathology: Proceedings,* Blandeau, R. J., Ed., S. Karger, Basel, 1975, 415.

Table 16
EFFECTS OF OLD AGE ON FETAL MORTALITY
AND THE INCIDENCE OF VARIOUS BIRTH
DEFECTS IN HUMANS

	Ref.
Perinatal mortality increases steadily with increasing maternal age	1, 2
A 42.8% fetal loss through abortion, still-birth, or neonatal death at maternal age 44 and over, as opposed to a total loss of 11.5% in younger gravidas	3
Birth weights tend to increase with maternal age to approximately 35 years, and then the trend reverses	2, 4
Maternal age-related disorders	
Increased incidence of	
Down's syndrome	2, 5—7
spina bifida	2
hypospadias	2
syndactyly	2
esophageal atresia	2
Edward's syndrome	8
Patau syndrome	8
Klinefelter Triple-x-syndrome	9
Chromosome defects especially trisomies are found in progeny of older mothers in disproportionate numbers	
Some evidence links higher rates of fetal death to older fathers	10, 11
Paternal age-related disorders	
Achondroplasia	12
Apert's syndrome	13, 14
Marfan's syndrome	15, 16
Fibrodysplasia ossificans progressiva	17

REFERENCES

1. **Law, R. G.,** The elderly primipara, in *Standards of Obstetric Care,* Law, R. G., Ed., E. and S. Livingston, London, 1967, 206.
2. **Mariona, F. G.,** Is pregnancy a risk in the elderly woman, in *Aging and Reproductive Physiology,* Hafez, E. S. E., Ed., Ann Arbor Science, Ann Arbor, Mich., 1976, 67.
3. **Wharton, R.,** Normal pregnancy with children in women past the age of fifty, *Am. J. Obstet. Gynecol.,* 90, 672, 1964.
4. **Israel, S. L. and Deutschberger, M. A.,** Relation of the mother's age to obstetric performance, *Obstet. Gynecol.,* 24, 411, 1964.
5. **Collman, R. D. and Stoller, A.,** A survey of mongoloid births in Victoria, Australia, 1942—1957, *Am. J. Public Health,* 52, 613, 1962.
6. **Koen, A. L.,** Maternal aging and chromosomal defects, in *Aging and Reproductive Physiology,* Vol. 2, Hafez, E. S. E., Ed., Ann Arbor Science, Ann Arbor, Mich., 1976, 75.
7. **Kram, D. and Schneider, E. L.,** An effect of reproductive aging: increased risk of genetically abnormal offspring, in *The Aging Reproductive System,* Schneider, E. L., Ed., Raven Press, New York, 1978, 237.
8. **Magenis, R. E., Hecht, F., and Milham, S.,** Trisomy 13(Dl) syndrome: studies on parental age, sex ratio, and survival, *J. Pediatr.,* 73, 222, 1968.
9. **Zuppinger, E., Engel, E., Forbes, A. P., Mantooth, L., and Claffey, J.,** Klinefelter's syndrome: a clinical and cytogenetic study in 24 cases, *Acta Endocrinol. Suppl.,* 113, 5, 1967.
10. **Sonneborn, T. M.,** The human early foetal death rate in relation to age of father, in *The Biology of Aging,* Strehler, B. L., Ed., American Institute of Biological Sciences, Washington, D.C., 1960, 288.
11. **Barrai, I., Cann, H. M., Cavalli-Sforza, L. L., and Nicola, P.,** The effect of parental age on rates of mutation for hemophilia and evidence for differing mutation rates for hemophilia A and B, *Am. J. Hum. Genet.,* 20, 175, 1968.

Table 16 (continued)
EFFECTS OF OLD AGE ON FETAL MORTALITY AND THE INCIDENCE OF VARIOUS BIRTH DEFECTS IN HUMANS

12. **Penrose, L. S.**, Parental age and mutation, *Lancet*, 2, 312, 1955.
13. **Blank, C. E.**, Apert's syndrome (a type of acrocephalosyndactyly) observation on a Britian Series of 39 cases, *Ann. Hum. Genet.*, 24, 151, 1960.
14. **Erickson, D. and Cohen, M. M.**, A study of parental effects on the occurance of fresh mutations for the Apert Syndrome, *Ann. Hum. Genet.*, 38, 89, 1974.
15. **Murdoch, J. L., Walker, B. A., and McKusick, V. A.**, Parental age effects on the occurrence of new mutations of the Marfan Syndrome, *Ann. Hum. Genet.*, 35, 331, 1971.
16. **Smith, C. A. B.**, Note on the estimation of parental age effects, *Ann. Hum. Genet.*, 35, 337, 1971.
17. **Tunte, W.**, Human mutations and paternal age, *Humangenetik*, 4, 320, 1967.

Table 17
EFFECTS OF AGE ON MAMMARY GLANDS

	Ref.
Human	
Decrease in size; become more flacid	1, 2
Shrinkage of glandular epithelium and a corresponding increase in subcutaneous fat	
Alveoli gradually disappear	
Ducts diminish in size and their epithelium becomes flattened	
Nipples decrease in size and lose their erectile character	
10% of women show an unexplained enlargement of the breast during and after the menopause	
Increased incidence of neoplasia	
Rat	
Increased incidence of mammary tumors	3
Cattle	
Decreased milk production and change in milk composition	4

REFERENCES

1. **Rakoff, A. E. and Nowroozi, K.**, The female climacteric, in *Geriatric Endocrinology*, Greenblatt, R. B., Ed., Raven Press, New York, 1978, 165.
2. **Masters, W. H. and Johnson, V. E.**, Eds., *Human Sexual Response*, Little, Brown, Boston, 1966, 233.
3. **Huang, H. H.**, Relation of Neuroendocrine System to Loss of Reproductive Function in Aging Female Rats, Ph.D. dissertation, Michigan State University, East Lansing, 1977.
4. **Smith, V. R.**, Ed., *Physiology of Lactation*, 5th ed., Iowa State University Press, Ames, 1959, 182.

Table 18
AGE-RELATED ALTERATION OF OVARIAN MORPHOLOGY

	Ref.
Women	
The ovary becomes progressively small and more fibrotic	1—3
The surface becomes grayish-yellow and relatively smooth	3
Diminution of primordial and graafian follicles (see Table 19), although follicles with normal oocytes are still present	4
Stromal hyperplasia seen in 30—40% of women 55 years or older	1—3
Thecal interstial glands, often well differentiated, persist well after menopause	1
Corpora albicantia, composed of collagen fibers, are numerous; derive both from regressing corpura lutea from the postmenopausal years and from relatively recent atretic follicles	1
Hyalinization of collagen elements common	5
Hilar cell hyperplasia occasionally observed	1, 3
Thickening of the tunica albuginea	2
Stroma calcification and/or hemorrhage may be encountered	2
Vessels of the hilus and medulla undergo severe arteriosclerosis	2
Increased incidence of neoplasia	1, 6, 7
Rats	
Decline in oocyte number with age, but exhaustion of oocytes does not appear to contribute to reproductive decline	8, 9
Presence of "deficiency cells" and "epithelial cellular cords" in old rats	10, 11
Presence of Sertoli adenomas or tubular adenomas	12
Irregular cycling	
Reduced number of nonatretic and atretic follicles	13
CL present	
Follicular cysts composed of elongated thecal cells	
Additional cysts of the rete ovarii origin	
Luteinization of follicles without ovulation	14
Constant estrus	
Characterized by numerous 1—3 mm fluid filled cysts	15—17
No CL but small preantral and medium antral follicles present	
Pseudopregnant-like	
Numerous large CL, medium antral and small prenatalfollicles are present; some alteration of CL morphology with age	15—17
Anestrus	
Atrophic ovaries — small with no antral follicles present	16, 17
Mice	
Decreased oocyte number with age	18, 19
Depletion of oocytes in the CBA mouse	
Luteinization of follicles without ovulation	20
Ovarian weight increases to 8 months then declines gradually	21
Pigmentation of interstitium along with nuclear and cytoplasmic changes	21
Generalized amyloydosis, pigment accumulation, rete hyperplasia, cysts, and sertoli-like elements increase with age	20, 22

Table 18 (continued)
AGE-RELATED ALTERATION OF OVARIAN MORPHOLOGY

Guinea pigs
Increasing incidence of cysts arising from the rete   23—25

REFERENCES

1. **Asch, R. H. and Greenblatt, R. B.** The aging ovary: morphological and endocrine correlations, in *Geriatric Endocrinology,* Greenblatt, R. B., Ed., Raven Press, New York, 1978, 141.
2. **Kuppe, G., Metzger, H. and Ludwig, H.,** Aging and structural changes in the female reproductive tract, in *Aging and Reproductive Physiology,* Vol. 2, Hafez, E. S. E., Ed., Ann Arbor Sciences, Ann Arbor, Mich., 1976, 21.
3. **Rakoff, A. E. and Nowroozi, K.,** The female climacteric, in *Geriatric Endocrinology,* Greenblatt, R. B., Ed., Raven Press, New York, 1978, 165.
4. **Costoff, A. and Mahesh, V. B.,** Primordial follicles with normal oocytes in the ovaries of postmenopausal women, *J. Am. Geriatr. Soc.,* 23, 193, 1975.
5. **Thung, P. J.,** Ageing changes in the ovary, in *Structural Aspects of Aging,* Bourne, J., Ed., Hafner, New York, 1961, 109.
6. **Julien, C. G., Goss, J., Blanchard, K., and Woodruff, J. D.,** Biologic behavior of primary ovarian malignancy, *Obstet. Gynecol.,* 44, 873, 1974.
7. **Rome, R. M., Lauerty, C. R., and Brown, J. B.,** Ovarian tumors in postmenopausal women clinicopathological features and hormonal studies, *J. Obstet. Gynaecol. Br. Commonw.,* 80, 984, 1973.
8. **Mandl, A. M. and Shelton, M.,** A quantitative study of oocytes in young and old nulliparous laboratory rats, *J. Endocrinol.,* 18, 444, 1959.
9. **Shelton, M.,** A comparison of the population of oocytes in nulliparous and multiparous senile laboratory rats, *J. Endocrinol.,* 18, 451, 1959.
10. **Crumeyrolle-Arsas, M., Scheib, D., and Aschheim, P.,** Light and electron microscopy of the ovarian interstial tissue in the senile rat. Normal aspect of response to HCG of "deficiency cells" and "epithelial cords", *Gerontology,* 22, 185, 1976.
11. **Wolfe, J. M.,** The effects of advancing age on the structure of the anterior hypophyses and ovaries of female rats, *Am. J. Anat.,* 72, 361, 1943.
12. **Engle, E. T.,** Tubular adenomas of testis-like tubules of the ovaries of aged rats, *Cancer Res.,* 6, 578, 1946.
13. **Peluso, J. J., Steger, R. W., Huang, H. H., and Meites, J.,** Alterations in the pattern of follicular development and steroidogenesis in the ovary of aging cycling rats, *Exp. Aging Res.,* 5, 319, 1979.
14. **Burack, E. and Wolfe, J. M.,** The effect of anterior hypophyseal administration on the ovaries of old rats, *Endocrinology,* 64, 676, 1959.
15. **Steger, R. W., Peluso, J. J., Huang, H. H., Hafez, E. S. E. and Meites, J.,** Gonadotropin binding sites in the ovary of aged rats, *J. Repro. Fertil.,* 48, 205, 1976.
16. **Huang, H. H.,** Relation of Neuroendocrine System to Loss of Reproductive Function in Aging Female Rats, Ph.D. dissertation, Michigan State University, East Lansing, 1977.
17. **Huang, H. H. and Meites, J.,** Reproductive capacity of aging female rats, *Neuroendocrinology,* 17, 289, 1975.
18. **Jones, E. C.,** The ageing ovary and its influence on reproductive capacity, *J. Reprod. Fertil. Suppl.,* 12, 17, 1970.
19. **Jones, E. C. and Krohn, P. L.,** The relationship between age number of oocytes and fertility in virgin and multiparous mice, *J. Endocrinol.,* 21, 469, 1961.
20. **Thung, P. L., Boot, L. M. and Muhlbook, O.,** Senile changes in the oestrous cycle and in ovarian structures in some inbred strains of mice, *Acta Endocrinol. (Copenhagen),* 23, 8, 1956.
21. **Green, James A.,** Some effects of advancing age on the histology and reactivity of the mouse ovary, *Anat. Rec.,* 129, 333, 1957.
22. **Leathem, J. H.,** The effects of aging on reproduction, in *The Endocrinology of Reproduction,* Velardo, J. T., Ed., Oxford University Press, New York, 1958, 315.
23. **Qualtropani, S. L.,** Serous cysts of the aging guinea pig ovary. I. Light microscopy and origins, *Anat. Rec.,* 188, 351, 1977.
24. **Qualtropani, S. L.,** Serous cysts of the aging guinea pig ovary. II. Scanning and transmission electron microscopy, *Anat. Rec.,* 190(2), 285, 1978.
25. **Rogers, J. B. and Taylor, R. C.,** Age changes in the uterus and ovary of the guinea pig, *Anat. Rec.,* 121, 448, 1955.

Table 19
RELATIONSHIP OF OOCYTE NUMBER TO REPRODUCTIVE DECLINE

	Ref.
General	
Most mammalian ovaries have obtained full complement of oocytes by time of birth and oocyte numbers decrease progressively	1
With the exception of CBA mice, most animals retain a large number of oocytes throughout their life-span	2—6
Several studies in laboratory animals have shown no relationship between oocyte population and reproductive decline	6—8
Women	
Occasional primordial follicles with intact oocytes can be found in the old ovary	9, 10
Reproductive cycles become irregular prior to oocyte depletion	10
Oocytes decline continually from birth with few oocytes remaining after 50	4, 5
Decreased follicular population with age	5
Rats	
Oocytes number and follicle population decrease with age but no effects of parity	6, 11
Oocytes still present at the end of the life-span	6
Follicle numbers decline, but not the ovulation rate	12
No decrease in age of last litter after unilateral ovariectomy	13
Mice	
Irradiated young mice with ovaries retaining only 100—200 oocytes are still fertile while old mice with 2000—3000 oocytes were not	6—8
Litter size does, however, decrease	
Unilateral ovariectomy does not prevent the maintenance of ovulation and pregnancy, although uterine overcrowding may cause premature uterine failure	2, 15, 16
Parity does not effect the age-related decrease in oocyte number	14
Some mice strains show oocyte exhaustion while others do not	2, 3, 14
Follicle number decreases with age, but not ovulation rate	17
Rabbits	
No decrease in age of last litter after unilateral ovariectomy	13
Hamsters	
Growing follicles decrease with age but are still present in the postreproductive period	18
Dogs	
Oocytes still present when reproduction ceases	19
Cows	
Oocytes still present when reproduction ceases	20

REFERENCES

1. Franchi, L. L., Mandl, A. M., and Zuckerman, S., The development of the ovary and the process of oogenesis, in *The Ovary*, Vol. 1, Zuckerman, S., Mandl, A. M., and Eckstein, P., Eds., Academic Press, London, 1962, 1.

Table 19 (continued)
RELATIONSHIP OF OOCYTE NUMBER TO REPRODUCTIVE DECLINE

2. **Jones, E. C.**, The ageing ovary and its influence on reproductive capacity, *J. Reprod. Fertil. Suppl.*, 12, 17, 1970.
3. **Krohn, P. L.**, Ageing processes in the female reproductive tract, *Lect. Sci. Basis Med.*, 7, 285, 1958.
4. **Novak, E. R.**, Ovulation after 50, *Obstet. Gynaecol.*, 30, 903, 1970.
5. **Block, E.**, A quantitative morphological investigation of the follicular system in women variations at different ages, *Acta. Anat.*, 14, 108, 1953.
6. **Mandl, A. M. and Shelton, M.**, A quantitative study of oocytes in young and old nulliparous laboratory rats, *J. Endocrinol.*, 18, 444, 1959.
7. **Ingram, D. L.**, Fertility and oocyte numbers after X-irradiation of the ovary, *J. Endocrinol.*, 17, 81, 1958.
8. **Arai, H.**, On the postnatal development of the ovary (albino rat) with especial reference to the number of ova, *Am. J. Anat.*, 27, 405, 1920.
9. **Costoff, A. and Mahesh, V. B.**, Primordial follicles with normal oocytes in the ovaries of postmenopausal women, *J. Am. Geriatr. Soc.*, 23, 193, 1975.
10. **Talbert, G. B.**, Effect of maternal age on reproductive capacity, *Am. J. Obstet. Gynecol.*, 102, 451, 1968.
11. **Shelton, M.**, A comparison of the population of oocytes in nulliparous and multiparous senile laboratory rats, *J. Endocrinol.*, 18, 451, 1959.
12. **Peluso, J. J., Steger, R. W., Huang, H. H., and Meites, J.**' Alterations in the pattern of follicular development and steroidogenesis in the ovary of aging cycling rats, *Exp. Aging Res.*, 5, 319, 1979.
13. **Adams, C. E.**, Ageing and reproduction in the female mammal with particular reference to the rabbit, *J. Reprod. Fertil. Suppl.*, 12, 1, 1970.
14. **Jones, E. C. and Krohn, P. L.**, The relationship between age number of oocytes and fertility in virgin and multiparous mice, *J. Endocrinol.*, 21, 469, 1961.
15. **Biggers, J. D., Finn, C. A., and McLaren, A.**, Long-term reproductive performance of female mice. I. Effect of removing one ovary, *J. Reprod. Fertil.*, 3, 303, 1962.
16. **Finn, C. A.**, Reproductive capacity and litter size in mice effect of age and environment, *J. Reprod. Fertil.*, 6, 205, 1963.
17. **Harman, S. M. and Talbert, G. B.**, The effect of maternal age on ovulation, corpora lutea of pregnancy and implantation failure in mice, *J. Reprod. Fertil.*, 23, 33, 1970.
18. **Rolle, G. K. and Charipper, H. A.**, The effect of advancing age upon the histology of the ovary, uterus and the vagina of female golden hamster *(caricetus aviatus)*, *Anat. Rec.*, 105, 281, 1949.
19. **Schottener, A.**, Veitrag zur Festellng der Eranzahl in verschiedenen altersperioden bei der Hundin, *Anat. Anz.*, 65, 177, 1928.
20. **Erickson, B. H.**, Development and senescence of the postnatal bovine ovary, *J. Anim. Sci.*, 25, 800, 1966.

Table 20
THE EFFECTS OF AGE ON OVARIAN GONADOTROPIN RESPONSES

	Ref.
Human	
The postmenopausal ovarian cortical stroma and hilus still bind ^{125}I-LH and FSH	1
Contradictory reports, but in general the ovary still responds to exogenous gonadotropin stimulation	2—4
50,000 I.U. HCG for 10 days increases urinary estrogen levels but not testosterone, androstenedione, nor total 17-ketosteroid, or 17-hydroxycorticoid secretion; also alters ovarian enzyme levels	5
10,000 I.U. HCG caused vaginal smear changes in postmenopausal, but not in ovariectomized women	6
5,000 I.U. HCG increases ovarian venous androstenedione and testosterone, but not estradiol	7
3,000 I.U. HCG had no effect on serum estradiol in postmenopausal women	7
Endogenous gonadotropin levels are elevated, although ovarian steroid output is low after the menopause (see Tables 21 and 27)	
Rats	
Transplants of young ovaries to old donors and old ovaries to young donors demonstrate the maintenance of ovarian function despite age	9, 10
Ovulation can be induced in old rats by many procedures (e.g., pituitary extracts, LH or HCG, progesterone, L-dopa, and GnRH)	9, 11—15
Normal or reduced ovarian compensatory hypertrophy, following unilateral ovariectomy	16—19
Mice	
Decreased weight gain in response to gonadotropins	20
Stimulation of Δ^5-3β hydroxysteroid dehydrogenase by PMS and HCG	21
Hamster	
Loss of reproductive capacity precedes decline in ovarian response to gonadotropins	22
Rabbit	
Decreased ovulatory response after HCG injection	23

REFERENCES

1. **Peluso, J. J., Steger, R. W., Jaszczak, S., and Hafez, E. S. E.,** Gonadotropin binding sites in the human post-menopausal ovary, *Fertil. Steril.,* 27, 789, 1976a.
2. **Paulsen, C. A., Leach, R. B., Sandberg, H., and Maddock, W. O.,** Function of the postmenopausal ovary, urinary estrogen excretion, and the response to administered FSH, *J. Clin. Endocrinol. Metab.,* 15, 846, 1955.
3. **Paulsen, C. A., Leach, R. B., Sandberg, H., Sheinfield, S., and Maddock, W. O.,** Function of the postmenopausal ovary. Comparison of urinary estrogen and gonadotropin excretion and response to administration of FSH in postmenopausal and ovariectomized women, *J. Am. Geriatr. Soc.,* 6, 803, 1958.
4. **Vermeulen, A.,** The hormonal activity of the postmenopausal ovary, *J. Clin. Endocrinol. Metab.,* 42, 247, 1976.
5. **Poliak, A., Jones, G., and Goldberg, B.,** Effect of human chorionic gonadotropin on postmenopausal women, *Am. J. Obstet. Gynecol.,* 101, 731, 1968.
6. **Mills, T. M. and Mahesh, V. B.,** Gonadotropin secretion in the menopause, *Clin. Obstet. Gynecol.,* 4(1), 71, 1977

Table 20 (continued)
THE EFFECTS OF AGE ON OVARIAN GONADOTROPIN RESPONSES

7. Greenblatt, R. B., Colle, M. L., and Mahesh, V. B., Ovarian and adrenal steroid production in the postmenopausal women, *Obstet. Gynecol.*, 47, 383, 1976.
8. Longcope, C., Effect of HCG on plasma steroid levels in young and old men, *Steroids*, 21, 583, 1973.
9. Aschheim, P., Aging in the hypothalamic-hypophyseal ovarian axis in the rat, in *Hypothalamus, Pituitary, and Aging*, Everitt, A. V. and Burgess, J. A., Ed., Charles C Thomas, Springfield, Ill., 1976, 376.
10. Peng, M. T. and Huang, H. H., Aging of hypothalamic-pituitary ovarian function in the rat, *Fertil. Steril.*, 23, 535, 1972.
11. Aschheim, P., Contenu hypophysaire en hormone luteinisante (LH) et reaction histophysiologique a la LH circulante du tissue interstitial ovarian chez divers bypes de ratte seniles, *C. R. Acad. Sci.*, 267, 1397, 1968.
12. Clemens, J. A., Amenomori, Y., Jenkins, T., and Meites, J., Effects of hypothalamic stimulation, hormones, and drugs on ovarian function in old female rats, *Proc. Soc. Exp. Biol. Med.*, 132, 561, 1969.
13. Everett, J. W., The restoration of ovulatory cycles and corporus luteum formation in persistant estrous rats, *Endocrinology*, 27, 681, 1940.
14. Ingram, D. L., The vaginal smear of senile laboratory rats, *J. Endocrinol.*, 19, 182, 1959.
15. Meites, J., Huang, H. H., and Simpkins, J. W., Recent studies on neuroendocrine control of reproductive senescence in rats, in *The Aging Reproductive System*, Schneider, E. L., Ed., Raven Press, New York, 1978, 213.
16. Howland, B. E. and Preiss, C., Effect of aging on basal levels of serum gonadotropins, ovarian compensatory hypertrophy, and hypersecretion of gonadotropins after ovariectomy in female rats, *Fertil. Steril.*, 26, 271, 1975.
17. Labhsetwar, A. P., Age-dependentant changes in the pituitary-gonadal relationship: a study of ovarian compensatory hypertrophy, *J. Endocrinol.*, 39, 387, 1967.
18. Labhsetwar, A. P., Aging changes in pituitary-ovarian relationships, *J. Reprod. Fertil. Suppl.*, 12, 99, 1970.
19. Peppler, R. D., Effects of unilateral ovariectomy on follicular development and ovulation in cycling, aged rats, *Am. J. Anat.*, 132, 423, 1971.
20. Green, J. A., Some effects of advancing age on the histology and reactivity of the mouse ovary, *Anat. Rec.*, 129, 333, 1957.
21. Albrecht, E. D., Koos, R. D., and Gottlieb, S. F., Pregnant mare serum and human chorionic gonadotropin stimulate ovarian Δ^5-3β hydroxysteroid dehydrogenase in aged mice, *Fertil. Steril.*, 28(7), 762, 1977.
22. Ortiz, E., The relation of advancing age to reactivity of the reproductive system in the female hamster, *Anat. Rec.*, 122, 517, 1955.
23. Adams, C. E., Ageing and reproduction in the female mammal with particular reference to the rabbit, *J. Reprod. Fertil. Suppl.*, 12, 1, 1970.

Table 21
STEROIDOGENESIS IN THE OLD OVARY

	Ref.
Human	
Ovariectomy in the postmenopausal patient results in a further reduction of already low serum estrogen levels in some cases but not others	1 2
Histochemical studies show the postmenopausal ovarian cortical stroma still possesses several of the enzymes necessary for steroid synthesis	3—5
The postmenopausal cortical stroma and hilus still bind ^{125}I-LH and ^{125}I-FSH	5
The postmenopausal ovary produces chiefly androgens	6—8
Major source of estrogens in the postmenopause is through peripheral conversion of androgens	6, 9, 10
Estrone becomes the most important estrogen during the postmenopausal years due to decreased estradiol production and increased conversion of precursors	11—14
Decreased metabolic clearance rate for serum steroids	15
The adrenal contributes significantly to serum steroid levels in the postmenopausal woman	16—20
Rats	
Decreased ovarian Δ^5-3β-hydroxysteroid dehydrogenase activity and altered substrate preference	21
Marked in vitro conversion of pregnenolone to androstenedione and testosterone in old rats	22
Steroidogenic response to HCG decreases with age	22
Mice	
Decreased ovarian Δ^5-3β-hydroxysteroid dehydrogenase and increased cholesterol with advancing age	23—25
Hamsters	
Altered Δ-3β-HSD activity	26
Rabbit	
No in vitro age effect on basal progesterone synthesis but LH stimulates progesterone synthesis in old ovaries but mainly 20α-hydroxyprogesterone in young ovaries	27

REFERENCES

1. **Paulsen, C. A., Leach, R. B., Sandberg, H., Sheinfield, S., and Maddock, W. O.,** Function of the postmenopausal ovary. Comparison of urinary estrogen and gonadotropin excretion and response to administration of FSH in postmenopausal and ovariectomized women, *J. Am. Geriatr. Soc.*, 6, 803, 1958.
2. **Procope, B. J.,** Studies on urinary excretion, biological effects and origin of oestrogens in postmenopausal women, *Acta Endocrinol. (Copenhagen) Suppl.*, 135, 1968.
3. **Brandau, H., Brandau, L., and Mestwerdt, W.,** Endocrine activity in postmenopausal ovaries, *Eur. J. Obstet. Gynecol.*, 4 (Suppl. 1), 5187, 1974.
4. **Novak, E. R., Goldberg, B., Jones, G. S., and O'Toole, R. V.,** Enzyme histochemistry of the postmenopausal ovary associated with normal and abnormal endometrium, *Am. J. Obstet. Gynecol.*, 93, 669, 1965.
5. **Peluso, J. J., Steger, R. W., Jaszczak, S., and Hafez, E. S. E.,** Gonadotropin binding sites in the human postmenopausal ovary, *Fertil. Steril.*, 27, 789, 1976a.
6. **Judd, H. L., Judd, G. E., Lucas, W. E., and Yen, S. S. C.,** Endocrine function of the postmenopausal ovary: concentration of androgens and estrogens in ovarian and peripheral vein blood, *J. Clin. Endocrinol. Metab.*, 39, 1020, 1974.
7. **Abraham, G. E., Lobotsky, J., and Lloyd, C. W.,** Metabolism of testosterone and androstenedione in normal and ovariectomized women, *J. Clin. Invest.*, 48, 696, 1969.
8. **Mattingly, R. F. and Haung, W. Y.,** Steroidogenesis of the menopausal and postmenopausal ovary, *Am. J. Obstet. Gynecol.*, 103, 679, 1969.

Table 21 (continued)
STEROIDOGENESIS IN THE OLD OVARY

9. **Longcope, C., Kats, T., and Horten, R.,** Conversion of blood androgens to estrogens in normal adult men and women, *J. Clin. Invest.*, 48, 2191, 169.
10. **Pourtman, J., Thijssen, J. H., and Schwartz, F.,** Androgen production and conversion to estrogens in normal postmenopausal women and in selected breast cancer patients, *J. Clin. Endocrinol. Metab.*, 37, 101, 1973.
11. **Judd, H. L., Lucas, W. E., and Yen, S. S. C.,** Serum 17β-estradiol and estrone levels in postmenopausal women with and without endometrial cancer, *J. Clin. Endocrinol. Metab.*, 43, 272, 1976.
12. **Asch, R. H. and Greenblatt, R. B.,** Steroidogenesis in the postmenopausal ovary, *Clin. Obstet. Gynecol.*, 4(1), 85, 1977.
13. **Asch, R. H. and Greenblatt, R. B.,** The aging ovary: morphological and endocrine correlations, in *Geriatric Endocrinology*, Greenblatt, R. B., Ed., Raven Press, New York, 1978, 141.
14. **Hemsell, D. L., Grodin, J. M., Brenner, P. F., Silteri, P. K., and MacDonald, P. C.,** Plasma precursors of estrogen. II. Correlation of the extent of conversion of plasma androstenedione to estrone with age, *J. Clin. Endocrinol. Metab.*, 38, 476, 1974.
15. **Longcope, C.,** Metabolic clearance and blood production of estrogens in postmenopaual women, *Am. J. Obstet. Gynecol.*, 111, 778, 1971.
16. **Baird, D. T. and Guevara, A.,** Concentration of unconjugated estrone and estradiol in peripheral plasma in non-pregnant women throughout the menstrual cycle, castrate and postmenopausal women and in men, *J. Clin. Endocrinol. Metab.*, 29, 879, 1969.
17. **Greenblatt, R. B., Colle, M. L., and Mahesh, V. B.,** Ovarian and adrenal steroid production in the postmenopausal woman, *Obstet. Gynecol.*, 47, 383, 1976.
18. **Greenblatt, R. B., Oettinger, M., and Bohler, C. S. S.,** Estrogen-androgen levels in aging men and women, *J. Am. Geriatr. Soc.*, 24, 173, 1976.
19. **Grodin, J. M., Silteri, P. K., and MacDonald, P. C.,** Source of estrogen production in postmenopausal women, *J. Clin. Endocrinol. Metab.*, 36, 207, 1973.
20. **Vermeulen, A.,** The hormonal activity of the postmenopausal ovary, *J. Clin. Endocrinol. Metab.*, 42, 247, 1976.
21. **Leathem, J. H. and Shapiro, B. H.,** Aging and ovarian Δ^5-3β-hydroxysteroid dehydrogenase in rats, *Proc. Soc. Exp. Biol. Med.*, 148, 793, 1975.
22. **Chan, S. W. C. and Leathem, J. H.,** Aging and ovarian steroidogenesis in the rat, *J. Gerontol.*, 32, 395, 1977.
23. **Albrecht, E. O., Koos, R. D., and Gottlieb, S. F.,** Pregnant mare serum and human chorionic gonadotropin stimulate ovarian Δ^5-3β hydroxysteroid dehydrogenase in aged mice, *Fertil. Steril.*, 28(7), 762, 1977.
24. **Albrecht, E. O., Koos, R. D., and Wehrenberg, W. B.,** Ovarian Δ^5-3β-hydroxysteroid dehydrogenase and cholesterol in the aged mouse during pregnancy, *Biol. Reprod.*, 13, 158, 1975.
25. **Wehrenberg, W. B., Gottlieb, S. F., Levine, D. and Ramsay, L.,** Ageing and ovarian Δ^5-3β, hydroxysteroid dehydrogenase in the pregnant mouse, *J. Endocrinol.*, 70, 183, 1976.
26. **Blaha, G. C. and Leavitt, W. W.,** Ovarian steroid dehydrogenase histochemistry and circulating progesterone in aged golden hamsters during the estrous cycle and pregnancy, *Biol. Reprod.*, 11, 156, 1974.
27. **Maurer, R. R. and Foote, R. H.,** Maternal ageing and embryonic mortality in the rabbit. II. Hormonal changes in young and ageing females, *J. Reprod. Fertil.*, 31, 15, 1972.

Table 22
SERUM STEROID LEVELS IN OLD FEMALE ANIMALS

Women (Postmenopausal)

Steroid	Level[a]	Ref.
Estradiol	1—10 pg/ml	1
	11—15 pg/ml	2—6
	16—20 pg/ml	7
	>20 pg/ml	9, 10
Estrone	0—30 pg/ml	1, 8
	<30 pg/ml	4, 11, 7
Progesterone	0—0.25 ng/ml	1, 7
	<0.25 ng/ml	2, 9, 10
Androstenedione	0—1.0/ml	2, 1
	<1 ng/ml	9, 10

Rats

Young	Estradiol (pg/ml)	Progesterone (ng/ml)	Testosterone (pg/ml)	
Estrus	19.2±1.9	14.0±2.2	77±2	12, 13
Proestrus a.m.	53.7±5.4	11.7±2.4	209±16	
p.m.	72.1±6.4	31.0±3.9	436±55	
Diestrus	29.0±2.0	16.7±2.6	142±21	
Old				
Constant estrus	33.6±3.3	15.5±2.8	150±29	
Pseudopregnant-like	28.7±4.8	25.2±6.5	106±16	
Anestrus	19.8±2.5	6.5±0.88	83±15	

[a] Levels average 150 pg/ml in young women.[5,6]

REFERENCES

1. **Longcope, C.**, Metabolic clearance and blood production of estrogens in postmenopausal women, *Am. J. Obster. Gynecol.*, 111, 778, 1971.
2. **Abraham, G. E., Lobotsky, J., and Lloyd, C. W.**, Metabolism of testosterone and androstenedione in normal and ovariectomized women, *J. Clin. Invest.*, 48, 696, 1969.
3. **Baird, D. T. and Guevara, A.**, Concentration of unconjugated estrone and estradiol in peripheral plasma in non-pregnant women throughout the menstrual cycle, castrate and postmenopausal women and in men, *J. Clin. Endocrinol. Metab.*, 29, 879, 1969.
4. **Rader, M. D., Flickiner, G. L., and deVilla, G. O.**, Plasma estrogens in postmenopausal women, *Am. J. Obstet. Gynecol.*, 116, 1069, 1973.
5. **Sherman, B. M. and Korenman, S. G.**, Hormonal characteristics of the human menstrual cycle throughout reproductive life, *J. Clin. Invest.*, 55, 699, 1975.
6. **Sherman, B. M., West, J. H., and Korenman, S. G.**, The menopausal transition: Analysis of LH, FSH, estradiol, and progesterone concentrations during menstrual cycles of older women, *J. Clin. Endocrinol. Metab.*, 42, 629, 1976.
7. **Judd, H. L., Lucas, W. E., and Yen, S. S. C.**, Serum 17β-estradiol and estrone levels in postmenopausal women with and without endometrial cancer, *J. Clin. Endocrinol. Metab.*, 43, 272, 1976.
8. **Judd, H. L., Judd, G. E., Lucas, W. E., and Yen, S. S. C.**, Endocrine function of the postmenopausal ovary: concentration of androgens and estrogens in ovarian and peripheral vein blood, *J. Clin. Endocrinol. Metab.*, 39 (Abstr.), 1020, 1974.
9. **Greenblatt, R. B., Colle, M. L., and Mahesh, V. B.**, Ovarian and adrenal steroid production in the postmenopausal woman, *Obstet. Gynecol.*, 47, 383, 1976.
10. **Greenblatt, R. B., Oettinger, M., and Bohler, C. S. S.**, Estrogen-androgen levels in aging men and women, *J. Am. Geriatr. Soc.*, 24, 173, 1976.
11. **Yen, S. S. C., Tsai, C. C., Naftolin, F., Vandenberg, G., and Judd, H.**, Circulating estradiol, estrone and gonadotropin levels following the administration of orally active 17β-estradiol in postmenopausal women, *J. Clin. Endocrinol. Metab.* 34, 671, 1972.
12. **Huang, H. H., Steger, R. W., Bruni, J., and Meites, J.**, Changes in patterns of sex steroid and gonadotropin secretion in aging female rats, *Endocrinology*, 103, 1855, 1978.
13. **Steger, R. W., Huang, H. H., and Meites, J.**, Relation of aging to hypothalamic LHRH content and serum gonadal steroids in female rats, *Proc. Soc. Exp. Biol. Med.*, 161, 251, 1979.

Table 23
GENERAL CONSIDERATION OF ROLE OF CORPORA LUTEA (CL) AND PROGESTERONE IN AGE-RELATED REPRODUCTIVE CHANGES

	Ref.
Decreased progesterone output is one of the earliest age-related ovarian changes and is possibly related to an increased frequency of anovulatory cycles and spontaneous abortions seen prior to menopause.	1
Decreased number of CL are found in old animals, but usually not until after litter size has declined	2—4
Progesterone administration increases the implantation rate but not subsequent embryo survival in aged mice.	5, 6
Improving the CL/embryo ratio by oviduct ligation prior to ovulation in the old mouse does not improve embryonic survival.	7

REFERENCES

1. **Talbert, G. B.**, Effect of maternal age on reproductive capacity, *Am. J. Obstet. Gynecol.*, 102, 451, 1968.
2. **Blaha, G. C.**, Reproductive senescence in the female golden hamster, *Anat. Rec.*, 150, 405, 1964.
3. **Jones, E. C.**, The ageing ovary and its influence on reproductive capacity, *J. Reprod. Fertil. Suppl.*, 12, 17, 1970.
4. **Labhsetwar, A. P.**, Aging changes in pituitary-ovarian relationships, *J. Reprod. Fertil. Suppl.*, 12, 99, 1970.
5. **Gosden, R. G.**, Corpus luteum adequacy in the aging pregnant mouse, *Eur. J. Obstet. Gynecol. Reprod. Biol.*, Suppl. S109, 411, 1974.
6. **Gosden, R. G.**, Ovarian support of pregnancy in ageing inbred mice, *J. Reprod. Fertil.*, 42, 423, 1975.
7. **Finn, C. A.**, Reproductive capacity and litter size in mice effect of age and environment, *J. Reprod. Fertil.*, 6, 205, 1963.

Table 24
CORPUS LUTEUM FUNCTION IN OLD FEMALES

	Ref.
Women	
Only corpora atretica or corpora albicantia remain in the postmenopausal ovary; these structures appear to be steroidogenically inactive	1, 2
Decreased luteal function in the perimenopause responsible for low progesterone levels, dysfunctional uterine bleeding, miscarriages, and changes in the pattern of basal body temperature	3—6
Rat	
Old luteal cells are morphologically altered	7
CL of old rats bind LH normally and show increased 3β-HSD activity	8
Substrate specificity for 3β-HSD is altered in the CL of old rats	9
Decreased number of CL seen in aged rat, but not until a decrease in litter size has taken place	10
Mice	
Altered structure of old CL	11—16
Decreased 3β-HSD in old CL	17
Alterations in corpora lutea function do not seem to be a cause of increased embryonic decline rates in old pregnant mice	19
	20
	12, 18
Other reports implicate declining CL function in the increase in embryonic decline	11, 13, 14

Table 24 (continued)
CORPUS LUTEUM FUNCTION IN OLD FEMALES

	Ref.
Hamster	
Reduced growth of CL in old pregnant hamsters	21
Rabbit	
Exogenous progesterone did not increase declining litter sizes in old rabbits	22

REFERENCES

1. **Asch, R. H. and Greenblatt, R. B.**, The aging ovary: morphological and endocrine correlations, in *Geriatric Endocrinology*, Greenblatt, R. B., Ed., Raven Press, New York, 1978, 141.
2. **Peluso, J. J., Steger, R W., Jaszczak, S., and Hafez, E. S. E.**, Gonadotropin binding sites in the human post-menopausal ovary, *Fertil. Steril.*, 27, 789, 1976a.
3. **Collett, M. E., Wertenberger, G. E., and Fiske, V. M.**, The effect of age upon the pattern of the menstrual cycle, *Fertil. Steril.*, 5, 437, 1954.
4. **Sherman, B. M. and Korenman, S. G.**, Hormonal characteristics of the human menstrual cycle throughout reproductive life, *J. Clin. Invest.*, 55, 699, 1975.
5. **Sherman, B. M., West, J. H., and Korenman, S. G.**, The menopausal transition: analysis of LH, FSH, estradiol, and progesterone concentrations during menstrual cycles of older women, *J. Clin. Endocrinol. Metab.*, 42, 629, 1976.
6. **Talbert, G. B.**, Effect of maternal age on reproductive capacity, *Am. J. Obstet. Gynecol.*, 102, 451, 1968.
7. **Mandl, A. M.**, Corpora lutea in senile virgin laboratory rats, *J. Endocrinol.*, 18, 438, 1959.
8. **Steger, R. W., Peluso, J. J., Huang, H. H., Hafez, E. S. E., and Meites, J.**, Gonadotropin binding sites in the ovary of aged rats, *J. Reprod. Fertil.*, 48, 205, 1976.
9. **Leathem, J. H. and Murono, E. P.**, Ovarian Δ^5-3β-hydroxysteroid dehydrogenase in aging rats, *Fertil. Steril.*, 26, 996, 1975b.
10. **Labhsetwar, A. P.**, Aging changes in pituitary-ovarian relationships, *J. Reprod. Fertil. Suppl.*, 12, 99, 1970.
11. **Gosden, R. G.**, Corpus luteum adequacy in the aging pregnant mouse, *Eur. J. Obstet. Gynecol. Reprod. Biol.*, Suppl. S109, 411, 1974.
12. **Gosden, R. G.**, Ovarian support of pregnancy in ageing inbred mice, *J. Reprod. Fertil.*, 42, 423, 1975.
13. **Harman, S. M. and Talbert, G. B.**, Structural changes in corpora lutea and decline of reproductive function in aging female mice, *Am. Zool.*, 7, 757, 1967.
14. **Harman, S. M. and Talbert, G. B.**, The effect of maternal age on ovulation corpora lutea of pregnancy and implantation failure in mice, *J. Reprod. Fertil.*, 23, 33, 1970.
15. **Jones, E. C.**, The ageing ovary and its influence on reproductive capacity, *J. Reprod. Fertil. Suppl.*, 12, 17, 1970.
16. **Loeb, L.**, Aging processes in the ovaries of mice belonging to strains differing in the indicence of mammary carcinoma, *Arch. Pathol.*, 46, 401, 1948.
17. **Albrecht, E. O., Koos, R. D. and Wehrenberg, W. B.**, Ovarian Δ^5-3β-hydroxysteroid dehydrogenase and cholesterol in the aged mouse during pregnancy, *Biol. Reprod.*, 13, 158, 1975.
18. **Finn, C. A.**, Reproductive capacity and litter size in mice effect of age and environment, *J. Reprod. Fertil.*, 6, 205, 1963.
19. **Parkening, T. A., Lau, I., Saksena, S. K., and Chang, M. C.**, Circulating plasma levels of pregnenolone, progesterone, estrogen, LH and FSH in young and aged C57BL/6 mice during various stages of pregnancy, *J. Gerontol.*, 33(2), 191, 1978.
20. **Talbert, G. B.**, Effect of maternal age on postimplantation reproduction failure in mice, *J. Reprod. Fertil.*, 24, 449, 1971.
21. **Thorneycroft, I. H. and Soderwell, A. L.**, The nature of the litter size loss in senescent hamsters, *Anat. Rec.*, 165, 343, 1969.
22. **Larson, L., Spilman, C. H., Dunn, H. O., and Foote, R. H.**, Reproductive efficiency in aged female rabbits given supplemental progesterone and estradiol, *J. Reprod. Fertil.*, 33, 31, 1973.

Table 25
PITUITARY MORPHOLOGY IN OLD ANIMALS IN RELATION TO CHANGES IN FEMALE REPRODUCTION

	Ref.
Human	
Decreased weight at the menopause	1, 2
8—10% increase in basophils; 40—50% decrease in acidophils	3, 4
Vacuolation of basophils	5
Decreased vascularity of anterior ptuitary after age 40—50	4
Increased connective tissue with age	2
Invasion of posterior pituitary by basophils	6
Rats	
Atypical areas of hypertrophic cells similar to adenomata	7, 8
Vacuolation of basophils	7, 8
Increased colloid, but relative proportion of cell types unchanged with age; increase in acidophils and chromophobes with age in virgin rats	7, 8
Decreased incidence of mitosis with age	7
Presence of adenoma-like lesions	7—9
Increase in number and thickness of reticular tissue fibers with age	10
Hamsters	
Increase in numbers of basophils with age	11
Vacuolation of basophils	
Degranulation of some cells	
Loss of regularity of the reticular network	
Mouse	
Decrease in size of gland cells	12
Increase in connective tissue	12
Decrease in frequency of mitosis; none seen after 21 months in male, slightly longer in the female (slight resumption between 27—31 months)	12, 13
Alteration of nucleus, mitochondria, and endoplasmic reticulum	13
Rabbit	
Increased pituitary weight with age	14

REFERENCES

1. Parson, R. J., *Medical Papers Dedicated to Henry Astbury Christian,* Waverly Press, Baltimore, 1935, 366.
2. Verzar, F., Anterior pituitary function in age, in in *The Pituitary Gland,* Harris, G. W. and Donovan, B. T., Eds., University of California, Press, Berkeley, Calif., 1966, 444.
3. Baggart, J. H., *Edinburgh Med. J.,* 42, 113, 1935.
4. Finn, C. A., Embryonic death in aged mice, *Nature (London),* 194, 499, 1962.
5. Timiras, P. S., *Developmental Physiology and Aging,* Macmillan, New York, 1972, 527.
6. Tessaurd, G., La senescence de l'hypophyse, *C. R. Soc. Fr. Gynecol.,* 22(4), 188, 1952.
7. Wolfe, J. M., The effects of advancing age on the structure of the anterior hypophyses and ovaries of female rats, *Am. J. Anat.,* 72, 361, 1943.
8. Wolfe, J. M., Bryan, R., and Wright, A. W., Histological observation on the anterior pituitary of old rats with particular reference to the spontaneous apparition of pituitary adenomata, *Am. J. Cancer,* 34, 352, 1938.
9. Sayten, J. A., The relation of age to the occurrence of adenoma-like lesions in the rat hypophysis and to their adenoma-like lesions in the rat hypophysis and to their growth after transplantation, *Cancer Res.,* 1, 227, 1941.
10. Lansing, W. and Wolfe, J. M., Changes in the fibrillar tissue of the anterior pituitary of the rat associated with advancing age, *Anat. Rec.,* 83, 355, 1942.
11. Spagnoli, H. H. and Charipper, H. A., The effects of aging on the histology and cytology of the pituitary gland of the golden hamster *(Cricetus auratus)* with brief reference to simultaneous changes in the thyroid and testis, *Anat. Rec.,* 121, 117, 1955.
12. Blumenthal, H. T., Aging processes in the endocrine glands of various strains of normal mice: relationship of hypophyseal activity to aging changes in other endocrine glands, *J. Gerontol.,* 10, 253, 1955.
13. Weiss, J. and Lansing, A. I., Age changes in the fine structure of anterior pituitary of the mouse, *Proc. Soc. Exp. Biol. Med.,* 82, 460, 1953.
14. Maurer, R. R. and Foote, R. H., Maternal ageing and embryonic mortality in the rabbit. II. Hormonal changes in young and ageing females, *J. Reprod. Fertil.,* 31, 15, 1972.

Table 26
PITUITARY GONADOTROPIN CONTENT IN FEMALES

	Ref.
Human	
Two- to threefold increase in LH content after the menopause (by radioimmunoassay)	1
Increased FSH, but not LH (by bioassay)	2
Immunohistochemical evidence of prolactin containing cells demonstrated in the postmenopausal pituitary	3
Altered forms of LH found in postmenopausal pituitaries	4
Rats	
Strain and age differences	
Early bioassay studies showed few aging changes	5
Constant estrus	
LH and FSH levels not significantly different than found in young females at estrus	6
FSH/LH ratio 1.4 in old rats, 2.2 in young rats (bioassay)	6
Higher pituitary FSH and prolactin levels than young rats, but no change in LH levels (bioassay)	7
Pseudopregnant-like	
Pituitary LH concentrations similar to young diestrous rats (bioassay)	6
Pituitary LH higher but prolactin lower than in old constant estrus rats (bioassay)	7
Pituitary LH similar but FSH higher than in younger rats	8, 9
Anestrus	
Similar LH levels, but markedly higher pituitary FSH levels than young diestrous rats (bioassay)	6
Irregular cycles	
Increased LH content	10
Rabbit	
Total LH content unchanged with age, but concentration is lower	11

REFERENCES

1. **Ryan, R. J.**, The luteinizing hormone content of human pituitaries. I. Variations with sex and age, *J. Clin. Endocrinol.*, 22, 300, 1965.
2. **Albert, A., Randall, R. V., Smith, R. A., and Johnson, C. E.**, Urinary excretion of gonadotropins as a function of age, in *Hormones and the Aging Process*, Engle, E. T. and Pincus, G., Eds., Academic Press, New York, 1956, 49.
3. **Kovacs, K., Ryan, N., Horvath, E., Pena, G., and Ezrin, C.**, Prolactin cells of the human pituitary gland in old age, *J. Gerontol.*, 32, 534, 1977.
4. **Prentice, L. G. and Ryan, R. J.**, LH and its subunits in human pituitary, serum, and urine, *J. Clin. Endocrinol. Metab.*, 40, 303, 1975.
5. **Larson, H. D., Golden, J. B., and Serringhaus, E. I.**, The gonadotropic content of the hypophysis throughout the life cycle of the normal female rat, *Am. J. Physiol.*, 125, 396, 1939.
6. **Pi, W. P., Huang, H. H., and Peng, M. T.**, Pituitary luteinizing hormone and follicle stimulating hormone concentrations to stalk median eminence LH-releasing factor and FSH-RF levels of old female rats, *J. Formosan Med. Assoc.*, 72, 485, 1973.
7. **Clemens, J. A. and Meites, J.**, Neuroendocrine status of old constant-estrus rats, *Neuroendocrinology*, 7, 249, 1971.
8. **Aschheim, P.**, Contenu hypophysaire en hormone luteinisante (LH) et reaction histophysiologique a la LH circulante du tissue interstitiel ovarian chez divers bypes de ratte seniles, *C. R. Acad. Sci.*, 267, 1397, 1968.
9. **Aschheim, P.**, Aging in the hypothalamic-hypophyseal ovarian axis in the rat, in *Hypothalamis, Pituitary and Aging*, Everitt, A. V. and Burgess, J. A., Eds., Charles C Thomas, Springfield, Ill., 1976, 376.
10. **Labhsetwar, A. P.**, Age dependent changes in the pituitary-gonadal relationship. II. A study of pituitary LH and FSH content in female rat, *J. Reprod. Fertil.*, 20, 21, 1969.
11. **Maurer, R. R. and Foote, R. H.**, Maternal ageing and embryonic mortality in the rabbit. II. Hormonal changes in young and ageing females, *J. Reprod. Fertil.*, 31, 15, 1972.

Table 27
THE EFFECTS OF AGE ON PITUITARY RESPONSIVENESS TO GONADOTROPIN RELEASING HORMONE IN THE FEMALE

	Ref.
Human	
Pituitary response to GnRH remains in patients up to 100 years of age despite high basal gonadotropin levels	1—4
150 ng GnRH causes an LH surge in postmenopausal women up to 100 years old	5
25 µg GnRH causes a sharp rise of LH and FSH in young women, but only a 3-fold rise in FSH and a slight rise in LH in postmenopausal women	6
GnRH elevated in the serum of postmenopausal patients	7
GnRH and LH peak every 1 or 2 hr in an inverse relationship in the postmenopause	8
Rats	
Reduced responsiveness of old constant estrus or pseudopregnant-like rats	9, 10
No age difference in responsiveness of old ovariectomized rats or intact constant estrus rats primed with estrogen	10, 11
Multiple GnRH injections in intact old CE rats can induce as much LH and more FSH than in young proestrus rats	12—14
In vitro GnRH response not affected by age	14, 15

REFERENCES

1. Dekretser, D. M., Burger, H. G., and Dumpys, R., Patterns of serum LH and FSH in response to 4 hour infusions of LHRH in normal women during menstrual cycle, on oral contraceptives and in postmenopausal state, *J. Clin. Endocrinol., Metab.*, 46(2), 227, 1978.
2. Hashimato, T., Miyai, K., and Izumi, K., Effect of clomiphene on basal and LRH-induced gonadotropin secretion in postmenopausal women, *J. Clin. Endocrinol.*, 42, 593, 1976.
3. Kuhaara, Y., Miyai, K., Hashimoto, T., and Onishi, T., Aging and anterior pituitary function-responses of PRL, TSH and gonadotropins and TRH and LH-RH in normal subjects, *J. Geriatr.*, 12, 363, 1975.
4. Scaglia, H., Medina, M., Pinto-Ferreira, A. L., Vazques, G., Gaul, C., and Perez-Palacios, G., Pituitary LH and FSH secretion and responsiveness in women of old age, *Acta Endocrinol. (Copenhagen)*, 81, 673, 1976.
5. Wagner, H., Bockel, K., Hrubesch, M., and Grote, G., Examination of the pituitary gonadotropin relationship in man with synthetic LH-FSH releasing hormones, in *Hypophysiotropic Hormones*, Gaul, G. and Rosenberg, D., Eds., Excerpta Medica, Amsterdam, 1973, 257.
6. Yen, S. S. C., Rebar, R., Vandenberg, G., Naftolin, F., Judd, H., Ehara, K., Ryan, K. J., Rivier, J., Amoss, M., and Guillemin, R., Clinical studies with synthetic LRF, in *Hypophysiotropic Hormones*, Gaul, G. and Rosenberg, O., Eds., Excerpta Medica, Amsterdam, 1973, 217.
7. Rosenblum, N. G. and Schlaff, S., Gonadotropin-releasing hormone radioimmunoassay and its measurement in normal human plasma, secondary amenorrhea and postmenopausal syndrome, *Am. J. Obstet. Gynecol.*, 124, 340, 1976.
8. Papanicolaou, A. D., Loraine, J. A., and Dove, G. A., Endocrine function in postmenopausal women, *J. Obstet. Gynaecol. Br. Commonw.*, 76, 317, 1969.
9. Howland, B. E., Reduced gonadotropin release in response to progesterone or gonadotropin releasing hormone (GnRH) in old female rats, *Life Sci.*, 19, 219, 1976.
10. Watkins, B. E., Meites, J., and Riegle, G. D., Age-related changes in pituitary responsiveness to LHRH in the female rat, *Endocrinology*, 97, 543, 1975.
11. Peluso, J. J., Steger, R. W., and Hafez, E. S. E., Regulation of LH secretion in aged female rats, *Biol. Reprod.*, 16, 212, 1977.
12. Huang, H. H., Relation of Neuroendocrine System to Loss of Reproductive Function in Aging Female Rats, Ph.D. dissertation, Michigan State University, East Lansing, 1977.
13. Miller, A. E. and Riegle, G. D., Serum LH levels following multiple LHRH injections in aging rats, *Proc. Soc. Exp. Biol. Med.*, 157(3), 494, 1978.
14. Riegle, G. D. and Miller, A. E., Aging effects on the hypothalamic-hypophyseal-gonadal control system in the rat, in *The Aging Reproductive System*, Schneider, E. L., Ed., Raven Press, New York, 1978, 159.
15. Tsai, Y. F., Peng, M. T., and Peng, Y. I., Responsiveness of old rat pituitaries to LH-RH *in vitro*, *J. Formosan Med. Assoc.*, 74, 389, 1975.

Table 28
THE EFFECTS OF AGE ON SERUM GONADOTROPIN LEVELS IN FEMALES

	Ref.
Women	
There is a marked elevation of serum LH and FSH levels after the menopause	1—15
FSH levels increase to a greater extent than do LH levels	9,13—15
Elevated gonadotropins are due to increased secretion since metabolic clearance is not radically altered	17—18
Elevated urinary gonadotropins	19,20
Serum LH normal and FSH usually elevated in the perimenopausal patients	14,15
Urinary gonadotropins elevated in the perimenopausal period	21
High gonadotropin levels suppressed by illness	22
Mice	
Parabiosis studies indirectly indicate increased gonadotropin levels in old mice	23
Rats	
As the rat ages, estrous cycles become irregular, then cease, at which time the female rats enter a period of constant estrous or repeated pseudopregnancies; occasionally, senescent rats progress into an anestrous state characterized by atrophic ovaries and uteri	24, 25
There is an absence of cyclic gonadotropin release in the old rats although each reproductive state is characterized by a somewhat different steriod and gonadotropin profile	26

		LH (ng LH-RP-1/ml)	FSH (ng LH-RP-1/ml)	
Young	De	25±2.5	46±8.5	26
a.m.	Pe	41±3.5	38±3.4	
p.m.	Pe	780±123	173±11.5	
	E	43±4.3	166±8.9	
Old	Ce	43±4.7	214±14	
	Pp	21±2.5	84±10.3	
	An	Undetectable	62±7.2	

	Ref.
Numerous reports confirm the loss of cyclic gonadotropin release, increased FSH, and decreased or no change in LH levels with age	24—31
Ovarian compensatory hypertrophy studies suggest a reduced gonadotropin level with age	32—34

REFERENCES

1. DeKretser, D. M., Burger, H. G., and Dumpys, R., Patterns of serum LH and FSH in response to 4 hour infusions of LHRH in normal women during menstrual cycle, on oral contraceptives, and in postmenopausal state, *J. Clin. Endocrinol. Metab.*, 46(2), 227, 1978.
2. Hashimoto, T., Miyai, K., and Izumi, K., Effect of clomiphene on basal and LRH-induced gonadotropin secretion in postmenopausal women, *J. Clin. Endocrinol.*, 42, 593, 1976.
3. Hashimoto, T., Miyai, K., Izumi, K., and Kumahara, Y., Gonadotropin response to synthetic LHRH in normal subjects correlation between LH and FSH, *J. Clin. Endocrinol. Metab.*, 37, 910, 1973.
4. Kuhahara, Y., Miyai, K., Hashimoto, T., and Onishi, T., Aging and anterior pituitary function-responses of PRL, TSH and gonadotropins and TRH and LH-RH in normal subjects, *J. Geriatr.*, 12, 363, 1975.
5. Lauritzen, C., The hypothalamic anterior pituitary system in the climacteric age period, *Front. Horm. Res.*, 3, 20, 1975.
6. Mills, T. M. and Mahesh, V. B., Gonadotropin secretion in the menopause, *Clin. Obstet. Gynecol.*, 4(1), 71, 1977.
7. Mills, T. M. and Mahesh, V. B., Pituitary function in the aged, in *Geriatric Endocrinology*, Greenblatt, R. B., Ed., Raven Press, New York, 1978, 1.
8. Monroe, S. E. and Menon, K. M., Changes in reproductive hormone secretion during the climacteric and postmenopausal periods, *Clin. Obstet. Gynecol.*, 20, 113, 1977.
9. Odell, W. D. and Swerdloff, R. S., Progesterone-induced luteinizing and follicle stimulating hormone surge in post-menopausal women: a simulated ovulatory peak, *Proc. Nat. Acad. Sci. U.S.A.*, 61, 529, 1968.

Table 28 (continued)
THE EFFECTS OF AGE ON SERUM GONADOTROPIN LEVELS IN FEMALES

10. Reyes, F. I., Winter, J. S. D., and Faiman, C., Pituitary-ovarian relationships preceding menopause. I. Cross-sectional study of serum follicle stimulating hormone, luteinizing hormone, prolactin, estradiol and progesterone levels, *Am. J. Obstet. Gynecol.*, 129(5), 557, 1977.
11. Wise, A. J., Gross, M. A., and Schlach, D. S., Quantitative relationships of the pituitary-gonadal axis in postmenopausal women, *J. Lab. Clin. Med.*, 81, 28, 1973.
12. Yen, S. S. C., Tsai, C. C., Naftolin, F., Vandenberg, G., and Judd, H., Circulating estradiol, estrone and gonadotropin levels following the administration of orally active 17β-estradiol in postmenopausal women, *J. Clin. Endocrinol. Metab.*, 34, 671, 1972.
13. Scaglia, H., Medina, M., Pinto-Ferreira, A. L., Vazques, G., Gaul, C., and Perez-Palacios, G., Pituitary LH and FSH secretion and responsiveness in women of old age, *Acta Endocrinol. (Copenhagen)*, 81, 673, 1976.
14. Sherman, B. M. and Korenman, S. G., Hormonal characteristics of the human menstrual cycle throughout reproductive life, *J. Clin. Invest.*, 55, 699, 1975.
15. Sherman, B. M., West, J. H., and Korenman, S. G., The menopausal transition: analysis of LH, FSH, estradiol and progesterone concentrations during menstrual cycles of older women, *J. Clin. Endocrinol. Metab.*, 42, 629, 1976.
16. Albert, A., RAndall, R. V., Smith, R. A., and Johnson, C. E., Urinary excretion of gonadotropins as a function of age, in *Hormones and the Aging Process*, Engle, E. T. and Pinus, G., Eds., Academic Press, New York, 1956, 49.
17. Coble, Y. D., Jr., Kohler, P. O., Cargille, C. M., and Ross, G. T., Production rates and metabolic clearance rates of human FSH in pre-menopausal and post-menopausal women, *J. Clin. Invest.*, 48, 359, 1969.
18. Kohler, P. O., Ross, G. T., and Odell, W. D., Metabolic clearance and production rates of human luteinizing hormone in pre- and postmenopausal woman, *J. Clin. Invest.*, 47, 38, 1968.
19. Albert, A., Human urinary gonadotropins, *Recent Prog. Horm. Res.*, 12, 266, 1956.
20. Papanicolaou, A. D., Loraine, J. A., and Dove, G. A., Endocrine function in postmenopausal women, *J. Obstet. Gynaecol. Br. Commonw.*, 76, 317, 1969.
21. Adamopoulos, D. A., Loraine, J. A. and Dove, G. A., Endocrinological studies in women approaching the menopause, *J. Obstet. Gynaecol. Br. Commonw.*, 78, 62, 1971.
22. Warren, M. P., Siris, E. S., and Petrovich, C., The influence of severe illness on gonadotropin secretion in the postmenopausal female, *J. Clin. Endocrinol. Metab.*, 45(1), 99, 1977.
23. Tagasuji, N., Gonadotropic activity of the anterior hypophysis of old female mice as demonstrated by parabiosis with young partners, *J. Fac. Sci. Univ. Tokyo Sect. 9*, 10, 193, 1963.
24. Huang, H. H., Relation of Neuroendocrine System to Loss of Reproductive Function in Aging Female Rats, Ph.D. dissertation, Michigan State University, East Lansing, 1977.
25. Huang, H. H. and Meites, J., Reproductive capacity of aging female rats, *Neuroendocrinology*, 17, 289, 1975.
26. Huang, H. H., Steger, R. W., Bruni, J., and Meites, J., Changes in patterns of sex steroid and gonadotropin secretion in aging female rats, *Endocrinology*, 103, 1855, 1978.
27. Finch, C. E., Jones, V., Wisner, J. R., Jr., Sinha, Y. N., DeVellis, J. S., and Swerdloff, R. S., Hormone production by the pituitary and testes of male C57BL/6J mice during aging, *Endocrinology*, 101, 1310, 1977.
28. Meites, J., Huang, H. H., and Riegle, G. D., Relation of the hypothalamo-pituitary-gonadal system to decline of reproductive functions in aging female rats, in *Hypothalamus and Endocrine Functions*, Labrie, F., Meites, J., and Pelletier, G., Eds., Plenum Publishing Corporation, New York, 1976, 3.
29. Meites, J., Huang, H. H., and Simpkins, J. W., Recent studies on neuroendocrine control of reproductive senescence in rats, in *The Aging Reproductive System*, Schneider, E. L., Ed., Raven Press, New York, 1978, 213.
30. Howland, B. E. and Preiss, C., Effect of aging on basal levels of serum gonadotropins, ovarian compensatory hypertrophy and hypersecretion of gonadotropins after ovariectomy in female rats, *Fertil. Steril.*, 26, 271, 1975.
31. Gosden, R. G. and Bancroft, L., Pituitary function in reproductive senescent female rats, *Exp. Gerontol.*, 11, 157, 1976.
32. Labhsetwar, A. P., Age-dependent changes in the pituitary-gonadal relationship: a study of ovarian compensatory hypertrophy, *J. Endocrinol.*, 39, 387, 1967.
33. Labhsetwar, S P., Aging changes in pituitary-ovarian relationships, *J. Reprod. Fertil. Suppl.*, 12, 99, 1970.
34. Peppler, R. D., Effects of unilateral ovariectomy on follicular development and ovulation in cycling, aged rats, *Am. J. Anat.*, 132, 423, 1971.

Table 29
THE EFFECTS OF AGE ON SERUM AND PITUITARY PROLACTIN LEVELS IN FEMALES

	Ref.
Women	
Serum prolactin declines with age in women but not men	1, 2
Serum prolactin decline parallels the fall in estrogens	3
Estrogen administration increases serum prolactin levels in postmenopausal women	4
Pituitary mammotropes decrease in size and number with age in one study and were shown not to change in another	5, 6
Sulpiride is still capable of increasing serum prolactin in postmenopausal patients	7
Pituitary responses to TRH is delayed but the surge is prolonged	1, 8
Rats	
Increased pituitary prolactin with advancing age	9, 10
High incidence of prolactin secreting pituitary tumors in old rats	11—17
Serum prolacting high in old constant-estrus (CE), and especially in anestrus (AN) rats; old pseudopregnant-like rats have prolactin levels equal to/or less than young diestrus rats	14, 18, 10
Ovariectomy lowers prolactin levels in old CE and PP, but not in old AN rats	14
Estrogen administration increases prolactin in old CE, PP, and AN rats	14, 20
L-Dopa injections cause less inhibition of prolactin release in aged rats	21

REFERENCES

1. **Yamaji, T., Shimamato, K., Ishibashi, M., Kosaka, K., and Orimo, H.,** Effect of age and sex on circulating and pituitary prolactin levels in human, *Acta Endocrinol. (Copenhagen),* 83, 711, 1976.
2. **Reyes, F. I., Winter, J. S. D., and Faiman, C.,** Pituitary-ovarian relationships preceeding menopause. I. Cross-sectional study of serum follicle stimulating hormone, luteinizing hormone, prolactin, estradiol, and progesterone levels, *Am. J. Obstet. Gynecol.,* 129(5), 557, 1977.
3. **Vekemens, M. and Robyn, C.,** Influence of age on serum prolactin levels in women and men, *Br. Med. J.,* 4, 738, 1975.
4. **Robyn, C. and Vekemans, M.,** Influence of low dose oestrogen on circulating prolactin, LH and FSH levels in post-menopausal women, *Acta Endocrinol., (Copenhagen),* 83, 9, 1976.
5. **Baker, B. L. and Ya-Yen, Y.,** An immunocytochemical study of human pituitary mammotropes from fetal life to old age, *Am. J. Anat.,* 148, 217, 1977.
6. **Kovacs, K., Ryan, N., Horvath, E., Pena, G., and Ezrin, C.,** Prolactin cells of the human pituitary gland in old age, *J. Gerontol.,* 32, 534, 1977.
7. **Dor, P., Muquardt, C., Lhermite, M., and Barkowski, A.,** Influence of corticotrophin and prolactin on steroid sex hormones and their precursors in postmenopausal women, *J. Endocrinol.,* 77(2), 263, 1978.
8. **Kuhahara, Y., Miyai, K., Hashimato, T., and Onishi, T.,** Aging and anterior pituitary function-responses of PRL, TSH and gonadotropins and TRH and LH-RH in normal subjects, *J. Geriatr.,* 12, 363, 1975.
9. **Clemens, J. A. and Meites, J.,** Neuroendocrine status of old constant-estrous rats, *Neuroendocrinology,* 7, 249, 1971.
10. **Shaar, C. J., Euker, J. S., Riegle, G. D., and Meites, J.,** Effects of castration and gonadal steroids on serum LH and prolactin in old and young rats, *J. Endocrinol. (Copenhagen)* 66, 45, 1975.
11. **Aschheim, P.,** Aging in the hypothalamic-hypophyseal ovarian axis in the rat, in *Hypothalamus, Pituitary and Aging,* Everitt, A. V. and Burgess, J. A., Eds., Charles C Thomas, Springfield, Ill., 1976, 376.
12. **Furth, J. and Clifton, K. H.,** Experimental pituitary tumors, in *The Pituitary Gland,* Vol. 2, Harris, G. W. and Donovan, B. T., Eds., Butterworth, London, 1966, 460.
13. **Huang, H. H.,** Relation of Neuroendocrine System to Loss of Reproductive Function in Aging Female Rats, Ph.D. dissertation, Michigan State University, East Lansing, 1977.
14. **Huang, H. H., Marshall, S., and Meites, J.,** Capacity of old versus young female rats to secrete LH, FSH, and prolactin, *Biol. Reprod.,* 14, 538, 1976.
15. **Huang, H. H. and Meites, J.,** Reproductive capacity of aging female rats, *Neuroendocrinology,* 17, 289, 1975.

Table 29 (continued)
THE EFFECTS OF AGE ON SERUM AND PITUITARY PROLACTIN LEVELS IN FEMALES

16. Meites, J., Relation of prolactin and estrogen to mammary tumorigenesis in the rat, *J. Natl. Cancer Inst.*, 48, 1217, 1972.
17. Wolfe, J. M., Bryan, R., and Wright, A. W., Histological observation on the anterior pituitary of old rats with particular reference to the spontaneous apparation of pituitary adenomata, *Am. J. Cancer,* 34, 352, 1938.
18. Kawashima, S., Asai, T., and Wakabayashi, K., Prolactin secretion in normal and neonatally estrogenized persistent-diestrous rats at advanced ages, in *Psychoneuroendocrinology Workshop Conf., Int. Soc. Psychoenuroendo.,* S. Karger, Basel, 1974, 128.
19. Wise, P. M., Ratner, A., and Peake, G. T, Effect of ovariectomy on serum prolactin concentrations in old and young rats, *J. Reprod. Fertil.,* 47, 363, 1976.
20. Ratner, A. and Peake, G. T., Maintenance of hyperprolactinemia by gonadal steroids in androgensterilized and spontaneously constant estrous rats, *Proc. Soc. Exp. Biol. Reprod.,* 146, 680, 1974.
21. Watkins, B. E., McKay, D. W., Meites, J., and Riegle, G. D., L-dopa effects on serum LH and prolactin in old and young female rats, *Neuroendocrinology,* 19, 331, 1975.

Table 30
NEGATIVE FEEDBACK RELATIONSHIPS IN OLD FEMALES

		Ref.
Women		
The postmenopausal endocrine profile is characterized by low steroid levels and high gonadotropin levels (see Tables 22 and 28)		
Steroid replacement in postmenopausal women lowers LH and FSH		1—6
Estradiol (50 µg infusion to young women, 400 µg to old women)	Lowered LH and FSH but higher doses needed to effect levels in old as compared to young women	7
Ethinyl estradiol (20—25 µg)	Lowered LH and FSH in peri- and postmenopausal women, but even 50 µg would not restore premenopausal levels	8
Estrogen pellets (50 mg) Serum levels obtained Estradiol (167 pg/mℓ) Estrone (110pg/mℓ)	Suppressed LH and FSH levels in young women, but even after 11 weeks gonadotropins were elevated in postmenopausal women	9
Diethylstilbesterol (15 mg/day)	Suppressed LH and FSH to approximately normal levels	10
Low doses of estrogen depress only FSH whereas higher doses depress LH and FSH		8
Rats		
Serum LH levels in old rats increase after ovariectomy but the increase is less than in young rats		11—16
Serum FSH also increases at a reduced rate and magnitude after ovariectomy		15, 16
Estrogen suppresses post-castration gonadotropin levels in old female rats		11, 15, 16
LH and FSH levels after ovariectomy increase more in old pseudopregnant rats than in old constant-estrus rats; no increase in old anestrus rats		15, 16

Table 30 (continued)
NEGATIVE FEEDBACK RELATIONSHIPS IN OLD FEMALES

REFERENCES

1. **Larsson-Cohn, U. and Wallentin, L.**, Metabolic and hormonal effects of post-menopausal oestrogen replacement treatment, *Acta Endocrinol., (Copenhagen)*, 86(3), 583, 1977; **Wallentin, L. and Larsson-Cohn, U.**, Metabolic and hormonal effects of post-menopausal oestrogen replacement treatment, *Acta Endocrinol. (Copenhagen)*, 86(3), 597, 1977.
2. **Nillius, S. J. and Wide, L.**, Effects of oestrogen on serum levels of LH and FSH, *Acta Endocrinol. (Copenhagen)*, 65, 583, 1970.
3. **Ricciardi, I., Bruni, G., Imparato, E., Marino, L., and Pesando, P.**, Effect of quinestral on plasma and urinary gonadotropins of post-menopausal women, *Horm. Metab. Res.*, 7, 323, 1975.
4. **Robyn, C. and Vekemans, M.**, Influence of low dose oestrogen on circulating prolactin, LH and FSH levels in post-menopausal women, *Acta Endocrinol. (Copenhagen)*, 83, 9, 1976.
5. **Wise, A. J., Grass, M. A., and Schlach, D. S.**, Quantitative relationships of the pituitary-gonadal axis in postmenopausal women, *J. Lab. Clin. Med.*, 81, 28, 1973.
6. **Yen, S. S. C., Tsai, C. C., Naftolin, F., Vandenberg, G., and Judd, H.**, Circulating estradiol, estrone and gonadotropin levels following the administration of orally active 17β-estradiol in postmenopausal women, *J. Clin. Endocrinol. Metab.*, 34, 671, 1972.
7. **Tsai, C. C. and Yen, S. S. C.**, Acute effects of intravenous infusion of 17β-estradiol on gonadotropin release in pre- and postmenopausal women. *J. Clin. Endocrinol. Metab.*, 32, 766, 1971.
8. **Franchimont, P., Legros, J. J., and Meurice, J.**, Effects of several estrogens on serum gonadotropin levels in postmenopausal women, *Horm. Metab. Res.*, 4, 288, 1972.
9. **Nagamani, M., Lin, T. J., McOonaugh, P. G., Watatani, H., McPherson, J. C., and Mahesh, V. B.**, Unpublished observations, cited in "Pituitary Function in the Aged," Mills, T. and Mahesh, V. B., in *Geriatric Endocrinology,* Greenblatt, R. B., Ed., Raven Press, New York, 1978, 7.
10. **Odell, W. D. and Swerdloff, R. S.**, Progesterone-induced luteinizing and follicle stimulating hormone surge in postmenopausal women: a simulated ovulatory peak, *Proc. Natl. Acad. Sci. U.S.A.*, 61, 529, 1968.
11. **Peluso, J. J., Steger, R. W., and Hafez, E. S. E.**, Regulation of LH secretion in aged female rats, *Biol. Reprod.*, 16, 212, 1977.
12. **Shaar, C. J., Euker, J. S., Riegle, G. D., and Meites, J.**, Effects of castration and gonadal steroids on serum LH and prolactin in old and young rats, *J. Endocrinol.*, 66, 45, 1975.
13. **Howland, B. E.**, Reduced gonadotropin release in response to progesterone or gonadotropin releasing hormone (GnRH) in old female rats, *Life Sci.*, 19, 219, 1976.
14. **Howland, B. E. and Preiss, C.**, Effect of aging on basal levels of serum gonadotropins, ovarian compensatory hypertrophy and hypersecretion of gonadotropins after ovariectomy in female rats, *Fertil. Steril.*, 26, 271, 1975.
15. **Huang, H. H.**, Relation of Neuroendocrine System to Loss of Reproductive Function in Aging Female Rats, Ph.D. dissertation, Michigan State University, East Lansing, 1977.
16. **Huang, H. H., Marshall, S., and Meites, J.**, Capacity of old versus young female rats to secrete LH, FSH, and prolactin, *Biol. Reprod.*, 14, 538, 1976.

Table 31
POSITIVE FEEDBACK RELATIONSHIPS IN OLD FEMALES

	Ref.
Women	
Intravenous infusions of E_2 induce small LH surges in pre- and postmenopausal women	1
Estradiol and/or 17-α-hydroxyprogesterone administration produced an increase in serum LH and FSH in postmenopausal patients	2
Progesterone can induce an ovulatory-like LH and FSH surge in estrogen primed post-menopausal or castrate women	3, 4
Rats	
Reduced positive feedback in old ovariectomized estrogen primed rats given a large dose of estrogen	5
Reduced positive feedback in old ovariectomized estrogen primed rats given a dose of progesterone	6—9

REFERENCES

1. **Tsai, C. C. and Yen, S. S. C.**, Acute effects of intravenous infusion of 17β-estradiol on gonadotrophin release in pre- and postmenopausal women, *J. Clin. Endocrinol. Metab.*, 32, 766, 1971.
2. **Kempers, R. B. and Ryan, R. J.**, Acute effects of intravenous infusion of 17β estradiol and 17α-hydroxyprogesterone on gonadotropin release, *Fertil. Steril.*, 28(6), 631, 1977.
3. **Odell, W. D. and Swerdloff, R. S.**, Progesterone-induced luteinizing and follicle stimulating hormone surge in post-menopausal women: a simulated ovulatory peak, *Proc. Natl. Acad. Sci. U.S.A.*, 61, 529, 1968.
4. **Wise, A. J., Grass, M. A., and Schlach, D. S.**, Quantitative relationships of the pituitary-gonadal axis in postmenopausal women, *J. Lab. Clin. Med.*, 81, 28, 1973.
5. **Peluso, J. J., Steger, R. W., and Hafez, E. S. E.**, Regulation of LH secretion in aged female rats, *Biol. Reprod.*, 16, 212, 1977.
6. **Howland, B. E.**, Reduced gonadotropin release in response to progesterone or gonadotropin releasing hormone (GnRH) in old female rats, *Life Sci.*, 19, 219, 1976.
7. **Gosden, R. G. and Bancroft, L.**, Pituitary function in reproductively senescent female rats, *Exp. Gerontol.*, 11, 157, 1976.
8. **Huang, H. H.**, Relation of Neuroendocrine System to Loss of Reproductive Function in Aging Female Rats, Ph.D. dissertation, Michigan State University, East Lansing, 1977.
9. **Lu, K. H., Huang, H. H., Chen, H.T., Kurcz, M., Mioduszewski, R., and Meites, J.**, Positive feedback by estrogen and progesterone on LH release in old and young rats, *Proc. Soc. Exp. Biol. Med.*, 154, 82, 1977.

Table 32
TESTICULAR CHANGES WITH AGE

I. Histology and Gross Morphology

	Ref.
Man	
No correlation between testicular weight and age after puberty	1
Thickening of the basement membrane and tunica propria of the seminiferous tubule	2
Decreased diameter or complete obliteration of the tubule lumen	2
Thinning of the germinal epithelium	2
Progressive intertubular fibrosis	3
Decreased number of capillaries	4, 5
Conflicting reports on Leydig's cells number	
No change	6
Decrease	7
Decreased lipid content of Leydig's cells after 35 years of age	8
Sertoli Cells retain high lipid content	8
Rat	
Weight of testes plateaus at 5 months then declines	9
Limited basement membrane thickening and tubular fibrosis in 22-month Wistar rats	10
Primary atrophy of testis is common	11
Mice	
No difference in testicular weight in 12- vs. 28-month-old C57BL/6J mice unless diseased	12, 13
Hamster	
Dedifferentiation and degeneration of aged testis, but sperm and normal tubules still present at 21 months	14

II. Spermatogenesis

Man	
Germ cells constantly replenished from puberty to extreme old age	
Presence of sperm in the ejaculate is decreased	15
Found in 68.5% of 60- to 70-year-old men	
Found in 59.5% of 70- to 80-year-old men	
Found in 48.0% of 80- to 90-year-old men	
Number of seminiferous tubules with spermatids is decreased	5
Found in 90% of tubules between 20- to 30-year-old men	
Found in 50% of tubules between 50- to 70-year-old men	
Found in 10% of tubules in men over 80 years	
Rats	
Most old males show no change in spermatogenesis	9
Spermatogenic cycle quantitatively similar to 40- and 20-month Wistar rats	
Testicular LH binding unchanged	10
Increase in undifferentiated spermatids intubules	10, 16

III. Steroidogenesis

Man	
Testosterone secretion	
Decline in mean circulating free testosterone (T) levels by 5th decade; mean plasma T at 55 years in low normal range (normal 5—12 ng/mℓ)	7 17—19
Increased T binding globulin (TeBG)	7, 17, 20, 21
Decline in total testosterone by 6th decade despite a considerable overlap of individual T values between old men (80—90 years) and young men	21—24, 17

Table 32 (continued)
TESTICULAR CHANGES WITH AGE

III. Steroidogenesis

	Ref.
Decreased T in spermatic vein blood	25
Decreased T production rate	26
Decreased metabolic clearance rate	20, 26, 22
Impaired Leydig's cell response to HCG with age	27, 28
Decreased T and 17β-estradiol response to gonadotropin administration although % increase over pre-injection level was similar	24
Decreased 3β-hydroxysteroid dehydrogenase activity in Leydig's cell of men over 72	29
Decreased desmolase activity	30
Androgen-binding protein in testis decreases with age	31
Decreased excretion of urinary testosterone glucoronide	32
Estrogen secretion	
Free and bound estradiol is significantly elevated in the elderly male	33
Estradiol averages between 21—24 pg/mℓ plasma in men over 65	19
	24
Estrone and estradiol both elevated because of increased peripheral androgen conversion (estradiol originates in equal amounts from testicular synthesis and from peripheral testosterone conversion)	19, 34

Rats

Decreased serum testosterone with age (3.2 ng/mℓ at 4 months and 0.64 ng/mℓ at 22 months in healthy Wistar rats)	10, 35—39
Decreased ability to synthesize testosterone and 5β-androstanediol; similar testicular response in old (20—30 month) and young (5—6 month) rats when HCG given for 7 days, although initial response decreased with age	37, 38, 40, 41
Decreased 3β-steroid dehydrogenase activity in Leydig cell of rats over 15 months; partially restored by HCG	42

Rabbit

Testosterone secretion in response to gonadotropin administration reduced in 36 month as compared to 18-month rabbit	43
Testicular perfusion with LH and FSH results in a smaller increase in T secretion in old as compared to young testes	43

Mouse

T decreases in old sick but not healthy C57BL/6J mice	13
In vivo and in vitro T output of testis after LH stimulation similar in 12- and 28-month-old C57BL/6J mice	12
No decrease in T levels in DBA/2J mice with age	44

REFERENCES

1. **Habitz, T. B.**, Testis weight and the histology of the prostate in elderly men. Analysis in an autopsy series, *Acta Pathol. Microbiol. Scand. A*, 81, 148, 1973a.
2. **Bishop, M. W. H.**, Ageing and reproduction in the male, *J. Reprod. Fertil. Suppl.*, 12, 65, 1970.
3. **Burgi, H. and Hedinger, C.**, Histologische hodenveränderugen im hohen alter, *Schweiz. Med. Wochenschr.*, 89, 1236, 1959.
4. **Sasano, N. and Ichijo, S.**, Vascular patterns of the human testis with special reference to its senile changes, *Tohoku J. Exp. Med.*, 99, 260, 1969.
5. **Suoranta, H.**, Changes in the small blood vessels of the adult human testis in relation to age and to some pathological conditions, *Virchow's Arch. Path. Anat. Physiol.*, 352, 165, 1971.
6. **Sokal, Z.**, Morphology of the human testes in various periods of life, *Folia Morphol. (Warsaw)*, 23, 102, 1964.

Table 32 (continued)
TESTICULAR CHANGES WITH AGE

7. **Harbitz, T. B.,** Morphometric studies of the Leydig Cells in elderly men with special reference to the histology of the prostate. An Analysis in an autopsy series, *Acta Pathol. Microbiol. Scand. A,* 81, 301, 1973b.
8. **Lynch, K. M. and Scott, W. W.,** The lipid content of the Leydig Cell and Sertoli Cell in the human testis as related to age, benign prostatic hyperplasia, and prostatic cancer, *J. Urol.,* 64, 767, 1950.
9. **Peng, M. T., Pi, W. P. and Peng, Y. M.,** The hypothalamic-pituitary-testicular function of the old rat, *J. Formosan Med. Assoc.,* 72, 495, 1973; *Index Medicus,* 15, 888, 1974.
10. **Steger, R. W., Peluso, J. J., Bruni, J. F., Hafez, E. S. E. and Meites, J.,** Gonadotropin binding and testicular function in old rats, *Endokrinologie,* 73, 1, 1979.
11. **Berg, B. N.,** Longevity studies in rats. II. Pathology of ageing rats, in *Pathology of Laboratory Rats and Mice,* Cotchin, E. and Roe, F. J., Eds., Davis, Philadelphia, 1967, 749.
12. **Finch, C. E., Jones, V., Wisner, J. R. Jr., Sinha, Y. N., DeVellis, J. S., and Swerdloff, R. S.,** Hormone production by the pituitary and testes of Male C57BL/6J mice during aging, *Endocrinology,* 101, 1310, 1977.
13. **Nelson, J. F., Latham, K. R., and Finch, C. E.,** Plasma testosterone levels in C57BL/6J male mice: effects of age and disease, *Acta Endocrinol. (Copenhagen),* 80, 744, 1976.
14. **Spagnoli, H. H. and Charipper, H. A.,** The effects of aging on the histoloty and cytology of the pituitary gland of the golden hamster *(Cricetus auratus)* with brief reference to simultaneous changes in the thyroid and testis, *Anat. Rec.,* 121, 117, 1955.
15. **Blum, V.,** Das problem des mannlichen klimacteriums, *Wien. Klin. Wochschr.,* 49, 1133, 1936.
16. **Humphreys, P. N.,** The histology of the testis in aging and senile rats, *Exp. Gerontol.,* 12, 27, 1977.
17. **Vermeulen, A., Reubens, R., and Verdonck, L.,** Testosterone secretion and metabolism in male senescence, *J. Clin. Endocrinol. Metab.,* 34, 730, 1972.
18. **Hallberg, M. C., Wieland, R. G., Zorn, E. M., Furst, B. H., and Wieland, J. M.,** Impaired Leydig Cell reserve and altered serum androgen binding in the aging male, *Fertil. Steril.,* 27, 812, 1976.
19. **Baker, H. W. G., Burger, H. G., Dekretser, D. M., Hudson, B., O'Conner, S., Wang, C., Micovics, A., Court, J., Dunlap, M., and Rennie, G. C.,** Changes in the pituitary-testicular system with age, *Clin. Endocrinol.,* 5, 349, 1976.
20. **Vermeulen, A., Verdonck, L., Van der Stracten, M., and Orie, N.,** Capacity of the testosterone binding globulin in human plasma and influence of specific binding of testosterone on its metabolic clearance role, *J. Clin. Endocrinol. Metab.,* 29, 1470, 1969.
21. **Pirke, K. M. and Doerr, P.,** Age-related changes and interrelationship between plasma testosterone, oestradiol, and testosterone binding globulin in normal adult males, *Acta Endocrinol. (Copenhagen),* 79, 792, 1974.
22. **Nieschlag, E., Kley, H., Wiegelmann, W., Solbach, H., and Kruskemper, H.,** Lebensalter und endokrine funktion der testes des erwachsenan mannes, *Dtsche. Med. Wochenschr.,* 98, 1281, 1973.
23. **Lewis, J. G., Ghanadian, R., and Chisholm, G. D.,** Serum 5α-dihydrotestosterone and testosterone changes with age in man, *Acta Endocrinol. (Copenhagen),* 82, 444, 1976.
24. **Longcope, C.,** Effect of HCG on plasma steroid levels in young and old men, *Steroids,* 21, 583, 1973.
25. **Hollander, N. and Hollander, V. P.,** The microdetermination of testosterone in human spermatic vein blood, *J. Clin. Endocrinol. Metab.,* 18, 966, 1958.
26. **Kent, J. Z. and Acone, A. B.,** Plasma testosterone levels and aging in males, in *Androgens in Normal and Pathological Conditions,* Vermeulen, A. and Exley, D., Eds., Excerpta Medica, Amsterdam, 1965, 31.
27. **Purvis, K., Clausen, P. F., and Hansson, V.,** Age-related changes in responsiveness of rat Leydig Cells for hCG, *J. Reprod. Fertil.,* 52(2), 379, 1978.
28. **Rubens, R., Dhont, M., and Vermeulen, A.,** Further studies on Leydig Cell function in old age, *J. Clin. Endocrinol. Metab.,* 39, 40, 1974.
29. **Piotti, L. E., Ghiringhelli, F., and Magrini, U.,** A propos de la fonction testiculaire du rieillard: observatiens histochiniques et biologiques, *Rev. Fr. Endocrinol. Clin.,* 8, 479, 1967.
30. **Axelrod, L.,** Metabolic patterns of steroid biosynthesis in young and aged human testis, *Biochim. Biophys. Acta,* 97, 551, 1965.
31. **Hsu, A. F., Nankin, N. R., and Troen, P.,** Androgen-binding protein in human testis: effect of age, in, *The Testis in Normal and Infertile Men,* Troen, P. and Nankin, H. R. Eds., Raven Press, New York, 1977, 421.
32. **Vermeulen, A.,** Urinary excretion of testosterone, in *Androgens in Normal and Pathological Conditions,* Vermeulen, A. and Exley, D., Eds., Excerpta Medica, Amsterdam, 1966, 71.

Table 32 (continued)
TESTICULAR CHANGES WITH AGE

33. **Albequx-Fernet, M., Bohler, C., and Karpas, A.**, Testicular function in the aging male, *Geriatric Endocrinology*, Greenblatt, R. B., Ed., Raven Press, New York, 1978, 201.
34. **Kley, H. K., Nieschlag, E., Wiegelmann, W., and Kruskemper, H. L.**, Sexual hormone biem alterdon mann, *Aktuel. Gerontol.*, 6, 1976.
35. **Bruni, J. F., Huang, H. H., Marshall, S., and Meites, J.**, Effects of single and multiple injections of synthetic GnRH on serum LH, FSH, and testosterone in young and old male rats, *Biol. Reprod.*, 17, 309, 1977.
36. **Ghanadian, R., Lewis, J. G., and Chisholm, G. D.**, Serum testosterone and dihydrotestosterone changes with age in rat, *Steroids*, 25, 753, 1975.
37. **Miller, A. E. and Riegle, G. D.**, Aging and testosterone secretion in the male rat, *Fed. Proc. Fed. Am. Soc. Exp. Biol.*, 36(3), 612, 1977.
38. **Miller, A. E. and Riegle, G. D.**, Serum testosterone response to HCG in young and aged male rats, *J. Gerontol.*, 33(2), 197, 1978.
39. **Riegle, G. D. and Miller, A. E.**, Aging effects on the hypothalamic-hypophyseal-gonadal control system in the rat, in *The Aging Reproductive System*, Schneider, E. L., Raven Press, New York, 1978, 159.
40. **Chan, S. W. C. and Leathem, J. H.**, Testicular function in aging rats, in *Prog. 9th Annu. Meet. Soc. Study Reproduction*, University of Pennsylvania, Philadelphia, 1976, 25.
41. **Chan, S. W. C., Leathem, J. H., and Esachi, T.**, Testicular metabolism and serum testosterone in aging male rats, *Endocrinology*, 101, 128, 1977.
42. **Leathem, J. H. and Albrecht, E. D.**, Effect of age on testis Δ^5-3β-hydroxysteroid dehydrogenase in the rats, *Proc. Soc. Exp. Biol. Med.*, 145, 1212, 1974.
43. **Ewing, L. L., Johnson, B. H., Desjardins, C., and Clegg, R.F.**, Effect of age upon the spermatogenic and steroidogenic elements of rabbit testis, *Proc. Soc. Exp. Biol. Med.*, 140, 907, 1972.
44. **Eleftheriou, B. E. and Lucas, L. A.**, Age-related changes in testes, seminal vesicles, and plasma testosterone levels in male mice, *Gerontologia*, 20, 231, 1974.

Table 33
AGE-RELATED CHANGES IN THE PROSTATE GLAND HISTOLOGY AND ANATOMY

	Ref.
Man[a]	
Increased interstitial tissue components	1, 2
Atrophy of smooth muscle (replaced by collagen)	
Deposition of pigment granules (lipofuscin) in epithelial cells	1, 2
Epithelial cells gradually change from columnar to cuboidal	3
Decreased blood supply with age principally due to periurethral arterial changes	4
Formation of laminated concretions, called corpora amylacea, in the acini; increase in size and number with age, especially after 65 years	5
Greatly increased incidence of benign hyperplasia after 50 years of age; possible genetic or environmental influences since hyperplasia very common in Caucasians and American Negroes but much less common in Chinese	3, 5, 6
Prostatic carcinoma increases greatly after age 50	
10% of men between 50—59	7
36% of men between 60—69	1, 2
50% of men over 80	
Mouse	
Disarrangement of prostatic epithelial cells	8
Increased cell rise	8
Decreased in vitro response to androgen stimulation	8
Alteration of basement membranes	9
Rats	
Atrophy; even if healthy tissue still present	10
Deposition of pigment	11, 5

[a] Changes are rarely uniform. Some lobules show more atrophic changes than others. After 60 years of age, all acini show some atrophic changes.

REFERENCES

1. **Harbitz, T. B.,** Morphometric studies of the Leydig Cells in elderly men with special reference to the histology of the prostate. An analysis in an autopsy series, *Acta Pathol. Microbiol. Scand. A,* 81, 301, 1973b.
2. **Harbitz, T. B. and Haugen, O. A.,** Histology of the prostate in elderly men, *Acta Pathol. Microbiol. Scand. A,* 80, 756, 1972.
3. **Moore, R. A.,** Male secondary sexual organs, *Cowdry's Problems of Ageing,* Lansing, A. I., Ed., William and Wilkins, Baltimore, 1952, 686.
4. **Leutert, G. and Jahn, K.,** Uber altersabhangige histologische und histochemische befunde an der prostata des menschen, *Acta Histochem.,* 37, 136, 1970.
5. **Brandes, D. and Garcia-Bunel, R.,** Aging of the male accessory organ, in *The Aging Reproductive System,* Schneider, E. L., Ed., Raven Press, New York, 1978, 127.
6. **Grayhack, J. T., Wilson, J. D., and Scherbenske, M. J.,** Benign Prostatic Hyperplasia, DHEW Publ. NO. 76-1113, National Institutes of Health, U.S. Department of Health Education and Welfare, Bethesda, 1975.
7. **Higginson, J. and Muir, C. S.,** Epidemiology, in *Cancer Medicine,* Holland, J. F. and Frei, E., Eds., Lea and Febiger, Philadelphia, 1973, 241.
8. **Franks, L. M.,** The effects of age on the structure and response to estrogens and testosterone of the mouse prostate in organ culture, *Br. J. Cancer,* 13, 59, 1959.
9. **Rowlat, C.,** Some effects of age and castration in the epithelial basal lamina of secondary sex organs in the mouse, *Gerontologia,* 16, 182, 1970.
10. **Peng, M. T., Pi, W. P., and Peng, Y. M.,** The hypothalamic-pituitary-testicular function of the old rat, *J. Formosan Med. Assoc.,* 72, 495, 1973.
11. **Mainwaring, W. I. P. and Brandes, D.,** Functional and structural changes in accessory sex organs during aging, in *Male Accessory Sex Organs: Structure and Function in Mammals,* Brandes, D., Ed., Academic Press, New York, 1974, 469.

Table 34
BIOCHEMICAL CHANGES IN THE OLD PROSTATE GLAND

	Ref.
Man	
Decreased total protein content after 60 years of age	1
Increased collagen content	1
Increased dihydrotestosterone content associated with benign hypertrophy	2
Mouse	
Decreased microsomal RNA content	3, 4
Decrease in DNA-primed RNA synthesis	3, 4
Reduced template activity for RNA polymerase	3, 4
Selective loss of nonhistone nuclear proteins	3, 4
Disaggregation of polysomes	3, 4
Increased levels of ribonuclease	3, 4
Decrease in androgen dependent citric acid synthesis	3, 4
Decreased total protein content	3, 4
Rats	
Decreased 5α-dihydrotestosterone binding in 80% of 10- to 14-month-old rats due to loss of high affinity binding sites	5
Decreased DHT binding in the ventral and lateral, but not in the dorsal and anterior prostate	6

REFERENCES

1. **Jahn, K., Leutert, G., and Rotzsch,** Age dependent morphological and biochemical examinations of the human prostate, *Z. Alternsforsch.,* 23, 323, 1971.
2. **Siiteri, P. K. and Wilson, J. D.,** Dihydrotestosterone in prostate hypertrophy, *J. Clin. Invest.,* 49, 1737, 1970.
3. **Mainwaring, W. I. P.,** The aging process in the mouse ventral prostate gland; a preliminary biochemical survey, *Gerontologia,* 13, 177, 1967.
4. **Mainwaring, W. I. P.,** Changes in the RNA metabolism of aging mouse tissue with particular reference to the prostate gland, *Biochem. J.,* 110, 79, 1968a.
5. **Shain, S. A. and Axelrod, L. R.,** Reduced high affinity 5-dihydrotestosterone receptor capacity in the ventral prostate of the aging rat, *Steroids,* 21, 801, 1973.
6. **Robinette, C. L. and Mawhinney, M. G.,** Cytosol binding of dihydrotestosterone in young and senile rats, *Fed. Proc. Fed. Am. Soc. Exp. Biol.,* 36, 3, 1977.

Table 35
AGE-RELATED CHANGES IN THE SEMINAL VESICLE

	Ref.
Man	
Decrease in fluid capacity from 5 ml in 21- to 60-year-old to 2.25 ml in man older than 60 years	1
Decrease in thickness of walls	1
Loss of mucosal folds	1
Decreased epithelial cell height	1
Replacement of muscle with connective tissue	1
Accumulation of amyloid	2
Accumulation of a "yellow pigment" in the columnar, but not in the basal cells of the epithelium	3
Mouse	
Decreased cellularity	4
Marked enlargement in 60% of C57BL mice over 28 months, due to fluid accumulation	4
Atrophic secretory epithelium	4
Rats	
Decreased weight with age	5
Fructose levels unchanged with age	6
Citric acid levels reach a maximum at 12—20 weeks, then decline gradually	6
No change in dihydrotestosterone binding up to 2 years	7
Decreased secretory activity	5

REFERENCES

1. **Nilsson, S.,** The human seminal vessicle. A morphogenetic and gross anatomic study with special regard to changes due to age and to prostatic adenoma, *Acta Chir. Scand. Suppl.,* 296, 5, 1962.
2. **Goldman, H.,** Amyloidosis of seminal vesicles and vas deferens, *Arch. Pathol.,* 75, 94, 1963.
3. **Andrew, W. G., Ed.,** *The Anatomy of Aging in Man and Animals,* Grune and Stratton, New York, 1971, 286.
4. **Finch, C. E. and Girgis, F. G.,** Enlarged seminal vesicles of senescent C57BL/6J mice, *J. Gerontol.,* 29, 134, 1974.
5. **Peng, M. T., Pi, W. P., and Peng, Y. M.,** The hypothalamic-pituitary-testicular function of the old rat, *J. Formosan Med. Assoc.,* 72, 495, 1973.
6. **Kruszel, T.,** Fructose and citric acid concentrations in the seminal vessicles of rats in relationship to age, *Endokrynol. Pol.,* 18, 287, 1967.
7. **Robinette, C. L. and Mawhinney, M. G.,** Cytosol binding of dihydrotestosterone in young and senile rats, *Fed. Proc. Fed. Am. Soc. Exp. Biol.,* 36, 3, 1977.

Table 36
EFFECTS OF ADVANCING AGE ON BASAL AND
POSTCASTRATION GONADOTROPIN SECRETION BY THE
MALE (NEGATIVE FEEDBACK)

	Ref.
Man	
Variable results have been reported	
Increased LH, but normal FSH levels	1, 2
Increased LH and FSH; FSH rise usually greater than the LH rise	3—7
Subpopulations exist in men over 50 with 1 group showing elevated LH and FSH and another group showing depressed LH and FSH levels	8
Increased urinary gonadotropins in men over 55	9
Increased urinary FSH/LH ratio although LH and FSH both rise significantly with age	10
Increased pituitary LH in old men	11
Rats	
Decreased serum LH and FSH	12—14
Impaired postcastration rise of LH	13
Old rats more responsive to negative feedback effect of low testosterone doses	13
Decreased pituitary LH levels with age	12, 15, 16
Decreased pituitary FSH levels with age	
Mice	
No differences in basal LH and FSH between 12-month and 28-month C57BL/6J mice	17
Attenuated postcastration LH rise but unimpaired FSH rise in 28- vs. 12-month-old C57BL/6J mice	17

REFERENCES

1. Schalch, D. D., Parlow, A. F., Boon, R. C., and Reichlin, S., Measurement of human LH in plasma by radioimmunoassay, *J. Clin. Invest.*, 47, 665, 1968.
2. Nieschlag, E., Kley, H., Wiegelmann, W., Solbach, H., and Kurskemper, H., Lebensalter and endokrine funktion der testes des erwachsenan mannes, *Dtsche Med. Wochenschr.*, 98, 1281, 1973.
3. Rubens R., Dhont, M., and Vermeulen, A., Further studies on Leydig Cell function in old age, *J. Clin. Endocrinol. Metab.*, 39, 40, 1974.
4. Baker, H. W. G., Burger, H. G., Dekretser, D. M., Hudson, B., O'Conner, S., Wang, C., Micovics, A., Court, J., Dunlop, M., and Rennie, G. C., Changes in the pituitary-testicular system with age, *Clin. Endocrinol.*, 5, 349, 1976.
5. Mazzi, C., Riva, L. R., and Bernasconi, D., Gonadotropins and plasma testosterone in senescence, in *The Endocrine Function of the Human Testes*, Vol. 2, James, V., Serio, M., and Martini, L., Academic Press, New York, 1974, 51.
6. Greenblatt, R. B., Oettinger, M., and Bohler, C. S. S., Estrogen-androgen levels in aging men and women, *J. Am. Geriatr. Soc.*, 24, 173, 1976.
7. Stearns, E. L., MacDonald, J. A., Kauffman, B. J., Lucman, T. S., Winters, J. S., and Faiman, C., Declining testicular function with age, *Am. J. Med.*, 57, 761, 1974.
8. Faiman, C. and Winter, D. S., Diurnal cycles in plasma FSH, testosterone, and cortisol in man, *J. Clin. Endocrinol.*, 33, 186, 1971.
9. Pedersen-Bjergaard, K. and Jonnesen, M., Sex hormone analysis: excretion of sexual hormones by normal males, impotent males, polyarthritic, and prostatics, *Acta Med. Scand. Suppl.*, 213, 284, 1948.
10. Albert, A., Randall, R. V., Smith, R. A., and Johnson, C. E., Urinary excretion of gonadotropins as a function of age, in *Hormones and the Aging Process*, Engle, E. T. and Pincus, G., Eds., Academic Press, New York, 1956, 49.
11. Ryank, R. J., The luteinizing hormone content of human pituitaries. I. Variations with sex and age, *J. Clin. Endocrinol.*, 22, 300, 1965.
12. Riegle, G. D. and Meites, J., Effects of aging on LH and prolactin after LHRH, L-dopa methyldopa, and stress in the male rat, *Proc. Soc. Exp. Biol. Med.*, 151, 507, 1976.
13. Shaar, C. J., Euker, J. S., Riegle, G. D., and Meites, J., Effects of castration and gonadal steroids on serum LH and prolactin in old and young rats, *J. Endocrinol.*, 66, 45, 1975.
14. Bruni, J. F., Huang, H. H., Marshall, S., and Meites, J. Effects of single and multiple injections of synthetic GnRH on serum LH, FSH, and testosterone in young and old male rats, *Biol. of Reprod.*, 17, 309, 1977.

Table 36 (continued)
EFFECTS OF ADVANCING AGE ON BASAL AND POSTCASTRATION GONADOTROPIN SECRETION BY THE MALE (NEGATIVE FEEDBACK)

15. Peng, M. T., Pi, W. P., and Peng, Y. M., The hypothalamic-pituitary-testicular function of the old rat, *J. Formosan Med. Assoc.*, 72, 495, 1973.
16. Riegle, G. D., Meites, J., Miller, A. E., and Wood, S. M., Effect of aging on hypothalamic LH-releasing and prolactin inhibiting activities and pituitary responsiveness to LHRH in the male laboratory rat, *J. Gerontol.*, 32, 13, 1977.
17. Finch, C. E., Jonec, V., Wisner, J. R., Jr., and Sinha, Y. N., Hormone production by the pituitary and testes of male C57BL/6J mice during aging, *Endocrinology*, 101, 1310, 1977.

Table 37
PITUITARY RESPONSE TO GnRH IN THE AGING MALE

	Ref.
Man	
No difference in LH and FSH levels after exogenous LHRH stimulation	1, 2
Absolute magnitude of pituitary response unchanged, but relative response decreased	3, 4
Rats	
Decreased absolute LH and FSH response, but similar relative increase in old male rats given a single GnRH injection	5
Diminished LH and FSH response to multiple GnRH injections	5
No difference in LH and FSH response to multiple GnRH injections in old vs. young rats	6, 7
Diminished in vitro LH and FSH response to GnRH	6, 8
Decreased pituitary LH levels in the old male rats, not affected by LHRH stimulation	6, 8
Mouse	
No age related difference in LH and FSH after LHRH stimulation in vitro or in vivo	9

REFERENCES

1. Vermeulen, A., Reubens, R., and Verdonck, L., Testosterone secretion and metabolism in male senescence, *J. Cin. Endocrinol. Metab.*, 34, 730, 1972.
2. Mazzi, C., Riva, L. R., and Bernasconi, D., Gonadotropins and plasma testosterone in senescence, in *The Endocrine Function of the Human Testes*, Vol. 2, James, V., Serio, M., and Martini, L., Academic Press, New York, 1974, 51.
3. Rubens, R., Dhont, M., and Vermeulen, A., Further studies on Leydig Cell function in old age, *J. Clin. Endocrinol. Metab.*, 39, 40, 1974.
4. Hashimoto, T., Miyai, K., Izumi, K., and Kumahara, Y., Gonadotropin response to synthetic LHRH in normal subjects correlation between LH and FSH, *J. Clin. Endocrinol. Metab.*, 37, 910, 1973.
5. Bruni, J. F., Huang, H. H., Marshall, S., and Meites, J., Effects of single and multiple injections of synthetic GnRH on serum LH, FSH, and testosterone in young and old male rats, *Biol. Reprod.*, 17, 309, 1977.
6. Riegle, G. D. and Meites, J., Effects of aging on LH and prolactin after LHRH, L-dopa, methyldopa and stress in the male rat, *Proc. Soc. Exp. Biol. Med.*, 151, 507, 1976.
7. Miller, A. E., and Riegle, G. D., Serum LH levels following multiple LHRH injections in aging rats, *Proc. Soc. Exp. Biol. Med.* 175(3), 494, 1978.
8. Riegle, G. D., Meites, J., Miller, A. E., and Wood, S. M., Effect of aging on hypothalamic LH-releasing and prolactin inhibiting activities and pituitary responsiveness to LHRH in the male laboratory rat, *J. Gerontol.*, 32, 13, 1977.
9. Finch, C. E., Jonec, V., Wisner, J. R., Jr., Sinha, Y. N., DeVellis, J. S., and Swerdloff, R. S., Hormone production by the pituitary and testes of male C57BL/6J mice during aging, *Endocrinology* 101, 1310, 1977.

ADRENAL MEDULLARY HORMONES AND SYMPATHETIC NEUROTRANSMITTER

J. T. Herlihy and J. Severson

Table 1
EFFECT OF AGE ON CATECHOLAMINE CONTENT AND METABOLISM

Tissue	Species	Findings	Ref.
Adrenal	Human, rat	Catecholamine content increases	1—5
	Rat	The activities of tyrosine hydroxylase, dopamine-β-hydroxylase, and phenylethanolamine-N-methyltransferase increase	4
Plasma	Human	Resting norepinephrine levels as well as elevation in the levels observed with stress increase	6—8
		Dopamine-β-hydroxylase activity has been reported to either remain unchanged or increase	8, 9
Adipose	Human, rat	Endogenous catecholamine content as well as the uptake of administered epinephrine do not change	10, 11
Cardiac muscle	Human, rat, rabbit, cat, mouse	Norepinephrine content decreases	12—15
		The uptake of administered epinephrine does not change, whereas norepinephrine uptake has been reported to either decrease or remain unchanged	11, 13, 16
		Monamine oxidase activity has been reported to increase or remain unchanged	13, 17—19
Thyroid	Mouse	The number of interfollicular sympathetic nerve terminals decreases	20
Vascular wall	Human	Vascular catecholamine fluorescence in human gingival tissue decreases with the age of the subject	21, 22

REFERENCES

1. Descovich, G. C., Gritti, F. M., Marangolo, M., and Bernardi, P., Senile hyperfunction of the adrenal medulla, *Schweiz. Med. Wochenschr.*, 100, 1689, 1970.
2. Eidelman, M. M., Maximov, S. V., and Tyagileva, V. P., The influence of vitamin B on age peculiarities of the sympathetoadrenal system functional state, Abstr. 9th Int. Cong. Gerontology, Kiev, 1972, 19.
3. Giorgino, R., Scardapane, R., Nardelli, G. M., and Tafaro, E., Adrenal glands and aging: aspects of medullary activity, *Folia Endocrinol.*, 22, 215, 1969.
4. Kvetňansky, R., Jahnová, E., Torda, T., Štrbák, V., Baláž, V., and Macho, L., Changes of adrenal catecholamines and their synthesizing enzymes during ontogenesis and aging in rats, *Mech. Ageing Dev.*, 7, 209, 1978.
5. Sotgiu, G., Cussini, G., Chierici, F., and Vancini, B., Senile adrenal hypermedullism, *Panminerva Med.*, 2, 1, 1960.
6. Christensen, N. J., Plasma noradrenaline and adrenaline in patients with thyrotoxicosis and myxoedema, *Clin. Sci. Mol. Med.*, 45, 163, 1973.
7. Ziegler, M. G., Lake, C. R., and Kopin, I. J., Plasma noradrenaline increases with age, *Nature (London)*, 261, 333, 1976.
8. Palmer, G. J., Ziegler, M. G., and Lake, C. R., Response of norepinephrine and blood pressure to stress increases with age, *J. Gerontol.*, 33, 482, 1978.

Table 1 (continued)
EFFECT OF AGE ON CATECHOLAMINE CONTENT AND METABOLISM

9. **Freedman, L. S., Ohuchi, T., Goldstein, M., Axelrod, F., Fish, I., and Dancis, J.,** Changes in serum dopamine-β-hydroxylase activity with age, *Nature (London),* 236, 310, 1972.
10. **Stuchlíková, E., Jelinková, M., Hrůza, Z., and Hrušková, J.,** The level of endogenous catecholamines in adipose tissue of old and obese persons, *Exp. Gerontol.,* 2, 57, 1967.
11. **Jelinková, M., Hrůza, Z., and Erdošova, R.,** The effect of the application of epinephrine on its level in the adipose tissue in rats of different age, *Exp. Gerontol.,* 2, 63, 1967.
12. **Frolkis, V. V., Bezrukov, V. V., Bogatskaya, L. N., Verkhratsky, N. S., Zamostian, V. P., Schevtchuk, V. G., and Shtchegoleva, I. V.,** Catecholamines in the metabolism and functions regulation in ageing, *Gerontologia,* 16, 129, 1970.
13. **Gey, K. F., Burkard, W. P., and Pletscher, A.,** Variation of the norepinephrine metabolism of the rat heart with age, *Gerontologia,* 11, 1, 1965.
14. **Roberts, J. and Goldberg, P. B.,** Changes in basic cardiovascular activities during the lifetime of the rat, *Exp. Aging Res.,* 2, 487, 1976.
15. **Weisfeldt, M. L.,** Function of cardiac muscle in aging rat, *Adv. Exp. Med. Biol.,* 61, 95, 1975.
16. **Hody, G., Jonec, V., Viliam, J., Morton-Smith, W., and Finch, C. E.,** Norepinephrine uptake by the myocardium of the senescent mouse in vitro, *J. Gerontol.,* 30, 275, 1975.
17. **Novick, W. J.,** The effect of age and thyroid hormones on the monamine oxidase of rat heart, *Endocrinology,* 69, 55, 1961.
18. **Studer, A., Baumgartner, H. R., and Reber, K.,** Histochemical evidence of monamine oxidase activity in rats of different ages, *Histochemie,* 4, 43, 1964.
19. **Lai, F. M., Berkowitz, B., and Spector, S.,** Influences of age on brain vascular and cardiovascular monamine oxidase activity in the rat, *Life Sci.,* 22, 2051, 1978.
20. **Melander, A., Sundler, F., and Westgren, U.,** Sympathetic innervation of the thyroid: variation with species and with age, *Endocrinology,* 96, 102, 1975.
21. **Frewin, D. B., Hume, W. R., Waterson, J. G., and Whelan, R. F.,** The histochemical localisation of sympathetic nerve endings in human gingival blood vessels, *Aust. J. Exp. Biol. Med. Sci.* 49, 573, 1971.
22. **Waterson, J. G., Frewin, D. B., and Soltys, J. S.,** Age-related differences in catecholamine fluorescence of human vascular tissue, *Blood Vessels,* 11, 79, 1974.

Table 2
EFFECT OF AGE ON THE RESPONSE OF TARGET ORGANS TO CATECHOLAMINE

Tissue	Species	Findings	Ref.
Whole organism	Rat	No change was observed in the plasma pyruvate and lactate response to infused epinephrine	1
	Rat	Older rats exhibit a smaller maximal oxygen consumption due to epinephrine administration than younger rats	2
Adipose	Human, rat	The lipolytic response of the organism to in vivo administration of epinephrine decreases	3, 4
	Human, rat	The epinephrine-stimulated lipolysis of isolated fat tissue and adipocytes has been reported to increase, decrease, or remain unchanged	3—12
	Rat	The biphasic response to epinephrine observed with the fat cells from young rats becomes a monophasic response in cells from old rats	6
	Rat	No change in the epinephrine-stimulated lipase enzymatic activity has been observed; the epinephrine-stimulated adenylate cyclase activity has been reported to decrease or remain unchanged	11, 13, 14
	Rat	The lipolytic response of old rats to in vivo administration of norepinephrine decreases	15
	Human, rat	The norepinephrine-stimulated lipolysis of isolated adipose tissue and cells decreases	10, 16—18
	Rat	The norepinephrine-stimulated adenylate cyclase activity of isolated adipocytes remains unchanged	16
Cardiovascular system	Human, rat, rabbit, cat	Some studies report a general increase in the sensitivity of the cardiovascular system to administered epinephrine and norepinephrine; one study, however, reports a decrease	19—22
Myocardium	Human, dog	The aged myocardium exhibits a decreased chronotropic response to norepinephrine and isoproterenol	23, 24
	Rat	The aged myocardium exhibits a decreased inotropic response to norepinephrine and isoproterenol	25
	Human	The sympathetic drive to the heart under strain of exercise diminishes	26
	Rat	The severity of isoproterenol-induced heart damage increases	27
Vascular smooth muscle	Rat	The aorta and microcirculation exhibit a decreased contractile response to norepinephrine	21, 28
		Aortas from old animals exhibit a decreased lipolytic response to epinephrine	29
		The aortas from old animals exhibit a decreased response in oxygen consumption to epinephrine	30

Table 2 (continued)
EFFECT OF AGE ON THE RESPONSE OF TARGET ORGANS TO CATECHOLAMINE

Tissue	Species	Findings	Ref.
	Rabbit	The β-receptor stimulated relaxation of isolated thoracic aorta and pulmonary artery decreases until the animal is 2 years of age	31, 32
Red blood cell	Rat	Neither the number of β-adrenergic receptors nor the catecholamine-stimulated adenylate cyclase activity changes	33—35
Lymphocyte	Human	Both the number and concentration of β-adrenergic receptors decreases	36, 37
Liver	Rat	Epinephrine-stimulated adenylate cyclase activity decreases	38
Salivary gland	Rat	Isoproterenol-stimulated DNA synthesis decreases	39
Tracheal smooth muscle	Rat	The β-receptor relaxation of tracheal smooth muscle has been reported to either remain unchanged or decrease	32, 40

REFERENCES

1. **Hruza, Z. and Jelinkova, M.**, Carbohydrate metabolism after epinephrine, glucose and stress in young and old rats, *Exp. Gerontol.*, 1, 139, 1965.
2. **Bunnell, I. L. and Griffith, F. R., Jr.**, Age and the calorigenic response to subcutaneously administered adrenaline in the rat, *Am. J. Physiol.*, 138, 669, 1943.
3. **Jelinkova-Tenorova, M. and Hruza, Z.**, The effect of epinephrine on fat metabolism in old rats, *Gerontologia*, 7, 168, 1963.
4. **Stuchlikova, E., Hruskova, J., Hruza, Z., Jelinkova, M., Nova, P., and Soukupova, K.**, The effect of adrenaline on lipolysis and glycogenolysis in relation to age and stress, *Exp. Gerontol.*, 2, 15, 1966.
5. **Altschuler, H., Lieberson, M., and Spitzer, J. J.**, Effect of body weight on free fatty acid release by adipose tissue in vitro, *Experientia*, 18, 91, 1962.
6. **Miller, E. A. and Allen, D. O.**, Hormone-stimulated lipolysis in isolated fat cells from "young" and "old" rats, *J. Lipid Res.*, 14, 331, 1973.
7. **Benjamin, W., Gellhorn, A., Wagner, M., and Kundel, H.**, Effect of aging on lipid composition and metabolism in the adipose tissue of the rat, *Am. J. Physiol.*, 201, 540, 1961.
8. **Dury, A.**, Relative insensitivity of adipose tissue of old rats to lipolytic action of epinephrine, *J. Gerontol.*, 16, 389, 1961.
9. **James, R. C., Burns, T. W., and Chase, G. R.**, Lipolysis of human adipose tissue cells: influence of donor factors, *J. Lab. Clin. Med.*, 77, 254, 1971.
10. **Mosinger, B., Kuhn, E., and Kujalova, V.**, Action of adipokinetic hormones on human adipose tissue in vitro, *J. Lab. Clin. Med.*, 66, 380, 1965.
11. **Masoro, E. J., Bertrand, H., Liepa, G., and Yu, B. P.**, Analysis and exploration of age-related changes in mammalian structure and function, *Fed. Proc. Fed. Am. Soc. Exp. Biol.*, 38, 1956, 1979.
12. **Zinder, O. and Shapiro, B.**, Effect of cell size on epinephrine- and ACTH-induced fatty acid release from isolated fat cells, *J. Lipid Res.*, 12, 91, 1971.
13. **Jelinkova, M., Stuchlikova, E., and Smrz, M.**, The effect of theophylline and adrenaline on the lipolytic response of rats of different age, *Exp. Gerontol.*, 5, 257, 1970.
14. **Cooper, B. and Gregerman, R. I.**, Hormone-sensitive fat cell adenylate cyclase in the rat. Influences of growth, cell size, and aging, *J. Clin. Invest.*, 57, 161, 1976.
15. **Jelinkova, M. and Hruza, Z.**, Decreased effect of norepinephrine and growth hormone on the release of free fatty acids in old rats, *Physiol. Bohemoslov.*, 13, 327, 1964.
16. **Hartman, A. D., Cohen, A. I., Richane, C. J., and Hsu, T.**, Lipolytic response and adenyl cyclase activity of rat adipocytes as related to cell size, *J. Lipid Res.*, 12, 498, 1971.
17. **Berger, M., Preiss, H., Hesse-Wortmann, C., and Gries, F. A.**, Age dependence of fat cell size and lipolytic activity in human adipose tissue, *Gerontologia*, 17, 312, 1971.
18. **Nakano, J., Gin, A. C., and Ishii, T.**, Effect of age on norepinephrine-, ACTH-, theophylline- and dibutryl cyclic AMP-induced lipolysis in isolated rat fat cells, *J. Gerontol.*, 26, 8, 1971.

Table 2 (continued)
EFFECT OF AGE ON THE RESPONSE OF TARGET ORGANS TO CATECHOLAMINE

19. Bender, A. D., The influence of age on the activity of catecholamines and related therapeutic agents, *J. Am. Geriatr. Soc.*, 18, 220, 1970.
20. Frolkis, V. V., The autonomic nervous system in the aging organism, *Triangle Engl. Ed.*, 8, 22, 1969.
21. Hruza, Z. and Zweifach, B. W., Effect of age on vascular reactivity to catecholamines in rats, *J. Gerontol.*, 22, 469, 1967.
22. Kelliher, G. J. and Stoner, S., Cardiovascular effects of norepinephrine (NE) and phenylephrine (PE) in Fischer 344 rats of different ages, *Gerontol. Soc.*, 18, 88, 1978.
23. Lakatta, E. G., Perspectives on the aged myocardium, *Adv. Exp. Med. Biol.*, 97, 147, 1978.
24. Yin, F. C., Spurgeon, H. A., Raizes, G. S., Greene, H. L., Weisfeldt, M. L., and Shock, N. W., Age associated decrease in chronotropic response to isoproterenol, *Circulation Suppl.*, 54(2), 167, 1976.
25. Lakatta, E. G., Gerstenblith, G., Angell, C. S., Shock, N. W., and Weisfeldt, M. L., Diminished inotropic response of aged myocardium to catecholamines, *Circ. Res.*, 36, 262, 1975.
26. Conway, J., Wheeler, R., and Sannerstedt, R., Sympathetic nervous activity during exercise in relation to age, *Cardiovasc. Res.*, 5, 577, 1971.
27. Rona, G., Chappel, C. I., Balazs, T., and Gaudry, R., The effect of breed, age, and sex on the myocardial necrosis produced by isoproterenol in the rat, *J. Gerontol.*, 14, 169, 1959.
28. Tuttle, R. S., Age-related changes in the sensitivity of rat aortic strips to norepinephrine and associated chemical and structural alterations, *J. Gerontol.*, 21, 510, 1966.
29. Jelinkova, M., Stuchlikova, E., Hruza, Z., Deyl, Z., and Smrz, M., Hormone-sensitive lipolytic activity of the aorta of different age groups of rats, *Exp. Gerontol.*, 7, 263, 1972.
30. Nakatari, M., Sasaki, T., Miyazaki, T., and Nakamura, M., Synthesis of phospholipid, *J. Atheroscler. Res.*, 7, 759, 1967.
31. Fleisch, J. H. and Hooker, C. S., The relationship between age and relaxation of vascular smooth muscle in the rabbit and rat, *Circ. Res.*, 38, 243, 1976.
32. Fleisch, J. H., Maling, H. M., and Brodie, B. B., Beta-receptor activity in aorta, *Circ. Res.*, 26, 151, 1970.
33. Bilezikian, J. P. and Gammon, D. E., The effect of age on Beta-adrenergic receptors and adenylate cyclase activity in rat erythrocytes, *Life Sci.*, 23, 253, 1978.
34. Bylund, D. B., Tellez-Inon, M. T., and Hollenberg, M. D., Age-related parallel decline in Beta-adrenergic receptors, adenylate cyclase and phosphodiesterase activity in rat erythrocyte membranes, *Life Sci.*, 21, 403, 1977.
35. Sheppard, H. and Burghardt, C. R., Age-dependent changes in the adenylate cyclase and phosphodiesterase activity of rat erythrocytes, *Biochem. Pharmacol.*, 22, 427, 1973.
36. Schocken, D. D. and Roth, G. S., Reduced β-adrenergic receptor concentrations in ageing man, *Nature (London)*, 267, 856, 1977.
37. Schocken, D. D. and Roth, G. S., Age-associated loss of Beta-adrenergic receptors from human lymphocytes in vivo, *Adv. Exp. Med. Biol.*, 97, 273, 1978.
38. Bitensky, M. W., Russell, V., and Blanco, M., Independent variation of glucagon and epinephrine responsive components of hepatic adenyl cyclase as a function of age, sex and steroid hormones, *Endocrinology*, 86, 154, 1970.
39. Roth, G. S. and Adelman, R. C., Possible changes in tissue sensitivity in the age-dependent stimulation of DNA synthesis in vivo, *J. Gerontol.*, 28, 298, 1973.
40. Aberg, G., Adler, G., and Ericsson, E., The effect of age on β-adrenoceptor activity in tracheal smooth muscle, *Br. J. Pharmacol.*, 47, 181, 1973.

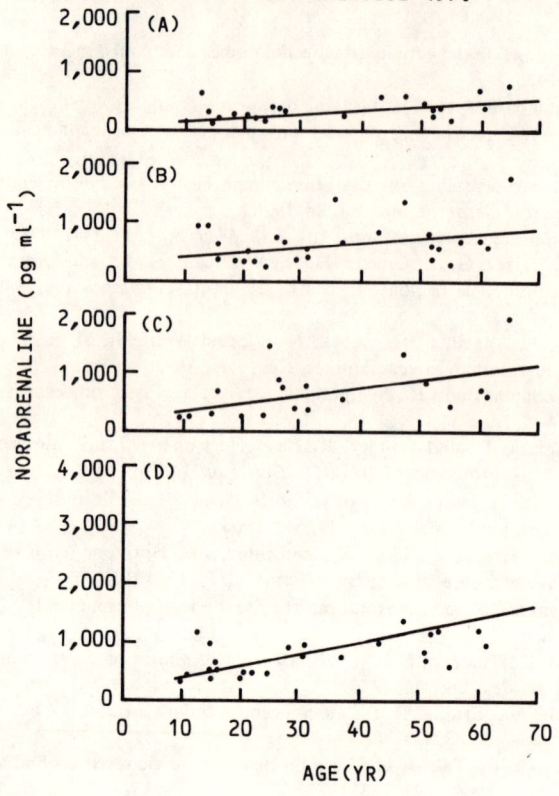

FIGURE 1. Plasma noradrenaline. (From Ziegler, M. G., Lake, C. R., and Kopin, I. J., *Nature (London)*, 261, 333, 1976. With permission.)

Table 3
URINARY MONOAMINE METABOLITES

Compound	Age group (years)	Sex (No.[a])	Urine vol (ml/24 hr)	Total 5-HIAA (ml/24 hr)	5-HIAA (μg/ml urine)
5-Hydroxyindole acetic acid (5-HIAA)	20—40	M + F (18)	1555	14.1 ± 5.2	9.07
	>80	F (30)	740	7.6 ± 2.5[b]	10.27

[a] Subjects were "healthy" and not given foods high in serotonin.
[b] Different from younger group, $P<0.001$.

From Foldes, I., Csötöntöle, L., and Beregi, E., *Gerontol. Clin.*, 7, 92, 1965. With permission.

PANCREATIC HORMONES

E. J. Masoro

Table 1
SERUM INSULIN LEVELS

Species	Findings	Ref.
Human	Some studies indicate that serum immunoreactive insulin levels increase with age in postabsorptive or fasting people; in another study this was not found to be the case	1, 2, 8
	Old people have higher postprandial insulin levels than do young people	3
	The serum immunoreactive proinsulin: immunoreactive insulin ratio increases with age	4, 5
Rats	The plasma insulin level of fasted 24-month-old rats is lower than that of fasted 8- to 12-month-old rats	6
	The concentration of insulin in the portal vein blood of fed or fasted rats decreases by 50—60% from 12 months of age to 24 months of age	7

REFERENCES

1. Chlouverakis, C., Jarrett, R. J., and Keen, H., Glucose tolerance, age, and circulating insulin, *Lancet*, 1, 806, 1967.
2. Kosaka, K., Haguro, R., and Odagiri, R., Aging and pancreatic secretion, *Clin. Endocrinol.*, 17, 863, 1969.
3. Metz, R., Surmaczynska, B., Berger, S., and Sobel, G., Glucose tolerance, plasma insulin, and free fatty acids in elderly subjects, *Ann. Intern. Med.*, 64, 1042, 1966.
4. Duckworth, W. C. and Kitabchi, A. E., Direct measurement of plasma proinsulin in normal and diabetic subjects, *Am. J. Med.*, 53, 418, 1972.
5. Duckworth, W. D. and Kitabchi, A. E., The effect of age on plasma proinsulin-like material after oral glucose, *J. Lab. Clin. Med.*, 88, 359, 1976.
6. Gatsko, G. G., Insulin activity of the blood plasma in adult and aged rats, determined by the manometric method, *Probl. Endokrinol. Gormonoter.*, 12, 95, 1966.
7. Freeman, C., Karoly, K., and Adelman, R. C., Impairments in availability of insulin to liver in vivo and in binding of insulin to purified hepatic plasma membrane during aging, *Biochem. Biophys. Res. Commun.*, 54, 1573, 1973.
8. Dudl, R. J. and Ensinck, J. W., Insulin and glucagon relationships during aging in man, *Metabolism*, 26, 33, 1977.

Table 2
EFFECTS OF AGE ON THE SECRETION OF INSULIN BY BETA CELLS OF PANCREATIC ISLETS OF LANGERHANS

Species	Findings	Ref.
Human	From studies in which plasma glucose was maintained constant at various concentrations for 2 hr, it was found that age does not influence insulin secretion in response to 300 mg glucose per dℓ but that with concentrations of glucose lower than this, the insulin secretion response is decreased in old subjects	1
	The response of serum insulin to oral glucose tolerance test in some studies indicates no age-related change in the insulin secretion system, but in one study it was found that after 50 years of age serum insulin response levels are increased and the data of another study were interpreted to indicate some impairment in the responsiveness of the insulin secretion system to the glucose stimulus	2—7
	The changes in serum insulin in the intravenous glucose tolerance test in one study indicate a decreased insulin secretion response with age; in other studies no effect of age on the insulin secretion response was noted	3, 8, 9, 20
	A combined oral glucose-intravenous tolbutamide, glucagon challenge resulted in a more sluggish, but more persistant increase in serum immunoreactive insulin levels in old subjects than in young subjects	10—13
	The response to the administration of a 20 g pulse of glucose intravenously indicates that age does not influence the ability to secrete insulin	14
	In one study, the response of the insulin secretion system to intravenously administered arginine was a decrease with increasing age and in another study, increasing age was found not to have an effect	15, 20
Rats	Rats 12 months of age and older respond to intravenously administered glucose with higher blood insulin levels than do those 3 months of age or younger	16—18
	The insulin secretion response to intragastrically administered glucose is delayed with increasing age	19
	The insulin secretion response of perifused Islets from 24-month-old rats to an increase in glucose concentration shows a different temporal pattern than that observed with Islets from 2-month-old rats	19

Table 2 (continued)
EFFECTS OF AGE ON THE SECRETION OF INSULIN BY BETA CELLS OF PANCREATIC ISLETS OF LANGERHANS

REFERENCES

1. Andres, R. and Tobin, J. D., Aging and the disposition of glucose, *Adv. Exp. Med. Biol.*, 61, 239, 1975.
2. Danowski, T. S., Tsai, C. T., Morgan, C. R., Sieracki, J. C., Alley, R. A., Robbins, T. J., Sabeh, G., and Sunder, J. H., Serum growth hormone and insulin in females without glucose intolerance, *Metabolism*, 18, 811, 1969.
3. Malherbe, C., DeGasparo, M., Berthet, P., DeHertogh, R., and Hoet, J. J., The pattern of plasma insulin response to glucose in patients with a previous myocardial infarction — the respective effects of age and disease, *Eur. J. Clin. Invest.*, 1, 265, 1971.
4. Martin, F. I. R., Pearson, M. J., and Stocks, A. E., Glucose tolerance and insulin insensitivity, *Lancet*, 1, 1285, 1968.
5. Welborn, T. A., Rubenstein, A. H., Haslan, R., and Fraser, R., Normal insulin response to glucose, *Lancet*, 1, 280, 1966.
6. Welborn, T. A., Stenhouse, N. S., and Johnstone, C. G., Factors determining serum-insulin response in a population sample, *Diabetologia*, 5, 263, 1969.
7. O'Sullivan, J. B., Mahan, C. M., Freedlander, A. E., and Williams, R. F., Effect of age on carbohydrate metabolism, *J. Clin. Endocrinol. Metab.*, 33, 619, 1971.
8. Crockford, P. M., Barbeck, R. J., and Williams, R. H., Influence of age on intravenous glucose tolerance and serum immunoreactive insulin, *Lancet*, 1, 465, 1966.
9. Feldman, J. M. and Plank, J. W., Effect of age on intravenous glucose tolerance and insulin secretion, *J. Am. Geriatr. Soc.*, 34, 1, 1976.
10. Jaffe, B. I., Binik, A. I., and Jackson, W. P. U., Insulin reserve in elderly subjects, *Lancet*, 1, 1292, 1969.
11. Kosaka, K., Studies on the relation between aging and endocrine secretion of pancreas and on the impairment of carbohydrate tolerance in the aged, *Folia Endocrinol. Jap.*, 45, 796, 1969.
12. Kosaka, K., Haguro, R., and Odagiri, R., Aging and pancreatic secretion, *Clin. Endocrinol.*, 17, 863, 1969.
13. Shimizu, Y., Hiramatsu, K., Miyake, K., Tomiyama, Y., Shimono, M., Fuchimoto, T., Sasaki, M., Harada, H., and Kibata, M., Insulin secretion and pancreatic exocrine secretion in the aged, *Jpn. J. Geriatr. Nihon Ronen Igakkai Zasshi*, 13, 8, 1976.
14. Palmer, J. and Ensinck, J. W., Acute-phase insulin secretion and glucose tolerance in young and aged normal men and diabetic patients, *J. Clin. Endocrinol. Metab.*, 41, 498, 1975.
15. Yoshie, Y., Suzuki, H., Takemura, Y., and Kobayashi, S., Proceedings: effects of aging on arginine induction of insulin secretion, *Folia Endocrinol. Jap.*, 50, 223, 1974.
16. Gommers, A. and deGasparo, M., Variation de l'insulinemie en fonction de l'age chez le rat male, *Gerontologia*, 18, 176, 1972.
17. Gommers, A., Jeanjeau, M., and Dehez-Delhaye, M., Problems in glycoregulation and senescence, *Probl. Actuels Endocrinol. Nutr. Ser.*, 17, 193, 1973.
18. Zierden, E., Wayner, H., and Hauss, W. H., Effect of run-training and run-stress on glucose assimilation and insulin release in rats of different age, *Aktval Vopr. Gerontol.*, 6, 47, 1976.
19. Gold, G., Karoly, K., Freeman, C., and Adelman, R. C., A possible role for insulin in the altered capability for hepatic enzyme adaptation during aging, *Biochem. Biophys. Res. Commun.*, 73, 1003, 1976.
20. Dudl, R. J. and Ensinck, J. W., Insulin and glucagon relationships during aging in man, *Metabolism*, 26, 33, 1977.

Table 3
EFFECTS OF AGE ON THE INTERACTIONS OF INSULIN WITH TARGET TISSUES

Species	Findings	Ref.
Human	In steady state in vivo studies, it was found that increasing age does not influence the responsiveness of the body to insulin	1, 2
	Intravenously administered insulin causes a less rapid fall in blood sugar, but a more prolonged hypoglycemia with advancing age	3—5
	The impairment in glucose tolerance with increasing age has been attributed to a relative insensitivity to endogenous insulin	6
	The sensitivity of adipose tissue to insulin is not impaired with advancing age	7
	The amount of insulin bound by cultured fibroblasts increases as the age of the donor increases	8
Rat	On the basis of glucose tolerance studies, it is concluded that 9-month-old rats are more resistant to endogenous insulin than 3-month-old rats	9
	The sensitivity to small doses of exogenous insulin is the same in 24-month-old rats as it is in 12-month-old rats	10
	The sensitivity of the diaphragm studied in vitro to the action of insulin is the same with tissue from young adults as it is with the tissue of old animals	11
	Serum antagonists to the in vitro action of insulin on diaphragm increase with age	12
	Some in vitro studies indicate that the responsiveness of adipose tissue to insulin decreases with age; another study indicates such is not the case; moreover, changes in insulin responsiveness when observed may be the result of increased adiposity rather than aging per se	13—15
	The capacity of purified hepatic plasma membranes to bind insulin decreases by 60% between 2 and 24 months of age	16
	Morphometric analysis of Islets of Langerhans does not reveal a decrease in the insulin content of the pancreas with increasing age	17
Mouse	The capacity of membranes prepared from liver and heart to bind insulin is not affected by increasing age nor is the dissociation constant	18

REFERENCES

1. Andres, R. and Tobin, J. D., Aging and the disposition of glucose, *Adv. Exp. Med. Biol.*, 61, 239, 1975.
2. Kimmerling, G., Javorski, W. C., and Reaven, G. M., Aging and insulin resistance in a group of nonobese male volunteers, *J. Am. Geriatr. Soc.*, 25, 349, 1977.
3. Muggeo, M., Fedele, D., Tiengo, A., Molinari, M., and Crepaldi, G., Human growth hormone and cortisol response to insulin stimulation in aging, *J. Gerontol.*, 30, 546, 1975.
4. Silverstone, F. A., Brandfonbrener, M., Shock, N. W., and Yiengst, M. J., Age differences in intravenous glucose tolerance tests and the response to insulin, *J. Clin. Invest.*, 36, 504, 1957.
5. Davidson, P. C. and Albrink, M. J., Insulin resistance in hyperglyceridemia, *Metabolism*, 14, 1059, 1965.
6. Hales, C. N., Greenwood, F. C., Mitchell, F. L., and Strauss, W. T., Blood-glucose, plasma-insulin and growth hormone concentrations of individuals with minor abnormalities of glucose tolerance, *Diabetologia*, 4, 73, 1968.
7. Schreuder, H. B., Influence of age on insulin secretion and lipid mobilization after glucose stimulation, *Isr. J. Med. Sci.*, 8, 832, 1972.
8. Rosenbloom, A. L., Goldstein, S., and Yip, C., Insulin binding to cultured human fibroblasts increases with normal and precocious aging, *Science*, 193, 412, 1976.
9. Bracho-Romero, E. and Reaven, G. M., Effect of age and weight on plasma glucose and insulin responses in the rat, *J. Am. Geriatr. Soc.*, 25, 299, 1977.
10. Gommers, A. and Genne, H., Effect of ageing on insulin and insulin-glucose sensitivity tests in rats, *Acta Diabetol. Lat.*, 12, 303, 1975.
11. Gommers, A., Dehez-Delhaye, M., and Jeanjeau, M., The effect of age on the in vitro response to insulin in the rat. I. Glucose metabolism on the diaphragm, *Gerontology*, 23, 134, 1977.
12. Gatsko, G. G. and Gulko, V. V., The effect of the serum of rats of various age on the insulin action in vitro, *Probl. Endokrinol.*, 16, 99, 1970.

Table 3 (continued)
EFFECTS OF AGE ON THE INTERACTIONS OF INSULIN WITH TARGET TISSUES

13. DiGirolamo, M. and Rudman, D., Variations in glucose metabolism and sensitivity to insulin of the rat's adipose tissue, in relation to age and body weight, *Endocrinology,* 82, 1133, 1968.
14. Moore, R. O., Effect of age of rats on the response of adipose tissue to insulin and the multiple forms of hexokinase, *J. Gerontol.*, 23, 45, 1968.
15. Jeanjeau, M., Dehez-Delhaye, M., and Gommers, A., The effect of age on the *in vitro* insulin response in the rat. II. Glucose metabolism in epididymal adipose tissue, *Gerontology,* 23, 127, 1977.
16. Freeman, C., Karoly, K., and Adelman, R. C., Impairment in availability of insulin to liver in vivo and in binding of insulin to purified hepatic plasma membrane during aging, *Biochem. Biophys. Res. Commun.*, 54, 1573, 1973.
17. Remacle, C., Hauser, N., Jeanjeau, M., and Gommers, A., Morphometric analysis of endocrine pancreas in old rats, *Exp. Gerontol.*, 12, 207, 1977.
18. Sorrentino, R. N. and Florini, J. R., Variations among individual mice in binding of growth hormone and insulin to membranes from animals of different ages, *Exp. Aging Res.*, 2, 191, 1976.

Table 4
EFFECTS OF AGE ON GLUCAGON CONCENTRATION, SECRETION, AND ACTION

Species	Findings	Ref.
Human	The postabsorptive serum level of glucagon is not influenced by age	1
	The secretion of glucagon in response to intravenously administered arginine is not influenced by age	1
	Subcutaneous adipose tissue from 20- to 30-year-old people responded in vitro to glucagon by an increased release of glycerol and a decreased release of free fatty acids, while in tissues from 50- to 70-year-old people, glucagon did not increase glycerol release, but did increase free fatty acid release	2
Rat	With increase in age during the first 20% of the life-span, there is a marked decrease in the lipolytic action of glucagon in isolated adipocytes; this loss in glucagon responsiveness can be prevented by restricting food intake to 60% of the *ad libitum* intake	3—5
	Loss of lipolytic responsiveness of adipocytes with age relates to a reduction in glucagon binding by adipocytes and to an increased adipocyte phosphodiesterase activity with age	5, 6
	The responsiveness of the adenylate cyclase activity of adipocyte ghosts to glucagon is lost between 1 and 12 months of age, a loss that can be modified by food restriction	7, 8
	The responsiveness of the adenylate cyclase activity of liver homogenates to glucagon increases slightly between 3 and 24 months of age	9

Table 4 (continued)
EFFECTS OF AGE ON GLUCAGON CONCENTRATION, SECRETION, AND ACTION

Species	Findings	Ref.
Rat	Glucagon subcutaneously administered inhibits glutamine synthetase activity in liver homogenate prepared from 3-month-old animals, but not from those prepared from 28-month-old animals	10
Goose	When expressed on the basis of rate of FFA or glycerol released per gram of adipose tissue, glucagon promoted lipolysis in vitro to a greater extent in 4- to 8-week-old animals than in animals over 1 year of age	11
	Glucagon increased plasma FFA levels to a greater extent when administered in vivo to geese over 1 year of age than to geese 4—8 weeks of age	11

REFERENCES

1. Dudl, R. J. and Ensinck, J. W., Insulin and glucagon relationships during aging in man, *Metabolism,* 26, 33, 1977.
2. Gries, F. A., Berger, M., Preiss, H., Liebermeister, H., and Johnke, K., Glucagon effect on human adipose tissue in vitro: dependence on body weight and age, *Verh. Dtsch. Ges. Inn. Med.,* 75, 796, 1969.
3. Manganiello, V. and Vaughan, M., Selective loss of adipose cell responsiveness to glucagon with growth in the rat, *J. Lipid Res.,* 13, 12, 1972.
4. Bertrand, H. A., Yu, B. P., and Masoro, E. J., Modulation of age-related loss of glucagon-induced lipolysis, *Fed. Proc. Fed. Am. Soc. Exp. Biol.,* 37, 632, 1978.
5. Livingston, J. N., Cuatrecasas, P., and Lockwood, D. H., Studies on glucagon binding and lipolytic capacity, *J. Lipid Res.,* 15, 26, 1974.
6. DeSantis, R. A., Gorenstein, T., Livingston, J. N., and Lockwood, D. H., Role of phosphodiesterase in glucagon resistance of large adipocytes, *J. Lipid Res.,* 15, 35, 1974.
7. Cooper, B. and Gregerman, R. I., Hormone-sensitive fat cell adenylate cyclase in rat. Influences of growth, cell size, and aging, *J. Clin. Invest.,* 57, 161, 1976.
8. Cooper, B., Weinblatt, F., and Gregerman, R. I., Enhanced activity of hormone-sensitive adenylate cyclase during dietary restriction in the rat. Dependence on age and relation to cell size, *J. Clin. Invest.,* 59, 567, 1977.
9. Kalish, M. I., Katz, M. S., Pineyro, M. A., and Gregerman, R. I., Epinephrine- and glucagon-sensitive adenylate cyclases of rat liver during aging. Evidence for membrane instability associated with increased enzymatic activity, *Biochim. Biophys. Acta,* 483, 452, 1977.
10. Wu, C., Enzyme regulation during development and aging, *Biochem. Biophys. Res. Commun.,* 75, 879, 1977.
11. Santos, P. G. and Grande, F., Age influence on lipolytic efect of glucagon in geese, *Proc. Soc. Exp. Biol. Med.,* 149, 652, 1975.

PARATHYROID HORMONE, CALCITONIN, AND VITAMIN D$_3$

Dike Kalu

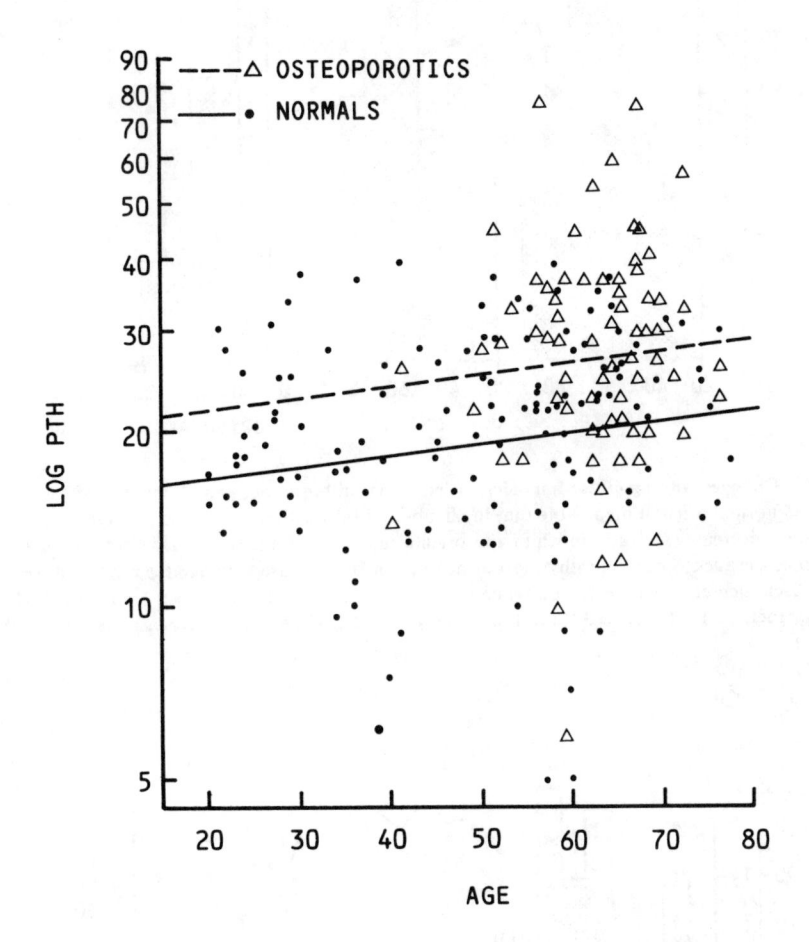

FIGURE 1. Serum immuno-parathyroid hormone levels (iPTH) in normal and osteoporotic patients in relation to age. Serum iPTH in normals (●) and patients with symptomatic osteoporosis (Δ) in relation to age. Plotted are the lines obtained when a common slope is assumed. Normals $\log_n$ iPTH = 2.7834 + 0.0039 × age (years). Osteoporotics $\log_n$ iPTH = 3.0595 + 0.0039 × age (years). The individual lines for —normals: $\log_n$ iPTH = 2.7930 + 0.0037 × age (years); —osteoporotics: $\log_n$ iPTH = 2.9414 + 0.0058 × age (years). (From Jowsey, J. O. M. and Offord, K. P., *Mechanisms of Localized Bone Loss*, Horton, E. J., Tarpley, J. M., and Davis, W. F., Eds., Information Retrieval, Arlington, Va., 1978, 345. With permission.)

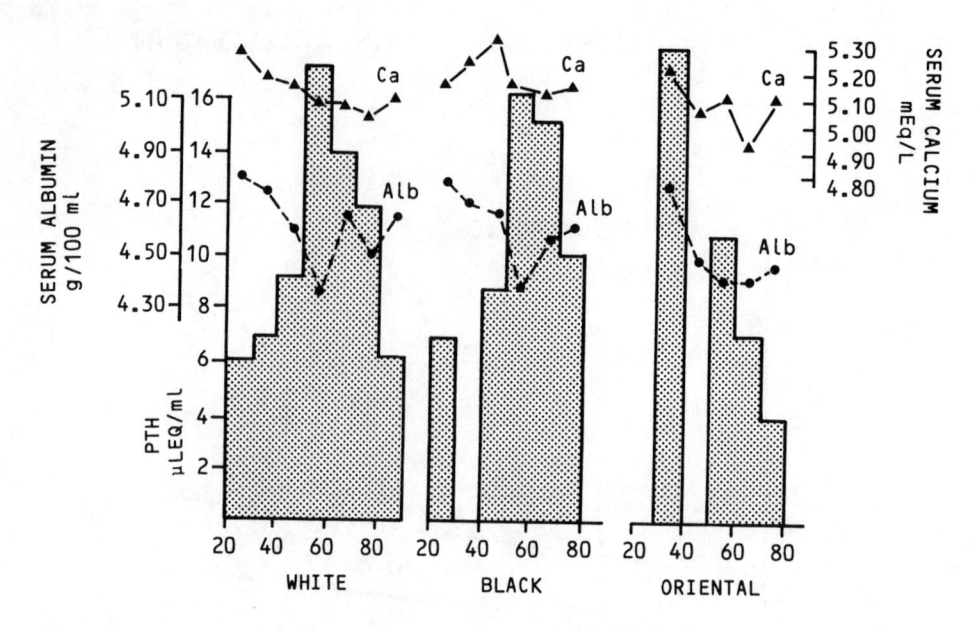

FIGURE 2. Changes with age in serum calcium, parathyroid hormone, and albumin in 382 white, 68 black, and 35 normal oriental men. Note that in all albumin falls with age until the 50-59 decade. Serum albumin slowly decreases with age in white and oriental men, but in black men rises from the 20 to 29 to the 40 to 49 decades. Serum parathyroid hormone seems to increase with age from 20 to 59 years in white and black men and then decreases, while in oriental men it steadily decreases from age 30. (From Roof, B. S., Piel, C. F., Hansen, J., and Fundenberg, H. H., *Mech. Ageing Dev.*, 5, 289, 1976. With permission.)

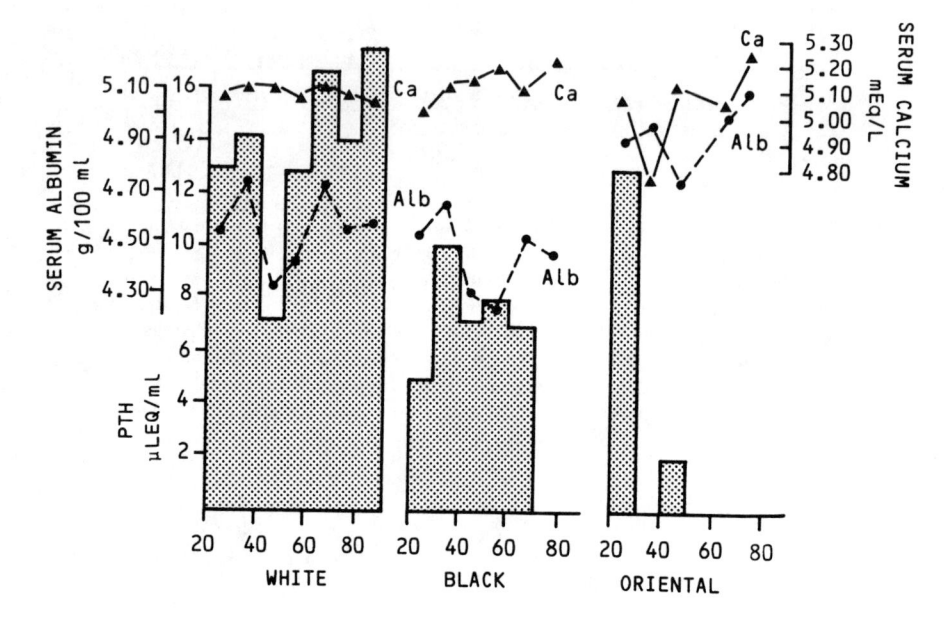

FIGURE 3. Changes with age in calcium, parathyroid hormone, and albumin in 375 white, 70 black, and 15 normal oriental women. Note that in black women serum calcium is higher and albumin and parathyroid hormone are lower than in white women. The rise in serum calcium with age is greater in black women than in white women. (From Roof, B. S., Piel, C. F., Hansen, J., and Fundenberg, H. H., *Mech. Ageing Dev.*, 5, 289, 1976. With permission.)

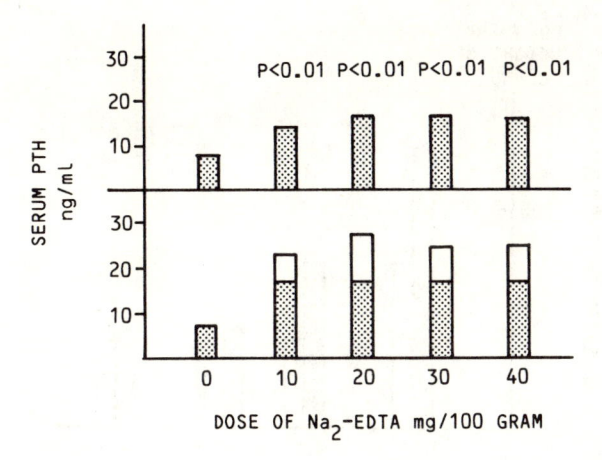

FIGURE 4. Parathyroid hormone secretion in response to induced hypocalcemia. Serum parathyroid hormone was measured following injection of Na$_2$-EDTA to 1-month (1M)- and 18-month (18M)-old rats. Serum parathyroid hormone is shown on the ordinate, and dose of Na$_2$-EDTA in mg/100 gm body weight on the abscissa. At each dose of Na$_2$-EDTA, serum parathyroid hormone was significantly higher in 1-month-old animals than in 18-month-old animals. (From Fujita, T., Ohata, M., Ota, K., Tsuda, T., Uezu, A., Okano, K., and Yoshikawa, M., *J. Gerontol.*, 31, 523, 1976. With permission.)

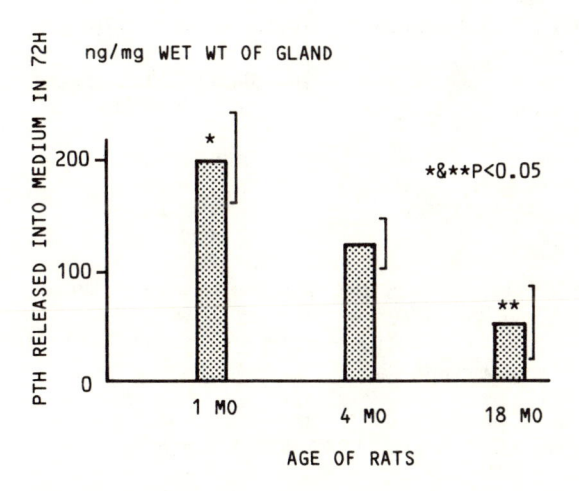

FIGURE 5. Release of parathyroid hormone from rat parathyroid glands in culture. The parathyroid glands from 18-month-old rats released significantly less parathyroid hormone than those from 1-month-old rats (p<0.05). (From Fujita, T., Ohata, M., Ota, K., Tsuda, T., Uezu, A., Okano, K., and Yoshikawa, M., *J. Gerontol.*, 31, 523, 1976. With permission.)

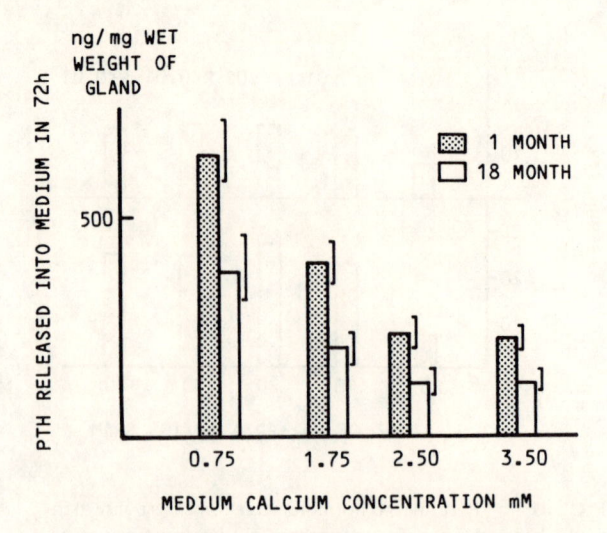

FIGURE 6. Release of parathyroid hormone from rat parathyroid glands in culture at various levels of concentration of calcium. At each level, the parathyroid glands from older rats released significantly less parathyroid hormone than those from the younger ones ($p<0.05$). (From Fujita, T., Ohata, M., Ota, K., Tsuda, T., Uezu, A., Okano, K., and Yoshikawa, M., *J. Gerontol.*, 31, 523, 1976. With permission.)

Table 1
DEGRADATION OF PARATHYROID HORMONE

Half-life of ^{125}I-labeled parathyroid hormone (^{125}I-PTH) in plasma of intact rats of various ages

Age (months)	No. of rats	Half-life of ^{125}I-PTH in plasma (min) mean ± SEM
1.5	5	19.2 ± 1.9(a)
6	4	24.0 ± 4.1
12	4	24.9 ± 4.1
24	5	25.3 ± 1.0(b)

Note: The calculation is based on ^{125}I-PTH levels in plasma 15, 30, 45, and 60 min after injection, with the use of the method of least squares. (b) is significantly larger than (a) with $p<0.05$.

From Fujita, T., Okano, K., Orimo, H., Ohata, M., and Yoshiwaka, M., *J. Gerontol*, 27, 25, 1972. With permission.

Table 2
CONCENTRATIONS OF CALCITONIN IN THE THYROID

Age (days)	Body weight[a] (g)	Thyroid weight[a] (mg)	TCT potency per mg thyroid tissue (% of 60-day-old rat) and 95% fiducial limits
5	10	1.12	10
15	30±1	2.96±0.11	42
30	62±3	4.47±0.34	120
60	192±7	9.05±0.54	100
120	317±19	13.13±0.26	112
360	568±49	21.06±1.74	93

[a] Values are means ±SEM, except 5-day-old rats, in which only the mean of pooled weights is shown. At 5 days of age the concentration of assayable thyrocalcitonin is only about 10% as high as in 30-day-old rats, but from 30 days on to as old as 1 year the concentration of thyrodial thyrocalcitonin remains essentially constant.

Modified from Frankel, S. and Yasumura, S., *Endocrinology*, 87, 602, 1970. With permission.

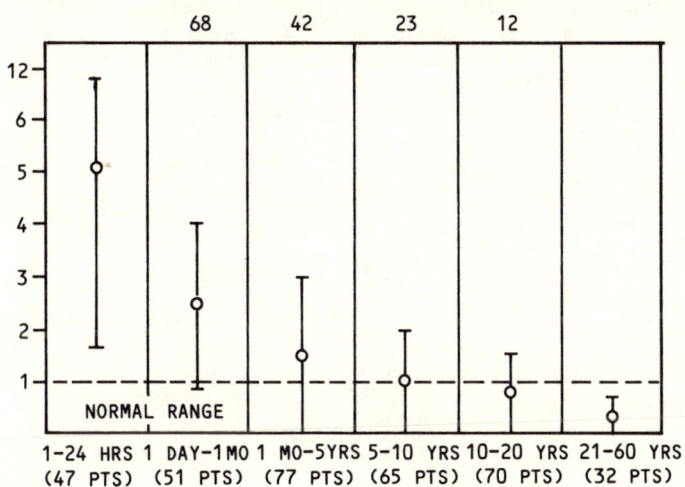

FIGURE 7. Serum immunoreactive calcitonin at different age groups in human subjects. The unit on the ordinate is ng/mℓ, the circles are mean ± SD and the number of subjects per age group is in parentheses. (From Samaan, N. A., Anderson, G. D., and Adam-Mayne, M. E., *Am. J. Obstet. Gynecol.*, 121, 622, 1975. With permission.)

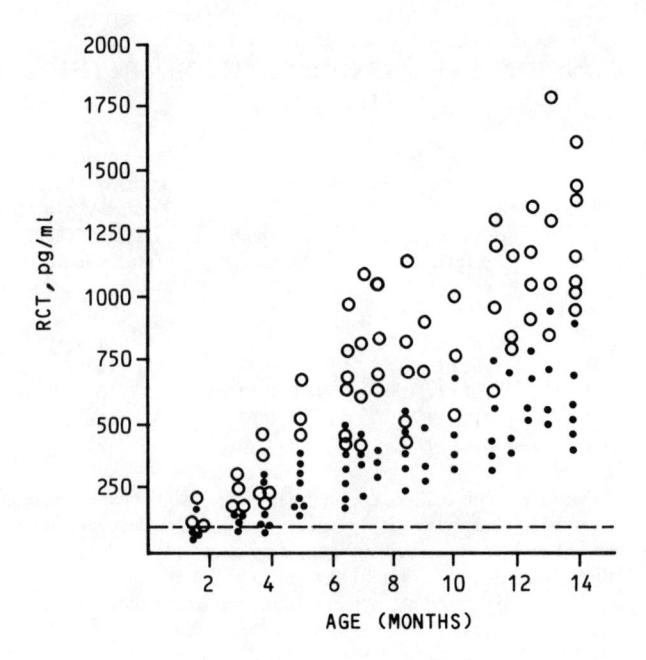

FIGURE 8. Serum calcitonin concentrations in rats. Serial plasma immunoreactive CT measurements during somatosexual maturation. Results were obtained by RIA (rCT standards) of 137 unextracted plasmas obtained by serial tail vein bleeding of 26 male (•) and 21 female (O) Wistar rats maintained on standard rat chow *(ad libitum)* for 15 months.(—-) Lower limit of detectability. Linear regression analysis of male and female data gave the following results: males, plasma CT = 43 (age in months) + 16 (r = 0.81; n = 70); females, plasma CT = 91 (age in months) − 12 (r = 0.86; n = 67). (From Roos, B. A., Cooper, C. W., Frelinger, A. L., and Deftos, L. J., *Endocrinology,* 103, 2180, 1978, The Endocrinology Society. With permission.)

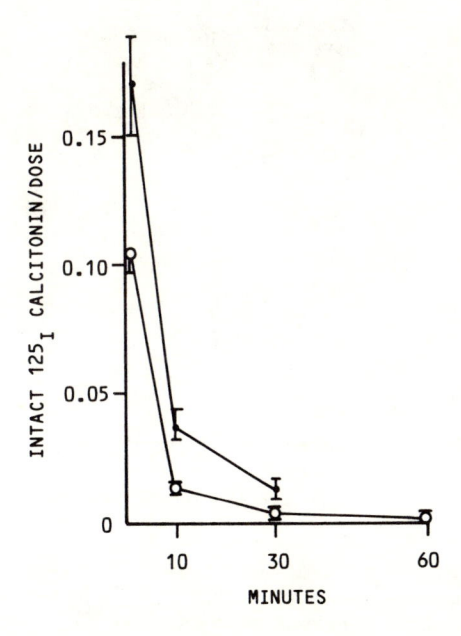

FIGURE 9. Degradation of calcitonin. The clearance of intact [^{125}I]iodocalcitonin from the serum of young rats (O) (24-day-old) and mature rats (•) (8-month-old). The unit of the ordinate is fraction of the dose remaining in serum. The zero-point for both groups of animals is 1.0. Intact calcitonin appears to clear the serum at a slower rate in the old animals compared to the young animals. There is significantly less [^{125}I]iodocalcitonin present at 10 ($P < 0.001$) and 30 min ($P < 0.05$) in the young animals compared to the old animals. The 1-min value for the young rats is an average of 2 rats. The 1-min value for the old rats is an average of 3 animals. The remaining values are the average of 4 rats. Vertical bars represent SE. (From Scarpace, P. J., Neuman, W. F., and Raisz, L. G., *Endocrinology*, 100, 1260, 1977. With permission.)

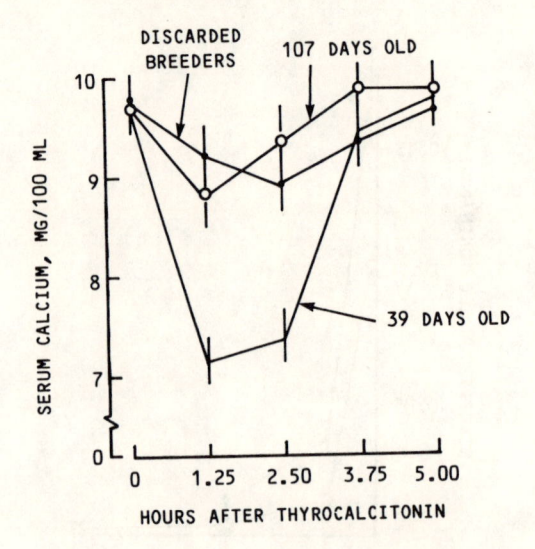

FIGURE 10. Hypocalcemic action of exogenous calcitonin. Duration and magnitude of the hypocalcemic response to thyrocalcitonin injected at 135 mU in 39-day-old, at 405 mU in 107-day-old, and at 1215 mU in 1-year-old (discarded breeders) female rats. Each point represents the mean value from 5 rats. Mean values of serum calcium of the 39-day-old rats were significantly different (p <0.001) from those of both 107-day-old and 1-year-old rats at 1.25 and 2.5 hr. (From Orimo, H. and Hirsch, P. F., *Endocrinology*, 93, 1206, 1973. With permission.)

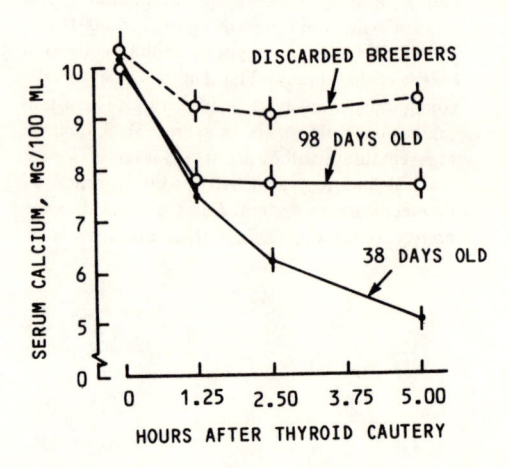

FIGURE 11. Hypocalcemic action of endogenous calcitonin. Effect of age on the hypocalcemic response of male rats to endogenous thyrocalcitonin released as a result of thyroid cautery. There was greater response to thyroid cautery in 38-day-old-rats compared to 98-day-old-rats and 1-year-old retired breeders. Serum calcium values were significantly different among the 3 groups at 2.5 and 5 hr (p < 0.001). Each point represents the mean value from 5 rats. (From Orimo, H. and Hirsch, P. F., *Endocrinology*, 93, 1206, 1973. With permission.)

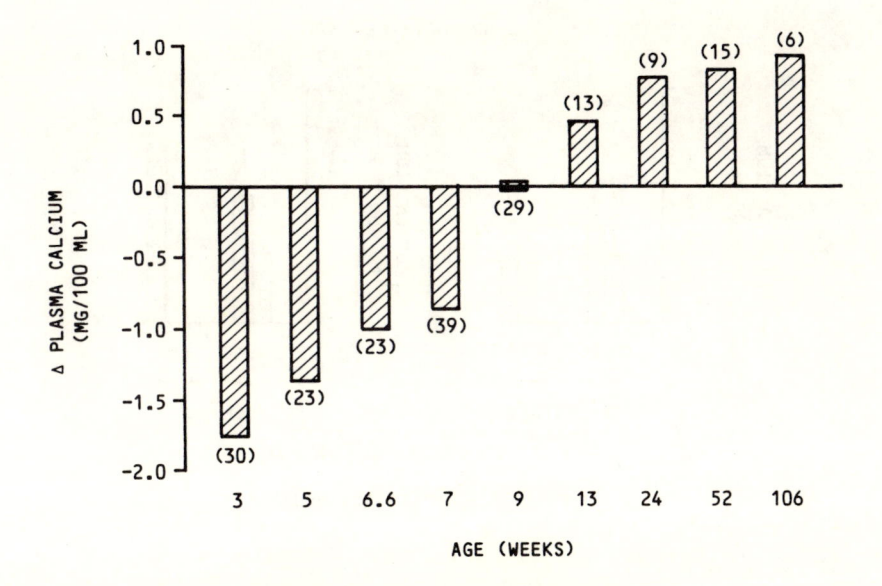

FIGURE 12. Changes in plasma calcium concentrations 3 hr after thyroparathyroidectomy in male rats of varying ages. Number of rats is in parentheses. Rats were fasted overnight and thyroparathyroidectomized or sham operated. (Modified from Kalu, D. N., Hadji-Georgopopoulos, A., Sarr, M. G., Solomon, B. A., and Foster, G. V., *Endocrinology*, 95, 1156, 1974; Kalu, D. N. and Foster, G. V., *Am. J. Physiol.*, 231, 1533, 1976; Kalu, D. N., *Horm. Metab. Res.*, 10, 72, 1978; Kalu, D. N., unpublished observations, 1979.)

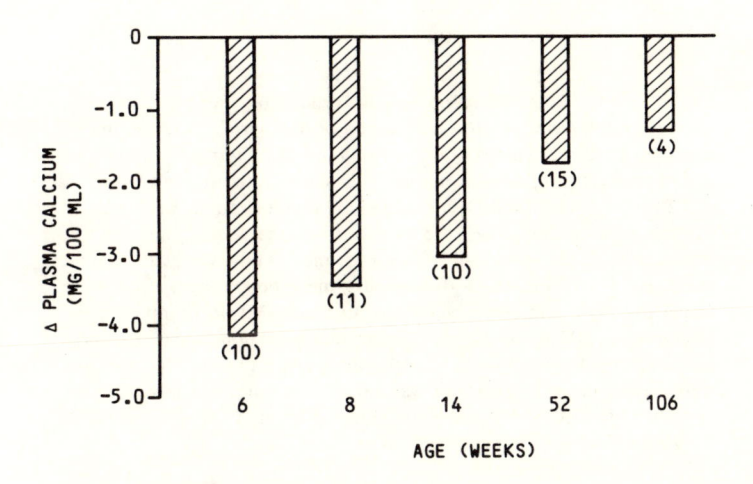

FIGURE 13. Changes in plasma calcium concentrations 24 hr after thyroparathyroidectomy in male rats of varying ages. Number of rats is in parentheses. Rats were fasted overnight and thyroparathyroidectomized or sham operated. (Modified from: Kalu, D. N., Hadji-Georgopoulos, A., Sarr, M. G., Solomon, B. A., and Foster, G. V., *Endocrinology*, 95, 1156, 1974; Kalu, D. N. and Foster, G. V., *Am. J. Physiol.*, 231, 1533, 1976; Kalu, D. N., *Horm. Metab. Res.*, 10, 72, 1978; Kalu, D.N., unpublished observations, 1979.)

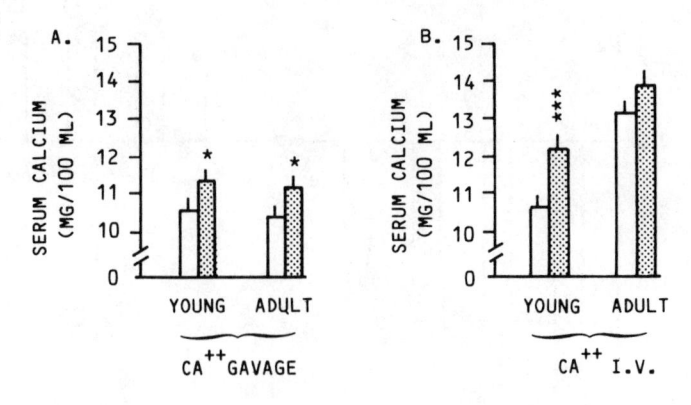

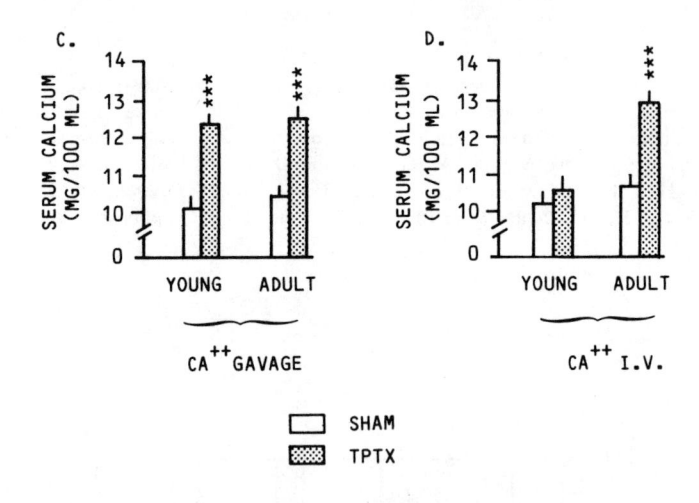

FIGURE 14. Role of calcitonin in promoting calcium tolerance. Changes with age in the protective action of the thyroid gland (source of calcitonin) against hypercalcemia induced in rats by intragastric (gavage) or intravenous (i.v.) administration of calcium. Rats were bled 1 hr (A and B), and 2 hr (C and D) after calcium administration. Each vertical bar represents mean value for 5 to 7 rats and the vertical lines are SE. Young rats (6- to 7-week-old female rats, mean body weight 135 g) and adult rats (4- to 7-month-old female rats, mean body weight 304 g) were fasted overnight and either sham operated (SHAM) or thyroparathyroidectomized (TPTX) just before calcium administration. The thyroid protected against hypercalcemia in both young and adult rats, but the protective effect after i.v. calcium was earlier in young than in adult rats. *p<0.05, **p<0.025, ***p<0.0005. (From Harper, C. and Toverud, S. U., *Endocrinology,* 93, 1354, 1973. With permission.)

Table 3
SERUM 25-HYDROXYCHOLECALCIFEROL (25-OH-VITAMIN D) IN NORMAL SUBJECTS OF VARYING AGES

Age (years)	Serum 25-OH-vitamin D (ng/mℓ)	Number	Sex	Race	Country	Month	Vitamin D intake	Ref.
9.9 ± 0.6 (SE)	23.6 ± 0.9 (SE)	51		26 B/25 W	U.S.	Between February and April	3520 ± 170 u/week	1
11—17	16.3 ± 1.6 (SE)	12	M		U.K.			2
23.7 ± 3.1 (SD)	22.9 ± 3.0 (SD)	5			U.S.			3
24—45	18.6 ± 7.9 (SD)	11	8 F/3 M	W	U.K.	December		4
	26.7 ± 7.1 (SD)					March		
	27.3 ± 11.3 (SD)					June		
	36.2 ± 9.2 (SD)					September		
30.2 ± 12.9 (SD)	27.3 ± 11.8 (SD)	40			U.S.	May and June		5
34.2 ± 2.1 (SE)	20.5 ± 1.0 (SE)	38	21 M/17 F	18 B/20 W	U.S.		1710 ± 170(SE) (u/week)	6
Adults	18.8 ± 7.63 (SD)	81		W	U.S.			7
Adults	15.2 ± 5.6	18	M/F		U.K.			
Adults	15.8 ± 1.4 (SE)	19			U.K.			2
55.5 ± 3.2 (SE)	21.4 (12.4—38.8)	27	9 M/19 F		U.S.	Between April and October		9

Note: SE = standard error; SD = standard deviation; M = male; F = female; B = black; W = white; U = units; and adults — age not specified.

REFERENCES

1. **Hahn, T. J., Hendin, B. A., Scharp, C. R., Boisseau, V. C., and Haddad, J. G.**, Serum 25-hydroxycalciferol levels and bone mass in children on chronic anticonvulsant therapy, *N. Engl. J. Med.*, 292, 550, 1975.
2. **Stamp, T. C. B., Round, J. M., Rowe, D. J. F., and Haddad, J. G.**, Plasma levels and therapeutic effect of 25-hydroxycholecalciferol in epileptic patients taking anticonvulsant drugs, *Br. Med. J.*, 4, 9, 1972.
3. **Jubiz, W., Haussler, M. R., McCain, T. A., and Tolman, K. G.**, Plasma 1,25-dihydroxyvitamin D levels in patients receiving anticonvulsant drugs, *J. Clin. Endocrinol. Metab.*, 44, 614, 1977.
4. **McLaughlin, M., Fairney, A., Lester, E., Raggat, P. R., Brown, D. J., and Wills, M. R.**, Seasonal variations in serum 25-hydroxycholecalciferol in healthy people, *Lancet*, 1 (Suppl. 1), 536, 1974.
5. **Haddad, J. G. and Chyu, K. J.**, Competitive protein-binding radioassay for 25-hydroxycholecalciferol, *J. Clin. Endocrinol. Metab.*, 33, 992, 1971.
6. **Hahn, T. J., Hendin, B. A., Scharp, C. R., and Haddad, J. G., Jr.**, Effect of chronic anticonvulsant therapy on serum 25-hydroxycalciferol levels in adults, *N. Engl. J. Med.*, 287, 900, 1972.
7. **Haddad, J. G. and Stamp, T. C. B.**, Circulating 25-hydroxyvitamin D in man, *Am. J. Med.*, 57, 57, 1974.
8. **Edelstein, S., Charman, M., Lawson, D. E. M., and Kodicek, E.**, Competitive protein-binding assay for 25-hydroxycholecalciferol, *Clin. Sci. Mol. Med.*, 46, 231, 1974.
9. **Klein, R. C., Arnaud, S. B., Gallagher, G. C., Deluca, H. F., and Riggs, B. L.**, Intestinal calcium absorption in exogenous hypercortisonism role of 25-hydroxyvitamin D and corticosteroid dose, *J. Clin. Invest*, 60, 253, 1977.

Body Composition — Metabolic System

METABOLIC RATE

E. J. Masoro

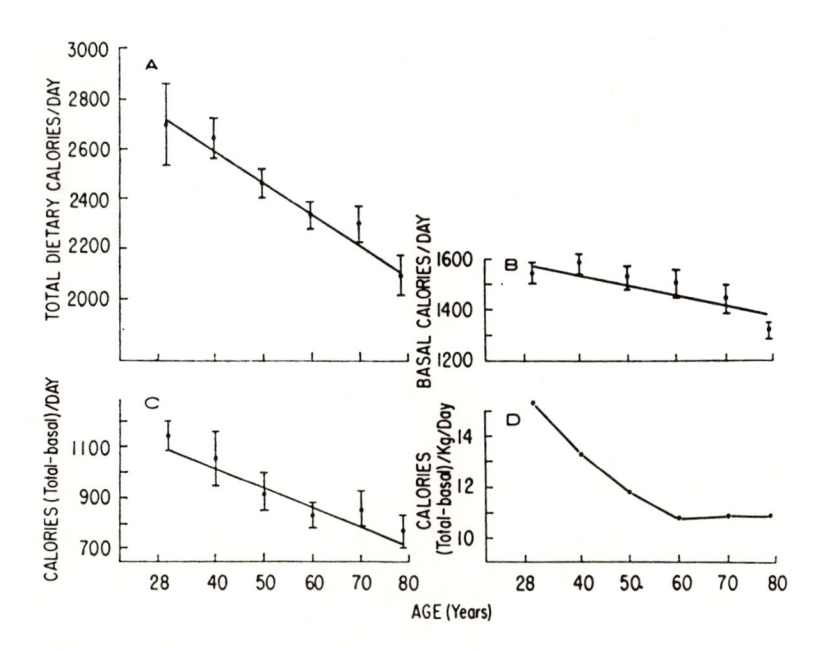

FIGURE 1. Effect of age on energy transformations in man. (A) Total dietary caloric intake; (B) basal caloric expenditure; (C) caloric expenditure due to activities other than basal activities; and (D) same as C but expressed on a per kilogram body mass basis. (From McGandy, R. B., Barrows, C. H., Jr., Spanias, A., Meredith, A., Stone, J. L., and Norris, A. H., *J. Gerontol.,* 21, 581, 1966. With permission.)

Table 1
METABOLIC RATE

Species	Findings	Ref.
Human	Basal metabolic rate falls with age, but the magnitude of the fall varies greatly from study to study; it is believed that the reason for this variation relates to increase in adipose mass relative to lean body mass with age — when based on lean body mass the reduction of basal metabolism with age is no more than 1—2% per decade	1—5
	There is a linear decrease in overnight O_2 consumption with age even though older people sleep less (i.e., awake more often) then younger people	6
	In a cross-sectional study, it was shown that the fall in muscle mass relative to total body mass may be wholly responsible for age-related decreases in BMR; subsequent longitudinal study confirms this conclusion	12, 13

Table 1 (continued)
METABOLIC RATE

Species	Findings	Ref.
Rat	Basal metabolic rate and minimal O_2 consumption rate decline with age	7
	In vitro studies with skin indicate the rate of O_2 consumption per gram dry weight or per mg DNA declines with age; glucose and galactose were used as substrates	8
	In vitro studies with cartilage indicate the rate of O_2 consumption declines with age; glucose and galactose were used as substrates	9
Mouse	O_2 consumption measured in vivo declines with age	10
Chicken	Oxygen consumption expressed per gram of homogenate nitrogen declines with increasing age in heart and liver homogenates, but not in kidney homogenates	11

REFERENCES

1. **Keys, A. Taylor, H. L., and Grande, F.,** Basal metabolism and age of adult man, *Metabolism*, 22, 579, 1973.
2. **Podlesch, I. and Ulmer, W. T.,** On the dependence of heart minute volume, heart index, stroke volume, stroke volume index, and oxygen consumption on age, *Arch. Kreislaufforsch.*, 48, 252, 1965.
3. **Bafitis, H. and Sargent, F., II,** Human physiological adaptability through the life sequence, *J. Gerontol.*, 32, 402, 1977.
4. **Robinson, S., Dill, D. B., Tzankoff, S. P., Wagner, J. A., and Robinson, R. D.,** Longitudinal studies of aging in 37 men, *J. Appl. Physiol.*, 38, 263, 1975.
5. **McGandy, R. B., Barrows, C. H., Jr., Spanias, A., Meredith, A., Stone, J. L., and Norris, A. H.,** Nutrient intake and energy expenditure in men of different ages, *J. Gerontol.*, 21, 581, 1966.
6. **Webb, P. and Hiestand, M.,** Sleep metabolism and age, *J. Appl. Physiol.*, 38, 257, 1975.
7. **Denckla, W. D.,** Role of the pituitary and thyroid glands in the decline of minimal O_2 consumption with age, *J. Clin. Invest.*, 53, 572, 1974.
8. **Patnaik, B. K. and Kanungo, M. S.,** Metabolic changes in the skin of rats of various ages. Oxygen consumption and uptake of glucose, *Biochem. J.*, 98, 374, 1966.
9. **Patnaik, B. K.,** Effect of age on the oxygen consumption and glucose uptake by the elastic cartilage of rat, *Gerontologia*, 13, 173, 1967.
10. **Pettegrew, R. K. and Ewing, K. L.,** Life history study of oxygen utilization in the C57BL/6 mouse, *J. Gerontol.*, 26, 381, 1971.
11. **Kment, A., Leibetseder, J., and Linder, G.,** Studies on the age dependency of tissue respiration (heart, kidney, and liver) in chickens, *Z. Alternsforsch.*, 20, 23, 1967.
12. **Tzankoff, S. P. and Norris, A. H.,** Effect of muscle mass decrease on age-related BMR changes, *J. Appl. Physiol.*, 43, 100, 1977.
13. **Tzankoff, S. P. and Norris, A. H.,** Longitudinal changes in basal metabolism in man, *J. Appl. Physiol.*, 45, 537, 1978.

LEAN BODY MASS

E. J. Masoro

Table 1
LEAN BODY MASS AND RELATED MEASUREMENTS

Species	Findings	Ref.
Human	Longitudinal studies with an American population during young adulthood and middle age shows the occurrence of an age-related loss in lean body mass of about 3 kg per decade of increasing age	1
	Longitudinal studies with a Chinese population shows no change in lean body mass during a 12-year span involving young adulthood and early middle age	2
	Longitudinal study of men in the 7th and 8th decade of life shows no change in lean body mass over an 8—10 year time period	3
	Cross-sectional studies indicate that lean body mass declines with increasing age and that the rate of decline is somewhat greater in men than women with the rate of decline increasing in the later years	4—6
	Cross-sectional studies indicate that cell mass decreases between 25 and 80 years of age in both sexes with the rate of decrease increasing after 45 years of age	5, 7
	Cross-sectional studies of body potassium content shows it to decrease between 18 and 85 years both when expressed as total potassium content and the amount of potassium per kilogram body mass	5, 8—11
	Cross-sectional studies of the K content per kg lean body mass shows it falls with age from a value of 72 meq/kg in men and 60 meq/kg in women at 20 years of age to 50 meq/kg in men and 47 meq/kg in women at 90 years of age	2, 12, 13
	Several cross-sectional studies based on a variety of techniques indicate that muscle mass declines with increasing age	9, 11, 14, 15
	Total body water (TBW) declines with age as does intracellular water (ICW) in accord with the following formula	16

Males

$$\frac{TBW_{(\ell)}}{Body\ weight_{(kg)}} \times 100 = 79.45 - 0.24\ (body\ weight) - 0.15\ age\ (years)$$

$$\frac{ICW}{TBW} \times 100 = 62.3 - 0.16\ age\ (years)$$

Females

$$\frac{TBW_{(\ell)}}{Body\ weight_{(kg)}} \times 100 = 69.81 - 0.26\ (body\ weight) - 0.12\ age\ (years)$$

$$\frac{ICW}{TBW} \times 100 = 52.3 - 0.07\ age\ (years)$$

Table 1 (continued)
LEAN BODY MASS AND RELATED MEASUREMENTS

Species	Findings	Ref.
	In males, the lean tissues of extremities decrease with age	19
Rat	Longitudinal studies show that lean body mass does not decline with age	17, 20
Mice	There is a loss of nitrogen content in the skinned carcass of male mice between 250 and 750 days of age, but not in those of female mice	18

REFERENCES

1. Forbes, G. B., The adult decline in lean body mass, *Hum. Biol.*, 48, 161, 1976.
2. Chien, S., Peng, M. T., Chen, K. P., Huang, T. F., Chang, C., and Fong, H., Longitudinal measurements of blood volume and essential body mass in human subjects, *J. Appl. Physiol.*, 39, 818, 1975.
3. Parizkova, J and Eiselt, E., A further study on changes in somatic characteristics and body composition of old men followed longitudinally for 8-10 years, *Hum. Biol.*, 43, 318, 1971.
4. Forbes, G. B. and Reina, J. C., Adult lean body mass declines with age; some longitudinal observations, *Metabolism*, 19, 653, 1970.
5. Novak, L., Aging, total body potassium, fat-free mass, and cell mass in males and females between ages 18 and 85 years, *J. Gerontol.*, 27, 438, 1972.
6. Weinsier, R. L., Fuchs, R. J., Kay, T. D., Triebwasser, J. H., and Lancaster, M. C., Body fat; its relationship to coronary heart disease, blood pressure, lipids and other risk factors measured in a large male population, *Am. J. Med.*, 61, 815, 1976.
7. Burmeister, W. and Bingert, A., Quantitative changes of the human cell mass between the 8th and 90th year of life, *Klin. Wochenschr.*, 45, 409, 1967.
8. Shukla, K. K., Ellis, K. J., Dombrowski, C. S., and Cohn, S. H., Physiological variation of total-body potassium in man, *Am. J. Physiol.*, 224, 271, 1973.
9. Malina, R. M., Quantification of fat, muscle and bone in man, *Clin. Orthop. Relat. Res.*, 65, 9, 1969.
10. Krzywicki, H. J. and Chinn, K. S. K., Body composition of a military population, Fort Carson, 1963, *Am. J. Clin. Nutr.*, 20, 708, 1967.
11. Cohn, S. H., Vaswani, A., Zanzi, I., Aloia, J. F., Roginsky, M. S., and Ellis, K. J., Changes in body chemical composition with age measured by total-body neutron activation, *Metabolism*, 25, 85, 1976.
12. Pierson, R. N., Lin, D. H. Y., and Phillips, R. A., Total-body potassium in health; effects of age, sex, height, and fat, *Am. J. Physiol.*, 226, 206, 1974.
13. Womersley, J., Durnin, J. V. G. A., Boddy, K., and Mahaffy, M., Influence of muscular development, obesity, and age on the fat-free mass of adults, *J. Appl. Physiol.*, 41, 223, 1976.
14. Bugyi, B., Age dependent changes of body constitution based on adipose tissue and musculature evaluation, *Z. Alternsforsch.*, 20, 327, 1967.
15. Matsuki, S. and Yoda, R., An evidence for the decrease of body muscle mass due to ageing by means of height, weight and upper arm circumference measurements, *Endocrinol. Jpn.*, 19, 401, 1972.
16. Randall, H. T., Fluid, electrolyte and acid-base balance, *Surg. Clin. North Am.*, 56, 1019, 1976.
17. Lesser, G. T., Deutsch, S., and Markofsky, J., Aging in the rat; longitudinal and cross-sectional studies of body composition, *Am. J. Physiol.*, 225, 1472, 1973.
18. Sobel, H., Hrubant, H. E., and Hewlett, M. J., Changes in the body composition of C57BL/6aa mice with age, *J. Gerontol.*, 23, 387, 1968.
19. Borkan, G. A. and Norris, A. H., Fat redistribution and the changing body dimensions of the adult male, *Hum. Biol.*, 49, 495, 1975.
20. Yu, B. P. and Masoro, E. J., Age-related changes in the total body mass, lean body mass and adipose tissue mass. II, *Gerontologist*, 18(5), 140, 1978.

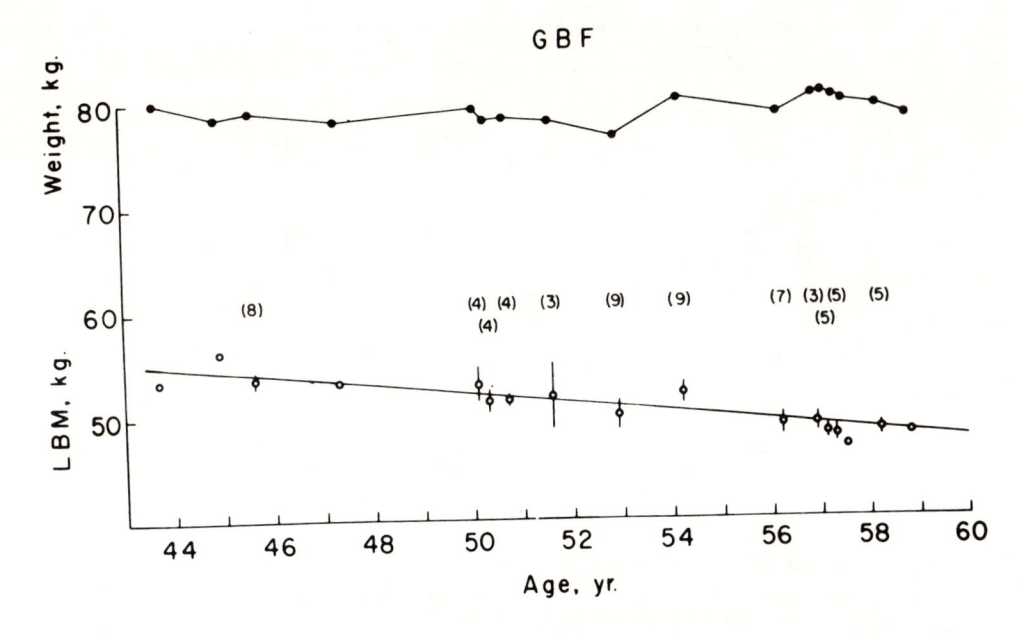

FIGURE 1. Change in lean body mass (LBM) and weight as a function of age in one male subject. Vertical bars indicate one standard deviation; number of runs in parentheses (the ultimate and antepenultimate points are averages of two runs each). (Reprinted from *Hum. Biol.*, 48, 161, 1976, by Forbes, G. B. By permission of the Wayne State Universty Press.)

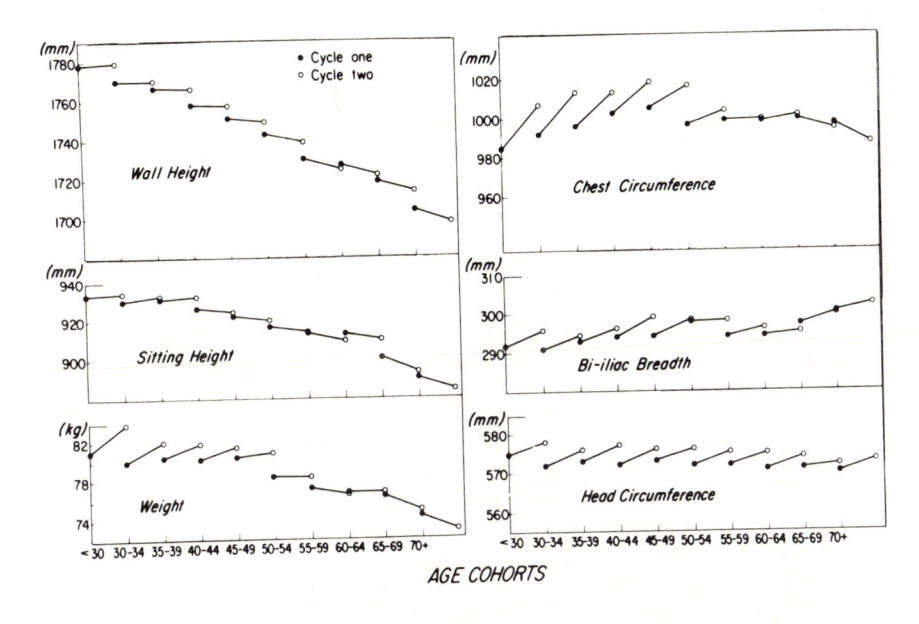

FIGURE 2. Five-year mean longitudinal changes for selected body structure measurements made on a group of 1813 healthy, white veterans living in the Boston, Mass. area. (Reprinted from *Hum. Biol.*, 49, 541, 1977, by Friedlaender, J. S., Costa, P. T., Jr., Bosse, R., Ellis, E., Rhoads, J. G., and Standt, H. W. By permission of the Wayne State University Press.)

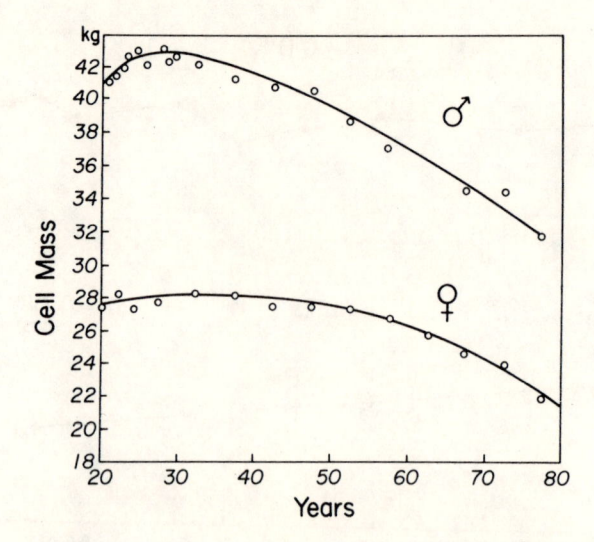

FIGURE 3. Age-changes in cell mass in men and women. (From Burmeister, W. and Bingert, A., *Klin. Wochenscher.*, 45, 409, 1967. With permission.)

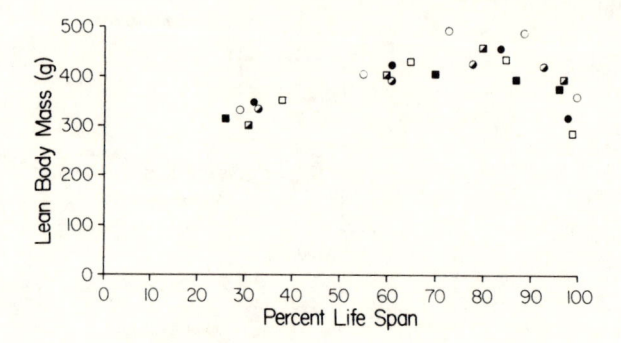

FIGURE 4. Lean body mass was measured in 14 Fischer 344 male rats in a longitudinal study. The data shown in the figure are for the 6 longest lived; similar results were obtained with the 8 shortest lived. Each symbol refers to a particular rat studied longitudinally. (From Yu, B. P. and Masoro, E. J., *Gerontologist*, 18(5), 140, 1978. With permission.)

ADIPOSE TISSUE

E. J. Masoro

Table 1
ADIPOSE TISSUE MASS AND RELATED MEASUREMENTS

Species	Findings	Ref.
Humans	In most studies, body fat content expressed as absolute mass has been found to increase with age until the 6th decade of life; after the 6th decade the findings have varied with reports of a continued increase, no further change, and some decrease in adipose mass	1—13
	Body density falls until the 6th decade of life; two studies show this decrease to continue with advancing age after the 6th decade and another study shows an increase in density after the 6th decade	3, 9, 14, 15
	The sum of 10 skinfold thickness measurements in Europeans shows increases up to 60 years of age in both sexes which indicates that the mass of subcutaneous fat increases with increasing age, a finding corroborated by roentgenographic analysis	3, 16, 17
	The triceps and subscapular skinfold thickness increase until the 6th decade of life after which they decrease in New Zealand Europeans	18
	In American men, skinfold thickness changes little with age over the adult life-span in the knee and chin, but large increases in subcutaneous fat masses occur in abdomen and chest during this time while in women there is a marked increase in subcutaneous fat in abdomen, chest, chin, and knee with increasing age, but the triceps skinfold changes little during the adult life-span	19
	In men, subcutaneous fat increases in the region of the greater trochanter but decreases in abdominal region through middle age	30
	In the Wajana Indians of Surinam, the skinfold thicknesses remain constant throughout the adult life-span	20
	The fat thickness of the extremities of Europeans increases until middle age after which it decreases	21
	Mean adipocyte mass in the epigastrial subcutaneous fat depot increases from 0.2 µg in young men to 0.6 µg in middle age men while the mean mass of the gluteal subcutaneous depot adipocyte increases from 0.28—0.65 µg; in women the increase in mean adipocyte mass from young adulthood to middle age is from 0.28—0.6 µg in the hypogastrial subcutaneous depot and from 0.25—0.65 µg in the femoral subcutaneous depot	22

Table 1 (continued)
ADIPOSE TISSUE MASS AND RELATED MEASUREMENTS

Species	Findings	Ref.
	Middle age women were found to have adipocytes of almost twice the size of young women, but to have a smaller total number of adipocytes than young women	23
	The fatty acid composition of the subcutaneous adipose tissue of the anterior abdominal wall changes very little during the adult life-span of of Negro and Caucasian people	24
Rat	In Osborne-Mendel strain, the perirenal fat depot increases in mass to a greater extent during most of the adult life-span than does body mass; after sexual maturity the increase in mass of the genital and subcutaneous fat depots is proportional to the increase in body mass	25
	In Fischer 344 strain, the epididymal fat depot increases markedly in mass until 52 weeks of age and remains relatively constant thereafter; the mean mass of the adipocyte population of this depot increases markedly until 52 weeks of age and remains constant until 104 weeks of age after which it decreases; the number of adipocytes in the depot increases between 26 and 52 weeks of age, remains constant between 52 and 104 weeks of age and increases again between 104 and 130 weeks of age	26
Mouse	In the C57B strain, the mass of the epididymal fat depot continuously increases between 1 and 18 months of age; the depots from young and old adult animals have the same number of adipocytes but the mean size of the adipocyte population is markedly larger in the old rats	27
	The multilocular fat cells of the brown adipose tissue show an age-dependent change to the unilocular fat cell type, a change which starts immediately after birth and continues throughout life	28
Guinea pig	The adipose mass increases markedly up to 10 months of age and continues to increase in mass at a slower rate until 20 months of age after which it is not certain as to whether it remains constant or declines in mass	29
Rat	In Fischer 344 male rats, perirenal fat depot increases markedly in mass from 6 through 18 months of age as the result of hyperplasia rather than hypertrophy	31
	In Fischer 344 male rats total adipose mass reaches a maximum between 50 and 70% of the life-span and decreases with increasing age	32

Table 1 (continued)
ADIPOSE TISSUE MASS AND RELATED
MEASUREMENTS

REFERENCES

1. **Novak, L.**, Aging, total body potassium, fat-free mass, and cell mass in males and females between ages 18 and 85 years, *J. Gerontol.*, 27, 438, 1972.
2. **Tran, M. H., Lellouch, J., and Richard, J. L.**, Fat body mass. II. Its relationships with some biological parameters, blood pressure, and physical training in a population of 8660 men aged 20 to 55, *Biomedicine*, 18, 499, 1973.
3. **Malina, R. M.**, Quantification of fat, muscle and bone in man, *Clin. Orthop. Relat. Res.*, 65, 9, 1969.
4. **Burmeister, W. and Bingert, A.**, Quantitative changes of the human cell mass between the 8th and 90th year of life, *Klin. Worchenschr.*, 45, 409, 1967.
5. **Mackova, E.**, Changes in functional and efficiency indicators between the 18th and 50th year in man, *Physiol. Bohemoslov.*, 17, 279, 1968.
6. **Bismark, H. D.**, On age-dependent changes in adipose tissue layers, *Z. Alternforsch.*, 20, 347, 1967.
7. **Weinsier, R. L., Fuchs, R. J., Kay, T. D., Thiebwasser, J. H., and Lancaster, M. C.**, Body fat; its relationship to coronary heart disease, blood pressure, lipids and other risk factors measured in a large male population, *Am. J. Med.*, 61, 815, 1976.
8. **Parizkova, J., Eiselt, E., Sprynarova, S., and Wachtlova, M.**, Body composition, aerobic capacity, and density of muscle capillaries in young and old men, *J. Appl. Physiol.*, 31, 323, 1971.
9. **Myhre, L. G. and Kessler, W. V.**, Body density and potassium 40 measurements of body composition as related to age, *J. Appl. Physiol.*, 21, 1251, 1966.
10. **Parizkova, J. and Eiselt, E.**, A further study on changes in somatic characteristics and body composition of old men followed longitudinally for 8—10 years, *Hum. Biol.*, 43, 318, 1971.
11. **Chien, S., Peng, M. T., Chen, K. P., Huang, T. F., Chang, C., and Fong, H.**, Longitudinal measurements of blood volume and essential body mass in human subjects, *J. Appl. Physiol.*, 39, 818, 1975.
12. **Brozek, J.**, Changes of body composition in man during maturity and their nutritional implications, *Fed. Proc. Fed. Am. Soc. Exp. Biol.*, 11, 784, 1952.
13. **Young, C. M., Blondin, J. Tensuan, R., and Fryer, J. H.**, Body composition of "older" women, *J. Am. Diet. Assoc.*, 43, 344, 1963.
14. **Krzywicki, H. J. and Chinn, K. S. K.**, Body composition of a military population, Fort Carson, 1963, *Am. J. Clin. Nutr.*, 20, 708, 1967.
15. **Ries, W., Jahn, K., Raue, I., and Sauer, I.**, Relationship between locomotion apparatus, aging and body weight, *Beitr. Orthop. Traumatol.*, 22, 570, 1975.
16. **Parizkova, J.**, Body composition and lipid metabolism, *Proc. Nutr. Soc.*, 32, 181, 1973.
17. **Garn, S. M. and Harper, R. V.**, Fat accumulation and weight gain in the adult male, *Hum. Biol.*, 27, 39, 1955.
18. **Evans, J. G., Prior, I. A. M., Davidson, F., and Morrison, R. B. I.**, The Carterton study; 2, height, weight and skinfold measurements in a sample of town-dwelling New Zealand Europeans, *N. Z. Med. J.*, 68, 318, 1968.
19. **Shephard, R. J., Jones, G., Ishu, K., Kaneko, M., and Olbrecht, A. J.**, Factors affecting body density and thickness of subcutaneous fat, *Am. J. Clin. Nutr.*, 22, 1175, 1969.
20. **Glanville, E. V. and Geerdink, R. A.**, Skinfold thickness, body measurements and age changes in Trio and Wajana Indians of Surinam, *Am. J. Phys. Anthropol.*, 32, 455, 1970.
21. **Bugyi, B.**, Age dependent changes of body constitution based on adipose tissue and musculature evaluation, *Z. Alternsforsch.*, 20, 327, 1967.
22. **Bjorntorp, P.**, Effects of age, sex and clinical conditions on adipose tissue cellularity in man, *Metabolism*, 23, 1091, 1974.
23. **Greenwood, M. R. C. and Johnson, P. R.**, Adipose tissue cellularity and its relationship to the development of obesity in females, *Curr. Concepts Nutr.*, 5, 119, 1977.
24. **Insull, W., Jr. and Bartsch, G. E.**, Fatty acid composition of human adipose tissue related to age, sex, and race, *Am. J. Clin. Nutr.*, 20, 13, 1967.
25. **Schemmel, R., Mickelsen, O., and Mostosky, U.**, Influence of body weight, age, diet and sex on fat depots in rats, *Anat. Rec.*, 166, 437, 1970.
26. **Stiles, J. W., Francendese, A. A., and Masoro, E. J.**, Influence of age on size and number of fat cells in the epididymal depot, *Am. J. Physiol.*, 229, 1561, 1975.
27. **Greenwood, M. R. C., Johnson, P. R., and Hirsch, J.**, Relationship of age and cellularity to metabolic activity in C57B mice, *Proc. Soc. Exp. Biol. Med.*, 133, 944, 1970.

Table 1 (continued)
ADIPOSE TISSUE MASS AND RELATED MEASUREMENTS

28. **Cameron, I. L.**, Age-dependent changes in the morphology of brown adipose tissue in mice, *Texas Rep. Biol. Med.,* 33, 391, 1975.
29. **Pitts, G. C., Bull, L. S., and Hollifield, G.**, Physiologic changes in composition and mass of total body adipose tissue, *Am. J. Physiol.,* 221, 961, 1971.
30. **Borkan, G. A. and Norris, A. H.**, Fat redistribution and the changing body dimensions of the adult male, *Hum. Biol.,* 49, 495, 1975.
31. **Bertrand, H. A., Masoro, E. J., and Yu, B. P.**, Increasing adipocyte number as the basis for perirenal depot growth in adult rats, *Science,* 201, 1234, 1978.
32. **Yu, B. P. and Masoro, E. G.**, Age-related changes in the total body mass, lean body mass and adipose tissue mass, II, *Gerontologist,* 18(5), 140, 1978.

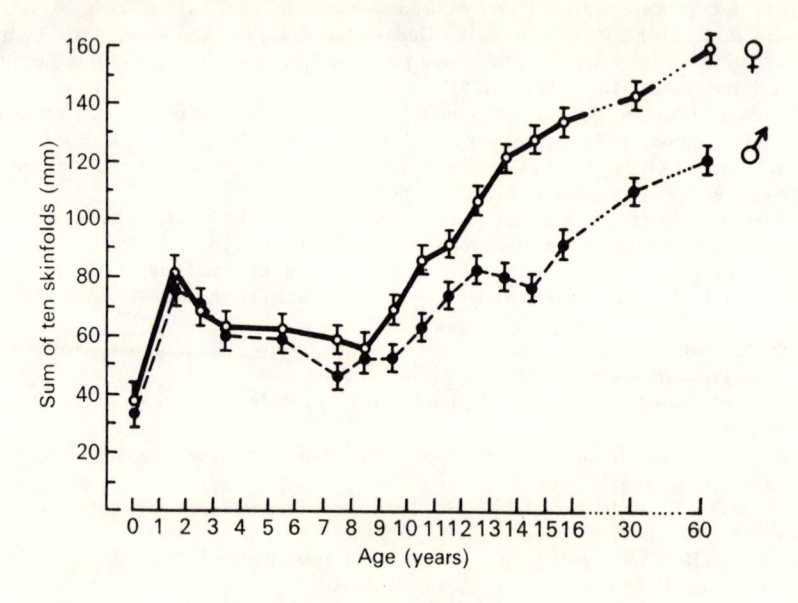

FIGURE 1. Age-related changes in skinfold thickness in men and women. (From Parizkova, J., Body composition and lipid metabolism, *Proc. Nutr. Soc.,* 32, 181, 1973, Cambridge University Press, New York. With permission.)

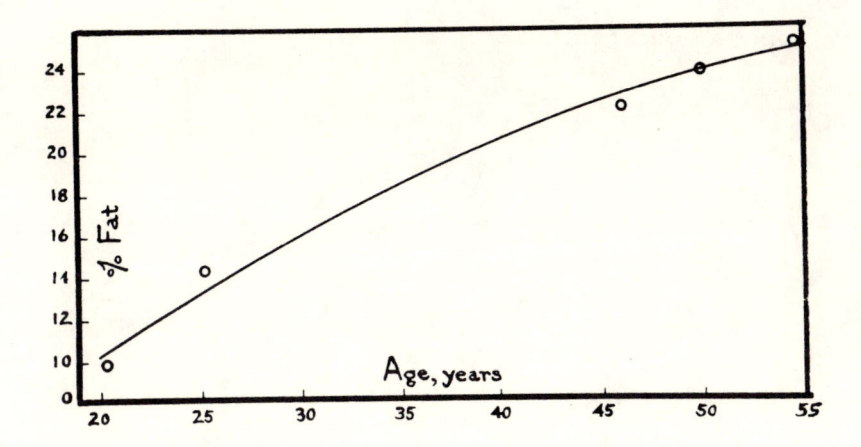

FIGURE 2. Changes in percent fat content of men with age. (From Brozek, J., *Fed. Proc. Fed. Am. Soc. Exp. Biol.*, 11, 784, 1952. With permission.)

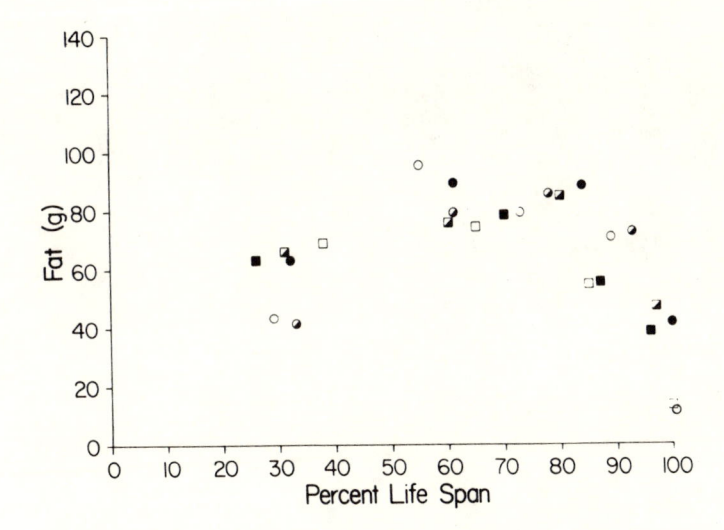

FIGURE 3. Fat content was measured in 14 Fischer 344 male rats in a longitudinal study. The data shown in the figure are for the 6 longest lived; similar results were obtained with most of the 8 shortest lived. Each symbol refers to a particular rat studied longitudinally. (From Yu, B. P. and Masoro, E. J., II., *Gerontologist*, 18(5), 140, 1978. With permission.)

BONE

Dike Kalu

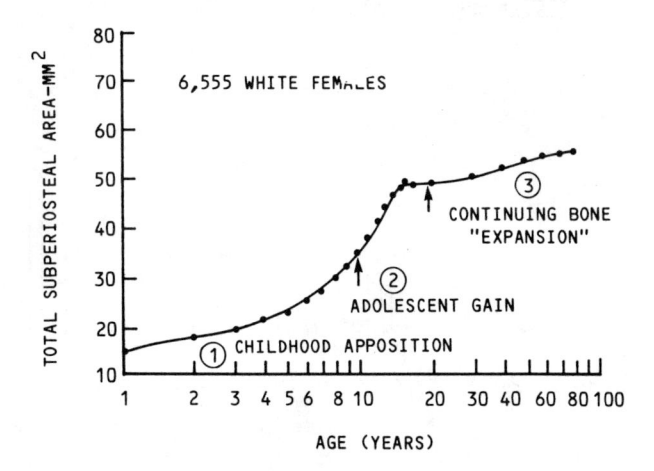

FIGURE 1. Subperiosteal appositional growth shown in 6555 white females and indicating the phase of childhood apposition (1), the period of adolescent gain (2), and continuing bone expansion after the third decade (3). (From Garn, S. M., *Orthop. Clin. North Am.*, 3, 503, 1972. With permission.)

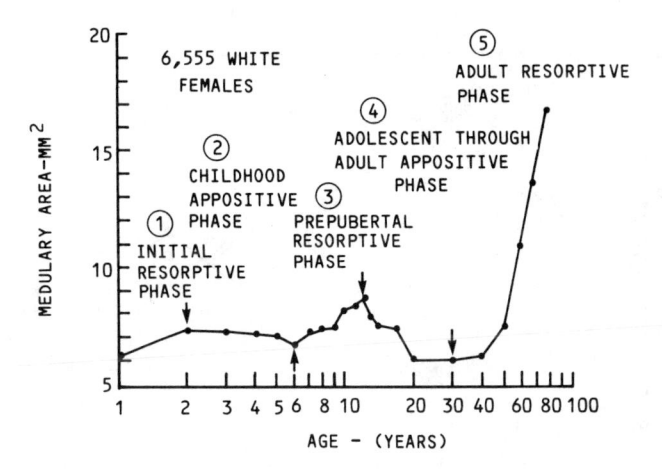

FIGURE 2. Bone growth and remodeling — endosteal surface changes. Changes at the endosteal surface (as reflected by medullary area). Shown is the resorptive phase of infancy (1), the childhood appositive phase: (2), the marked prepubertal resorptive phase (3), the adolescent-through adulthood appositive phase (4), and finally the adult resorptive phase (5) during which as much as 30% of compact bone may be lost. (From Garn, S. M., *Orthop. Clin. North Am.*, 3, 503, 1972. With permission.)

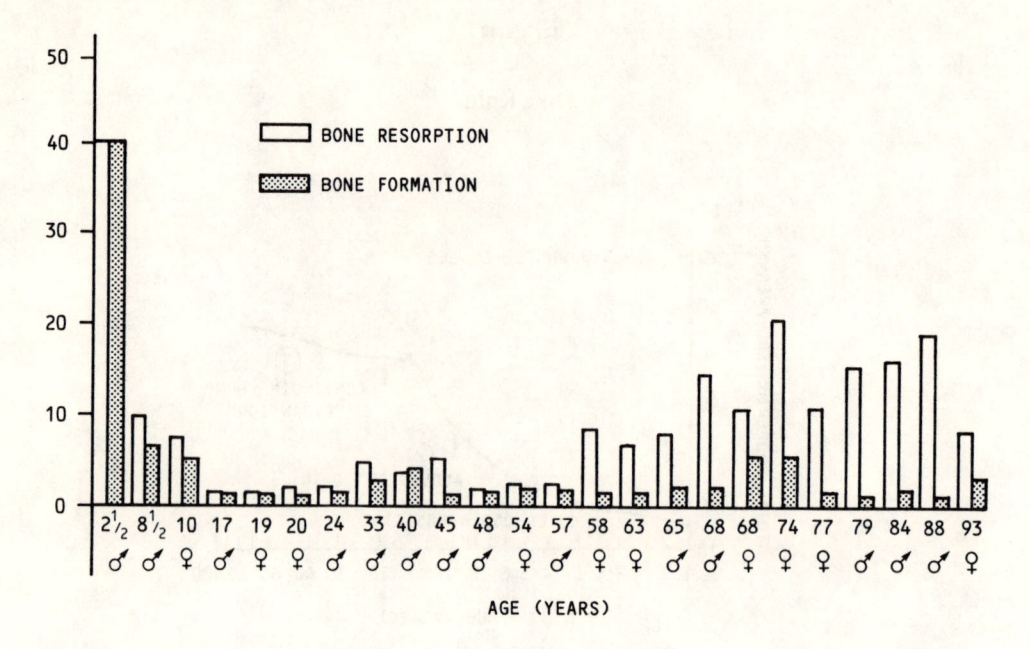

FIGURE 3. Changes with age in haversian bone of the human femoral cortex. Bone formation and resorption were measured by contact microradiography. (From Jowsey, J., Ed., *Metabolic Diseases of Bone*, W. B. Saunders, Philadelphia, 1977, 44. With permission.)

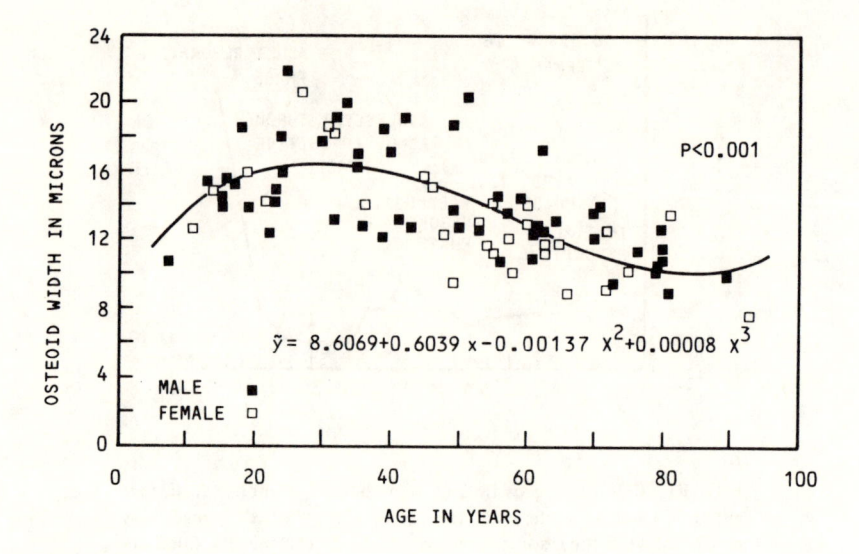

FIGURE 4. Variations in the width of osteoid tissue in normal men and women of different ages. The mean for a 20-year old is 16 microns; at age 80 mean osteoid width had decreased to 10 microns. (From Johnson, K. A., Riggs, B. L., Kelley, P. J., and Jowsey, J., *J. Clin. Endocrinol. Metab.*, 33, 745, 1971. With permission.)

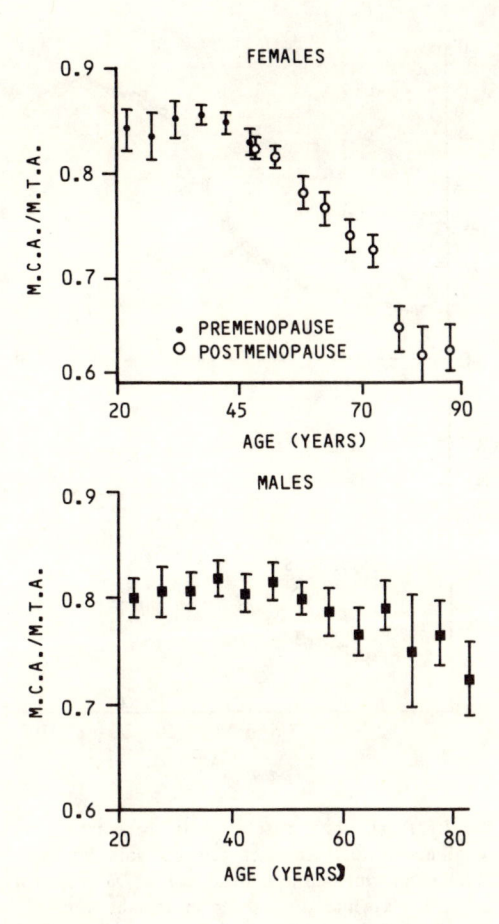

FIGURE 5. Bone changes in men and women during aging. M.C.A./M.T.A. is metacarpal cortical area/metacarpal total area ratios plotted as mean ± standard error. (From Nordin, B. E. C., *Br. Med. J.,* 1, 571, 1971. With permission.)

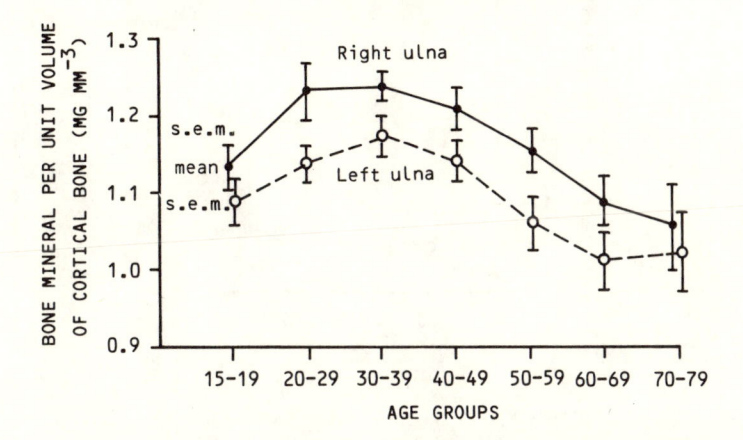

FIGURE 6. Mineral density of cortical bone in women. The highest values for both ulnae are in the 30-39 age group. The values for the right ulnae are significantly higher than those for the left ulnae. The reduction in mineral density in cortical bone between 40-49 and 60-69 parallels the fall in average mineral concentration. (From Doyle, F. H., *Sci. Basis Med. Annu. Rev.,* 8, 133, 1969. Reproduced with the permission of Professor F. H. Doyle and of the British Postgraduate Medical Federation.)

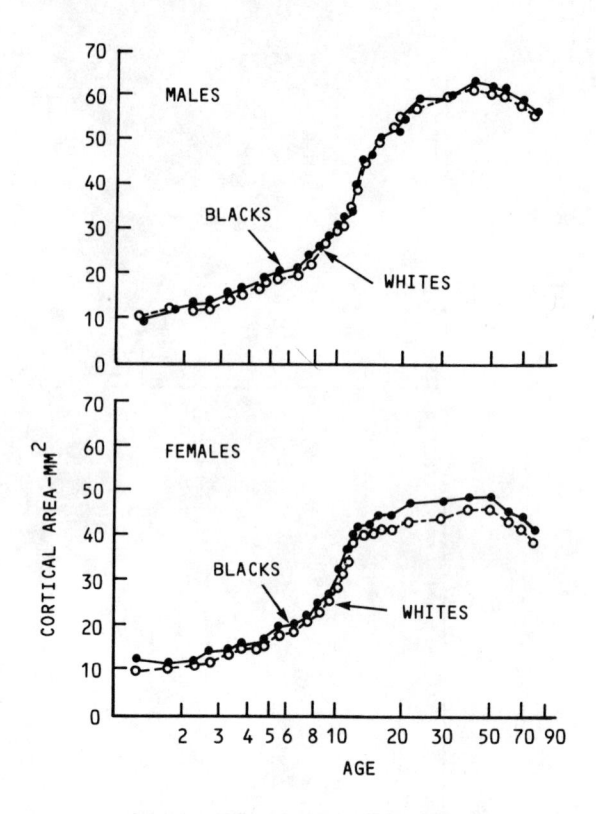

FIGURE 7. Black-white differences in metacarpal cortical area. At all ages, American black subjects (solid line) tend to exceed American white subjects (dashed line), with systematically larger black-white differences in females throughout. (From Garn, S. M., *Orthop. Clin. North Am.*, 3, 503, 1972. With permission.)

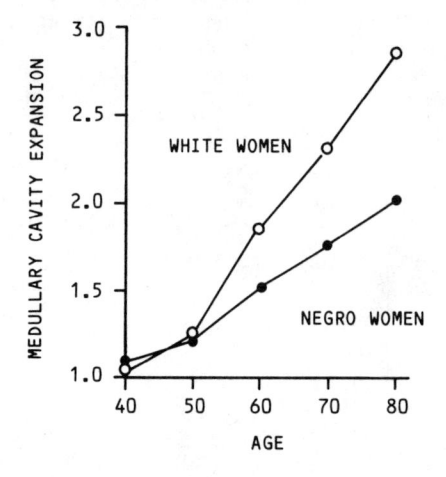

FIGURE 8. Comparative bone-loss as indicated by medullary cavity expansion in white and black women. Black women lose less bone both relatively and absolutely. (From Garn, S. M., *The Physiology and Pathology of Human Aging*, Goldman, R. and Rockstein, M., Eds., Academic Press, New York, 1975, 47. With permission.)

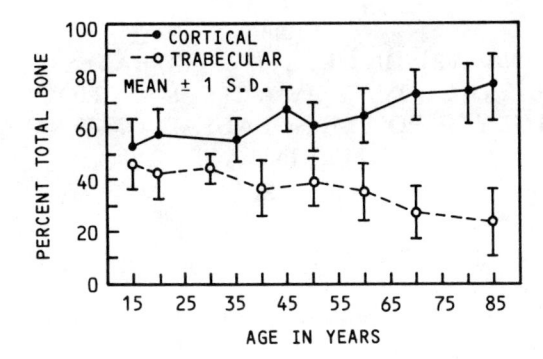

FIGURE 9. Percent of cortical and trabecular bone in the human iliac crest. Before skeletal maturity, the volumes of these two types are nearly the same; by the age of 65, the majority is cortical bone. (From Jowsey, J., Ed., *Metabolic Disease of Bone,* W. B. Saunders, Philadelphia, 1977, 44. With permission.)

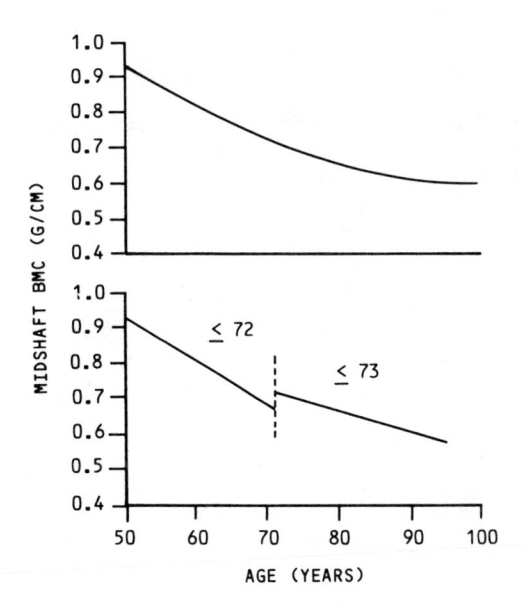

FIGURE 10. Loss of bone mineral in the right radius of women at the midshaft. Cross sectional measuree measurements on 530 women. (Top) The regression curve of bone mineral measurements of 530 women aged 50-96 years. (Bottom). The two regression lines were obtained when the population was divided by age into a younger group, aged 50-72 years and an older group aged 73-96 years. (From Smith, D. M., Khairi, M. R. A., Norton, J., and Johnston, C. C., Jr., *J. Clin. Invest.,* 58, 716, 1976. With permission.)

Table 1
COMPARISON OF ESTIMATED RATES OF
MINERAL LOSS FROM A CROSS-SECTIONAL
STUDY OF POSTMENOPAUSAL WOMEN OF
DIFFERING AGES

	Younger	Older
Mean age (year)	57 (50—72)[a]	81 (73—96)[a]
No. of subjects	264	266
Estimated rate of loss (g/cm/year)	−0.0114	−0.0055
SE	±0.0014	±0.0017

[a] Numbers in parentheses refer to range.

From Smith, D. M., Khairi, M. R. A., Norton, J., and Johnston, C. C., Jr., *J. Clin. Invest.*, 58, 716, 1976. With permission.

Table 2
COMPARISON OF RATES OF MINERAL LOSS
FROM A LONGITUDINAL STUDY OF
POSTMENOPAUSAL WOMEN OF DIFFERING
AGES

	Younger	Older
Mean age (year)	57 (51—64)[a]	81 (70—91)[a]
No. of subjects	33	38
Mean follow-up period (year)	4.5	3.8
No. of visits (mean/subject)	16	31
Mean rate of loss (g/cm/year)	−0.00990	−0.00020
SE	±0.00107	±0.00236

[a] Numbers in parentheses refer to range.

From Smith, D. M., Khairi, M. R. A., Norton, J., and Johnston, C. C., Jr., *J. Clin. Invest.*, 58, 716, 1976. With permission.

Table 3
MEAN MECHANICAL PROPERTY VALUES FOR WET EMBALMED TIBIAL CORTICAL BONE IN DIFFERENT 20-YEAR AGE GROUPS

Property	No.	20—39 years	No.	40—59 years	No.	60—79 years	No.	80—99 years	Unit of measurement
Tensile strength[a]	46	15,873 ± 2,568	45	14,854 ± 2,201	87	11,803 ± 2,041	14	11,552 ± 2,578	lbf/in.^{2}
		11.16 ± 1.81		10.44 ± 1.55		8.30 ± 1.43		8.12 ± 1.81	kgf/mm^2
% elongation[a]	45	2.29 ± 0.79	41	1.68 ± 0.81	75	1.53 ± 0.59	13	1.5 ± 0.73	
Modulus of elasticity[a]	46	2.46 ± 0.43	45	2.68 ± 0.47	84	2.08 ± 0.39	13	1.91 ± 0.35	×10^{6}lbf/in.^{2}
		1.73 ± 0.30		1.88 ± 0.33		1.46 ± 0.27		1.34 ± 0.25	×10^{3}kgf/mm^2
Single shear strength[b]	24	11,358 ± 2,321	45	11,693 ± 737	46	11,308 ± 904			lbf/in.^{2}
		7.98 ± 1.63		8.22 ± 0.52		7.95 ± 0.64			kgf/mm^2
Rockwell superficial hardness	24	15.2 ± 14.1	45	14.1 ± 8.3	46	7.1 ± 7.97			

[a] Parallel to long axis of bone.
[b] Perpendicular to long axis of bone.

From Evans, F. G., Mechanical Properties of Bone, 1973, 226. Courtesy of Charles C Thomas, Publisher, Springfield, Ill.

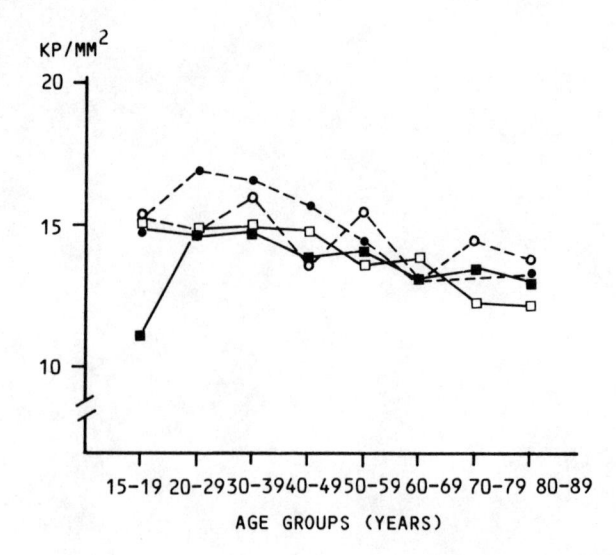

FIGURE 11. The variation of the mean ultimate strength with age for the femur and humerus of men and women. (From Lindhal, O. and Lindgren, A. G. H., *Acta Orthop. Scand.*, 38, 141, 1967. With permission.)

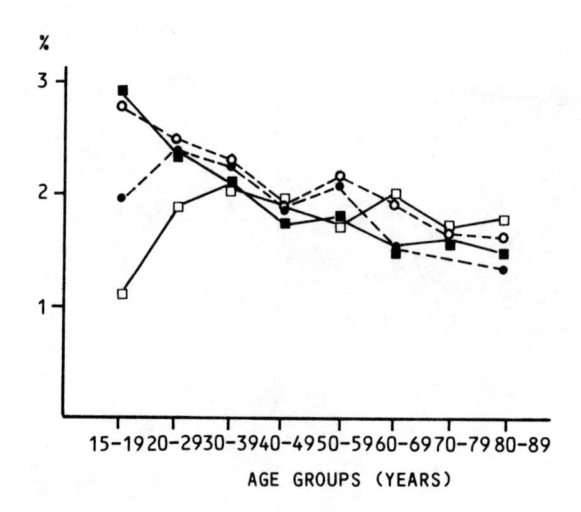

FIGURE 12. The variation of the mean deformation at failure with age for femur and humerus of men and women. (From Lindahl, O. and Lindgren, A. G. H., *Acta Orthop. Scand.*, 38, 141, 1967. With permission.)

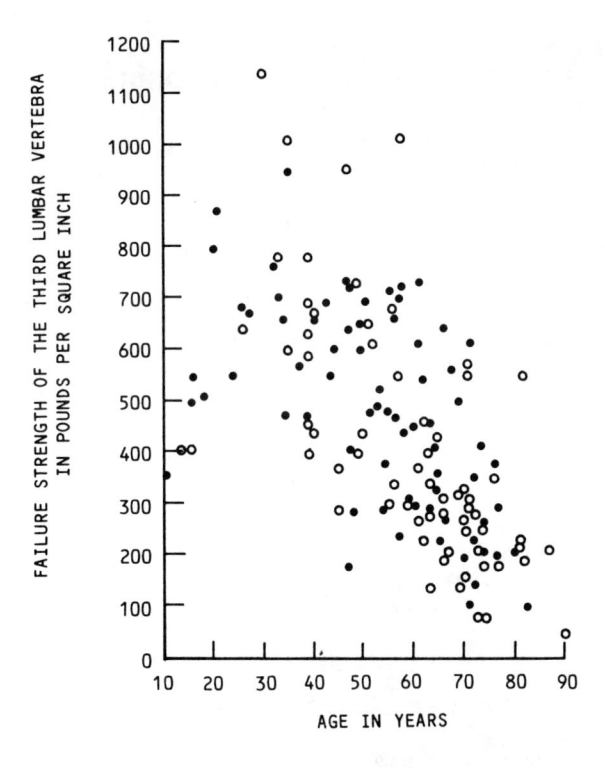

FIGURE 13. The change in vertebral compressive strength with advancing age in 137 cadavera (O indicates female, ● indicate male). There appears to be a relatively rapid increase in compressive strength up to the age of thirty and a gradual decrease in strength after the age of forty. There appears to be a broader range of normality in the middle age groups. (From Weaver, J. K. and Chalmers, J., *J. Bone Jt. Surg.*, 48-A, 289, 1966. With permission.)

Table 4
EFFECTS OF AGING ON BONE OF FEMALE RATS

Mean age (days)	Mean body weight (g)	Tibial length Mean ± SD (cm)	No. of animals
31	58	2.31 ± 0.160	10
51	145	3.21 ± 0.080	14
71	155	3.41 ± 0.090	10
79	178	3.57 ± 0.044	6
108	192	3.74 ± 0.040	11
176	220	3.90 ± 0.042	10
357	238	3.93 ± 0.058	26
585	271	3.96 ± 0.088	14
801	279	3.99 ± 0.086	33, 37

Modified from Berg, B. N. and Harmison, C. R., *J. Gerontol.*, 12, 370, 1957. With permission.

Table 5
EFFECTS OF AGING ON BONE OF MALE RATS

Mean age (days)	Mean body weight (g)	Tibial length Mean ± SD (cm)	No. of animals
31	60	2.37 ± 0.100	10
48	154	3.17 ± 0.110	13
67	225	3.65 ± 0.130	15
100	328	4.13 ± 0.140	10
162	380	4.38 ± 0.056	12
242	400	4.43 ± 0.067	10
328	438	4.50 ± 0.050	10
522	486	4.58 ± 0.077	20
622	456	4.56 ± 0.090	15
681	474	4.61 ± 0.089	18

From Berg, B. N. and Harmison, C. R., *J. Gerontol.*, 12, 370, 1957. With permission.

Table 6
SKELETAL EPIPHYSES IN RATS

Most unite by about day 120
Some persist till death
One epiphysis in each major long bone persists till senescence
Caudal vertebral epiphyses are patent throughout life
Osteogenic activity decreases with aging in the proximal tibial epiphysis of the rat in spite of persistent epiphysial cartilage

Modified from Berg, B. N. and Harmison, C. R., *J. Gerontol.*, 12, 370, 1957. With permission.

CONNECTIVE TISSUE

R. R. Kohn

Table 1
QUANTITATIVE CHANGES IN COLLAGEN DURING AGING

Tissue	Species	Change	Ref.
Myocardium	Man	Remains constant	1—3
	Rat	Increases	4
Aortic media	Man	Increases	5
	Rat	Increases	6
Cerebral arteries	Pig	Increases	7
Arterioles, capillaries	Man, rat	Increases	8
Kidney, lung, liver	Rat	Increases	9
Skin	Man	Decreases	10
Uterus	Rat	Increases	11

REFERENCES

1. **Kohn, R. R. and Rollerson, E.**, Age-changes in swelling properties of human myocardium, *Proc. Soc. Exp. Biol. Med.,* 100, 253, 1959.
2. **Montfort, I. and Perez-Tamayo, R.**, The muscle-collagen ratio in normal and hypertrophic human hearts, *Lab. Invest.,* 11, 463, 1962.
3. **Sasaki, R., Ichikawa, S., Yamagiwa, H., Ito, H., and Yamagata, S.**, Aging and hydroxyproline content in human heart muscle, *Tohoku J. Exp. Med.,* 118, 11, 1976.
4. **Tomanek, R. J., Taunton, C. A., and Liskop, K. S.**, Relationship between age, chronic exercise, and connective tissue of the heart, *J. Gerontol.,* 27, 33, 1972.
5. **Feldman, S. A. and Glagov, S.**, Transmedial collagen and elastin gradients in human aortas: reversal with age, *Atherosclerosis,* 13, 385, 1971.
6. **Cliff, W. J.**, The aortic tunica media in aging rats, *Exp. Mol. Pathol.,* 13, 172, 1970.
7. **Nanda, B. S. and Getty, R.**, Age related histomorphological changes in the cerebral arteries of domestic pig, *Exp. Gerontol.,* 6, 453, 1971.
8. **Casarett, G. W.** Acceleration of aging by ionizing radiation, in *The Biology of Aging,* Strehler, B., Ed., American Institute of Biological Sciences, Washington, D.C., 1960, 147.
9. **Schaub, M. C.**, Qualitative and quantitative changes of collagen in parenchymatous organs of the rat during aging, *Gerontologia,* 8, 114, 1963.
10. **Shuster, S., Raffle, E. J. and Bottoms, E.**, Skin collagen in rheumatoid arthritis and the effect of corticosteroids, *Lancet,* 1, 525, 1967.
11. **Kao, K. T. and Hitt, W. E.** The intermolecular cross-links in rat uterine collagen, *Biochim. Biophys. Acta,* 371, 501, 1974.

Table 2
CHANGES IN COLLAGEN PROPERTIES DURING AGING

Tissue	Species	Change	Ref.
Tendon	Rat	Force of thermal contraction increases	1
	Rat	Becomes resistant to enzymatic digestion	2
	Rat	Breaking time in urea increases	3
	Man	Loses swelling ability	4
	Man	Becomes resistant to enzymatic digestion	5
Myocardium	Man	Becomes resistant to enzymatic digestion	6
	Man	Becomes insoluble	7
Chordae tendineae	Man	Extensibility, waviness, decrease	8
Cornea	Man	Fibers break down, interfibriller distance decreases	9
Skin	Man	Becomes insoluble	10
Bone, cartilage	Man	Becomes insoluble	11
Uterus	Rat	Becomes insoluble	12

REFERENCES

1. **Verzár, F.**, The aging of collagen fibers, *Experientia Suppl.*, 4, 35, 1956.
2. **Schaub, M. C.**, Degradation of young and old collagen by extracts of various organs, *Gerontologia*, 9, 52, 1964.
3. **Delbridge, L. and Everitt, A. V.**, The effect of hypophysectomy and age on the stabilization of labile cross-links in collagen, *Exp. Gerontol.*, 7, 413, 1972.
4. **Kohn, R. R. and Rollerson, E.**, Studies of the effect of heat and age in decreasing ability of human collagen to swell in acid, *J. Gerontol.*, 14, 11, 1959.
5. **Hamlin, C. R. and Kohn, R. R.**, Evidence for progressive age-related structural changes in post mature human collagen, *Biochim. Biophys. Acta*, 236, 458, 1971.
6. **Zwolinski, R. J., Hamlin, C. R., and Kohn, R. R.** Age-related alteration in human heart collagen, *Proc. Soc. Exp. Biol. Med.*, 152, 362, 1976.
7. **Sasaki, R., Ichikawa, S., Yamagiwa, H., Ito, A., and Yamagata, S.**, Aging and hydroxyproline content in human heart muscle, *Tohoku J. Exp. Med.*, 118, 11, 1976.
8. **Lim, K. O. and Boughner, D. R.**, Morphology and relationship to extensibility curves of human mitral valve chordae tendineae, *Circ. Res.*, 39, 580, 1976.
9. **Kanai, A. and Kaufman, H. E.**, Electron microscopic studies of corneal stroma: aging changes of collagen fibers, *Ann. Ophthalmol.*, 5, 285, 1973.
10. **Bakerman, S.**, Quantitative extraction of acid-soluble human skin collagen with age, *Nature (London)*, 196, 375, 1962.
11. **Fujii, K., Yoshinori, K., and Sasaki, S.**, Aging of human bone and articular cartilage collagen: changes in the reducible cross-links and their precursors, *Gerontology*, 22, 363, 1976.
12. **Kao, K. T. and Hitt, W. E.**, The intermolecular cross-links in rat uterine collagen, *Biochim. Biophys. Acta*, 371, 501, 1974.

Table 3
CHANGES IN CHEMISTRY OF COLLAGEN DURING AGING

Tissue	Species	Change	Ref.
Tendon	Man	Flourescent material increases	1
	Rat	Allysine residues decrease	2
	Rat	Aldehydes decrease	3
Skin	Rat, hamster, cat	Semicarbizide cleavage decreases	4
	Man	Glycosylation of hydroxylysine increases	5
	Bovine	Dityrosine increases	6
Aorta	Rat	Lysyl oxidase decreases	3
Bone, cartilage	Man	Schiff bases decrease, hexitollysine increases	7
Uterus	Rat	Dehydrodihydroxylysinonorleucine/dehydrohydroxylysinonorleucine ratio decreases	8

REFERENCES

1. LaBella, F. S. and Paul, G., Structure of collagen from human tendon as influenced by age and sex, *J. Gerontol.,* 20, 54, 1965.
2. Davison, P. F. and Patel, A., Age-related changes in aldehyde location on rat tail tendon collagen, *Biochem. Biophys. Res. Commun.,* 65, 983, 1975.
3. Howarth, D. and Everitt, A. V., Effect of age, hypophysectomy, cortisone, and growth hormone on amine (lysyl) oxidase activity in rat aorta, *Gerontologia,* 20, 27, 1974.
4. Vancikova, O. and Deyl, Z., Aging of connective tissue: solubilisation of collagen from animals varying in age and species by reagents capable of splitting aldimine bonds, *Exp. Gerontol.,* 8, 297, 1973.
5. Murai, A, Miyahara, T., and Shiozawa, S., Age-related variations in glycosylation of hydroxylysine in human and rat skin collagens, *Biochim. Biophys. Acta,* 404, 345, 1975.
6. Waykole, P. and Heidemann, E., Dityrosine in collagen, *Connect. Tissue Res.,* 4, 219, 1976.
7. Fujii, K., Kuboki, Y., and Sasaki, S., Aging of human bone and articular cartilage collagen: changes in the reducible cross-links and their precursors, *Gerontology,* 22, 363, 1976.
8. Kao, K-Y.T. and Hitt, W. E., The intermolecular cross-links in rat uterine collagen, *Biochim. Biophys. Acta,* 371, 501, 1974.

Table 4
ELASTIN CHANGES AND PROPERTIES DURING AGING

Tissue	Species	Change or property	Ref.
Artery	Man	Contains more calcium	1
	Man	Binds more calcium	2
	Man	Reverses concentration gradient	3
	Man	Becomes fragmented	4
Artery, lung	Man	Isodesmosine, desmosine, decrease	5
	Man	Carbohydrate content increases	5
Lung	Man	Concentration increases	6—8
Artery	Rat	Is metabolically inert	9
	Rat	Decreases in lamina, increases around cells	10

REFERENCES

1. **Lansing, A. I.**, Elastic tissue in atherosclerosis, in *Connecive Tissue, Thrombosis, and Atherosclerosis*, Page, I. H., Ed., Academic Press, New York, 1959, 167.
2. **Eisenstein, R., Ayer, J., Papajiannis, S., Hass, G., and Ellis, H.**, Mineral binding by human arterial elastic tissue, *Lab. Invest.*, 13, 1198, 1964.
3. **Feldman, S. A. and Glagov, S.**, Transmedial collagen and elastic gradients in human aortas: reversal with age, *Atherosclerosis*, 13, 385, 1971.
4. **Blumenthal, H. T., Lansing, A. L., and Gray, S. H.** The interrelation of elastic tissue and calcium in the genesis of arteriosclerosis, *Am. J. Pathol.*, 26, 989, 1950.
5. **John, R. and Thomas, J.**, Chemical compositions of elastins isolated from aortas and pulmonary tissues of humans of different ages, *Biochem. J.*, 127, 261, 1972.
6. **Briscoe, A. M. and Loring, W. E.**, Elastin content of the human lung, *Proc. Soc. Exp. Biol. Med.*, 99, 162, 1958.
7. **FitzPatrick, M. and Hospelhorn, V. D.**, Studies on human pulmonary connective tissue. I. Amino acid composition of elastins isolated by alkaline digestion, *J. Lab. Clin. Med.*, 60, 799, 1962.
8. **Pierce, J. A. and Hocott, J. B.**, Studies on the collagen and elastin content of the human lung, *J. Clin. Invest.*, 39, 8, 1960.
9. **Walford, R. L., Carter, P. K., and Schneider, R. B.**, Stability of aortic elastic tissue with age and pregnancy in the rat, *Arch. Pathol.*, 78, 43, 1964.
10. **Cliff, W. J.**, The aortic tunica media in aging rats, *Exp. Mol. Pathol.*, 13, 172, 1970.

Table 5
CHANGES IN GLYCOSAMINOGLYCANS DURING AGING

Tissue	Species	Change	Ref.
Skin	Man	Soluble glycosaminoglycans decrease	1
	Man	Dermatan sulfate plus heparan sulfate decrease	2
	Rat	Hyaluronic acid/chondroitin sulfate ratio decreases	3
	Mouse	Chondroitin sulfate, hyaluronic acid, decrease	4
Cartilage	Man	Chondroitin sulfate decreases	5, 6
	Man	Keratan sulfate plus glycoprotein/chondroitin sulfate ratio increases	7
Aorta	Man	Hyaluronic acid, chondroitin sulfate C decrease	8
	Man	Chondroitin sulfate B, heparitan sulfate increase	8
Aortic intima	Man	Glycosaminoglycans decrease	9
Heart valves	Man	Acid mucopolysaccharides increase	10
Lung	Man	Glycosaminoglycans decrease, glycoproteins increase	11
Nucleus pulposus	Rabbit	Keratosulfate/chondroitin sulfate C ratio increases	12

REFERENCES

1. Fleischmajer, R., Perlish, J. S., and Bashey, R. I., Human dermal glycosaminoglycans and aging, *Biochim. Biophys. Acta*, 279, 265, 1972.
2. Van Lis, J. M. J., Kruiswijk, T., Mager, W. H., and Kalsbeek, G. L., Glycosaminoglycans in human skin, *Br. J. Dermatol.*, 88, 355, 1973.
3. Prodi, G., The effect of age on acid mucopolysaccharides in rat dermis, *J. Gerontol.*, 19, 128, 1964.
4. Sobel, H., Hewlett, M. J., and Hrubant, H. E., Collagen and glycosaminoglycans in skin of aging mice, *J. Gerontol.*, 25, 102, 1970.
5. Kaplan, D. and Meyer, K., Aging of human cartilage, *Nature (London)*, 183, 1267, 1959.
6. Stidworthy, G., Masters, Y. F., and Shetlar, M. R., The effect of aging on mucopolysaccharide composition of human costal cartilage as measured by hexosamine and uronic acid content, *J. Gerontol.*, 13, 10, 1958.
7. Hjertquist, S-O. and Lemperg, R., Identification and concentration of the glycosaminoglycans of human articular cartilage in relation to age and osteoarthritis, *Calcif. Tissue Res.* 10, 223, 1972.
8. Kaplan, D. and Meyer, K., Mucopolysaccharides of aorta at various ages, *Proc. Soc. Exp. Biol. Med.*, 105, 78, 1960.
9. Berenson, G. S., Dalferes, E. R., Jr., Robin, R., and Strong, J. P., Mucopolysaccharides and atherosclerosis, in *Evolution of the Atherosclerotic Plaque*, Jones, R. J., Ed., University of Chicago Press, Chicago, 1963, 139.
10. Sames, K., Stegmann, T., and Rebel, W., Age-related changes in concentrations of acid mucopolysaccharides in human heart valves, *Gerontologia*, 20, 69, 1974.
11. Buddecke, E. and Ruff-Lichtenstein, E., Anionic polysaccharides and glycoproteins of human lung connective tissue in relation to age and silicosis, *Beitr. Silikose-Forsch.*, Suppl. 5, 173, 1963.
12. Davidson, E. A. and Small, W., Metabolism in vivo of connective-tissue mucopolysaccharides. I. Chondroitin sulfate C and keratosulfate of nucleus pulposus, *Biochim. Biophys. Acta*, 69, 445, 1963.

Table 6
CHANGES IN CONNECTIVE TISSUE HEXOSES DURING AGING

Tissue	Species	Change	Ref.
Skin, tendon	Rat	Hexosamine/collagen ratio decreases	1, 2
Aorta, myocardium, skin	Man	Hexosamine/collagen ratio decreases	3, 4
	Man	Hexuronic acid/collagen ratio decreases	5
Bone, cartilage	Rat	Hexosamine/collagen ratio increases	2
Cartilage	Man	Sulfate/hexuronic acid ratio increases	6
	Man	Galactosamine/glucosamine ratio decreases	7
Nucleus pulposus	Man	Hexosamine decreases	8

REFERENCES

1. **Kao, K. T., Hilker, D. M., and McGavak, T. H.,** Connective tissue. III. Collagen and hexosamine content of tissues of rats of different ages, *Proc. Soc. Exp. Biol. Med.*, 104, 359, 1960.
2. **McGavack, T. H. and Kao, K. T.,** Aging in connective tissue: a dynamic process, *J. Am. Geriatr. Soc.*, 11, 1024, 1963.
3. **Clausen, B.,** Influence of age on connective tissue: hexosamine and hydroxyproline in human aorta, myocardium, and skin, *Lab. Invest.*, 11, 229, 1962.
4. **Sobel, H., Gabay, S., Wright, E., Lichtenstein, I., and Nelson, N. H.,** The influence of age upon the hexosamine collagen ratio of dermal biopsies from men, *J. Gerontol.*, 13, 128, 1958.
5. **Clausen, B.,** Influence of age on connective tissue: uronic acid and uronic acid-hydroxyproline ratio in human aorta, myocardium, and skin, *Lab. Invest.*, 11, 1340, 1962.
6. **Hjertquist, S.-O. and Lemperg, R.,** Identification and concentration of the glycosaminoglycans of human articular cartilage in relation to age and osteoarthritis, *Calcif. Tissue Res.*, 10, 223, 1972.
7. **Saltzman, H. A., Sieker, H. O., and Green, J.,** Hexosamine and hydroxyproline content in human bronchial cartilage from aged and diseased lungs, *J. Lab. Clin. Med.*, 62, 78, 1963.
8. **Hallén, H.,** The collagen and ground substance of human intervertebral disc at different ages, *Acta Chem. Scand.*, 16, 705, 1962.

Table 7
CHANGES IN PROPERTIES AND COMPOSITION OF CONNECTIVE TISSUE-RICH STRUCTURES DURING AGING

Tissue	Species	Change	Ref.
Lung	Man	Becomes stiffer	1, 2
Arteries	Man, rat	Becomes stiffer	3—9
	Man	Calcium increases	10
Heart	Rat	Becomes stiffer	11
Cartilage	Rabbit	Permeability decreases	12
	Man	Fatigue properties decrease	13
Skin	Man	Becomes stiffer	14
	Man	Permeability decreases	15
Artery, tendon, dura, fascia, sclera, skin	Man	Lipids increase	16—19

REFERENCES

1. **Niewoehner, D. E., Kleinerman, J., and Liotta, L.**, Elastic behavior of postmortem human lung: effects of aging and mild emphysema, *J. Appl. Physiol.*, 39, 943, 1975.
2. **Radford, E. P., Jr.**, Static mechanical properties of lungs in relation to age, in *Aging of the Lung*, Cander, L. and Moyer, J. M., Eds., Grune and Stratton, New York, 1964, 152.
3. **Bader, H.**, Dependence of wall stress in the human thoracic aorta on age and pressure, *Circ. Res.*, 20, 354, 1967.
4. **Band, W., Goedhard, W. J. A., and Knoop, A. A.**, Effects of aging on viscoelastic properties of the rat's thoracic aorta, *Pfluegers Arch.*, 331, 357, 1972.
5. **Gozna, E. R., Marble, A. E., Shaw, A., and Holland, J. G.**, Age-related changes in the mechanics of the aorta and pulmonary artery of man, *J. Appl. Physiol.*, 36, 407, 1974.
6. **Mozersky, D. J., Sumner, D. S., Hokanson, D. E., and Strandness D. E.**, Transcutaneous measurement of the elastic properties of the human femoral artery, *Circulation*, 46, 948, 1972.
7. **Nakashima, T. and Tanikawa, J.**, A study of human aortic distensibility with relation to atherosclerosis and aging, *Angiology*, 22, 477, 1971.
8. **O'Rourke, M. F., Blazek, J. V., Morreels, C. L., and Kravetz, L. J.**, Pressure wave transmission along the human aorta, *Circ. Res.*, 23, 567, 1968.
9. **Roach, M. R. and Burton, A. C.**, The effect of age on the elasticity of human iliac arteries, *Can. J. Biochem. Physiol.*, 37, 557, 1959.
10. **Bertelsen, S. V.**, Alterations in human aorta and pulmonary artery with age, *Acta Pathol. Microbiol. Scand.*, 51, 206, 1961.
11. **Weisfeldt, M. L., Loeven, W. A., and Shock, N. W.**, Resting and active mechanical properties of trabeculae carnae from aged male rats, *Am. J. Physiol.*, 220, 1921, 1971.
12. **Stockwell, R. H. and Barnett, C. H.**, Changes in permeability of articular cartilage with age, *Nature (London)*, 201, 835, 1964.
13. **Weightman, B.**, Tensile fatigue of human articular cartilage, *J. Biomech.*, 9, 193, 1976.
14. **Sanders R.**, Torsional elasticity of human skin in vivo, *Pfluegers Arch. Eur. J. Physiol.*, 342, 255, 1973.
15. **Aschner, B. M.**, Intradermal salt solution test in elderly persons, *Exp. Med. Surg.*, 18, 17, 1960.
16. **Adams, C. and Bayliss, O.**, Acid mucosubstances underlying lipid deposits in aging tendons and atherosclerotic arteries, *Atherosclerosis*, 18, 191, 1973.
17. **Adams, C. W. M., Bayliss, O. B., Baker, R. W. R., Abdulla, Y. H., and Hunter-Craig, C. J.**, Lipid deposits in aging human arteries, tendons and fascia, *Atherosclerosis*, 19, 429, 1974.
18. **Broekhuyse, R. M.**, Lipids in tissues of the eye. VII. Changes in concentration and composition of sphingomyelins, cholesterol esters, and other lipids in aging sclera, *Biochim. Biophys. Acta*, 280, 637, 1973.
19. **Crouse, J. R., Grundy, S. M., and Ahrens, E. H., Jr.**, Cholesterol distribution in the bulk tissues of man: variation with age, *J. Clin. Invest.*, 51, 1292, 1972.

Exercise

SURVEY OF EXERCISE AND AGING

N. W. Bolduan and S. M. Horvath

Table 1
GENERAL CHANGES WITH AGE IN EXERCISE PHYSIOLOGY

	Ref.
Exercise tolerance and performance decrease with age	1—7
Declines in physical working capacity, largely take place beyond age 50 or age 60	2—4, 8
Active older subjects demonstrate aerobic capacities far in excess of their sedentary counterparts and superior to sedentary young subjects	9
Reaction and movement times for older active subjects are faster than those exhibited by young and old nonactive individuals, and more like those of younger active subjects than either of the nonactive groups	10, 11
Physiological processes known to decline with aging that have been reported to be modifiable by exercise and physical conditioning include cardiac efficiency, arterial distensibility, pulmonary function, and bone calcium	9, 12—14

REFERENCES

1. **Robinson, S., Dill, D. B., Tzankoff, S. P., Wagner, J. A., and Robinson, R. D.,** Longitudinal studies of aging in 37 men, *J. Appl. Physiol.*, 38, 263, 1975.
2. **Drinkwater, B. L., Horvath, S. M., and Wells, C. L.,** Aerobic power of females ages 10 to 68, *J. Gerontol.*, 30, 385, 1975.
3. **Asmussen, E., Fruensbaard, K., and Norgaard, S.,** A follow-up longitudinal study of selected physiologic function in former physical education students — after forty years, *J. Am. Geriatr. Soc.*, 23, 442, 1975.
4. **Atomi, Y. and Miyashita, M.,** Effects of moderate recreational activities on the aerobic work capacity of middle-aged women, *J. Sports Med. Phys. Fitness*, 16, 261, 1976.
5. **Brunner, D.,** Physical exercise and cardiovascular fitness, in *Guide to Fitness After Fifty*, Harris, R. and Frankel, L. J., Eds., Plenum Press, New York, 1977, 143.
6. **Fischer, A. A. and Parizkova, J.,** A follow-up study of the effect of physical activity on the decline of working capacity and maximal O_2 consumption in the senescent male, in *Guide to Fitness After Fifty*, Harris, R. and Frankel, L. J., Eds., Plenum Press, New York, 1977, 67.
7. **Hartung, G. H. and Farge, E. J.,** Personality and physiological traits in middle-aged runners and joggers, *J. Gerontol.*, 32, 541, 1977.
8. **Pollock, M. L., Miller, H. S., and Wilmore, J.,** Physiological characteristics of champion American track athletes 40 to 75 years of age, *J. Gerontol.*, 29, 645, 1974.
9. **Wilmore, J. H., Miller, H. L., and Pollock M. L.,** Body composition and physiological characteristics of active endurance athletes in their eighth decade of life, *Med. Sci. Sports*, 6, 44, 1974.
10. **Spirduso, W. W.,** Reaction and movement time as a function of age and physical activity level, *J. Gerontol.*, 30, 435, 1975.
11. **Spirduso, W. W. and Clifford, P.,** Replication of age and physical activity effects on reaction and movement time, *J. Gerontol.*, 33, 26, 1978.
12. **Webb, J. L., Urner, S. C., and McDaniels, J.,** Physiological characteristics of a champion runner: age 77, *J. Gerontol.*, 32, 286, 1977.
13. **Montoye, H. J., Ed.,** *Physical Activity and Health: An Epidemiologic Study of an Entire Community*, Prentice-Hall, Englewood Cliffs, N.J., 1975.
14. **Sidney, K. H., Shephard, R. J., and Harrison, J. E.,** Endurance training and body composition of the elderly, *Am. J. Clin. Nutr.*, 30, 326, 1977.

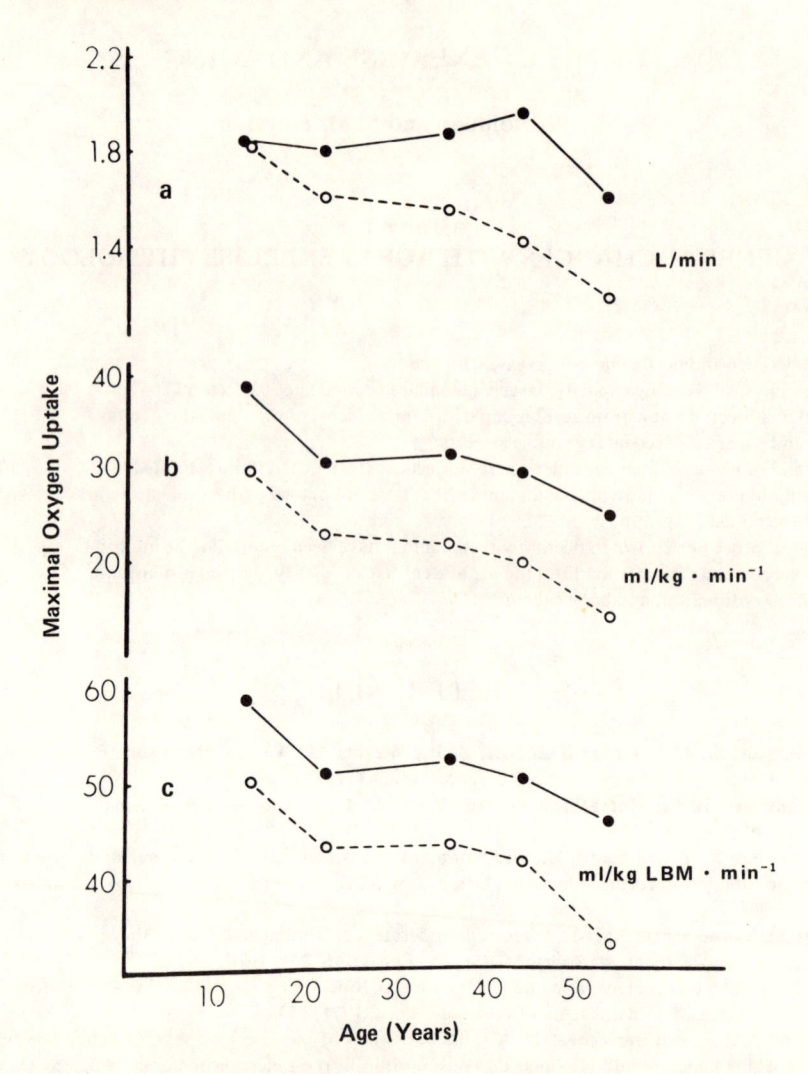

FIGURE 1. Maximal aerobic power of males and females related to chronological age (max $\dot{V}_{O_2}$ expressed in l/min, $ml/kg \cdot m^{-1}$ and ml/kg lean body mass $\cdot m^{-1}$). (Data from the Institute of Environmental Stress, University of California, Santa Barbara. With permission.)

Table 2
WORK CAPACITY

	Ref.
Maximum aerobic capacity decreases with age	1—5
Maximal O₂ uptake is a highly reproducible variable	6
For accurate analysis of max aerobic power there is no alternative to measuring $\dot{V}_{O_2\,max}$ directly; asymptote of HR vs. $\dot{V}_{O_2}$ is a limiting factor in predicting	7
Balke treadmill method preferred for exercise testing	8
Voluntary max fatigue is the safest endpoint; 85% of heart rate at max $\dot{V}_{O_2}$ also safe	9
Submaximal work is not useful to project maximal capacity at different ages	10
A battery of tests ($\dot{V}_{O_2\,max}$, muscle strength, neuromuscular coordination, reaction time) is more accurate than single tests for predicting performance by age	11
Age is a sufficient but not a necessary cause for diminishing physical power	12, 13
Max capacity in normal children is related to size and sex; females require a higher pulse rate to accomplish the same level of effort as males	14
Superior capacity of young males over females to run in desert heat related to increased aerobic capacity — not better temperature regulation	15
Max aerobic power in males and females is the same when related to lean body weight	16
Age produces a loss in functional ability despite maintenance of dimensional capacity of youth	17
Aerobic power shows a progressive decline throughout the span of working life; by age 60 many men, and almost all women, are unlikely to sustain an 8-hr load at three times the resting level of energy expenditure without fatigue	18
Length of exercise endurance dependent on level of work; 8 hr tolerated at HR 120 and only 2 hr at HR 160	19, 20
Capacity for light to moderate work is grossly independent of age; with hard exhaustive work it is strongly age dependent	21

REFERENCES

1. Grimby, G. and Saltin, B., Physiologic analysis of physically well-trained middle aged and older individuals, *Acta Med. Scand.*, 179, 513, 1966.
2. Wessel, J., Small, A., Van Hess, W. D., Anderson, D. J., and Cedarquick, D. C., Age and physiologic responses to exercise in females 20-69 years, *J. Gerontol.*, 23, 269, 1968.
3. Wyndham, C. H. and Sluis-Creme, G., Capacity for physical work of white miners in South Africa, *S. Afr. Med. J.* 42, 43, 1968; 1969.
4. McCurdy, J. H. and Larson, L., Age and organic efficiency, *Mil. Surg.*, 85(2), 93, 1939.
5. Dill, D. B., Fitness of Harvard men (20) after 22 years, in *Proc. Duke University Comm. Gerontol. Seminars*, Duke University Press, Durham, N.C., 1961-1965.
6. Clausen, J. P., Effect of physical training on cardiovascular adjustments in man, *Physiol. Rev.*, 57, 779, 1977.
7. Davies, C. T. M., Limitations to prediction of $\dot{V}_{O_2\,max}$ from heart rate, *J. Appl. Physiol.*, 24, 700, 1968.
8. Dill, D. B., Influence of Age on performance, as shown by exercise tests, *Pediatrics*, 32, 653, 1958.
9. Cumming, G., Yield of ischemic exercise ECG in relation to exercise intensity in a normal population, *Br. Heart J.*, 34, 919, 1972.
10. Åstrand, I., Physical work capacity of workers 50-64 years old, *Acta Physiol. Scand.* 42, 73, 1958; Acat Med. Scand., 162, 1958.
11. Åsmussen, E., Correlation Between Various Physiologic Test Results in Handicapped Persons, No. 27, Danish National Association for Infantile Paralysis, Copenhagen, 1968.
12. Barry, A. J., Daly, J. W., Pruett, E. D. R., Steinmetz, J. R., Page, H. F., Birkhead, N. C., and K. Rodahl, Effects of physical conditioning on older individuals, *J. Gerontol.*, 21, 182, 1965.
13. Diem, C., Exercise benefits against aging, Lecture at 18th German Team Physician Congress, Hamburg, July 1957.
14. Godfrey, S., Davies, C. T. M., Wozniak, E., and Barnes, C., Cardiorespiratory response to exercise in normal children, *Clin. Sci.*, 40, 419, 1971; Clin. Sci., 40, 433, 1971.
15. Dill, D. B., Soholt, L. F., McLean, D., Drost, T. F., and Longhorm, M., Capacity of young males and females to run in desert heat, *Med. Sci. Sports*, 9, 137, 1977.

Table 2 (continued)
WORK CAPACITY

16. Steplock, D. A., Veicsteinas, A., and Mariani, M., Maximal aerobic power and stroke volume of the heart in a sub-alpine population, *Int. Z. Angew. Physiol. Einschl. Arbeitsphysiol.*, 29, 203, 1971.
17. Davies, C. T. M., O$_2$ transporting system in relation to age, *Clin. Sci.*, 42, 1, 1972.
18. Buskirk, E. R. and Councilman, J., Special exercise problems in middle age, in *Science and Medicine of Exercise and Sports*, Ridehsun, W., Ed., Harper, New York, 1960, 24.
19. Michael, E., Hutton, K., and Horvath, S. M., Cardiorespiratory responses during prolonged exercise, *J. Appl. Physiol.*, 16, 997, 1961.
20. Hollmann, W., Changes in capacity for maximal and continuous effort in relation to age, in *Book review — Summary of Investigations in Cologne*, J. A. Bartl, Munich, 1963, 128.
21. Henschel, A., Effects of age on work capacities, *Am. Ind. Hyg. Assoc. J.*, 31, 430, 1970.

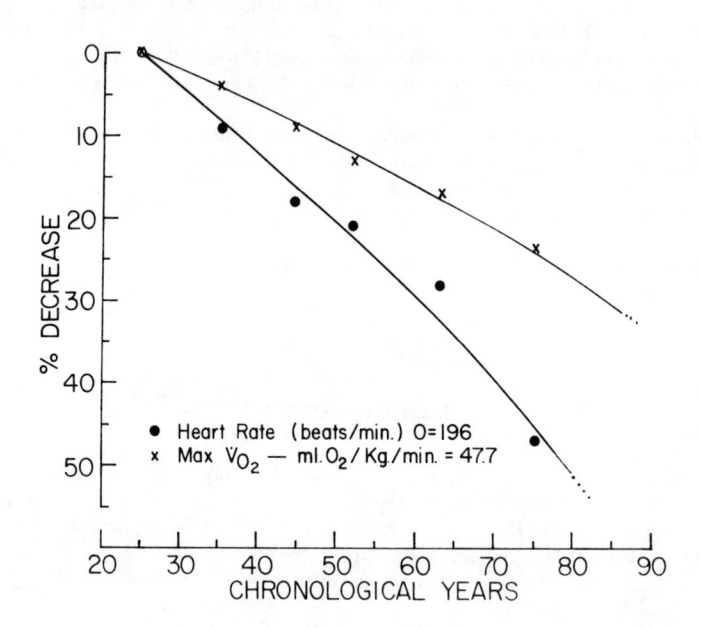

FIGURE 2. Percent decrease in maximum heart rates and maximal aerobic capacity of male subjects in relation to age. (Data from the Institute of Environmental Stress, University of California, Santa Barbara. With permission.)

Table 3
CARDIOVASCULAR RESPONSES TO EXERCISE

	Ref.
Cardiac output	1
Athletes 36 ℓ/min at BP 116 systolic	
Middle-aged men 11.5 ℓ/min at BP 164 systolic	
Maximum heart rate decreases with age	2—6
Stroke volume decreases in older males	2—6
Heart volume/$\dot{V}_{O_2\,max}$ increased in active older athletes	2
Return of heart rate to pre-exercise rate is delayed with age	3, 7, 8
Circulatory system of well-trained athletes has extreme ability to reduce peripheral resistance rather than increase blood pressure	1, 9
Vascular beds most affected in hypertension do not take part in dilatation of exercise	10
Muscle blood flow diminishes at sub max after physical conditioning	11
Skin blood flow increases up to 50—60% $\dot{V}_{O_2\,max}$ with physical conditioning	11

REFERENCES

1. Clausen, J. P., Effect of physical training on cardiovascular adjustments in man, *Physiol. Rev.*, 57, 779, 1977.
2. Grimby, G. and Saltin, B., Physiologic analysis of physically well-trained middle aged and older individuals, *Acta Med. Scand.*, 179, 513, 1966.
3. Wessel, J., Small, A., Van Hess, W. D., Anderson, D. J., and Cedarquick, D. C., Age and physiologic responses to exercise in females 20—69 years, *J. Gerontol.*, 23, 269, 1968.
4. Wyndham, C. H. and Sluis-Creme, G., Capacity for physical work of white miners in South Africa, *S. Afr. Med. J.*, 42, 43, 1968; 1969.
5. McGurdy, J. H. and Larson, L., Age and organic efficiency, *Mil. Surg.*, 85, 93, 1939.
6. Dill, D. B., Fitness of Harvard men (20) after 22 years, in *Proc. Duke University Comm. Gerontol. Seminars*, Duke University Press, Durham, N.C., 1961—1965.
7. Montoye, H. J., Willis, P. W., and Cunningham, D. J., Heart rate response to submaximal exercise: age and sex, *J. Gerontol.*, 23, 127, 1968.
8. Falls, H. B., Ismail, A. H., and MacLeod, D. F., Physical working capacity and motor fitness in relation to age of American University Faculty, *J. Assoc. Phys. Ment. Rehabilitation*, 20, 184, 1966.
9. Amery, A., Julius, S., Whitlock, L. S., and Conway, J., Influence of hypertension on the hemodynamic response to exercise, *Circulation*, 36, 231, 1967.
10. Julius, S., Amery, A., Whitlock, L. S., and Conway, J., Effect of age on hemodynamic response to exercise, *Circulation*, 36, 222, 1967.
11. Saltin, B., Kilborn, Å., and Åstrand, I., Physical conditioning in older subjects, *Scand. J. Clin. Lab. Invest.*, 24, 305, 1969.

Table 4
INFLUENCE OF TRAINING

	Ref.
The adaptation to physical training which improves performance involves multiple reactions involving skeletal muscle fibers, nervous system, and circulatory system	1
Physical conditioning is associated with adaptation of a neuroregulatory mechanism to a higher level of functioning	1, 2
Improvement in physical performance from physical training is an example of long-term adaptation to increased chronic stress	1, 3
Training is the adaptive response to stress of exercise	1, 4
Exercise preserves youth	5
Effective response to training programs has been observed in middle-aged and older individuals	6
More active men performed at a higher level of work load on a bicycle ergometer when pushed to exhaustion	7
Maximum cardiac output rises with physical conditioning in older subjects; sustained physical training is of value in preventive cardiology	3, 8—12
Improvement in diminution of $\dot{V}_{O_2 max}$ with age is associated with increase in activity and decrease in smoking	13

REFERENCES

1. **Clausen, J. P.,** Effect of physical training on cardiovascular adjustments in man, *Physiol. Rev.,* 57, 779, 1977.
2. **Barry, A. J., Daly, J. W., Pruett, E. D. R., Steinmetz, J. R., Page, H. F., Birkhead, N. C., and Rodahl, K.,** Effects of physical conditioning on older individuals, *J. Gerontol.,* 21, 182, 1965.
3. **Amery, A., Julius, S., Whitlock, L. S., and Conway, J.,** Influence of hypertension on hemodynamic response to exercise, *Circulation,* 36, 231, 1967.
4. **Dill, D. B., Phillips, E. E., and MacGregor, D.,** Training: youth and age, *Ann. N.Y. Acad. Sci.,* 134, 760, 1966.
5. **Fischer, A., Parizkova, J., and Roth, Z.,** The effects of systemic physical activity on maximum performance and functional capacity in senescent men, *Int. Z. Angew. Physiol Einschl. Arbeitsphysiol.,* 21, 269, 1965.
6. **Opie, L. H. and Noakes, T. D.,** Heart disease in marathon runners, *N. Engl. J. Med.,* 298, 1031, 1978.
7. **Shepard, R. J.,** Working capacity of the older employee, *Arch. Environ. Health,* 18, 982, 1969.
8. **Saltin, B., Kilborn, Å., and Åstrand, I.,** Physical conditioning in older subjects, *Scand. J. Clin. Lab. Invest.,* 24, 305, 1969.
9. **Lester, M., Sheffield, L. T., Trammell, P., and Reeves, T. J.,** Effect of age and athlete training on max heart rate during exercise, *Am. Heart J.,* 76, 370, 1968.
10. **Jokl, E., Jokl-Ball, M., Jokl, P., and Frankel, L.,** Notation of exercise. Method for describing and standardizing exercise regimes in normal and hypertensive males, *Environ. Health,* 5, 1968.
11. **Shepard, J.,** Age factor in sports, *Sport Age,* 1971.
12. **Schnorhr, P. J.,** Investigation of previous athletes, *J. Sports Med.,* 8, 245, 1968.
13. **Robinson, S., Dill, D. B., Tzankoff, S. P., Wagner, J. A., and Robinson, R. D.,** Longitudinal studies of aging in 37 men, *J. Appl. Physiol.,* 38, 263, 1975.

Table 5
EFFECTS OF AGE ON OTHER EXERCISE RESPONSES

	Ref.
Activity in rats diminishes with age but increases with experience	1
Grip strength and grip strength endurance peaks about age 20 then diminishes with age	2, 3
Workers over age 40 carry a substantial amount of body fat; they have diminished muscle strength which increases their liability to fatigue	4
Measurement of working capacity in the factory should include tests of aerobic power, obesity, and strength	4
Motivation and training can modify work responses after age 30	5—7
Cardiac performance in the presence of coronary disease is impaired by reserve inadequacy due to impaired systolic ejection and failure to increase mechanical efficiency with exercise	8
High levels of physical fitness do not guarantee the absence of noteworthy heart disease	9
When exertional ST segment depression occurs, it is result of hemodynamic response to exercise; physical training produces no ST depression at $\dot{V}_{O_2 max}$.	10
Peripheral circulatory impairment must be differentiated from left ventricular impairment in evaluating age and cardiovascular disease in max exercise	11—13
Acid-base mechanism slows up in older men, and may affect exercise response	14—16
When resting O_2 is expressed as $ml/kg/min$ there is no significant correlation with age	17, 18
Sweat chloride increases with age; wide differences at same age may be genetic; plasma volume decreased in youth and altitude (increased with age)	19
Age changes in psychomotor capacity represent compensation by adaptation; "complex" activities deteriorate	20—23

REFERENCES

1. Jones, D. C., Kimeldorf, D. J., Rubadeau, D. O., and Castanera, T. J., Relationship between volitional activity and age in the male rat, *Am. J. Physiol.*, 172, 109, 1953.
2. Burke, W. E., Tuttle, W. W., Thompson, C. W., Janney, C. D., and Weber, R. J., Relation of grip strength and grip strength endurance to age, *J. Appl. Physiol.*, 5, 628, 1953.
3. Fisher, M. B. and Birren, J., Age and strength, *J. Appl. Psychol.*, 31(5), 1947.
4. Buskirk, E. R. and Councilman, J., Special exercise problems in middle age, in *Science and Medicine of Exercise and Sports*, Ridehsun, W., Ed., Harper, New York, 1960, 24.
5. Carver, R. P. and Winsman, F. P., Relationship between physical work performance and age, *Ergonomics*, 13, 247, 1970.
6. Falls, H. B., Ismail, A. H., and MacLeod, D. F., Physical working capacity and motor fitness in relation to age of American University Faculty, *J. Assoc. Phys. Ment. Rehabilitation*, 20, 184, 1966.
7. Diem, C., Exercise benefits against aging, Lecture at 18th German Team Physician Congress, Hamburg, July 1957.
8. Messer, J. V., Levine, H. J., Wagman, R., and Gorlin, R., Effect of exercise on cardiac performance in human subjects with coronary disease, *Circulation*, 28, 404, 1963.
9. Eiselt, E., Work performance, caloric consumption, and work efficiency in old age, *Z. Alternsforsch.*, 21, 223, 1968.
10. Detry, J. M. and Bruce, R. A., Effect of physical training on exertional ST depression in coronary heart disease, *Circulation*, 44, 390, 1971.
11. Bruce, R. A., Fisher, L. D., Cooper, M. N., Separation of effects of cardiovascular disease and age on ventricular function with max exercise, *Am. J. Cardiol.*, 34, 757, 1974.
12. Ferguson, R. J., Petitclerc, R., Choquetta, G., Effect of physical training on treadmill exercise capacity on collateral circulation and progression of coronary disease, *Am. J. Cardiol.*, 34, 764, 1974.
13. Amery, A., Julius, S., Whitlock, L. S., and Conway, J., Influence of hypertension on hemodynamic response to exercise, *Circulation*, 36, 231, 1967.
14. Dill, D. B., Phillips, E. E., and MacGregor, D., Training: youth and age, *Ann. N. Y. Acad. Sci.*, 134, 760, 1966.
15. Bowlings, A., Bool, J., Binkhorst, R. A., and Van Leewin, P., Metabolic acidosis of exercise in healthy males, *J. Appl. Physiol.*, 21, 1040, 1966.
16. Simonson, E., Physical fitness of older men, *Geriatrics*, 2, 110, 1947.
17. Wessel, J., Small, A., Van Hess, W. D., Anderson, D. J., and Cedarquick, D. C., Age and physiologic responses to exercise in females 20—69 years, *J. Gerontol.*, 23, 269, 1968.

Table 5 (continued)
EFFECTS OF AGE ON OTHER EXERCISE RESPONSES

18. Wyndham, C. H., Work capacity of rural and urban Bantu in South Africa, *S. Afr. Med., J.*, 47, 1239, 1973.
19. Dill, D. B., Hall, E. G., and van Beaumont, W., Sweat chloride concentration: sweat rate, metabolic rate, skin temperature and age, *J. Appl. Physiol.*, 21, 99, 1966.
20. Kleemeier, R. W., Age changes in psychomotor capacity and productivity, *J. Bus.*, 27(2), 1954.
21. Griew, S., Uncertainty as a determinant of performance in relation to age, *Gerontologia*, 2, 284, 1958.
22. Miles, W. R., Abilities of older men, *Personnel J.*, 11, 352, 1932/33.
23. Clay, H. M., Time, accuracy and age on tasks of ranging complexity, *Gerontologia*, 1, 41, 1957.

Table 6
REGRESSION EQUATIONS FOR CHANGES IN $\dot{V}_{O_2 MAX}$ (EXPRESSED IN Ml/KG/MIN) WITH AGE

Active men	$\dot{V}_{O_2 max}$ = 69.7 − 0.612 (years of age) (r = −0.704)
Sedentary men	$\dot{V}_{O_2 max}$ = 57.8 − 0.445 (years of age) (r = −0.659)
Active women	$\dot{V}_{O_2 max}$ = 44.4 − 0.343 (years of age) (r = −0.631)
Sedentary women	$\dot{V}_{O_2 max}$ = 41.2 − 0.343 (years of age) (r = −0.720)

From Bruce, R. A., Kusumi, F., and Hosmer, D., Maximal oxygen intake and nomographic assessment of functional aerobic impairment in cardiovascular disease, *Am. Heart J.*, 85, 546, 1973. With permission.

Table 7
MAXIMAL OXYGEN INTAKE OF UNTRAINED MALE SUBJECTS CLASSIFIED BY NATIONAL GROUPINGS AND AGE

National grouping		16—17	18—19	20—30	30—40	40—50	50—60	60—70	70—80
Canada	No.	167	124	88	24	65	16	~8	—
	$\dot{V}_{O_2}$	3.44	3.44	3.55	3.20	3.00	3.02	1.91	—
		(3.16—3.53)	(3.38—3.75)	(2.58—4.01)	(2.65—3.47)	(2.91—3.29)	(2.74—3.29)	(1.91)	
	$\dot{V}_{O_2}$/kg	52.5	51.2	48.0	40.8	39.1	39.5	25.1	
		(48.2—54.4)	(51.1—51.8)	(35.7—5.7)	(35.4—43.5)	(36.5—43.0)	(36.2—42.7)	(25.1)	
U.S.	No.	21	10	1005	333	112	11	16	3
	$\dot{V}_{O_2}$	2.92	2.21	2.73	2.84	2.83	2.51	2.32	1.71
		(2.17—3.61)	(2.21)	(2.20—3.97)	(2.44—3.42)	(2.81—2.94)	(2.36—2.57)	(2.31—2.33)	(1.71)
	$\dot{V}_{O_2}$/kg	43.9	33.2	37.6	36.2	35.7	35.7	32.1	25.5
		(34.2—52.8)	(33.2)	(29.5—55.0)	(30.0—43.1)	(35.3—39.2)	(30.5—37.6)	(30.6—34.1)	(25.5)
Scandinavia	No.	9	—	511	57	377	176	6	—
	$\dot{V}_{O_2}$	3.94	—	4.11	3.23	3.38	2.61	2.23	
		(3.94)		(3.38—4.34)	(2.68—3.43)	(3.20—3.88)	(2.35—2.88)	(2.23)	
	$\dot{V}_{O_2}$	61.6	—	59.1	43.7	44.6	34.5	33.2	
		(61.6)		(46.4—63.6)	(42.2—46.3)	(41.9—44.6)	(31.8—37.1)	(33.2)	
Other countries	No.	87	565	767	370	186	203	166	25
	$\dot{V}_{O_2}$	2.71	2.80	2.90	2.84	2.68	2.34	1.86	1.46
		(2.33—3.19)	(2.71—3.63)	(2.43—3.32)	(2.42—3.47)	(2.51—3.14)	(1.96—2.60)	(1.62—2.09)	(1.46)
	$\dot{V}_{O_2}$/kg	42.4	42.2	44.9	40.1	35.1	30.4	24.6	20.3
		(36.7—49.8)	(41.3—52.4)	(32.5—48.6)	(36.4—46.4)	(33.0—41.1)	(25.5—33.6)	(22.1—27.5)	(20.3)
All countries	No.	284	699	2371	784	690	406	196	28
	$\dot{V}_{O_2}$	3.19	2.91	3.11	2.88	3.11	2.49	1.91	1.49
		(2.17—3.94)		(2.20—4.34)	(2.42—3.47)	(2.51—3.38)	(1.96—3.29)	(1.62—2.33)	(1.46—1.71)
	$\dot{V}_{O_2}$/kg	49.0	43.7	45.0	38.7	36.3	32.7	25.5	20.9
		(34.2—61.6)	(33.2—52.4)	(29.5—62.6)	(30.0—46.4)	(33.0—44.6)	(25.5—42.7)	(22.1—34.1)	(20.3—25.8)

Note: Mean for all authors and range of means for individual authors shown.   From Shephard, J., *Arch. Environ. Health*, 13, 664, 1966. With permission.

Table 8
MAXIMAL OXYGEN INTAKE OF ACTIVE AND ATHLETIC MALE SUBJECTS CLASSIFIED BY NATIONAL GROUPINGS AND AGE

National grouping		16—17	18—19	20—30	30—40	40—50	50—60	60—70	70—80	80—90
Active subjects										
Canada	No.	—	—	38	—	—	—	—	—	—
	$\dot{V}_{O_2}$	—	—	4.01						
				(3.63—4.18)						
	$\dot{V}_{O_2}/kg$	—	—	55.1						
				(47.3—60.2)						
U.S.	No.	—	—	152	—	6	—	—	—	—
	$\dot{V}_{O_2}$	—	—	3.68	—	3.99				
				(3.20—39.9)		(3.99)				
	$\dot{V}_{O_2}/kg$	—	—	51.5	—	51.3				
				(48.3—54.6)		(51.3)				
Scandinavia	No.	20	21	123	24	—	6	—	—	—
	$\dot{V}_{O_2}$	3.87	4.30	4.07	3.42	—	3.00			
		(3.22—4.22)	(4.14—4.45)	(3.64—4.42)	(3.21—3.53)		(3.00)			
	$\dot{V}_{O_2}/kg$	58.8	65.8	58.5	53.6	—	47.1			
		(50.5—63.3)	(65.6—65.9)	(52.4—63.0)	(50.7—55.0)		(47.1)			
Other countries	No.	—	—	170	127	—	—	36	20	3
	$\dot{V}_{O_2}$	—	—	3.04	4.38	—	—	1.82	1.73	1.18
				(2.29—3.39)	(4.38)			(1.82)	(1.73)	(1.18)
	$\dot{V}_{O_2}/kg$	—	—	47.2	59.1	—	—	25.0	24.7	21.9
				(45.1—47.7)	(59.1)			(25.0)	(24.7)	(21.9)
All countries	No.	20	21	483	151	6	6	36	20	3
	$\dot{V}_{O_2}$	3.87	4.30	3.58	4.23	3.99	3.00	1.82	1.73	1.18
		(3.22—4.22)	(4.14—4.45)	(2.29—4.42)	(3.21—4.38)	(3.99)	(3.00)	(1.82)	(1.73)	(1.18)
	$\dot{V}_{O_2}/kg$	58.8	65.8	52.0	58.2	51.3	47.1	25.0	24.7	21.9
		(50.5—63.3)	(65.6—65.9)	(45.1—63.0)	(50.7—59.1)	(51.3)	(47.1)	(25.0)	(24.7)	(21.9)

Athletes	No.	No data	50	No data	188	No data	No data	No data
	$\dot{V}_{O_2}$		4.62		3.54			
			(3.69—5.48)		(3.42—3.66)			
	$\dot{V}_{O_2}/kg$		69.1		51.3			
			(60.6—80.2)		(50.3—52.3)			

From Shephard, J., *Arch. Environ. Health*, 13, 664, 1966. With permission.

Table 9
HEART RATES BEFORE, DURING, AND AFTER EXERCISE (BEATS/MIN)[a]

Age group

	10—11 M SD	12—13 M SD	14—15 M SD	16—17 M SD	18—19 M SD	20—29 M SD	30—39 M SD	40—49 M SD	50—59 M SD	60—69 M SD
Males										
Resting (reclining) before exercise	85 13	82 13	78 12	76 12	73 13	76 12	75 11	76 11	75 12	74 10
Terminal (3′) exercise	132 13	129 13	125 13	125 13	123 12	125 14	122 13	122 13	122 14	117 19
30 sec postexercise (sitting)	98 16	94 16	88 15	91 16	92 14	97 15	97 14	101 15	101 17	100 15
1 min postexercise (sitting)	90 16	86 15	82 15	84 15	84 15	88 16	88 14	91 14	92 14	89 14
3 min postexercise sitting)	93 14	90 14	84 13	86 13	84 14	86 14	84 13	86 14	87 14	84 13
5 min postexercise (sitting)	92 13	89 13	85 12	85 13	85 13	86 13	84 12	86 12	85 13	83 11
N =	193	171	147	161	84	365	428	334	148	50
Females										
Resting (reclining) before exercise	90 14	88 13	83 14	80 12	80 12	78 11	78 11	78 11	77 12	76 8
Terminal (3′) exercise	141 14	141 14	143 16	142 14	142 12	138 14	134 15	135 15	135 17	129 17
30 sec postexercise (sitting)	108 18	107 17	109 18	110 17	112 16	108 16	108 16	109 16	111 15	108 16
1 min postexercise (sitting)	99 18	98 16	98 20	97 18	99 14	96 16	97 16	98 16	100 17	97 13
3 min postexercise (sitting)	101 15	98 15	96 16	95 16	94 13	91 14	90 15	90 15	90 15	88 10
5 min postexercise (sitting)	100 15	96 14	95 15	94 13	93 13	91 13	90 14	90 14	88 14	84 10
N =	157	167	143	135	84	413	453	302	120	28

[a] Data from the Institute of Environmental Stress.

Table 10
MEAN MAXIMUM VALUES OF PHYSICAL WORKING CAPACITY IN RELATION TO SEX AND AGE

Age	Males kg	Max O₂ intake (ml/min/kg)	Maximum heart rate	L max ventilation (BTPS)	Females kg	Max O₂ intake (ml/min/kg)	Maximum heart rate	L max ventilation (BTPS)
4	20.5	48.2	201	41.2	17.7	44.7	195	32.3
5	18.2	52.9	205	37.5	18.1	50.4	208	32.8
6	23.8	46.2	206	40.3	19.7	47.2	207	37.4
7	25.2	58.7	203	50.0	22.8	56.0	209	49.6
8	30.1	56.0	218	60.7	29.9	52.3	205	57.6
9	32.5	56.8	206	65.7	27.6	56.4	215	60.5
10	36.2	55.1	215	70.5	30.6	51.8	206	58.3
11	36.7	56.9	207	70.6	34.1	52.9	210	63.5
12	39.4	56.4	196	67.7	43.4	51.0	207	70.7
13	47.3	56.5	213	82.0	49.5	48.7	208	87.7
14	53.5	59.2	204	103.0	52.8	47.7	202	88.9
15	65.5	59.7	202	122.9	58.7	44.7	202	87.1
16	57.1	59.0	199	102.5	56.6	47.0	207	93.9
17	65.6	58.2	201	107.7	60.4	47.9	201	93.6
18	69.8	55.6	205	120.8				
20	70.1	60.3	201	132.1	59.5	48.4	193	93.5
21					60.8	48.7	198	94.3
22	68.7	58.9	190	121.6	60.8	46.5	201	89.9
23					60.8	49.7	201	93.9
24	68.5	60.4	192	119.3	58.0	47.8	196	88.2
25	70.1	58.5	201	131.6				
26	72.4	58.8	200	125.1				
28	74.8	58.5	192	127.8				
29	75.0	51.2	196	115.3				
30	68.8	58.3	188	112.4				
32	69.4	57.4	198	116.5				
Mean		56.5	201			49.5	204	
Range		43.2—67.4	171—237			42.4—59.6	176—225	

ᵃ Åstrand, P.-O., *Exp. Studies*, 1954. With permission.

HUMAN DATA FROM SEATTLE HEART WATCH AND NETWORK REGISTERIES, 1971-1977

R. A. Bruce

PREFACE TO USE OF TABLES AND FIGURES
(Variations in Aerobic and Cardiovascular Responses to Maximal Exercise in Relation to Sex, Physical Activity Status, and Age in Health and to Restrictions Imposed by Cardiovascular Disease in Men*)

The range of aerobic metabolic activities extends from the basal metabolic requirements to the maximal oxygen uptake ($\dot{V}_{O_2}$ max), or functional limits of the cardiovascular system during dynamic exercise involving large muscle masses. Physiologically, $\dot{V}_{O_2}$ max equals the product of cardiac output and arterial-mixed venous oxygen difference at symptom-limited maximal exercise.[1] The limits of $\dot{V}_{O_2}$ max vary widely with sex, age, habitual activity status of each individual, and are reduced by cardiovascular disease, especially coronary heart disease (CHD).[2] Since the primary causes of morbidity and mortality in middle-aged persons are hypertension (HT) and CHD, respectively, it is appropriate to consider the effects of these diseases on exercise performance. In order to describe the salient physical characteristics of the selected subgroups, resting observations on several variables are included, along with responses to symptom-limited maximal exercise. The latter are not determined by any arbitrary "target heart rates", which are impossible for all to attain, and which represent deterrents of unknown magnitude in others who can readily exceed these artificial endpoints. Because of the importance of conventional risk factors, i.e., familial history of HT and/or CHD, HT as diagnosed by physicians, cholesterol of 250 mg/dℓ or higher and/or cigarette smoking, the prevalences are reported. Similarly, age-specific prevalences of exertional arrhythmia, ischemic ST depression to maximal exertion, and the high incidence of CHD morbidity and mortality within 3 years, these additional items are also included. In industrially developed countries these diseases accentuate the physiologic effects of aging in men because the restrictions to functional cardiovascular limits of aerobic metabolism are largely additive to those of aging.** Although the absolute oxygen requirements, weight-adjusted, remain the same for any given level of ordinary submaximal exertion, the relative aerobic requirement, or percent of each individual's $\dot{V}_{O_2}$ max, increases with aging and, particularly, with disabling cardiovascular disease.

Data sources — Seattle Heart Watch and Network Registries,*** 1971-1977.[3-6] Clinical classifications of Caucasian persons are based upon preliminary examinations, i.e., history, physical, chest X-ray, and 12-lead electrocardiograms, by over 50 participating physicians. Observations represent a community experience involving industrial or nonmedical and clinical cohorts of ambulatory persons. Data on annual rates of change in the primary non-invasive variables when maximal exercise testing is repeated 1 to 5 years later are reported elsewhere.

Definitions — *Normål* (NL) means that no symptoms or signs of cardiovascular disease were detected prior to exercise testing. *Hypertensive* (HT) means elevated rest-

---

* Summarized by R. A. Bruce, M. D., Professor of Medicine, Co-Director, Division of Cardiology RG-20; T. A. DeRouen, Associate Professor of Biostatistics; with technical assistance of F. Kusumi and V. Hofer; University of Washington, Seattle, 98195.
** Corresponding data for an oriental population sample have been published elsewhere.[9]
***These studies have been supported by NHLI Contract, HU-12474, research grants HL-13517 from the National Heart, Lung and Blood Institute and MB-00184 from the Bureau of Health Resources Development.

ing blood pressure as classified by the physician, whether or not it was treated. *Coronary heart disease* (CHD) means history of prior clinical manifestations of typical angina pectoris, myocardial infarction and/or sudden cardiac arrest with resuscitation by defibrillation of the heart. *Active* means history of vigorous exercise, long enough to induce sweating, at least once a week, regularly each week; *sedentary* refers to those who do not qualify as "active". CHD morbidity is defined by admission to hospital primarily because of CHD; mortality refers to all death from cardiac causes, whether or not they were sudden. *Exertional arrhythmia* means the occurrence of two or more premature beats, paroxysmal tachycardia or complex arrhythmias occurring during or within 5 min after exercise testing to maximal effort. *ST depression* refers to visual observation of 1 mm or more horizontal or downsloping "ischemic" depression of the ST segment in a left precordial ECT lead from V_5 position to the inferior tip of the right scapula during initial recovery from maximal exercise. ST_B refers to mean voltage, after computer averaging of 100-beat samples of the ST interval from 50 to 69 msec after the nadir of S. The measurement at 1 min after maximal exercise is selected because this represents the greatest differentiation (P <0.0001) between normal subjects and cardiac patients in the time course of exercise and recovery observations. *ACP* refers to atypical chest pain syndromes, specifically not angina pectoris.

Derived variables — *Relative weight* refers to percentage relationship of observed to predicted weights, where predicted is derived by regression on height as follows:[2]

$$-60.7 + 0.79 \text{ (height in cm) for men}$$
$$-68.2 + 0.79 \text{ (height in cm) for women}$$

Estimated maximal oxygen uptake ($\dot{V}_{O_2}$ max) is derived by regression on duration of multistage treadmill test of symptom-limited maximal exercise according to the Bruce protocol as follows:[2]

$$= 3.88 + 0.056 \text{ (duration in sec) for men}$$
$$= 1.06 + 0.056 \text{ (duration in sec) for women}$$

An independent comparative study of $\dot{V}_{O_2}$ max by this and three other protocols in 51 normal men has been published.[8]

Morbidity refers to hospital admission for cardiac reasons; mortality refers to death from cardiac causes; both number of events and adjusted rates cited permit determination of confidence intervals.

Variations in relation to age are greater for the limits of aerobic metabolism than for the limits of circulatory responses to maximal exercise. The commonly observed increments in resting blood pressure with aging are less than usually reported; presumably this reflects greater care in exclusion of hypertensive persons. The majority of patients with cardiovascular disease and within the range of 45 to 64 years of age exhibit responses to maximal exercise which are within the 95% confidence intervals for healthy subjects. For a given individual of known classification, the percentile relationship of exercise responses may be ascertained from the cumulative percent distribution curves of each variable. The amount of aerobic, myocardial, and chronotropic impairment, each corrected for age, may be ascertained from the corresponding indices; the complementary variables of percent of age-adjusted, average normal aerobic, chronotropic, and myocardial capacities are scaled at the top of the graphs.

How to Use the Tables and Graphs

To aid interpretation of responses to maximal exercise in any given individual, select the table which corresponds with the preliminary clinical classification before the exercise test is done. For example, a sedentary male of 51 years of age with a history of prior myocardial infarction is classified as "normotensive CHD patient of 45 to 64 years of age." Referring to Table 6: the average age of 763 such men is 54.1 ± 5.3 years; relative weight 101.5 ± 13.1%, and cholesterol concentration 253 ± 46%. About 52% have one or more conventional risk factors, 32% are smokers, 6.7% have cardiomegaly, and nearly one-third exhibit at least 1 mm of ST depression after maximal exercise which lasts 384 sec (6-⅓ min), with a heart rate of 148 per minute, and blood pressure at peak exercise of 166/82 mm Hg. Two or more premature beats occur in 44% of such patients.

To understand how the information contained in the graphs may be used, first convert the observed duration of exercise of 384 sec to estimated $\dot{V}_{o_2}$ max by use of the regression equation stated above:

$$\dot{V}_{o_2} \text{ max} = 3.88 + (0.056 \times 384) = 3.88 + 21.5 = 25.4 \text{ m}\ell/(\text{kg} \times \text{min})$$

This value, 25.4 mℓ/(kg × min) intersects the cumulative percent distribution curve for CHD men about 68%. Thus, two-thirds of such patients have lower values; one-third have higher values. Similarly, for HR max of 148, about 48% of CHD patients have lower values; for SBP max of 166, only 48% of such patients have lower values; and for DBP max of 82, 50% of patients have lower values. For the same values of these variables, the percentiles for a normal population would be the 7th percentile for $\dot{V}_{o_2}$ max, 4th percentile for HR max, 15th percentile for SBP max, and 62nd percentile for DBP max.

REFERENCES

1. **Mitchell, J. H., Sproule, B. J., and Chapman, C. V.,** The physiological meaning of a maximal oxygen intake tests, *J. Clin. Invest.*, 37, 538, 1958.
2. **Bruce, R. A., Kusumi, F., and Hosmer, D.,** Maximal oxygen intake and nomographic assessment of functional aerobic impairment in cardiovascular disease, *Am. Heart J.*, 85, 546, 1973.
3. **Bruce, R. A., Gey, G. O., Cooper, M. N., Fisher, L. D., and Peterson, D. R.,** The Seattle Heart Watch: initial clinical, circulatory and electrocardiographic responses to maximal exercise, *Am. J. Cardiol.*, 33, 450, 1974.
4. **Bruce, R. A., Fisher, L. D., Cooper, M. N., and Gey, G. O.,** Separation of effects of cardiovascular disease and age on ventricular function with maximal exrcise, *Am. J. Cardiol.*, 34, 757, 1974.
5. **Bruce, R. A., DeRouen, T., Peterson, D. R., Irving, J. B., Chinn, N., Blake, B., and Hofer, V.,** Non-invasive predictors of sudden cardiac death in men with coronary disease, *Am. J. Cardiol.*, 39, 833, 1977.
6. **Irving, J. B., Bruce, R. A., and DeRouen, R. A.,** Variations in and significance of systolic pressure during maximal treadmill testing, *Am. J. Cardiol.*, 39, 841, 1977.
7. **Bruce, R. A. and DeRouen, T. A.,** Comparison of longitudinal responses to maximal exercise, in *Environmental Stress, Individual Human Adaptations*, Folbinbee, L. J., Wagner, J. A., Borgia, J. F., Brinkwater, B. A., Eds., Academic Press, New York, 1978, 205.
8. **Pollack, M. L., Bohannon, R. L., Cooper, K. H., Ayres, J. J., Ward, A., White, S. R., and Linnerud, A. C.,** A comparative analysis of four protocols for maximal treadmill stress testing, *Am. Heart J.*, 92, 39, 1976.
9. **Bruce, R. A., Pao, Y-l., Ting, N., Chiang, B. N., Li, Y-b., Chiang, S. T., Alexander, E. R., Beasley, R. P., and Fisher, L. D.,** Seven-year follow-up of cardiovascular study of Chinese men, *Circulation*, 51, 890, 1975.

Table 1
NORMAL SUBJECTS OF 25—34 YEARS OF AGE

Physical status variables	Men Active N	Means	±SD	Men Sedentary N	Means	±SD	Women Active N	Means	±SD	Women Sedentary N	Means	±SD
Age (years)	100	31.5	2.0	111	31.3	2.3	10	31.3	1.8	12	32.1	2.6
Height (cm)	107	179.5	7.4	106	180.1	7.6	9	165.2	7.3	11	164.5	6.1
Weight (kg)	106	79.4	9.4	107	81.2	11.4	9	57.4	6.1	11	62.1	20.5
Relative weight (%)	98	98.2	10.4	99	99.5	11.2	7	92.6	7.8	8	105.8	35.9
Cholesterol (mg/dℓ)	21	230.0	44.0	14	232.0	30.0	3	221.0	28.0	2	180.0	64.0
Resting												
Heart rate (b/min)	110	68	11	111	76[a]	11	10	90	17	12	87	13
Systolic pressure (mm Hg)	110	124	12	111	122	13	10	116	10	12	113	10
Diastolic pressure (mm Hg)	110	77	9	111	77	10	10	74	8	12	73	12
ST_B (mv)	79	0.060	0.122	89	0.065	0.060	7	−0.040	0.068	10	0.027	0.040
Maximal exercise												
Duration (sec)	110	758	92	111	655[a]	100	10	567	82	12	465[b]	114
Estimate $\dot{V}_{O_2}$ max [mℓ/(kg × min)]	110	42.5	5.1	111	36.7[a]	5.6	10	31.7	4.6	12	26.1[b]	6.4
Heart rate (b/min)	110	186	10	111	189[b]	8	10	184	8	12	176	13
Systolic pressure (mm Hg)	104	189	23	109	183[b]	21	10	153	13	12	152	20
Diastolic pressure (mm Hg)	101	63	22	103	72[c]	16	8	78	13	9	77	11
HR × SBP × 10^{-2}	104	354	45	109	347	45	10	284	26	12	267	35
At 1 min recovery [ST_n,(mV)]	78	0.077	0.066	88	0.054[b]	0.064	7	−0.011	0.047	10	0.008	0.037
Prevalences (%)												
Conventional risk factors (≥ 1)		28.2			34.2			30.0			33.3	
Smoking		14.6			27.0			30.0			33.3	
Cardiomegaly		0.0			0.0			0.0			0.0	
Exertional arrhythmia		14.6			12.6			0.0			16.7	
Chest pain with max exertion		0.0			1.8			10.0			0.0	
ST depression (≥ 1 mm)		1.8			8.1			0.0			0.0	
Subsequent annual incidences/1000 persons at risk												
Morbidity	1	2.4		0	0.0		0	0.0		0	0.0	
Mortality	0	0.0		0	0.0		0	0.0		0	0.0	

[a] $P < 0.001$ — comparison of active vs. sedentary individuals.
[b] $P < 0.05$ — comparison of active vs. sedentary individuals.
[c] $P < 0.01$ — comparison of active vs. sedentary individuals.

Table 2
NORMAL SUBJECTS OF 35—44 YEARS OF AGE

	Men Active			Men Sedentary			Women Active			Women Sedentary		
Physical status variables	N	Means	±SD	N	Means	±SD	N	Means	±SD	N	Means	±SD
Age (years)	380	40.0	2.7	592	39.7	2.9	21	39.0	3.1	53	40.2	2.8
Height (cm)	370	178.8	6.6	584	179.0	6.5	20	164.3	7.8	53	165.4	7.9
Weight (kg)	368	79.5	8.6	585	81.8[a]	10.3	20	59.0	8.3	53	621.0	8.1
Relative weight (%)	347	99.0	9.6	564	101.4	11.2	17	96.5	9.5	47	100.3	12.7
Cholesterol (mg/dℓ)	99	229.0	47.0	120	223.0[a]	41.0	7	233.0	41.0	8	233.0	48.0
Resting												
Heart rate (b/min)	380	70	11	592	76[b]	11	21	84	10	53	82	13
Systolic pressure (mm Hg)	380	123	13	592	121[c]	12	21	110	14	53	111	12
Diastolic pressure (mm Hg)	380	78	9	591	78	9	21	71	13	53	73	9
ST_H (mV)	287	0.064	0.066	481	0.055	0.057	9	0.009	0.042	35	0.025	32
Maximal exercise												
Duration (sec)	380	711	96	592	618[b]	76	21	533	95	53	431[a]	58
Estimate $\dot{V}_{O_2}$ max [mℓ/(kg × min)]	380	39.9	5.4	592	36.6	4.3	21	29.9	5.3	53	24.1[a]	3.2
Heart rate (b/min)	380	182	10	592	184[d]	11	21	178	14	53	177	12
Systolic pressure (mm Hg)	376	188	22	587	182[a]	21	21	156	20	53	155	18
Diastolic pressure (mm Hg)	353	69	18	565	71	17	18	77	13	47	74	15
HR × SBP × 10^{-2}	376	343	43	587	337[c]	45	21	280	46	53	273	37
At 1 min recovery [ST_H (mV)]	275	0.036	0.082	467	0.026	0.061	9	0.002	0.073	35	0.002	0.051
Prevalences (%)												
Conventional risk factors (≥1)		26.6			31.8			38.1			22.6	
Smoking		11.3			25.2			28.6			18.9	
Cardiomegaly		0.0			0.0			0.0			0.0	
Exertional arrhythmia		18.7			21.0			9.5			17.0	
Chest pain with max exertion		0.5			1.0			0.0			5.7	
ST depression, (≥1 mm)		10.5			9.6			9.5			7.5	
Subsequent annual incidences/1000 persons at risk												
Morbidity	3	2.0		4	1.7		0	0.0		0	0.0	
Mortality	0	0.0		0	0.0		0	0.0		0	0.0	

[a] $P < 0.001$ — comparison of active vs. sedentary individuals.
[b] $P < 0.0001$ — comparison of active vs. sedentary individuals.
[c] $P < 0.05$ — comparison of active vs. sedentary individuals.
[d] $P < 0.01$ — comparison of active vs. sedentary individuals.

Table 3
NORMAL SUBJECTS OF 45—54 YEARS OF AGE

Physical status variables	Men Active N	Men Active Means	Men Active ±SD	Men Sedentary N	Men Sedentary Means	Men Sedentary ±SD	Women Active N	Women Active Means	Women Active ±SD	Women Sedentary N	Women Sedentary Means	Women Sedentary ±SD
Age (years)	373	48.9	2.8	556	49.3[a]	2.7	15	49.6	2.7	76	48.8	2.6
Height (cm)	367	178.2	6.0	547	178.4	6.4	13	166.4	4.9	73	164.1	5.4
Weight (kg)	368	79.5	8.4	548	81.0[a]	9.7	13	58.1	6.2	74	62.7	9.0
Relative weight (%)	354	99.2	8.7	535	100.9[a]	10.6	13	92.1	10.1	62	101.6[a]	12.4
Cholesterol (mg/dℓ)	112	235.0	48.0	170	238.0		5	237.0	30.0	14	240.0	35.0
Resting												
Heart rate (b/min)	373	70	12	556	74[b]	11	15	82	10	76	79	13
Systolic pressure (mm Hg)	373	125	14	556	123	14	15	115	16	76	121	14
Diastolic pressure (mm Hg)	373	79	9	556	80	9	15	74	12	76	77	8
ST_B (vM)	298	0.051	0.054	435	0.041[a]	0.051	11	0.030	0.048	63	0.015	0.048
Maximal exercise												
Duration (sec)	373	659	95	556	584[b]	84	15	493	110	76	412[c]	72
Estimate $\dot{V}_{O_2}$ max [mℓ/(kg × min)]	373	37.0	5.3	556	32.7[b]	4.7	15	27.6	6.2	76	23.1[c]	4.0
Heart rate (b/min)	373	176	12	556	176	12	15	173	10	76	175	14
Systolic pressure (mm Hg)	366	192	25	551	187[d]	22	15	161	19	73	170	21
Diastolic pressure (mm Hg)	357	72	17	538	76[c]	15	15	79	10	65	79	10
HR × SBP × 10^{-2}	366	341	51	551	332[d]	45	15	279	36	73	299	48
At 1 min recovery [ST_B (mV)]	293	0.001	0.086	426	−0.002	0.062	11	0.013	0.049	63	−0.020	0.053
Prevalences (%)												
Conventional risk factors (>1)		28.4			34.2			33.3			34.2	
Smoking		8.7			114.0			30.0			33.3	
Cardiomegaly		0.3			1.0			0.0			0.0	
Exertional arrhythmia		26.2			170.0			0.0			16.7	
Chest pain with max exertion		0.5			1.1			.0			1.3	
ST depression (≥1 mm)		13.1			11.3			6.7			15.8	
Subsequent annual incidences/1000 persons at risk												
Morbidity	1	0.6			4.4		0	0.0		2	6.5	
Mortality	0	0.0		3	1.3		0	0.0		0	0.0	

[a] $P < 0.05$ — comparison of active vs. sedentary individuals.
[b] $P < 0.0001$ — comparison of active vs. sedentary individuals.
[c] $P < 0.001$ — comparison of active vs. sedentary individuals.
[d] $P < 0.01$ — comparison of active vs. sedentary individuals.

Table 4
NORMAL SUBJECTS OF 55—64 YEARS OF AGE

Physical status variables	Men Active N	Means	± SD	Men Sedentary N	Means	± SD	Women Active N	Means	± SD	Women Sedentary N	Means	± SD
Age (years)	83	57.9	2.6	153	57.8	2.5	3	57.3	1.5	46	57.9	2.5
Height (cm)	76	177.6	6.7	151	176.4	6.8	3	165.0	4.4	46	163.7	5.6
Weight (kg)	77	77.7	8.2	151	78.5	9.2	3	65.7	5.5	46	64.8	10.8
Relative weight (%)	73	99.3	9.0	144	99.9	8.8	2	103.0	5.7	40	105.7	14.8
Cholesterol (mg/dℓ)	17	240.0	36.0	40	225.0	45.0	1	197.0	0.0	12	250.0	40.0
Resting												
Heart (b/min)	83	69	11	153	73[a]	11	3	60	9	46	81[b]	11
Systolic pressure (mm Hg)	83	128	13	153	129	15	3	127	14	46	128	15
Diastolic pressure (mm Hg)	83	78	8	153	81	9	3	75	13	46	79	6
ST_B (mV)	65	0.041	0.045	112	0.034	0.047	1	0.009	0	29	0.009	0.038
Maximal exercise												
Duration (sec)	83	593	79	153	532[c]	86	3	530	83	46	360[d]	77
Estimate $\dot{V}_{O_2}$ max [mℓ/(kg × min)]	83	33.3	4.4	153	29.8[c]	4.8	3	29.7	4.7	46	20.2[d]	4.3
Heart rate (b/min)	83	169	12	153	169	13	3	162	11	46	169	14
Systolic pressure (mm Hg)	81	191	22	151	192	22	3	169	16	45	177	24
Diastolic pressure (mm Hg)	79	75	14	144	81	12	2	70	14	40	81	11
HR × SBP × 10⁻²	81	323	45	151	326	42	3	274	16	45	301	50
At 1 min recovery [STB (mV)]	63	−0.023	0.066	112	−0.024	0.080						
Prevalences (%)												
Conventional risk factors (>1)		24.1			37.9			33.3			41.3	
Smoking		7.2			17.6			0.3			13.3	
Cardiomegaly		0.0			0.0			0.0			0.0	
Exertional arrhythmia		40.0			36.0			0.0			38.8	
Chest pain with max exertion		1.2			0.6			0.0			2.2	
ST depression (>1 mm)		24.4			15.8			66.7			23.9	
Subsequent annual incidences/1000 persons at risk												
Morbidity	2	6.8		5	8.2		0	0.0		0	0.0	
Mortality	1	3.4		2	3.3		0	0.0		0	0.0	

[a] $P < 0.05$ — comparison of active vs. sedentary individuals.
[b] $P < 0.01$ — comparison of active vs. sedentary individuals.
[c] $P < 0.0001$ — comparison of active vs. sedentary individuals.
[d] $P < 0.001$ — comparison of active vs. sedentary individuals.

Table 5
HYPERTENSIVE PERSONS OF 45—64 YEARS OF AGE

Physical status variables	Men Active N	Men Active Means	Men Active ±SD	Men Sedentary N	Men Sedentary Means	Men Sedentary ±SD	Women Active N	Women Active Means	Women Active ±SD	Women Sedentary N	Women Sedentary Means	Women Sedentary ±SD
Age (years)	135	52.5	4.7	326	53.3	5.1	9	59.0	4.4	114	54.3	4.6
Height (cm)	127	178.0	6.7	310	177.6	6.6	7	161.9	5.6	108	163.1	6.0
Weight (kg)	127	81.3	9.2	308	85.5[a]	12.4	8	66.0	8.5	108	67.4	12.4
Relative weight (%)	124	101.7	11.1	291	107.2[a]	13.9	9	107.4	9.2	101	110.7	18.9
Cholesterol (mg/dl)	55	244.0	42.0	140	248.0	44.0	5	247.0	48.0	50	250.0	46.0
Resting												
Heart rate (b/min)	135	73	14	326	79[a]	15	9	71	10	114	82	15
Systolic pressure (mm Hg)	135	140	18	326	140	18	9	139	20	114	143	21
Diastolic pressure (mm Hg)	135	87	12	326	90[b]	11	9	79	15	113	87	12
ST_n (mV)	100	0.016	0.107	225	0.005	0.104	4	−0.022	0.028	77	−0.021	0.069
Maximal exercise												
Duration (sec)	135	588	134	326	485[a]	128	9	441	127	114	329[a]	106
Estimate $\dot{V}_{O_2}$ max [ml/(kg × min)]	135	33.0	7.5	326	27.2[a]	7.2	9	24.7	7.1	114	18.5[b]	6.0
Heart rate	135	168	16	326	163[c]	20	9	154	12	114	157	15
Systolic pressure (mm Hg)	134	202	29	314	198	29	9	169	25	112	188	30
Diastolic pressure (mm Hg)	132	86	14	302	90[b]	16	8	74	33	104	89[b]	12
HR × SBP × 10⁻²	134	343	62	302	90[b]	16	9	262	39	112	297	55
At 1 min recovery [ST_n (mV)]	99	−0.037	0.116	222	−0.033	0.092	4	−0.052	0.046	75	−0.050	0.066
Prevalences												
Conventional risk factors (≥1)		63.7			62.6			77.8			66.4	
Smoking		18.5			20.6			44.4			35.1	
Cardiomegaly		2.2			5.8			11.1			7.0	
Exertional arrhythmia		48.9			47.2			33.3			35.1	
Chest pain with max exertion		1.5			4.3			.0			12.4	
ST depression (≥1 mm)		26.7			22.5			33.3			20.2	
Subsequent annual incidences/1000 persons at risk												
Morbidity		9.3			7.7			31.1			9.9	
Mortality		1.9			9.5			0.0			5.0	

[a] $P < 0.001$ — comparison of active vs. sedentary individuals.
[b] $P < 0.01$ — comparison of active vs. sedentary individuals.
[c] $P < 0.05$ — comparison of active vs. sedentary individuals.

Table 6
NORMOTENSIVE CHD PATIENTS OF 45—64 YEARS OF AGE

Physical status variables	Men Active N	Means	±SD	Men Sedentary N	Means	±SD	Women Active N	Means	±SD	Women Sedentary N	Means	±SD
Age (years)	186	53.7	5.3	763	54.1	5.3	24	56.7	3.6	142	53.8[a]	5.1
Height (cm)	175	176.4	8.2	694	176.5	7.1	24	164.0	6.5	133	162.6	7.0
Weight (kg)	176	79.2	10.9	701	79.7	11.3	24	62.4	6.6	138	64.6	12.0
Relative weight (%)	160	101.2	13.4	645	101.5	13.1	23	102.6	16.6	118	107.8	16.9
Cholesterol (mg/dℓ)	71	244.0	44.0	294	253.0	46.0	12	246.0	52.0	62	254.0	54.0
Resting												
Heart rate (b/min)	186	73	13	761	77	13	24	77	10	140	81	15
Systolic pressure (mm Hg)	186	124	16	763	125	17	24	135	19	142	128	21
Diastolic pressure (mm Hg)	186	79	10	763	79	11	24	80	10	142	80	10
ST_n (mV)	118	0.020	0.069	420	0.009	0.084	17	−0.052	0.051	94	−0.018[b]	0.060
Maximal exercise												
Duration (sec)	186	466	158	763	384[c]	152	23	358	132	141	295[b]	124
Estimate $\dot{V}_{O_2}$ max [mℓ/(kg × min)]	186	26.1	8.8	763	21.5[c]	8.5	23	20.0	7.4	141	16.5[b]	7.0
Heart rate (b/min)	186	152	22	763	148[b]	22	24	149	22	141	148	22
Systolic pressure (mm Hg)	182	166	27	739	166	29	24	169	21	141	163	29
Diastolic pressure (mm Hg)	172	83	15	708	82	12	23	80	18	121	83	13
HR × SBP × 10⁻²	182	254	59	739	249	65	24	255	53	140	244	58
At 1 min recovery [ST_n (mV)]	116	−0.055	0.149	422	−0.064	0.117	17	−0.110	0.082	95	−0.066	0.088
Prevalences (%)												
Conventional risk factors (≥1)		46.8			52.6			62.5			54.9	
Smoking		26.2			32.0			12.5			33.1	
Cardiomegaly		5.0			6.7			4.2			10.1	
Exertional arrhythmia		42.5			44.0			62.5			28.9	
Chest pain with max exertion		30.8			40.7			33.3			32.5	
ST depression (>1 mm)		39.2			32.6			58.3			36.2	
Subsequent annual incidences/1000 persons at risk												
Morbidity	18	27.6		100	39.1		5	53.3		27	49.8	
Mortality	17	26.1		88	34.9		0	0.0		4	7.4	

[a] $P < 0.01$ — comparison of active vs. sedentry individuals.
[b] $P < 0.05$ — comparison of active vs. sedentary individuals.
[c] $P < 0.001$ — comparison of active vs. sedentary individuals.

Table 7
HYPERTENSIVE CHD PATIENTS OF 45—64 YEARS OF AGE

Men

Physical status variables	Active N	Means	±SD	Sedentary N	Means	±SD
Age (years)	52	54.5	5.9	339	54.6	5.0
Height (cm)	47	175.5	7.1	302	176.3	7.0
Weight (kg)	48	81.3	11.2	303	84.0	13.7
Relative weight (%)	44	105.2	15.3	277	106.6	14.8
Cholesterol (mg/dℓ)	22	262.0	42.0	124	253.0	52.0
Resting						
Heart rate 339	52	79	15	8	78	10
Systolic pressure (mm Hg)	52	139	22	339	140	20
Diastolic pressure (mm Hg)	52	89	12	339	89	11
ST_B (mV)	31	−0.025	0.162	197	−0.009	0.092
Maximal exercise						
Duration (sec)	52	434	126	339	357[a]	137
Estimate $\dot{V}_{O_2}$ max [mℓ/(kg × min)]	52	24.3	7.1	339	20.0[a]	7.7
Heart rate (b/min)	52	153	21	338	148	23
Systolic pressure (mm Hg)	52	184	27	327	183	31
Diastolic pressure (mm Hg)	48	92	14	303	92	15
HR × SBP × 10⁻²	52	284	61	328	274	68
At 1 min recovery [ST_B (mV)]	31	−0.088	0.092	195	−0.085	0.149
Prevalences (%)						
Conventional risk factors (≥ 1)		63.5			65.8	
Smoking		23.5			32.4	
Cardiomegaly		9.8			12.2	
Exertional arrhythmia		50.0			47.9	
Chest pain with max exertion		36.5			44.5	
ST depression (≥ 1 mm)		38.5			33.1	
Subsequent annual incidence/1000 persons at risk						
Morbidity	5	27.2		52	47.3	
Mortality	4	21.7		31	28.2	

Women

Physical status variables	Active N	Means	±SD	Sedentary N	Means	±SD
Age (years)	8	52.6	4.9	101	55.1	1.2
Height (cm)	8	165.5	5.2	96	162.6	6.7
Weight (kg)	8	71.0	10.2	97	65.2	10.9
Relative weight (%)	6	116.8	20.3	90	108.2	16.2
Cholesterol (mg/dℓ)	4	203.0	20.0	51	261.0	61.0
Resting						
Heart rate	101	84	16	100	142	23
Systolic pressure (mm Hg)	8	136	29	100	142	23
Diastolic pressure (mm Hg)	8	84	14	100	87	12
ST_B (mV)	5	−0.024	0.044	59	−0.041	0.072
Maximal exercise						
Duration (sec)	8	406	124	100	295[b]	119
Estimate $\dot{V}_{O_2}$ max [mℓ/(kg × min)]	8	22.7	6.9	100	16.5	6.6
Heart rate (b/min)	8	156	22	101	152	22
Systolic pressure (mm Hg)	7	166	35	99	185	29
Diastolic pressure (mm Hg)	6	85	13	93	88	14
HR × SBP × 10⁻²	7	262	53	99	286	68
At 1 min recovery [ST_B (mV)]	6	−0.175	0.202	58	−0.083	0.100
Prevalences (%)						
Conventional risk factors (≥ 1)		37.5			71.3	
Smoking		37.5			36.6	
Cardiomegaly		0.0			11.3	
Exertional arrhythmia		50.0			36.7	
Chest pain with max exertion		25.0			38.6	
ST depression (≥ 1 mm)		37.5			41.6	
Subsequent annual incidence/1000 persons at risk						
Morbidity	2	76.2		14	40.3	
Mortality	0	0.0		5	14.4	

[a] $P < 0.001$ — comparison of active vs. sedentary individuals.
[b] $P < 0.05$ — comparison of active vs. sedentary individuals.

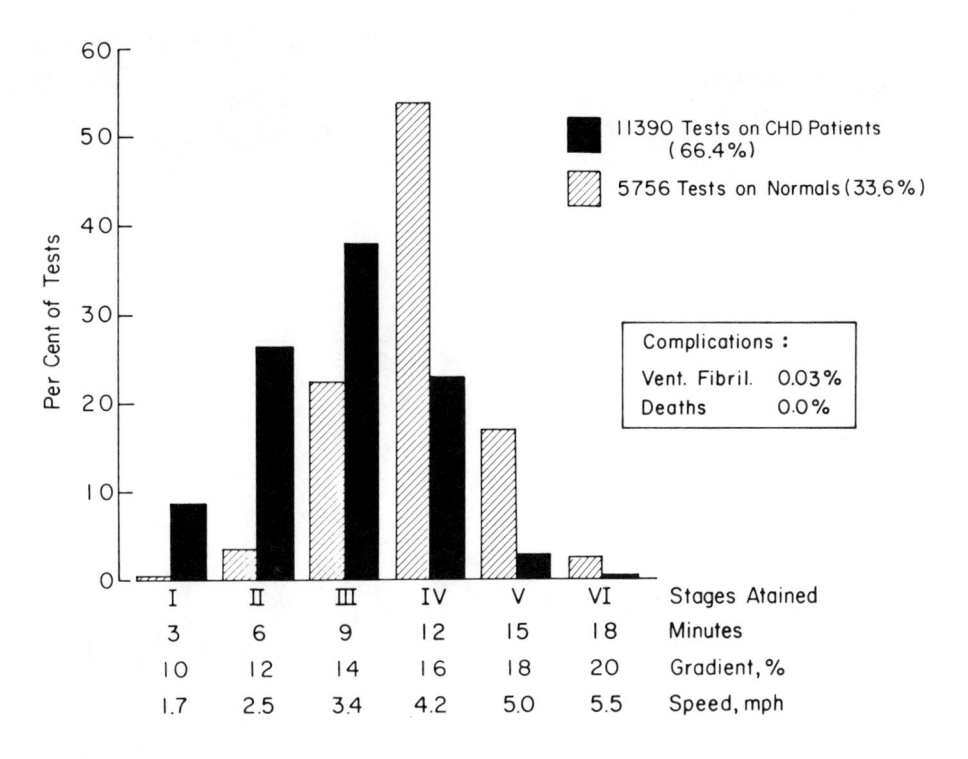

FIGURE 1. 17146 Multistage treadmill tests of symptom-limited maximal exercise (Seattle Experience, 6 years, 7/71 to 6/77).

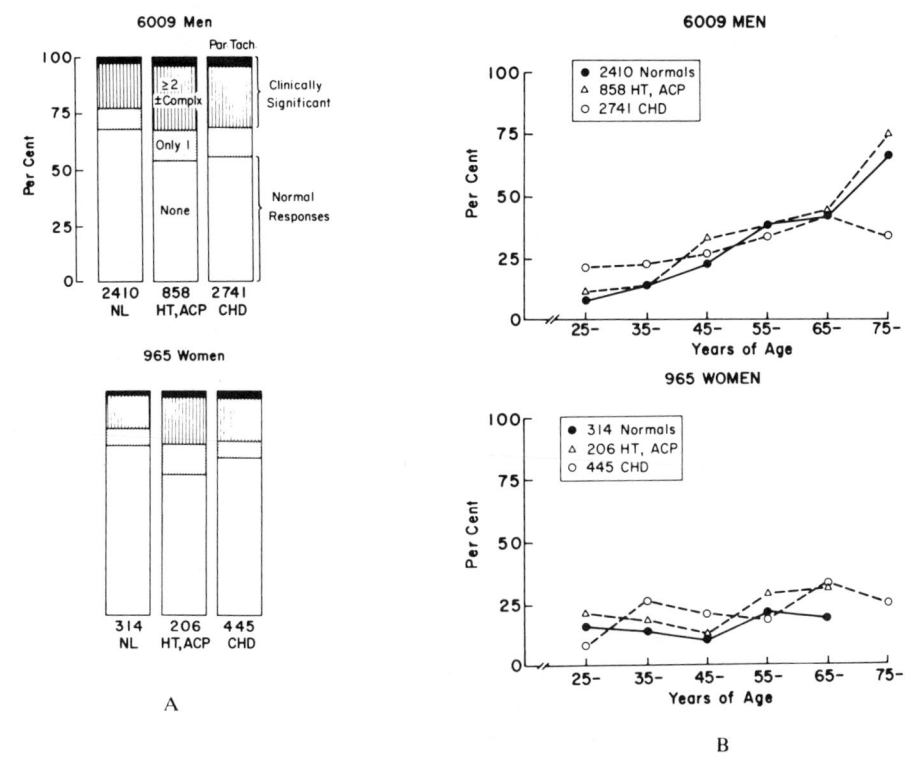

FIGURE 2. Arrhythmias in relation to exercise. (A) Arrhythmias during or after maximal exercise; (B) age-specific prevalences of two or more premature beats during and after maximal ST depression in relation to exercise.

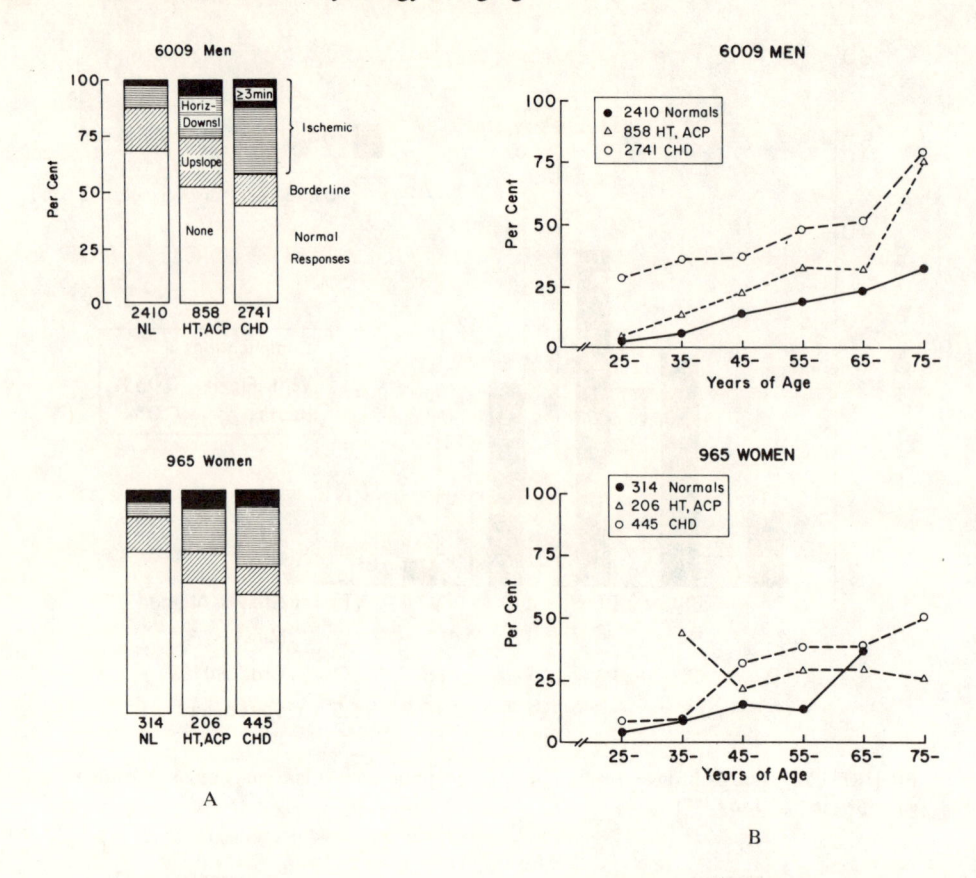

FIGURE 3. (A) ST depression ≥1 mm after maximal exercise; (B) ischemic ST depression (≥1 mm, horiz/downslope) after maximal exercise.

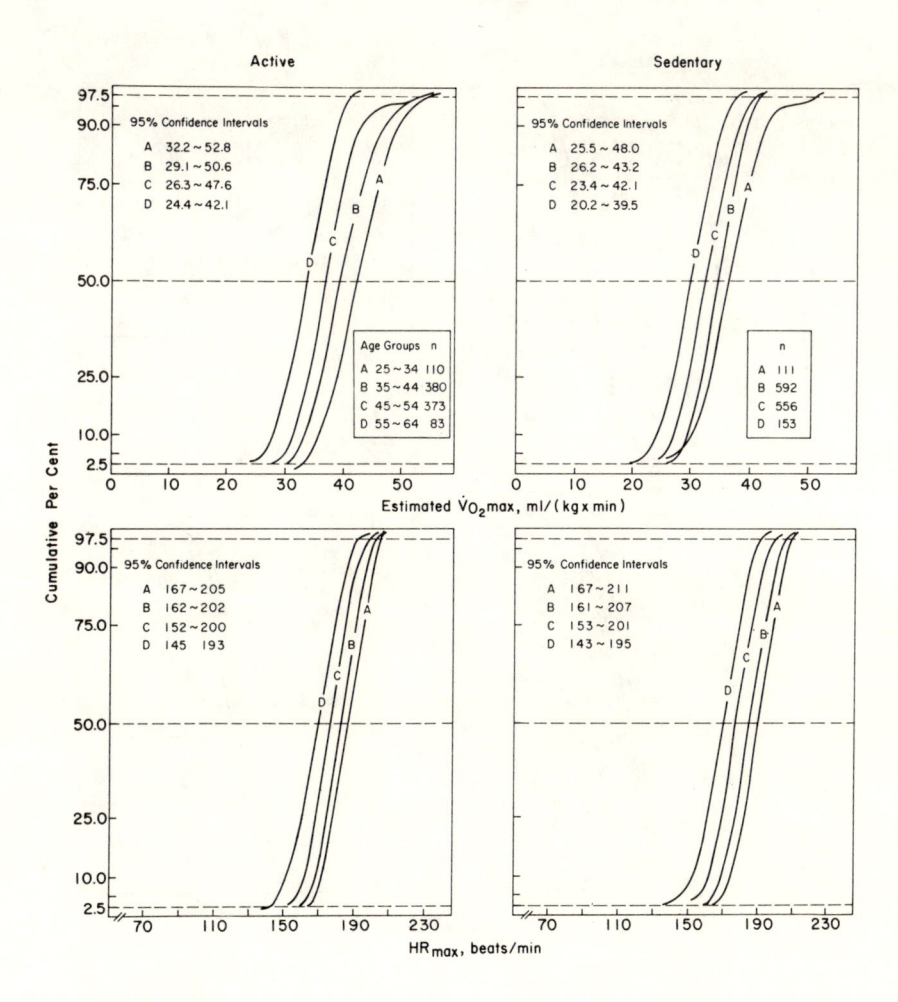

FIGURE 4. Effects of age and physical status on maximal O_2 consumption and maximal heart rate.

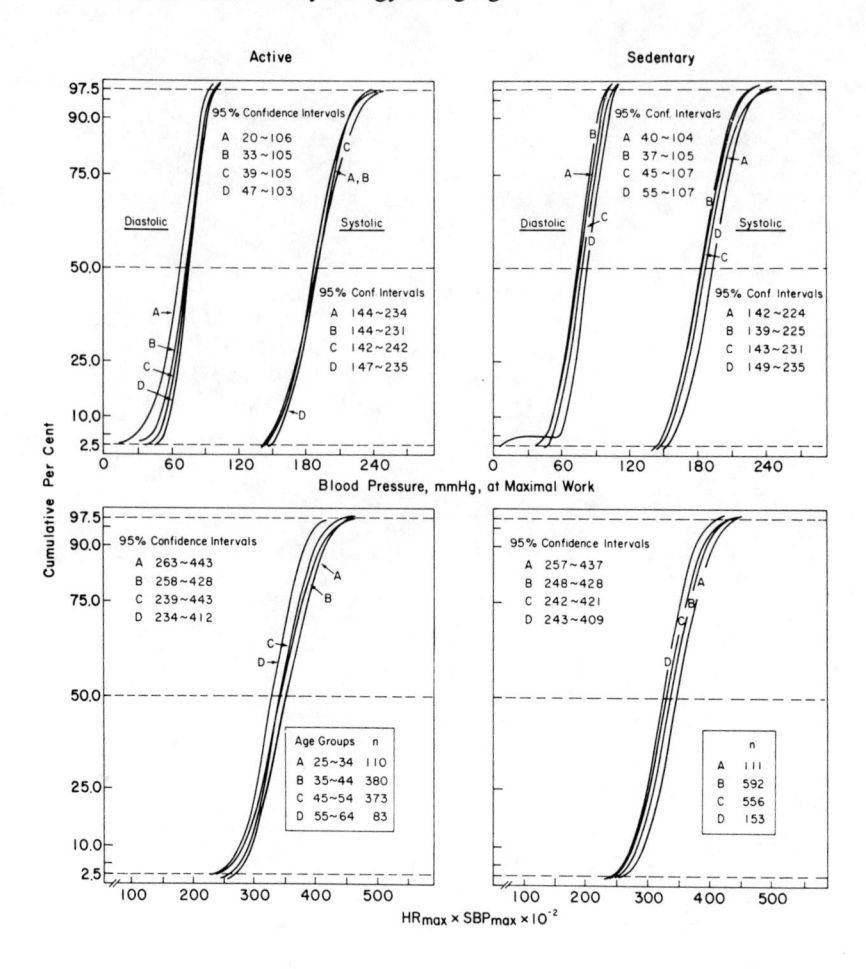

FIGURE 5. Effects of age and physical status on blood pressure at maximal work and on maximal heart rate-blood pressure product.

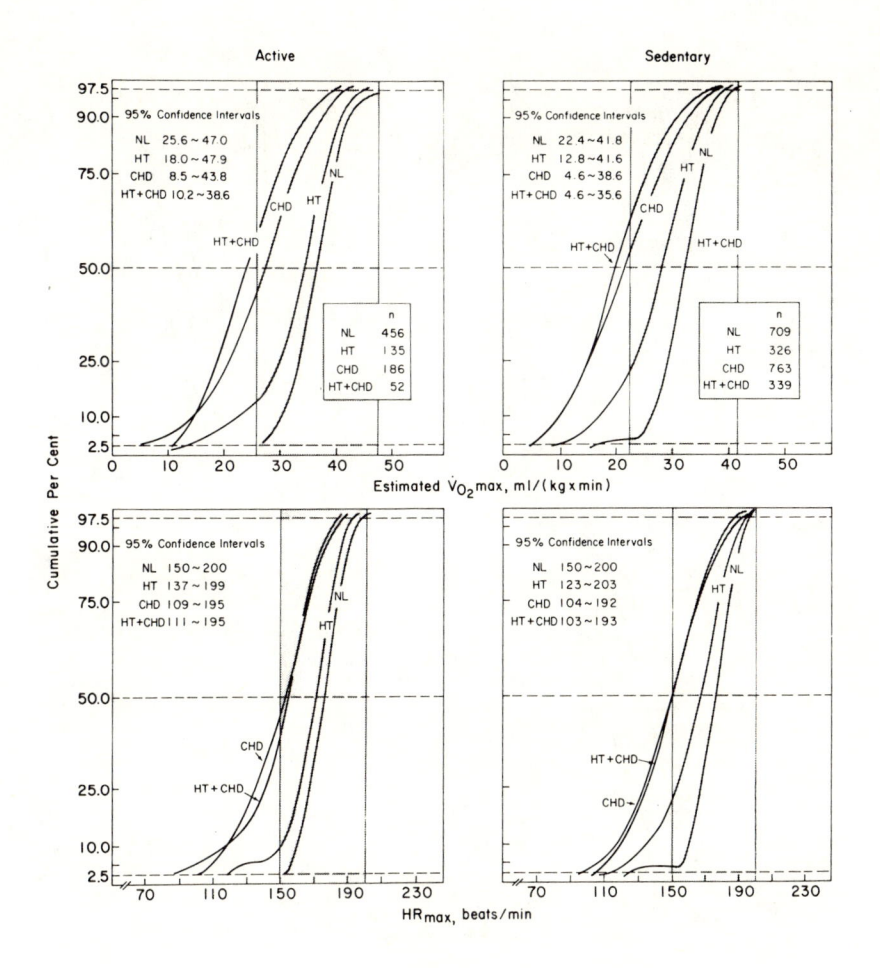

FIGURE 6. Effects of cardiovascular diseases in men of 45-64 years of age on maximal oxygen consumption and on maximal heart rate.

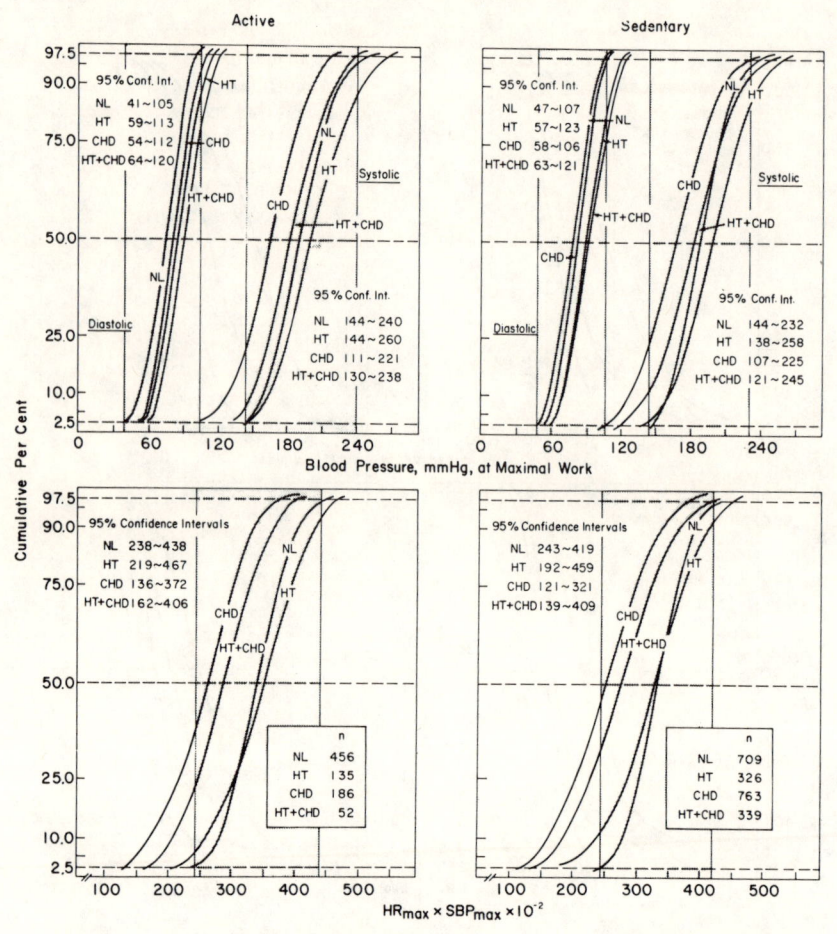

FIGURE 7. Effects of cardiovascular diseases in men of 45-64 years of age on blood pressure at maximal work and on maximal heart rate-systolic blood pressure product.

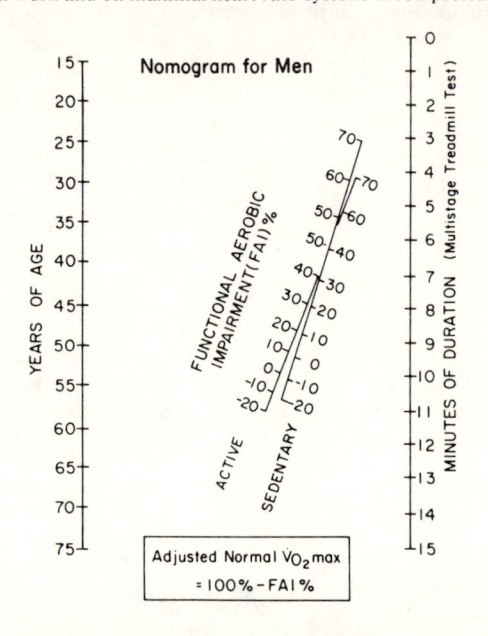

FIGURE 8. Relationship of age to functional aerobic impairment.

Temperature Regulation

TERMS, CONSTANTS, SYMBOLS, AND EQUATIONS USED IN THERMAL PHYSIOLOGY

D. Dubey and E. Y. Yunis

Table 1
SYMBOLS AND UNITS OF PHYSICAL QUANTITIES USED IN THERMAL PHYSIOLOGY

Fundamental units	Symbol	Unit	Abbreviation of unit
Length	L	Meter	m
Mass	m	Kilogram	kg
Time	t	Second	sec
Temperature	T	Degree kelvin	K
Absorptance (radiation)	α	Dimensionless	—
Area	A	Square meter	m²
Conductivity (thermal)	k	Watt per meter and °C	W/(m °C)
Density	ϱ	Kilogram per cubic meter	kg/m³
Emittance (radiation)	ε	Dimensionless	—
Heat (rate of exchange)	H	Watt per square meter	W/m²
Heat (latent)	λ	Joule per kilogram	J/kg
Heat (quantity; energy)	J	Joule	J
Heat transfer coefficient (total surface conductance)	h	Watt per square meter and °C	W/(m² °C)
Irradiance (incident radiant flux density)	I	Watt per square meter	W/m²
Mass transfer rate	$\dot{m}$	Kilogram per second	kg/sec
Pressure	P	Newton per square meter or millimeter of mercury	N/m² or mmHg
Reflectance (radiation)	ϱ	Dimensionless	—
Resistance, thermal (insulation)	R; I	°C and square meter per watt	(°C m²)/W
Specific heat	c	Joule per kilogram and °C	J/(kg °C)
Transmittance (radiation)	T	Dimensionless	—
Ventilation rate	$\dot{V}$	Cubic meter per second; liter per second	m³/sec; ℓ/sec
Velocity (linear)	v	Meter per second	m/sec
Volume	V	Cubic meter, liter, milliliter	m³, ℓ, mℓ
Work rate	W	Watt, joule per second	W, J/sec

From Committee of the American Physiological Society, *J. Appl. Physiol.*, 27(3), 439, 1969. With permission.

Table 2
COMMONLY USED CONSTANTS AND SYMBOLS USED IN THERMAL PHYSIOLOGY

Name or term	Symbol	Value or example
Avogadro constant	N_A	6.0225×10^{23} mol^{-1}
Boltzmann constant	k	1.38×10^{-23} J/K
Gas constant	R	8.3143 J/(K mol)
Gravitational constant	G	6.670×10^{-11} (N m^2)/kg^2
Stefan-Boltzmann constant	σ	5.67×10^{-8} W/ (m^2 K^4)
Ambient	a	T_a = ambient or dry bulb temperature
Arterial	ar	T_{ar} = arterial temperature
Body	b	T_b = mean body temperature
Blood	bl	$\dot{m}_{bl}$ = blood flow
Conductive	k	h_k = conductive heat transfer coefficient
Convective	c	h_c = convective heat transfer coefficient
Diffusion	D	h_D = mass transfer coefficient by diffusion
Emitting source	i	T_i = temperature of emitting source
Evaporative	e	h_e = evaporative heat transfer coefficient
Expired	ex	T_{ex} = temperature of expired air
Hypothalamic	hy	T_{hy} = hypothalamic temperature
Inspired	in	T_{in} = temperature of inspired air
Oral	or	T_{or} = oral temperature
Pressure (constant)	P	c_p = specific heat at constant pressure
Projected	$\overline{P}$	A_p = projected area
Radiation (radiative)	r	h_r = linear radiation heat transfer coefficient
Rectal	re	T_{re} = rectal temperature
Skin	s	$\overline{T}_s$ = mean skin temperature
Spectral wave length	λ	F_λ = spectral radiant flux intensity in wavelength intervals
Tympanic	ty	T_{ty} = tympanic temperature
Venous	ve	T_{ve} = venous temperature
Volume (constant)	V	c_V = specific heat at constant volume
Water vapor	w	P_w = partial pressure of water vapor
Wet bulb	wb	T_{wb} = wet bulb temperature

From Committee of the American Physiological Society, *J. Appl. Physiol.*, 27(3), 439, 1969. With permission.

Table 3
MATHEMATICAL FORMULAS COMMONLY USED IN THERMOREGULATION STUDIES

Radiation transfer	$R = \sigma(\overline{T}s^4 - \overline{T}r^4)\, Ar/A_D$
Radiation heat transfer $(\overline{T}s - \overline{T}r) < 20°\,K$	$R = \dfrac{4\sigma Ar \overline{T}^3}{A_D}(\overline{T}s - \overline{T}r)$
Convective heat transfer	$C = hc\,(\overline{T}s - Ta)$
Evaporative heat transfer	$E = E_{ex} + E_{sw}$
Heat loss by expired air	$Ex = \dot{V}(\rho ex - \phi_a \rho in) Ar/A_D$
Heat loss by sweating	$Esw = hc(Pws - \phi_a Pwa) Aw/A_D$
Body heat content	$S = (0.1\Delta \overline{T}s + 0.9\Delta T_{ty}) M_b C_b / A_D / \Delta t$
Heat balance equation	$M = E + h(\overline{T}s - Ta) - Hr$ where $Hr = hr(\overline{T}r - Ta)$
Heat transfer coefficient by evaporation	$he = \dfrac{h_D \lambda}{RwT},\ T = \dfrac{(Ta + \overline{T}a)}{2}$
Evaporative heat loss	$E = he \cdot \Delta P\, \dfrac{Aw}{A_D}$

From Gagge, A. P., Hardy, J. D., and Rapp, G. M., *J. Appl. Physiol.*, 27, 439, 1969. With permission.

GLOSSARY OF SOME IMPORTANT TERMS USED IN THERMAL PHYSIOLOGY

Area, DuBois (A_D) — The total surface area in square meters in a nude human as estimated by the formula of DuBois based on the height, $H_{(m)}$, and weight $W(kg)$

$$A_D = 0.202 \cdot W^{0.425} \cdot H^{0.725}$$

Area, effective radiating (Ar) — The surface area of a body that exchanges radiant energy with the environment through a solid angle of 4π steraians

Area, total body (A_b) — The area of the outer surface of a body, assumed smooth

Body heat balance equation — A mathematical expression that describes the net rate at which a body generates and exchanges heat with its environment

$$S = M \pm E - (\pm W) \pm R \pm C \pm K$$

where S = rate of storage of body heat, M = metabolic free energy production (always +), E = evaporative heat transfer (− for net loss), W = work (+ for positive work against external forces), R = radiant heat exchange (+ for net gain), C = convective heat transfer (+ for net gain), and K = conductive heat transfer (+ for net gain)

Clo — A unit to express the relative thermal insulation values of various clothing assemblies

$$1 \text{ clo} = 0.18°C \text{ m}^2 \cdot \text{hr} \cdot \text{kcal}^{-1} = 0.155°C \text{ m}^2 \text{ w}^{-1}$$

Conductive heat transfer (K) — The net rate of total heat transfer by conduction between an organism and its environment, usually expressed in terms of unit area of the total body surface

Evaporative heat gain (+ E) — The rate of total heat gain due to condensation of vapor on the skin and/or the surfaces of the respiratory tract, expressed in terms of unit area of total body surface

Evaporative heat loss (−E) — The rate of total heat loss by evaporation of water from the skin and the surface of the respiratory tract, usually expressed in terms of unit area of total body surface (−E)

Heat loss, nonevaporative — The sum of heat losses by radiation, convection, and conduction per unit area of body surface in units time

Heat storage, change in — The gain or loss of heat associated with change in body temperature or body mass

Heat transfer coefficient, combined nonevaporative (h) — The ratio of total rate of heat transfer per unit area by radiation, convection, and conduction due to the temperature difference between the surface and operative temperature of the environment

$$h = hr + h_c + h_R$$

Heat transfer (conduction) coefficient (hk) — The net rate of heat transfer by conduction per unit area between a surface and a solid or stationary fluid in contact with the surface per unit temperature difference between the surface and the substance with which it is in contact:

$$L_K = K\Delta T^{-1}$$

Heat transfer coefficient, convection (hc) — The net rate of heat transfer per unit area between a surface and a moving fluid per unit temperature difference (ΔT) between the surface and the fluid:

$$hc = C\Delta T^{-1}$$

Heat transfer coefficient, evaporative (e) — The rate of heat exchange per unit vapor pressure gradient caused by the evaporation of water from a unit area of wet surface or by the condensation of water vapor in a unit area of body surface. The driving force is the vapor pressure gradient from Pws (on the surface) to Pwa (of the ambient gas)

$$he = -E(Pws - Pwa)^{-1} \text{ or } + E(Pwa - Pws)^{-1}$$

The evaporative heat transfer coefficient (he) can be expressed in terms of latent heat (λ) of water, the constant of water vapor Rw, the mean temperature (T) of the medium in K, and mass transfer coefficient (h_D)

$$he = h_D\, Rw^{-1}\, T^{-1}$$

Latent heat of vaporization (λ) — The quantity of heat released (or absorbed) in the reversible process of evaporation (or condensation) of unit mass of liquid (or vapor) under isobaric and isothermal equilibrium conditions

Mass transfer coefficient (diffusion) (h_D) — The rate of mass transfer ($\dot{m}$) from a vaporizing liquid (usually water) to a moving gas (usually air) in contact with it, per unit area (A) of the liquid surface and per unit difference between the vapor density (saturated) at the surface (Pwa) and the vapor density of the ambient gas (Pwa), expressed in the equation:

$$h_D = \dot{m}A^{-1}(Pws - Pwa)^{-1}$$

GLOSSARY OF SOME IMPORTANT TERMS USED IN THERMAL PHYSIOLOGY (continued)

Metabolic free energy production (M) — The rate of transformation of chemical energy into heat and mechanical work by aerobic and anaerobic metabolic activities within an organism, usually expressed in terms of unit area of the total body surface; the quantity M in the Body heat balance equation

Metabolic heat production (H) — Rate of transformation of chemical energy into heat in an organism, usually expressed in terms of unit area of the total body surface; the quantity $M - (+W)$ in the body heat balance equation

Metabolic level — The heat production measured under standard conditions during a 24-hr period divided by the metabolic body size

Metabolic rate, basal (BMR) — The rate of metabolic free energy production calculated from measurements of heat production or oxygen consumption in an organism in a rested, awake, fasting, and thermoneutral state (a particular case of standard metabolic rate)

Temperature core — The mean temperature of the tissues at a depth below that which is affected directly by a change in the temperature gradient through peripheral tissues; mean core temperature cannot be measured accurately, and is generally represented by a specified core temperature, i.e., that of the rectum; synonym: temperature, deep body

Temperature, dry bulb (T_{db}) — The temperature of a gas or mixture of gases indicated by a thermometer shielded from radiation; synonym: temperature, ambient

Temperature, effective (T_{eff}) — An arbitrary index which combines in a single value the effect of temperature, humidity, and air movement on the sensation of warmth or cold felt by human subjects; the numerical value is that of the temperature of "still" air saturated with water vapor which would induce an identical sensation

Temperature, mean body ($\bar{T}_b$) — The sum of the products of the heat capacity and temperature of all the tissues of the body divided by the total heat capacity of the organism

$$\bar{T}_b = \Sigma(c_i \cdot T_i)/\Sigma c_i$$

Temperature, mean radiant ($\bar{T}_r$) — The temperature of an imaginary isothermal "black" enclosure in which a solid body or occupant would exchange the same amount of heat by radiation as in the actual nonuniform enclosure

Temperature, mean skin ($\bar{T}_{sk}$) — The sum of the products of the area of each regional surface element (A_i) and its mean temperature (T_i) divided by the total area of body surface

$$\bar{T}_{sk} = (\Sigma A_i \cdot \bar{T}_i)/Ab$$

Temperature, operative ($\overline{T}_o$)	The temperature of a uniform (isothermal) "black" enclosure in which a solid body or occupant would exchange the same amount of heat by radiation and convection as in the actual nonuniform environment
Temperature regulation	The maintenance of the temperature or temperatures of a body within a restricted range under conditions involving variable internal and/or external heat loads; biologically, the existence of some degree of body temperature regulation by autonomic or behavioral means
Temperature regulation, autonomic	The regulation of body temperature by autonomic (i.e., involuntary) responses to heat and cold which modify the rates of heat production and heat loss (i.e., by sweating, thermal tachypnea, shivering, and variations in peripheral vasomotor tone and basal metabolism)
Temperature regulation, physiological	Both autonomic and behavioral temperature regulation (preferred); synonym for autonomic temperature regulation
Temperature, wet bulb (T_{wb})	The thermodynamic wet bulb temperature of a sample of air is the lowest temperature to which it can be cooled by evaporating water adiabatically
Thermal conductance, tissue	The rate of heat transfer per unit area during steady state when a temperature difference of 1°C is maintained across a layer of tissue
Thermal conductivity (k)	A property of a material defined by the flow of heat by conduction through unit thickness of the material per unit area and per unit temperature difference maintained at right angles to the direction of heat flow
Thermal insulation, clothing (I_{cl})	The intrinsic insulation of a clothing assembly; the effective insulation of clothing is (I_{cl} + I_a) where I_a is the reciprocal of the thermal conductance of the ambient environment; (I_{cl} + I_a) is usually measured as the temperature gradient from the surface of a heated man-sized manikin to the ambient air divided by the heat production per unit area of manikin surface; the value is sometimes expressed in Clo units
Thermogenesis, nonshivering (NST)	An increase in the rate of heat production during cold exposure due to processes which do not involve contractions of voluntary muscles, i.e., increased heat production by processes other than tone, microvibrations, or clonic contractions of skeletal muscles
Thermogenesis, shivering	An increase in the rate of heat production during cold exposure due to processes which do not involve contractions of voluntary muscles, i.e., increased heat production by processes other than tone, microvibrations, or clonic contractions of skeletal muscles
Thermoneutral zone (TNZ)	The range of ambient temperature within, which temperature regulation is achieved by nonevaporative physical processes alone
Total heat production	The rate of transformation of chemical energy into heat in an organism (metabolic heat production) plus any heat liberation within the body resultig from work done on the organism by an external force

From Bligh, J. and Johnson, K. G., *J. Appl. Physiol.*, 35, 941, 1973. With permission.

AGE-RELATED CHANGES IN THERMAL PHYSIOLOGY

D. Dubey and E. J. Yunis

Table 1
CHANGES WITH AGE IN THERMOREGULATORY FUNCTIONS OF RESTING MAN

			Ref.
I.	Thermoneutral environment		
	A.	Rectal or tympanic temperature is highest in prepubertal boys (10—14 years) and declines in young adults and older men (15—74 years); mean rectal temperature of female is more than male in the age range (19—34 years)	1, 2 6, 10
	B.	The difference in rectal and skin temperatures (Tre-Ts) increases with age (15—67 years)	6, 13
	C.	Metabolic rate is high among young boys and gradually decreases with age (15—74 years)	6, 13, 14
	D.	There is a gradual decline in body heat storage with age (15—67 years)	13
	E.	Young men (15—29 years) have higher finger blood flow than prepubertal and older persons (46—70 years)	1, 11, 13
II.	During an exposure to cold environment		
	A.	Rectal temperatures of pre- and post-pubertal boys increases after an initial fall; the rate of increase in temperature reduces with age; in elderly people, the fall in core temperature continues throughout cold exposure	1, 8, 13
	B.	There is a gradual decline in mean skin temperature in young pre- and post-pubertal boys, but changes more rapidly for adults and aged	1, 8, 13
	C.	Metabolic rate is reduced with increasing age; total heat loss is constant with respect to age	13
	D.	Peripheral vascular reactivities decrease with increasing age (14—67 years); the observed coefficient of heat conductance in the cold environment (15 °C) is independent of age	1, 13
	E.	Heat conduction is increased in older group (45—67 years) in cold environment (15 °C) than in thermoneutral atmosphere (30 °C) for the same group	1, 12, 13
III.	During an exposure to hot environment (35—49°C)		
	A.	The core temperature rises significantly with age (20—67 years)	3, 5, 6, 14
	B.	Metabolic rate remains constant with age	14
	C.	Heat conductance is reduced with increasing age	14
	D.	Evaporative heat loss is not significantly affected with age (20—67 years)	14
	E.	There is no significant increase in forearm blood flow with age (20—67 years)	14
	F.	The finger blood flow rate is reduced with age (20—87 years)	5, 14
	G.	There is a significant increase in the threshold temperature with age (20—89 years) for the start of sweating	1, 5
	H.	No significant difference in the threshold temperature for vasodilation with age has been reported	3

REFERENCES

1. Collins, K. J., Dore, C., Exton-Smith, A. N., Fox, R. H., MacDonald, I. C., and Woodward, P. M., Accidental hypothermia and impaired temperature hemeostasis in the elderly, *Br. Med. J.*, 1, 353, 1977.
2. Craig, F. N., Effects of atropine, work and heat on heart rate and sweat production in man, *J. Appl. Physiol.*, 4, 826, 1952.

Table 1 (continued)
CHANGES WITH AGE IN THERMOREGULATORY FUNCTIONS OF RESTING MAN

3. Crowe, J. P. and Moore, R. E., Physiological and behavioural responses of aged men to passive heating, *J. Physiol. (London),* 236, P43P, 1974.
4. Drinkwater, B. L., Kupprat, J. C., Denton, J. E., Crist, J. L., and Horvath, S. M., Response of prepubertal girls and college women to work in the heat, *J. Appl. Physiol.,* 43, 1946, 1977.
5. Fennell, W. H. and Moore, R. E., Responses of aged men to passive heating, *J. Physiol. (London),* 231, P118, 1973.
6. Fox, R. H., Even-Paz, Z., Woodward, P. M., and Jack, J. W., A study of temperature regulation in Yemenite and Kurdish Jews in Israel. VIII, *Philos. Trans. R. Soc. (London) Ser. B,* 266, 149, 1973.
7. Horvath, S. M., Radcliffe, C. E., Hutt, B. K., and Spurr, G. B., Metabolic responses of old people to a cold environment, *J. Appl. Physiol.,* 8, 145, 1955.
8. Hayward, J. S., Eckerson, J. D., and Collis, M. L., Thermoregulatory heat production in man: prediction equation based on skin and core temperatures, *J. Appl. Physiol.,* 42, 377, 1977.
9. Johnson, R. H. and Park, D. M., Intermittent hypothermia independence of central and reflex thermoregulatory mechanisms, *J. Neurol. Neurosurg. Psychiatry,* 36, 411, 1973.
10. Paolone, A. M., Wells, C. L., and Kelly, G. T., Sexual variations in thermoregulation during heat-stress, *Aviat. Space Environ. Med.,* 49, 715, 1978.
11. Ring, G. C., Kurbatov, T., and Shannon, G. J., Changes in central pulse and finger plethysmography during aging, *J. Gerontol.,* 14, 189, 1959.
12. Spurr, G. B., Hutt, B. K., and Horvath, S. M., The effects of age on finger temperature responses to local cooling, *Am. Heart J.,* 50, 551, 1955.
13. Wagner, J. A., Robinson, S., and Morino, R. P., Age and temperature regulation of humans in neutral and cold environment, *J. Appl. Physiol.,* 37, 562, 1974.

Table 2
BODY TEMPERATURE VARIATION WITH AGE IN RESTING MAN

Age	Sex	No. subjects	State	Ambient temp (°C)	Time of measurement	Surface temp (°C)	Core temp (°C)	Ref.
40 [a]	M/F	10	Nude	32—33	N.M.		R 37.1±0.2	1
7 days	M/F	10	Nude	32—33	N.M.		R 36.7±0.1	1
12.0 years [b]	F	5	Partially clothed	28	A.M.	S 33.4±0.2	R 37.1±0.1	2
20.6±0.7 years	F	5	Partially clothed	28	A.M.	S 33.7±0.3	R 37.0±0.1	2
24.6±4.0 years	F	7	Partially clothed	25—30	A.M.	S 34.31±0.22	A 37.09±0.08	3
25.7±4.2 years	M	9	Partially clothed	25—30	A.M.	S 34.29±0.30	A 36.77±0.07	3
25.2±3.2 years	F	6	Partially clothed	25—30	A.M.	S 34.84±0.22	A 36.97±0.11	3
26.1±3.7 years	M	10	Partially clothed	25—30	A.M.	S 34.48±0.17	A 36.86±0.06	3
74.0±4.0 years	M/F	29	Lightly clothed	30	A.M.	S 33.45±0.60	A 36.87±0.20	4

Note: Body temperatures show circadian variation, most of the values reported here were measured in morning times under controlled ambient temperatures. Body core temperatures were measured by thermistor temperature measuring device inserted deep into the rectum (R) or in the external auditory meatus of each ear. (A) = All measurements made on normal volunteers. N.M. = not mentioned; A.M. = morning; S = skin; R = rectal; and A = ear.

[a] Weight 2.99 to 3.69 kg (kept in incubator before temperature measurement).
[b] Weight at measurement 2.11 to 4.0 kg (kept in incubator before temperature measurement).

Table 2 (continued)
BODY TEMPERATURE VARIATION WITH AGE IN RESTING MAN

REFERENCES

1. **Rylander, E.**, Age dependent reactions of rectal and skin temperatures of infants during exposure to cold, *Acta Paediatr. Scan.*, 61, 597, 1972.
2. **Drinkwater, B. L., Kupprat, I. C., Denton, J. E., Crist, J. L., and Horvath, S. M.**, Response of prepubertal girls and college women to work in the heat, *J. Appl. Physiol.*, 43, 1046, 1977.
3. **Fox, R. H., Even-Paez, Z., Woodward, P. M., and Jack, J. W.**, A study of temperature regulation in Yemenite and Kurdish Jews in Israel, VIII, *Philos. Trans. R. Soc. (London) Ser. B*, 266, 149, 1973.
4. **Collins, K. J., Dore, C., Exton-Smith, A. N., Fox, R. H., MacDonald, I. C., and Woodward, P. M.**, Accidental hypothermia and impaired temperature hemoestasis in the elderly, *Br. Med. J.*, 1, 353, 1977.

Table 3
TEMPERATURE CHANGE IN RESTING HUMANS IN COLD ENVIRONMENT

Age	Sex	No. subjects	Ambient temp (°C)	State	Temp °C (duration of exposure)	Temp °C Before exposure	Temp °C After exposure	Response	Comments	Ref.
40'—70'	M/F	10	33—35	Nude	23°(30')	R 37.1±0.2	R 36.0±0.1	Fall in T$_{re}$ 0.40°C/min cooling	Values refer to last 15' exposure to cold	1
145'	M/F	8	33—35	Nude	23°(30')	R 36.5±0.1	R 36.1±0.2	Fall in T$_{re}$ 0.01°C/min cooling	Values refer to last 15' exposure to cold	1
7d	M/F	10	32—35ª	Nude	23°(30')	R 36.7±0.1	R 36.6±0.1	No change in T$_{re}$ temp	Kept in incubator at 32—33°C for 30'; recorded temp measured during last 15' exposure to cold	1
10—13 years	M	9	30(15)	Partially clothed	16—17°(30')	see Table 2		After initial decline T$_{re}$ increases during exposure	MR increases	2

14—16 years	M	7	30(15)	Partially clothed		see Table 2	MR increases	2
19—26 years	M	10	30(15)	Partially clothed	16—17°(30')	see Table 2	No change in T_{rc}	MR increases	2
21—26 years	M	8	25—26	Partially clothed	10°(45—60')[a]		Continue fall in T_{rc} at rate of 2.1°C/hr during cold immersion (45—60')	MR increases with time during immersion	3
19—29 years	F	3	25—30	Partially clothed		R 36.99±0.16 R 38.00±0.01[b]		4
21—34 years	M	7	25—30	Partially clothed		T 36.83±0.13 T 38.02±0.01[b]		4
46—67 years	M	7	30(15)	Partially clothed	16—17°(30')	see Table 2		3
74±4 years	M/F	29	30	Partially clothed	15°(16')	A 36.87±0.2 T 36.91±0.21		5

Note: T_{rc} = rectal temperature; T_s = skin temperature; R = rectal site; A = tympanic site (auditory meatus); and MR = metabolic rate.

[a] Temperatures measured after water immersion in cold water at 10°C.
[b] All temperature measurements performed in the morning.

REFERENCES

1. **Rylander, E.**, Age dependent reactions of rectal and skin temperatures of infants during exposure to cold, *Acta Paediatr. Scan.*, 61, 597, 1972.
2. **Wagner, J. A., Robinson, S., and Marino, R. P., Jr.**, Age and temperature regulation of humans in neutral and cold environment, *J. Appl. Physiol.*, 37, 562, 1974.
3. **Hayward, J. S., Eckerson, J. D., and Collis, M. L.**, Thermoregulatory heat production in man: prediction equation based on skin and core temperatures, *J. Appl. Physiol.*, 42, 377, 1977.
4. **Fox, R. H., Even-Paz, Z., Woodward, P. M., and Jack, J. W.**, A study of temperature regulation in Yemenite and Kurdish Jews in Israel, VIII, *Philos. Trans. R. Soc. (London) Ser.B*, 266, 149, 1973.
5. **Collins, K. J., Dore, C., Exton-Smith, A. N., Fox, R. H., MacDonald, I. C., and Woodward, P. M.**, Accidental hypothermia and impaired temperature hemoestasis in the elderly, *Br. Med. J.*, 1, 353, 1977.

Table 4
THERMOREGULATORY RESPONSES OF RESTING BOYS AND ADULTS DURING COLD EXPOSURE (16—17°C)

Age group (years)	No. subjects	m²/kg	Metabolic rate (kcal/m²/hr²)	Heat storage loss(kcal/m² hr²)	Total heat loss(kcal/m² hr²)	$T_{rec}-T_{sk}$ (°C)	Heat conduction
10—13	9	0.034	55.2±1.7	−63.2±6.6	118.4±6.3	8.6±0.2	12.8±0.8
14—16	7	0.033	53.8±1.0	−58.6±9.1	112.4±9.4	7.6±0.3	13.7±1.3
19—26	10	0.026	47.9±2.7	−69.7±6.5	117.6±5.6	7.1±0.3	15.6±0.8
46—67	7	0.025	39.2±3.6	−77.7±8.0	116.9±9.7	7.4±0.5	15.0±1.0

Note: All parameters were measured during the last 15 min of a 30-min exposure to cold environment. Heat loss values calculated by partitional heat balance equations.

From Wagner, J. A., Robinson, S., and Marino, R. P., Age and temperature regulation of humans in neutral and cold environment, *J. Applied Physiol.*, 37, 562, 1974. With permission.

Index

INDEX

A

Abdominal aorta, 105, 109, 123, 128
Absorption
    of calcium, 273—275
    of carbohydrates, 277—278
    of cholesterol, 285
    of ions, 273—275
    of lead, 275
    of lipids, 285
    of phosphorus, 275
    of strontium, 275
    of vitamins, 283—284
    of water-soluble vitamins, 283—284
Acetanillide, 4
Acetylcholinesterase, 45
N-Acetyl-β-D-glucosaminidase, 135
Acid-base balance, 191, 449
Acid carboxypeptidase, 135
Acidophils, 365
ACTH, 4, 302, 314
Adenohypophysis, 289—294
Adenosine triphosphatase (ATP-ase), 48
Adenylate cyclase, 395
Adenyl cyclase, 128
ADH, see Antidiuretic hormone
Adipocytes, 418
Adipose tissue, see also Fat, 383, 385, 417—421
Adrenal, 383
Adrenal cortex, 295—316
    function of, 315, 316
    stimulation of, 305—308
Adrenaline, 153
Adrenal medullary hormones, 383—389
Adrenocortical steroid hormones, 295—296, 302, 304
Aerobic capacity, 445
Aerobic impairments, 472
Aerobic metabolic activities, 457
Alanine, 54, 279
Aluminum ions, 4
Alzheimer's disease, 4
Amino acids, 54, 279—281
D-Amphetamine, 31
Amyloid, 4, 380
Androgen-binding protein, 375
Androstenedione, 362
Antidiuretic hormone (ADH), 179, 325
Aorta, 83, 105, 109, 113, 116, 123, 128, 133—135, 433, 435, 437, 438
    dimensions of, 84—85, 87
    elastic properties of, 90, 92—94
    mechanical properties of, 129
    regression equations of changes in, 95
    thoracic properties of, 129
Aqueous humor, 19
Arcus senilis, 18
Arginine, 54, 280
Arginine vasopressin, 179

Arrhythmias, 151, 467
Arterial blood pressure, 137—145
Arterial distensibility, 443
Arterial lesions, 160
Arteries, 94, 99, 101—103, 105, 117, 119, 126, 128, 130, 134, 135, 160, 436, 439
    brain, 37
    calcium in, 123—124
    cerebral, 433
    collagen in, 109
    coronary, 101, 117, 134, 160
    elastin in, 109
    iliac, 105, 123
    lipid in, 119
    muscle in, 109
    muscular, 104
    pulse wave velocity in, 106, 108
    viscoelastic properties of, 105
Arterioles, 126, 433
Arteriosclerosis, 126
Ascorbic acid, 284
Aspartic acid, 54
Astigmatism, 18
Astrocytes, 39
Atherogenesis, 126
Atherosclerosis, 37
Atherosclerotic lesions, 160
ATP-ase, 48
Atrophy
    of muscles, 47
    of nerves, 16
    of olfactory glomeruli, 16
Atropine, 151
Auditory sensitivity tests, 25
Auditory system changes, 25
Axon myeliation, 7, 8
Axoplasmic flow, 4
Axoplasmic transport, 45

B

Baboons, reproductive life-span in, 334
Balke treadmill, 445
Baroreceptor
    reactivity of, 128
    sensitivity of, 126, 135
Baroreflexes, 154
Basal gonadotropin secretion, 381
Basal metabolic rate (BMR), 411, 412, 457, 480
Basophils, 365
Beagles
    cardiac performance in, 76
    flow characteristics in, 149
Bears, reproductive life-span in, 335
Bicarbonate, 191
Biogenic amine, 330
Birth defects, 352

Bladder, 193
Blood, see also Plasma, 189
   clotting of, 63
   coagulation factors in, 65
   pH of, 191
Blood flow, 161, 164, 168—170, 177, 447, 483
   cerebral, 33
Blood oxygen affinity, 218
Blood pressure, 137—145, 149
Blood vessels, see also Coronary, 25, 83—135
   composition of, 130—131
   elastic modulus of, 128
   enzyme activities in, 126
   mucopolysaccharides in, 113
   nonfibrous elements of, 116
B lymphocytes, 62
BMR, see Basal metabolic rate
Body density, 417
Body fluids, 189—190
Body heat
   balance of, 477, 478
   conductance coefficient for, 483
   conduction of, 483
   content of, 477, 478
   dolorimetry for, 9
   loss of, 477, 478, 483
   production of, 481
   storage of, 478
   transfer of, 477—479
Body temperature, 7, 10, 483
   variations in, 485—487
Body temperature core, 483
Bone, see also specific bones, 423—432, 434, 435, 438
   calcium in, 443
   cortical, 425, 427, 429
   formation of, 424
   growth of, 423
   loss of, 426
   mean deformation of, 430
   mean ultimate strength of, 430
   minerals in, 427
   remodeling of, 423
Bovines
   collagen in, 435
   skin in, 435
Brain, 35, 222
Brain arteries, 37
Brain vasculature, 37
Brown adipose tissue, 418
Buffalo, reproductive life-span in, 334

C

Cadmium, 117
Calcitonin, 397—408
   degradation of, 403
Calcium, 131, 189, 405, 436, 439, 443
   absorption of, 273—275
   in arteries, 123—124

   binding of, 126
   tolerance of, 406
   in viens, 123—124
Calcium-activated myosin ATP-ase, 48
Calf blood flow, 170
cAMP, 128
Capillaries, 155, 169, 433
   density of, 170
Carbohydrate absorption, 277—278
Carcinoma, prostatic, 378
Cardiac anatomy, see also Heart, 81
Cardiac muscle, 383
Cardiac performance, see also Heart, 69, 70, 74, 76, 77, 79, 146—148, 447, 449
   efficiency of, 443
   regulation of, 152
Cardiovascular diseases, 470, 471
Cardiovascular reflexes, 154
Cardiovascular system, 82, 385
   humoral regulation of, 151—158
   neural regulation of, 151—158
   response of to exercise, 447
Carotid artery, 105, 130
Carotid sinus, 100
   hypersensitivity of, 154
Cartilage, 434, 435, 437—439
Cartilagenous tissues, 25
Catecholamine, 330, 383, 385—386
Cathepsin D, 135
Cats
   cardiac muscle in, 383
   cardiovascular system in, 385
   collagen in, 435
   skin in, 435
Cattle
   aorta in, 133
   blood vessels in, 135
   lungs in, 200
   thorax in, 200
Cells
   endometrial, 347
   epithelial, 258
   ganglion, 7
   giant, 126
   glial, 39—40
   intestinal epithelial, 258
   Leydig, 374, 375
   mass of, 413, 416
   microglia, 39
   proliferation of, 39
   receptor, 29
   sertoli, 374
Central nervous system
   integrative functions of, 31—33
   non-neuronal elements of, 35—40
   remyelination of tissue in, 39
Central visual pathways, 20
Centrophenoxine, 3
Cephalin, 121
Cerebral arteries, 433
Cerebral blood flow, 33, 164
Cerebral circulation, 164—165

Cerebral cortex, 3, 36, 39
Cervix, 342, 344
CFF, see Critical flicker frequency
Chest wall, 207—208, 210
Chickens, metabolic rate in, 412
Chimpanzees, reproductive life-span in, 334
Chloride, 189, 449
Cholesterol, 119, 134
  absorption of, 285
  in red blood cells, 55, 59
Cholesterol ester, 119
Choline acetyltransferase, 45
Chondroitin sulfate, 113, 135, 437
Chordae tendineae, 434
Choroid, 19
Choroidal vessels, 37
Chritae, 29
Chromatic aberration, 20
Chromium, 117
Chronic stress, 448
Ciliary epithelium, 19
Ciliary muscle, 19
Circulation
  cerebral, 164—165
  cutaneous, 170
  hepatic, 168
  impairment of, 449
  limb, 170
  renal, 161—162
  skeletal muscle, 169
  splanchnic, 168
Circumvallate papilla, 13
CL, see Corpus luteum
Closure judgements, 21
Coagulation factors, 65
Cochleo-saccular tissues, 29
Collagen, 83, 126, 128, 130, 135, 346, 349, 354, 378, 379, 433—435, 438
  in arteries, 109
Colon, 232
Color vision, 20
Compensatory renal hypertrophy, 184
Concentrating ability, 179
Conductive heat transfer, 478
Confusion, 33
Conjunctiva, 18, 172
Connective tissue, 433—439
Connective tissue hexoses, 438
Contextual effects, 21
Convective heat transfer, 477
Copper, 117, 189
Core temperature, 483
Cornea, 9, 18, 434
Coronary anatomy, see also Blood vessels, 160
Coronary arteris, 101, 117, 134, 160
Coronary circulation, 159—160
Coronary flow capacity, 159
Coronary heart disease, 465
Coronary vasculature, 159
Corpuscles, 8
Corpus luteum function, 363—364
Cortical bone, 425, 427, 429

Cows
  adrenocortical stimulation in, 308
  calcium absorption in, 275
  oocyte number in, 356
  oxytocin secretion in, 327
  pituitary function in, 327
  plasma glucocorticoid response in, 299, 308
  posterior pituitary function in, 327
  reproductive life-span in, 334
  resting plasma glucocorticoids in, 299
Creatine, 111
Creatine phosphokinase, 126
Critical flicker frequency (CFF), 20
Curare, 45
Cutaneous circulation, 170
Cutaneous tactile receptors, 7
Cysteine, 280
Cystine, 54
Cystometrograms, 193

D

Dark adaptation thresholds, 20
Decision criteria, 25
Dendritic spines, 3
Denervation of muscles, 47
Dental pain threshold, 10
6-Deoxy-D-glucose, 277
Dermatan sulfate, 113, 135, 437
Desmosine, 436
Diaphragm, 45
Diet, 47
Dihydrotestosterone, 379, 380
Diphosphoglycerate (DPG), 218
2,3-Diphosphoglycerate (2,3-DPG), 58, 218
Distensibility of aorta, 83
DNA, 111, 130, 135, 348
Dogs
  adrenocortical stimulation in, 308
  arterial blood pressure in, 145
  blood vessels in, 135
  calcium absorption in, 275
  cardiac performance in, 76
  chest wall in, 210
  flow characteristics in, 149
  gas exchange in, 216
  lungs in, 200, 205, 210
  lung volume in, 205
  myocardium in, 385
  oocyte number in, 356
  plasma glucocorticoid response in, 300, 308
  resting plasma glucocorticoids in, 300
  thorax in, 200
  ventilation in, 213
Dopamine, 330
Dopamine β-hydroxylase, 153, 331
Down's syndrome, 352
DPG, see Diphosphoglycerate
Dura, 439

E

Edward's syndrome, 352
EEG patterns, 33
Eighth nerve, 29
Elastic fibers, 126
Elastic lamellae, 83
Elastic laminae, 128
Elastic modulus
   of aorta, 94
   of blood vessels, 88, 128
Elastic properties of aorta, 90, 92—93
Elastic tissue, calcium binding in, 123
Elastin, 83, 123, 126, 128, 130, 131, 346, 436
   in arteries, 109
Electroconvulsive shock, 31
Electrolyte concentrations, 189
Elephants, reproductive life-span in, 335
Embryonic mortality, 338
Endogenous calcitonin, 404
Endometrium, 344
   cells of, 347
Endoplasmic reticulum membrane, 135
Endothelium of blood vessels, 126
   cells of, 135
Endplate potentials, 45, 47
Enzymes
   fibrinolytic, 65
   hepatic, 249—251
   in blood vessels, 126
Epididymal fat, 418
Epididymal fat depot, 418
Epithelium
   ciliary, 19
   olfactory, 16
   pigment, 19
Erythrocytes, see Red blood cells
Erythropoiesis, 55
Esophagus, 232, 239—240
   atresia of, 352
Estradiol, 348, 358, 362, 371, 373, 375
17-β-Estradiol, 375
Estrogen, 193, 348, 370, 371, 375
Estrone, 362, 371, 375
Evaporative heat gain, 478
Evaporative heat loss, 477, 483
Evaporative heat transfer, 477
Evoked responses, 33
Exercise, 151, 160, 169, 170, 443—472
   cardiovascular responses to, 447
   endurance of, 445
   heart rate and, 454
   tolerance of, 443
Exocrine pancrease, 272
Exogenous calcitonin, 404
Extracellular fluid, 189
Extraocular muscles, 18
Eyelids, 18

F

Facial nerve nucleus, 3
Fascia, 439
Fast-twitch, 47
Fat, see also Adipose tissue, 417, 418, 421
Fatigue, 445
Female reproductive tract, 338
Femoral artery, 105
Femoral cortex bone, 424
Fetal abnormalities, 338
Fetal mortality, 352
Fiber, 47
Fibrinolytic enzyme levels, 65
Filtration fraction, 177
Finger blood flow, 170, 513
Fluorogens, 19
Foliate papillae, 13
Follicles, 354, 356
Follicle stimulating hormone (FSH), 358, 366, 367, 369, 371, 373, 381, 382
Foot blood flow, 170
Forearm blood flow, 170
Free cholesterol, 119, 134
FSH, see Follicle stimulating hormone
Fumarse, 126
Functional aerobic impairment, 472

G

Galactosamine, 113, 438
Galactose, 277
Gametes, 351
Ganglion cells, 7
Gas exchange, 214, 216
Gas transport, 217
Gastric gland secretion, 270, 271
Gastrocnemius muscles, 47
Gastrointestinal motility, 231—233
Gastrointestinal secretion, 267—272
Geese, glucagon in, 386
Giant cells, 126
Glare sensitivity, 20
Glaucoma, 19
Glial cells, 39—40
Glial fibers, 39
Gliosis, 35
Glomerular filtration rate, 177
Glomerular permeability, 181
Glucagon, 395—396
Glucocorticoids, 298—300, 305—308
Glucosamine, 113, 438
Glucose, 277
Glucose tolerance, 392
Glucuronidase, 126
β-D-Glucuronidase, 135
Glutamic acid, 54
Glyceraldehyde-3-phosphate dehydrogenese, 117
Glycerides, 285
Glycerol, 54
Glycero phosphate dehydrogenese, 118
Glycine, 54, 279
Glycogen, 47
Glycogen phosphorylase, 126

Glycoproteins, 437
Glycosaminoglycans, 437
GnRH, see Gonadotropin-releasing hormone
Goats
    adrenocortical stimulation in, 308
    plasma glucocorticoid response in, 300, 308
    reproductive life-span in, 334
    resting plasma glucocorticoids in, 300
Gonadotropin, 358, 366, 368, 381
    levels of, 371
    secretion of, 330
Gonadotropin-releasing hormone (GnRH), 329, 367, 382
Graafian follicles, 354
Grip strength, 449
Growth hormone, 289
Guinea pigs
    adipose tissue in, 418
    blood vessels in, 135
    cardiac performance in, 76
    ovaries in, 355
    reproductive life-span in, 335
    uterus in, 344
Gustation, 13

H

Hamsters
    cardiac performance in, 76
    collagen in, 435
    corpus luteum in, 364
    glomerular permeability in, 181
    oocyte number in, 356
    ovarian gonadotropin responses in, 358
    ovaries in, 360
    oviduct in, 349
    pituitary morphology in, 365
    reproductive life-span in, 335
    skin in, 435
    testicular changes in, 374
    uterus in, 348
Haversian bone, 424
Hearing, 25
Heart, see also Cardiac anatomy, performance; Coronary arteries, 72, 81, 221, 439
Heart disease, 449
Heart rate, 447, 454
    regulation of, 151
Heart valves, 437
Heart volume, 447
Heat, see Body heat
Hematocrit, 57
Hemodynamics, 137—149
Hemoglobin, 57, 218
Heparan sulfate, 437
Heparin, 114
Heparitan sulfate, 113, 135, 437
Hepatic circulation, 168
Hepatic enzymes, 249—251
Hepatic metabolism, see also Liver, 249—251

Hexosamine, 113, 438
Hexuronic acid, 438
5-HIAA, see 5-Hydroxyindole acetic acid
Hirano's bodies, 4
Histidine, 54
Hormones
    adrenal medullary, 383—389
    adrenocortical steroid, 295—296, 302, 304
    antidiuretic (ADH), 179, 325
    follicle stimulating (FSH), 358, 366, 367, 369, 371, 373, 381, 382
    gonadotropin-releasing (GnRH), 329, 367, 382
    growth, 289
    luteinizing (LH), 358, 366—368, 371, 373, 374, 381, 382
    pancreatic, 391—396
    parathyroid, 397—408
    steroid, 295—296, 302, 304, 362, 371
    thyroid stimulating (TSH), 290, 291
    thyrotrophin-releasing (TRH), 291
Horses
    aorta in, 133
    lungs in, 200
    reproductive life-span in, 334
    thorax in, 200
Houseflies
    brain in, 3
    diet of, 47
    mitochondria in, 47
Humoral regulation of cardiovascular system, 151—158
Hyalinosis, 126
Hyaluronate, 113
Hyaluronic acid, 113, 135, 437
Hyaluronidase, 135
25-Hydroxycholecalciferol, 407
5-Hydroxyindole acetic acid (5-HIAA), 389
3β-Hydroxysteroid dehydrogenase, 358, 363, 375
Hypercapnia, 165, 225
Hypertension, 351, 464, 466
Hypocalcemic action of calcitonin, 404
Hypospadias, 352
Hypotension, 154
Hypothalamic biogenic amine, 330
Hypothalamic-hypophysial system, 329—330
Hypoxia, 151, 165, 170, 225

I

ICW, see Intracellular water
IHR, see Intrinsic heart rate
Iliac artery, 94, 105, 123
Imagery, 31
Immuno-parathyroid hormone levels (IPTH), 397
Immunoreactive calcitonin, 401
Implantation rate, 340
Inactivity of muscles, 47
Inferior olivary nucleus, 3
Information extraction time, 21
Innervation ratio, 45

Insulin, 391, 392
    interactions of with target tissues, 394
Integrative functions of nervous system, 31
Internal pyramidal layer of cerebral cortex, 39
Intestinal epithelial cells, 258
Intestines, 20, 255—261, 263—265
Intracellular membranes, 135
Intracellular volume, 189
Intracellular water (ICW), 413
Intraocular pressure, 19
Intrapartum performance, 351
Intrinsic heart rate (IHR), 151
Iodine, 319
Ion absorption, 273—275
IPTH, see Immuno-parathyroid hormone
Iris, 19
Iron absorption, 275
Ischemic exercise, 169
Isodesmosine, 436
Isoleucine, 54
Isoproterenol, 128, 135, 153

K

Kavain, 4
Keratan sulfate, 114, 437
Keratosulfate, 437
Kidneys, see also Renal function, 175—187, 433
Kinesthesia, 7, 10
Klinefelter triple-x-syndrome, 352

L

Langhans cells, 126
Large intestine, 20, 263—265
Latent heat of vaporization, 479
LBM, see Lean body mass
Lead, 117
    absorption of, 275
Lean body mass (LBM), 413—416
Lecithin, 121
Left ventricular impairment, 449
Leg blood flow, 170
Lens, 19
Leucine, 54, 279
Leukocytes, 61
Leydig cells, 374, 375
LH, see Luteinizing hormone
Light scatter, 18, 19, 20
Limb circulation, 170
Lipid phosphorus in red blood cells, 59
Lipids, 126, 130, 134, 135
    absorption of, 285
    in arteries, 119
    in platelets, 64
Lipofuscin, 3, 8, 378
Lithium, 117
Liver, see also Hepatic, 221, 243—261, 386, 433
    blood flow in, 168

Locus ceruleus, 3, 33
Luminance thresholds, 20
Lungs, see also Pulmonary function, 197—216,
    433, 436, 437, 439
Lung volume, 202—203, 205
Luteinizing hormone (LH), 358, 366—368, 371,
    373, 374, 381, 382
Lymphocytes, 61, 386
Lymph system, 155—158
Lysine, 54, 280, 281

M

Maculae, 29
Magnesium, 189
Magnesium arotate, 4
Mammary glands, 353
Mammary tumors, 353
Manganese, 117
Mass transfer coefficient, 479
Maternal mortality, 351
Maximal oxygen utilization, 451, 452, 457
Maximum aerobic capacity, 445
Maximum tubular transport capacity, 177
Maximum urine concentrating ability, 179
Maximum urine diluting ability, 179
MCH, see Mean corpuscular hemoglobin
MCHC, see Mean corpuscular hemoglobin
    concentration
MCV, see Mean corpuscular volume
Mean adipocyte mass, 417
Mean corpuscular hemoglobin (MCH), 55
Mean corpuscular hemoglobin concentration
    (MCHC), 55
Mean corpuscular volume (MCV), 55
Mean transit time (MTT), 164
Mechanical stimuli, 10
Mecholyl, 154
Medullary cavity expansion, 426
Meissner corpuscles, 7, 8
Membrane, 45
Membrane potential, 47
Memory, 31
Merkel corpuscles, 8
Mesenteric arteries, 128
Metabolic free energy production, 480
Metabolic heat production, 480
Metabolism
    hepatic, 249—251
    rate of, 411—412, 480, 483
Metacarpal cortical area, 425, 426
Methionine, 54, 280
3-Methyl-glucose, 277
Mice
    adipose tissue in, 418
    adrenocortical function in, 316
    adrenocortical stimulation in, 305—307
    cardiac muscle in, 383
    corpus luteum in, 363
    6-deoxy-D-glucose absorption in, 277

esophagus in, 239
glomerular permeability in, 181
glycosaminoglycans in, 437
gonadotropin levels in, 368
gonadotropin-releasing hormone (GnRH) in, 382
hepatic metabolism in, 250, 251
implantation rate in, 340
insulin in, 394
large intestine in, 263
lean body mass in, 414
leukocyte counts in, 62
liver in, 245
lungs in, 200
metabolic rate in, 412
negative feedback in, 381
oocyte number in, 356
ovarian gonadotropin responses in, 358
ovaries in, 354, 360
oviduct in, 349
pituitary morphology in, 365
pituitary response to GmRH in, 382
plasma glucocorticoid response in, 307—308
plasma growth hormone in, 289
prostate gland in, 378, 379
reproductive life-span in, 335
resting plasma glucocorticoids in, 299
seminal vesicle in, 380
skin in, 437
small intestine in, 255—256
steroidogenesis in, 375
testicular changes in, 374, 375
thorax in, 200
thyroid hormones in, 324
thyroid stimulating hormone in, 290, 291
thyrotrophin-releasing hormone in, 291
uterus in, 344, 348
Microcirculation, 155—158
Microglia, 39
Microglia cells, 39
Micturition, 193—216
Minerals, 126, 427
  density of, 425
  loss of, 428
Miniature-endplate potentials, 47
Mitochondria, 48
Monkeys
  arteries in, 134
  lead absorption in, 275
  lungs in, 200
  reproductive life-span in, 334
  resting plasma glucocorticoids in, 300
  thorax in, 200
  vestibular apparatus in, 29
Monoamine metabolites, 389
Motility, 231—233
Motor nerve fibers, 47
Motor unit, 45
MTT, see Mean transit time
Mucopolysaccharides, 126, 135
  in blood vessels, 113
Muscles, see also specific muscles, 7, 221, 231

arteries, 104, 109
atrophy of, 47
blood flow in, 169, 170, 447
cardiac, 383
ciliary, 19
extraocular, 18
gastrocnemius, 47
mass of, 413
skeletal, 47—48, 169
slow, 47
smooth, 111, 126, 128, 135, 385—386
soleus, 45, 47
tracheal smooth, 386
vascular smooth, 385—386
Muscular arteries, 104
Myelinated axons, 7, 8
Myocardium, 71, 385, 433, 434, 438
Myogenic foam cells, 126
Myometrium, 344

N

Negative feedback, 371, 381
Neoplasia, 353
Nerve terminals, 45
Nervous system
  integrative functions of, 31—33
  non-neuronal elements of, 35—40
Neural cellular changes, 3—4
Neural regulation of cardiovascular system, 151—158
Neuroblastoma, 3
Neurofibrillary tangles, 4, 8
Neurohypophysis, 325—331
Neuromuscular junction, 45
Neurotransmitters, 31
Niacin, 283
Nickel, 117
Nisil substance, 3
Nitrogen, 116, 414
Nitroglycerine, 128, 135
Nonfibrous elements of blood vessels, 116
Nonneural tissue, 7, 8
Non-neuronal elements of central nervous system, 35—40
Nonshivering thermogenesis (NST), 481
Norepinephrine, 153, 330
Normotensive coronary heart disease, 465
NST, see Nonshivering thermogenesis
5'-Nucleotidase, 126
Nucleus pulposus, 437, 438
Nystagmic responses, 29

O

Olfaction, 16
Olfactory epithelium, 16
Olfactory glomeruli and nerve atrophy, 16
Olfactory sensitivity, 16
Olfactory thresholds, 18

Oligodendrocytes, 39
Oligodendroglia, 39
Olivary nucleus, 3
Oocytes, 349, 354, 356
Optic nerve, 20
Oral cavity, 8
Oral mucosa, 236
Ornithine, 54
Osmolality, 179
Ossicles, 25
Osteoid tissue, 424
Otoconia, 29
Ova, 338, 349
Ovarian gonadotropin responses, 358
Ovaries, 354—355, 358
  steroidogenesis in, 360
Oviduct, 349
Ovulation, 358
Oxygen
  affinity of, 218
  consumption of, 48, 412
  extraction of, 160
  utilization of, 33, 221—222, 451, 452, 457
Oxytocin secretion, 327

P

Pacinian corpuscles, 8
Pain, 7
Pain threshold, 7, 9—10
Pancreas, 272
Pancreatic hormones, 391—396
Pancreatic islets of Langerhans, 392
Papillae, 13
Papillary latency, 19
Parasympathetic blockade, 151
Parathyroid hormone, 397—408
Patau syndrome, 352
Paternal-age related disorders, 352
Perceptual changes, 21
Perceptual closure judgments, 21
Perchlorphenazine, 4
Perfusion, 211
Pericytes, 36
Peripheral circulatory impairment, 449
Peripheral resistance, 146
Peripheral sensory axons, 88
Peripheral vascular reactivities, 513
Perirenal fat depot, 418
pH, 191
Phagocytes, 36
Phagocytosis, 39
Phenylalanine, 54, 281
Phosphate, 116
Phosphodiesterase activity, 128, 395
Phosphoglucomutase, 126
Phospholipid, 119, 135
  in red blood cells, 59
Phospholipid phosphorus, 130
Phosphorus absorption, 275
Physical conditioning, 447

Physical training, 448
PIF, see Prolactin-inhibiting factor
Pigment epithelium, 19
Pigs
  cerebral arteries in, 433
  lungs in, 200
  reproductive life-span in, 334
  thorax in, 200
  uterus in, 344
Pituitary
  function of, 327
  morphology of, 365
  prolactin levels of, 370
  responsiveness to gonadotropin releasing
    hormone, 367, 382
Pituitary gonadotropin, 366
Plasma, see also Blood, 189, 383
  adrenocortical steroids in, 302
  components of, 53
  flow in, 161
  glucocorticoid response to adrenocortical
    stimulation in, 305—308
  growth hormone in, 289
  lipids in, 54
  renin activities in, 182
  volume of, 153, 449
Plasma membrane, 128, 135
  proliferation of, 134
Platelets, 63
  lipid composition of, 64
Pollutants, 16
Portal vein, 135
Positive feedback, 373
Postcastration gonadotropin secretion, 381
Posterior pituitary function, 327
Postjunctional membrane, 45
Postprandial insulin, 301
Postural hypotension, 154
Potassium, 117, 189, 413
  in red blood cells, 58
Prenatal complications, 351
Prenatal mortality, 338
Presbycusis, 25
Presbyopia, 19
Pressure-volume diagram for aorta, 83
Preventive cardiology, 448
Primary taste qualities, 13
Primordial follicles, 354, 356
Progesterone, 348, 362, 363, 373
Prolactin, 370
Prolactin-inhibiting factor (PIF), 329
Proline, 54, 281
Propranolol, 151
Prostate, 193, 378, 379
Prostatic carcinoma, 378
Protein, 130
  absorption of, 279—281
  androgen-binding, 375
Protein-bound iodine, 319
Psychomotor capacity, 449
Pulmonary arteries, see also Lungs, 99, 109, 113,
    116, 119, 123, 126, 128, 135

Pulmonary function, 443
Pulmonary trunk, 97—98
Pulse wave velocity in arteries, 106, 108
Pure tone intensity thresholds, 25

Q

Quantal content of endplate potential, 45

R

Rabbits
　blood vessels in, 135
　cardiac muscle, in, 383
　cardiac performance in, 76
　cardiovascular system in, 385
　cartilage in, 439
　chest wall in, 210
　connective tissue in, 439
　corpus luteum in, 364
　glycosaminoglycans in, 437
　lungs in, 200, 210
　lung volume in, 205
　nucleus pulposus in, 437
　oocyte number in, 356
　ovarian gonadotropin responses in, 358
　ovaries in, 360
　pituitary gonadotropin in, 366
　pituitary morphology in, 365
　reproductive life-span in, 335
　steroidogenesis in, 375
　testicular changes in, 375
　thorax in, 200
　uterus in, 348
　vascular smooth muscle in, 385
　ventilation in, 213
Radiation heat transfer, 477
Radius, 427
Rats
　adipose tissue in, 383, 385, 418
　adrenal in, 383
　adrenocortical function in, 316
　adrenocortical stimulation in, 305—308
　alanine absorption in, 279
　amino acid absorption in, 279—281
　aorta in, 435
　arginiine absorption in, 280
　arteries in, 436
　arterioles in, 433
　blood vessels in, 128, 130—131
　bone in, 431, 432, 438
　calcitonin in, 402
　calcium absorption in, 273—275
　capillaries in, 433
　cardiac muscle in, 383
　cardiac performance in, 69, 70, 74
　cardiovascular system in, 385
　cartilage in, 438
　catecholamine in, 385
　cerebral cortex in, 36
　chest wall in, 210
　cholesterol absorption in, 285
　collagen in, 434, 435
　connective tissue, 439
　connective tissue hexoses in, 438
　corpus luteum in, 363
　cysteine absorption in, 280
　diaphragm in, 45
　elastin in, 436
　estradiol in, 362
　gas exchange in, 216
　glomerular permeability in, 181
　glucagon in, 385
　glucocorticoid response in, 305—308
　glucose absorption in, 277
　glycerol in, 54
　glycine absorption in, 279
　glycosaminoglycans in, 437
　gonadotropin in, 330, 368
　gonadotropin releasing hormone in, 367, 382
　heart in, 72, 439
　hepatic metabolism in, 249—251
　hypothalamic biogenic amine in, 330
　insulin in, 391, 392, 394
　iron absorption in, 275
　kidney in, 433
　large intestine in, 263
　lead absorption in, 275
　lean body mass in, 414
　leucine absorption in, 279
　lipids in, 54
　liver in, 243, 245, 246, 386, 433
　lungs in, 200, 210, 433
　lysine absorption in, 280, 281
　metabolic rate in, 412
　myocardium in, 385, 433
　negative feedback in, 371, 381
　olfactory degeneration in, 16
　oocyte number in, 356
　ovarian gonadotropin responses in, 358
　ovaries in, 354, 360
　oviduct in, 349
　oxytocin secretion in, 317
　pericytes in, 36
　phenylalanine absorption in, 281
　phosphorlipid composition in red blood cells of, 59
　pituitary in, 365, 367, 370, 382
　pituitary function in, 327
　pituitary gonadotropin in, 366
　pituitary response to GmRH in, 382
　plasma glucocorticoid response in, 305—308
　plasma lipids in, 54
　positive feedback in, 373
　posterior pituitary function in, 327
　progesterone in, 362
　proline absorption in, 281
　prostate gland in, 378, 379
　protein absorption in, 279—281
　red blood cells in, 59, 386
　reproductive life-span in, 335

resting plasma glucocorticoids in, 298
saliva in, 269
salivary gland in, 386
seminal vesicle in, 380
skeletal epiphyses in, 432
skin in, 435, 437, 438
slow muscles in, 47
small intestine in, 255—256, 261
smooth muscle in, 385
soleus muscle in, 47
spermatogenesis in, 374
steroid levels in, 362
steroidogenesis in, 375
strontium absorption in, 275
tendon in, 434, 435, 438
testicular changes in, 374, 375
testosterone in, 362
thorax in, 200
thyroid function in, 322
thyroid hormones in, 324
thyroid stimulating hormone in, 291
thyrotrophin-releasing hormone in, 291
tracheal smooth muscle in, 386
tryptophan absorption in, 281
uterus in, 344, 348, 433—435
valine absorption in, 281
vascular smooth muscle in, 385
ventilation in, 213
vitamin absorption in, 283
Reaction time, 443
Receptor cells, 29
Receptors, 20, 29
Rectal temperature, 483
Red blood cells, 55, 386
 cholesterol in, 55, 59
 count of, 57
 lipid phosphorus in, 59
 potassium in, 58
 sedimentation rates in (ESR), 59
 sodium in, 58
Refractory peroids, 45
REM sleep, 33
Remyelination in CNS tissue, 39
Renal blood flow, 161
Renal circulation, 161—162
Renal function, see also Kidneys, 177
Renal hypertrophy, 184
Renal morphology, 175—176
Renal pathophysiology, 183
Renal plasma, 161, 177
Reproduction, 333—382
Respiratory activity, 48
Resting membrane potential, 47
Resting plasma adrenocortical steroid levels, 295—296
Resting plasma glucocorticoids, 298—300
Resting skeletal muscle, 169
Reticular activating system, 31
Retina, 20
Retinal vessels, 37
Rhesus monkeys
 arteries in, 134

reproductive life-span in, 334
Riboflavin, 283
RNA, 348, 379
Rodents, see also specific rodents
 hypothalamic biogenic amine in, 330

S

Saliva composition, 269
Salivary glands, 267, 386
Sclera, 18, 439
Seat chloride, 449
Seattle Heart Watch and Network Registries, 457
Seminal vesicle, 380
Seminiferous tubules, 374
Senile miosis, 19, 20
Senile muscular atrophy, 47
Senile plaques, 4
Sensation thresholds, 7
Senses, see also specific senses, 13—29
Sensory axons, 7, 8
Serine, 54
Serotonin, 330
Sertoli cells, 374
Serum sodium, 189
Sheep
 blood vessels in, 135
 reproductive life-span in, 334
Shivering thermogenesis, 481
Signal detection theory, 7
Silver, 117
Sinus arrhythmia, 151
Skeletal epiphyses, 432
Skeletal muscle, 47—48
 circulation in, 169
Skin, 7, 8, 433—435, 437—439
 blood flow in, 170
 temperature of, 483
Skinfold thickness, 417, 420
Sleep, 33
Sleep apnea, 33
Sleep spindle, 33
Slow muscles, 47
Slow-twitch, 47
Slow-wave sleep, 33
Small intestine, 255—261
Smoking, 448
Smooth muscles, 111, 126, 128, 135, 386
Sodium, 189
 conservation of, 182
 in red blood cells, 58
Sodium nitrite, 128
Soleus muscle, 45, 47
Somatic receptors, 7
Somatosensory mechanisms, 7—10
Somatosensory receptors, 8
Speech discrimination, 25
Sperm, 374
Spermatogenesis, 374
Sphingomyelin, 120, 134
Spina bifida, 352

Spinal ganglia, 8
Splanchnic circulation, 168
Spontaneous transmitter release, 45
3β-Steroid dehydrogenase, 375
Steroid hormones, 295—296, 302, 304, 362, 371
Steroidogenesis, 374—375
    in ovaries, 360
Steropsis, 20
Stomach, 232, 241—242
Stress, 128, 448
    and cardiac function, 79
Striatum, 39
Stroke volume, 447
Strontium, 117
    absorption of, 275
Subcutaneous fat, 417
Sulfate, 438
Sulfur, 116
Superiosteal, 423
Sweating, 477, 483
Sympathetic blockade, 151
Sympathetic neurotransmitter, 383—389
Syndactyly, 352
Systemic hypoxia, 170

T

Tactile receptors, 7
Tangential stress, 128
Taste buds, 13
Taste sensitivity, 13
Taste thresholds, 15—16
Taurine, 54
T binding globulin (TeBG), 374
TBW, see Total body water
Tearing, 18
TeBG, see T binding globulin
Teeth
    composition of, 235
    structure of, 235
Temperature core, 480
Temporal cortex, 25
Tendons, 7, 434, 435, 438, 439
Tension, 128
Testes, 222, 375
Testicular changes, 374—375
Testosterone, 374, 375, 381
Tetanus toxin, 4
Thermal conductivity, 481
Thermal insulation, 481
Thermal physiology, 475—481, 483—488
Thermogenesis, 481
Thermoneutral atmosphere, 483
Thermoneutral zone (TNZ), 481
Thermoregulation, 477, 488
Thiamine, 283
Thoracic aorta, 109, 123, 128
    chemical properties of, 129
    mechanical properties of, 129
Thoracic arteries, 105
Thorax, 197—216

Threonine, 54
Thresholds
    dark adaptation, 20
    dental pain, 10
    exercise, 443, 445
    luminance, 20
    olfactory, 18
    pain, 7, 9—10
    pure tone intensity, 25
    sensation, 7
    taste, 15—16
    temperature, 483
    two-point, 9
Thromboenbolic disease, 351
Thyroid, 317—324, 383
    function of, 322—323
    uptake by, 321
Thyroid stimulating hormone (TSH), 290
    response of to thyrotrophin-releasing hormone, 2
Thyroparathyroidectomy, 405
Thyrotrophin-releasing hormone (TRH), 291
    pituitary response to, 370
Thyroxine, 318
Tibia, 431
Tilting, 151
Tin, 117
Tissue, see also specific tissues
    cartilagenous, 25
    degeneration of, 25
    thermal conductance in, 511
TNZ, see Thermoneutral zone
Tone intensity thresholds, 25
Total body water (TBW), 413
Total heat loss, 483
Total heat production, 481
Touch, 7—9
Toxemia, 351
Trabecular bone, 427
Tracheal smooth muscle, 386
Training, 448
Transmitter release, 45
Transverse tubular system, 47
TRH, see Thyrotrophin-releasing hormone
Triglyceride, 120, 135
Triiodothyronine, 317
Tryptophan, 281
TSH, see Thyroid stimulating hormone
Tumors, mammary, 353
Twitch, 47
Two-point discrimination, 7
Two-point threshold, 9
Tympanic membrane, 25
    temperature of, 483
Tyrosine, 54

U

Ultrastructural degeneration, 47
Unmyelinated sensory axons, 7
Urethra, 193

Urinary adrenocorticosteroid excretion, 310—314
Urinary aldosterone excretions, 182
Urinary gonadotropins, 368, 381
Urinary monoamine metabolites, 389
Urine, 193
Urine concentrating ability, 179
Urine diluting ability, 179
Uterus, 343, 344, 347, 433—435
   biochemical responses of, 348
   circulation in, 172
   collagen in, 346

V

Vagina, 338, 340, 341
Valine, 54, 281
Valsalva maneuver, 151
Vascular beds, 447
Vascular smooth muscle, 385—386
Vascular system, 126
Vascular wall, 383
Vasculature
   brain, 37
   coronary, 159
Vasopressin, 179
Veins, 102—103, 117, 121, 126, 128, 135
   calcium in, 123—124
Vena cava, 117, 121
Vena femoralis, 121
Ventilation, 211, 213
   chemical regulation of, 225
Ventral cochlear nucleus, 3
Ventricular impairment, 449
Vertebral compressive strength, 431
Vertigo, 29

Vestibular function, 29
Vestibular ganglia, 29
Vibration, 7, 9
Virus particles, 4
Viscera, circulation in, 168
Visual field, 20
Visual function, 18—21
Visual masking studies, 21
Visual persistence, 21
Visual sensitivity tests, 20
Vitamins
   D, 397—408
   E, 4
   water-soluble, 283—284
Vitreous body, 20
Volume elastic modulus, 83
Vulva, 339

W

Wall stress of aorta, 83
Wandering, 33
Water, 413
Water-soluble vitamins, 283—284
Working capacity, 445, 449, 455
Working life span, 445

X

Xylose, 278

Z

Zinc, 117, 189